Why Do You Need This New Edition?

If you're wondering why you should buy this new edition of *The Conscious Reader*, here are five good reasons!

1. A **new Part I on visual literacy, Reading Images**, encourages you to "read" both classic and contemporary art in a variety of media and includes essays about visual literacy that underline the importance of understanding the arguments in the images that you confront every day.

2. **Thirty-seven new selections**—almost a third of the book—offer models of good persuasive writing on a range of compelling contemporary topics including political issues like the "Great Recession," the wars in the Middle East, and rabidly partisan politics; the future of higher education; and the transformative effects that new technologies may soon have on all of our lives.

3. New readings in Parts II and IV wrestle honestly with **the challenges of learning in a technology-saturated world** and offer guidance about how your own interactions with technology—in-class texting, for example, or your use of Wikipedia and other online research sources—may impact your role as a student.

4. The chapter on **popular culture** includes **texts on topics rooted in today's cultural context**: robot toys (including Transformers and Furbys), ethics in sports (steroids in baseball), male-bashing in sitcoms and commercials, and the surprising resurgence of popularity of vampires, from the romantic (*Twilight, True Blood*) to the more horrific and violent (*30 Days of Night, Daybreakers, Let the Right One In*).

5. **An array of exciting new Notebooks**—collections of related readings at the beginning of most parts—bring together persuasive texts on controversial issues and offer you fresh opportunities to add your own voice to contemporary debates.

The
Conscious Reader

TWELFTH EDITION

CAROLINE SHRODES
Late, The Union Institute

MICHAEL SHUGRUE
The College of Staten Island of the City University of New York

MARC DiPAOLO
Oklahoma City University

CHRISTIAN J. MATUSCHEK

Longman

Boston   Columbus   Indianapolis   New York   San Francisco   Upper Saddle River
Amsterdam   Cape Town   Dubai   London   Madrid   Milan Munich   Paris   Montreal   Toronto
Delhi   Mexico City   São Paulo   Sydney   Hong Kong   Seoul   Singapore   Taipei   Tokyo

Senior Sponsoring Editor: Virginia L. Blanford
Senior Marketing Manager: Sandra McGuire
Assistant Editor: Rebecca Gilpin
Senior Supplements Editor: Donna Campion
Production Coordinator: Scarlett Lindsay
Project Coordination, Text Design, and Electronic Page Makeup: PreMediaGlobal
Cover Designer/Manager: Wendy Ann Fredericks
Cover Photo: © Slow Images/Getty Images
Photo Researcher: Linda Sykes
Senior Manufacturing Buyer: Roy L. Pickering, Jr.
Printer and Binder: RR Donnelley/Crawfordsville
Cover Printer: RR Donnelley/Crawfordsville

Library of Congress Cataloging-in-Publication Data

The conscious reader / [edited by] Caroline Shrodes, Michael Shugrue, Marc
Dipaolo, Christian J. Matuschek. — 12th ed.
    p. cm.
  ISBN-13: 978-0-205-80328-6
  ISBN-10: 0-205-80328-8
    1. College readers.   2. English language — Rhetoric — Problems, exercises,
etc.   I. Shrodes, Caroline.   II. Shugrue, Michael Francis.   III. Di Paolo, Marc.
IV.   Matuschek, Christian   J.
  PE1122.C586 2011
  808'.0427—dc22
                                                                    2010029098

Longman
is an imprint of

1 2 3 4 5 6 7 8 9 10—DOC—13 12 11 10
ISBN-13: 978-0-205-80328-6
www.pearsonhighered.com   ISBN-10:   0-205-80328-8

BRIEF CONTENTS

DETAILED CONTENTS

I. Reading Images

II. Conscious Reading, Intelligent Writing

NOTEBOOK

PERSONAL WRITING

III. Personal Values and Relationships

∾∾∾

IV. Education

꙳꙳꙳

V. Popular Culture

꙳꙳꙳

VI. Art and Society

ESSAYS

FICTION

POETRY

VII. Science and Civilization

NOTEBOOK

PERSONAL WRITING

ESSAYS

FICTION

POETRY

~~~~~

VIII. Freedom and Human Dignity

~~~~~

IX. Globalism, Nationalism, and Cultural Identity

RHETORICAL CONTENTS

The following arrangement of expository essays suggests ways in which readers can approach the selections. The classifications are not rigid, and many selections might fit as easily into one category as into another.

ANALYSIS

ARGUMENT AND PERSUSASION

COMPARISON / CONTAST

DEFINITION

N A R R A T I O N

PREFACE

> *. . . the unexamined life is not worth living.*
>
> —PLATO, *The Apology*

For eleven editions, the editors of *The Conscious Reader* have brought together the past and the present through a rich variety of classic and cutting-edge texts. The selections range across genres, including essays, poems, short stories, and plays that will encourage students to read carefully and think critically.

As we point out in the introduction to Part II of this edition, we are concerned that reading is becoming a lost art, buried beneath the weight of new electronics. Yet research suggests, almost counterintuitively, that today's students are actually *writing* more than previous generations did—writing in the form of text messages, blogs, electronic posts, and so on. Even that kind of writing—or perhaps that kind of writing most of all—needs to be informed by an understanding of what makes good writing. The ability to write clearly, concisely, and with an efficient command of the rules of our language may be more important to a potential employer than any other skill. And learning to write well means learning to read well. That's what *The Conscious Reader* is all about.

What's New in This Edition

- **A newly re-imagined opening section on visual literacy**, *Reading Images*, showcases a color art portfolio of classic and contemporary works rendered in a variety of media, and also includes essays about visual literacy that raise questions about the role of art in society, the intent of the artist, and the possible reactions of the audience. Discussion questions and writing assignments throughout the book, identified by a leaf symbol ॐ, create pedagogical links between selected essays and accompanying images.

- **Thirty-seven new selections** include readings that confront contemporary political issues (the Great Recession, the wars in the Middle East, rabidly partisan politics), consider the future of higher education and include predictions concerning the transformative effect new technologies may soon have upon all of our lives.
  - New selections in Parts II and IV wrestle honestly with **the challenges of teaching college students in a technology-saturated world**, portraying a learning environment in which many students text-message in class nonstop, knowingly or unknowingly plagiarize their papers from the Web, and do most of their research on Wikipedia. No bullet-proof solutions are offered, but students and teachers who read these selections together may find opportunities to discuss these issues openly, understand one another more completely, and learn to reconcile their conflicting perspectives and expectations.
  - Students may be more excited about Part V on **popular culture**, which includes texts on robot toys (including Transformers and Furbys), ethics in sports, male-bashing in sitcoms and commercials, and the surprising resurgence in the popularity of vampires, from the romantic (*Twilight, True Blood, Dark Shadows*) to the more horrific and violent (*30 Days of Night, Daybreakers, Let Me In*).
- **An array of exciting new Notebooks** collect related writings at the start of each chapter, offering arguments that may be read against one another, debated in class, or synthesized by students, who are given the opportunity to add their own voices to some of the most important debates of our time. These Notebooks address compelling contemporary topics including war (*Globalism, Nationalism, and Cultural Identity*), the economy (*Freedom and Human Dignity*), technology (*Science and Civilization*), censorship (*Art and Society*), multitasking (*Education*), and the effects of divorce (*Personal Values and Relationships*).
- **New synthesis discussion questions** throughout the book offer students opportunities to analyze and synthesize both texts and images by suggesting relationships between selections. For example, all of the Essays in Part II, *Conscious Reading, Intelligent Writing*, deal with issues surrounding the practicalities of researching and writing a paper; those in *Education* all ask what comprises a proper education; and the Personal Writings showcased in *Art and Society* concern music therapy. Paired essays by Salman Rushdie and Chris Hedges in the Personal Writing section of *Globalism, Nationalism, and Cultural Identity* explore the cultural clash between fundamentalist and progressive forces within organized religion, and the battles between secular and religious forces in contemporary society.

~~~~~

The Heart of
The Conscious Reader

As central as contemporary and avant-garde selections are to this text, one of the key strengths of *The Conscious Reader* is that it continues to include classic selections like Plato's "Allegory of the Cave," which dates from ancient Athens, and Oscar Wilde's nineteenth-century British tract, "The Soul of Man Under Socialism." While these works are challenging reads, they are classics for a reason, and their merits will be self-evident to any students who take the time to read them. They are included here partly because American public education, sadly, often no longer requires students to read classic works of nonfiction, literature, and philosophy, and many students either encounter such texts while taking a course in the common core curriculum their freshman year in college or *do not encounter them at all.* Consequently, we are pleased to include texts by authors such as William Shakespeare, Willa Cather, George Orwell, William Faulkner, Virginia Woolf, Anton Chekhov, and even classical music composer Ludwig von Beethoven.

In addition to these canonical texts, we have selected essays by the most erudite and gifted contemporary artists, be they world leaders (Barack Obama), established literary figures (Edwidge Danticat), or distinguished commentators (Susan Sontag). Many of these writers and thinkers are often unknown to students who get much of their information from television and the Internet. We encourage enterprising instructors to bring these demanding and important works to life for modern-day visual learners.

~~~~~

How This Book Is Organized

The Conscious Reader is divided into nine parts. In addition to Parts I and II, *Reading Images* and *Conscious Reading, Intelligent Writing,* six other parts cover subjects we hope you will find compelling.

- *Personal Values and Relationships* is replete with personal stories from a variety of people who share their private pains, their dreams, their victories, and their defeats, as well as the relationships that help define their lives.

- The lifelong intellectual development of the individual, beginning in early child development, moving through high school, college, and afterwards is examined in *Education.*
- *Popular Culture* and *Art and Society* consider the influence of populist and "highbrow" art on American culture, and the importance of both.
- Essays in *Science and Civilization* explore some of the most pressing topics of our time—climate change, the evolution debate, "the end of oil"—and also offer thoughts on such diverse topics as the extinction of the dinosaurs and the potential reality of time travel.
- *Freedom and Human Dignity* reprints classic speeches and declarations of principles that argue for individual freedoms and democratic ideals, but it also includes essays that consider times when society has failed to protect the rights of the individual and has tolerated, or actively committed, injustices and acts of genocide against marginalized groups.
- The final section, *Globalism, Nationalism, and Cultural Identity,* deals primarily with contemporary border disputes, civil wars, and the clash of globalist and nationalist forces. It is especially concerned with the "war on terror" and the immigration debate, all the while offering the hope that peaceful solutions may be found to the bitterest of conflicts in the international community.

Each section of *The Conscious Reader* begins with a brief introduction, placing the various anthologized texts in context with one another; an image, serving as a "visual appetizer" to the overall theme of the new section; as well as a Notebook that groups several common-themed pieces together to be read in tandem. Individual texts include headnotes and suggestions for discussion and writing to help students explore multiple levels of understanding. The suggestions invite students to pay careful attention to thought and structure and to compare their experience with the vision of life expressed in the selections. Exploring cultural patterns both similar and alien to one's own should encourage a continuing dialectic in classroom discussion as well as in writing.

If there is a dominant theme in these readings, it is that neither understanding of the past nor projections of the future can eliminate conflict from our lives and that opposing forces in the self and society are a part of the human condition. Indeed, it is vital that these forces contend. For it is primarily through conscious recognition and expression of these conflicting forces that we may find our way to a tolerant worldview and to an increased freedom of choice.

Resources for Instructors and Students

An Instructor's Manual is available either in print or online. This extensive resource provides teaching guides, sample syllabi, and additional writing and discussion prompts.

Pearson's **MyCompLab** is available packaged with this text at no additional cost and offers a wealth of resources for grammar review, research guidance, and writing, including a "writing space" program that allows students and instructors to manage all the writing assignments in a composition course in one easy-to-use site.

Acknowledgments

We extend our thanks to Virginia Blanford for her gracious, artful, expert editorial guidance.

We thank Rebecca Gilpin for her constant, good-natured assistance.

We thank Marc Lucht and Victoria Williams for their suggestions for new selections.

Thanks to the following reviewers: Sandra Mayfield; Christine Mitchell; Pauline T. Newton; Jan Stahl; and Julie Townsend as well as Michael E. Barrett, Moberly Area Community College; Emanuel di Pasquale, Middlesex County College; Rich DuRocher, St. Olaf College; Iain Ellis, University of Kansas; Curtis Harrell, NorthWest Arkansas Community College; Jayne Marek, Franklin College; James McNamara, Marquette University; Bernie Prokop, Colorado Christian University; Jennifer Rich, Hofstra University; and Jennifer Viereck, Midlands Technical College.

ABOUT THE EDITORS

Michael Shugrue, professor and dean emeritus at The College of Staten Island, the City University of New York, has written widely about Eighteenth Century and Cultural Studies. He earned his PhD from Duke University.

Marc DiPaolo wrote *Emma Adapted: Jane Austen's Heroine from Book to Film* and has authored chapters for *A Century of the Marx Brothers, Beyond Adaptation,* and *The Encyclopedia of Religion and Film.* He writes the blogs *Bedford Falls Movie House* and *The Adventures of Italian-American Man.* He has a PhD in English from Drew University and is an Assistant Professor of English and Film at Oklahoma City University. His next book, *War, Politics, and Superheroes: Ethics and Propaganda in Comics and Film,* will be published in 2011.

Christian J. Matuschek, M.Div/M.Th, is a German visual artist and theologian whose work has gained attention in Germany and the United States and is part of permanent collections, including the Christopher Isherwood Foundation (Santa Monica, California) and the Sheldon Memorial Art Gallery (Lincoln, Nebraska). Mr. Matuschek has taught both undergraduates and adult learners and, having lived and worked in New York City, considers himself bi-cultural.

The
Conscious
Reader

Reading Images

✺✺✺

Works of art, in my opinion, are the only objects in the material universe to possess internal order, and that is why, though I don't believe that only art matters, I do believe in Art for Art's sake.

— E. M. FORSTER, "Art for Art's Sake"

When we abstract images through cartooning we're not so much eliminating details as we are focusing on specific details. By stripping down an image to its essential "meaning," an artist can amplify that meaning in a way that realistic art can't. Film critics will sometimes describe a live-action film as a "cartoon" to acknowledge the stripped-down intensity of a simple story or visual style. Though the term is often used disparagingly, it can be equally well applied to many time-tested classics. Simplifying characters and images toward a purpose can be an effective tool for storytelling in any medium. Cartooning isn't a way of drawing. It's a way of seeing.

— SCOTT McCLOUD, "The Language of Comics"

CHRISTIAN J. MATUSCHEK

"headmaster"

c-print, 2010

© Christian J. Matuschek/www.foto-lounge.de

INTRODUCTION

Discussing images as texts presents certain problems. It is difficult, sometimes impossible, to discover the intent of the visual artist or the "argument" of the painting or photograph. Moreover, students may be unaware of how much the piece's content derives from the traditions of its form. A number of contemporary artists find any attempt to explicate their work as repugnant. The contemporary artist Georg Baselitz goes so far as to contend that a painting never projects ideas and that no statements, information, or opinions are communicated publicly through visual art.

We respectfully disagree. The editors of *The Conscious Reader* believe that paintings and photographs not only inspire emotions but also communicate ideas. Further, we believe that, since we are all surrounded every day with images, we must develop critical skills to "read" their messages, just as we need to be able to read text. We hope that the ideas the following images suggest, while accounting for only a part of their total impact, may well provoke useful discussion and writing. Therefore, we offer these works of visual art in the hope—even the expectation—that you will find them exciting and be moved to talk and write about them in ways even beyond the ones that we suggest. The glossy color pages towards the beginning of this chapter feature a variety of striking works of art. Biographies of the artists, discussion questions, and writing prompts designed to accompany these pictures appear at the beginning of this chapter.

Supplementing the color art portfolio is a series of essays concerning visual literacy. These essays were chosen by the editors to help you interpret the specific images contained throughout this text, and to help you better analyze and appreciate the far broader canvas of the material universe in its entirety, including the natural world, multiple digital realities, and the rural, urban, and suburban landscapes we occupy.

David Wall examines how stereotyped imagery in advertising and politics distorts public opinion, while Margaret Atwood argues that pornography is more about violence and power relations than it is about romance, sex, and "harmless" erotica. The psychological effects of the mass media and American consumer culture are also central to essays by Susan Sontag and Peggy Orenstein. Sontag meditates on the wider moral and ethical implications of war and the human impulse to be fascinated by suffering and pain on the news, while in "What's Wrong with Cinderella?" Orenstein argues that the fairy tale worldview, especially the one represented by the Disney Princess line of merchandise, may do serious psychological damage to young girls. Meanwhile,

Chris Suellentrop examines the birth of the multigenerational phenomenon of the Transformers, the ultimate "boy's toys."

Working in a medium often considered disreputable, Scott McCloud offers in his graphic novel a discourse on iconography and visual literacy. The piece may look cute, but its content is serious, and this juxtaposition may cause us to rethink our definitions of *art* and *popular culture*. Art does not breed easy definitions. Is art valuable primarily—or even only—for its own sake (a concept that E. M. Forster explores) or because of the way it interacts or provokes? Who are the real "artists" in contemporary society? Those who are paid to produce elite art by universities, museums, or private donors? Those who make products to sell, such as movies, toys, or other merchandise? Or does every individual who takes photos with a cell phone or makes a YouTube video, or doodles in a notebook count as an artist? These questions and more are raised in the Suggestions for Writing and Suggestions for Discussion accompanying the texts and works of art featured in this section, and we hope they provide food for thought for students and professors alike.

∿∿∿∿

RENÉ MAGRITTE

La Condition Humaine
Oil on canvas, 1933

Belgian artist René Magritte (1898–1967), a widely admired surrealist painter and a poster and advertisement designer by trade, achieved great popular appeal through the frequent reproduction of his works as affordable prints. Magritte's works are known for their sense of humor, as well as for their striking oddity; they often evoke a sense of mystery opposed to any attempt at reasoning. As a consequence, Magritte's imagery has had a considerable influence on pop and minimalist art, as well as on a variety of conceptual artists.

Suggestions for Discussion

1. Examine the painting carefully. What do you see? What *don't* you see? How do the seen and unseen elements work together?

2. Christian J. Matuschek—photographer, visual artist, and one of the co-authors of this reader—states: "The whole world can be considered a gallery with an ever-changing program." How does this idea compare with the central theme of Magritte's painting, "La Condition Humaine" as you see it? Do you agree that art can be "found" anywhere? Once again, what is art? Does art exist as accidental discovery? Does art exist apart from a skillful technique? After discussing these ideas, ask yourself: How do I define art?

Suggestions for Writing

1. Find Magritte's painting titled "The Treachery of Images," which is discussed in Scott McCloud's "The Language of Comics." Compare "The Treachery of Images" to "La Condition Humaine," shown here. Write a brief essay responding to McCloud. Do you agree or disagree with him? Is the object depicted a pipe—or isn't it?

2. Write about a dream that you remember in detail. If you don't remember a dream, make one up! Be imaginative.

SANDRO BOTTICELLI

Portrait of a Young Woman
Tempera on wood, 1480–1485

Sandro Botticelli, born in 1445 in Florence, began as a goldsmith but soon moved on to painting, studying with the Fra Filippo Lippi, famous for his use of color. Soon Botticelli developed his own style and was able to open his own workshop, under the patronage of the powerful Medici family. Probably best known are his large paintings "Primavera" and "The Birth of Venus." Botticelli's portraits of women, whether derived from Christianity, Greco-Roman mythology, or portraits of noble contemporaries, often appear to be idealized figures with introverted, slightly sad or melancholic expressions. His use of line and detail seems to bring his characters to life. Although one of the most distinct and esteemed early Italian Renaissance artists of his time, his work was forgotten for many centuries and was rediscovered late in the nineteenth century by a group of artists in England known as the Pre-Raphaelites. Botticelli died in 1510.

Suggestions for Discussion

1. Describe this woman's features, clothes, expression. Pay special attention to her hair. Consider her pose, her eyes, and the fact that her head is slightly tilted towards the onlooker. What can we infer about her personality? Her position in society?

2. How does the background of this painting contrast with the background featured in the self-portrait by Frida Kahlo? What tone does the background and the use of light and color give this painting? What might it tell you about "beauty from within"?

Suggestion for Writing

How can classic works of art remain intriguing for modern American college students? What would bring them to life best? Knowing more about the time periods? The life of the artist? The subject? Understanding art history better? What is the value of studying "old" art? How does knowing history and valuing classical works of art, music, and literature help us live life fuller in the present, with its emphasis on the new, the transient, and the now? Write an essay in which you consider these questions.

FRIDA KAHLO

Self-Portrait with Necklace and Hummingbird
Oil on canvas, 1940

Frida Kahlo (1907–1954) created her autobiography in scenes of her own life cycle—from conception to birth to marriage, surgeries, miscarriages, and dreams of her own death. She was born to a religious Catholic mother of Indian and Spanish parentage and to an agnostic father, a German Jew of Hungarian origin. She vowed as a teenager to bear a child to the famous Mexican painter Diego Rivera, twenty years her senior, before she had ever met him. She did indeed marry him at age 22, after she had been left with a limp from polio and had almost died in a horrifying accident that destroyed much of her body and forced her to abandon her medical studies. Kahlo and Rivera were political activists, affiliated with the Communist party, as well as with the patriotic "Mexicanidad" movement founded to restore pride in indigenous Mexican art that had been eclipsed by imported colonial values. Rivera was a womanizer, and Kahlo eventually took both male and female lovers. The two were divorced the year of this self-portrait, but later remarried. Although Kahlo had seen little surrealist art, her work often demonstrates an interest in dreams, the unconscious, eroticism, pain, and death, and contains many seemingly unrelated elements. Kahlo's body of work is considered unique, not part of any particular movement, style, or school.

Suggestions for Discussion

1. Examine Kahlo's "costume," her coiffure, her jewels, the pet monkey (who appears in other paintings), and the cat on either side of her. Explore her use of color. What is the effect of the overall composition? What sensations does it engender in you?

RENÉ MAGRITTE

La Condition Humaine

Oil on canvas, 1933

Private collection. Photo credit: Herscovici

Art Resource, New York

SANDRO BOTTICELLI

Portrait of a Young Woman

Tempera on wood, 1480–1485

© U. Edelmann/Städel Museum, Frankfurt/Artothek

10

FRIDA KAHLO

Portrait with a Necklace and Hummingbird

Oil on canvas, 1940

Nickolas Muray Collection, Harry Ransom Humanities Research, The University of Austin

© 2007 Banco de Mexico Diego Rivera & Frida Kahlo Museums Trust

11

DUANE HANSON

Queenie II

Life-size polychromed bronze,
with accessories, 1988
© Estate of Duane Hanson
Licensed by VAGA,
New York, NY

PATRICIA WATWOOD

The Boxer

Oil on canvas, 1999
Private collection
Photo credit: Stefan Hagen

12

EDWARD HOPPER

Room in New York

Oil on canvas, 1932

Sheldon Museum of Art, University of Nebraska-Lincoln

EDWARD HOPPER

Room in Brooklyn

Oil on canvas, 1932

Erich Lessing/Art Resource, NY

ROY LICHTENSTEIN

Girl with Beach Ball III

PABLO PICASSO

*Seated Woman with
Crossed Arms*

MEL SMOTHERS

"I Painted Over Andy Warhol (Montauk)#14"

Oil on canvas, 2007

Courtesy of the artist

ANDY WARHOL

Brillo Boxes

Acrylic silkscreen on wood, 1969

Norton Simon Museum. © Andy Warhol Foundation for the Visual Arts

Artists Rights Society

BANKSY

Untitled

Stencil on wall, 2007

Digital photograph: Courtesy of Sandrine Geith

2. How does Kahlo seem to see herself in this picture? What does her expression reveal of herself? Is the portrait realistic or symbolic? What do you think she wants to show us? How successful is the portrait as autobiography? If Kahlo is both subject and object in this painting, then what is the function of the viewer?

3. Watch the film *Frida*, starring Selma Hayek as Frida Kahlo. What does viewing this film reveal to you about Kahlo's life, values, and art?

Suggestions for Writing

1. Synthesis: Compare Kahlo's self-portrait with Botticelli's "Portrait of a Young Woman." Organize your essay around one of the following points of consideration: Male vision of a female body vs. female vision of a female body; portrait of a young woman vs. self-portrait of a woman; "inner beauty"; dream vs. vision.

2. How might the "Portrait of a Young Woman" have been different if it had been intended as a self-portrait of the subject? How might Kahlo have been painted differently by Botticelli? Support your position with specific details from the paintings.

DUANE HANSON, *Queenie II*
Life-sized polychromed bronze, with accessories, 1988

PATRICIA WATWOOD, *The Boxer*
Oil on canvas, 1999

Duane Hanson (1925–1996) produced life-size, hyperrealistic sculptures in bronze, resin, and fiberglass that often represented "unremarkable" blue-collar people overlooked by society at large. Hanson was one of the most influential American sculptors of his time. Exhibitions of his work often consisted of casually posed figures scattered strategically throughout the museum or gallery, so that viewers sometimes "mistook" them for "real people."

Patricia Watwood (b. 1971) is primarily concerned with the human figure, drawing inspiration from the old masters. She began as a scenic designer with productions in regional theaters across the U.S. and in Germany during her college years. Watwood's reputation as a figurative artist continues to grow, and key collectors have begun to acquire her work.

Suggestions for Discussion

1. What similarities and differences do you see between the two images? What thoughts do these images evoke in you?

2. Do these images represent stereotypes? Consider sex, race, and society in your response. Do you find either of these images offensive? Support your opinion.

3. In what ways would these two images be different if they were color photographs rather than a painting and sculpture? How does the medium chosen by the artist alter your point of view on the subject matter being portrayed?

Suggestion for Writing

Look carefully at the eyes of the persons portrayed as they confront or avoid your gaze. How would you start a conversation with each of them? What would you like to ask them? What would they ask you?

EDWARD HOPPER

Room in New York
Room in Brooklyn
Both oil on canvas, 1932

Aside from notable trips to Paris, Mexico, and New England, Edward Hopper (1882–1967) spent most of life in New York City, living and working quietly in the same small, sparsely furnished apartment in Greenwich Village from 1913 until his death. Educated at the New York School of Art, Hopper worked as a commercial artist to support himself until he was able to become a full-time artist at 42. While he did paint landscapes, seascapes, and villages, Hopper seems to have been fascinated with the city—its restaurants, theaters, offices, and apartments glimpsed through open windows. When he left the city as subject, it was often to study the impermanent elements of travel: trains, filling stations, deserted country roads, hotel lobbies, and motel rooms. In Paris, Hopper became fascinated by the quality of light in the city, and the glorious interplay of light and shadow in Impressionist paintings. Afterwards light—especially a harsh, "spotlight"-like light—became a staple of his art.

Suggestions for Discussion

1. Examine both paintings carefully. What is the role of light in these paintings? What and where is the source of the light? What is the emotional effect of the paintings? How do these paintings differ from each other?

2. Describe these apartments, based on what you can see, and what you can infer that remains unseen. How do they differ? Do these seem to you like good places to live?

3. Describe the figures in these paintings. What do their personalities seem like? Their inner lives? Relationships to others? To each other?

4. What portrait do these paintings offer of New York? How much does modern New York resemble the city of Hopper's era? Consider the infrastructure, architecture, and inhabitants.

Suggestions for Writing

1. In an interview, Hopper said, "Great art is an outward expression of the inner life in the artist, and the inner life will result in his personal vision of the world." Write an essay discussing the relevance of this statement to the pictures shown here. How are these paintings "personal" and what might they reveal about Hopper's "inner life"? Why has Hopper chosen these settings? What adjectives describe the feelings of these scenes? Would a voyeur be welcome in these rooms?

2. Compose a short story based on Hopper's *Room in New York* titled *In the Silence of our Hearts–A Dialogue Unspoken.*

ROY LICHTENSTEIN

Girl with Beach Ball III

Oil and magna on canvas, 1977

Painter Roy Lichtenstein (1923–1997) found his inspiration and themes in comic books and bubblegum wrappers. In 1962 he had his first solo show of cartoon painting. Critics sneered, but the public was enchanted with his work, which was seen as an integral part of the Pop Art movement. Pop Art was hailed as the New Realism because it dealt directly with the contemporary life of the 1960s, an age of consumerism fostered by government economic policies, industrial expansion, and the coming of age of mass media, particularly television. Advertisements promoted a standardized version of men and women as bland as cartoon images. Lichtenstein found fodder for his satirical art in second-hand comic shops, where he would pull one key action panel from a longer strip, sketch an enlarged and altered version of it, and paint it through a screen in a pixilated style evocative of newspaper BenDay dots, until he had created a work of his own from another's template.

PABLO PICASSO

Seated Woman with Crossed Arms
Oil on canvas, 1937

Through thousands of paintings, prints, sculptures, and ceramics no other artist is probably more associated with the term Modern Art than Pablo Ruiz Picasso, born on October 25, 1881, in Málaga, Spain. For some the product of the greatest genius, for others that of a gifted charlatan, Picasso's work and vision certainly left an influential mark on the art of the twentieth century. Picasso went through different "periods" of characteristic painting styles (the Blue Period; the Rose Period; Cubism—along with George Braque and Juan Gris; Classicism; and Surrealism). Picasso did not consider these periods as part of an ongoing evolution, but merely as the sheer expression of the moment. For Picasso, constant travel—and womanizing—may have also been ways of expressing the moment and of staying young. Mass media turned Picasso into a celebrity. He is also remembered as a vigorous activist of the Peace Movement, deeply distraught by the horrors of war. His mural *Guernica* has become a part of the collective consciousness of the twentieth century. Picasso died on April 8, 1973, at the age of 92.

Suggestions for Discussion

1. Examine Lichtenstein's work. How does the girl look: her features, her hair, her body? Does her expression indicate her situation? What are her emotions? How does this compare to traditional comic strips in newspapers, or more avant-garde art found in graphic novels marketed to adults?

2. Examine Picasso's work. What can you make out? Gender? Expression? Emotion? How? Why does there appear to be "mistakes" in this picture, such as bleeding color, jagged lines, and uneven coloring? What effect do you think that creates?

3. Compare the two images. Describe the use of shape and color in both works. How are they similar and how do they differ from each other? What do the particular images tell us about the figures portrayed that a more realistic portrait might or could not?

Suggestion for Writing

Our *Reading Images* section features, in paintings by Botticelli, Kahlo, Lichtenstein, and Picasso, four different ways of portraying women, four different versions of the female, and four different takes on female beauty. If "beauty lies in the eye of the beholder," how do you think each artist would respond to the question of beauty and the female body—that is, what makes a woman beautiful? Write four possible answers considering each artist's work represented.

MEL SMOTHERS, *"I Painted Over Andy Warhol (Montauk) #14"*
Oil on canvas, 2007

ANDY WARHOL, *Brillo Boxes*
Acrylic silkscreen on wood, 1969

Mel Smothers (b. 1947) began his "Painting Over" series by observing how many painters in the past—including Lichtenstein, Matisse, Max Ernst, and Dali—have acknowledged influences and included them in their work. According to Smothers, "My painting needs to awaken the viewers' imagination and give them a break from the material world, just as it does for me."

Andy Warhol (1928–1987), the founding father of Pop Art, is probably best remembered for presenting multiplied representations of mass-produced objects, as well as multiple portraits of celebrities like Marilyn Monroe and Mao Tse-dong, themselves omnipresent "manufactured" images of celebrity, that were identical except for their coloring. Warhol's own celebrity was assured by his 1968 prediction that "In the future, everyone will be world-famous for fifteen minutes."

Suggestions for Discussion

1. Warhol's "Brillo Boxes" is considered to be a milestone in American art and even in the history of art itself. Research the Pop Art phenomenon. What claim do banal objects like Brillo pads have to being considered pieces of art? Have an informed discussion over your findings.

2. How does the "quoting" of Warhol's "Brillo Boxes" and the painting over by another image alien to the original (here the flying swan) alter the original and the story happening with the image?

Suggestions for Writing

1. Write the lyrics to a song based on these images. Be imaginative.

2. If a soap pad can be considered "found art," then should a person be able to lift language from random text, such as the Yellow Pages, and present it as "found literature"? Create your own original piece of "found text." Bring your text to class, along with a brief written explanation of what inspired you to highlight this particular text. What is literary about it? How does the new context you've put the words in make it art? How did you transform it?

B A N K S Y

Untitled
Graffiti art/stencil

The political activist and street artist Banksy was probably born in Bristol, England, in 1974 or 1975 but keeps his identity anonymous. Most of his graffiti are found in London, but Banksy "works" all over Europe and beyond. His chosen topics include politics, ethics, and culture. His stencils are just as skillful as they are thoughtful and witty. His "public interventions" are oftentimes considered illegal. Banksy does not work for any monetary profit and is not represented by any commercial art gallery. Nevertheless, his work has gained substantial respect within the international art scene and photographic reproductions have been shown in numerous galleries. On several occasions he has sneaked some of his work into well-known art museums including London's Tate Gallery and the Museum of Modern Art in New York, where he has placed his works among other works of art on display—in a sense, an "art robbery" in reverse.

Suggestions for Discussion

1. Examine the image sprayed onto the West Bank Barrier in Bethlehem, a wall designed to keep Israelis and Palestinians apart from each other. Does this image surprise you in any way? How so? What makes it unusual? What story is this graffiti trying to tell?

2. What effect does the "role-reversal" have? Why do you think a little Caucasian girl in a pink dress is featured rather than a more stereotypical figure normally associated with an enemy combatant?

3. How is this art "political"? What commentary is it making on war? Power? Crime? Security? Imperialism? Mass media?

4. Read the essays included in the Notebook of the *Globalism, Nationalism, and Cultural Identity* section. How does Banksy's work fit into the broader conversation about war that is taking place in those pieces?

Suggestions for Writing

1. Banksy's graffiti could be seen as an intervention into public space, or as an act of beautification, protest, political activism. It could be seen as an act of self-expression or moral obligation, or simply as vandalism. Is it art or graffiti? Is graffiti art? Support your argument through research.

2. With the essays included in the Notebook of the *Globalism, Nationalism, and Cultural Identity* in mind, compose a critical newspaper commentary on the role of mass media as "weapons of mass distraction."

SCOTT McCLOUD

The Language of Comics

Artist, literary theorist, and cultural critic Scott McCloud (b. 1960) has written the definitive critical treatments of the comic book as an art form, *Understanding Comics* (1993) and *Reinventing Comics* (2000). A lifelong comic book enthusiast, the Boston native created the intellectual super-hero comic *Zot!* (1984), and contributed stories to *Superman: Adventures of the Man of Steel* during the mid-1990s. He has also contributed articles to *Wired, Computer Gaming World, Wizard,* and *Publishers' Weekly.* In addition to being highly regarded by comic book fans, McCloud ranks with Art Spiegelman, Will Eisner, Alan Moore, and Marjane Satrapi as one of the few graphic novelists whose work is respected in the academe.

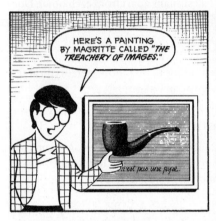

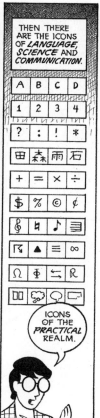

WHY-- --ARE-- --WE-- --SO-- --INVOLVED?

WHY WOULD *ANYONE,* YOUNG OR OLD, RESPOND TO A CARTOON AS MUCH OR MORE THAN A *REALISTIC IMAGE?*

WHY IS OUR CULTURE *SO IN THRALL* TO THE *SIMPLIFIED REALITY* OF THE *CARTOON?*

DEFINING THE CARTOON WOULD TAKE UP AS MUCH SPACE AS DEFINING *COMICS,* BUT FOR *NOW,* I'M GOING TO EXAMINE CARTOONING AS A FORM OF *AMPLIFICATION THROUGH SIMPLIFICATION.*

WHEN WE *ABSTRACT* AN IMAGE THROUGH *CARTOONING,* WE'RE NOT SO MUCH *ELIMINATING* DETAILS AS WE ARE *FOCUSING* ON *SPECIFIC DETAILS.*

BY *STRIPPING DOWN* AN IMAGE TO ITS ESSENTIAL *"MEANING,"* AN ARTIST CAN *AMPLIFY* THAT MEANING IN A WAY THAT REALISTIC ART *CAN'T.*

FILM CRITICS WILL SOMETIMES DESCRIBE A *LIVE-ACTION* FILM AS A "CARTOON" TO ACKNOWLEDGE THE STRIPPED-DOWN *INTENSITY* OF A SIMPLE STORY OR VISUAL STYLE.

THOUGH THE TERM IS OFTEN USED *DISPARAGINGLY,* IT CAN BE EQUALLY WELL APPLIED TO MANY *TIME-TESTED CLASSICS.* SIMPLIFYING CHARACTERS AND IMAGES TOWARD A *PURPOSE* CAN BE AN EFFECTIVE TOOL FOR STORYTELLING IN *ANY* MEDIUM.

CARTOONING ISN'T JUST A WAY OF *DRAWING,* IT'S A WAY OF *SEEING!*

FOLLOW! FOLLOW!

THE ABILITY OF CARTOONS TO *FOCUS* OUR ATTENTION ON AN IDEA IS, I THINK, AN IMPORTANT PART OF THEIR SPECIAL POWER, BOTH IN COMICS AND IN DRAWING GENERALLY.

ONE | A FEW | THOUSANDS | MILLIONS | (NEARLY) ALL

ANOTHER IS THE *UNIVERSALITY* OF CARTOON IMAGERY. THE MORE CARTOONY A FACE IS, FOR INSTANCE, THE MORE PEOPLE IT COULD BE SAID TO *DESCRIBE.*

BUT I BELIEVE THERE'S SOMETHING *MORE* AT WORK IN OUR MINDS WHEN WE VIEW A CARTOON--ESPECIALLY OF A HUMAN FACE--WHICH WARRANTS FURTHER INVESTIGATION.

WHAT

ARE YOU

REALLY

SEEING?

THE FACT THAT YOUR MIND IS *CAPABLE* OF TAKING A *CIRCLE,* TWO DOTS AND A *LINE* AND TURNING THEM INTO A *FACE* IS NOTHING SHORT OF *INCREDIBLE!*

BUT STILL *MORE* INCREDIBLE IS THE FACT THAT YOU CANNOT *AVOID* SEEING A FACE HERE. YOUR MIND WON'T *LET* YOU!

ASK A FRIEND TO DRAW YOU SOME SHAPES ON A PIECE OF PAPER. THEY SHOULD BE *CLOSED CURVES*, BUT *OTHERWISE* CAN BE AS *WEIRD* AND *IRREGULAR* AS HE OR SHE *WANTS*.

LET'S SAY THE RESULTS LOOK SOMETHING LIKE *THIS*.

NOW -- YOU'LL FIND THAT NO MATTER WHAT THEY *LOOK* LIKE, EVERY SINGLE *ONE* OF THOSE SHAPES *CAN* BE MADE INTO A FACE WITH ONE SIMPLE ADDITION.

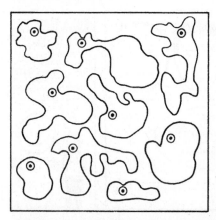

YOUR MIND HAS NO TROUBLE AT ALL CONVERTING SUCH SHAPES INTO FACES, YET WOULD IT EVER MISTAKE *THIS*--

--FOR *THIS?*

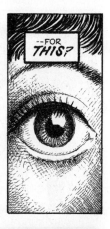

WE HUMANS ARE A SELF-CENTERED RACE.

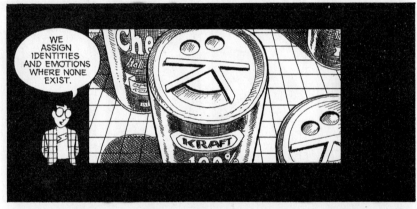

EACH ONE *ALSO* SUSTAINS A CONSTANT AWARENESS OF HIS OR HER *OWN* FACE, BUT *THIS* MIND-PICTURE IS NOT NEARLY SO VIVID; JUST A SKETCHY ARRANGEMENT... A SENSE OF SHAPE... A SENSE OF *GENERAL PLACEMENT.*

SOMETHING AS *SIMPLE* AND AS *BASIC*--

--AS A *CARTOON.*

THUS, WHEN YOU LOOK AT A PHOTO OR REALISTIC DRAWING OF A FACE--

--YOU SEE IT AS THE FACE OF *ANOTHER.*

BUT WHEN YOU ENTER THE WORLD OF THE *CARTOON*--

-- YOU SEE *YOURSELF.*

I BELIEVE THIS IS THE *PRIMARY CAUSE* OF OUR CHILDHOOD FASCINATION WITH *CARTOONS,* THOUGH OTHER FACTORS SUCH AS *UNIVERSAL IDENTIFICATION, SIMPLICITY* AND THE *CHILDLIKE FEATURES* OF MANY CARTOON CHARACTERS ALSO PLAY A PART.

THE CARTOON IS A *VACUUM* INTO WHICH OUR *IDENTITY* AND *AWARENESS* ARE *PULLED...*

...AN *EMPTY SHELL* THAT WE INHABIT WHICH *ENABLES* US TO TRAVEL IN *ANOTHER REALM.*

WE DON'T JUST *OBSERVE* THE CARTOON, WE *BECOME* IT!

THAT'S WHY I DECIDED TO *DRAW* MYSELF IN SUCH A SIMPLE *STYLE.*

WOULD YOU HAVE *LISTENED* TO ME IF I LOOKED LIKE *THIS*??

Suggestions for Discussion

1. Why does McCloud believe that we relate more strongly to cartoon characters and smiley faces than realistic characters and detailed portraits?

2. Consider the current popularity of cartoons like *The Simpsons* and *Family Guy* and the boom of superhero-themed movies and television shows. Do you think that this essay provides part of the explanation for their popularity? Why or why not?

3. Magritte's painting expresses the famous sentiment "This is not a pipe." Argue for and against viewing the object as a pipe.

4. How does McCloud use the terms *icons*, *symbols*, and *pictures*? How do his definitions of these terms help him make his argument? Could he have just as easily defined these terms in a different way? Would you? Explain.

Suggestions for Writing

1. Consider the artwork in *The Conscious Reader*. Is McCloud correct in his assertion that viewers are more apt to relate to "cartoony" art than realistic art? Consider the more detailed pictures. The gritty and realistic ones. The ones that anger, confuse, or alienate you. What is the virtue of contemplating such difficult pictures? How might it be a more rewarding (emotional, intellectual, and artistic) experience challenging yourself by confronting an "other" figure than merely enjoying looking at a cartoon that reminds you of yourself? Write a journal entry in which you consider these ideas.

2. Compare this treatment of the visual arts to the essay, "It Is and It Isn't: Stereotype, Advertising, and Narrative." Write an essay in which you synthesize the two theses into a broader whole that incorporates ideas from both works.

3. How do McCloud's observations help us understand the hypnotic power of advertising? How can we best resist the pull to be a compulsive consumer?

E. M. F O R S T E R

Art for Art's Sake

Edward Morgan Forster (1879–1970) was a British novelist educated at King's College, Cambridge. He lived for a time in Italy, was a member of the Bloomsbury Group of writers and artists in London, and spent the major part of his life in Cambridge. His works include *Where Angels Fear to Tread* (1905), *A Room with a View* (1908), and *A Passage to India* (1924). In this essay from *Two Cheers for Democracy* (1951), Forster explains the importance of art as a source of comfort and order in a troubled society.

I believe in art for art's sake. It is an unfashionable belief, and some of my statements must be of the nature of an apology. Sixty years ago I should have faced you with more confidence. A writer or a speaker who chose "Art for Art's Sake" for his theme sixty years ago could be sure of being in the swim, and could feel so confident of success that he sometimes dressed himself in aesthetic costumes suitable to the occasion—in an embroidered dressing-gown, perhaps, or a blue velvet suit with a Lord Fauntleroy collar; or a toga, or a kimono, and carried a poppy or a lily or a long peacock's feather in his mediaeval hand. Times have changed. Not thus can I present either myself or my theme today. My aim rather is to ask you quietly to reconsider for a few minutes a phrase which has been much misused and much abused, but which has, I believe, great importance for us—has, indeed, eternal importance.

Now we can easily dismiss those peacock's feathers and other affectations—they are but trifles—but I want also to dismiss a more dangerous heresy, namely the silly idea that only art matters, an idea which has somehow got mixed up with the idea of art for art's sake, and has helped to discredit it. Many things besides art matter. It is merely one of the things that matter, and high though the claims are that I make for it, I want to keep them in proportion. No one can spend his or her life entirely in the creation or the appreciation of masterpieces. Man lives, and ought to live, in a complex world, full of conflicting claims, and if we simplified them down into the aesthetic he would be sterilised. Art for art's sake does not mean that only art matters and I would also like to rule out such phrases as, "The Life of Art," "Living for Art," and "Art's High Mission." They confuse and mislead.

What does the phrase mean? Instead of generalising, let us take a specific instance—Shakespeare's *Macbeth*, for example, and pronounce the words, "*Macbeth* for *Macbeth*'s sake." What does that mean? Well, the play has several aspects—it is educational, it teaches us something about legendary Scotland, something about Jacobean England, and a good deal about human nature and its perils. We can study its origins, and study and enjoy its dramatic technique and the music of its diction. All that is true. But *Macbeth* is furthermore a world of its own, created by Shakespeare and existing in virtue of its own poetry. It is in this aspect *Macbeth* for *Macbeth*'s sake, and that is what I intend by the phrase "art for art's sake." A work of art—whatever else it may be—is a self-contained entity, with a life of its own imposed on it by its creator. It has internal order. It may have external form. That is how we recognise it.

Take for another example that picture of Seurat's which I saw two years ago in Chicago—"*La Grande Jatte*." Here again there is much to study and to enjoy: the pointillism, the charming face of the seated girl, the nineteenth-century Parisian Sunday sunlight, the sense of motion in immobility. But here again there is something more; "*La Grande Jatte*" forms a world of its own, created by Seurat and existing by virtue of its own poetry: "*La Grande Jatte*" pour "*La Grande Jatte*": *l'art pour l'art*. Like *Macbeth* it has internal order and internal life.

It is to the conception of order that I would now turn. This is important to my argument, and I want to make a digression, and glance at order in daily life, before I come to order in art.

In the world of daily life, the world which we perforce inhabit, there is much talk about order, particularly from statesmen and politicians. They tend, however, to confuse order with orders, just as they confuse creation with regulations. Order, I suggest, is something evolved from within, not something imposed from without; it is an internal stability, a vital harmony, and in the social and political category, it has never existed except for the convenience of historians. Viewed realistically, the past is really a series of *dis*orders, succeeding one another by discoverable laws, no doubt, and certainly marked by an increasing growth of human interference, but disorders all the same. So that, speaking as a writer, what I hope for today is a disorder which will be more favourable to artists than is the present one, and which will provide them with fuller inspirations and better material conditions. It will not last—nothing lasts—but there have been some advantageous disorders in the past—for instance, in ancient Athens, in Renaissance Italy, eighteenth-century France, periods in China and Persia—and we may do something to accelerate the next one. But let us not again fix our hearts where true joys are not to be found. We were promised a new order after the first world war through the League of Nations. It did not come, nor have I faith in present promises, by whomsoever endorsed. The implacable offensive of Science forbids. We cannot reach social and political stability for the reason that we continue to make scientific discoveries and to apply them, and thus to destroy the arrangements which were based on more elementary discoveries. If Science would discover rather than apply—if, in other words, men were more interested in knowledge than in power—mankind would be in a far safer position, the stability statesmen talk about would be a possibility, there could be a new order based on vital harmony, and the earthly millennium might approach. But Science shows no signs of doing this: she gave us the internal combustion engine, and before we had digested and assimilated it with terrible pains into our social system, she harnessed the atom, and destroyed any new order that seemed to be evolving. How can man get into harmony with his surroundings when he is constantly altering them? The future of our race is, in this direction, more unpleasant than we care to admit, and it has sometimes seemed to me that its best chance lies through apathy, uninventiveness, and inertia. Universal exhaustion might promote that Change of Heart which is at present so briskly recommended from a thousand pulpits. Universal exhaustion would certainly be a new experience. The human race has never undergone it, and is still too perky to admit that it may be coming and might result in a sprouting of new growth through the decay.

I must not pursue these speculations any further—they lead me too far from my terms of reference and maybe from yours. But I do want to emphasize that order in daily life and in history, order in the social and political category, is unattainable under our present psychology.

Where is it attainable? Not in the astronomical category, where it was for many years enthroned. The heavens and the earth have become terribly alike since Einstein. No longer can we find a reassuring contrast to chaos in the night sky and look up with George Meredith to the stars, the army of unalterable law, or listen for the music of the spheres. Order is not there. In the entire universe there seem to be only two possibilities for it. The first of them—which again lies outside my terms of reference—is the divine order, the mystic harmony, which according to all religions is available for those who can contemplate it. We much admit its possibility, on the evidence of the adepts, and we must believe them when they say that it is attained, if attainable, by prayer. "O thou who changest not, abide with me," said one of its poets. "*Ordina questo amor, o tu che m'ami,*" said another: "Set love in order thou who lovest me." The existence of a divine order, though it cannot be tested, has never been disproved.

The second possibility for order lies in the aesthetic category, which is my subject here: the order which an artist can create in his own work, and to that we must now return. A work of art, we are all agreed, is a unique product. But why? It is unique not because it is clever or noble or beautiful or enlightened or original or sincere or idealistic or useful or educational—it may embody any of those qualities—but because it is the only material object in the universe which may possess internal harmony. All the others have been pressed into shape from outside, and when their mold is removed they collapse. The work of art stands up by itself, and nothing else does. It achieves something which has often been promised by society, but always delusively. Ancient Athens made a mess—but the *Antigone* stands up. Renaissance Rome made a mess—but the ceiling of the Sistine got painted. James I made a mess—but there was *Macbeth*. Louis XIV—but there was *Phedre*. Art for art's sake? I should just think so, and more so than ever at the present time. It is the one orderly product which our muddling race has produced. It is the cry of a thousand sentinels, the echo from a thousand labyrinths; it is the lighthouse which cannot be hidden: *c'est le meilleur témoignage que nous puissions donner de notre dignité. Antigone* for *Antigone*'s sake, *Macbeth* for *Macbeth*'s, "*La Grande Jatte*" *pour* "*La Grande Jatte.*"

If this line of argument is correct, it follows that the artist will tend to be an outsider in the society to which he has been born, and that the nineteenth century conception of him as a Bohemian was not inaccurate. The conception erred in three particulars: it postulated an economic system where art could be a full-time job, it introduced the fallacy that only art matters, and it overstressed idiosyncracy and waywardness—the peacock-feather aspect—rather than order. But it is a truer conception than the one which prevails in official circles on my side of the Atlantic—I don't know about yours: the conception which treats the artist as if he were a particularly bright government advertiser and encourages him to be friendly and matey with his fellow citizens, and not to give himself airs.

Estimable is mateyness, and the man who achieves it gives many a pleasant little drink to himself and to others. But it has no traceable connection with the creative impulse, and probably acts as an inhibition on it. The artist who is seduced by mateyness may stop himself from doing the one thing which he, and he alone, can do—the making of something out of words or sounds or paint or clay or marble or steel or film which has internal harmony and presents order to a permanently disarranged planet. This seems worth doing, even at the risk of being called uppish by journalists. I have in mind an article which was published some years ago in the London *Times*, an article called "The Eclipse of the Highbrow," in which the "Average Man" was exalted, and all contemporary literature was censured if it did not toe the line, the precise position of the line being naturally known to the writer of the article. Sir Kenneth Clark, who was at that time director of our National Gallery, commented on this pernicious doctrine in a letter which cannot be too often quoted. "The poet and the artist," wrote Clark, "are important precisely because they are not average men; because in sensibility, intelligence, and power of invention they far exceed the average." These memorable words, and particularly the words "power of invention," are the Bohemian's passport. Furnished with it, he slinks about society, saluted now by a brickbat and now by a penny, and accepting either of them with equanimity. He does not consider too anxiously what his relations with society may be, for he is aware of something more important than that—namely the invitation to invent, to create order, and he believes he will be better placed for doing this if he attempts detachment. So round and round he slouches, with his hat pulled over his eyes, and maybe with a louse in his beard, and—if he really wants one—a peacock's feather in his hand.

If our present society should disintegrate—and who dare prophesy that it won't?—this old-fashioned and démodé figure will become clearer: the Bohemian, the outsider, the parasite, the rat—one of those figures which have at present no function either in a warring or a peaceful world. It may not be dignified to be a rat, but many of the ships are sinking, which is not dignified either—the officials did not build them properly. Myself, I would sooner be a swimming rat than a sinking ship—at all events I can look around me for a little longer—and I remember how one of us, a rat with particularly bright eyes called Shelley, squeaked out, "Poets are the unacknowledged legislators of the world," before he vanished into the waters of the Mediterranean.

What laws did Shelley propose to pass? None. The legislation of the artist is never formulated at the time, though it is sometimes discerned by future generations. He legislates through creating. And he creates through his sensitiveness and power to impose form. Without form the sensitiveness vanishes. And form is as important today, when the human race is trying to ride the whirlwind, as it ever was in those less agitating days of the past, when the earth seemed solid and the stars fixed, and the discoveries of science were made slowly, slowly. Form is not tradition. It alters from generation to generation. Artists always seek a new technique, and will continue to do so as long as their work excites them. But form of some kind is imperative. It is the surface crust of the internal harmony, it is the outward evidence of order.

My remarks about society may have seemed too pessimistic, but I believe that society can only represent a fragment of the human spirit, and that another fragment can only get expressed through art. And I wanted to take this opportunity, this vantage ground, to assert not only the existence of art, but its pertinacity. Looking back into the past, it seems to me that that is all there has ever been: vantage grounds for discussion and creation, little vantage grounds in the changing chaos, where bubbles have been blown and webs spun, and the desire to create order has found temporary gratification, and the sentinels have managed to utter their challenges, and the huntsmen, though lost individually, have heard each other's calls through the impenetrable wood, and the lighthouses have never ceased sweeping the thankless seas. In this pertinacity there seems to me, as I grow older, something more and more profound, something which does in fact concern people who do not care about art at all.

In conclusion, let me summarise the various categories that have laid claim to the possession of Order.

1. The social and political category. Claim disallowed on the evidence of history and of our own experience. If man altered psychologically, order here might be attainable: not otherwise.
2. The astronomical category. Claim allowed up to the present century, but now disallowed on the evidence of the physicists.
3. The religious category. Claim allowed on the evidence of the mystics.
4. The aesthetic category. Claim allowed on the evidence of various works of art, and on the evidence of our own creative impulses, however weak these may be or however imperfectly they may function. Works of art, in my opinion, are the only objects in the material universe to possess internal order, and that is why, though I don't believe that only art matters, I do believe in Art for Art's Sake.

Suggestions for Discussion

1. Why does Forster make clear that the belief in art for art's sake does not mean a belief that only art matters?
2. Where does art stand, for Forster, in the list of things that matter?
3. Explain Forster's phrase, "*Macbeth* for *Macbeth*'s sake." How does he use it to explain his main argument?

4. Explain Forster's comparison of the order of art with order in life. How does this comparison function in his argument?

5. What does Forster mean by claiming that a work of art is a unique product?

6. Examine Forster's categories that have laid claim to the possession of order. Why does he reject all but the religious and aesthetic categories?

Suggestions for Writing

1. Write a paper explaining Forster's defense of art.

2. Obviously, many people feel differently from Forster about the autonomy of art. In Marxist countries, for example, art is often considered to be a servant of the state. Write a paper in which you argue for or against Forster's position.

SUSAN SONTAG

Regarding the Pain of Others

Social commentator, author, and director Susan Sontag (1933–2004) is best known for writing incisive philosophical examinations of contemporary issues. The native New Yorker earned M.A.s in English literature and philosophy from Harvard University in 1954 and 1955 and published her first novel, *The Benefactor*, in 1963. Other works include *Against Interpretation* (1966), *On Photography* (1977), *Illness as Metaphor* (1978), *AIDS and Its Metaphors* (1988), and *In America* (2002), winner of the National Book Award. Sontag won the Montblanc de la Culture Award for her humanitarian efforts in Sarajevo and was listed as one of *Life* magazine's "Women Who Shook the World." The following reflections are drawn from *Regarding the Pain of Others* (2003).

One can feel obliged to look at photographs that record great cruelties and crimes. One should feel obliged to think about what it means to look at them, about the capacity actually to assimilate what they show. Not all reactions to these pictures are under the supervision of reason and conscience. Most depictions of tormented, mutilated bodies do arouse a prurient interest. (*The Disasters of War* is notably an exception: Goya's images cannot be looked at in a spirit of prurience. They don't dwell on the beauty of the human body; bodies are heavy, and thickly clothed.) All images that display the violation of an attractive body are to a certain degree, pornographic. But images of the repulsive can also allure. Everyone knows that what slows down highway traffic going past a horrendous car crash is not only curiosity. It is also, for many, the wish to see something gruesome. Calling such wishes "morbid" suggests a rare aberration, but the attraction to such sights is not rare, and is a perennial source of inner torment.

Indeed, the very first acknowledgment (as far as I am aware) of the attraction of mutilated bodies occurs in a founding description of mental conflict. It is a passage in *The Republic*, Book IV, where Plato's Socrates describes how our reason may be overwhelmed by an unworthy desire, which drives the self to become angry with a part of its nature. Plato has been developing a tripartite theory of mental function, consisting of reason, anger or indignation, and appetite or desire—anticipating the Freudian schema of superego, ego, and id (with the difference that Plato puts reason on top and conscience, represented by indignation, in the middle). In the course of this argument, to illustrate how one may yield, even if reluctantly, to repulsive attractions, Socrates relates a story he heard about Leontius, son of Aglaion:

> On his way up from the Piraeus outside the north wall, he noticed the bodies of some criminals lying on the ground, with the executioner standing by them. He wanted to go and look at them, but at the same time he was disgusted and tried to turn away. He struggled for some time and covered his eyes, but at last the desire was too much for him. Opening his eyes wide, he ran up to the bodies and cried, "There you are, curse you, feast yourselves on this lovely sight."

Declining to choose the more common example of an inappropriate or unlawful sexual passion as his illustration of the struggle between reason and desire, Plato appears to take for granted that we also have an appetite for sights of degradation and pain and mutilation.

Surely the undertow of this despised impulse must also be taken into account when discussing the effect of atrocity pictures.

At the beginning of modernity, it may have been easier to acknowledge that there exists an innate tropism toward the gruesome. Edmund Burke observed that people like to look at images of suffering. "I am convinced we have a degree of delight, and that no small one, in the real misfortunes and pains of others," he wrote in *A Philosophical Enquiry into the Origin of Our Ideas of the Sublime and Beautiful* (1757). "There is no spectacle we so eagerly pursue, as that of some uncommon and grievous calamity." William Hazlitt, in his essay on Shakespeare's Iago and the attraction of villainy on the stage, asks, "Why do we always read the accounts in the newspapers of dreadful fires and shocking murders?" Because, he answers, "love of mischief," love of cruelty, is as natural to human beings as is sympathy.

One of the great theorists of the erotic, Georges Bataille, kept a photograph taken in China in 1910 of a prisoner undergoing "the death of a hundred cuts" on his desk, where he could look at it every day. (Since become legendary, it is reproduced in the last of Bataille's books published during his lifetime, in 1961, *The Tears of Eros*.) "This photograph," Bataille wrote, "had a decisive role in my life. I have never stopped being obsessed by this image of pain, at the same time ecstatic and intolerable." To contemplate this image, according to Bataille, is both a mortification of the feelings and a liberation of tabooed erotic knowledge—a complex response that many people must find hard to credit. For most, the image is simply unbearable: the already armless sacrificial victim of several busy knives, in the terminal stage of being flayed—a photograph, not a painting; a real Marsyas, not a mythic one—and still alive in the picture, with a look on his upturned face as ecstatic as that of any Italian Renaissance Saint Sebastian. As objects of contemplation, images of the atrocious can answer to several different needs. To steel oneself against weakness. To make oneself more numb. To acknowledge the existence of the incorrigible.

Bataille is not saying that he takes pleasure at the sight of this excruciation. But he is saying that he can imagine extreme suffering as something more than just suffering, as a kind of transfiguration. It is a view of suffering, of the pain of others, that is rooted in religious thinking, which links pain to sacrifice, sacrifice to exaltation—a view that could not be more alien to a modern sensibility, which regards suffering as something that is a mistake or an accident or a crime. Something to be fixed. Something to be refused. Something that makes one feel powerless.

What to do with such knowledge as photographs bring of faraway suffering? People are often unable to take in the sufferings of those close to them. (A compelling document on this theme is Frederick Wiseman's film *Hospital*.) For all the voyeuristic lure—and the possible satisfaction of knowing, This is not happening to *me*, I'm not ill, I'm not dying, I'm not trapped in a war—it seems normal for people to fend off thinking about the ordeals of others, even others with whom it would be easy to identify.

A citizen of Sarajevo, a woman of impeccable adherence to the Yugoslav ideal, whom I met soon after arriving in the city the first time in April 1993, told me: "In October 1991 I was here in my nice apartment in peaceful Sarajevo when the Serbs invaded Croatia, and I remember when the evening news showed footage of the destruction of Vukovar, just a couple of hundred miles away, I thought to myself, 'Oh, how horrible,' and switched the channel. So how can I be indignant if someone in France or Italy or Germany sees the killing taking place here day after day on their evening news and says, 'Oh, how horrible,' and looks for another program. It's normal. It's human." Wherever people feel safe—this was her bitter, self-accusing point—they will be indifferent. But surely a Sarajevan might have another motive for shunning images of terrible events taking place in what was then, after all, another part of her own country than did those abroad who were turning their backs on Sarajevo. The dereliction of the foreigners, to whom she was so charitable, was also a consequence of the feeling that nothing could be done. Her unwillingness to engage with these premonitory images of nearby war was an expression of helplessness and fear.

People can turn off not just because a steady diet of images of violence has made them indifferent but because they are afraid. As everyone has observed, there is a mounting level of acceptable violence and sadism in mass culture: films, television, comics, computer games. Imagery that would have had an audience cringing and recoiling in disgust forty years ago is watched without so much as a blink by every teenager in the multiplex. Indeed, mayhem is entertaining rather than shocking to many people in most modern cultures. But not all violence is watched with equal detachment. Some disasters are more apt subjects of irony than others.*

It is because, say, the war in Bosnia didn't stop, because leaders claimed it was an intractable situation, that people abroad may have switched off the terrible images. It is because a war, any war, doesn't seem as if it can be stopped that people become less responsive to the horrors. Compassion is an unstable emotion. It needs to be translated into action, or it withers. The question is what to do with the feelings that have been aroused, the knowledge that has been communicated. If one feels that there is nothing "we" can do—but who is that "we"?—and nothing "they" can do either—and who are "they"?—then one starts to get bored, cynical, apathetic.

And it is not necessarily better to be moved. Sentimentality, notoriously, is entirely compatible with a taste for brutality and worse. (Recall the canonical example of the Auschwitz commandant returning home in the evening, embracing his wife and children, and sitting at the piano to play some Schubert before dinner.) People don't become inured to what they are shown— if that's the right way to describe what happens—because of the *quantity* of images dumped on them. It is passivity that dulls feeling. The states described as apathy, moral or emotional anesthesia, are full of feelings; the feelings are rage and frustration. But if we consider what emotions would be desirable,

---

*Tellingly, that connoisseur of death and high priest of the delights of apathy, Andy Warhol, was drawn to news reports of a variety of violent deaths (car and plane crashes, suicides, executions). But his silk-screened transcriptions excluded death in war. A news photo of an electric chair and a tabloid's screaming from page, "129 Die in Jet," yes. "Hanoi Bombed," no. The only phototgraph Warhol silk-screened that refers to the violence of war is one that had become iconoic; that is, a cliché: the mushroom cloud of an atomic bomb, repeated as on a sheet of postage stamps (like the faces of Marilyn, Jackie, Mao) to illustrate its opaqueness, it fascination, its banality.

it seems too simple to elect sympathy. The imaginary proximity to the suffering inflicted on others that is granted by images suggests a link between the faraway sufferers—seen close-up on the television screen—and the privileged viewer that is simply untrue, that is yet one more mystification of our real relations to power. So far as we feel sympathy, we feel we are not accomplices to what caused the suffering. Our sympathy proclaims our innocence as well as our impotence. To that extent, it can be (for all our good intentions) an impertinent—if not an inappropriate—response. To set aside the sympathy we extend to others beset by war and murderous politics for a reflection on how our privileges are located on the same map as their suffering, and may—in ways we might prefer not to imagine—be linked to their suffering, as the wealth of some may imply the destitution of others, is a task for which the painful, stirring images supply only an initial spark.

Suggestions for Discussion

1. Discuss your response to a gruesome scene depicted on television. Why was your curiosity raised? Analyze your responses to the event and the coverage.

2. Discuss Sontag's assertion that passivity dulls feeling.

Suggestions for Writing

1. Consider Edmund Burke's observation that we "have a degree of delight . . . in the real misfortunes and pains of others."

2. What does Sontag mean when she writes that compassion "needs to be translated into action, or it withers"?

DAVID WALL

It Is and It Isn't: Stereotype, Advertising, and Narrative

British born art historian and visual culture scholar David Wall is the director of the Cultural Studies Program at the Batley School of Art and Design (UK). After completing an M.A. in American Studies at Nottingham, Wall studied abroad in the United States, and earned a Ph.D. in American Culture Studies from Bowling Green State University, Ohio. A specialist in nineteenth- and twentieth-century American culture, his doctoral thesis was entitled *Subject to Disorder: Carnival and the Grotesque Body in Antebellum Literature and Culture.* He returned to Great Britain in 2002 and has contributed cultural studies articles to several academic journals. The following essay was originally published in *The Journal of Popular Culture*, Vol. 41, Issue 6, in 2008.

In the run-up to the 2005 general election in Britain controversy was generated over a Labour party election poster featuring the Conservative politicians Michael Howard and Oliver Letwin (both of whom are Jewish) portrayed as flying pigs (Figure 1). Broadly speaking there were two (somewhat predictable) responses. The Labour party's ad team (headed by Trevor Beattie of the infamous FCUK campaign) argued that the poster was clearly and explicitly designed only to link the phrase "when pigs fly" with the likelihood of the Conservatives being able to produce some kind of convincing economic strategy. Critics of the poster said that as both Howard and Letwin are Jewish, to portray them as pigs is at best insulting and at worst anti-Semitic.

This controversy occurred at a moment when issues of race and racism were once again firmly in the center of the British social and political landscape. Over the previous couple of years explicitly anti-immigration parties such as the British Nationalist Party (BNP) and United Kingdom Independence Party (UKIP), with the routine and regular assistance of some sections of the tabloid press, made significant inroads into popular consciousness if not government. Black English football players were racially abused while playing in a "friendly" against the Spanish national team (whose coach had earlier referred to the Arsenal player Thierry Henry as "a black shit"); TV pundit Ron Atkinson, thinking his microphone was turned off, called the French football star Marcel Desailly "a fucking lazy nigger" live on air; and in the

FIGURE 1. LABOUR PARTY CAMPAIGN POSTER FOR 2005 BRITISH GENERAL ELECTION.

weeks leading up to the general election, both major parties scurried shame-fully to demonstrate their "robustness" on immigration and asylum seeking.

Nevertheless, I think we can safely assume that Labour as a party had no deliberate or overt anti-Semitic agenda. Consequently this means that their policy makers—at all levels—were guilty of either an appalling lack of sensitivity or an appalling ignorance of history (or perhaps both). For while it is obvious that the poster is just a visual gag employing a well-known (if not clapped out and clichéd) idiomatic expression it is also, at the same time, an image that ties in to profoundly anti-Semitic discourses that have been articulated throughout European culture for nearly two thousand years. It seems almost inconceivable that as the poster was going through its various committees and boardrooms and onto mock-up stages and final approvals no one made the connection. Or maybe the connection was made. Perhaps the questions were asked and then dismissed. But while these are interest-ing considerations the significance of the event lies less in the specifics of that process than in what it reveals about the ubiquitous presence and suc-cess of stereotypes within the visual media.

Part of the powerful dynamic of the visual image—especially within the context of advertising and political campaigning—is its amenability to mul-tivalent readings. In the 1970s and 1980s Maidenform ran a series of adver-tisements, which saw their models in a variety of traditionally male-oriented scenarios such as arriving on a Manhattan heliport or standing among a group of downtown businessmen. Regardless of their location, however, the women wore nothing other than an open overcoat and their Maidenform lingerie. Steeped as they are in the fantasies of post-1970s women's lib and 1980s Gecko-finance madness, there seem to be two possible, though con-tradictory, ways of reading these advertisements. On the one hand these young women have broken free of the bounds of convention and succeeded in the male-dominated environment of corporate business. They embody power, wealth, ruthlessness, and determination, all traditionally wholly mas-culine characteristics. At the same time, dressed only in their flimsy lingerie, they are clearly just "bits of fluff" on sexual display for the pleasure and pleasing of men. The first reading turns traditional lumpen sexism on its head; the second reading simply reinforces it. A third reading might suggest a more nuanced articulation of sexual politics in which the predictability and mundanity of male desire is appropriated in order to subvert the social and ideological structures that are designed to shape those male fantasies of sex and power in the first place.

Avoiding the kind of simplistic binary reading whereby an image must mean either one thing or another we can see immediately that there is not necessarily a "right" reading of the Maidenform image. Images can and do mean many things and often all at the same time. Equally often, responses to an image such as this can potentially be affected by any number of contingent social and personal factors such as gender, race, age, or nationality. However, this is not to imply that any particular subject-position gives an *a priori* greater insight into understanding an image or indeed that all interpretations of any particular image are equally valid. Meaning can only be generated within the cultural and historical contexts that serve as our surrounding sense-making structures. So, while there are multiple ways of analyzing and assessing the Maidenform ad, there are clearly limits to the number of possible readings. It makes sense, for example, to read this ad in terms of its use of sexuality within the context of a culture that routinely portrays women as sexual objects for consumption by men. It would not make any sense to read it as a warning of impending alien invasion.

So, does it make sense that considering the historical context of European anti-Semitism the Labour election poster could upset, offend, and—albeit unintentionally—*function* as a piece of anti-Semitic propaganda? Would not that be one valid reading of that particular visual text? That it was intended *only* as a joke does not undermine this reading but in fact serves to underline the multivalent flexibility of the image. And, intentional or not, the "animalizing" of Howard and Letwin is part of a continuum of anti-Semitic propaganda in which Jews have been represented for centuries as verminous and unclean.

The popular drama series *24* came in for similar criticisms over its portrayal of terrorists as Muslim extremists. Apologists for the show have rooted their defense in the twofold argument that firstly while not all Muslims are terrorists, the vast majority of contemporary terrorists are Muslims and secondly *24* is a fiction and therefore "not real." Putting to one side the problematic notion of defining the term "terrorist," we are confronted here by an argument that seems to justify itself—at one and the same time—by holding two completely opposing positions: that the program is both "real" (most terrorists *are* Muslims) and "unreal" (it is *just* a story).

Whether the first point is statistically supportable is of no consequence. The significance here lies in the implications and importance of the relationship between the two arguments. A show like *24*, while dealing in realism is not dealing in reality and would rightly make no claims to documentary. But realism as a narrative visual form has always had a "claim to reality" because it so looks like the world we recognize. So while realism is merely a rhetorical or narrative technique there is an implicit claim to objectivity in the form of its representation. Hence, *24*'s realism gives the show a powerful and compelling dynamic which makes it appear "real." So even if the first argument is not statistically true, *24* might encourage an audience to believe that it is. The supposed reflection of reality is inseparable from the construction of that reality articulated as it is through the discourse of realism.

Just as with the Labour poster, *24* can offer its consumers a multiplicity of intentions, consequences, and meanings at one and the same time, dependent on culture, context, and audience. And to criticize it on the grounds that it misrepresents Muslims does not get us very far. While *24* is undeniably the product of a set of wider cultural politics, which routinely represents Muslims and Islam negatively, we should remember that the media also generates some positive images of Islam. But to engage in the sort of analysis whereby we trawl the media and simply count off each negative image against a positive one and see what total we end up with is missing the broader point. If this kind of misrepresentation were the main problem then the only corrective necessary would simply be to make lots of television shows featuring Muslims as special needs teachers or acrobats. A show such as *24* needs to be assessed not in terms of the supposed accuracy or inaccuracy of its representations but in terms of what Ella Shohat and Robert Stam (1994) call "a specific orchestration of ideological discourses" (180). In other words, how are those representations arranged and how do they reimagine, rearticulate, and reinstate wider cultural politics?

The modern-day stereotype of Muslims as radical religious extremists willing to kill themselves and others to further their fundamentalist beliefs has a long history, but it is also undeniably connected to contemporary political, religious, and cultural conflict. But the fact that Islamic suicide bombers exist in reality is not the issue here. For most of us in Western Europe or the United States, access to the suicide bomber is available only through media representations where—depending on the particular outlet—they are likely to be portrayed across the spectrum from fanatical terrorists to glorious martyrs for the cause. And those representations exist in a realm of image and fantasy that, while it might look like reality, functions wholly apart from it. And just as an analysand's dreams would tell us only about herself and not the objects of her fantasies, so we can be sure that an analysis of these images and stereotypes will tell us much mote about those doing the representing than those who are being represented.

The media, it might be argued, sometimes seems driven by its own fantasy of realizing a Lear-like state of power without responsibility, and if we assess a drama such as *24* only in terms of its mimetic accuracy then we give in to that. It is not that stereotypes are not relevant or do not inflict great damage, but in order to understand their strength we need to move our assessment from the categorical oppositions of true/false and see them ideologically and discursively as elements within much wider tropes of representation. Our imperative should be to shift focus from the "stereotypes and distortions" or "equal time" analysis and begin to engage the image as an "utterance, an act of contextualized interlocution between socially situated producers and receivers" (Shohat and Stam 180).

Nowhere is that "act of contextualized interlocution" performed more obviously, and nowhere is the contingent relationship between truth, reality, realism, and representation articulated more explicitly, than within the world of advertising. In terms of our understanding and awareness of the visual and aesthetic techniques of advertising—as well as standard articulations of narrative—we are certainly more sophisticated than we were even forty years ago, when the technologies of production, persuasion, and communication were so profoundly and ubiquitously fused through the medium of television. But in the twenty-first century we are still no less subject to the emotionally inflected manipulations that have always targeted such primal drives as fear, sexual desire, and the need for community.

When the modern consumer looks at an advertisement such as that for Listerine from the 1920s (Figure 2) they will be most likely struck by the apparently archaic nature of the graphic layout and odd overemphasis on text. Similarly, the ad's effort to generate a deep and abiding anxiety that halitosis will render one worthless appears crude and heavy handed.[1] The ploy seems so laughably obvious that it is easy to dismiss this miss who is missing her mister. But if we look at a contemporary advert (Figure 3) we can see that those same anxious discourses of desire and rejection are being

FIGURE 2. ADVERT FOR *LISTERINE* MOUTHWASH, 1920s (USA).

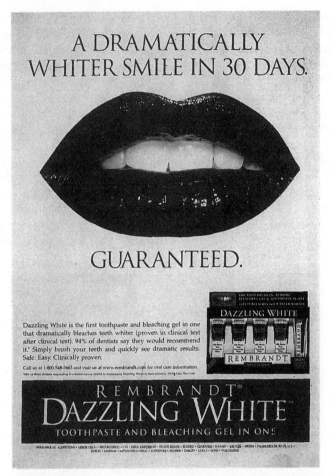

FIGURE 3. ADVERT FOR *REMBRANDT* TOOTHPASTE, 1990s (USA).

rearticulated albeit using slightly different visual codes. There is, for instance, an explicitly sexual emphasis in the Rembrandt advert that is merely implicit in the earlier image, with the full and pouting red lips signaling a sexual aggression and confidence unimaginable to Listerine's lonely, rheumy-eyed and pasty-faced pre-Raphaelite virgin. But underlying it all, still, is the implicit threat of rejection and loneliness.

Visually, the Rembrandt ad fits in seamlessly with contemporary significations of health, desire, and beauty and, therefore, to the contemporary eye remains unremarkable. It is a form of visual narrative no less structured or contrived than a painting by Rembrandt von Rijn himself, and while we should not ask "is it real" of the ad any more than we can ask it of, for instance, *The Feast of Belshazzar*, we can bring critical and analytical tools to both visual texts to assess them for meaning. As far as the advert is concerned, we might say that the appropriation of the name "Rembrandt" is an effort to connect the product to fantasies of sophistication and status implicitly represented by classical art and "high" culture; and the presentation of informational phrases ("clinical tests," "94% of dentists") invoke a pseudoscientific discourse suggesting that there is a basis in factual evidence for the claims being implicitly made. But just as the power of a stereotype derives precisely from the fact that it is neither informational nor, consequently, susceptible to categorizations of truth or falsity so those categories of truth or falsity do not apply to advertising images.

Ads such as that for Old Milwaukee beer which featured two young men who, when they opened their beers, were suddenly met by the "Swedish Bikini Team"—a group of bikini-clad Nordic beauties— parachuting into their living room, or the acne cream commercial featuring a teenage boy whose friends did not want to sit with him because of his "pizza face" are, it should go without saying, not meant to be taken literally. We know that there is no cause-and-effect relationship between the fantasies in the commercial and our own lives. We know that no matter how many bottles of Old Milwaukee we open the Swedish Bikini Team will not appear. And the advertisers know it too. They also know that we know. What the advertisers are relying upon with this "act of contextualized interlocution" is not an exchange of information but the manipulation of the roiling emotions of desire and anxiety.

There is a structural simplicity to commercials suggesting a broad but limited series of "strategies of persuasion" into which all advertising falls.[2] By concentrating on primal drives such as sex, fear, and the need for community adverts are deliberately designed to force the suspension of any intellectual or critical sensibility and to generate a visceral response from the most elemental of human emotions. It is not only that ads are not designed to make us think but that they are expressly designed to make us *not think*. And because advertising exists in a realm of feeling and desire, the images used must inevitably be as compelling and seductive as possible (which surely goes some way to explaining the ubiquitous use of sexual images to sell everything from breakfast cereals to lawnmowers). In constructing an entire emotional identity for the product, a process of symbolic transference—what Marx calls "reification"—ensures that the product itself then becomes the embodiment of happiness, contentment, freedom, etc., and the conduit to an altered, implicitly paradisiacal, state of being. Stereotypes work similarly as the reified symbolic embodiments of a whole set of feelings that routinely target the basic elements of primal human response. The stereotype's "strategy of persuasion," focusing as it usually does on metaphors of disruption and disease, usually embodies simplistic characteristics such as violence or contamination. But just as, for instance, the Rembrandt ad functions as a symbolic narrative for working out rejection anxieties, so stereotypes of the Other are narratives we articulate in order to structure a sense of self.

Let us consider some dominant stereotypes in contemporary British and American culture. The French are stereotyped as being arrogant, over-sexed, and unclean, while the Germans are supposedly humorless and overdisciplined. The Scots are cheap, and the Swedish are sex mad. And blondes, of course, are dumb. Notwithstanding the claim made in many sociology textbooks that stereotyping often has a "kernel" of truth at its center there is nothing within these stereotypes which has anything to do with reality. As I have already stated, categories of "truth" or "falsity" are simply not applicable to the way stereotypes function any more than they are relevant to the way advertising or narrative functions. We would not assess *Persuasion* or *Moby Dick* by applying analytical or investigative strategies of "truth" or "falsity" any more than we would to *The House at Pooh Corner* or an ad for Cadbury's chocolate.

Stereotyping is not an analytical process of statistical assessment but a form of narrative which utilizes figures of difference in order to structure narratives about the self. That there may be instances when some of these things are true of individuals is coincidental and of no relevance. Some French people are doubtlessly unclean and arrogant. But so are some English people. And surely some Scottish people are tight with their money. But then so are some Swedish people. And there are undoubtedly humorless well-disciplined Italians just as there are excitable Germans. Stereotypes are not an issue of reality but representation and concerned not with difference itself but with the narrativizing of differences.

To return to the issue of whether stereotypes have a kernel of truth at their center, Gill Branston and Roy Stafford (2003) claim that stereo-types have enduring strength because "they can point to features that apparently have a grain of truth" (92). Illustrating their argument by linking some particular black stereotypes with their supposed origins in American slavery they suggest that a stereotypical "shuffling" gait might be a result of the fact that "slaves . . . had their calf muscles cut if they tried to run away." Similarly, they argue that the basis of the Mammy stereotype is that enslaved women were treated as breeding stock with the consequence that "their bodies were perhaps enlarged by repeated pregnancies" (93).

To suggest any kind of causal, one-to-one relationship between a stereo-type and the social reality of slavery—even if only at source—implies that originally the image was merely a neutral descriptor that has somehow become distorted. But as I have mentioned above in regards to the issue of positive versus negative representations in *24*, this kind of distortion analy-sis is unproductive. One of the fundamentals that underpins both visual communications and cultural studies is that there is no such thing as a neutral image and that even the "innocent" family snapshot is inevitably striated by the micropolitics of everyday life. And clearly images associated with and generated from slavery can never be neutral. Stereotypes *are* profoundly rooted in social reality but not in the kind of causal-behaviorist way suggested by Branston and Stafford. The way to understand the connection between social reality and stereotype is to return to Shohat and Stam's "specific orchestration of ideological discourses" and consider who benefits from the existence of those images and ask what purpose those stereotypes serve and how are they related to the wider exercise of social, political, and cultural power?

As the work undertaken by writers such as David Roediger (1991) and Eric Lott (1995) has demonstrated the imaginative construction or "trope" of blackness—within which racial stereotyping played (and plays) a crucial role—was used by whites in order to both legitimize the institution of slavery and structure their own racial and social identity. The precise origins of the shuffling "Steppin Fetchit" stereotype are, of course, questionable. Some scholars have argued, for instance, that shuffling originated in legislations against dancing—with dancing being defined as crossing the feet—in response to which slaves developed an alternative "shuffling" form of dance.[3] Whatever the case may be, the stereotype emerges only by removing the activity itself from any supposed grounding it may have had in codes of behavior to the realm of the social imaginary where it clearly then assumes a "second-order of signification"[4] as a symbol, in this case, of listlessness, backwardness, and childlike dependence.

Similarly, some female slaves may have been obese, and they may have been so as a consequence of repeated pregnancies (though contemporaneous photographs of enslaved women seem to indicate that physically they covered the spectrum of body shape and size that might be expected within any other social grouping from schoolteachers to factory workers). But, again, to analyze for distortion in this way is to accept the debate on the stereotype's own terms. We must shift the parameters of analysis by repeating that this stereotype too has no cause-and-effect relationship to the social reality of enslaved black women's lives. To understand the stereotype we must look at the Mammy as a narrativized figure within the wider discourse of racial politics and identity. As a figure that was nurturing, accommodating, entirely asexual, and wholly supportive of the white family the Mammy stereotype served (in every sense) as a positive endorsement of the institution of slavery. In the image's emphasis on the Mammy's asexuality it also, and not incidentally, worked to disguise the sexual violence and exploitation routinely carried out by white male slave masters upon their black female slaves. So this kind of discursive analysis of stereotypes can help us to understand the social reality of slavery not because we can make any kind of mundane causal connection between activity and image but because by analyzing the image as a feature and function of discourse we can reveal the elisions and articulations that performed the supportive work of racial identity under slavery.

This is evident also from the change in dominant black stereotypes in response to a shift in the social and cultural context of post-Civil War America. Before the Civil War, when the overriding imperative for the south was to demonstrate that slavery was an essentially benign institution that benefited slaves as much as slave owners, dominant stereotypes of blacks focused on their supposed docility, dependence, frivolity, and feck-lessness—they were essentially characterized as children who needed the guiding hand of responsible whites to look after them. After the Civil War, once the institution of slavery had been outlawed and could no longer be relied upon to control the black population (and with blacks demanding access to the same constitutional and political rights as whites) the empha-sis in stereotypes changed and became dominated by images of violence and power. Blacks were now portrayed as violent and uncontrolled beasts that needed to be contained. These changes occurred not because "black behavior" (as if such a meaningless and nebulous category could even be identified!) had changed but because the social and political circumstances of black and white relationships—the origin of the stereotypes—had changed.[5]

Stereotypes respond to social reality because ideology and social real-ity are mutually constitutive, and it is the cultural, racial, and ideological construction of social reality and social relationships that is being articu-lated through stereotypes. Stereotypes are an effort to both promote and mask the complicated social realities of the inequitable distribution of political power by invoking "higher" discourses of God, history, or nature. And the consequences of stereotyping are critically related to the exercise of social, cultural, and political power. As I mentioned at the beginning of this article the issues of immigration and asylum seeking are currently in the forefront of political and social debate in both Europe and the United States. This contentious issue offers another explicit example of the stereo-type as a narrativized figure of negative difference and its consequence for the exercise of cultural and political power.

The immigrant stereotype has always embodied invasion anxieties and fear of the unknown and is ubiquitously associated with disease no less in Britain today than, for instance, in the United States in the nine-teenth century. Scare stories such as "Asylum Seeker AIDS Con" (*Scottish Daily Record* 3, December 2000) and "Struggling schools swamped with asylum seekers" (*Mail on Sunday*, 5, May 2002) that appear regularly in the tabloid press construct the immigrant body as diseased and threatening and "our" nation state consequently as a healthy body under siege. Mainstream British political parties such as Labour and Conservative and fringe organizations such as UKIP or even the BNP are all most likely to couch their anti-immigration sentiment within the "rational" parameters of a debate over "resources" or "economics." However, they are no less reliant on the propagation of a racial and ethnic stereotype than was the explicit racism of Enoch Powell or the ultraright wing National Front in the 1970s.

There has been a narrative collapsing of the immigrant/asylum seeker/refugee into one figurative bundle that embodies a threat not only to health and resources but also to the successful maintenance of the demarcation lines of national identity and order. In the article "Whites Quitting Cities"[6] the political correspondent Nic Cecil uncritically reports the claim by anti-immigrant group Migration Watch UK that "Tens of thousands of white families are pouring out of UK cities as immigrants move in" and that this "exodus is creating an increasingly divided society." He further states:

> [The report] found that 600,000 more people left London for the regions between 1993–2002 than arrived in the capital from elsewhere in Britain. Those moving out were believed to be mainly white. In the same decade, the number of immigrants arriving in London went up by 726,000.

There is—as always—a kind of apocalyptic quality to this kind of report, in terms of the logistical and statistical implications as well as the invoking of the biblical notion of exodus and the image of 600,000 Londoners all streaming out of the capital in an effort to escape the invasion ("plague"?). This is underpinned by the categorical juxtaposing of "white" and "immigrant" that defines all immigrants implicitly as people of color thereby—again implicitly—further delegitimizing their presence. The tabloid press seem peculiarly—though by no means exclusively—comfortable with generating and propagating this kind of public rhetoric of anti-immigrant fear and panic through which all social problems are attributed to the corrosive presence of the "foreign body."

With the narrative of the threatening alien constructed in this way, it then becomes difficult to not situate any individual identified as an immigrant, asylum seeker, or refugee within the parameters of that construction. A figure such as the infamous Muslim cleric Abu Hamza is a dream for the tabloids because, with his hooked hand and milky glazed eye, he so clearly displays the visual signifiers of destructive and threatening difference. He is the crackling phobic presence of the Other, whose image is so powerful visually that he has become the central body around which the discourse and narrative of fear and rejection revolve. With Hamza literally as the poster boy for the stereotype of the immigrant/asylum seeker/refugee it has become almost impossible to divorce any image from the destructive narrative of this stereotype. And the ubiquity of Hamza's image means that when we see an image such as that of an "ordinary" immigrant it is almost inevitably drawn into Hamza's orbit. Needless to say, none of this is to either defend Hamza or to deny that he seems to be a particularly unpleasant individual. But we must not forget that it is the popular media, and specifically the tabloid press, which has created and constructed the visual image of Hamza—"Hook"—in a particular way to fit in with wider panicky fantasies about the supposed negative consequences of immigration.

A corrective response might be to state that statistically most immigrants and asylum seekers are white and/or European; that immigrants always benefit their host countries economically; and that the president of the National Farmers' Union recently underlined the importance of migrant labor to Britain's agriculture industry.[7] However, the stereotype, as it is propagated by the tabloid press, is not related to statistical reality. It performs a different function, namely that of a narrative construction of a racial and religious Other through which a populist sensibility of legitimate "Britishness" can be articulated.

It is not difference that is at the root of this problem but how we culturally choose to narrativize difference and, in doing so, how we then represent the Other for the purposes of constructing our own social, cultural, and racial identity. Visual stereotypes are merely a kind of cultural *trompe l'oeil* that are convincing, compelling, and seductive in their familiarity because they play such a profound role in the structural formation of that identity. There is an extraordinary example of this at work in a Kaloderma shaving foam advertisement from the 1920s (Figure 4).

This advertisement is both an instructive example of racial stereotyping and a visual expression—for a European audience of course—of the social relationships established under imperialism. While histories of imperialism demonstrate that members of indigenous populations routinely performed the menial tasks forced upon them by the colonizing population this image speaks much more deeply to the structural underpinnings of the colonial enterprise. It obviously articulates a relationship between Africa and Europe in which Africa is characterized as the serving child and Europe as the mature adult preparing himself for the daily responsibilities of governance. The portrayal of Africa as a needful and dependent child was ubiquitous in European popular culture and functioned as the structural foundation for the self-serving narrative of "the white man's burden." Underlining this attitude is the overt juxtaposition of the unclothed (uncivilized) with the clothed (civilized) that again became a widespread feature of the imperial narrative.[8]

FIGURE 4. ADVERT FOR *KALODERMA* SHAVING FOAM, 1920s (GERMANY).

But the image is also revealing in a less obvious way in that it expresses the profound way in which European identity is structured by its relationship to, and construction of, Africa. As Africa holds up the mirror, Europe looks toward Africa but in true narcissistic fashion sees nothing other than its own gloriously reflected self (a self-construct as the highest embodiment of beauty and culture). Europe blithely refuses to acknowledge both the African presence and the profound debt it owes Africa for its sense of self-hood. Without African labor (in every sense) Europe would be unable to not only *see* but *to be* itself. In short this ad is a visual distillation of the entire history of empire.

There is no greater fantasy than that of empire (to be, as the ad positions the white European, "over all") and advertising was crucial to its success. In this image we see combined the processes of advertising and the articulation of stereotypes as part of a wider narrative of self-hood and the two impulses fusing into one whereby advertising is not only the model for, but also the medium through which, stereotyping works. As I have tried to demonstrate, stereotypes work much as advertising works—by projecting negative or positive fantasies that particular constituencies are expected to project themselves toward or away from. Stereotypes are like ads because they target our deepest human emotions such as fear and desire, and they appear "real" because they are part of a political, cultural, and aesthetic landscape—the separate spheres of which touch and merge at crucial points—that reinforces their believability. Difficult though it is to see beyond these horizons it is not impossible. We need to understand the enormous power possessed by the visual media to develop and promote stereotypes but also that the visual text can be assessed and analyzed in ways which reveal the wider politics that produces it. Raymond Williams once referred to advertising as a "magic system," and we can see stereotyping as a similarly illusory process. To learn the language of analysis is to allow us to see beyond the smoke and mirrors and sleights of hand and to dispel what Jan Nederveen Pieterse refers to as the "enchantment" of stereotypes and to understand the visual stereotype as a form of cultural "advertisement for the self" that is inseparable from the wider cultural narratives that create it.

Notes

1. Many of today's ads are no less crude and heavy handed although the emergence of reality advertising and the self-reflexive irony of much contemporary advertising reveals a degree of audience sophistication in terms of narrative, if nothing else.
2. See Jack Solomon's "Masters of Desire" for a compelling structural analysis of advertising.
3. Lenwood Sloan interview in *Ethnic Notions*.
4. See Roland Barthes, *Mythologies*.
5. Marlon Riggs' *Ethnic Notions* is both a fascinating and informative analysis of the progression of black stereotypes in nineteenth and twentieth century America and details quite clearly the post-Civil War development of popular images of blacks in white American popular culture.
6. *The Sun*, February 10, 2005.
7. Interview on BBC Radio 4's *Today* program, February 21, 2005.
8. See John M. McKenzie (Ed.) *Imperialism and Popular Culture* for the significance of popular cultural forms in the construction of concepts of race, empire, and "Britishness."

Works Cited

Barthes, Roland. *Mythologies*. New York: Noonday Press, 1972.

Branston, Gill, and Roy Stafford. *The Media Student's Book*. 3rd ed. London: Routledge, 2003.

Ethnic Notions. (Video) Dir. Marlon Riggs. Berkeley: California Newsreel. 1987. VHS. 58 mins.

Lott, Eric. *Love and Theft: Blackface Minstrelsy and the American Working Class.* New York: Oxford UP, 1995.

McKenzie, John., ed. *Imperialism and Popular Culture.* Manchester: Manchester UP, 1998.

Pieterse, Jan Nederveen. *White on Black: Images of Africa and Blacks in Western Popular Culture.* New Haven: Yale UP, 1994.

Roediger, David. *Wages of Whiteness: Race and the Making of the American Working Class.* London: Verso, 1991.

Shohat, Ella, and Robert Stam. *Unthinking Eurocentrism: Multiculturalism and the Media.* London: Routledge, 1994.

Solomon, Jack. "Masters of Desire: The Culture of American Advertising." *Entry Points.* Ed. Elizabeth Alvarado and Barbara Cully. New York: Addison Wesley Longman, 1999. 10–17.

Williams, Raymond. "Advertising: the Magic System." *Problems in Materialism and Culture.* London: Verso, 1980.

Suggestions for Discussion

1. How and why does advertising encourage the onlooker to *not think*?

2. Wall suggests several strikingly different possible readings of a Maidenform advertisement. How could they all be considered accurate? Why does he suggest that the "alien invasion" reading is definitely not accurate? *Could* it be a legitimate reading? When does one know that an interpretation is truly groundless, or that one reading might be more valid than another?

3. Wall says it isn't important whether a given stereotype is "true," "false," or "partly true." Why isn't this kind of analysis of stereotypes important? What *is* important, to Wall?

4. What is the relationship between advertising, stereotypes, and political power struggles?

Suggestions for Writing

1. Choose an advertisement that appears to be particularly effective. Using techniques similar to those demonstrated by Wall, analyze what message the advertisement is sending, both overtly and more subtly. Consider what social assumptions are being made by the advertisers and how the ad reinforces existing power bases and cultural expectations. Write your findings in an essay.

2. Compose an essay in which you compare and contrast Wall's treatment of the stereotyping of women in advertising to Peggy Orenstein's handling of the issue in "What's Wrong with Cinderella?"

ᘯᘯᘯᘯᘯ

PEGGY ORENSTEIN

What's Wrong with Cinderella?

Peggy Orenstein (b. 1961) writes often about topics that affect girls and women in today's society. She has served in an editorial capacity at *Mother Jones, 7 Days, Manhattan, Inc.*, and *Esquire.* Orenstein is the author of a number of books, including her memoir *Waiting for Daisy: A Tale of Two Continents, Three Religions, Five Infertility Doctors, An Oscar, An Atomic Bomb, A Romantic Night, and One Woman's Quest to Become a Mother* (2006). She has also published *Schoolgirls: Young Women, Self-Esteem, and the Confidence Gap* (1994) and *FLUX: Women on Sex, Work, Kids, Love, and Life in a Half-Changed World* (2000), and she has contributed to publications such as *Vogue, Elle, Discover, More, Glamour, Mother Jones, Salon, Parenting, O: The Oprah Magazine*, the *New York Times*, and the *New Yorker*. The following article appeared in the *New York Times*.

I finally came unhinged in the dentist's office—one of those ritzy pediatric practices tricked out with comic books, DVDs and arcade games—where I'd taken my 3-year-old daughter for her first exam. Until then, I'd held my tongue. I'd smiled politely every time the supermarket-checkout clerk greeted her with "Hi, Princess"; ignored the waitress at our local breakfast joint who called the funny-face pancakes she ordered her "princess meal"; made no comment when the lady at Longs Drugs said, "I bet I know your favorite color" and handed her a pink balloon rather than letting her choose for herself. Maybe it was the dentist's Betty Boop inflection that got to me, but when she pointed to the exam chair and said, "Would you like to sit in my special princess throne so I can sparkle your teeth?" I lost it.

"Oh, for God's sake," I snapped. "Do you have a princess drill, too?"

She stared at me as if I were an evil stepmother.

"Come on!" I continued, my voice rising. "It's 2006, not 1950. This is Berkeley, Calif. Does every little girl really have to be a princess?"

My daughter, who was reaching for a Cinderella sticker, looked back and forth between us. "Why are you so mad, Mama?" she asked. "What's wrong with princesses?"

Diana may be dead and Masako disgraced, but here in America, we are in the midst of a royal moment. To call princesses a "trend" among girls is like calling Harry Potter a book. Sales at Disney Consumer Products, which started the craze six years ago by packaging nine of its female characters under one royal rubric, have shot up to $3 billion, globally, this year, from $300 million in 2001. There are now more than 25,000 Disney Princess items. "Princess," as some Disney execs call it, is not only the fastest-growing brand the company has ever created; they say it is on its way to becoming the largest girls' franchise on the planet.

Meanwhile in 2001, Mattel brought out its own "world of girl" line of princess Barbie dolls, DVDs, toys, clothing, home décor and myriad other products. At a time when Barbie sales were declining domestically, they became instant best sellers. Shortly before that, Mary Drolet, a Chicago-area mother and former Claire's and Montgomery Ward executive, opened Club Libby Lu, now a chain of mall stores based largely in the suburbs in which girls ages 4 to 12 can shop for "Princess Phones" covered in faux fur and attend "Princess-Makeover Birthday Parties." Saks bought Club Libby Lu in 2003 for $12 million and has since expanded it to 87 outlets; by 2005, with only scant local advertising, revenues hovered around the $46 million mark, a 53 percent jump from the previous year. Pink, it seems, is the new gold.

Even Dora the Explorer, the intrepid, dirty-kneed adventurer, has ascended to the throne: in 2004, after a two-part episode in which she turns into a "true princess," the Nickelodeon and Viacom consumer-products division released a satin-gowned "Magic Hair Fairytale Dora," with hair that grows or shortens when her crown is touched. Among other phrases the bilingual doll utters: "Vámonos! Let's go to fairy-tale land!" and "Will you brush my hair?"

As a feminist mother—not to mention a nostalgic product of the Grranimals era—I have been taken by surprise by the princess craze and the girlie-girl culture that has risen around it. What happened to William wanting a doll and not dressing your cat in an apron? Whither Marlo Thomas? I watch my fellow mothers, women who once swore they'd never be dependent on a man, smile indulgently at daughters who warble "So This Is Love" or insist on being called Snow White. I wonder if they'd concede so readily to sons who begged for combat fatigues and mock.

More to the point, when my own girl makes her daily beeline for the dress-up corner of her preschool classroom—something I'm convinced she does largely to torture me—I worry about what playing Little Mermaid is teaching her. I've spent much of my career writing about experiences that undermine girls' well-being, warning parents that a preoccupation with body and beauty (encouraged by films, TV, magazines and, yes, toys) is perilous to their daughters' mental and physical health. Am I now supposed to shrug and forget all that? If trafficking in stereotypes doesn't matter at 3, when does it matter? At 6? Eight? Thirteen?

On the other hand, maybe I'm still surfing a washed-out second wave of feminism in a third-wave world. Maybe princesses are in fact a sign of progress, an indication that girls can embrace their predilection for pink without compromising strength or ambition; that, at long last, they can "have it all." Or maybe it is even less complex than that: to mangle Freud, maybe a princess is sometimes just a princess. And, as my daughter wants to know, what's wrong with that?

The rise of the Disney princesses reads like a fairy tale itself, with Andy Mooney, a former Nike executive, playing the part of prince, riding into the company on a metaphoric white horse in January 2000 to save a consumer-products division whose sales were dropping by as much as 30 percent a year. Both overstretched and underfocused, the division had triggered price wars by granting multiple licenses for core products (say, Winnie-the-Pooh undies) while ignoring the potential of new media. What's more, Disney films like "A Bug's Life" in 1998 had yielded few merchandising opportunities— what child wants to snuggle up with an ant?

It was about a month after Mooney's arrival that the magic struck. That's when he flew to Phoenix to check out his first "Disney on Ice" show. "Standing in line in the arena, I was surrounded by little girls dressed head to toe as princesses," he told me last summer in his palatial office, then located in Burbank, and speaking in a rolling Scottish burr. "They weren't even Disney products. They were generic princess products they'd appended to a Halloween costume. And the light bulb went off. Clearly there was latent demand here. So the next morning I said to my team, 'O.K., let's establish standards and a color palette and talk to licensees and get as much product out there as we possibly can that allows these girls to do what they're doing anyway: projecting themselves into the characters from the classic movies.'"

Mooney picked a mix of old and new heroines to wear the Pantone pink No. 241 corona: Cinderella, Sleeping Beauty, Snow White, Ariel, Belle, Jasmine, Mulan and Pocahontas. It was the first time Disney marketed characters separately from a film's release, let alone lumped together those from different stories. To ensure the sanctity of what Mooney called their individual "mythologies," the princesses never make eye contact when they're grouped: each stares off in a slightly different direction as if unaware of the others' presence.

It is also worth noting that not all of the ladies are of royal extraction. Part of the genius of "Princess" is that its meaning is so broadly constructed that it actually has no meaning. Even Tinker Bell was originally a Princess, though her reign didn't last. "We'd always debate over whether she was really a part of the Princess mythology," Mooney recalled. "She really wasn't." Likewise, Mulan and Pocahontas, arguably the most resourceful of the bunch, are rarely depicted on Princess merchandise, though for a different reason. Their rustic garb has less bling potential than that of old-school heroines like Sleeping Beauty. (When Mulan does appear, she is typically in the kimonolike hanfu, which makes her miserable in the movie, rather than her liberated warrior's gear.)

The first Princess items, released with no marketing plan, no focus groups, no advertising, sold as if blessed by a fairy godmother. To this day, Disney conducts little market research on the Princess line, relying instead on the power of its legacy among mothers as well as the instant-read sales barometer of the theme parks and Disney Stores. "We simply gave girls what they wanted," Mooney said of the line's success, "although I don't think any of us grasped how much they wanted this. I wish I could sit here and take credit for having some grand scheme to develop this, but all we did was envision a little girl's room and think about how she could live out the princess fantasy. The counsel we gave to licensees was: What type of bedding would a princess want to sleep in? What kind of alarm clock would a princess want to wake up to? What type of television would a princess like to see? It's a rare case where you find a girl who has every aspect of her room bedecked in Princess, but if she ends up with three or four of these items, well, then you have a very healthy business."

Every reporter Mooney talks to asks some version of my next question: Aren't the Princesses, who are interested only in clothes, jewelry and cadging the handsome prince, somewhat retrograde role models?

"Look," he said, "I have friends whose son went through the Power Rangers phase who castigated themselves over what they must've done wrong. Then they talked to other parents whose kids had gone through it. The boy passes through. The girl passes through. I see girls expanding their imagination through visualizing themselves as princesses, and then they pass through that phase and end up becoming lawyers, doctors, mothers or princesses, whatever the case may be."

Mooney has a point: There are no studies proving that playing princess directly damages girls' self-esteem or dampens other aspirations. On the other hand, there is evidence that young women who hold the most conventionally feminine beliefs—who avoid conflict and think they should be perpetually nice and pretty—are more likely to be depressed than others and less likely to use contraception. What's more, the 23 percent decline in girls' participation in sports and other vigorous activity between middle and high school has been linked to their sense that athletics is unfeminine. And in a survey released last October by Girls Inc., school-age girls overwhelmingly reported a paralyzing pressure to be "perfect": not only to get straight A's and be the student-body president, editor of the newspaper and captain of the swim team but also to be "kind and caring," "please everyone, be very thin and dress right." Give those girls a pumpkin and a glass slipper and they'd be in business.

At the grocery store one day, my daughter noticed a little girl sporting a Cinderella backpack. "There's that princess you don't like, Mama!" she shouted.

"Um, yeah," I said, trying not to meet the other mother's hostile gaze.

"Don't you like her blue dress, Mama?"

I had to admit, I did.

She thought about this. "Then don't you like her face?"

"Her face is all right," I said, noncommittally, though I'm not thrilled to have my Japanese-Jewish child in thrall to those Aryan features. (And what the heck are those blue things covering her ears?) "It's just, honey, Cinderella doesn't really do anything."

Over the next 45 minutes, we ran through that conversation, verbatim, approximately 37 million times, as my daughter pointed out Disney Princess Band-Aids, Disney Princess paper cups, Disney Princess lip balm, Disney Princess pens, Disney Princess crayons and Disney Princess notebooks—all cleverly displayed at the eye level of a 3-year-old trapped in a shopping cart— as well as a bouquet of Disney Princess balloons bobbing over the checkout line. The repetition was excessive, even for a preschooler. What was it about my answers that confounded her? What if, instead of realizing: Aha! Cinderella is a symbol of the patriarchal oppression of all women, another example of corporate mind control and power-to-the-people! my 3-year-old was thinking, Mommy doesn't want me to be a girl?

According to theories of gender constancy, until they're about 6 or 7, children don't realize that the sex they were born with is immutable. They believe that they have a choice: they can grow up to be either a mommy or a daddy. Some psychologists say that until permanency sets in kids embrace whatever stereotypes our culture presents, whether it's piling on the most spangles or attacking one another with light sabers. What better way to assure that they'll always remain themselves? If that's the case, score one for Mooney. By not buying the Princess Pull-Ups, I may be inadvertently communicating that being female (to the extent that my daughter is able to understand it) is a bad thing.

Anyway, you have to give girls some credit. It's true that, according to Mattel, one of the most popular games young girls play is "bride," but Disney found that a groom or prince is incidental to that fantasy, a regrettable necessity at best. Although they keep him around for the climactic kiss, he is otherwise relegated to the bottom of the toy box, which is why you don't see him prominently displayed in stores.

What's more, just because they wear the tulle doesn't mean they've drunk the Kool-Aid. Plenty of girls stray from the script, say, by playing basketball in their finery, or casting themselves as the powerful evil stepsister bossing around the sniveling Cinderella. I recall a headline-grabbing 2005 British study that revealed that girls enjoy torturing, decapitating and microwaving their Barbies nearly as much as they like to dress them up for dates. There is spice along with that sugar after all, though why this was news is beyond me: anyone who ever played with the doll knows there's nothing more satisfying than hacking off all her hair and holding her underwater in the bathtub. Princesses can even be a boon to exasperated parents: in our house, for instance, royalty never whines and uses the potty every single time.

"Playing princess is not the issue," argues Lyn Mikel Brown, an author, with Sharon Lamb, of "Packaging Girlhood: Rescuing Our Daughters From Marketers' Schemes." "The issue is 25,000 Princess products," says Brown, a professor of education and human development at Colby College. "When one thing is so dominant, then it's no longer a choice: it's a mandate, cannibalizing all other forms of play. There's the illusion of more choices out there for girls, but if you look around, you'll see their choices are steadily narrowing."

It's hard to imagine that girls' options could truly be shrinking when they dominate the honor roll and outnumber boys in college. Then again, have you taken a stroll through a children's store lately? A year ago, when we shopped for "big girl" bedding at Pottery Barn Kids, we found the "girls" side awash in flowers, hearts and hula dancers; not a soccer player or sailboat in sight. Across the no-fly zone, the "boys" territory was all about sports, trains, planes and automobiles. Meanwhile, Baby GAP's boys' onesies were emblazoned with "Big Man on Campus" and the girls' with "Social Butterfly"; guess whose matching shoes were decorated on the soles with hearts and whose sported a "No. 1" logo? And at Toys "R" Us, aisles of pink baby dolls, kitchens, shopping carts and princesses unfurl a safe distance from the "Star Wars" figures, GeoTrax and tool chests. The relentless resegregation of childhood appears to have sneaked up without any further discussion about sex roles, about what it now means to be a boy or to be a girl. Or maybe it has happened in lieu of such discussion because it's easier this way.

Easier, that is, unless you want to buy your daughter something that isn't pink. Girls' obsession with that color may seem like something they're born with, like the ability to breathe or talk on the phone for hours on end. But according to Jo Paoletti, an associate professor of American studies at the University of Maryland, it ain't so. When colors were first introduced to the nursery in the early part of the 20th century, pink was considered the more masculine hue, a pastel version of red. Blue, with its intimations of the Virgin Mary, constancy and faithfulness, was thought to be dainty. Why or when that switched is not clear, but as late as the 1930s a significant percentage of adults in one national survey held to that split. Perhaps that's why so many early Disney heroines—Cinderella, Sleeping Beauty, Wendy, Alice-in-Wonderland—are swathed in varying shades of azure. (Purple, incidentally, may be the next color to swap teams: once the realm of kings and N.F.L. players, it is fast becoming the bolder girl's version of pink.)

It wasn't until the mid-1980s, when amplifying age and sex differences became a key strategy of children's marketing (recall the emergence of "'tween"), that pink became seemingly innate to girls, part of what defined them as female, at least for the first few years. That was also the time that the first of the generation raised during the unisex phase of feminism—ah, hither Marlo!—became parents. "The kids who grew up in the 1970s wanted sharp definitions for their own kids," Paoletti told me. "I can understand that, because the unisex thing denied everything—you couldn't be this, you couldn't be that, you had to be a neutral nothing."

The infatuation with the girlie girl certainly could, at least in part, be a reaction against the so-called second wave of the women's movement of the 1960s and '70s (the first wave was the fight for suffrage), which fought for reproductive rights and economic, social and legal equality. If nothing else, pink and Princess have resuscitated the fantasy of romance that that era of feminism threatened, the privileges that traditional femininity conferred on women despite its costs—doors magically opened, dinner checks picked up, Manolo Blahniks. Frippery. Fun. Why should we give up the perks of our sex until we're sure of what we'll get in exchange? Why should we give them up at all? Or maybe it's deeper than that: the freedoms feminism bestowed came with an undercurrent of fear among women themselves—flowing through "Ally McBeal," "Bridget Jones's Diary," "Sex and the City"—of losing male love, of never marrying, of not having children, of being deprived of something that felt essentially and exclusively female.

I mulled that over while flipping through "The Paper Bag Princess," a 1980 picture book hailed as an antidote to Disney. The heroine outwits a dragon who has kidnapped her prince, but not before the beast's fiery breath frizzles her hair and destroys her dress, forcing her to don a paper bag. The ungrateful prince rejects her, telling her to come back when she is "dressed like a real princess." She dumps him and skips off into the sunset, happily ever after, alone.

There you have it, "Thelma and Louise" all over again. Step out of line, and you end up solo or, worse, sailing crazily over a cliff to your doom. Alternatives like those might send you skittering right back to the castle. And I get that: the fact is, though I want my daughter to do and be whatever she wants as an adult, I still hope she'll find her Prince Charming and have babies, just as I have. I don't want her to be a fish without a bicycle; I want her to be a fish with another fish. Preferably, one who loves and respects her and also does the dishes and half the child care.

There had to be a middle ground between compliant and defiant, between petticoats and paper bags. I remembered a video on YouTube, an ad for a Nintendo game called Super Princess Peach. It showed a pack of girls in tiaras, gowns and elbow-length white gloves sliding down a zip line on parasols, navigating an obstacle course of tires in their stilettos, slithering on their bellies under barbed wire, then using their telekinetic powers to make a climbing wall burst into flames. "If you can stand up to really mean people," an announcer intoned, "maybe you have what it takes to be a princess."

Now here were some girls who had grit as well as grace. I loved Princess Peach even as I recognized that there was no way she could run in those heels, that her peachiness did nothing to upset the apple cart of expectation: she may have been athletic, smart and strong, but she was also adorable. Maybe she's what those once-unisex, postfeminist parents are shooting for: the melding of old and new standards. And perhaps that's a good thing, the ideal solution. But what to make, then, of the young women in the Girls Inc. survey? It doesn't seem to be "having it all" that's getting to them; it's the pressure to be it all. In telling our girls they can be anything, we have inadvertently demanded that they be everything. To everyone. All the time. No wonder the report was titled "The Supergirl Dilemma."

The princess as superhero is not irrelevant. Some scholars I spoke with say that given its post-9/11 timing, princess mania is a response to a newly dangerous world. "Historically, princess worship has emerged during periods of uncertainty and profound social change," observes Miriam Forman-Brunell, a historian at the University of Missouri-Kansas City. Francis Hodgson Burnett's original "Little Princess" was published at a time of rapid urbanization, immigration and poverty; Shirley Temple's film version was a hit during the Great Depression. "The original folk tales themselves," Forman-Brunell says, "spring from medieval and early modern European culture that faced all kinds of economic and demographic and social upheaval—famine, war, disease, terror of wolves. Girls play savior during times of economic crisis and instability." That's a heavy burden for little shoulders. Perhaps that's why the magic wand has become an essential part of the princess get-up. In the original stories—even the Disney versions of them—it's not the girl herself who's magic; it's the fairy godmother. Now if Forman-Brunell is right, we adults have become the cursed creatures whom girls have the thaumaturgic power to transform.

In the 1990s, third-wave feminists rebelled against their dour big sisters, "reclaiming" sexual objectification as a woman's right—provided, of course, that it was on her own terms, that she was the one choosing to strip or wear a shirt that said "Porn Star" or make out with her best friend at a frat-house bash. They embraced words like "bitch" and "slut" as terms of affection and empowerment. That is, when used by the right people, with the right dash of playful irony. But how can you assure that? As Madonna gave way to Britney, whatever self-determination that message contained was watered down and commodified until all that was left was a gaggle of 6-year-old girls in belly-baring T-shirts (which I'm guessing they don't wear as cultural critique). It is no wonder that parents, faced with thongs for 8-year-olds and Bratz dolls' "passion for fashion," fill their daughters' closets with pink sateen; the innocence of Princess feels like a reprieve.

"But what does that mean?" asks Sharon Lamb, a psychology professor at Saint Michael's College. "There are other ways to express 'innocence'— girls could play ladybug or caterpillar. What you're really talking about is sexual purity. And there's a trap at the end of that rainbow, because the natural progression from pale, innocent pink is not to other colors. It's to hot, sexy pink—exactly the kind of sexualization parents are trying to avoid."

Lamb suggested that to see for myself how "Someday My Prince Will Come" morphs into "Oops! I Did It Again," I visit Club Libby Lu, the mall shop dedicated to the "Very Important Princess."

Walking into one of the newest links in the store's chain, in Natick, Mass., last summer, I had to tip my tiara to the founder, Mary Drolet: Libby Lu's design was flawless. Unlike Disney, Drolet depended on focus groups to choose the logo (a crown-topped heart) and the colors (pink, pink, purple and more pink). The displays were scaled to the size of a 10-year-old, though most of the shoppers I saw were several years younger than that. The decals on the walls and dressing rooms—"I Love Your Hair," "Hip Chick," "Spoiled"—were written in "girlfriend language." The young sales clerks at this "special secret club for superfabulous girls" are called "club counselors" and come off like your coolest baby sitter, the one who used to let you brush her hair. The malls themselves are chosen based on a company formula called the G.P.I., or "Girl Power Index," which predicts potential sales revenues. Talk about newspeak: "Girl Power" has gone from a riot grrrrl anthem to "I Am Woman, Watch Me Shop."

Inside, the store was divided into several glittery "shopping zones" called "experiences": Libby's Laboratory, now called Sparkle Spa, where girls concoct their own cosmetics and bath products; Libby's Room; Ear Piercing; Pooch Parlor (where divas in training can pamper stuffed poodles, pugs and Chihuahuas); and the Style Studio, offering "Libby Du" makeover choices, including 'Tween Idol, Rock Star, Pop Star and, of course, Priceless Princess. Each look includes hairstyle, makeup, nail polish and sparkly tattoos.

As I browsed, I noticed a mother standing in the center of the store holding a price list for makeover birthday parties—$22.50 to $35 per child. Her name was Anne McAuliffe; her daughters—Stephanie, 4, and 7-year-old twins Rory and Sarah—were dashing giddily up and down the aisles.

"They've been begging to come to this store for three weeks," McAuliffe said. "I'd never heard of it. So I said they could, but they'd have to spend their own money if they bought anything." She looked around. "Some of this stuff is innocuous," she observed, then leaned toward me, eyes wide and stage-whispered: "But . . . a lot of it is horrible. It makes them look like little prostitutes. It's crazy. They're babies!"

As we debated the line between frivolous fun and JonBenét, McAuliffe's daughter Rory came dashing up, pigtails haphazard, glasses askew. "They have the best pocketbooks here," she said breathlessly, brandishing a clutch with the words "Girlie Girl" stamped on it. "Please, can I have one? It has sequins!"

"You see that?" McAuliffe asked, gesturing at the bag. "What am I supposed to say?"

On my way out of the mall, I popped into the "'tween" mecca Hot Topic, where a display of Tinker Bell items caught my eye. Tinker Bell, whose image racks up an annual $400 million in retail sales with no particular effort on Disney's part, is poised to wreak vengeance on the Princess line that once expelled her. Last winter, the first chapter book designed to introduce girls to Tink and her Pixie Hollow pals spent 18 weeks on The New York Times children's best-seller list. In a direct-to-DVD now under production, she will speak for the first time, voiced by the actress Brittany Murphy. Next year, Disney Fairies will be rolled out in earnest. Aimed at 6-to 9-year-old girls, the line will catch them just as they outgrow Princess. Their colors will be lavender, green, turquoise—anything but the Princess's soon-to-be-babyish pink.

To appeal to that older child, Disney executives said, the Fairies will have more "attitude" and "sass" than the Princesses. What, I wondered, did that entail? I'd seen some of the Tinker Bell merchandise that Disney sells at its theme parks: T-shirts reading, "Spoiled to Perfection," "Mood Subject to Change Without Notice" and "Tinker Bell: Prettier Than a Princess." At Hot Topic, that edge was even sharper: magnets, clocks, light-switch plates and panties featured "Dark Tink," described as "the bad girl side of Miss Bell that Walt never saw."

Girl power, indeed.

A few days later, I picked my daughter up from preschool. She came tearing over in a full-skirted frock with a gold bodice, a beaded crown perched sideways on her head. "Look, Mommy, I'm Ariel!" she crowed, referring to Disney's Little Mermaid. Then she stopped and furrowed her brow. "Mommy, do you like Ariel?"

I considered her for a moment. Maybe Princess is the first salvo in what will become a lifelong struggle over her body image, a Hundred Years' War of dieting, plucking, painting and perpetual dissatisfaction with the results. Or maybe it isn't. I'll never really know. In the end, it's not the Princesses that really bother me anyway. They're just a trigger for the bigger question of how, over the years, I can help my daughter with the contradictions she will inevitably face as a girl, the dissonance that is as endemic as ever to growing up female. Maybe the best I can hope for is that her generation will get a little further with the solutions than we did.

For now, I kneeled down on the floor and gave my daughter a hug.
She smiled happily. "But, Mommy?" she added. "When I grow up, I'm
still going to be a fireman."

Suggestions for Discussion

1. Discuss what Orenstein finds problematic with the Cinderella image as
   portrayed to young girls.

2. What effect does Orenstein feel the worship of the princess figure will have
   on shaping and evolving the meaning of girlhood?

3. What position does the author have at the end of the article? Is it the same
   as where she started?

4. Are there any positive elements to the princess phenomenon? What, if anything, can young girls learn from princesses as role models?

Suggestions for Writing

1. Choose one question from above and write a two-paragraph essay exploring the topic further.

2. Research a boyhood trend (e.g., superheroes, sports figures). What effect
   does that trend have on shaping boyhood in the United States. Compare
   your analysis with Orenstein's article.

CHRIS SUELLENTROP

Transformers

Chris Suellentrop (b. 1975) is a story editor for *The New York Times
Magazine.* He founded "The Opinionator" blog for *The New York Times*
in 2006, making him the first person paid by the *Times* only to blog. He
previously worked as a staff editor for the Op-Ed page at the *Times.* He
has written feature articles for *The New York Times Magazine, Wired, New
York, Legal Affairs,* and *The Wilson Quarterly.* He covered the 2004 presidential campaign for *Slate,* where he spent five years in the Washington,
D.C., bureau as a writer and editor. His essays, reviews, and columns have
appeared in, among other publications, *The New York Times Book
Review, The Washington Post, The Los Angeles Times,* and *Washington*

Monthly. He graduated from Tulane University and the Missouri School of Journalism. He was born in Louisiana, grew up in Kansas, and lives with his wife and daughter in New York City. The following article first appeared in *Wired Magazine* on June 26, 2007.

Hasbro organized the robots into a narrative: Autobots fighting Decepticons. It was an intricate (if clichéd) epic. **So many things we cherished in the 1980s** sprang from dazzling collaborations between two giants. Apple: Steve Jobs and Steve Wozniak. Physical fitness: Jane Fonda and Olivia Newton-John. Wham!: George Michael and Andrew Ridgeley. And for the beloved toys called Transformers, you can thank Ronald Reagan and George Lucas. Not literally, of course. The Gipper and the father of *Star Wars* never actually sat down in a room together, downing Mountain Dew and brainstorming until Optimus Prime burst from their skulls like Athena. Although that would have been cool.

No, what happened was more subtle, but it explains why fanboys this summer are alternately slobbering over and scoffing at *Transformers,* the first blockbuster film to be based on a line of toys.

It wouldn't have happened without Uncle George's deft licensing of the rights to make *Star Wars* dolls or Ronnie's deregulation of television advertising to children. And we wouldn't have had the movie had toymaker Hasbro not become a purveyor of must-have accoutrements for the hip and happening 13-year-old at the dawn of the modern Nerd Era.

Next time you're in a cubicle farm, take a look around. You'll see your Nerf guns and your lightsabers, your Spider-Men and your Vulcan ideological iconography. But that's mostly over in IT. Among the straights—the non-Jedi crowd—you'll see Transformers. A Constructicon here, a Dinobot there. And everyone can sing the theme song.

That's not by accident. *Transformers* is a movie in 2007 because of the toy-media industrial complex invented in the 1980s. That's when sprawling lines of figures started to be marketed as characters in a ready-mixed narrative, making them must-have collectibles. This new way to play would be supported by ads, yes, but also by entire TV series. And the toys would be aimed not just at nerds but at everyone. If you are deeply psyched to see a live-action Optimus Prime beat up a live-action Megatron, you are not necessarily a sci-fi dweeb. It simply means that everything went exactly according to plan.

New toys don't come along very often. New ways to play—what people in the business call play patterns—are even rarer. In 1959, Barbie introduced a new play pattern for American girls: a doll that was a glamorous woman to be emulated instead of an infant or child to be mothered. The 1964 introduction of G.I. Joe by Hasbro was another. As toy historian Gary Cross puts it: "Between 1900 and World War II, boys played with machines, girls played with dolls." Then G.I. Joe arrived, and boys had dolls, too. Oh, sorry: "action figures."

༄

Transformers Episode 1

Joe was a 12-inch-tall tough-guy loner (scar, beard). The rest of the action-figure market was dominated by a company called Mego, which made 8-inch-tall versions of everyone else. Comics characters. *Star Trek* characters. Apes from the Planet of same. It was a consolidation of licensed properties that could never happen today.

In 1976, Mego passed on the *Star Wars* license. Bad move.

An upstart company called Kenner grabbed it. But in the late 1970s, the price of oil was rising and the toys were made of vinyl—a petroleum product. Kenner was afraid it couldn't sell enough giant figures, vehicles, and play sets (X-wings, TIE fighters, Death Stars), to recoup costs. The exact size of the first *Star Wars* toys, according to the book *Toyland*, was determined when Kenner president Bernie Loomis turned to one of his designers with his thumb and index finger about 4 inches apart and said, "Luke Skywalker should be this big." That made them cheap enough that every character, no matter how minor, would have a figure. Kids bought them all.

Meanwhile, G.I. Joe was on life support, outgunned and outsold. Hasbro took the line in for repairs. "Our whole approach was learned from *Star Wars*," says Kirk Bozigian, Hasbro's product manager for the revamped G.I. Joe in 1982. The new figures—dozens of characters—were highly poseable, stood 3.75 inches tall, and had gear Darpa would shoot a puppy for. And there were bad guys—a vast terrorist conspiracy called Cobra. "Kids were looking to buy more than one figure," Bozigian says. "They wanted the vehicles and play sets that encompassed this whole world."

Hasbro had figured out what worked: lots of characters with an easy-to-follow backstory. For the introduction of Transformers in 1984, Hasbro used the same approach. It bought brand rights from several Japanese companies that made relatively generic toys with one real novelty: They unfolded from familiar vehicles into robot action figures.

The company knew that kids (and nerds) are fanatic completists. It's the baseball card model—or maybe, retrospectively, the Pokemon effect. "You gotta have the whole series," Bozigian says. "We were appealing to the kids' acquisitiveness—the more I get, the cooler I am. You know, he who dies with the most toys wins. That was our marketing philosophy for boys' action." To make every toy a must-have, Hasbro organized the robots into a narrative: Autobot heroes fighting Decepticon villains. Each box came with a description of the character—this isn't just a robot who is also a Walther P38. This is Megatron, villainous mastermind of the evil Decepticons. As it had with G.I. Joe, Hasbro was selling a far-reaching, intricate (if clichéd) epic.

More than that, though, Transformers let boys play with dolls and machines at the same time. Transformable toys were new to American kids— vehicles, action figures, and puzzles all in one. Bozigian's team had lucked into a new play pattern. Something about that degree of control over the toy, about an object that became another object, made it irresistible. An Autobot like Jazz (a Porsche) managed to be both Michael Knight and KITT. Except in this case, Michael Knight was a giant robot instead of David Hasselhoff. Yet another improvement. In the first year, Transformers made $100 million. Within eight years, the line generated $1 billion in sales—$333 million in 1985 alone, more than a quarter of Hasbro's entire revenue that year.

Still, sales wouldn't have spiked without the power of a fully operational battle station: television. For years, broadcasting-industry guidelines and the Federal Communications Commission prohibited the toy industry from making television shows about its products. In 1983, the rules changed. Beginning with Mattel's *He-Man and the Masters of the Universe*, toymakers could reap benefits from TV shows starring their characters. *He-Man*, the TV show, helped to sell 125 million action figures by fall 1985. It was the exact reverse of the Mego model—from now on, toys would lead to TV. And, eventually, movies.

Transformers lived in the interregnum—the quiet period between the beeps of Simon and the arrival of Nintendo—and no toy since has duplicated their success. It's morning in America any time Transformers are back, but the decade they came from feels like a galaxy far, far away.

Suggestions for Discussion

1. How does Suellentrop suggest that the popularity of the original Transformers toy line and multimedia narrative were the result of Reagan-era legislation and 1980s advertising strategies?

2. Does knowing the history of the creation of the Transformers "brand" help us understand the success of the recent *Transformers* movies? Is the modern science fiction narrative similar and different? How does the "business model" of the Transformers of today seem similar to and/or different from the marketing initiatives of the 1980s?

3. Synthesis: Compare and contrast this article to Peggy Orenstein's "What's Wrong with Cinderella?"

Suggestion for Writing

Synthesis: Sherry Turkle's essay, "Cuddling Up to Cyborg Babies," touches on similar issues. Write a brief paper in which you consider the arguments in this essay alongside those of Turkle.

ᴄᴜᴄᴜᴄᴜ

MARGARET ATWOOD

Pornography

Margaret Atwood was born in 1939 in Ottawa, Canada, and was educated at Victoria College of the University of Toronto, Radcliffe College, and Harvard University. Her novels include *Bodily Harm* (1982), *The Hand-maid's Tale* (1986), *Cat's Eye* (1989), *Alias Grace* (1996), and *The Robber Bride* (1994). She has also written a controversial study of Canadian literature, *Survival* (1972), and compiled *The New Oxford Book of Cana-dian Verse in English* (1983). She earned a Booker Prize for *The Blind Assasin* (2000), and her recent work includes *Payback* (2008) and *The Year of the Flood* (2009). Her *Selected Poems*, originally published in 1976, has appeared in several editions, the latest in 1992. In this essay, from *Chatel-aine* (1988), she attempts to explain clearly why pornography is intoler-able and why discussions of banning it have created much confusion.

When I was in Finland a few years ago for an international writers' con-ference, I had occasion to say a few paragraphs in public on the subject of pornography. The context was a discussion of political repression, and I was suggesting the possibility of a link between the two. The immediate result was that a male journalist took several large bites out of me. Prudery and pornography are two halves of the same coin, said he, and I was clearly a prude. What could you expect from an Anglo-Canadian? Afterward, a cou-ple of pleasant Scandinavian men asked me what I had been so worked up about. All "pornography" means, they said, is graphic depictions of whores, and what was the harm in that?

Not until then did it strike me that the male journalist and I had two entirely different things in mind. By "pornography," he meant naked bod-ies and sex. I, on the other hand, had recently been doing the research for my novel *Bodily Harm*, and was still in a state of shock from some of the material I had seen, including the Ontario Board of Film Censors' "out-takes." By "pornography," I meant women getting their nipples snipped off with garden shears, having meat hooks stuck into their vaginas, being dis-emboweled; little girls being raped; men (yes, there are some men) being smashed to a pulp and forcibly sodomized. The cutting edge of pornogra-phy, as far as I could see, was no longer simple old copulation, hanging from the chandelier or otherwise: it was death, messy, explicit and highly sadis-tic. I explained this to the nice Scandinavian men. "Oh, but that's just the

United States," they said. "Everyone knows they're sick." In their country, they said, violent "pornography" of that kind was not permitted on television or in movies; indeed, excessive violence of any kind was not permitted. They had drawn a clear line between erotica, which earlier studies had shown did not incite men to more aggressive and brutal behavior toward women, and violence, which later studies indicated did.

Some time after that I was in Saskatchewan, where, because of the scenes in *Bodily Harm*, I found myself on an open-line radio show answering questions about "pornography." Almost no one who phoned in was in favor of it, but again they weren't talking about the same stuff I was, because they hadn't seen it. Some of them were all set to stamp out bathing suits and negligees, and, if possible, any depictions of the female body whatsoever. God, it was implied, did not approve of female bodies, and sex of any kind, including that practised by bumblebees, should be shoved back into the dark, where it belonged. I had more than a suspicion that *Lady Chatterley's Lover*, Margaret Laurence's *The Diviners*, and indeed most books by most serious modern authors would have ended up as confetti if left in the hands of these callers.

For me, these two experiences illustrate the two poles of the emotionally heated debate that is now thundering around this issue. They also underline the desirability and even the necessity of defining the terms. "Pornography" is now one of those catchalls, like "Marxism" and "feminism," that have become so broad they can mean almost anything, ranging from certain verses in the Bible, ads for skin lotion and sex texts for children to the contents of *Penthouse*, Naughty '90s postcards and films with titles containing the word *Nazi* that show vicious scenes of torture and killing. It's easy to say that sensible people can tell the difference. Unfortunately, opinions on what constitutes a sensible person vary.

But even sensible people tend to lose their cool when they start talking about this subject. They soon stop talking and start yelling, and the name-calling begins. Those in favor of censorship (which may include groups not noticeably in agreement on other issues, such as some feminists and religious fundamentalists) accuse the others of exploiting women through the use of degrading images, contributing to the corruption of children, and adding to the general climate of violence and threat in which both women and children live in this society; or, though they may not give much of a hoot about actual women and children, they invoke moral standards and God's supposed aversion to "filth," "smut" and deviated *perversion*, which may mean ankles.

The camp in favor of total "freedom of expression" often comes out howling as loud as the Romans would have if told they could no longer have innocent fun watching the lions eat up Christians. It too may include segments of the population who are not natural bedfellows: those who proclaim their God-given right to freedom, including the freedom to tote guns, drive when drunk, drool over chicken porn and get off on videotapes of women being raped and beaten, may be waving the same anticensorship banner as responsible liberals who fear the return of Mrs. Grundy, or gay groups for whom sexual emancipation involves the concept of "sexual theatre." *Whatever turns you on* is a handy motto, as is *A man's home is his castle* (and if it includes a dungeon with beautiful maidens strung up in chains and bleeding from every pore, that's his business).

Meanwhile, theoreticians theorize and speculators speculate. Is today's pornography yet another indication of the hatred of the body, the deep mind-body split, which is supposed to pervade Western Christian society? Is it a backlash against the women's movement by men who are threatened by uppity female behavior in real life, so like to fantasize about women done up like outsize parcels, being turned into hamburger, kneeling at their feet in slavelike adoration or sucking off guns? Is it a sign of collective impotence, of a generation of men who can't relate to real women at all but have to make do with bits of celluloid and paper? Is the current flood just a result of smart marketing and aggressive promotion by the money men in what has now become a multibillion-dollar industry? If they were selling movies about men getting their testicles stuck full of knitting needles by women with swastikas on their sleeves, would they do as well, or is this penchant somehow peculiarly male? If so, why? Is pornography a power trip rather than a sex one? Some say that those ropes, chains, muzzles and other restraining devices are an argument for the immense power female sexuality still wields in the male imagination: you don't put these things on dogs unless you're afraid of them. Others, more literary, wonder about the shift from the 19th-century Magic Women or Femme Fatale image to the lollipop-licker, airhead or turkey-carcass treatment of women in porn today. The proporners don't care much about theory: they merely demand product. The anti-porners don't care about it in the final analysis either: there's dirt on the street, and they want it cleaned up, now.

It seems to me that this conversation, with its *You're-a-prude/You're-a-pervert* dialectic, will never get anywhere as long as we continue to think of this material as just "entertainment." Possibly we're deluded by the packaging, the format: magazine, book, movie, theatrical presentation. We're used to thinking of these things as part of the "entertainment industry," and we're used to thinking of ourselves as free adult people who ought to be able to see any kind of "entertainment" we want to. That was what the First Choice pay-TV debate was all about. After all, it's only entertainment, right? Entertainment means fun, and only a killjoy would be antifun. What's the harm?

This is obviously the central question: *What's the harm?* If there isn't any real harm to any real people, then the antiporners can tsk-tsk and/or throw up as much as they like, but they can't rightfully expect more legal controls or sanctions. However, the no-harm position is far from being proven.

(For instance, there's a clear-cut case for banning—as the federal government has proposed—movies, photos and videos that depict children engaging in sex with adults: real children are used to make the movies, and hardly anybody thinks this is ethical. The possibilities for coercion are too great.)

To shift the viewpoint, I'd like to suggest three other models for looking at "pornography"—and here I mean the violent kind.

Those who find the idea of regulating pornographic materials repugnant because they think it's Fascist or Communist or otherwise not in accordance with the principles of an open democratic society should consider that Canada has made it illegal to disseminate material that may lead to hatred toward any group because of race or religion. I suggest that if pornography of the violent kind depicted these acts being done predominantly to Chinese, to blacks, to Catholics, it would be off the market immediately, under the present laws. Why is hate literature illegal? Because whoever made the law thought that such material might incite real people to do real awful things to other real people. The human brain is to a certain extent a computer: garbage in, garbage out. We only hear about the extreme cases (like that of American multimurderer Ted Bundy) in which pornography has contributed to the death and/or mutilation of women and/or men. Although pornography is not the only factor involved in the creation of such deviance, it certainly has upped the ante by suggesting both a variety of techniques and the social acceptability of such actions. Nobody knows yet what effect this stuff is having on the less psychotic.

Studies have shown that a large part of the market for all kinds of porn, soft and hard, is drawn from the 16-to-21-year-old population of young men. Boys used to learn about sex on the street, or (in Italy, according to Fellini movies) from friendly whores, or, in more genteel surroundings, from girls, their parents, or, once upon a time, in school, more or less. Now porn has been added, and sex education in the schools is rapidly being phased out. The buck has been passed, and boys are being taught that all women secretly like to be raped and that real men get high on scooping out women's digestive tracts.

Boys learn their concept of masculinity from other men: is this what most men want them to be learning? If word gets around that rapists are "normal" and even admirable men, will boys feel that in order to be normal, admirable and masculine they will have to be rapists? Human beings are enormously flexible, and how they turn out depends a lot on how they're educated, by the society in which they're immersed as well as by their teachers. In a society that advertises and glorifies rape or even implicitly condones it, more women get raped. It becomes socially acceptable. And at a time when men and the traditional male role have taken a lot of flak and men are confused and casting around for an acceptable way of being male (and, in some cases, not getting much comfort from women on that score), this must be at times a pleasing thought.

It would be naïve to think of violent pornography as just harmless entertainment. It's also an educational tool and a powerful propaganda device. What happens when boy educated on porn meets girl brought up on Harlequin romances? The clash of expectations can be heard around the block. She wants him to get down on his knees with a ring, he wants her to get down on all fours with a ring in her nose. Can this marriage be saved?

Pornography has certain things in common with such addictive substances as alcohol and drugs: for some, though by no means for all, it induces chemical changes in the body, which the user finds exciting and pleasurable. It also appears to attract a "hard core" of habitual users and a penumbra of those who use it occasionally but aren't dependent on it in any way. There are also significant numbers of men who aren't much interested in it, not because they're undersexed but because real life is satisfying their needs, which may not require as many appliances as those of users.

For the "hard core," pornography may function as alcohol does for the alcoholic: tolerance develops, and a little is no longer enough. This may account for the short viewing time and fast turnover in porn theatres. Mary Brown, chairwoman of the Ontario Board of Film Censors, estimates that for every one mainstream movie requesting entrance to Ontario, there is one porno flick. Not only the quantity consumed but the quality of explicitness must escalate, which may account for the growing violence: once the big deal was breasts, then it was genitals, then copulation, then that was no longer enough and the hard users had to have more. The ultimate kick is death, and after that, as the Marquis de Sade so boringly demonstrated, multiple death.

The existence of alcoholism has not led us to ban social drinking. On the other hand, we do have laws about drinking and driving, excessive drunkenness and other abuses of alcohol that may result in injury or death to others.

This leads us back to the key question: what's the harm? Nobody knows, but this society should find out fast, before the saturation point is reached. The Scandinavian studies that showed a connection between depictions of sexual violence and increased impulse toward it on the part of male viewers would be a starting point, but many more questions remain to be raised as well as answered. What, for instance, is the crucial difference between men who are users and men who are not? Does using affect a man's relationship with actual women, and, if so, adversely? Is there a clear line between erotica and violent pornography, or are they on an escalating continuum? Is this a "men versus women" issue, with all men secretly siding with the proporners and all women secretly siding against? (I think not; there *are* lots of men who don't think that running their true love through the Cuisinart is the best way they can think of to spend a Saturday night, and they're just as nauseated by films of someone else doing it as women are.) Is pornography merely an expression of the sexual confusion of this age or an active contributor to it?

Nobody wants to go back to the age of official repression, when even piano legs were referred to as "limbs" and had to wear pantaloons to be decent. Neither do we want to end up in George Orwell's *1984*, in which pornography is turned out by the State to keep the proles in a state of torpor, sex itself is considered dirty and the approved practise is only for reproduction. But Rome under the emperors isn't such a good model either.

If all men and women respected each other, if sex were considered joyful and life-enhancing instead of a wallow in germ-filled glop, if everyone were in love all the time, if, in other words, many people's lives were more satisfactory for them than they appear to be now, pornography might just go away on its own. But since this is obviously not happening, we as a society are going to have to make some informed and responsible decisions about how to deal with it.

Suggestions for Discussion

1. Identify the following in the essay: D. H. Lawrence's *Lady Chatterley's Lover*, Margaret Laurence's *The Diviners*, Mrs. Grundy, the Marquis de Sade.

2. Summarize Atwood's major argument against pornography. What action does she believe society should take against it?

3. How do the Scandinavian countries deal with pornography? How do they define it?

4. Is Atwood too pessimistic about the ability of people who watch or read pornography to resist translating it into action themselves?

Suggestions for Writing

1. Write a paper in which you express your agreement or disagreement with Atwood's definition of pornography.

2. Does Atwood's position result in censorship? Are you opposed to censorship? Write a paper in which you discuss censorship and pornography as defined by Atwood.

3. Is pornography an issue for women or is it important to both sexes? Write a paper in which you explain your opinion.

Conscious Reading,
Intelligent Writing

∽∽∽∽∽

Reading is the creative center of a writer's life. I take a book with me everywhere I go and find there are all sorts of opportunities to dip in. The trick is to teach yourself to read in small sips as well as long swallows.

—STEPHEN KING, *On Writing*

Has this ever happened to you?
You work very horde on a paper for English clash
And then get a very glow raid (like a D or even a D=)
and all because you are the word's liverwurst spoiler.
Proofreading your peppers is a matter of the the utmost impotence

—TAYLOR MALI, *The The Impotence of Proofreading*

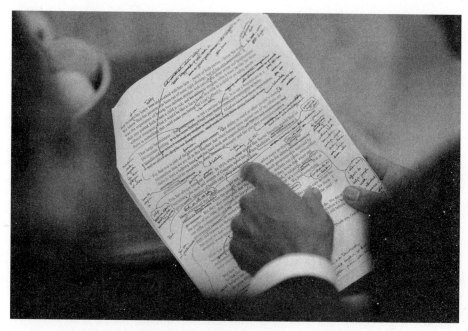

Twitter page of President Obama's handwritten edits of his September 9, 2009, speech to Congress about health care reform. Courtesy of the White House.

INTRODUCTION

This book is called *The Conscious Reader*—so a discussion of what we mean by that seems like a good place to start. A conscious reader is one who reads seriously and critically. But, above all, a conscious reader is one who *reads*. First, we must read.

Excuses abound for not reading: busy schedules, traffic, distracting phone calls and text messages, kids, great shows on cable TV. A report from the National Endowment for the Arts (19 November 2007) argues that reading test scores for young learners are dropping sharply—and their math and science skills are suffering as well—because they spend less time reading for fun. Anecdotal evidence also suggests that fewer books are being assigned in schools, from elementary school through graduate school. Employers complain that many of their new employees lack basic reading and writing skills. (Not surprisingly, related studies suggest that those who read often are more likely to get better jobs than those who read infrequently or not at all.)

Why don't we read? Amazon.com founder and CEO Jeff Bezos argues that reading simply can't compete in the digital world because it is less "sexy" than video games, DVDs, messaging, and other new media. "Books are the last bastion of analog," according to Bezos (*Newsweek*, 26 November 2007). In response, Bezos sponsored the creation of what he saw as the next generation of books, the Kindle, a wireless, portable device that allows readers to access more than 300,000 books, blogs, magazines, and newspapers, and many others including Barnes and Noble, Sony, and Apple have followed suit. Perhaps Kindle and products like it will make reading "cool" again. We certainly hope so.

The editors of this "analog" volume believe strongly that reading increases knowledge, enhances wisdom, and provides us with a unique sense of fulfillment. Reading—*conscious* reading—also makes us better writers. The more we understand about how written texts are constructed, the better we will be at applying that to our own writing. Also, reading and writing well will make us many things—more employable, better citizens, and better parents and friends, among them.

The following selections suggest methods for reading with comprehension and, because good readers make good writers, writing intelligently. We begin with a very successful writer, Stephen King, who talks compellingly about why we need to read and write at every opportunity. The essays that follow by Malcolm X and Flannery O'Connor—two people who could hardly be more different—together argue for the power of reading in changing lives.

A classic selection by Virginia Woolf offers personal thoughts about the question of what it means to be a female writer—an issue she wrestled with throughout her career.

The Essays section offers both guidance on writing well (and persuasively) from admired stylists and teachers and thoughts on the experience of reading from essayist and creative nonfiction forerunner Henry David Thoreau. A timely essay about the pervasive problem of plagiarism considers the causes of plagiarism and how it can be avoided and exposed, while an article about Instant Messaging considers why academic and business writing should be more formal than chatty, slang-filled missives sent to friends via an iPhone or Facebook chat feature. Finally, slam poetry celebrity and veteran K–12 English, history, and math teacher Taylor Mali provides sound advice about reading, editing, and revising one's own work before submitting it to the teacher. To drive his point home, he uses language that will offend many readers who are bothered by swear words, but his poem "The The Impotence of Proofreading" is as convincing as it is amusing, if read in the right spirit.

All in all, we have chosen texts that we hope will challenge you to think, enrich your self-awareness, and broaden your worldview. The texts between these covers are intended to be read carefully, with the reader's full attention—and ideally to be reread, for a deeper and richer understanding. We expect readers to think seriously about the arguments that each text makes; we hope you will not dismiss too quickly those texts that represent a worldview different from your own, or those that seem outright *weird*, or even offensive. After all, those moments when we confront the different, the weird, or the offensive are often the very moments when we are granted unique opportunities to grow in knowledge, understanding, and tolerance.

NOTEBOOK

❧❧❧❧

STEPHEN KING

On Writing

Stephen King (b. 1947), the famous horror novelist, has written scores of books in the genre, many of which were made into highly successful motion pictures. Critics have noted that his protagonists, both in his horror works and his dramas, are often children or intellectual young men who find themselves pitted against sinister authority figures. The Bangor, Maine, resident is best known for the novels *Carrie, The Shining, Salem's Lot, The Stand, Misery, Cujo*, and *The Dead Zone*. King also wrote a book of essays on the gothic genre called *Danse Macabre* (1980), and his most acclaimed forays outside of the supernatural are the dramatic novellas *Rita Hayworth and the Shawshank Redemption* and *Stand By Me* (also known as *The Body*), both of which appeared in his 1982 book *Different Seasons*. His recent works include *Under the Dome* (2009), *Duma Key* (2008), and *On Writing* (2000), a combination memoir and guidebook to aspiring writers, from which the following passage is reprinted.

If you want to be a writer, you must do two things above all others: read a lot and write a lot. There's no way around these two things that I'm aware of, no shortcut.

I'm a slow reader, but I usually get through seventy or eighty books a year, mostly fiction. I don't read in order to study the craft; I read because I like to read. It's what I do at night, kicked back in my blue chair. Similarly, I don't read fiction to study the art of fiction, but simply because I like stories. Yet there is a learning process going on. Every book you pick up has its own lesson or lessons, and quite often the bad books have more to teach than the good ones.

When I was in the eighth grade, I happened upon a paperback novel by Murray Leinster, a science fiction pulp writer who did most of his work during the forties and fifties, when magazines like *Amazing Stories* paid a penny a word. I had read other books by Mr. Leinster, enough to know that the quality of his writing was uneven. This particular tale, which was about mining in the asteroid belt, was one of his less successful efforts. Only that's too kind. It was terrible, actually, a story populated by paper-thin characters and driven by outlandish plot developments. Worst of all (or so it seemed to me at the time), Leinster had fallen in love with the word *zestful*.

Characters watched the approach of ore-bearing asteroids with *zestful smiles*. Characters sat down to supper aboard their mining ship with *zestful anticipation*. Near the end of the book, the hero swept the large-breasted, blonde heroine into a *zestful embrace*. For me, it was the literary equivalent of a smallpox vaccination: I have never, so far as I know, used the word *zestful* in a novel or a story. God willing, I never will.

Asteroid Miners (which wasn't the title, but that's close enough) was an important book in my life as a reader. Almost everyone can remember losing his or her virginity, and most writers can remember the first book he/she put down thinking: *I can do better than this. Hell, I am doing better than this!* What could be more encouraging to the struggling writer than to realize his/her work is unquestionably better than that of someone who actually got paid for his/her stuff?

One learns most clearly what not to do by reading bad prose—one novel like *Asteroid Miners* (or *Valley of the Dolls, Flowers in the Attic,* and *The Bridges of Madison County,* to name just a few) is worth a semester at a good writing school, even with the superstar guest lecturers thrown in.

Good writing, on the other hand, teaches the learning writer about style, graceful narration, plot development, the creation of believable characters, and truth-telling. A novel like *The Grapes of Wrath* may fill a new writer with feelings of despair and good old-fashioned jealousy—"I'll never be able to write anything that good, not if I live to be a thousand"—but such feelings can also serve as a spur, goading the writer to work harder and aim higher. Being swept away by a combination of great story and great writing—of being flattened, in fact—is part of every writer's necessary formation. You cannot hope to sweep someone else away by the force of your writing until it has been done to you.

So we read to experience the mediocre and the outright rotten; such experience helps us to recognize those things when they begin to creep into our own work, and to steer clear of them. We also read in order to measure ourselves against the good and the great, to get a sense of all that can be done. And we read in order to experience different styles.

You may find yourself adopting a style you find particularly exciting, and there's nothing wrong with that. When I read Ray Bradbury as a kid, I wrote like Ray Bradbury—everything green and wondrous and seen through a lens smeared with the grease of nostalgia. When I read James M. Cain, everything I wrote came out clipped and stripped and hard-boiled. When I read Lovecraft, my prose became luxurious and Byzantine. I wrote stories in my teenage years where all these styles merged, creating a kind of hilarious stew.

This sort of stylistic blending is a necessary part of developing one's own style, but it doesn't occur in a vacuum. You have to read widely, constantly refining (and redefining) your own work as you do so. It's hard for me to believe that people who read very little (or not at all in some cases) should presume to write and expect people to like what they have written, but I know it's true. If I had a nickel for every person who ever told me he/she wanted to become a writer but "didn't have time to read," I could buy myself a pretty good steak dinner. Can I be blunt on this subject? If you don't have time to read, you don't have the time (or the tools) to write. Simple as that.

Reading is the creative center of a writer's life. I take a book with me everywhere I go, and find there are all sorts of opportunities to dip in. The trick is to teach yourself to read in small sips as well as in long swallows. Waiting rooms were made for books—of course! But so are theater lobbies before the show, long and boring checkout lines, and everyone's favorite, the john. You can even read while you're driving, thanks to the audiobook revolution. Of the books I read each year, anywhere from six to a dozen are on tape. As for all the wonderful radio you will be missing, come on—how many times can you listen to Deep Purple sing "Highway Star"?

Reading at meals is considered rude in polite society, but if you expect to succeed as a writer, rudeness should be the second-to-least of your concerns. The least of all should be polite society and what it expects. If you intend to write as truthfully as you can, your days as a member of polite society are numbered, anyway.

Where else can you read? There's always the treadmill, or whatever you use down at the local health club to get aerobic. I try to spend an hour doing that every day, and I think I'd go mad without a good novel to keep me company. Most exercise facilities (at home as well as outside it) are now equipped with TVs, but TV—while working out or anywhere else—really is about the last thing an aspiring writer needs. If you feel you must have the news analyst blowhards on CNN while you exercise, or the stock market blowhards on MSNBC, or the sports blowhards on ESPN, it's time for you to question how serious you really are about becoming a writer. You must be prepared to do some serious turning inward toward the life of the imagination, and that means, I'm afraid, that Geraldo, Keith Olbermann, and Jay Leno must go. Reading takes time, and the glass teat takes too much of it.

Once weaned from the ephemeral craving for TV, most people will find they enjoy the time they spend reading. I'd like to suggest that turning off that endlessly quacking box is apt to improve the quality of your life as well as the quality of your writing. And how much of a sacrifice are we talking about here? How many *Frasier* and *ER* reruns does it take to make one American life complete? How many Richard Simmons infomercials? How many whiteboy/fatboy Beltway insiders on CNN? Oh man, don't get me started. Jerry-Springer-Dr.-Dre-Judge-Judy-Jerry-Falwell-Donny-and-Marie, I rest my case.

When my son Owen was seven or so, he fell in love with Bruce Spring-steen's E Street Band, particularly with Clarence Clemons, the band's burly sax player. Owen decided he wanted to learn to play like Clarence. My wife and I were amused and delighted by this ambition. We were also hopeful, as any parent would be, that our kid would turn out to be talented, perhaps even some sort of prodigy. We got Owen a tenor saxophone for Christmas and lessons with Gordon Bowie, one of the local music men. Then we crossed our fingers and hoped for the best.

Seven months later I suggested to my wife that it was time to discontinue the sax lessons, if Owen concurred. Owen did, and with palpable relief—he hadn't wanted to say it himself, especially not after asking for the sax in the first place, but seven months had been long enough for him to realize that, while he might love Clarence Clemons's big sound, the saxophone was simply not for him—God had not given him that particular talent.

I knew, not because Owen stopped practicing, but because he was practicing only during the periods Mr. Bowie had set for him: half an hour after school four days a week, plus an hour on the weekends. Owen mastered the scales and the notes—nothing wrong with his memory, his lungs, or his eye-hand coordination—but we never heard him taking off, surprising himself with something new, blissing himself out. And as soon as his practice time was over, it was back into the case with the horn, and there it stayed until the next lesson or practice-time. What this suggested to me was that when it came to the sax and my son, there was never going to be any real playtime; it was all going to be rehearsal. That's no good. If there's no joy in it, it's just no good. It's best to go on to some other area, where the deposits of talent may be richer and the fun quotient higher.

Talent renders the whole idea of rehearsal meaningless; when you find something at which you are talented, you do it (whatever *it* is) until your fingers bleed or your eyes are ready to fall out of your head. Even when no one is listening (or reading, or watching), every outing is a bravura performance, because you as the creator are happy. Perhaps even ecstatic. That goes for reading and writing as well as for playing a musical instrument, hitting a baseball, or running the four-forty. The sort of strenuous reading and writing program I advocate—four to six hours a day, every day—will not seem strenuous if you really enjoy doing these things and have an aptitude for them; in fact, you may be following such a program already. If you feel you need permission to do all the reading and writing your little heart desires, however, consider it hereby granted by yours truly.

The real importance of reading is that it creates an ease and intimacy with the process of writing; one comes to the country of the writer with one's papers and identification pretty much in order. Constant reading will pull you into a place (a mind-set, if you like the phrase) where you can write

eagerly and without self-consciousness. It also offers you a constantly growing knowledge of what has been done and what hasn't, what is trite and what
is fresh, what works and what just lies there dying (or dead) on the page.
The more you read, the less apt you are to make a fool of yourself with your
pen or word processor.

Suggestions for Discussion

1. Why does King feel that reading bad books can have a positive effect on a
   budding writer? What effect can the reading of good writing have?

2. According to King, why is it so necessary to read a lot and to write a lot in
   order to be a good writer?

3. What kinds of sacrifices does King believe a writer must make if he or she
   expects to succeed at becoming a good writer?

Suggestion for Writing

Take a dreadful story, poem, play, or screenplay and extensively rewrite it to
make it great.

MALCOLM X

A Homemade Education

Malcolm X (1925–1965), born Malcolm Little, became a Muslim while
serving a prison sentence and was an early minister of the Nation of
Islam's mosque in New York. Before his assassination, he was a spiritual
leader, writer, lecturer, and political activist who worked for worldwide
African-American unity and equality. The following selection is taken
from his powerful *Autobiography of Malcolm X* (1965).

It was because of my letters that I happened to stumble upon starting
to acquire some kind of a homemade education.

I became increasingly frustrated at not being able to express what
I wanted to convey in letters that I wrote, especially those to Mr. Elijah
Muhammad. In the street, I had been the most articulate hustler out
there—I had commanded attention when I said something. But now,

trying to write simple English, I not only wasn't articulate, I wasn't even functional. How would I sound writing in slang, the way I would say it, something such as, "Look, daddy, let me 'pull your coat about a cat, Elijah Muhammad—"

Many who today hear me somewhere in person, or on television, or those who read something I've said, will think I went to school far beyond the eighth grade. This impression is due entirely to my prison studies.

It had really begun back in the Charlestown Prison, when Bimbi first made me feel envy of his stock of knowledge. Bimbi had always taken charge of any conversations he was in, and I had tried to emulate him. But every book I picked up had few sentences which didn't contain anywhere from one to nearly all of the words that might as well have been in Chinese. When I just skipped those words, of course, I really ended up with little idea of what the book said. So I had come to the Norfolk Prison Colony still going through only book-reading motions. Pretty soon, I would have quit even these motions, unless I had received the motivation that I did.

I saw that the best thing I could do was get hold of a dictionary—to study, to learn some words. I was lucky enough to reason also that I should try to improve my penmanship. It was sad. I couldn't even write in a straight line. It was both ideas together that moved me to request a dictionary along with some tablets and pencils from the Norfolk Prison Colony school.

I spent two days just riffling uncertainly through the dictionary's pages. I'd never realized so many words existed! I didn't know which words I needed to learn. Finally, just to start some kind of action, I began copying.

In my slow, painstaking, ragged handwriting, I copied into my tablet everything printed on that first page, down to the punctuation marks.

I believe it took me a day. Then, aloud, I read back, to myself, everything I'd written on the tablet. Over and over, aloud, to myself, I read my own handwriting.

I woke up the next morning, thinking about those words—immensely proud to realize that not only had I written so much at one time, but I'd written words that I never knew were in the world. Moreover, with a little effort, I also could remember what many of these words meant. I reviewed the words whose meanings I didn't remember. Funny thing, from the dictionary first page right now, that "aardvark" springs to my mind. The dictionary had a picture of it, a long-tailed, long-eared, burrowing African mammal, which lives off termites caught by sticking out its tongue as an anteater does for ants.

I was so fascinated that I went on—I copied the dictionary's next page. And the same experience came when I studied that. With every succeeding page, I also learned of people and places and events from history. Actually the dictionary is like a miniature encyclopedia. Finally the dictionary's A section had filled a whole tablet—and I went on into the B's. That was the way I started copying what eventually became the entire dictionary. It went a lot faster after so much practice helped me to pick up handwriting speed. Between what I wrote in my tablet, and writing letters, during the rest of my time in prison I would guess I wrote a million words.

I suppose it was inevitable that as my word-base broadened, I could for the first time pick up a book and read and now begin to understand what the book was saying. Anyone who has read a great deal can imagine the new world that opened. Let me tell you something: from then until I left that prison, in every free moment I had, if I was not reading in the library, I was reading on my bunk. You couldn't have gotten me out of books with a wedge. Between Mr. Muhammad's teachings, my correspondence, my visitors—usually Ella and Reginald—and my reading of books, months passed without my even thinking about being imprisoned. In fact, up to then, I never had been so truly free in my life.

The Norfolk Prison Colony's library was in the school building. A variety of classes was taught there by instructors who came from such places as Harvard and Boston universities. The weekly debates between inmate teams were also held in the school building. You would be astonished to know how worked up convict debaters and audiences would get over subjects like "Should Babies Be Fed Milk?"

Available on the prison library's shelves were books on just about every general subject. Much of the big private collection that Parkhurst had willed to the prison was still in crates and boxes in the back of the library— thousands of old books. Some of them looked ancient: covers faded; old-time parchment-looking binding. Parkhurst, I've mentioned, seemed to have been principally interested in history and religion. He had the money and the special interest to have a lot of books that you wouldn't have in general circulation. Any college library would have been lucky to get that collection.

As you can imagine, especially in a prison where there was heavy emphasis on rehabilitation, an inmate was smiled upon if he demonstrated an unusually intense interest in books. There was a sizable number of well-read inmates, especially the popular debaters. Some were said by many to be practically walking encyclopedias. They were almost celebrities. No university would ask any student to devour literature as I did when this new world opened to me, of being able to read and understand.

I read more in my room than in the library itself. An inmate who was known to read a lot could check out more than the permitted maximum number of books. I preferred reading in the total isolation of my own room.

When I had progressed to really serious reading, every night at about ten P.M. I would be outraged with the "lights out." It always seemed to catch me right in the middle of something engrossing.

Fortunately, right outside my door was a corridor light that cast a glow into my room. The glow was enough to read by, once my eyes adjusted to it.

So when "lights out" came, I would sit on the floor where I could continue reading in that glow.

At one-hour intervals the night guards paced past every room. Each time I heard the approaching footsteps, I jumped into bed and feigned sleep. And as soon as the guard passed, I got back out of bed onto the floor area of that light-glow, where I would read for another fifty-eight minutes—until the guard approached again. That went on until three or four every morning. Three or four hours of sleep a night was enough for me. Often in the years in the streets I had slept less than that.

The teachings of Mr. Muhammad stressed how history had been "whitened"—when white men had written history books, the black man simply had been left out. Mr. Muhammad couldn't have said anything that would have struck me much harder. I had never forgotten how when my class, me and all of those whites, had studied seventh-grade United States history back in Mason, the history of the Negro had been covered in one paragraph, and the teacher had gotten a big laugh with his joke, "Negroes' feet are so big that when they walk, they leave a hole in the ground."

This is one reason why Mr. Muhammad's teachings spread so swiftly all over the United States, among all Negroes, whether or not they became followers of Mr. Muhammad. The teachings ring true—to every Negro. You can hardly show me a black adult in America—or a white one, for that matter—who knows from the history books anything like the truth about the black man's role. In my own case, once I heard of the "glorious history of the black man," I took special pains to hunt in the library for books that would inform me on details about black history.

I can remember accurately the very first set of books that really impressed me. I have since bought that set of books and I have it at home for my children to read as they grow up. It's called *Wonders of the World*. It's full of pictures of archaeological finds, statues that depict, usually, non-European people.

I found books like Will Durant's *Story of Civilization*. I read H. G. Wells' *Outline of History*. *Souls of Black Folk* by W. E. B. Du Bois gave me a glimpse into the black people's history before they came to this country. Carter G. Woodson's *Negro History* opened my eyes about black empires before the black slave was brought to the United States, and the early Negro struggles for freedom.

J. A. Rogers' three volumes of *Sex and Race* told about race-mixing before Christ's time; about Aesop being a black man who told fables; about Egypt's Pharaohs; about the great Coptic Christian Empires; about Ethiopia, the earth's oldest continuous black civilization, as China is the oldest continuous civilization.

Mr. Muhammad's teaching about how the white man had been created led me to *Findings in Genetics* by Gregor Mendel. (The dictionary's

G section was where I had learned what "genetics" meant.) I really studied this book by the Austrian monk. Reading it over and over, especially certain sections, helped me to understand that if you started with a black man, a white man could be produced; but starting with a white man, you never could produce a black man—because the white chromosome is recessive. And since no one disputes that there was but one Original Man, the conclusion is clear.

During the last year or so, in the *New York Times*, Arnold Toynbee used the word "bleached" in describing the white man. (His words were: "White [i.e., bleached] human beings of North European origin. . . .") Toynbee also referred to the European geographic area as only a peninsula of Asia. He said there is no such thing as Europe. And if you look at the globe, you will see for yourself that America is only an extension of Asia. (But at the same time Toynbee is among those who have helped to bleach history. He won't write that again. Every day now, the truth is coming to light.)

I never will forget how shocked I was when I began reading about slavery's total horror. It made such an impact upon me that it later became one of my favorite subjects when I became a minister of Mr. Muhammad's. The world's most monstrous crime, the sin and the blood on the white man's hands, are almost impossible to believe. Books like the one by Frederick Olmstead opened my eyes to the horrors suffered when the slave was landed in the United States. The European woman, Fannie Kimball, who had married a Southern white slaveowner, described how human beings were degraded. Of course I read *Uncle Tom's Cabin*. In fact, I believe that's the only novel I have ever read since I started serious reading.

Parkhurst's collection also contained some bound pamphlets of the Abolitionist Anti-Slavery Society of New England. I read descriptions of atrocities, saw those illustrations of black slave women tied up and flogged with whips; of black mothers watching their babies being dragged off, never to be seen by their mothers again; of dogs after slaves, and of the fugitive slave catchers, evil white men with whips and clubs and chains and guns. I read about the slave preacher Nat Turner, who put the fear of God into the white slavemaster. Nat Turner wasn't going around preaching pie-in-the-sky and "nonviolent" freedom for the black man. There in Virginia one night in 1831, Nat and seven other slaves started out at his master's home and through the night they went from one plantation "big house" to the next, killing, until by the next morning 57 white people were dead and Nat had about 70 slaves following him. White people, terrified for their lives, fled from their homes, locked themselves up in public buildings, hid in the woods, and some even left the state. A small army of soldiers took two months to catch and hang Nat Turner. Somewhere I have read where Nat Turner's example is said to have inspired John Brown to invade Virginia and attack Harper's Ferry nearly thirty years later, with thirteen white men and five Negroes.

I read Herodotus, "the father of History," or, rather, I read about him. And I read the histories of various nations, which opened my eyes gradually, then wider and wider, to how the whole world's white men had indeed acted like devils, pillaging and raping and bleeding and draining the whole world's non-white people. I remember, for instance, books such as Will Durant's *The Story of Oriental Civilization*, and Mahatma Gandhi's accounts of the struggle to drive the British out of India.

Book after book showed me how the white man had brought upon the world's black, brown, red, and yellow peoples every variety of the sufferings of exploitation. I saw how since the sixteenth century, the so-called "Christian trader" white man began to ply the seas in his lust for Asian and African empires, and plunder, and power. I read, I saw, how the white man never has gone among the non-white peoples bearing the Cross in the true manner and spirit of Christ's teachings—meek, humble, and Christlike.

I perceived, as I read, how the collective white man had been actually nothing but a piratical opportunist who used Faustian machinations to make his own Christianity his initial wedge in criminal conquests. First, always "religiously," he branded "heathen" and "pagan" labels upon ancient non-white cultures and civilizations. The stage thus set, he then turned upon his non-white victims his weapons of war.

I read how, entering India—half a billion deeply religious brown people—the British white man, by 1759, through promises, trickery and manipulations, controlled much of India through Great Britain's East India Company. The parasitical British administration kept tentacling out to half of the subcontinent. In 1857, some of the desperate people of India finally mutinied—and, excepting the African slave trade, nowhere has history recorded any more unnecessary bestial and ruthless human carnage than the British suppression of the non-white Indian people.

Over 115 million African blacks—close to the 1930s population of the United States—were murdered or enslaved during the slave trade. And I read how when the slave market was glutted, the cannibalistic white powers of Europe next carved up, as their colonies, the richest areas of the black continent. And Europe's chancelleries for the next century played a chess game of naked exploitation and power from Cape Horn to Cairo.

Ten guards and the warden couldn't have torn me out of those books. Not even Elijah Muhammad could have been more eloquent than those books were in providing indisputable proof that the collective white man had acted like a devil in virtually every contact he had with the world's collective non-white man. I listen today to the radio, and watch television, and read the headlines about the collective white man's fear and tension concerning China. When the white man professes ignorance about why the Chinese hate him so, my mind can't help flashing back to what I read, there in prison, about how the blood forebears of this same white man raped

China at a time when China was trusting and helpless. Those original white "Christian traders" sent into China millions of pounds of opium. By 1839, so many of the Chinese were addicts that China's desperate government destroyed twenty thousand chests of opium. The first Opium War was promptly declared by the white man. Imagine! Declaring war upon someone who objects to being narcotized! The Chinese were severely beaten, with Chinese-invented gunpowder.

The Treaty of Nanking made China pay the British white man for the destroyed opium: forced open China's major ports to British trade; forced China to abandon Hong Kong; fixed China's import tariffs so low that cheap British articles soon flooded in, maiming China's industrial development.

After a second Opium War, the Tientsin Treaties legalized the ravaging opium trade, legalized a British–French–American control of China's customs. China tried delaying that Treaty's ratification; Peking was looted and burned.

"Kill the foreign white devils!" was the 1901 Chinese war cry in the Boxer Rebellion. Losing again, this time the Chinese were driven from Peking's choicest areas. The vicious, arrogant white man put up the famous signs, "Chinese and dogs not allowed."

Red China after World War II closed its doors to the Western white world. Massive Chinese agricultural, scientific, and industrial efforts are described in a book that *Life* magazine recently published. Some observers inside Red China have reported that the world never has known such a hate-white campaign as is now going on in this non-white country where, present birthrates continuing, in fifty more years Chinese will be half the earth's population. And it seems that some Chinese chickens will soon come home to roost, with China's recent successful nuclear tests.

Let us face reality. We can see in the United Nations a new world order being shaped, along color lines—an alliance among the non-white nations. America's U.N. Ambassador Adlai Stevenson complained not long ago that in the United Nations "a skin game" was being played. He was right. He was facing reality. A "skin game" is being played. But Ambassador Stevenson sounded like Jesse James accusing the marshal of carrying a gun. Because who in the world's history ever has played a worse "skin game" than the white man?

Mr. Muhammad, to whom I was writing daily, had no idea of what a new world had opened up to me through my efforts to document his teachings in books.

When I discovered philosophy, I tried to touch all the landmarks of philosophical development. Gradually, I read most of the old philosophers, Occidental and Oriental. The Oriental philosophers were the ones I came to prefer; finally, my impression was that most Occidental philosophy had largely been borrowed from the Oriental thinkers. Socrates, for instance, traveled in Egypt. Some sources even say that Socrates was initiated into some of the Egyptian mysteries. Obviously Socrates got some of his wisdom among the East's wise men.

I have often reflected upon the new vistas that reading opened to me. I knew right there in prison that reading had changed forever the course of my life. As I see it today, the ability to read awoke inside me some long dormant craving to be mentally alive. I certainly wasn't seeking any degree, the way a college confers a status symbol upon its students. My homemade education gave me, with every additional book that I read, a little bit more sensitivity to the deafness, dumbness, and blindness that was afflicting the black race in America. Not long ago, an English writer telephoned me from London, asking questions. One was, "What's your alma mater?" I told him, "Books." You will never catch me with a free fifteen minutes in which I'm not studying something I feel might be able to help the black man.

Yesterday I spoke in London, and both ways on the plane across the Atlantic I was studying a document about how the United Nations proposes to insure the human rights of the oppressed minorities of the world. The American black man is the world's most shameful case of minority oppression. What makes the black man think of himself as only an internal United States issue is just a catch-phrase, two words, "civil rights." How is the black man going to get "civil rights" before first he wins his human rights? If the American black man will start thinking about his human rights, and then start thinking of himself as part of one of the world's great peoples, he will see he has a case for the United Nations.

I can't think of a better case! Four hundred years of black blood and sweat invested here in America, and the white man still has the black man begging for what every immigrant fresh off the ship can take for granted the minute he walks down the gangplank.

But I'm digressing. I told the Englishman that my alma mater was books, a good library. Every time I catch a plane, I have with me a book that I want to read—and that's a lot of books these days. If I weren't out here every day battling the white man, I could spend the rest of my life reading, just satisfying my curiosity—because you can hardly mention anything I'm not curious about. I don't think anybody ever got more out of going to prison than I did. In fact, prison enabled me to study far more intensively than I would have if my life had gone differently and I had attended some college. I imagine that one of the biggest troubles with colleges is there are too many distractions, too much panty-raiding, fraternities, and boola-boola and all of that. Where else but in a prison could I have attacked my ignorance by being able to study intensely sometimes as much as fifteen hours a day?

Suggestions for Discussion

1. Discuss the significance of the essay's title, "A Homemade Education."
2. Explain how Malcolm X used his dictionary to improve his education.
3. Discuss his observation that "the ability to read awoke inside me some long dormant craving to be mentally alive."
4. Comment on his assertion that his "alma mater was books."
5. What details help make clear his passion for learning?

Suggestions for Writing

1. Compare and contrast "A Homemade Education" with another section of Malcolm X's *Autobiography*.
2. Write about one or more books that have played an important role in shaping your thinking, attitudes, and behavior.

FLANNERY O'CONNOR

The Teaching of Literature

Flannery O'Connor (1925–1964), born in Georgia, was educated in Georgia schools and at the University of Iowa. She received three O. Henry first prizes for her short fiction and a Ford Foundation grant in 1959. Her books include the novels *Wise Blood* (1952) and *The Violent Bear It Away* (1960). Her collection of short stories, *Everything that Rises Must Converge*, and book of essays, *Mystery and Manners: Occasional Prose*, were both published posthumously. In these selections from *Mystery and Manners*, O'Connor argues that fewer and fewer Americans read novels because many are too timid to challenge themselves with realistic books rather than escapist ones, and because American schools don't really teach students how to read properly.

Every now and then the novelist looks up from his work long enough to become aware of a general public dissatisfaction with novelists. There's always a voice coming from somewhere that tells him he isn't doing his duty, and that if he doesn't mend his ways soon, there are going to be no more fiction readers—just as, for all practical purposes, there are now no more poetry readers.

Of course, of all the various kinds of artists, the fiction writer is most deviled by the public. Painters and musicians are protected somewhat since they don't deal with what everyone knows about, but the fiction writer writes about life, and so anyone living considers himself an authority on it.

I find that everybody approaches the novel according to his particular interest—the doctor looks for a disease, the minister looks for a sermon, the poor look for money, and the rich look for justification; and if they find what they want, or at least what they can recognize, then they judge the piece of fiction to be superior.

In the standing dispute between the novelist and the public, the teacher of English is a sort of middleman, and I have occasionally come to think about what really happens when a piece of fiction is set before students. I suppose this is a terrifying experience for the teacher.

I have a young cousin who told me that she reviewed my novel for her ninth-grade English class, and when I asked—without a trace of gratitude— why she did that, she said, "Because I had to have a book the teacher wouldn't have read." So I asked her what she said about it, and she said, "I said 'My cousin wrote this book.'" I asked her if that was all she said, and she said, "No, I copied the rest off the jacket."

So you see I do approach this problem realistically, knowing that perhaps it has no solution this side of the grave, but feeling nevertheless that there may be profit in talking about it.

I don't recall that when I was in high school or college, any novel was ever presented to me to study as a novel. In fact, I was well on the way to getting a Master's degree in English before I really knew what fiction was, and I doubt if I would ever have learned then, had I not been trying to write it. I believe that it's perfectly possible to run a course of academic degrees in English and to emerge a seemingly respectable Ph.D. and still not know how to read fiction.

The fact is, people don't know what they are expected to do with a novel, believing, as so many do, that art must be utilitarian, that it must do something, rather than be something. Their eyes have not been opened to what fiction is, and they are like the blind men who went to visit the elephant—each feels a different part and comes away with a different impression.

Now it's my feeling that if more attention, of a technical kind, were paid to the subject of fiction in the schools, even at the high-school level, this situation might be improved.

Of course, I'm in a bad position here. So far as teaching is concerned, I am in a state of pristine innocence. But I do believe that there is still a little common ground between the writer of English and the teacher of it. If you could eliminate the student from your concern, and I could eliminate the reader from mine, I believe that we should be able to find ourselves enjoying a mutual concern, which would be a love of the language and what can be done with it in the interests of dramatic truth. I believe that this is actually the primary concern of us both, and that you can't serve the student, nor I the reader, unless our aim is first to be true to the subject and its necessities. This is the reason I think the study of the novel in the schools must be a technical study.

It is the business of fiction to embody mystery through manners, and mystery is a great embarrassment to the modern mind. About the turn of the century, Henry James wrote that the young woman of the future, though she would be taken out for airings in a flying-machine, would know nothing of mystery or manners. James had no business to limit the prediction to one sex; otherwise, no one can very well disagree with him. The mystery he was talking about is the mystery of our position on earth, and the manners are those conventions which, in the hands of the artist, reveal that central mystery.

Not long ago a teacher told me that her best students feel that it is no longer necessary to write anything. She said they think that everything can be done with figures now, and that what can't be done with figures isn't worth doing. I think this is a natural belief for a generation that has been made to feel that the aim of learning is to eliminate mystery. For such people, fiction can be very disturbing, for the fiction writer is concerned with mystery that is lived. He's concerned with ultimate mystery as we find it embodied in the concrete world of sense experience.

Since this is his aim, all levels of meaning in fiction have come increasingly to be found in the literal level. There is no room for abstract expressions of compassion or piety or morality in the fiction itself. This means that the writer's moral sense must coincide with his dramatic sense, and this makes the presentation of fiction to the student, and particularly to the immature student, very difficult indeed.

I don't know how the subject is handled now, or if it is handled at all, but when I went to school I observed a number of ways in which the industrious teacher of English could ignore the nature of literature, but continue to teach the subject.

The most popular of these was simply to teach literary history instead. The emphasis was on what was written when, and what was going on in the world at that time. Now I don't think this is a discipline to be despised. Certainly students need to know these things. The historical sense is greatly in decay. Perhaps students live in an eternal present now, and it's necessary to get across to them that a Viking ship was not equipped like the *Queen Mary* and that Lord Byron didn't get to Greece by air. At the same time, this is not teaching literature, and it is not enough to sustain the student's interest in it when he leaves school.

Then I found that another popular way to avoid teaching literature was to be concerned exclusively with the author and his psychology. Why was Hawthorne melancholy and what made Poe drink liquor and why did Henry James like England better than America? These ruminations can take up endless time and postpone indefinitely any consideration of the work itself. Actually, a work of art exists without its author from the moment the words are on paper, and the more complete the work, the less important it is who wrote it or why. If you're studying literature, the intentions of the writer have to be found in the work itself, and not in his life. Psychology is an interesting subject but hardly the main consideration for the teacher of English.

Neither is sociology. When I went to school, a novel might be read in an English class because it represented a certain social problem of topical interest. Good fiction deals with human nature. If it uses material that is topical, it still does not use it for a topical purpose, and if topics are what you want anyway, you are better referred to a newspaper.

But I found that there were times when all these methods became exhausted, and the unfortunate teacher of English was faced squarely with the problem of having to teach literature. This would never do, of course, and what had to be done then was simply to kill the subject altogether. Integrate it out of existence. I once went to a high school where all the subjects were called "activities" and were so well integrated that there were no definite ones to teach. I have found that if you are astute and energetic, you can integrate English literature with geography, biology, home economics, basketball, or fire prevention—with anything at all that will put off a little longer the evil day when the story or novel must be examined simply as a story or novel.

Failure to study literature in a technical way is generally blamed, I believe, on the immaturity of the student, rather than on the unpreparedness of the teacher. I couldn't pronounce upon that, of course, but as a writer with certain grim memories of days and months of just "hanging out" in school, I can at least venture the opinion that the blame may be shared. At any rate, I don't think the nation's teachers of English have any right to be complacent about their service to literature as long as the appearance of a really fine work of fiction is so rare on the best-seller lists, for good fiction is written more often than it is read. I know, or at least I have been given to understand, that a great many high-school graduates go to college not knowing that a period ordinarily follows the end of a sentence; but what seems even more shocking to me is the number who carry away from college with them an undying appreciation for slick and juvenile fiction.

I don't know whether I am setting the aims of the teacher of English too high or too low when I suggest that it is, partly at least, his business to change the face of the best-seller list. However, I feel that the teacher's role is more fundamental than the critic's. It comes down ultimately, I think, to the fact that his first obligation is to the truth of the subject he is teaching, and that for the reading of literature ever to become a habit and a pleasure, it must first be a discipline. The student has to have tools to understand a story or a novel, and these are tools proper to the structure of the work, tools proper to the craft. They are tools that operate inside the work and not outside it; they are concerned with how this story is made and with what makes it work as a story.

You may say that this is too difficult for the student, yet actually, to begin with what can be known in a technical way about the story or the novel or the poem is to begin with the least common denominator. And you may ask what a technical understanding of a novel or poem or story has to do with the business of mystery, the embodiment of which I have been careful to say is the essence of literature. It has a great deal to do with it, and this can perhaps best be understood in the act of writing.

In the act of writing, one sees that the way a thing is made controls and is inseparable from the whole meaning of it. The form of a story gives it meaning which any other form would change, and unless the student is able, in some degree, to apprehend the form, he will never apprehend anything else about the work, except what is extrinsic to it as literature.

The result of the proper study of a novel should be contemplation of the mystery embodied in it, but this is a contemplation of the mystery in the whole work and not of some proposition or paraphrase. It is not the tracking-down of an expressible moral or statement about life. An English teacher I knew once asked her students what the moral of *The Scarlet Letter* was, and one answer she got was that the moral of *The Scarlet Letter* was, think twice before you commit adultery.

Many students are made to feel that if they can dive deep into a piece of fiction and come up with so edifying a proposition as this, their effort has not been in vain.

I think, to judge from what the nation reads, that most of our effort in the teaching of literature has been in vain, and I think that this is even more apparent when we listen to what people demand of the novelist. If people don't know what they get, they at least know what they want. Possibly the question most often asked these days about modern fiction is why do we keep on getting novels about freaks and poor people, engaged always in some violent, destructive action, when actually, in this country, we are rich and strong and democratic and the man in the street is possessed of a general good-will which overflows in all directions.

I think that this kind of question is only one of many attempts, unconscious perhaps, to separate mystery from manners in fiction, and thereby to make it more palatable to the modern taste. The novelist is asked to begin with an examination of statistics rather than with an examination of conscience. Or if he must examine his conscience, he is asked to do so in the light of statistics. I'm afraid, though, that this is not the way the novelist uses his eyes. For him, judgment is implicit in the act of seeing. His vision cannot be detached from his moral sense.

Readers have got somewhat out of the habit of feeling that they have to drain off a statable moral from a novel. Now they feel they have to drain off a statable social theory that will make life more worth living. What they wish to eliminate from fiction, at all costs, is the mystery that James foresaw the loss of. The storyteller must render what he sees and not what he thinks he ought to see, but this doesn't mean that he can't be, or that he isn't, a moralist in the sense proper to him.

It seems that the fiction writer has a revolting attachment to the poor, for even when he writes about the rich, he is more concerned with what they lack than with what they have. I am very much afraid that to the fiction writer the fact that we shall always have the poor with us is a source of satisfaction, for it means, essentially, that he will always be able to find someone like himself. His concern with poverty is with a poverty fundamental to man. I believe that the basic experience of everyone is the experience of human limitation.

One man who read my novel sent me a message by an uncle of mine. He said, "Tell that girl to quit writing about poor folks." He said, "I see poor folks every day and I get mighty tired of them, and when I read, I don't want to see any more of them."

Well, that was the first time it had occurred to me that the people I was writing about were much poorer than anybody else, and I think the reason for this is very interesting, and I think it can perhaps explain a good deal about how the novelist looks at the world.

The novelist writes about what he sees on the surface, but his angle of vision is such that he begins to see before he gets to the surface and he continues to see after he has gone past it. He begins to see in the depths of himself, and it seems to me that his position there rests on what must certainly be the bedrock of all human experience—the experience of limitation or, if you will, of poverty.

Kipling said if you wanted to write stories not to drive the poor from your doorstep. I think he meant that the poor live with less padding between them and the raw forces of life and that for this reason it is a source of satisfaction to the novelist that we shall always have them with us. But the novelist will always have them with him because he can find them anywhere. Just as in the sight of God we are all children, in the sight of the novelist we are all poor, and the actual poor only symbolize for him the state of all men.

When anyone writes about the poor in order merely to reveal their material lack, then he is doing what the sociologist does, not what the artist does. The poverty he writes about is so essential that it needn't have anything at all to do with money.

Of course Kipling, like most fiction writers, was attracted by the manners of the poor. The poor love formality, I believe, even better than the wealthy, but their manners and forms are always being interrupted by necessity. The mystery of existence is always showing through the texture of their ordinary lives, and I'm afraid that this makes them irresistible to the novelist.

A sense of loss is natural to us, and it is only in these centuries when we are afflicted with the doctrine of the perfectibility of human nature by its own efforts that the vision of the freak in fiction is so disturbing. The freak in modern fiction is usually disturbing to us because he keeps us from forgetting that we share in his state. The only time he should be disturbing to us is when he is held up as a whole man.

That this happens frequently, I cannot deny, but as often as it happens, it indicates a disease, not simply in the novelist but in the society that has given him his values.

Every novelist has his preoccupations, and none can see and write everything. Partial vision has to be expected, but partial vision is not dishonest vision unless it has been dictated. I don't think that we have any right to demand of our novelists that they write an *American* novel at all. A novel that could be described simply as an American novel and no more would be too limited an undertaking for a good novelist to waste his time on. As a fiction writer who is a Southerner, I use the idiom and the manners of the country I know, but I don't consider that I write *about* the South. So far as I am concerned as a novelist, a bomb on Hiroshima affects my judgment of life in rural Georgia, and this is not the result of taking a relative view and judging one thing by another, but of taking an absolute view and judging all things together; for a view taken in the light of the absolute will include a good deal more than one taken merely in the light provided by a house-to-house survey.

People are always complaining that the modern novelist has no hope and that the picture he paints of the world is unbearable. The only answer to this is that people without hope do not write novels. Writing a novel is a terrible experience, during which the hair often falls out and the teeth decay. I'm always highly irritated by people who imply that writing fiction is an escape from reality. It is a plunge into reality and it's very shocking to the system. If the novelist is not sustained by a hope of money, then he must be sustained by a hope of salvation, or he simply won't survive the ordeal.

People without hope not only don't write novels, but what is more to the point, they don't read them. They don't take long looks at anything, because they lack the courage. The way to despair is to refuse to have any kind of experience, and the novel, of course, is a way to have experience. The lady who only read books that improved her mind was taking a safe course—and a hopeless one. She'll never know whether her mind is improved or not, but should she ever, by some mistake, read a great novel, she'll know mighty well that something is happening to her.

Suggestions for Discussion

1. According to O'Connor, what is fiction? Why does she say that people, even those highly educated, have a difficult time knowing "how" to read fiction?

2. What does O'Connor mean when she describes the reading of fiction as a plunge "into" reality?

3. What methods does O'Connor cite that teachers have used to get around teaching literature? What did they have to do once these methods were expired? How does O'Connor suggest that English teachers should approach the teaching of literature?

4. What does O'Connor mean when she exhorts teachers to improve the quality of books found on the bestseller list. What, in her point of view, is wrong with bestsellers?

5. How does O'Connor's view of reading compare to Malcolm X's?

Suggestions for Writing

1. Read one of O'Connor's short stories. Write an essay in which you compare the story to this excerpt. Consider to what extent her writing lives up to her own definition of *good* literature. Also consider how her tone and writing style are different in fiction from nonfiction writing such as this essay.

2. Choose your favorite novel and write a paper discussing the methods you would use in teaching it to a class of literature students. What would you focus on? What would you leave out? Are your methods similar to O'Connor's?

3. How do you read fiction? Write an essay discussing your understanding of fiction and how one should approach reading it. What merits does your method have?

PERSONAL WRITING

∾∾∾

VIRGINIA WOOLF

The Angel in the House

Virginia Woolf (1882–1941) was an English novelist and critic known for her experimentation with the novel's form. Her works include *The Voyage Out* (1915), *Night and Day* (1919), *Jacob's Room* (1922), *Mrs. Dalloway* (1925), *To the Lighthouse* (1927), *Orlando: A Biography* (1928), *The Waves* (1931), *The Years* (1937), *Between the Acts* (1941), and several collections of essays, including *The Death of the Moth and Other Essays* (1942), in which this essay appeared. With her husband, Leonard Woolf, she founded the Hogarth Press.

MARY E. FREY, *Women and Children during Coffee Break (From the series Domestic Rituals, 1979–83)*. Gelatin silver print. Courtesy of the artist.

When your secretary invited me to come here, she told me that your Society is concerned with the employment of women and she suggested that I might tell you something about my own professional experiences. It is true I am a woman; it is true I am employed; but what professional experiences have I had? It is difficult to say. My profession is literature; and in that profession there are fewer experiences for women than in any other, with the exception of the stage—fewer, I mean, that are peculiar to women. For the road was cut many years ago—by Fanny Burney, by Aphra Behn, by Harriet Martineau, by Jane Austen, by George Eliot—many famous women, and many more unknown and forgotten, have been before me, making the path smooth, and regulating my steps. Thus, when I came to write, there were very few material obstacles in my way. Writing was a reputable and harmless occupation. The family peace was not broken by the scratching of a pen. No demand was made upon the family purse. For ten and sixpence one can buy paper enough to write all the plays of Shakespeare—if one has a mind that way. Pianos and models, Paris, Vienna, and Berlin, masters and mistresses, are not needed by a writer. The cheapness of writing paper is, of course, the reason why women have succeeded as writers before they have succeeded in the other professions.

But to tell you my story—it is a simple one. You have only got to figure to yourselves a girl in a bedroom with a pen in her hand. She had only to move that pen from left to right—from ten o'clock to one. Then it occurred to her to do what is simple and cheap enough after all—to slip a few of those pages into an envelope, fix a penny stamp in the corner, and drop the envelope into the red box at the corner. It was thus that I became a journalist; and my effort was rewarded on the first day of the following month—a very glorious day it was for me—by a letter from an editor containing a cheque for one pound ten shillings and sixpence. But to show you how little I deserve to be called a professional woman, how little I know of the struggles and difficulties of such lives, I have to admit that instead of spending that sum upon bread and butter, rent, shoes and stockings, or butcher's bills, I went out and bought a cat—a beautiful cat, a Persian cat, which very soon involved me in bitter disputes with my neighbours.

What could be easier than to write articles and to buy Persian cats with the profits? But wait a moment. Articles have to be about something. Mine, I seem to remember, was about a novel by a famous man. And while I was writing this review, I discovered that if I were going to review books I should need to do battle with a certain phantom. And the phantom was a woman, and when I came to know her better I called her after the heroine of a famous poem. The Angel in the House. It was she who used to come between me and my paper when I was writing reviews. It was she who bothered me and wasted my time and so tormented me that at last I killed her. You who come of a younger and happier generation may not have heard of her—you may not know what I mean by the Angel in the House. I will describe her as shortly as I can. She was intensely sympathetic. She was immensely charming. She was utterly unselfish. She excelled in the difficult arts of family life. She sacrificed herself daily. If there was chicken, she took the leg; if there was a draught she sat in it—in short she was so constituted that she never had a mind or a wish of her own, but preferred to sympathize always with the minds and wishes of others. Above all—I need not say it—she was pure. Her purity was supposed to be her chief beauty—her blushes, her great grace. In those days—the last of Queen Victoria—every house had its Angel. And when I came to write I encountered her with the very first words. The shadow of her wings fell on my page; I heard the rustling of her skirts in the room. Directly, that is to say, I took my pen in hand to review that novel by a famous man, she slipped behind me and whispered: "My dear, you are a young woman. You are writing about a book that has been written by a man. Be sympathetic; be tender; flatter; deceive; use all the arts and wiles of our sex. Never let anybody guess that you have a mind of your own. Above all, be pure." And she made as if to guide my pen. I now record the one act for which I take some credit to myself, though the credit rightly belongs to some excellent ancestors of mine who left me a certain sum of money—shall we say five hundred pounds a year?—so that it was not necessary for me to depend solely on charm for my living. I turned upon her and caught her by the throat. I did my best to kill her. My excuse, if I were to be had up in a court of law, would be that I acted in self-defense. Had I not killed her she would have killed me. She would have plucked the heart out of my writing. For, as I found, directly I put pen to paper, you cannot review even a novel without having a mind of your own, without expressing what you think to be the truth about human relations, morality, sex. And all these questions, according to the Angel in the House, cannot be dealt with freely and openly by women; they must charm, they must conciliate, they must—to put it bluntly—tell lies if they are to succeed. Thus, whenever I felt the shadow of her wing or the radiance of her halo upon my page, I took up the inkpot and flung it at her. She died hard. Her fictitious nature was of great assistance to her. It is far harder to kill a phantom than a reality. She was always creeping back when I thought I had despatched her. Though I flatter myself that I killed her in the end, the struggle was severe; it took much time that had better have been spent upon learning Greek grammar; or in roaming the world in search of adventures. But it was a real experience; it was an experience that was bound to befall all women writers at that time. Killing the Angel in the House was part of the occupation of a woman writer.

But to continue my story. The Angel was dead; what then remained? You may say that what remained was a simple and common object—a young woman in a bedroom with an inkpot. In other words, now that she had rid herself of falsehood, that young woman had only to be herself. Ah, but what is "herself"? I mean, what is a woman? I assure you, I do not know. I do not believe that you know. I do not believe that anybody can know until she has expressed herself in all the arts and professions open to human skill. That indeed is one of the reasons why I have come here—out of respect for you, who are in process of showing us by your experiments what a woman is, who are in process of providing us, by your failures and successes, with that extremely important piece of information.

But to continue the story of my professional experiences. I made one pound ten and six by my first review; and I bought a Persian cat with the proceeds. Then I grew ambitious. A Persian cat is all very well, I said; but a Persian cat is not enough. I must have a motor car. And it was thus that I became a novelist—for it is a very strange thing that people will give you a motor car if you will tell them a story. It is a still stranger thing that there is nothing so delightful in the world as telling stories. It is far pleasanter than writing reviews of famous novels. And yet, if I am to obey your secretary and tell you my professional experiences as a novelist, I must tell you about a very strange experience that befell me as a novelist. And to understand it you must try first to imagine a novelist's state of mind. I hope I am not giving away professional secrets if I say that a novelist's chief desire is to be as unconscious as possible. He has to induce in himself a state of perpetual lethargy. He wants life to proceed with the utmost quiet and regularity. He wants to see the same faces, to read the same books, to do the same things day after day, month after month, while he is writing, so that nothing may break the illusion in which he is living—so that nothing may disturb or disquiet the mysterious nosings about, feelings round, darts, dashes and sudden discoveries of that very shy and illusive spirit, the imagination. I suspect that this state is the same both for men and women. Be that as it may, I want you to imagine me writing a novel in a state of trance. I want you to figure to yourselves a girl sitting with a pen in her hand, which for minutes, and indeed for hours, she never dips into the inkpot. The image that comes to my mind when I think of this girl is the image of a fisherman lying sunk in dreams on the verge of a deep lake with a rod held out over the water. She was letting her imagination sweep unchecked round every rock and cranny of the world that lies submerged in the depths of our unconscious being. Now came the experience, the experience that I believe to be far commoner with women writers than with men. The line raced through the girl's fingers. Her imagination had rushed away. It had sought the pools, the depths, the dark places where the largest fish slumber. And then there was a smash. There was an explosion. There was foam and confusion. The imagination had dashed itself against something hard. The girl was roused from her dream. She was indeed in a state of the most acute and difficult distress. To speak without figure she had thought of something, something about the body, about the passions which it was unfitting for her as a woman to say. Men, her reason told her, would be shocked. The consciousness of what men will say of a woman who speaks the truth about her passions had roused her from her artist's state of unconsciousness. She could write no more. The trance was over. Her imagination could work no longer. This I believe to be a very common experience with women writers—they are impeded by the extreme conventionality of the other sex. For though men sensibly allow themselves great freedom in these respects, I doubt that they realize or can control the extreme severity with which they condemn such freedom in women.

These then were two very genuine experiences of my own. These were two of the adventures of my professional life. The first—killing the Angel in the House—I think I solved. She died. But the second, telling the truth about my own experiences as a body, I do not think I solved. I doubt that any woman has solved it yet. The obstacles against her are still immensely powerful—and yet they are very difficult to define. Outwardly, what is simpler than to write books? Outwardly, what obstacles are there for a woman rather than for a man? Inwardly, I think, the case is very different; she has still many ghosts to fight, many prejudices to overcome. Indeed it will be a long time still, I think, before a woman can sit down to write a book without finding a phantom to be slain, a rock to be dashed against. And if this is so in literature, the freest of all professions for women, how is it in the new professions which you are now for the first time entering?

Those are the questions that I should like, had I time, to ask you. And indeed, if I have laid stress upon these professional experiences of mine, it is because I believe that they are, though in different forms, yours also. Even when the path is nominally open—when there is nothing to prevent a woman from being a doctor, a lawyer, a civil servant—there are many phantoms and obstacles, as I believe, looming in her way. To discuss and define them is I think of great value and importance; for thus only can the labor be shared, the difficulties be solved. But besides this, it is necessary also to discuss the ends and the aims for which we are fighting, for which we are doing battle with these formidable obstacles. Those aims cannot be taken for granted; they must be perpetually questioned and examined. The whole position, as I see it—here in this hall surrounded by women practising for the first time in history I know not how many different professions—is one of extraordinary interest and importance. You have won rooms of your own in the house hitherto exclusively owned by men. You are able, though not without great labor and effort, to pay the rent. You are earning your five hundred pounds a year. But this freedom is only a beginning; the room is your own, but it is still bare. It has to be furnished; it has to be decorated; it has to be shared. How are you going to furnish it, how are you going to decorate it? With whom are you going to share it, and upon what terms? These, I think, are questions of the utmost importance and interest. For the first time in history you are able to ask them; for the first time you are able to decide for yourselves what the answers should be. Willingly would I stay and discuss those questions and answers—but not tonight. My time is up; and I must cease.

Suggestions for Discussion

1. What are the characteristics of this phantom, the Angel in the House? Do they persist today?

2. Why does the author say she had to kill the Angel?

3. What remaining obstacles to truth did she find? In what ways may women still encounter these obstacles?

4. What are the implications in the concluding paragraph concerning relationships with men?

5. How does the photograph by Mary E. Frey accompanying this selection reflect the concepts expressed in Virginia Woolf's writing?

Suggestions for Writing

Note the absence of men in this picture. Comment on the shortage of male role models at home and in grammar schools, in light of Frey's picture and Dan Quayle's essay "Restoring Basic Values."

ESSAYS

ᘐᘐᘐ

JOSEPH M. WILLIAMS
AND GREGORY G. COLOMB

Argument, Critical Thinking, and Rationality

Joseph M. Williams (1933–2008), long a professor in English at the University of Chicago, is widely recognized as an expert on writing well. Together with Gregory Colomb, Williams developed innovative instructional materials for advanced writers in the academy and the professions known as *The Little Red Schoolhouse* in the early 1970s, and, since 1980, Williams and Colomb have run Clearlines, a consulting firm helping writers in corporations, law firms, and consulting groups to write clearly and concisely. The following essay is from their textbook, *The Craft of Argument.*

Critical thinking is simply good problem solving. We can practice it silently, in our minds, as we size up a problem and try to solve it. But often, we must do more than analyze a problem and figure out how to solve it; we must then explain to others why we think our solution is worth their consideration. To that end, we have to make a case for our views, a case that we call an argument. Many of us think of argument as a hostile exchange between two people, each trying to coerce agreement from the other. But at its best, argument is a way to cooperate with others in finding and agreeing on good solutions to tough problems—call it cooperative critical thinking. Even when our arguments fail to achieve that agreement, they succeed if they help us know why we and others differ, in a way that creates mutual understanding and respect.

ᘐ

What Is Argument?

How many arguments have you heard or read today? Probably more than you noticed, perhaps more than you wanted. Television and talk radio have made nasty argument a national sport, and civic discourse seems to have been hijacked by those who shrilly advocate narrow causes in ways that sacrifice not only civility but truth and good sense. Meanwhile, advertisers make arguments that pander to our emotions with slick images and exaggerated claims to support their implied demand, "Buy this!" Hostile or pandering, such arguments might make a thoughtful person wonder whether argument hasn't become too repugnant for good people to engage in at all.

But that's argument at its worst. In an age that increasingly depends on sorting out good ideas from bad, we need good arguments more than ever. On the job, employers increasingly complain that they cannot find good thinkers who can judge others' claims critically and, more importantly, communicate their own conclusions clearly and persuasively. In the civic arena, we have seen in recent debates about ensuring our national security how much our democracy depends on officials and citizens who can judge not just claims but the quality of their supporting evidence. Many states now even require colleges to teach students how to think critically by analyzing the arguments of others and making sound ones of their own.

At their best, arguments are civil, even amiable ways to reach sound decisions. But even when they do become heated, good arguments differ from other forms of persuasion by both their process and their goal. When we engage one another *cooperatively* in arguments, we aim not to coerce or seduce others into mindless agreement, but to enlist them in helping us to find the best, most reasonable solution to a shared problem. We do not attack or pander; we exchange and test claims, assessing the reasons and supporting facts on all sides of the issue.

In this sense, argument isn't always about issues as momentous as national security. We all make countless little ones every day:

- Your friend says she doesn't want to eat Japanese, but you want vegetarian, so you talk it over and compromise on Indian.
- Your teacher rejects a claim that apes can count because it is based on flawed data.
- You complain to your boss that the new software she wants you to use can't generate up-to-date sales reports.
- You tell your friend that he cannot turn in a paper he copied-and-pasted from Web sites because it is unfair to everyone who did the work for themselves.

Even if you spent the day alone reading, you probably had silent arguments with your authors. You read "TV has degraded the quality of public argument" and think, *Wait a minute. What about PBS? I wonder what they would say about the arguments on "The News Hour."* You may even have argued with yourself when you tried to work through a personal issue in your mind: *So what do I do about my chem class? I have no shot at med school if I don't get a B. But can I? It would mean no social life. But do I really want to be a doctor . . . ?*

So as you think about argument, put aside the nasty exchanges, the political battles, and pandering ads, at least for now. Forget that we often talk about argument as though it were a form of close combat: *advancing* our claims, *marshalling* our evidence, *undermining* others' positions and *attacking* their claims, while we *defend* ours from *counterattack*. Forget that even the best of us sometimes argue as though we belong on *Jerry Springer*. Try to think not of *having* arguments with enemies but of *making* them with allies in order to find the best solution to a problem you all share.

∾

The Origin of the Word Argument

Occasionally, we'll discuss the original meaning of an important term, because earlier meanings can illuminate current ones. The original meaning of argument, for example, was to "make clear." The Latin word for silver, *argentum*, comes from the same root: what is clear often shines.

∾

What Good Is Argument?

Argument so pervades our thinking that it would be impossible to identify all of its uses, but two stand out:

- to convince others to think or do as we say
- to decide for ourselves what we should think or do

We usually think of argument as primarily a way to convince others. But the best, most critical thinkers also use argument to develop and test their own thinking by questioning their own ideas as severely as they do those of others. Through argument, we are able to make our thinking not only reflect our own experiences and beliefs but respond to those of others as well.

Arguments Help Us Think Critically

Philosophers have long celebrated rational thinking as our crowning human achievement, as one thing that distinguishes us from other creatures. But it is easier to say what rationality is not than what it is. It is not knowing lots of facts or rules of logic. It does not require formal education. It doesn't even mean knowing the truth, because we can rationally believe what we later find is false. For thousands of years it was rational to think the world is flat, because that's what the best evidence of our senses told us. Only when we had more facts and a larger perspective to reason from did we prove ourselves wrong.

We start to become rational thinkers almost from birth, when we first begin to interact with others. Toddlers show signs of rationality when they ask why they should do or think as others tell them to and, soon after, give reasons for what they want from others. We learn early not to accept others' claims and reasons blindly, but to question them in light of our experience and beliefs. But it takes some maturity before we learn to question our own thinking, our own reasons for believing what we do. As our critical judgment matures, we learn that just as others will not accept our claims and reasons without testing them, neither should we.

To make those mature judgments, we have to adopt an intellectual stance that questions what we want to believe, a stance that encourages us to pause before we leap to a conclusion just because we like it. To do that, we have to develop the self-control to slow down our thinking, so that we can not only examine our reasons for our beliefs but also investigate whether we have good evidence to accept them. In that pause, we can exercise other rational competencies:

- the patience to gather all the information that the situation allows—from remembered experience, direct observation, or active research
- the skepticism not to accept that information at face value, but instead to question whether it is factual
- the logical ability to use those facts as evidence in reasoning step-by-step to a conclusion

But that is not yet the crowning achievement of full rationality. To be fully rational, we must be able not only to reason to a conclusion but to reflect on and test the quality of that reasoning. For that, we must learn to

- seek out facts that might **contradict** our conclusions
- change our minds when the facts weigh against our beliefs
- imagine alternative ways of thinking about the problem, the facts, our conclusions
- recognize and question assumptions, inconsistencies, and contradictions

These last steps can challenge even the most careful thinkers, especially when we have reached a conclusion that we *want* to be true. That's when a sound argument is most helpful. The best help is a complete argument that we spell out in writing:

1. *Writing slows us down, giving us time to consider and reconsider.* What we think in an instant takes time to say; and what feels clear and compelling in a private thought often proves murky and uncertain in the public light of words.

2. *It gives us a mental checklist of matters we must consider.* The parts of argument lead us to question our own thinking: Are my reasons really backed up by facts? Are there facts that contradict them? Is my logic sound?

3. *It gives us the benefit of interacting with other minds.* Two heads may not always be better than one, but we usually think better when we consider all available ideas, not just our own. Even if we create it in our own minds, only for ourselves, an argument helps us think as critically as we do when we share our ideas with others who need good reasons before they agree. We have to ask questions about what those others might think, which leads us to consider facts, reasons, beliefs, and other views that we might ignore without the discipline of making an explicit argument.

∿

The Origin of the Word Critic and the Spirit of Critical Thinking

Some students and teachers are put off by the term *critical thinking*, because it sounds mean-spirited. As one young man put it, "First you tell us to make nice by writing arguments that are cooperative rather than hostile and then you tell us to be critical. They don't go together." But just as those who abuse argument have given it an undeserved bad name, so has criticism gotten a bad name from those who use it only negatively.

The word *critic* comes from the Greek *kritikos*, someone able to make judgments; that noun comes from the verb *krinein*, to separate or decide. And that's what good critical thinking does: it helps us judge an idea by separating out all the reasons and evidence that support or contradict it from all the feelings, hopes, and self-interest we attach to it.

That's why the most important tool of critical thinking is to ask good questions, including the five questions of argument. To be sure, when we ask questions, we can make people uncomfortable who *don't* want to examine their own ideas. And it can irritate those in power. After all, one of the earliest critical thinkers was Socrates, and we know what happened to him when he asked those in power more questions than they wanted to answer.

But in our world, not only do we have the right to ask questions and think for ourselves; we have an obligation to do so. That means not only asking lots of critical questions of others, but also answering theirs. And if that sounds difficult to you, that's all the more reason for you to learn to question and answer in ways that are civil, amiable, and constructive—which is to say, in service of finding the answers that everyone agrees are sound.

How Argument Supports Critical Thinking

When you use argument to think critically, you test old ideas and develop new ones in three "stages" or "levels." They involve increasingly difficult questions, not just about *what* you think but about your *basis* for thinking it. Since we normally judge others' ideas more critically than our own, we'll start with the kinds of questions you ask others (they are the same ones your readers will ask you). They are also the questions you must eventually learn to ask yourself before you submit your argument to others.

Level 1:   Is your idea or plan **supportable***? Or is it just opinion, insight, intuition, or some other quick response whose basis you can't really explain? Can you support it with reasons and facts showing that, all things considered, you can make a good case for your claims?*

Level 2:   Is your belief in your idea or plan **defensible***? Will others think that it is rational to believe it? Have you subjected your supporting reasons and facts to the scrutiny of others? Might someone know other reasons or facts that would contradict it? Have you considered all relevant possibilities?*

Level 3:   Is your belief in your idea or plan **logical***? Do you base it on principles of reasoning that are valid? Can you explain how the reasons and facts support your belief?*

When the ideas you are testing are your own, the questions are harder to answer: *Can I support my ideas with reasons and facts? Can I show that I have considered all other relevant views and alternatives? Can I explain my principles of reasoning?* Not only do these questions force you to consider new possibilities, but they can be disturbing when they upset familiar ways of thinking or challenge ideas that you *want* to be true.

By learning to make good arguments, you develop an attitude, a frame of mind that is always ready to listen to or can imagine another questioning voice that helps you separate out your ideas and reasons for believing them from the buzzing complexity of your mind and state them clearly. It's easiest when others ask those questions, but when they don't, you have to imagine an inner voice murmuring insistently, *But wait. How good is your evidence? Is it from a reliable source? Do you think your conclusion is right because you want it to be? What would you say to someone who said . . . ?* Once you learn to question yourself and think critically about your own ideas, you'll also learn to welcome the inevitable questions of others.

ॐ

How Common Are Critical Thinkers?

When one researcher investigated how well people critically reflect on their beliefs, she found that few were able to. She questioned 160 people about problems such as unemployment and school dropouts. They ranged from ninth graders to college graduates to experts in the problems she posed. When someone offered a cause of the problem, she asked questions like these:

- How do you know that is the cause? What evidence would you offer?
- How might someone disagree with you? What evidence might he offer?
- What would you say to that person to show he was wrong?
- Can you imagine evidence that would show your own view to be wrong?
- Could more than one point of view be right?

Fewer than half could think of any evidence to support their views. Though two out of three could think of an alternative view, fewer than half could think of an argument that might support it, and when offered a counterargument, fewer than half could think of an answer to it. In other words, most of those questioned could not imagine another point of view based on sound reasoning, or think of any good evidence to support their own! Even college graduates were not consistently good critical thinkers.

Source: Deanna Kuhn, *The Skills of Argument* (New York: Cambridge University Press, 1991).

Arguments Help Us Sustain Communities

Because rational thinking is inherently social, arguments are crucial for living and working with others whose views may differ from your own. So if you hope to be a member of a community of critical thinkers, you must be able not only to *think* critically about your own ideas and plans, but to *explain* your thinking, to give others reason to believe that your views deserve if not their agreement, then at least their respect. In fact, it's when we cannot agree that rational communities need cooperative arguments most—so that in the face of our differences, we can *understand* why others believe as they do, without dismissing their ideas as mere opinion or, worse, nonsense.

Rational argument is especially difficult, but also especially important, when communities include people from different cultures. Claims and reasons that seem reasonable to those of one background can seem wholly irrational to others, not because they disagree about the facts but because they base their claims on incompatible values and principles of reasoning. When we disagree over fundamental values, we often struggle to get beyond simply trading dogmatic claims. In those moments, arguments can become combative rather than cooperative, disrupting rather than supporting rational thinking.

Does that mean that people of different cultures can never agree? On some issues, perhaps not, especially when values are so deeply buried that they have to be excavated before they can even be identified, much less understood. But if cooperative arguments can't settle such issues, they can at least help us understand why not—so long as we can reach the second and third stages of critical thinking that explicitly put our ideas in dialogue with those of others. To succeed, a society of diverse values like ours needs more than goodwill and tolerance. We need amiable, civil ways to explain why we hold the values we do and to understand why others hold theirs. Argument is an essential tool for maintaining the fabric of a culturally diverse society.

Arguments Define Academic and Professional Communities

Thoughtful and civil arguments are also the lifeblood of academic and professional communities. Scientists, engineers, agricultural agents, college professors, and countless others—they all make arguments to find and support solutions to the problems in their fields. They formulate those arguments first in their own minds, then in conversations with colleagues, then often in writing for their wider community.

Most professional communities make arguments to address problems that can be solved only if someone *does* something:

Problem: Binge drinking in college has become a health problem.
Solution: We should devote time in orientation week discussing its dangers.

We call these *practical* problems, problems that, left unsolved, have tangible costs that we can't tolerate. To eliminate those costs, we propose a plan to *do* something.

In academic communities, on the other hand, researchers more often dig into a problem not to fix it directly, but to help us better *understand* something about it:

Problem: We do not understand the psychological factors that cause students to binge.
Solution: An important one is an attraction to risky behavior.

Academic researchers call an issue like this a *problem*, but it is a special kind of problem—it is a *conceptual* problem that we can phrase as a question: *How big is the universe? Do birds really descend from dinosaurs? What causes students to binge?*

Conceptual problems concern the world, but their solutions tell us not how to change it, but how to understand it better. Of course, before we can solve some practical problems, we have to understand them better. And academic researchers believe that the more we learn about the world, the better we can deal with all of its problems. But in the short run, the aim of most academic research is simply better understanding.

Whether a writer poses a practical or conceptual problem, however, she has to support her solution with an argument so that others in her community can reflect on it, test it, and maybe improve it before they accept it. Both require all the skills of sound critical thinking.

Questions and Answers
in Your Education

Researchers have found that many new college students differ from teachers in how they value questions and answers. Some students think their goal is to answer questions by reporting facts they have learned. But most teachers want not those pat answers but more questions—critical thinking about what their students hear and read, a willingness to test claims against alternatives and evidence. That difference confuses many first year students. Here is a test to find out how closely your thinking matches that of your teachers. Do you agree with the following?

1. Once you have the facts, most questions have only one right answer.
2. The best thing about science is that problems have only one right answer.
3. It wastes time to work on problems with no clear-cut answer.
4. Educators should know whether lecture or discussion is the better teaching method.
5. A good teacher keeps students from wandering off the right track.
6. If professors stuck to facts and theorized less, I'd get more out of college.

If you mostly agree, your educational values conflict with those of most of your teachers, and you may be puzzled why they ask you so many questions and give you so few answers. The theme in most of these questions concerns a critical cast of mind, one that emphasizes not settled facts but open questions, not rote knowledge but skeptical inquiry.

Source: M. P. Ryan, "Monitoring Text Comprehension: Individual Differences in Epistemological Standards," *Journal of Educational Psychology* 76 (1984): 250.

Arguments Enable Democracy

Critical thinking and good arguments are also at the heart of this messy way of governing ourselves that we call *democracy*. Dictators do not have to make arguments, because no one dares question their claims, much less their reasons. But in a democracy, those who govern us are, at least in theory, obliged to answer our questions.

In fact, we elect representatives to ask questions, make arguments, and analyze others' arguments on our behalf; and we pay journalists and political analysts to test the arguments and actions of those in power. Our designated questioners might not ask the questions we want them to; often we don't even know what questions they should ask. But democracy is served whenever an official is questioned on our behalf. One of the greatest risks to democracy is for officials to think that they can have their way without giving us sound reasons supported by reliable facts.

Of course, even the best arguments don't always succeed, especially when they threaten the interests of the powerful. Some even claim that rational argument is futile because what counts in politics is not logic and evidence but power and influence. But that view ignores occasions when good arguments have prevailed and, worse, excuses those who exercise power from having to justify its arbitrary use. Even if those in power sometimes get their way without our consent, we at least hold them to the principle that our critical assent is the source of that power.

ॐ

Developing Democracy Means More Arguments

Here's a news report about democracy in Thailand:

> Sumalee Limpaovart thought she was simply a mother protecting her child. But she found herself a warrior in the front lines of a struggle for democratic openness that is being fought today in Thailand and across East Asia. When her six-year-old daughter was rejected by an exclusive government school earlier

this year, Mrs. Sumalee did something that would have been unthinkable here only a few years ago: She challenged the decision, using a new freedom of information law to demand the test scores of the other children. In the end, Mrs. Sumalee found what she had suspected: One-third of the students admitted had failed the entrance exam but had been accepted because of their families' status or gifts to the school.

It was just one of the many small, sharp battles that have multiplied in recent years as a bolder, better-educated middle class begins to rise up against the paternalistic order of the past. As they do so, a society built on harmony and civility is becoming increasingly argumentative, confrontational, and noisy.[a]

The historian Robert Conquest makes the same point on a larger scale. He describes the suppression of critical thinking by all three twentieth-century totalitarian regimes—communism, fascism, and nazism:

> "Scientific" totalitarianism, which appears to be the rational, ordered form [of society], contains greater elements of irrationality than does the civic culture . . . [because civic culture] contains the element of debate and argument. . . . The totalitarian state contains within itself all of the elements of a more extreme irrationality: the elimination of real debate and criticism.[b]

ಌ

What's Not an Argument?

Three Forms of Persuasion That Are Not Arguments

Argument is often equated with persuasion, especially by those who think that they have to win an argument to succeed. But argument and persuasion are not the same. Not only can one make a successful argument without fully persuading readers, but there are forms of persuasion that are not arguments. Here are three kinds of persuasion that look like arguments but lack a key quality of sound and fair ones: (1) negotiation, (2) propaganda, and (3) coercion.

Negotiation feels like argument when you and another person trade claims and reasons about, say, the price of a car. But when you *negotiate*, you can offer any reason you want, even one you would not accept for yourself, so long as you reach an outcome that both sides can live with. You ought not lie, but you are not obliged (or even expected) to be candid—or complete. So you are not unethical when you do not reveal the highest price you are willing to pay. But when you make an argument, you are obligated to be

---

[a] *New York Times*, August 10, 1999.
[b] Robert Conquest, *Reflections on a Ravaged Century* (New York: Norton, 2001): 83–84.

candid and as informative as possible, and that includes *not* omitting information relevant to your claims or offering reasons you think are bogus.

Propaganda sometimes resembles argument when it offers claims and reasons, but propagandists don't care whether their reasons are any good, only whether they work, usually by exploiting the emotions of their audience. Nor do they care what others think, except to know what beliefs they have to defeat. Least of all do they care whether another point of view should change their own. A fair argument offers only good reasons and is obligated to acknowledge and respond to the beliefs of others.

Coercion solves problems by threat, by making the cost of rejecting a claim intolerable: *Agree or suffer!* Though we think of coercion as a stick, a carrot can also coerce when it's a bribe: *Agree and I will reward you.* Those who present themselves as authorities seek to coerce if they argue *Agree because I know better than you do.* So do those who try to shame us into agreement: When Princess Leia of *Star Wars* pleads, *Help me Obi-Wan Kenobi, you're my only hope,* he must either help or betray his deepest values.

Negotiation, propaganda, and coercion are not always irrational, or even unethical. When we coerce, propagandize, and negotiate with children, we call it parenting. Nor would anyone be irrational to threaten or negotiate with terrorists holding hostage a school bus full of students. Our challenge is to know what form of discourse best serves the cause of a civil and just community. That's usually a fair and candid argument.

∞

Arguments Persuade with Reasons

When Colomb was a boy, his school had a vice principal called the "Prefect of Discipline" who had a paddle called "The Persuader." It influenced Colomb's thinking and occasionally his actions, but getting paddled was not a form of argument, any more than are the insults of those who shout others into silence.

Arguments and Explanations

Some sets of claims and reasons look like arguments but are not.

Tanya: I have to go home. ₍claim₎ I'm so tired I'm making mistakes. ₍reason₎

In her first sentence, Tanya makes a claim and in the second offers a reason, but we cannot know whether they constitute an argument until we know Tanya's intention:

Ron: Leaving? About time. You've been working for hours.

Tanya: I have to go home. ₍claim₎ I'm so tired I'm making mistakes. ₍reason₎

Tanya offers Ron a reason not to *convince* him that she should go home (he seems to think she should), but to *explain* why she must. Contrast this:

Ron: You're not leaving, are you? We need you!

Tanya: I have to go home. _{claim} I'm so tired I'm making mistakes. _{reason}

Tanya offers the same claim and reason, but now to *convince* Ron to accept a claim that he will not accept just because she says it. That's not an explanation; it's an argument.

For an exchange to be an argument, it must meet two criteria:

- The first concerns its form. An argument consists of a claim (a statement saying what you want someone to believe or do), and at least one reason (a statement giving that person a basis for agreeing).
- The second concerns the intention of its participants. To make an argument, you must think that the other person will accept your claim *only if* you give her good reason to do so.

For an exchange to be a *thoughtful* argument, one based on all three stages of critical thinking, it has to be more than a one-sided offer of reasons:

- You make an argument that is both sound and fair when you also acknowledge and respond to views that might qualify or contradict your own. Tanya should respond to Ron if he said, "But you promised to stay!"

We use explanations and arguments for different ends, but we usually weave them together. You might argue that the campus bookstore should not sell clothing made in third world sweatshops, but in doing that, you would also have to explain that country's economic conditions.

Arguments and Stories

Stories are as old as arguments, probably older. They often seem like arguments, but they appeal to a kind of reasoning that is not always compatible with sound critical thinking, indeed that sometimes contradicts it.

- Told well, a story can make listeners feel awe, fear, pleasure, disgust. A good argument may give them a sense of intellectual pleasure, but that's less viscerally compelling than anger or delight.
- A vivid story seems to describe what "really" happened so that its truth seems self-evident to the mind's eye. An argument offers patterns of abstract reasons and evidence that lead to the truth more reliably, but much less vividly.
- When you tell a story, you hope listeners will, at least for a time, suspend their critical judgment so that they will not think, *Wait a minute,*

that can't be! but instead wonder only *What happened next?* In fact, we seem offensive when we question a story told as a personal experience, because we seem to doubt the story teller's truthfulness. When we write a thoughtful argument, however, we invite a critical response. We should want readers to question our reasons, our evidence, our logic, even the need for an argument at all.

When we tell stories, we want readers to suspend disbelief so that they can *experience* our words; when we make arguments, we welcome readers' doubts so that they *think about* our words.

Inexperienced writers sometimes think that a good story is enough to make a good argument. And some great stories do imply a point so clearly that we can infer their implicit claim. But a story alone can never itself offer a claim or even a reason. That's why so many moral tales end with a message like, *Be careful what you wish for.* Used as evidence, however, good stories can support a reason or claim with great power.

Arguments and Visual Images

Arguments require words, but they can also harness the power of images. With new digital tools, you have more ways than ever to create images that make your evidence, and so your argument, come alive for your readers. (For more on the visual presentation of evidence, see Chapter 6.) New digital tools have even made it possible to create arguments that blend the power of words with the power of moving images. When you can present evidence as a visual story, you can harness its vividness and emotional power to make your argument very persuasive.

But just as a story does not make an argument, neither does a visual image alone: arguments always need words that state at least a claim and supporting reasons. We cannot help but be moved when we see a TV commercial or print advertisement showing starving children. The image seems to cry out for us to do something. But what? Join the Peace Corps? Tell Congress to forgive third world debts? Stop globalization? Send money?—to whom? We know *what* this image wants us to do only when a text or voice-over tells us—Send money to Feed the Children (claim), because we can feed these children for pennies a day (reason).

∾

Logic, Character, Emotion/Logos, Ethos, Pathos

Rational argument is not an exercise in pure logic. Some philosophers exclude emotion from reasoning, but cognitive science has proved that feelings are crucial to human rationality. No rational person could write an argument about the Holocaust or slavery and be unmoved. And we have all acted on conclusions that seemed logical but felt wrong, then regretted ignoring our feelings.

But we cannot support a claim based on feelings alone. We can't justify a claim simply by saying how strongly we feel about it. We have to explain our claims—and our feelings—in ways that seem rational. And that means with reasons and evidence.

Those who write about arguments distinguish three kinds of force in them:

- When we appeal to our readers' logic, we rely on a force we call *logos*—the topic of most of this book.

But two other kinds of force depend on the ability to elicit feelings in readers:

- When we appeal directly to their feelings of pity, anger, fear, and so on, we appeal to their *pathos*.
- When we project a trustful, open-minded character, we hope readers will be moved by our *ethos*. (We discuss that force throughout this book.)

We can separate these appeals for analysis, but in practice they are so intertwined that to distinguish them is often just splitting hairs.

∾

Writing Process
Argument and Critical Thinking

It is crucial to learn to write sound arguments, but the habits of many inexperienced writers hinder them from doing that. Once they have a claim to make, they plunge into drafting and go where chance takes them. Others plan in painful detail, then write up their argument exactly according to plan, ignoring opportunities to discover something new. Experienced writers know they have to think and plan before they draft, but also that they are likely to change their minds as they draft and revise.

∾

Thinking and Talking

Your mind begins working on an argument long before you write anything. And if you let it, your unconscious mind will keep working on it even when you're thinking about other things. In this section, we show you how to work on your argument even when you're not reading or writing, from the moment you get an assignment until you turn it in.

Tell Your Elevator Story

Expert writers know that the more and the sooner they talk about what they plan to write, the better that first plan will be. Student writers, on the other hand, often keep their developing ideas to themselves, because they are afraid to look foolish by sharing unformed ones. To help yourself start talking about your ideas right away, you can do what professionals do: tell your elevator story. Imagine that as you step into an elevator headed to the fifth floor, you run into your teacher who says, "So, tell me what are you going to write in your paper." You don't have long, so you need to say what's interesting about your argument in just a few sentences.

Of course, you won't have much to say if you are still looking for a problem to write about. For an elevator story, you must already have a general idea about an issue you want to address, either because it was assigned or is important to you. But that's how just about every argument begins, with a rough sense that you believe something that others don't and that you have some reasons to support your claim. Once you have that, an elevator story will help you develop that rough sense into a responsible and plausible argument.

A good elevator story has four elements, each of which is only one or two sentences long:

1. the question or problem your argument will address
    I'm writing about the question/problem of. . . .
2. why that problem or question is important or interesting
    I chose that question or problem because. . . .
3. your current best guess at an answer, if you have one; otherwise, your best guess about where one can be found
    I think the answer/solution is. . . .
    I think the answer/solution has something to do with. . . .
4. where you expect to find evidence to support your answer
    I think the best evidence is. . . .

A good elevator story includes all four elements:

> I'm writing about the question of how actual families differed from the way they were depicted in 1950s sitcoms, because I think those depictions created expectations that a lot of people thought they should live up to, but couldn't. I think I can show that TV families were idealized and that actual families were much more varied. I can find evidence about TV families in the videotape collection of the media studies library, and there is a government database with statistics on actual families.

For now, just describe each element as best you can.

Don't put off formulating your elevator story until you have all the answers. Create one as soon as you can, and practice it as often as your friends will listen. Your story—and your ideas—will get better each time you tell it.

Think About Your Readers

As you tell your elevator story, keep in mind that what you count as an important problem others might not, and what you think are good reasons and evidence, others might reject. You might think there's a problem with rising college tuition, but a recent graduate might not care one bit. So once you understand what problem or question you want your argument to address, you must try to imagine how your readers will react to it.

When you think about readers, don't imagine yourself behind a podium reading your argument to a faceless crowd in a dark auditorium; imagine your readers as amiable but feisty friends sitting across the kitchen table, interrupting you with hard questions, objections, and their own views. In that situation, you have to respond to their questions and objections, especially questions like *So what? Why should I care?*

Real Versus Stipulated Readers   You may face a challenge if your teacher tells you to address readers different from the ones who will actually read your paper—a teacher, grader, or classmate: You are a researcher at Ace Advertising, working on the new V-Sport Vehicle account, and your manager wants an analysis of how Ford and Chrysler ads appeal to consumers under twenty-five. No ad manager will read your paper, but your writing teacher will judge it as if she were one. So you have an actual reader (your teacher) and a stipulated reader (the imagined manager). If you know about ad managers, you may be able to anticipate their questions. If not, all you can do is imagine yourself in their shoes, then decide whether your real reader will imagine the same thing.

If your assignment stipulates that your reader is "the general public," you have an even bigger challenge because there is no such reader. But if that's your assignment, assume (though it is not true) that this "general public" reads publications such as the *New York Times, National Review*, or *Scientific American*. Alternatively, assume that the "general public" is someone like yourself. They have read what you have but have not discussed it and want to hear more.

Talk to Readers If You Can   The best way to learn about readers is to talk to them. It's what experts do.

- Before an architect draws up a proposal, she finds out everything she can about her clients, from their finances to their living habits.
- Before a lawyer drafts a pleading, he checks out the judge who will hear the case by reading her decisions and asking other lawyers about her.

You might not be able to do that kind of detailed research, but it is a good idea to find out what your readers know and believe.

- Suppose Elena is preparing a proposal for a Center for English Language Studies to help students whose first language is not English. She could visit administrators to find out what they know about ESL students, whether they have dealt with the issue before, who will have a say in approving her proposal, and so on.

It's also wise to find out how readers react to your argument before you write it:

- Once Elena has a proposal, she could visit readers to gauge their reactions to it. Do they think there is a problem? Do they think resources should be invested in other services? Do they have a cheaper alternative? Readers often judge an argument more generously when they are familiar with it before they read it.

Of course, for most students, talking to readers means talking to their teacher. But that's not a bad thing. Not only will it help you anticipate your teacher's responses, but it will prepare her to read your argument more generously by giving her a stake in seeing it succeed. When you can't talk to readers directly, imagine someone who is smart, amiable, and open-minded, but inclined to disagree with you; write to that person.

ॐ

Preparing and Planning

Expert writers plan an argument in many ways, but they know that the more they plan, the faster they write and the better the argument they make. In time, you'll discover what rituals of preparing and planning work best for you—what you have to write out, what you can do in your head, and what you don't even have to think about. Nothing replaces experience, but what you practice now mechanically, you'll do automatically later.

Focus on Your Problem   Start planning your argument by deciding what you want it to achieve. What do you gain if readers agree with your solution? What do you lose if they don't? Do you propose ways to improve the world or just ways to understand it better?

- Your problem is *conceptual* if you solve it by getting readers simply to *understand* something better. What do you want readers to *understand* about Super-Kmart and Wal-Mart?

  Mega stores force small family stores out of business, replacing the intimate spaces of small stores where neighbors could meet with huge impersonal barns where everyone is a stranger, thereby eroding community values.

- Your problem is *practical* if you solve it by getting readers to *do* something or to support an *action* by others. What do you want readers to *do* about mega stores?

  Because large mega stores erode the quality of community life, this county should pass zoning laws to keep mega stores out of small towns.

Even if you are not yet certain what specific question or problem you will address, decide as soon as you can whether you want to make a claim about what your readers should think or what they should do. In most cases, your teacher will expect you to address a conceptual problem, since that is what most academic writing does and there are few serious practical problems you can solve in a few pages. So even if you feel that it's important to *do* something about those mega stores, consider building your argument around a question whose answer might be one step toward that goal.

ॐ

In A Nutshell
About Your Argument . . .

We do not define an argument by its abrasive tone, the belligerent attitudes of arguers, or by the desire to coerce an audience into accepting a claim. Instead, we define an argument by two criteria:

- Two (or more) people want to solve a problem but don't agree on a solution.
- They exchange reasons and evidence that they think support their respective solutions and respond to one another's questions, objections, and alternatives.

You make an argument not just to settle a disagreement. Good arguments help you explore questions and explain your beliefs, so that even when you and your readers can't agree, you can at least understand why.

ॐ

. . . and About Writing It

Your first task in writing an argument is to understand the problem that occasions it. Why (other than the fact that your teacher assigned it) are you writing it? What do you want it to achieve?

- Do you want your readers just to understand something, with no expectation that they will act? If so, why is that understanding important?

- Do you want your readers to act? If so, what do you expect them to accomplish? What problem will that action solve?

Once you understand your problem, try out a few solutions, pick one that seems promising, then list reasons that would encourage readers to agree. You can use that list as a scratch outline or, if you wish, expand it into a formal one.

Draft in whatever way feels comfortable: quick and messy, or slow and careful. If you are quick, start early and leave time to revise. If you are slow, plan carefully and get it right the first time, because you may not have time to fix it.

Suggestions for Discussion

1. How do arguments help us think critically? Why do Williams and Colomb suggest that it is important to think of an argument as the search for "a solution to a shared problem" as opposed to a battle that must be won over an opponent?

2. Why are good arguments "crucial for living and working with others whose views may differ from your own"?

3. Why is it important for mature critical thinkers to be willing to test their own personal beliefs and admit the possibility that they are wrong? How might one test his or her own beliefs successfully?

4. Paraphrase (that is, put in your own words) the definitions presented here for the following terms: *negotiation, propaganda, coercion.* How are these *not* arguments?

5. According to Williams and Colomb, what is the difference between a story and an argument?

6. What elements does a good "elevator story" contain?

Suggestions for Writing

1. Consider this essay alongside Howard Gardner's essay "Leading Beyond the Nation-State." Compare and contrast the perspectives represented by the two texts. To what extent do you agree with the models of communication and argument represented by these authors? Write your findings in a one-page essay.

2. Williams and Colomb's essay lays out a method of testing the validity of a line of argument. In the essay by Stephen Jay Gould, "Sex, Drugs, Disasters, and the Extinction of the Dinosaurs," Gould evaluates the relative merits of

three different scientific theories about why the dinosaurs became extinct. How do his methods of deconstructing the arguments of others compare to the methods shown in Williams and Colomb's essay? Does Gould do a good job evaluating the arguments of other scientists? Does he present his own argument successfully? Write your findings in a three-page essay.

∾∾∾∾

PATRICIA KUBIS AND ROBERT M. HOWLAND

How to Develop a Good Style

Patricia Kubis (b. 1928) is an author and educator whose novels, including *One More Time* and *Ocean's Edge*, were published under the pseudonym Casey Scott. Kubik is coauthor with Robert Howland of a number of books on the process of writing, including *Writing Fiction and Nonfiction and How to Publish* (1984), and *The Complete Guide to Writing Fiction and Nonfiction and Getting It Published* (1990), from which this selection is taken.

Style is the unique expression of a writer—the *way* he or she says a thing. Can style be developed? Yes and no. In one sense, style is not developed from something that is not there in the first place; perhaps it is more correct to say that style can be *revealed*. For every writer has a definite personality, a definite manner of expression. What must happen is that the writer's style be cleared of impediments so the personality can shine through the writing in a natural, vital way.

∾

Impediments That Prevent
Good Style

The major things that weaken style are the use of language and punctuation. First of all, any writer who is serious about writing should be sure of his or her grammar skills. Editors have always been and will always be sophisticated and well educated. In today's competitive writing market, the writer must have *top skills*. You can't write well if you can't spell or punctuate. You need language skills to communicate. If they are less than adequate, admit it and take a remedial English class at your local high school or college; evening classes are generally available. Don't hide your head in a basket and think that editors will overlook your writing skills. They won't—and they won't have a copy editor go over your entire manuscript and correct it, either. In today's market, your work will have to be as perfect as possible to even get an editor to *look* at it.

∞

What Exactly Do We Mean by "The Use of Language"?

Simply, the writer must be able to use words effectively to evoke in the reader the events and mood he or she wants to convey. Naturally, spelling and punctuation errors mar the effect the author wants to achieve. But many elements enter into the use of language.

The Generalization Trap

One of the main mistakes a new writer often makes is *generalizing* too much. A new writer is often inclined to describe the heroine as a "beautiful" woman. But what is a beautiful woman? If I ask you to close your eyes right now and then tell me what you see, you will find that you don't *see* anything—or, if you do, you are probably visualizing a woman whom you know or have seen; but *that* woman is not what the writer had in mind. Then, if you turn that new writer's page, you discover that he or she has added some further description, and the woman is indeed different from what you had imagined. This discrepancy usually jogs the reader out of the book and leaves him or her annoyed.

The great trick in writing is to keep the reader wholly involved in the book, for once the reader puts the book down he or she is unlikely to pick it up again. What every writer should strive for is to excite the reader so that the book is so good it can't be put down.

To keep the reader involved, the writer must use specific language that gives visual pictures and involves the reader's emotions. The writer must create a word picture so that the reader can *see* what the writer means, feel what the writer feels.

Rather than using a catch-all phrase like "beautiful," the writer should actively describe the woman so that the reader understands the woman is beautiful: "She had leaf-green eyes, black, black hair, and that peculiar translucent skin known only to the Irish. A faint blush reddened her high cheekbones, and her lips were full and soft."

Paint a picture in words of what you see.

If you get nothing more out of this book than the idea that "a picture is worth a million words," you will have learned a great deal about being a good writer.

A good exercise is to take a descriptive paragraph you've just written and analyze it for specific detail. Several years ago, a student asked for advice on his writing. The first part of his descriptive sketch read:

> A steady stream of water fell over the beautiful rocks to the bottom of the falls where it traveled on till soaked up by the ocean or the ground.

When I asked him what he meant by "beautiful" rocks, he quickly answered in specifics: red volcanic rock. Upon being prodded as to the shape of the rock, he replied: a ridge of red volcanic rock. When prodded further about the "color" of the water, he thought a moment and then said that it "frosts white," and he added that it fell to a shadowed streambed below. Now if you put what he actually *saw* in words, it would read:

> The water frosts white over the ridge of red volcanic rock, falling to the shadowed streambed below.

If you compare the two paragraphs, it is obvious which is the stronger. The point is that every writer sees detail quite clearly; yet in the case of many new writers, that information stays *in their heads* and never makes it to the written page. But the reader is not in your head and does not have your experience; all the reader can do is get impressions from the words you have written—and if your words are not "true," then the picture will not be true. Obviously, the greatest of challenges for a writer is to get what he or she has experienced out of the head and onto the page.

In a beginning writing class, if you asked the students to go down to the ocean and watch the ferry come in, many of the sketches would read: "Some gulls were flying over the dock as the ferry came in."

But here's how John Dos Passos wrote such a description in *Manhattan Transfer*:

> Three gulls wheel above the broken boxes, orange rinds, spoiled cabbage heads that heave between the splintered plank walls, the green waves spume under the round bow as the ferry, skidding on the tide, crashes, gulps the broken water, slides, settles slowly into the slip. Handwinches whirl with jingle of chains. Gates fold upwards, feet step out across the crack, men and women press through the manure-smelling wooden tunnel of the ferryhouse, crushed and jostling like apples fed down a chute into a press.

Compare the "generalized" description to Dos Passos' "specific" description. Again, which is stronger? In the first instance the new writer tells us about "some gulls"; but it's hard to visualize "some" gulls.

Notice that Dos Passos writes, "three gulls," and the number engages the mind and enables the mind to create an image. He also shows the three gulls "wheeling" in flight. He creates a word picture. He shows, too, the water: green, littered with broken boxes and orange rinds. His image conveys "garbage," and the "spoiled cabbage heads" and the "orange rinds" engages not only appeals to the sense of seeing but also that of smelling: you can *smell* the garbage.

"Splintered plank walls" engages the sense of touch. "Handwinches whirl with jingle of chains" engages the sense of hearing. Dos Passos uses words like *spume, crashes*, and *gulps*, to give a sense of motion. He uses alliteration—the ferry "slides, settles slowly into the slip"—to make the reader *feel* the motion of the ferry. Moreover, all of the images together create a tone, a mood of *pessimism*. This is not going to be a happy book—not with all the garbage and people crushed like apples, their blood being drained from them.

Notice, too, how every word in this passage contributes not only to a specific visual picture but also to a central mood. The point is that no writer can afford to describe randomly or to use generalizations that cause flat writing.

Generalizations are always caused by not really looking at what you see. "Freshness" in writing is always achieved by writing *exactly* what you see, by using the precise words that capture the experience. In Galway Kinnell's poem "The Avenue Bearing the Initial of Christ into the New World," note the precise imagery in this stanza:

> In the pushcart market on Sunday
> A crate of lemons discharges light like a battery.
> Icicle-shaped carrots that through black soil
> Wove away lie like flames in the sun.
> Onions with their shirts ripped seek sunlight. . . .

Images like these make most writers bang their heads in despair and say, "Why didn't I think of that?" It looks so easy, so obvious. What else is a carrot but an icicle, and of course it looks like a "flame in the sun." Onions *do* look as if they have their "shirts ripped." Unfortunately, the gift of concrete observation is usually a stamp of genius. Too many writers either never see what is "true" or they overuse words and destroy the truth of what they saw.

The Trap of Excess Adjectives

Many new writers pepper their sentences with adjectives, trying to capture what they saw, but excess adjectives weaken a sentence and take its force away. Rather than adjectives, Hemingway advocated the use of nouns and verbs; and he said that verbs were the "guts" of the English language.

Note how he artfully combines nouns, actions verbs, and a few well-chosen adjectives in this paragraph from *A Farewell to Arms*:

> In the late summer of that year we lived in a house in a village that looked across the river and the plain to the mountains. In the bed of the river there were pebbles and boulders, dry and white in the sun, and the water was clear and swiftly moving and blue in the channels. Troops went by the house and down the road and the dust they raised powdered the leaves of the trees. The trunks of the trees too were dusty and the leaves fell early that year and we saw the troops; marching along the road and the dust rising, and leaves, stirred by the breeze, falling and the soldiers marching and afterward the road bare and white except for the leaves.

In this passage, too, the very rhythm of the sentences achieves the flow of water in the riverbed and the "marching" of the troops. The repetition of the word *dust* gives the reader a hot, dusty feeling, and the repetition of the word *white* in conjunction with *dry and white* and *bare and white* conveys the hidden image of dry, white bones—and death.

The problem with overusing adjectives is that the reader is inundated with modifying words and ends up getting lost in the adjectives so that the real meaning of the sentence is either not grasped or felt. If Hemingway had used adjectives wholesale, his famous passage might have read:

> In the late hot summer of that terrible year we lived in a two-story Normandy cottage with green shutters and a tile roof in a small village that looked across the mighty Seine and the great vast plain to the towering purple mountains. Small, round white pebbles and great boulders glistened dry and white in the lemon-yellow sun, and the water was clear, cool, turbulent, falling in little rills here and there, and it was sparkling blue in the channels.

Obviously if Hemingway's novel had been written this way, it would never have been published. The writing is too cluttered, and the mind can't assimilate all of the description so that the paragraph has one central emotion. While a writer must be precise with description, he or she must also learn the right *balance*—how much description is needed to achieve the desired emotional effect.

The Trap of Excess Adverbs

Not only do adjectives weaken prose, but so do adverbs—modifiers which usually end in *-ly*. One adverb per paragraph is plenty. Consider the following passage:

> He looked at her smilingly as she joyfully rose and walked to him liltingly. He kissed her passionately, and she sighed wonderingly. They were happily and marvelously in love—and arm in arm they walked ecstatically (and sickeningly) on the sand.

The point is, don't overuse adjectives and adverbs to pad sentences in which nouns and verbs haven't been precisely chosen. Rather, look for the *right* noun and verb and let them carry the weight of the sentence.

The Cliché Trap

Clichés—trite, overused phrases—also rob the paragraph of its power. The phrase "her cheeks were red as roses" is such a phrase. The very first time it was used (probably 3000 B.C.), it perhaps evoked a powerful image—skin textured like a soft, velvety flower petal, delicately veined—but the image has been used so often that the reader's mind is no longer stimulated to make that comparison. A common cliché that most new writers use is "chills ran up and down my spine," and when told it is a cliché they usually reply: "But that's what happens, isn't it?" The answer in most cases is no. The writer has just read that phrase somewhere. The best way to avoid clichés is to: (1) be aware of what they are, (2) avoid *any* phrase that comes to mind too easily, (3) and try to write exactly how *you* feel in that given situation. Rather than use a catch-all phrase, note exactly how you react when you're extremely frightened. It might be something like: "He trembled, listening to the pounding of his heart." What *you* see, what *you* feel, will always be more original than what another writer "saw" or "felt" years ago.

Today we are inundated by clichés on the radio, on TV, and in movies and in the newspaper. The only way to free yourself from clichés is to tune into yourself and to honestly write what *you* experience—in much the same way as an artist sets up an easel near the ocean and paints what *he or she* sees.

Children have a remarkable ability to see truly. Two-year-olds drop marvelous phrases—for example, saying that twigs look like "witches' fingers." Of course, twigs look like that. But why can't *we* see so clearly? Well, we probably once did; but the media and the writing of other people put a veneer over our own thinking. Yet the writer, if he or she means to construct powerful prose, must strip that veneer away.

It is true, however, that sometimes one can play off a cliché by revising it or adding to it. For example, "He looked gentle as a lamb, only he was really a pit bull." A cliché can also be used ironically, "Who does she think she is, the Queen of Sheba?"

The Trap of Archaic Words

Archaic words also weaken prose. Generally, people who enjoy reading period literature often fall into this trap. They read writers like Longfellow, Wordsworth, and James Fenimore Cooper and pick up words that are now out of date: *ere, oft, forsooth, whilst, whence.* However, one of the main tasks of writing is to try to capture the time in which you live, and so you should use the language of your time. Even in historical writing archaic words will strangle your writing. Remember that it's very hard for a twentieth-century reader to identify with archaic language; in fact, he or she may very well have never even heard of those words—which in effect will probably make your sentences meaningless.

It's good advice to write the way you talk—what words do *you* use? When was the last time you heard someone actually say "whence" or "albeit"? If you argue that in historical novels such words are regularly used, you will find that the better writers seldom use archaic words. Rather, they are more likely to sprinkle a few well-chosen expressions of the time (unusual ones) to give a flavor of the period. They also try, through cadence, to catch that flavor. Note in this paragraph from Fabian Davenport's Regency novel *The Rose of Devon* how the language catches the stilted flavor of the Regency period:

> "Aye, that I do," Lang'l agreed. "That missus of mine could talk the horns off a tin bull. But she's a fine lady."

Note, too, that the name *Lang'l* helps to establish the time of the novel.

Another archaic word to avoid is "thus," even in term papers. Try to find a fresher connective term.

The Trap of Inflated Language

Some writers are proud of their vocabularies and like to show them off. But inflated language—the use of words that are beyond the average reader's comprehension—does not impress the reader. Instead, such language turns the reader off, and he or she stops reading. The sentence "As he cogitated, he saw her shining countenance image in a phantasmal diorama in his mind" might be better understood by the reader if it were put more simply: "As he reflected, her shining face imaged in his mind."

Remember that if a reader doesn't understand a word, you might as well write *bltfzkkk* for all the meaning it will convey. One of the most important tasks of writing is to select the *exact* word that will convey the desired emotion. No writer can afford to use words that only a very few people understand. As Mark Twain and Hemingway both said: "Why use a quarter word when you can use a nickel one instead?"

The Slang Trap

It's a good idea to avoid slang, too. Slang not only dates a work, but often its meaning is lost over the years. Mark Twain tried to faithfully reproduce the actual slang the miners used during the gold rush; however, the modern reader is not able to understand the slang, and so some of Twain's short stories and novels are incomprehensible. Yet his *Huckleberry Finn* and *Tom Sawyer*, which were written in simple, unadorned English, remain classics.

The Flat-Phrase Trap

Flat phrases are ready-made phrases which do not evoke any new ideas or sensations. The flat phrase is made up of clichés:

> Amy Harrison is back from her trip, tired but happy and glad to be back. She visited many lovely spots of interest and historical sites in our great land—majestic mountains, the great rivers of the United States, and the great battle-fields where history was made.

The writer, by using catch-all phrases, has not told the reader anything. "Tired but happy," "glad to be back," "many lovely spots of interest" are all clichéd phrases. Where *exactly* did Amy go? Did she visit Mount Shasta, Gettysburg? Mountains are always majestic, and many rivers are great—but what else can you say about them? Be specific!

The Surface-Glaze Trap

Less obvious than the flat phrase is the surface glaze. At first reading, the surface glaze seems professional—until you realize that the writer hasn't really said anything.

> John walked through the fields. Birds flew overhead, and clouds drifted by in the sunshine. Around him was the smell of hay. Beyond the wood he saw the outlines of the village, and he began to think of Ann, of their past life, of all the things they had done.

In the surface glaze, the style is more flowing, and the words fit with one another; but the words form a veneer that hides the lack of meaning. The words do not evoke any reaction from us. There aren't any new perceptions regarding the landscape or the character's mood. The words are not specific enough to create any new insights or to evoke any feelings in us. How *many* birds flew overhead; what kind of birds were they? Clouds have shapes; also, what kind of clouds were they—dark rain clouds, high cumulous clouds, clouds that sailed by like battleships? What does hay smell like? What kind of village is the hero going toward—a New England village, a small western village of weathered-board stores, a Mexican village with red tile roofs, an Indian village of dusty adobe houses? Each of these villages has a different kind of architecture. If you examine this passage closely, you'll see how devoid of meaning it is.

The Purple-Patch Trap

Of all the traps, the one most writers jump joyously into is the purple patch. This paragraph or page is the one the writer loves most. He's spent hours, days, weeks, rewriting it. He adores every word. The problem is—it's overwritten.

Stephen went to the canvas. He examined it carefully. It was a portrait of a harlequin—elongated, beautifully done, broadly stroked. The background was black. The head was a ghostly greenish-white scarred by thick red lips that twisted ominously, frighteningly. The satin costume of diamonds had a diabolic snake-like quality, sinuous and gleaming. But Stephen's eyes kept returning to the face—the black, beady eyes sunk in the decaying flesh . . . hypnotic eyes . . . serpent eyes. Yet the hellish thing was the human quality imbued in the features—the incongruity of the ruffled neckpiece. And down in the right-hand corner—blood. All the more awful because it was not flaming crimson that oozed from the clenched hand, but three drops of gray— blood from the soul.

The purple patch needs to be ruthlessly pruned of excess description. Hemingway once said that if you've spent an inordinate amount of time writing what you believe to be a superlative passage, the best thing you can do is to write a big X over it. If you don't, your editor most certainly will.

The purple patch is guilty of *sentimentality*. "Purple" does not necessarily mean "sickeningly sweet" but rather that the writing is weakly emotional and overstresses the feeling that the author meant to convey. Often editors and teachers will scrawl "Too much" over the offending paragraph.

The Punctuation Trap

Too many writers try to depend on punctuation for effect, rather than let the sentence itself convey the meaning; also, some writers do not understand punctuation devices such as the ellipsis, the dash, the exclamation point, and comma structure.

Ellipses   The ellipsis has three dots (. . .), and when it is used at the end of a sentence it has three dots plus the period that would have ended the sentence(. . . .). In dialogue, ellipses indicates the voice falling off. "Oh, Joel . . . don't go." (**Note, too, the white spaces around the ellipsis**. The ellipsis is like a word and needs spacing between it and the preceding and following words.) Don't get into the habit of filling up your dialogue with ellipses. Many fine writers never use them at all.

The dash   Another overused punctuation device is the dash. Some writers have "dash-itis." The dash is very showy punctuation, and here a little goes a long way. In dialogue, the dash indicates that the voice is broken off sharply: "Joel, don't—" Here, it indicates emotional intensity. It can also indicate that the speaker is interrupted. The dash is also used to connect phrases. "Joel, please—put down the gun!" In exposition, a sentence might read: "The flames licked up—a flaming spear fell at his feet." Note that **the**

dash connects the word before it to the word after it. Leave no white spaces around the dash. One dash per paragraph is plenty, and some writers feel that one per page is too much. In a typed manuscript use two dashes to indicate a dash. The dashes will be set as a solid line when material is typeset. One dash is a hyphen. Example: Twenty-four.

The exclamation point   The exclamation point is used to signify strong emotion, but it becomes boring when overused: "'Oh, James!' Lizzy cried. 'I'm so happy to see you!' She gestured to the sofa. 'Oh, darling! Do sit down; I want so to talk with you! I can't tell you how much I've missed you!'" This kind of writing wears the reader out. Lizzy sounds like a jumping jack. Actually, the sentences would convey her joy at seeing James if the exclamation points were removed. The exclamation point should be saved to show extreme emotion and should be only rarely used.

The comma   In the main, commas are used to connect a phrase to a sentence, to separate items in a series, and to set off elements (such as names) that interrupt the structure of the sentence. Commas should not be used arbitrarily to signify pauses in the sentence that the writer wants to indicate. Some writers put ten to twelve commas in a sentence, wherever they feel pauses are needed. If you have a comma problem, study a grammar handbook for advice on the various uses of the comma. But perhaps an old journalistic trick can be of some immediate help. Note the sentence: "The sea, blue, green, is quiet." The adjectives *blue* and *green* modify *sea* and are "nonrestrictive" in that they occur between the first and last comma in the sentence. If the sentence is constructed correctly, this nonrestrictive material can be deleted, and the remaining words should make a complete sentence: "The sea [, blue, green,] is quiet" = "The sea is quiet." You can test your sentences by making sure that the phrase before the first comma and the phrase after the last comma makes a complete sentence. For example, consider this sentence: "She went to the door, her heart fluttering, her mouth dry, her hands trembling, and her fingers closed on the doorknob." The sentence tests out. If you like to write long sentences, this simple technique may help.

The semicolon   Another punctuation device often misused is the semicolon. Its primary use is to connect two complete sentences to each other: "He went into the department store; it was musty inside." Do not use the semicolon to connect a phrase to a complete sentence: "He was hungry; very hungry" (incorrect). In this instance a comma, a dash, or ellipses could have been used to connect the phrase "very hungry"—depending on whether the writer felt a normal pace, an intense pace, or a slower pace should be emphasized.

The semicolon can also be used to separate items in a long series, for example:

> My favorite novels are Dostoyevski's *Crime and Punishment*, a novel that emphasizes moral responsibility; Fowles' *The Magus*, which discusses the alchemic transformation of man; and Conrad's *Lord Jim*, which explores the nature and consequences of evil.

The semicolons act as "breakers" between the itemized novels and also the internal commas, which might confuse the reader.

This brief discussion of punctuation is not meant to take the place of an English handbook, but it may help to clean up any glaring punctuation problems.

The Sentence Monotony Trap

A writer should also be aware of sentence lengths in a paragraph. If the sentences are too long, the paragraph will put the reader to sleep; if they are too short, the reader will feel a stacatto affect, although you definitely want short, pithy sentences for action scenes, especially fight scenes. To avoid monotony, *balance* your paragraphs by combining a long sentence with a medium sentence and then a short sentence.

Also, don't construct all of your sentences in the same way. Vary the placement of your subjects and verbs so that the monotony is broken up.

The Was *and* Were Trap

One of the best ways to strengthen prose is to eliminate the words *was* and *were*. They are paragraph killers and cause the events to be told. The author is talking *about* something or someone. By substituting an action verb, the writer is *showing* what is happening in action. It is better to say "I walked" than "I was walking." On the other hand, if you want to slow the pace of a paragraph you might wish to deliberately use *was*.

For example, if you were writing a short story about a very old man with a cane, you might say: "He was walking very slowly, he was leaning on his cane, and his chest was pumping up and down." Here the *wases* emphasize the slowness associated with age.

Be conscious of *was* and *were*. Prune them out. It's a good exercise to take a page or two of your writing and circle all the verbs *was* and *were*; then substitute action verbs and see how much stronger your writing reads. As a writing teacher and former agent, I have observed that this single polishing technique remarkably improves the work of most writers trying to publish.

Unfortunately, many new writers and professional writers in fields such as technical writing have learned to use the passive voice instead of the active voice. The active voice is strong and has a vitality. For example: "He shot the terrorist." Here, the subject (*he*) acted. The object (*terrorist*) received the action. The verb (*shot*) expresses that action. But in the passive voice, the subject *receives* the action: "The terrorist was shot by him." Analyze which statement is stronger.

If you use the passive voice, you should have a definite reason for doing so. Sometimes a writer may not want to reveal *who* the subject is. For example, if the X Oil Company made a $5 million profit last year, a writer who isn't interested in the name of the company might write: "A profit of millions of dollars was made last year by a comparatively small oil company."

In essence, the use of passive voice is often a definite evasion of responsibility, for in passive voice, one often doesn't know *who* did something. Consider these examples:

> The cost of the production was miscalculated.
> A letter to the school will be written.
> The suggestion was made that the department was top heavy and the work force needed to be cut.
> It was ruled that higher taxes needed to be assessed.
> It was reported that water and electric bills will go up.

Of course, the reader of the evasive passive wants to shout *who* is the one causing or doing these things? The evasive passive gets committee members off the hook, and that very reason encourages its use in various reports and announcements.

Consistent use of the passive voice will definitely weaken your style. Readers do not want to muddle through a story and not know who is doing what to whom. They also prefer a character who is involved in direct action rather than an intrusive author who is *telling* them events in flat prose that uses passive verbs.

ᏟᏞ

Other Devices to Improve Prose

Sentence Rhythm

A good writer uses language to give action to his or her writing and uses specific words to create the actual movement of what is happening. For example, note how the words in the following sentence simulate the movement of the action: "He dove under the giant waves and came to the surface gulping." Remember that the use of short stacatto sentences creates tension. Use short, pithy sentences for fight scenes:

> He jumped me from behind, I turned, smashing my fist into his stomach. I saw the raised knife and jerked back. A chain-link fence with barbed wire loomed ahead. He lumbered toward me. I kicked. He folded in two, clutched his groin. I ran past him.

Note, too, the absence of the passive verbs *was* and *were*, which would have slowed the action scene.

Dorothy Faeder, in her novel *The Queen of San Francisco*, matches sentence rhythms to the lightning storm being described:

> A second later, lightning struck the fir tree. The ground rumbled. The huge tree split in half. Searing flames ran down the forked trunk. The tree blazed, the earth trembling. Matt grabbed Fritz and they both ran, bent over, half crawling, away from the burning tree. The next blast of thunder knocked them down again. A bolt of lightning hit the big pine rooted in the pond. The trunk cracked, bursting into flames. Tongues of fire leaped and skimmed over the top of the pond, red devils writhing, careening, then sank with hissing steam into the sizzling water. The storm blazed on, the lightning going south. Thunder tagged it like a baying hound. The lightning struck further and further away now, great pillars of smoke and flame furling up into the sky, and the torrents of rain eased to a sprinkle.

Here, the words create the *passage* of the lightning storm as it blazes its way across the countryside. The first sentences are stacatto, capturing the shock of a lightning storm, and the sentences at the end of the paragraph lengthen out to show the intensity of the storm lessening.

It is also effective to combine action with dialogue, emotion, and as much characterization as possible:

> I heard the wind whipping the canvas. My God, I thought, the tent is going to go! Outside, the wind sounded like the rumble of a train engine. Then I saw the kerosene lamp tip, the flame licking out and up into the canvas. I tried to put it out, but it flared into a wall of flame. I dove under the canvas and outside. The wind caught the fire tongues and the next tent exploded into flames. I stood in the middle of an inferno. Nothing could stop it. I ran to the small clearing where other carnies gathered, and watching the tents burn I felt the angry tears in the corners of my eyes. I saw everything I'd worked for, my whole life, burning to ashes.

Note how the thoughts act as dialogue, reinforcing the action and giving the character's emotional responses to what is happening. Note too, that even in this long paragraph, no *was* is necessary.

Simile and Metaphor

You can also give additional dimension to your work by using simile and metaphor, methods of comparison. A simile uses the terms *like, as, as if,* and *seemed.* For example, "She was tall, long-legged, *like* a Las Vegas showgirl." Simile introduces an additional image that gives more depth to what is being said. In the previous description, the woman is not only tall, but it is implied that she is as striking as a Las Vegas showgirl. Simile is fairly direct, but metaphor is more subtle.

Metaphor links two dissimilar things together to form a new insight, a new feeling. Aristotle once said that it took a genius to be a master of metaphor. A metaphor does not say that something is *like* something else; it says, rather, that the thing you're discussing *is* something else:

> My thirteen-year-old daughter is a garbage disposal. Hamburgers, hot dogs, potato chips, pretzels, ice cream, candy bars, all slide in an endless stream down that yawning maw. Even now I can hear her grinding jaws.

Metaphor, because of its picture-evoking quality, is able to convey a deeper emotional feeling than words that are used in a less dramatic fashion.

Summary

When you're writing, strive for clarity of perception. Don't try to "impress" the reader with your large vocabulary and intricate sentence structure. If you do, you may be writing for yourself. Aim for simplicity of expression, but don't be childish. *Write what you see, what you feel.* Originality results from an honest, individual, thoughtful interpretation of life. Analyze what you see and be careful of the "too obvious" interpretation. The genius-writer looks at life, head cocked a little to one side, and he or she sees life differently from the way anyone else does. Develop that quality.

If you are content to look at life superficially, to use flat phrases, surface glazes, archaic expressions, inflated language, clichés, purple patches, and poor language skills, you will probably never be published. So work at your style until it is clean and powerful—until you are able to use it as an effective tool to truly **write what you see.** As Hemingway said: **"Find the authentic language of your own unique experience."**

Suggestions for Discussion

1. How can sensory descriptions, as opposed to flat generalizations, help create a tone, or mood, in a piece of writing?

2. What did Hemingway mean when he said that verbs were the "guts" of the English language? What do they do for a piece of writing?

Suggestion for Writing

As the authors suggest in the discussion of the *was* and *were* trap, take a piece of your own writing and circle all of the *was* and *were* verbs, replacing them with stronger action verbs. Observe what this act has done for your selection of writing. Has it improved? How?

∽∽∽∽

MARTHA BROCKENBROUGH

Does IM Make U Dum?

Seattle-based writer and teacher Martha Brockenbrough (b. 1970) has contributed columns to MSN and Encarta on topics as varied as motherhood, literacy, and family-friendly films. Upset by the mangling of the English language committed by celebrities and public figures, she founded The Society for the Promotion of Good Grammar in 2004. Her books include *It Could Happen To You: Diary of a Pregnancy and Beyond* (2002), *Things That Make Us (Sic): The Society for the Promotion of Good Grammar Takes on Madison Avenue, Hollywood, the White House, and the World* (2008), and the upcoming *The Dinosaur Tooth Fairy*. Brockenbrough has also contributed a chapter to the book *It's a Girl: Women Writers on Raising Daughters* (2006) and currently writes a parenting blog at Cozi.com.

B4 the Net, it wuz unheard of 2 use shorthand like this, unless U were writing a classified ad.

As you can see, I'm not very good at these abbreviations, probably "coz" in Internet years, I'm about 287 years old. It's a miracle my gnarled hands can type at all.

My own decrepitude aside, kids and hipsters everywhere regularly insert abbreviations, acronyms, and other Internetisms into their writing—even when they're offline.

Does this mean our language is going to LOL all the way to its doom? Does it mean that instant message (oops, I mean IM) abbreviators are dopes? Or are folks like me the real dummies because we can't bring ourselves to type "coz," except as a joke?

I know the answer, and it's not what you might think.

The best way to understand it is to imagine a guy wearing a very small, tight swimsuit. I know. Close your eyes and do it anyway. Now that you're thinking of that suit and its wearer, imagine a place where that person is standing.

If your swimsuit guy is standing in, say, a shopping center, then it's probably not too hard to imagine the next people entering the landscape of your imagination are police officers, ready to arrest him for indecent exposure.

But if your swimsuit guy is standing alongside an Olympic-size swimming pool, waiting for his event to begin, then you've imagined a context where the image fits right in. No one looks at a competitive swimmer in his little swimsuit and says, "Hey buddy, put some pants on!"

So the key with Internetisms is to know when it's okay to use them, when it's not okay, and when not using them will make you look clueless.

When It's Okay to Abbreviate

We use language shortcuts all the time, sometimes without even knowing it. Even fancy people who don't even use contractions when they're talking will sometimes take shortcuts with their speech and writing.

The last time you hailed a taxi, for example, you used a shortcut. And I'm not just talking about shortening taxicab to taxi. The unabbreviated term for it is taximeter cab. A taximeter is the thing in the cab that keeps track of your fare. Even "cab" is an abbreviation, for "cabriolet."

So anyone who tells you it's never okay to crunch down language into more easily chewable pieces had better be willing to holler "taximeter cabriolet" the next time he's in New York. My guess is that anyone who does that won't catch anything more than puzzled looks.

Just as you'd sound crazy saying, "taximeter cabriolet!" the truth is, you run the risk of sounding hopelessly out of touch if you're in a chat room or using instant messaging software and you don't shorten things here and there.

Imagine the agony of chatting with someone who wrote, "What you just typed was very funny. I am at this moment laughing out loud," instead of LOL.

You can communicate more information in less time by adopting Internetisms. The same goes for emoticons, those little sideways facial expressions made out of punctuation marks. When you're having a quick chat online, these tools help you communicate quickly and clearly when you're joking and when you're miffed. Later versions of the software even let you insert symbols that let a person know you're happy, sad, on the phone, or feeling a little bit romantic. For all these reasons, and even more that I'll get to later, it's A-OK to use Internetisms when chatting and sending instant messages.

Anywhere else, though, and watch out.

Your Webbish ways can sometimes make you look dumb. But don't just take my word for it, ask Jonathan Alexander, an associate professor of English at the University of Cincinnati. Alexander teaches courses in writing and technology. The same day I talked to him, he got this e-mail from a student:

"do u still have those blank postcards cuz i need to put my final postcard on one . . . if u do can u bring it to class on friday?"

Alexander, whose facial hair belies his own Internet-hipness, is a big fan of technology. He even holds class discussions in chat rooms, to enable his students to spend more time writing and to encourage the shy speakers to contribute to the discussion. But even this technophile thought the e-mail from his student was a bit much.

Why? Because he's the teacher. Students are supposed to impress teachers with what they know. If you look smart, you get a good grade. That's how it works.

To someone who is used to seeing a more formal writing style, this e-mail looks like it's one notch up from a cave scratching.

How much time could the student have saved by abbreviating "you" and "because"? Or by skipping the uppercase letters? My guess is about two seconds. Was it worth looking like a bonehead?

The point is, there are times and places where shortcuts are okay, just as there are times and places where tiny swimsuits don't look ridiculous. If you're chatting with or messaging a friend or peer, it's okay to abbreviate. It's probably okay in e-mail, though you never know where that's going to get forwarded or printed out.

But in anything else, it's a bad idea. This includes an e-mail to a boss, teacher, or anyone you want to impress. It includes term papers, cover letters, and even your private diary that you're hoping will some day be discovered like Anne Frank's was, thus earning global adoration for your sly wit and sensitive soul.

The reason Internetisms and other acronyms, abbreviations, and shortcuts have emerged is that people are creative.

Rich Epstein, an assistant professor of linguistics at Rutgers University, says people constantly seek "new ways of saying the same thing. It gets boring to always say it—or write it—the same way . . . People also like to say or write things as quickly as possible, so they seek out shortcuts."

Even though some teachers might disagree, this sort of change isn't going to ruin our mother tongue. It's still useful for communication, Epstein says, even if someone writes B4 when she means before.

The risk happens when the line between formal and informal writing gets crossed. When you write something, you have to consider its effect on the reader. It doesn't matter if the reader knows you mean "before." To her, it may be distracting. People need to learn the languages that are used in multiple contexts.

Bill Lutz, a professor of English at Rutgers, says this learning can be a double-edged sword. For example, if you're on the Internet and you don't use the catchphrases and abbreviations, you're going to stand out in a bad way.

"You're going to be suspect immediately," he says. "People will think, 'What are you, a narc?'"

In addition to just being more convenient, slang marks the language of a group. It not only identifies group members, Lutz says, it serves to keep out the riffraff.

This is probably one reason that so many young Internet users have adopted so many shortcuts like "wuz." It's the same number of letters as the word it replaces, but it sends the message, "I'm a kid. If you don't like it, go back to your rocking chair, gramps."

This isn't always the message a kid means to send. Lutz says the key to succeeding, whether in a chat room or in a more formal context, is this: Pay attention to your language.

"It's like air," he says. "We don't pay attention to it until it's really dirty. The more we pay attention, the more we learn, understand, and use it appropriately."

I couldn't have said it better myself.

Suggestions for Discussion

1. Under what circumstances might Instant Messaging lingo make a person seem unintelligent? When might the use of scrupulously correct grammar, spelling, and language make a person seem absurd?

2. Why is "context" so central to Brockenbrough's argument?

3. Synthesis: How does Brockenbrough's argument compare to that of George Orwell in "Politics and the English Language" (*Art and Society*)? Where might these two writers agree? Where might they disagree?

Suggestions for Writing

1. You are not feeling well enough to get up today, and you need to inform a variety of people that you will not be seeing them today, including your mother, a professor, a friend, your boss, and your romantic partner. Who gets a phone or Skype call, a text-message, an e-mail, or a Facebook post? How do you word each message? Craft each of these messages, and explain why you chose the wording and the communications medium for each person.

2. Synthesis: Read the following essays: Julie J.C.H. Ryan's "Student Plagiarism in an Online World," Samuel G. Freedman's "New Class(room) War: Teacher versus Technology," Maggie Jackson's "Distracted: The Erosion of Attention

and the Coming Dark Age," Steven Levy's "Facebook Grows Up" and Pete Rojas' "Bootleg Culture." Based on what you read in these selections—and your own thinking—write about the ways in which modern technology might enhance and/or undermine the quality of a college student's educational experience.

∿∿∿

KATIE HAFNER

Seeing Corporate Fingerprints in Wikipedia Edits

San Franciscan Katie Hafner (b. 1957) examines the social, legal, and psychological issues related to technological innovation. Formerly a technology correspondent for *The New York Times* and *Newsweek*, Hafner is now a full-time freelance journalist who has written for *Wired, The New Republic,* and *Esquire.* Her books include *The House at the Bridge: A Story of Modern Germany* (1995), *The WELL: A Story of Love, Death and Real Life in the Seminal Online Community* (2001), and *A Romance on Three Legs: Glenn Gould's Obsessive Quest for the Perfect Piano* (2008). She has also coauthored *Cyberpunk: Outlaws and Hackers on the Computer Frontier* (1991) with John Markoff, and *Where Wizards Stay Up Late: The Origins of the Internet* (1996) with Matthew Lyon. Her next book, *Mother Daughter Me,* is slated for publication in 2011. Hafner also appears in the documentary films *Freedom Downtime* (2001) and *Miracle in a Box* (2009). The following article appeared in *The New York Times* on August 19, 2007.

Last year a Wikipedia visitor edited the entry for the SeaWorld theme parks to change all mentions of "orcas" to "killer whales," insisting that this was a more accurate name for the species.

There was another, unexplained edit: a paragraph about criticism of SeaWorld's "lack of respect toward its orcas" disappeared. Both changes, it turns out, originated at a computer at Anheuser-Busch, SeaWorld's owner.

Dozens of similar examples of insider editing came to light last week through WikiScanner, a new Web site that traces the source of millions of changes to Wikipedia, the popular online encyclopedia that anyone can edit.

The site, wikiscanner.virgil.gr, created by a computer science graduate student, cross-references an edited entry on Wikipedia with the owner of the computer network where the change originated, using the Internet protocol address of the editor's network. The address information was already available on Wikipedia, but the new site makes it much easier to connect those numbers with the names of network owners.

Since Wired News first wrote about WikiScanner last week, Internet users have spotted plenty of interesting changes to Wikipedia by people at nonprofit groups and government entities like the Central Intelligence Agency. Many of the most obviously self-interested edits have come from corporate networks.

Last year, someone at PepsiCo deleted several paragraphs of the Pepsi entry that focused on its detrimental health effects. In 2005, someone using a computer at *Diebold* deleted paragraphs that criticized the company's electronic voting machines. That same year, someone inside Wal-Mart Stores changed an entry about employee compensation.

Jimmy Wales, founder of the Wikimedia Foundation, which runs Wikipedia, says the site discourages such "conflict of interest" editing. "We don't make it an absolute rule," he said, "but it's definitely a guideline."

Internet experts, for the most part, have welcomed WikiScanner. "I'm very glad that this has been exposed," said Susan P. Crawford, a visiting professor at the University of Michigan Law School. "Wikipedia is a reliable first stop for getting information about a huge variety of things, and it shouldn't be manipulated as a public relations arm of major companies."

Most of the corporate revisions did not stay posted for long. Many Wikipedia entries are in a constant state of flux as they are edited and re-edited, and the site's many regular volunteers and administrators tend to keep an eye out for bias.

In general, changes to a Wikipedia page cannot be traced to an individual, only to the owner of a particular network. In 2004, someone using a computer at ExxonMobil made substantial changes to a description of the 1989 Exxon Valdez oil spill in Alaska, playing down its impact on the area's wildlife and casting a positive light on compensation payments the company had made to victims of the spill.

Gantt Walton, a spokesman for the company, said that although the revisions appeared to have come from an ExxonMobil computer, the company has more than 80,000 employees around the world, making it "more than a difficult task" to figure out who made the changes.

Mr. Walton said ExxonMobil employees "are not authorized to update Wikipedia with company computers without company endorsement."

The company's preferred approach, he said, would be to use Wikipedia's "talk" pages, a forum for discussing Wikipedia entries.

Mr. Wales also said the "talk" pages are where Wikipedia encourages editors with a conflict of interest to suggest revisions.

"If someone sees a simple factual error about their company, we really don't mind if they go in and edit," he said. But if a revision is likely to be controversial, he added, "the best thing to do is log in, go to the 'talk' page, identify yourself openly, and say, 'I'm the communications person from such and such company.' The community responds very well, especially if the person isn't combative."

Mike Sitrick, a longtime public relations consultant in Los Angeles, agreed. "I'm a big believer that if you're going to correct it, correct it with a name," he said. "Otherwise it hurts your credibility."

An Anheuser-Busch employee eventually took responsibility for the changes to the SeaWorld page—but only after being challenged about them twice by another user. A person identifying himself as Fred Jacobs, communications director for the company's theme park unit, said on the entry's "talk" page that discussion of the ethics of keeping sea creatures captive "belongs in an article devoted to that subject."

Mr. Jacobs referred questions about the editing to another company office, which did not respond to requests for comment.

The SCO Group, a software maker in Salt Lake City, made changes to product information in its own entry this year. The company has been involved in legal disputes over the rights to some open-source software.

Craig Bushman, the company's vice president for marketing, said he had told a public relations manager to make the changes. "The whole history of SCO had been written by someone who doesn't know the history of SCO," he said.

An hour after the changes were made, he said, they disappeared. The company e-mailed Wikipedia administrators, who replied that the changes had been rejected because of a lack of objectivity.

In the case of the Wal-Mart revisions, David Tovar, a company spokesman, said that while he was not aware of anyone within Wal-Mart who had asked to contribute to Wikipedia, the changes could have been made by any of its workers, who are called associates. "We consider our associates our best ambassadors," he said, "and sometimes they speak out to set the record straight."

At Dell, the computer maker, employees are told that they need to identify their employer if they write about the company online. "Whether it's Wikipedia, Twitter or MySpace, our policy is you have to let someone know you're from Dell," said Bob Pearson, a Dell spokesman.

Before that policy was put in place a year ago, changes to parts of Dell's Wikipedia entry discussing its offshore outsourcing of customer service were made by someone from the Dell corporate network.

Most people using company networks to edit Wikipedia entries dabble in subjects that appear to have little to do with their work, although sometimes they cannot resist a silly dig at the competition.

Last year, someone using a computer at the *Washington Post* Company changed the name of the owner of a free local paper, *The Washington Examiner*, from Philip Anschutz to Charles Manson. A person using a computer at CBS updated the page on Wolf Blitzer of CNN to add that his real name was Irving Federman. (It is actually Wolf Blitzer.)

And *The New York Times* Company is among those whose employees have made, among hundreds of innocuous changes, a handful of questionable edits. A change to the page on President Bush, for instance, repeated the word "jerk" 12 times. And in the entry for Condoleezza Rice, the secretary of state, the word "pianist" was changed to "penis."

"It's impossible to determine who did any of these things," said Craig R. Whitney, the standards editor of *The Times*. "But you can only shake your head when you see what was done to the George Bush and Condoleezza Rice entries."

WikiScanner is the work of Virgil Griffith, 24, a cognitive scientist who is a visiting researcher at the Santa Fe Institute in New Mexico. Mr. Griffith, who spent two weeks this summer writing the software for the site, said he got interested in creating such a tool last year after hearing of members of Congress who were editing their own entries.

Mr. Griffith said he "was expecting a few people to get nailed pretty hard" after his service became public. "The yield, in terms of public relations disasters, is about what I expected."

Mr. Griffith, who also likes to refer to himself as a "disruptive technologist," said he was certain any more examples of self-interested editing would come out in the next few weeks, "because the data set is just so huge."

Mr. Wales, who called the scanner "a very clever idea," said he was considering some changes to Wikipedia to help visitors better understand what information is recorded about them.

"When someone clicks on 'edit,' it would be interesting if we could say, 'Hi, thank you for editing. We see you're logged in from *The New York Times*. Keep in mind that we know that, and it's public information,'" he said. "That might make them stop and think."

Suggestions for Discussion

1. Would you want control over a Wikipedia entry about you? Why or why not?

2. Why is it important for researchers to know where their information is coming from?

3. When can researchers be fairly confident that the sources they are using are reliable? What kinds of sources might typically be most reliably objective and accurate?

4. How did Wikipedia respond to the issues Hafner raises in her article? Were the steps they took appropriate? Were they enough?

5. For many researchers, the best part about a given Wikipedia entry is the source list and links featured at the bottom of the page. Why might some of these sources be considered more important than the entry itself?

Suggestions for Writing

1. In late 2009, Wikipedia founder Jimmy Wales posted an open letter online requesting donations to help Wikipedia stay in business. His Web site, he wrote, is "one of the world's five most popular web properties," with an ultimate goal of creating "a world in which every single person on the planet is given free access to the sum of all human knowledge." But its service is free, and it requires $6 million a year to operate. Wales was seeking donations rather than selling advertising, as most sites do: "Like a national park or a school, we don't believe advertising should have a place in Wikipedia." Do you agree that Wikipedia is worth supporting? Would you donate to it? Support your argument.

2. Synthesis: The Web site Conservapedia was created as a conservative Christian alternative to Wikipedia and describes itself as "anti-intellectual." (See its mission statement on the Web page *How Conservapedia Differs from Wikipedia*.) Compare the entries for "liberal" and "conservative" on Conservapedia with those for "liberalism" and "conservatism" on Wikipedia. You might also compare the entries on each for other terms "evolution," "Ronald Reagan," "global warming," and "Barack Obama." Describe the differences between the two Web sites, evaluating their mission statements, sources, reliability, and political biases.

J U L I E   J . C . H .   R Y A N

Student Plagiarism in an Online World

Julie J. C. H. Ryan, associate professor of Engineering Management and Systems Engineering at George Washington University, researches and teaches in the area of information security management and information warfare. She is an expert on plagiarism and other academic integrity issues. Ryan has served in the U.S. Air Force as a signals intelligence officer, in the Defense Intelligence Agency as a military intelligence officer, and in various corporations as a consultant and scientist. She has participated with the National Research Council in advanced technology studies. Ryan coauthored the book *Defending Your Digital Assets Against Hackers, Crackers, Spies, and Thieves* (2000) with Randall Nichols and Daniel J. Ryan. This paper first appeared in the December 1998 issue of *Prism Magazine*, the journal of the American Society for Engineering Education.

VEIT METTE, *Deutschstunde 2002.* © www.veitmette.de.

In academe, the consequences of plagiarism are clear: Using someone else's words or ideas without attribution is grounds for failed assignments, suspension, or expulsion. For some students, however, breaking the rules seems to be an irresistible challenge. And so the game goes: Students continually look for (and find) ways to cheat, and teachers remain on the alert for purloined paragraphs, pages, and even entire papers.

Plagiarized work used to be generated through frat house recycling efforts, purchased from local ghost writers, or simply copied from campus library reference materials—all clumsy efforts readily detectable by educators familiar with their course material. But the World Wide Web and other electronic resources have changed the game and left educators scrambling to keep abreast of plagiarists' new methods.

∾

Abusing Electronic Media

Before the world was linked by the Internet, hard-to-detect plagiarism required ingenuity and skill. But today, with the click of a mouse, even technologically inept students have access to vast information resources in cyberspace without having to leave the comfort of their dorm rooms.

A few words typed into a Web search engine can lead a student to hundreds, sometimes thousands, of relevant documents, making it easy to "cut and paste" a few paragraphs from here and a few more from there until the student has an entire paper-length collection. Or a student can find a research paper published in one of the hundreds of new journals that have gone online over the past few years, copy the entire text, turn it into a new document, and then offer it up as an original work without having to type anything but a cover page. Even recycling efforts and ghost writers have gone global, with Web sites offering professionally or student-written research papers for sale, some even with a money back guarantee against detection.

Facing the New Plagiarism Reality

I ran headlong into these new practices during the fall 1997 semester as my husband and I each taught an introductory information security concepts course for George Washington University. When students turned in their required research papers, we were initially surprised at how well they seemed to have mastered the course material. But when we looked closer, we realized that in many cases we were not looking at original student work.

Consider the following extract from one of the student-submitted papers:

> Both the government and the healthcare unions agree that electronic health records must be at least as well protected as paper ones; the Data Protection

> Act makes physicians and others responsible for the security of personal health information that they collect; and a recent Directive obliges the government to prohibit the processing of health data except where the data subject has given his explicit consent, and in certain other circumstances.

The level of erudition, education, and sophistication evidenced in this extract (and the entire document) made it immediately suspect—the student was, after all, taking an introductory course in information security concepts. To satisfy his curiosity, my husband asked me to research the paper content for possible plagiarism. I did so using the tool most readily available, the Internet. It didn't take me long to find an exact match.

I used the AltaVista Search engine to conduct a search for specific phrases (or strings) in the paper. To search for an exact match, I used quotation marks around the string. If quotations marks are not used, the results will include Web pages that contain some or all of the words in the string.

I also could have performed a category search using one of the comprehensive listing services that index Web sites by category. Yahoo! is one of the most popular sites of this type. Comprehensive list sites give you two search options. You can choose a category from the site's standing lists, or you can type a few words into the search box and the site's internal search engine will retrieve a list of categories and Web site that include the words in your search parameters. I found the following extract in an online journal article by Ross J. Anderson, a distinguished University of Cambridge computer researcher. The differences from the previous extract are underlined:

> Both the government and the healthcare unions <u>are</u> agree<u>d</u> that electronic health records must be at least as well protected as paper ones; the Data Protection Act makes *GPs* and others responsible for the security of personal health information that they collect; and a recent <u>EU</u> Directive obliges the government to prohibit the processing of health data except where the data subject has given his explicit consent, and in certain other circumstances [<u>EU95</u>].

It took me five minutes on the Internet to determine the probable source of the paper, and another 10 minutes to confirm word-for-word plagiarism. The entire paper, including the title, table of contents, and bibliography, was plagiarized. An open-and-shut case.

Once I caught the first plagiarism, I decided to check every paper. I discovered that seven of 42 students plagiarized most or all of their papers, and four others turned in papers with footnotes that could charitably be called substandard.

In the spring 1998 semester I discovered that the same percentage of students—one out of every six—plagiarized their entire papers. Also, as in the previous semester, several students' papers had inadequate footnotes.

ℒ

To Catch a Plagiarist

The World Wide Web provides plagiarists with a rich library of material from which to gather information, but it also provides professors with a powerful tool to check sources and catch the word thieves.

The laziness that prompts students to cheat can also prompt them to do a terrible job with their plagiarism. Being able to copy electronic source material rids them of the chore of retyping the paper, and some students don't even bother to proofread the results. These halfhearted efforts can easily be detected if you know what to look for.

Context Change

Students try to camouflage copying by changing the context of the original paper. For example, I received a paper purported to be a draft information security policy for an institute in Korea. The references to Massachusetts law were, therefore, somewhat startling. It turned out that the paper was an almost complete copy of Harvard University's information security policy.

Missing Footnotes

One technique that seems to appeal to plagiarists is to skip footnotes altogether. This is presumably done with the notion that when challenged, the student can point to a bibliography and claim ignorance regarding proper footnoting procedure. I have, in fact, had students try this defense. To counter this, sit down with the student and ask him or her about the subject matter of the paper and the cited bibliographic references. If the student doesn't understand or can't discuss the ideas presented in the paper, or doesn't know the subject matter of the books referenced, then it's safe to assume the student didn't write the paper.

False References

Citing nonexistent books or journal articles, or refering to sources unrelated to the subject matter is also common. Usually sparsely identified, these references tend to list overview or general subject texts, as opposed to the much more specific sources found in legitimate papers.

For example, a false footnote from a spring 1998 paper:

Pfleeger, Charles P. (1997) *Security in Computing.* New Jersey

A real footnote from a legitimate paper that same semester:

Denning, Dorothy E., *Encryption Policy and Market Trends,* http://www.cs.georgetown.edu/~denning/crypto, March 14, 1998.

True footnotes explain the source of data or some technicality in the text, while false footnotes may stand out because of their placement.

An example from a spring 1998 paper:

> Encryption systems fall into two broad classes (Fites & Kratz, 1993). Conventional or symmetric cryptosystems—those in which an entity with the ability to encrypt also has the ability to decrypt and vice versa—are the systems under consideration in this paper. . . . All known public key cryptosystems, however, are subject to shortcut attacks and must therefore use keys ten or more times the length of those discussed here to achieve an equivalent level of security.

Note several things about the reference—it is placed where it appears to substantiate the purported fact that there are two broad classes of encryption systems. However, this is a widely held piece of knowledge that does not warrant footnoting except by the most compulsive of students. The sentences following that, however, are quite different. They do, in fact, warrant footnoting in that they convey specific information that is not in the realm of what may be purported to be common knowledge. And yet there is no footnote.

Further, an examination of the Fites & Kratz reference reveals it to be a general purpose text of some age (in an era when information technology turns over generationally every 18 months or so, even a few years can have dramatic effects on the content of a text). As referenced: Fites, Philip & Kratz, Martin P. J., (1993). *Information Systems Security*. New York.

Online bookstores provide book descriptions and reviews, and information on availability, all of which can be used to make sure a reference book is appropriate for the subject matter. Using the online bookstore Amazon.com revealed that the true title of the above-mentioned text to be *Information Systems Security: A Practitioner's Reference*, and that it is out of print. A search on the Internet using the AltaVista search engine revealed a source with more information on the subject matter of the text:

> *Information Systems Security: A Practitioner's Reference.* Philip Fites and Martin P. J. Kratz
>
> You will refer to this valuable resource again and again. There are chapters on countermeasures, designing secure systems, software, accounting and auditing controls. Operations and physical security in fire prevention, libraries and database protection, waste disposal and storage are all discussed. All-encompassing and up-to-date, it's a vital reference tool! 471 pp., 1993 SCVR (http://www.asisonline.org/catcomputer.html#infosecurity, 13 May 1998)

Clearly the text, while useful, is not a cryptography reference. In this case, the false footnote actually highlighted the suspect nature of the text. Other suspect elements of this passage include the reference to "systems under consideration in this paper." As the paper was purportedly an analysis on electronic terrorism, this phrase seemed odd.

A string search on the Internet, again using the AltaVista search engine, revealed the true source of the material:

Minimal Key Lengths for Symmetric Ciphers to Provide Adequate Commercial Security: A Report by an Ad Hoc Group of Cryptographers and Computer Scientists, January 1996, by Matt Blaze et al.

This paper is published on the Internet at multiple locations.

Cyberspace Cooperation

While AltaVista and other search engines are excellent resources, they are of little or no use if the source text was not electronically published. In this case, an investigator can occasionally find clues in a paper that can point to the true author. An example of this occurred in a paper that appeared to be scanned in from a source text. The following is a quote from that student-submitted paper:

NetBill, a system under development at Carnegie Mellon University (CMU), Pittsburgh, in joint action with Mellon Bank Corp., also in Pittsburgh, is accelerated for delivering such information goods as text, images, and software over the Internet. Its developers, including the author, have stressed the significance of securing that consumers receive the information they pay for. For that reason, consumers are not charged until the information has actually been delivered to them.

This paper initially frustrated me, because I had a very strong suspicion that it was plagiarized but couldn't find the source of this text using either a string or category search.

However, the conjunction of references to "the author" and to what seemed to be a proprietary product of Carnegie Mellon University—NetBill—led me to the Carnegie Mellon University Web site. I used the site's internal search engine to find references to NetBill. In doing so, I discovered that Marvin Sirbu is leader of the NetBill project. The search also provided Sirbu's e-mail address.

I immediately sent an e-mail to Sirbu, inquiring as to whether he found that text extract familiar. Sirbu's reply included both the source identification and a URL from which the original document was available. When I compared the original with the student paper, I discovered that the entire paper was plagiarized, including the section headings.

If the Carnegie Mellon site had not provided Sirbu's e-mail address, I could have tried a string search of his name or used one of the many "phone book"-type search engines to hunt down the information.

These search tools may be new to you, but all are relatively easy to use. Most Web search sites have "Help" sections that provide information on using their specific search engines, and there are several sites dedicated to search instruction, including Search Insider.

☙

Why Cheating Still Matters

The papers that are the subject of this article were out-and-out forgeries, with inadequate, nonexistent, or false footnotes. In many cases the plagiary attempts were so patently obvious they were insulting.

The attempted deception is particularly disturbing because the class was an overview of information security concepts and practices. The curriculum focused on the value and protection of information, and specific readings and lectures addressed copyright law and other relevant topics. These students will go on to computer-related careers where they have to deal with information security issues on a regular basis, yet they showed no regard for information's basic value.

Also disturbing was students' reactions when caught. Instead of expressing shame or remorse, reactions included denial (even in the face of overwhelming evidence) and defiance. One student even exclaimed: "You can't do this to me—I'm on a scholarship!" A response from another student caught plagiarizing is immortalized in the following e-mail:

> Hi prof.
>
> I just wanted to tell you something. I called all my friends and asked them how they usually do their papers. Most of them told me that they do the same thing. They didn't know it is illegal and they can't do that. Can you believe it?
>
> Anyway, I told some of them what I did and what happened to me and they were shocked. They didn't know that what they do is wrong . . .
>
> That's why, I did that without knowing it's wrong. Also, I talked to my advisor in the writing center who reviewed my paper. He told me that he didn't notice that, even though I gave him all the articles I used in my paper . . . All I want to say is that I wanted to get an A in your class and I wanted to give you a good paper. . . .

Several other students made similar ignorance pleas when confronted, despite the fact that we emphasized acceptable footnoting practices for research papers during both semesters. In spring 1998, the emphasis on proper procedure was naturally even higher than it had been in fall 1997, and the repercussions from the preceding semester were still a subject of gossip within the student population. Thus it was quite startling to yet again see students attempt to pass off other people's works as their own.

Conclusion

Often lost in the discussion of plagiarism is the interest of the students who don't cheat. They do legitimate research and write their own papers. They work harder (and learn more) than the plagiarists, yet their grades may suffer when their papers are judged and graded against papers that are superior but stolen material. Students have a right to expect fairness in the classroom. When teachers turn a blind eye to plagiarism, it undermines that right and denigrates grades, degrees, and even institutions.

Plagiarism is alive and well on campuses and in cyberspace. But educators should take some solace in the fact that while the Internet is a useful resource for plagiarists, it is also an excellent tool to use against them.

Suggestions for Discussion

1. According to Ryan, why does cheating matter?

2. Why do you think so many students plagiarize?

3. How can students who actually do the work be encouraged to continue to work hard and challenge themselves in the face of rampant plagiarism among their peers?

4. Synthesis: Pete Rojas' essay in his book, *Bootleg Culture*, suggests that some "plagiarizing" is legitimately artistic. What is the distinction between the kind of remixed music he is writing about and homework copied and pasted out of Wikipedia? Is there a distinction?

Suggestions for Writing

1. How can students use the Internet to improve their education, rather than as a means of avoiding learning? Write a brief essay in which you advise your professor how to best approach teaching students of the Internet generation.

2. Helene Hegemann, a 17-year-old German author, admittedly copied some parts of her debut novel from another writer, but far from trying to hide it, Hegemann explains that what she was doing was not plagiarism, but *remixing*. "I wasn't lying, I was just *fibbing*," she argues. The book is a finalist for a $20,000 prize in the Leipzig Book Fair—and one of the prize jurors has said the panel was fully aware of the plagiarism charges *before* making the selection. "Remixing" is, in fact, one theme of the novel, which is set against the backdrop of a German youth culture that celebrates the remix as one of its premier forms of creativity. What's going on here? Write an essay explaining why you agree or disagree with Hegemann's argument.

CREATIVE NONFICTION

∾∾∾∾

HENRY DAVID THOREAU

Reading

Henry David Thoreau (1817–1862) was a philosopher and poet-naturalist whose independent spirit led him to the famous experiment recorded in *Walden, or Life in the Woods* (1854). Thoreau's passion for freedom and his lifetime resistance to conformity in thought and manners are force-fully present in his famous essay, "On the Duty of Civil Disobedience." In the following chapter from *Walden*, Thoreau explains what he loves to read and why.

With a little more deliberation in the choice of their pursuits, all men would perhaps become essentially students and observers, for certainly their nature and destiny are interesting to all alike. In accumulating property for our-selves or our posterity, in founding a family or a state, or acquiring fame even, we are mortal; but in dealing with truth we are immortal, and need fear no change nor accident. The oldest Egyptian or Hindoo philosopher raised a corner of the veil from the statue of the divinity; and still the trem-bling robe remains raised, and I gaze upon as fresh a glory as he did, since it was I in him that was then so bold, and it is he in me that now reviews the vision. No dust has settled on that robe; no time has elapsed since that divin-ity was revealed. That time which we really improve, or which is improv-able, is neither past, present, nor future.

My residence was more favorable, not only to thought, but to serious reading, than a university; and though I was beyond the range of the ordi-nary circulating library, I had more than ever come within the influence of those books which circulate round the world, whose sentences were first written on bark, and are now merely copied from time to time on to linen paper. Says the poet Mîr Carnar Uddîn Mast, "Being seated to run through the region of the spiritual world; I have had this advantage in books. To be intoxicated by a single glass of wine; I have experienced this pleasure when I have drunk the liquor of the esoteric doctrines." I kept Homer's Iliad on my table through the summer, though I looked at his page only now and then. Incessant labor with my hands, at first, for I had my house to finish and my beans to hoe at the same time, made more study impossible. Yet I sustained myself by the prospect of such reading in future. I read one or two shallow books of travel in the intervals of my work, till that employment made me ashamed of myself, and I asked where it was then that *I* lived.

The student may read Homer or Æschylus in the Greek without danger of dissipation or luxuriousness, for it implies that he in some measure emulate their heroes, and consecrate morning hours to their pages. The heroic books, even if printed in the character of our mother tongue, will always be in a language dead to degenerate times; and we must laboriously seek the meaning of each word and line, conjecturing a larger sense than common use permits out of what wisdom and valor and generosity we have. The modern cheap and fertile press, with all its translations, has done little to bring us nearer to the heroic writers of antiquity. They seem as solitary, and the letter in which they are printed as rare and curious, as ever. It is worth the expense of youthful days and costly hours, if you learn only some words of an ancient language, which are raised out of the trivialness of the street, to be perpetual suggestions and provocations. It is not in vain that the farmer remembers and repeats me few Latin words which he has heard. Men sometimes speak as if the study of the classics would at length make way for more modern and practical studies; but the adventurous student will always study classics, in whatever language they may be written and however ancient they may be. For what are the classics but the noblest recorded thoughts of man? They are the only oracles which are not decayed, and there are such answers to the most modern inquiry in them as Delphi and Dodona never gave. We might as well omit to study Nature because she is old. To read well, that is, to read true books in a true spirit, is a noble exercise, and one that will task the reader more than any exercise which the customs of the day esteem. It requires a training such as the athletes underwent, the steady intention almost of the whole life to this object. Books must be read as deliberately and reservedly as they were written. It is not enough even to be able to speak the language of that nation by which they are written, for there is a memorable interval between the spoken and the written language, the language heard and the language read. The one is commonly transitory, a sound, a tongue, a dialect merely, almost brutish, and we learn it unconsciously, like the brutes, of our mothers. The other is the maturity and experience of that; if that is our mother tongue, this is our father tongue, a reserved and select expression, too significant to be heard by the ear, which we must be born again in order to speak. The crowds of men who merely *spoke* the Greek and Latin tongues in the middle ages were not entitled by the accident of birth to *read* the works of genius written in those languages; for these were not written in that Greek or Latin which they knew, but in the select language of literature. They had not learned the nobler dialects of Greece and Rome, but the very materials on which they were written were waste paper to them, and they prized instead a cheap contemporary literature. But when the several nations of Europe had acquired distinct though rude written languages of their own, sufficient for the purposes of their rising literatures, then first learning revived, and scholars were enabled to discern from that remoteness the treasures of antiquity. What the Roman and Grecian multitude could not *hear*, after the lapse of ages a few scholars *read*, and a few scholars only are still reading it.

However much we may admire the orator's occasional bursts of eloquence, the noblest written words are commonly as far behind or above the fleeting spoken language as the firmament with its stars is behind the clouds. *There* are the stars, and they who can may read them. The astronomers forever comment on and observe them. They are not exhalations like our daily colloquies and vaporous breath. What is called eloquence in the forum is commonly found to be rhetoric in the study. The orator yields to the inspiration of a transient occasion, and speaks to the mob before him, to those who can *hear* him; but the writer, whose more equable life is his occasion, and who would be distracted by the event and the crowd which inspire the orator, speaks to the intellect and heart of mankind, to all in any age who can *understand* him.

No wonder that Alexander carried the Iliad with him on his expeditions in a precious casket. A written word is the choicest of relics. It is something at once more intimate with us and more universal than any other work of art. It is the work of art nearest to life itself. It may be translated into every language, and not only be read but actually breathed from all human lips;— not be represented on canvas or in marble only, but be carved out of the breath of life itself. The symbol of an ancient man's thought becomes a modern man's speech. Two thousand summers have imparted to the monuments of Grecian literature, as to her marbles, only a maturer golden and autumnal tint, for they have carried their own serene and celestial atmosphere into all lands to protect them against the corrosion of time. Books are the treasured wealth of the world and the fit inheritance of generations and nations. Books, the oldest and the best, stand naturally and rightfully on the shelves of every cottage. They have no cause of their own to plead, but while they enlighten and sustain the reader his common sense will not refuse them. Their authors are a natural and irresistible aristocracy in every society, and, more than kings or emperors, exert an influence on mankind. When the illiterate and perhaps scornful trader has earned by enterprise and industry his coveted leisure and independence, and is admitted to the circles of wealth and fashion, he turns inevitably at last to those still higher but yet inaccessible circles of intellect and genius, and is sensible only of the imperfection of his culture and the vanity and insufficiency of all his riches, and further proves his good sense by the pains which he takes to secure for his children that intellectual culture whose want he so keenly feels; and thus it is that he becomes the founder of a family.

Those who have not learned to read the ancient classics in the language in which they were written must have a very imperfect knowledge of the history of the human race; for it is remarkable that no transcript of them has ever been made into any modern tongue, unless our civilization itself may be regarded as such a transcript. Homer has never yet been printed in English, nor Æschylus, nor Virgil even,—works as refined, as solidly done, and as beautiful almost as the morning itself; for later writers, say what we will of their genius, have rarely, if ever, equalled the elaborate beauty and finish and the lifelong and heroic literary labors of the ancients. They only talk of forgetting them who never knew them. It will be soon enough to forget them when we have the learning and the genius which will enable us to attend to and appreciate them. That age will be rich indeed when those relics which we call Classics, and the still older and more than classic but even less known Scriptures of the nations, shall have still further accumulated when the Vaticans shall be filled with Vedas and Zendavestas and Bibles, with Homers and Dantes and Shakspeares, and all the centuries to come shall have successively deposited their trophies in the forum of the world. By such a pile we may hope to scale heaven at last.

The works of the great poets have never yet been read by mankind, for only great poets can read them. They have only been read as the multitude read the stars, at most astrologically, not astronomically. Most men have learned to read to serve a paltry convenience, as they have learned to cipher in order to keep accounts and not be cheated in trade; but of reading as a noble intellectual exercise they know little or nothing; yet this only is reading, in a high sense, not that which lulls us as a luxury and suffers the nobler faculties to sleep the while, but what we have to stand on tiptoe to read and devote our most alert and wakeful hours to.

I think that having learned our letters we should read the best that is in literature, and not be forever repeating our a b abs, and words of one syllable, in the fourth or fifth classes, sitting on the lowest and foremost form all our lives. Most men are satisfied if they read or hear read, and perchance have been convicted by the wisdom of one good book, the Bible, and for the rest of their lives vegetate and dissipate their faculties in what is called easy reading. There is a work in several volumes in our Circulating Library entitled Little Reading, which I thought referred to a town of that name which I had not been to. There are those who, like cormorants and ostriches, can digest all sorts of this, even after the fullest dinner of meats and vegetables, for they suffer nothing to be wasted. If others are the machines to provide this provender, they are the machines to read it. They read the nine thousandth tale about Zebulon and Sephronia, and how they loved as none had ever loved before, and neither did the course of their true love run smooth,—at any rate, how it did run and stumble, and get up again and go on! how some poor unfortunate got up on to a steeple, who had better never have gone up as far as the belfry; and then, having needlessly got him up there, the happy novelist rings the bell for all the world to come together and hear, O dear! how he did get down again! For my part, I think that they had better metamorphose all such aspiring heroes of universal noveldom into man weather-cocks, as they used to put heroes among the constellations, and let them swing round there till they are rusty, and not come down at all to bother honest men with their pranks. The next time the novelist rings the bell I will not stir though the meeting-house burn down. "The Skip of the Tip-Toe-Hop, a Romance of the Middle Ages, by the celebrated author of 'Tittle-Tol-Tan,' to appear in monthly parts; a great rush; don't all come together." All this they read with saucer eyes, and erect and primitive curiosity, and with unwearied gizzard, whose corrugations even yet need no sharpening, just as some little four-year-old bencher his two-cent gilt-covered edition of Cinderella,—without any improvement, that I can see, in the pronunciation, or accent, or emphasis, or any more skill in extracting or inserting the moral. The result is dulness of sight, a stagnation of the vital circulations, and a general deliquium and sloughing off of all the intellectual faculties. This sort of gingerbread is baked daily and more sedulously than pure wheat or rye-and-Indian in almost every oven, and finds a surer market.

The best books are not read even by those who are called good readers. What does our Concord culture amount to? There is in this town, with a very few exceptions, no taste for the best or for very good books even in English literature, whose words all can read and spell. Even the college-bred and so called liberally educated men here and elsewhere have really little or no acquaintance with the English classics; and as for the recorded wisdom of mankind, the ancient classics and Bibles, which are accessible to all who will know of them, there are the feeblest efforts any where made to become acquainted with them. I know a woodchopper, of middle age, who takes a French paper, not for news as he says, for he is above that, but to "keep himself in practice," he being a Canadian by birth; and when I ask him what he considers the best thing he can do in this world, he says, beside this, to keep up and add to his English. This is about as much as the college bred generally do or aspire to do, and they take an English paper for the purpose. One who has just come from reading perhaps one of the best English books will find how many with whom he can converse about it? Or suppose he comes from reading a Greek or Latin classic in the original, whose praises are familiar even to the so called illiterate; he will find nobody at all to speak to, but must keep silence about it. Indeed, there is hardly the professor in our colleges, who, if he has mastered the difficulties of the language, has proportionally mastered the difficulties of the wit and poetry of a Greek poet, and has any sympathy to impart to the alert and heroic reader; and as for the sacred Scriptures, or Bibles of mankind, who in this town can tell me even their titles? Most men do not know that any nation but the Hebrews have had a scripture. A man, any man, will go considerably out of his way to pick up a silver dollar; but here are golden words, which the wisest men of antiquity have uttered, and whose worth the wise of every succeeding age have assured us of;—and yet we learn to read only as far as Easy Reading, the primers and classbooks, and when we leave school, the "Little Reading," and story books which are for boys and beginners; and our reading, our conversation and thinking, are all on a very low level, worthy only of pygmies and manikins.

I aspire to be acquainted with wiser men than this our Concord soil has produced, whose names are hardly known here. Or shall I hear the name of Plato and never read his book? As if Plato were my townsman and I never saw him,—my next neighbor and I never heard him speak or attended to the wisdom of his words. But how actually is it? His Dialogues, which contain what was immortal in him, lie on the next shelf, and yet I never read them. We are under-bred and low-lived and illiterate; and in this respect I confess I do not make any very broad distinction between the illiterateness of my townsman who cannot read at all, and the illiterateness of him who has learned to read only what is for children and feeble intellects. We should be as good as the worthies of antiquity, but partly by first knowing how good they were. We are a race of tit-men, and soar but little higher in our intellectual flights than the columns of the daily paper.

It is not all books that are as dull as their readers. There are probably words addressed to our condition exactly, which, if we could really hear and understand, would be more salutary than the morning or the spring to our lives, and possibly put a new aspect on the face of things for us. How many a man has dated a new era in his life from the reading of a book. The book exists for us perchance which will explain our miracles and reveal new ones. The at present unutterable things we may find somewhere uttered. These same questions that disturb and puzzle and confound us have in their turn occurred to all the wise men; not one has been omitted; and each has answered them, according to his ability, by his words and his life. Moreover, with wisdom we shall learn liberality. The solitary hired man on a farm in the outskirts of Concord, who has had his second birth and peculiar religious experience, and is driven as he believes into silent gravity and exclusiveness by his faith, may think it is not true; but Zoroaster, thousands of years ago, travelled the same road and had the same experience; but he, being wise, knew it to be universal, and treated his neighbors accordingly, and is even said to have invented and established worship among men. Let him humbly commune with Zoroaster then, and, through the liberalizing influence of all the worthies, with Jesus Christ himself, and let "our church" go by the board.

We boast that we belong to the nineteenth century and are making the most rapid strides of any nation. But consider how little this village does for its own culture. I do not wish to flatter my townsmen, nor to be flattered by them, for that will not advance either of us. We need to be provoked,—goaded like oxen, as we are, into a trot. We have a comparatively decent system of common schools, schools for infants only; but excepting the half-starved Lyceum in the winter, and latterly the puny beginning of a library suggested by the state, no school for ourselves. We spend more on almost any article of bodily aliment or ailment than on our mental aliment. It is time that we had uncommon schools; that we did not leave off our education when we begin to be men and women.

It is time that villages were universities, and their elder inhabitants the fellows of universities, with leisure—if they are indeed so well off—to pursue liberal studies the rest of their lives. Shall the world be confined to one Paris or one Oxford forever? Cannot students be boarded here and get a liberal education under the skies of Concord? Can we not hire some Abelard to lecture to us? Alas! what with foddering the cattle and tending the store, we are kept from school too long, and our education is sadly neglected. In this country, the village should in some respects take the place of the nobleman of Europe. It should be the patron of the fine arts. It is rich enough. It wants only the magnanimity and refinement. It can spend money enough on such things as farmers and traders value, but it is thought Utopian to propose spending money for things which more intelligent men know to be of far more worth. This town has spent seventeen thousand dollars on a town-house, thank fortune or politics, but probably it will not spend so much on living wit, the true meat to put into that shell, in a hundred years. The one hundred and twenty-five dollars annually subscribed for a Lyceum in the winter is better spent than any other equal sum raised in the town. If we live in the nineteenth century, why should we not enjoy the advantages which the nineteenth century offers? Why should our life be in any respect provincial? If we will read newspapers, why not skip the gossip of Boston and take the best newspaper in the world at once?—not be sucking the pap of "neutral family" papers, or browsing "Olive-Branches" here in New England. Let the reports of all the learned societies come to us, and we will see if they know any thing. Why should we leave it to Harper & Brothers and Redding & Co. to select our reading? As the nobleman of cultivated taste surrounds himself with whatever conduces to his culture,—genius—learning—wit—books—paintings—statuary—music—philosophical instruments, and the like; so let the village do,—not stop short at a pedagogue, a parson a sexton, a parish library, and three selectmen, because our pilgrim forefathers got through a cold winter once on a bleak rock with these. To act collectively is according to the spirit of our institutions; and I am confident that, as our circumstances are more flourishing, our means are greater than the nobleman's. New England can hire all the wise men in the world to come and teach her, and board them round the while, and not be provincial at all. That is the *uncommon* school we want. Instead of noblemen, let us have noble villages of men. If it is necessary, omit one bridge over the river, go round a little there, and throw one arch at least over the darker gulf of ignorance which surrounds us.

Suggestions for Discussion

1. According to Thoreau, why is the studying of Classic literature a noble exercise?

2. Why doesn't Thoreau like fairy tales, newspapers, or best-selling novels? Why does he consider Americans who read only such texts, plus a little

of the Bible, functionally illiterate? Do you agree with his opinions? Explain.

3. Thoreau believes that "reading well . . . requires a training such as the athletes underwent." What kind of training does he believe will help us become better readers?

Suggestions for Writing

1. Write a letter in response to Thoreau in which you defend the virtues of fairy tales, novels, newspapers, and other elements of popular culture using arguments and reasoning that Thoreau might respect.

2. If Thoreau considered the people of his time illiterate, what would he think of contemporary Americans? Would you pass his literacy test? What encounters have you and those you know had with the Classics? Do you desire to read any of the texts that Thoreau recommends that you have not yet encountered? What did you learn from those books you *did* read? Write a personal reflection paper in which you consider these issues in light of your own opinions and experience, and considering the central arguments Thoreau makes.

POETRY

TAYLOR MALI

The The Impotence of Proofreading

Poet Taylor Mali (b. 1965) came to prominence as a member of the poetry slam movement and is best known for championing teachers and the fundamental value of education. A former teacher himself, Mali taught K–12 English, history, and math courses for nine years in New York and Massachusetts. He graduated with a B.A. in English from Bowdoin College in 1987, with an M.A. in Creative Writing from Kansas State University in 1993, and studied acting at Oxford with members of The Royal Shakespeare Company. The New York City native is the author of two books of poetry, *What Learning Leaves* (2002) and *The Last Time As We Are* (2009), and four CDs of spoken word. He has been featured in the series *Russell Simmons Presents DefPoetry* and the documentaries *SlamNation* (1998) and *Slam Planet* (2006), and has done commercial voiceover work and narrated several books on tape. "The The Impotence of Proofreading" is based on a comedy routine Mali created.

Has this ever happened to you?
You work very horde on a paper for English clash
And then get a very glow raid (like a D or even a D=)
and all because you are the word's liverwurst spoiler.
Proofreading your peppers is a matter of the the utmost impotence.

This is a problem that affects manly, manly students.
I myself was such a bed spiller once upon a term
that my English teacher in my sophomoric year,
Mrs. Myth, said I would never get into a good colleague.
And that¹s all I wanted, just to get into a good colleague.
Not just anal community colleague,
because I wouldn¹t be happy at anal community colleague.
I needed a place that would offer me intellectual simulation,
I really need to be challenged, challenged dentally.
I know this makes me sound like a stereo,
but I really wanted to go to an ivory legal colleague.

173

So I needed to improvement
or gone would be my dream of going to Harvard, Jail, or Prison
(in Prison, New Jersey).

So I got myself a spell checker
and figured I was on Sleazy Street.

But there are several missed aches
that a spell chukker can¹t can¹t catch catch.
For instant, if you accidentally leave a word
your spell exchequer won¹t put it in you.
And God for billing purposes only
you should have serial problems with Tori Spelling
your spell Chekhov might replace a word
with one you had absolutely no detention of using.
Because what do you want it to douch?
It only does what you tell it to douche.
You¹re the one with your hand on the mouth going clit, clit, clit.
It just goes to show you how embargo
one careless clit of the mouth can be.

Which reminds me of this one time during my Junior Mint.
The teacher read my entire paper on A Sale of Two Titties
out loud to all of my assmates.
I¹m not joking, I¹m totally cereal.
It was the most humidifying experience of my life,
being laughed at pubically.
So do yourself a flavor and follow these two Pisces of advice:
One: There is no prostitute for careful editing.
And three: When it comes to proofreading,
the red penis your friend.

Suggestions for Discussion

1. Proofread a piece of your own recent writing. Did you find errors? Share your most embarrassing mistakes with your classmates.

2. With a classmate, list the common writing mistakes that Mali makes fun of in his poem. What strategies you can use to avoid making similar mistakes in your paper?

3. Why might an educator use potentially offensive language as a teaching tool? What might Mali say to a critic who argues that the use of such language is unprofessional?

4. As a performance artist, Taylor Mali often recites his work to a live audience. Watch videos of his performance of this poem, as well as "What Teachers Make" (available on YouTube). What difference is there between watching Mali perform his work and reading it in this text? Does the medium of delivery make a difference?

Suggestions for Writing

1. Synthesis: Taylor Mali's Web site proudly declares him to be "one of the few people in the world to have no job other than that of poet." Read Andrea Frasier's essay "Why I Would Rather Have a Day Job" (*Art and Society*), which looks at why full-time poets are such a rare breed. Using Frasier's essay and Mali's Web site, write a brief essay considering the same question: Why is writing poetry a tough job in today's world? (Remember to proofread your essay before submitting it!)

2. Mali's poem uses language that some find offensive, especially in the context of a classroom. Is it possible to rewrite "The The Impotence of Proofreading" without the curses and sexual references? Try rewriting the piece and replacing the offensive language with different kinds of spelling and grammar errors, "Rated G for General Audiences." Does your rewrite of Mali's work get its message across as effectively? Is it as funny? Much art is "sanitized" in this way before it reaches the public. Write an argument discussing the broader implications of sanitized art.

3. Synthesis: Read Charles Taylor's essay "The Morality Police" (*Art and Society*). What do you think Taylor would think of your efforts to sanitize Mali's piece. How do you feel?

Personal Values and Relationships

I was raised in a family that never felt constrained by their poverty or by their race. So I never really knew I was supposed to feel in some way constrained by being an inner-city, public school black kid, the son of immigrants. I just went into the army and I found an organization that said no, no, no, we've changed, we're ahead of the rest of society. We don't care if you're black or blue, we only care if you're a good green soldier. And, if you do your best, you watch, you'll be recognized. If you don't do your best, you'll be punished. And I started out as a black lieutenant but I became a general who was black.

—COLIN POWELL, "The Good Soldier"

Love is affirmation; it motivates the yes response and sense of wider communication. Love casts out fear, and in the security of this togetherness we find contentment, courage. We no longer fear the age-old haunting questions: "Who am I?" "Why am I?" "Where am I going?" and having cast out fear, we can be honest and charitable.

—CARSON MCCULLERS,
"Loneliness . . . an American Malady"

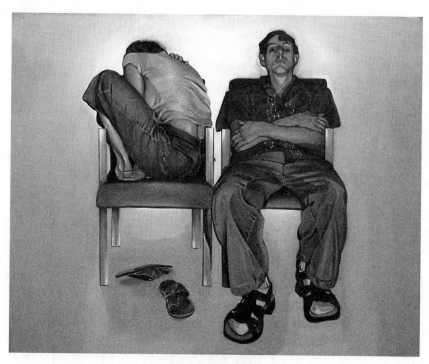

JULIE UNRUH

Bus to Istanbul

Acrylic on canvas, 2004

© Julie Unruh

INTRODUCTION

The questions are familiar ones: Who am I? How have my family and my family history contributed to making me who I am? What else in life has influenced me to become who I am? How do I compare to other people around me? How do I become happy with who I am? Where do I go from here?

All of these questions are likely to be ongoing intellectual and emotional preoccupations for you as a college student. The reading you do as part of your formal education may help you confront these questions and learn more about yourself by introducing you to other people's experiences and ideas about individual and community identity. The works in this section have two common themes: how selfhood develops, and how we relate to others. We learn from the writers' reminiscences that, through the process of ego formation, people travel many psychological and philosophical roads. We also learn that the search for self seldom occurs in isolation. Although each of us spends time alone thinking about ourselves, the search for answers about *who, what,* and *how* we should be is influenced by family at home; by peers everywhere; by leaders and role models in religious, political, and public service institutions; and by educators at school.

This section's Notebook offers two essays about the role of family in the formation of a child's character and moral values. Former United States Vice President Dan Quayle argues that divorce can undermine a child's development, and that the high number of broken homes in the United States has been a major cause of crime and economic hardship for urban communities in particular. Constance Matthiessen's personal tale about the effect a Harry Potter story had on her relationship with her son acts as a response to Quayle's perspective, and argues that there are many kinds of families that children can grow up in—not just the traditional nuclear family of one father, one mother, and 2.5 children.

Predictably, this section is heavy with personal writing that explores the many influences, both internal and external, that affect our sense of self. Gender is a key determiner of self in Kate Chopin's "A Respectable Woman" and in the poem by Anne Sexton. The extent to which the behavior of young people is determined by the social class into which they are born is the primary concern of Alfred Lubrano's "Blue-Collar Roots, White-Collar Dreams," while religion and politics are primary in an essay about pacifism by Mohandas K. Gandhi. Victorian arch-patriot and colonialist Rudyard Kipling sets his own ethical code to paper in *If*, a conservative manifesto that praises the British "stiff upper lip" and expresses a philosophy that may resonate with parents, teachers, and many others to this day.

Our sense of self is particularly volatile in childhood and adolescence, as we attempt to find our place in the world. Contemporary essayist Benoit Denizet-Lewis looks at the "friends with benefits" phenomenon (sex without emotional attachment) among American youth and wonders if sex with no emotional ties (or scars) is truly possible. This essay stands in stark contrast with the poetry selections, which consider—in the classic language of romance—how love can be exuberant (Shakespeare's *Sonnets*) and tragically ridiculous (T. S. Eliot's *The Love Song of J. Alfred Prufrock*).

We are also influenced in our sense of self by how we look, both to ourselves and to the world. In "On Being a Cripple," Nancy Mairs explores the way her physically challenged self influences her internal world. Race and nationality both affect a person's self-image as well and can be—but do not need to be—mighty factors in the search for self, as examined in the writings of Colin Powell, Judith Ortiz Cofer, and Jhumpa Lahiri. Carson McCullers, meanwhile, considers how many Americans live in isolation and do not share bonds of familial and romantic intimacy with *anyone,* and how they feel empty and lonely as a consequence.

In this postmodern era, the concept of the self is an embattled one. Many realities compete; the powerful emergence of virtual reality with its avatars and hidden identities presents many challenges to a traditional notion of self. Thus, the "search for self" explored in this section is perhaps more urgent than ever, and it informs the works throughout the book. For defining yourselves has always been a large part of what you do as college students—and that isn't going to change.

NOTEBOOK

DAN QUAYLE

Restoring Basic Values

Former Vice President James Danforth Quayle (b. 1947) served under President George H. W. Bush from 1989 to 1992. Before that, Quayle, a Republican, represented Indiana in the U.S. Senate (1981–1989) and the House of Representatives (1977–1981). His books include *Standing Firm* (1994) and *Worth Fighting For* (1999), and with Diane Medved, *The American Family* (1996). A graduate of DePauw University (1969) and Indiana University School of Law at Indianapolis (1974), Quayle now lives in Arizona and has served as chairman of Cerberus Global Investments. Quayle has long championed "family values," blaming high divorce and illegitimacy rates for urban poverty, violence, and social degeneration as he did in the speech reprinted here from May 1992. Sometimes derisively referred to as "The Murphy Brown Speech," this address has been criticized for narrowly defining the American family and appearing to blame the 1992 Los Angeles riots on a TV sitcom. However, several commentators have asserted that the core of Quayle's argument is accurate, including Democratic President Bill Clinton, the man who defeated Quayle and Bush in their bid for a second term in the White House.

I have been asked many times about the recent events in Los Angeles. What happened? Why? And how do we prevent it in the future?

Our response has been predictable: Instead of denouncing wrongdoing, some have shown tolerance for rioters; some have enjoyed saying "I told you so," and some have simply made excuses for what happened. All of this has been accompanied by pleas for more money.

I'll readily accept that we need to understand what happened. But I reject the idea we should tolerate or excuse it.

When I have been asked during these last weeks who caused the riots and the killing in L.A., my answer has been direct and simple: Who is to blame for the riots? The rioters are to blame. Who is to blame for the killings? The killers are to blame. Yes, I can understand how people were shocked and outraged by the verdict in the Rodney King trial. But there is simply no excuse for the mayhem that followed. To apologize or in any way to excuse what happened is wrong. It is a betrayal of all those people equally outraged and equally disadvantaged who did not loot and did not riot—and who were in many cases victims of the rioters. No matter how much you may disagree with the verdict, the riots were wrong. And if we as a society don't condemn what is wrong, how can we teach our children what is right?

But after condemning the riots, we do need to try to understand the underlying situation.

In a nutshell: I believe the lawless social anarchy which we saw is directly related to the breakdown of family structure, personal responsibility and social order in too many areas of our society. For the poor the situation is compounded by a welfare ethos that impedes individual efforts to move ahead in society, and hampers their ability to take advantage of the opportunities America offers.

If we don't succeed in addressing these fundamental problems, and in restoring basic values, any attempt to fix what's broken will fail. But one reason I believe we won't fail is that we have come so far in the last 25 years.

'When families fail, society fails.'

There is no question that this country has had a terrible problem with race and racism. The evil of slavery has left a long legacy. But we have faced racism squarely, and we have made progress in the past quarter-century. The landmark civil rights bills of the 1960s removed legal barriers to allow full participation by blacks in the economic, social and political life of the nation. By any measure the America of 1992 is more egalitarian, more integrated, and offers more opportunities to black Americans—and all other minority group members—than the America of 1964. There is more to be done. But I think that all of us can be proud of our progress.

And let's be specific about one aspect of this progress: This country now has a black middle class that barely existed a quarter-century ago. Since 1967, the median income of black two-parent families has risen by 60 percent in real terms. The number of black college graduates has skyrocketed. Black men and women have achieved real political power—black mayors head 48 of our largest cities, including Los Angeles. These are achievements.

But as we all know, there is another side to that bright landscape. During this period of progress, we have also developed a culture of poverty—some call it an underclass—that is far more violent and harder to escape than it was a generation ago.

The poor you always have with you, Scripture tells us. And in America we have always had poor people. But in this dynamic, prosperous nation, poverty has traditionally been a stage through which people pass on their way to joining the great middle class. And if one generation didn't get very far up the ladder—their ambitious, better-educated children would.

But the underclass seems to be a new phenomenon. It is a group whose members are dependent on welfare for very long stretches, and whose men are often drawn into lives of crime. There is far too little upward mobility, because the underclass is disconnected from the rules of American society. And these problems have, unfortunately, been particularly acute for black Americans.

Let me share with you a few statistics on the difference between black poverty in particular in the 1960s and now.

In 1967, 68 percent of black families were headed by married couples. In 1991, only 48 percent of black families were headed by both a husband and wife. In 1965, the illegitimacy rate among black families was 28 percent. In 1989, 65 percent—two thirds—of all black children were born to never-married mothers. In 1951, 9.2 percent of black youth between 16–19 were unemployed. In 1965, it was 23 percent. In 1980, it was 35 percent. By 1989, the number had declined slightly, but was still 32 percent. The leading cause of death of young black males today is homicide. It would be overly simplistic to blame this social breakdown on the programs of the Great Society alone. It would be absolutely wrong to blame it on the growth and success most Americans enjoyed during the 1980s. Rather, we are in large measure reaping the whirlwind of decades of changes in social mores.

The intergenerational poverty that troubles us so much today is predominantly a poverty of values. Our inner cities are filled with children having children; with people who have not been able to take advantage of educational opportunities; with people who are dependent on drugs or the narcotic of welfare. To be sure, many people in the ghettos struggle very hard against these tides—and sometimes win. But too many feel they have no hope and nothing to lose. This poverty is, again, fundamentally a poverty of values.

'This poverty is a poverty of values. Unless we change the basic rules of society, we cannot expect anything else to change.'

Unless we change the basic rules of society in our inner cities, we cannot expect anything else to change. For the government, transforming underclass culture means that our policies and programs must create a different incentive system. Our policies must be premised on, and must reinforce, values such as: family, hard work, integrity and personal responsibility.

I think we can all agree that government's first obligation is to maintain order. We are a nation of laws, not looting. If a single mother raising her children in the ghetto has to worry about drive-by shootings, drug deals, or whether her children will join gangs and die violently, her difficult tasks becomes impossible.

Safety is absolutely necessary. But it's not sufficient. Our urban strategy is to empower the poor by giving them control over their lives. Empowering the poor will strengthen families. And right now, the failure of our families is hurting America deeply. When families fail, society fails. The anarchy and lack of structure in our inner cities are testament to how quickly civilization falls apart when the family foundation cracks. Children need love and discipline. They need mothers and fathers. A welfare check is not a husband. The state is not a father. It is from parents that children learn how to behave in society; it is from parents above all that children come to understand values and themselves as men and women, mothers and fathers.

And for those concerned about children growing up in poverty, we should know this: Marriage is probably the best anti-poverty program of all. Among families headed by married couples today, there is a poverty rate of 5.7 percent. But 33.4 percent of families headed by a single mother are in poverty today.

The system perpetuates itself as these young men father children whom they have no intention of caring for, by women whose welfare checks support them. Teenage girls, mired in the same hopelessness, lack sufficient motive to say no to this trap.

Answers to our problems won't be easy.

We can start by dismantling a welfare system that encourages dependency and subsidizes broken families. We can attach conditions—such as school attendance, or work—to welfare. We can limit the time a recipient gets benefits. We can stop penalizing marriage for welfare mothers. We can enforce child support payments. Ultimately, however, marriage is a moral issue that requires cultural consensus and social sanctions. Bearing babies irresponsibly is, simply, wrong. We must be unequivocal about this.

It doesn't help matters when primetime TV has Murphy Brown—a character who supposedly epitomizes today's intelligent, highly paid, professional woman—mocking the importance of fathers, by bearing a child alone, and calling it just another "lifestyle choice."

I know it is not fashionable to talk about moral values, but we need to do it. Even though our cultural leaders in Hollywood, network TV, the national newspapers routinely jeer at them, I think that most of us in this room know that some things are good, and other things are wrong. Now it's time to make the discussion public.

It's time to talk again about family, hard work, integrity and personal responsibility. We cannot be embarrassed out of our belief that two parents, married to each other, are better in most cases for children than one. That honest work is better than handouts—or crime. That we are our brothers' keepers. That it's worth making an effort, even when rewards aren't immediate.

So I think the time has come to renew our public commitment to our Judeo-Christian values—in our churches and synagogues, our civic organization and our schools. We are, as our Children recite each morning, "one nation under God." That's a useful framework for acknowledging a duty and an authority higher than our own pleasures and personal ambitions.

If we lived more thoroughly by these values, we would live in a better society. For the poor, renewing these values will give people the strength to help themselves by acquiring the tools to achieve self-sufficiency, a good education, job training, and property. Then they will move from permanent dependence to dignified independence.

Though our hearts have been pained by the events in Los Angeles, we should take this tragedy as an opportunity for self-examination and progress. So let the national debate roar on. I, for one, will join it. The president will lead it. The American people will participate in it. And as a result, we will become an even stronger nation.

Suggestions for Discussion

1. What are the "family values" that Quayle appears to champion in this speech? Are these values your values? Your parents'? How do they differ from yours, if they do?

2. Statistics play an important role in Quayle's argument. How might you go about checking these numbers for accuracy, determining if Quayle interpreted the data correctly, and finding out how these figures have changed since 1992?

3. Synthesis: Consider how Constance Matthiessen's essay "Harry Potter and Divorce Among the Muggles" deals with issues of divorce and the integrity of the American family. How might Matthiessen's argument function as a response to Quayle's perspective? Is it a convincing response?

4. Synthesis: Michael Albernethy's "Male-Bashing on TV" and Peggy Orenstein's "What's Wrong with Cinderella?" also express concern over how sitcoms represent the American family. On the other hand, Charles Taylor's "The Morality Police" criticizes the tendency for moralists to worry over the content of art and popular culture. What happens when a person's moral sensibilities are offended by a television show, book, film, or work of art?

Suggestion for Writing

Synthesis: For a paper exploring the accuracy of Quayle's claims, research the historical circumstances surrounding the Los Angeles riots and the Rodney King trial referenced in this speech. Then read one of the essays in this book by Cornel West, Colin Powell, Malcolm X, Earl Shorris, or Martin Luther King, Jr. Using your research, Quayle's essay, and the additional essay you have read, make your own argument about whether Quayle's speech was an accurate assessment of the riots and of the problems facing African Americans in the 1990s.

ανανανω

CONSTANCE MATTHIESSEN

Harry Potter and Divorce among the Muggles

Constance Matthiessen is a San Francisco-based writer and journalist. The following piece was originally published in a shortened form in the *San Francisco Chronicle* and was later published as part of a 2005 anthology entitled *Because I Said So: 33 Mothers Write about Children, Sex, Men, Aging, Faith, Race and Themselves.*

We were listening to a tape of the most recent Harry Potter volume, *Harry Potter and the Order of the Phoenix*, on the way back from the beach, my three children and I. It was late, and everyone was sunburned and sandy, stunned into peaceful silence. The car was warm and rapt, and no one said a word as we hurtled down the highway, over the Golden Gate Bridge and across the city to our house.

The house was a new home for us, just five minutes away from our old one. We had only just moved in: boxes were everywhere, and a painter was scheduled to come in the morning. This new house was smaller, with no parking and one bathroom instead of two. But the biggest difference, the one that none of us had yet gotten used to, was that David, my husband, was living in an apartment in another part of the city.

By then *Harry Potter and the Order of the Phoenix* had been out for several months, and we'd heard rumors that someone close to Harry dies in the book. My nine-year-old, Aidan, had even discovered who the victim was, having wheedled the name out of his cousin. I wouldn't let him tell, but he had been dropping heavy, persistent hints to his younger brother and me.

But none of us, not even Aidan, was prepared for the shock of Sirius Black's death, and it hit hard that night in our dark little car. We reached home soon after Bellatrix Lestrange knocked Sirius down with a wand blow to the chest, and I couldn't find a parking place near the house. I finally found a spot a few blocks away, but couldn't face the walk up the hill, or the prospect of lugging the wet towels and swimming suits, the cooler with its grim picnic leftovers and sandy drinks.

So we all just sat there and listened as Jim Dale continued to spin out the story of Sirius's death and its aftermath. Harry Potter had trusted and adored Sirius: since his mother and father were both dead, Sirius was a substitute parent. And Harry's grief was compounded by guilt because, through a complicated series of circumstances, Sirius died trying to save Harry's life.

At that moment, I felt keenly the weight of my new single parenthood. Both boys were fighting sleep, and getting anyone to help me carry the bags was going to be a struggle. Julia, my four-year-old, appeared to be asleep, and would either wake up and wail when I picked her up or remain in a dead-weighted slumber. Either way, she would have to be carried. The walk to the house would likely rouse all of them and then I'd have to coax three grumpy children into bed. I was the only grown-up, I was exhausted, and I was in charge.

David and I had decided to separate the previous fall, and over the last six months I'd marched us through the house sale (which took a tortuously long time), found us a new home, orchestrated the move, and packed up everything we owned. Finally we were settled—David and I in different houses at last—yet I'd never felt so unsettled in my life. Some days were wonderful: to be living in a house with no undertones of anger was an enormous relief. On those days, I was optimistic that David and I could be good co-parents—better apart, in fact, than we had been when we were together. I envisioned our becoming friends in the months and years to come, as we both went on to happier lives.

At other times, I looked at our little family, and the kids seemed ragged, the grown-ups flailing, and this new life appeared lonely and sad. Huddled in the car on that chilly autumn night—miles, it seemed, from home—our little family seemed simply broken.

The tape was finally over, and the tape machine clicked off. "Why did Sirius have to die?" Dylan wailed out of the silence.

"Now Harry has nobody," Julia said drowsily, not asleep after all. "Lord Voldemort killed his parents when he was just a little baby."

"We know that, Julia," Aidan said scornfully. He was sarcastic to all of us these days. "Mom? Hello? Are we going to sit here in the car all night?"

After we reached the house Aidan told me he wasn't tired, that he needed to do something before going to bed. Later, when the other two were asleep, I went to look for him. I found him at my desk, hunched over a piece of paper. He'd been doing a lot of drawing lately: mostly strange, freakish figures on skateboards, or elaborate underground tunnels filled with the same freakish figures, or freakish figures caught in battle. Aidan has red hair and freckles and the rakish good looks of a boy in a Norman Rockwell painting, but he suffers from monumental feelings and a passionate heart.

"How are you doing, Aidee?" I asked him now. I knew he was missing his dad. He shrugged.

"Tired?"

"I hate her," he said fiercely, drawing thick black lines on the piece of paper, scratching out his drawing. "Why did she make Sirius die?"

"Who, Bellatrix?"

"No, the author, J. K. Rowling. She's an idiot."

I ruffled his hair, feeling futile. At that moment I kind of hated J. K. Rowling myself. Couldn't she have left Harry his beloved godfather, since he'd lost everyone else? Didn't she realize that this year had been hard enough already?

He looked so sad, my little nine-year-old, so fierce and knobby-kneed and heartbroken, that I ventured a foolish, hopeful thought. "Maybe he isn't really dead. Maybe he'll come back in one of the next books."

Aidan snorted in disgust. "He's dead, Mom, totally dead. He's never coming back."

Later that night, after Aidan had fallen asleep, I sat for a while in the boys' bedroom, listening to their peaceful breathing. I was tired, but I knew I wouldn't be able to sleep. On the nights when I could fall asleep, I would be roused at some point by my worries. Another writer I'd learned to dread during that difficult period—far more than J. K. Rowling—was psychologist Judith Wallerstein, whose warnings about the effects of divorce on children are the stuff of every parent's nightmares.

Wallerstein has spent years following the children of divorce and reporting on their lives in the years after their parents split up. Her conclusion, reiterated in her most recent book on the subject, *The Unexpected Legacy of Divorce*, is that these children carry the scars of their experience well into adulthood.

Wallerstein's most wrenching message is that parents *should* stay together for the sake of the children. It is in fact not true, she insists, that children are happier when their parents are happier. She writes, "Many adults who are trapped in very unhappy marriages would be surprised to learn that their children are relatively content. They don't care if Mom and Dad sleep in different beds as long as the family is together."

Julia, my youngest, clearly felt that way. Particularly in the beginning, she had a hard time going back and forth from my house to David's. One day, when we were driving through a dreary San Francisco fog, she said, "Mama? I think you and Daddy are both going to be sad until you get back together."

"I *am* sad that we aren't together," I said, fumbling for the right thing to say. "I think that Dad is too. But we seem to have trouble getting along when we are together. We make each other really angry. So, for now, this seems to be better for everyone."

Julia thought for a moment, then suggested practically, "I know what to do. If Dad says something you don't like, just pretend you didn't hear."

Most days, I could stand up to Wallerstein, and make the case that I was doing the right thing. At night, however, she prodded me awake, and I was defenseless. If she is right, then divorce becomes a Hobbesian choice between one's child's happiness and one's own. And as a cautionary tale, Wallerstein's message doesn't allow for happy endings. She gives parents advice for how to make divorce easier for children, but makes it obvious that she doesn't think there is any way to split without causing lasting damage.

Many people have challenged Wallerstein's conclusions, and her methodology continues to come under fire. Still, her message endures, probably because it hits a parental nerve. Divorce is not a fate any parent would choose for his or her child. It is not a future I ever imagined or hoped for—for my children or myself.

So, like every other divorced or divorcing parent I know, I find myself scrutinizing my children all the time, wondering if they are okay—and exactly what is okay? They ought to be sad, right? Their lives are being ripped in two. They have a right to be sad and angry and devastated. But how much is too much? What is normal, and will I recognize irreparable damage if I see it?

A few weeks after we'd told the children we were going to separate, Dylan and I were at a café together, while Julia was at dance class. I asked Dylan how he was feeling about the separation.

He was eating a cookie and playing with two little knight figures. The knights were jousting, periodically knocking each other to the floor. He shrugged, stopping the game for a minute. "Sad. Bad. *Really* bad."

I tried to respond as the parenting books advise, and made a noise that I hoped was sympathetic and encouraging.

"Are you and Dad going to get divorced?"

"We don't know, honey. We are going to try and work things out, but if we can't, then yes, we'll get divorced."

Dylan put his head down on the table. "That is *so* sad," he said. He kept his head there for a while as I stroked his hair. After a minute or so, he sat up again and resumed the jousting. I started to say something, and he said, "Mom, I don't want to talk about it anymore right now, if that's okay with you."

But after the separation actually happened, Dylan grew increasingly melancholy. He developed some minor physical problems that puzzled the pediatrician, and claimed to be tired all the time. One day, on the way home from school, he said wistfully, "If you were a bus or a car, you wouldn't have to worry about anything, because you wouldn't have a brain. Or if you were a rock."

"Do you have a lot of worries, Dylan?" I asked.

"Yes," he said simply.

"What do you worry about, honey?"

"I don't feel like telling you right now, Mom," he said wearily. "It's too long a list."

Of course, this is just the beginning of the rest of my life as a parent. I will wonder forever, I know. In the years to come I will ask myself, is that why she is failing in school? Is that why he is getting a divorce? Dropping out of college? Drinking too much? For the rest of my life, I will search for the roots of their disappointments and failures in the decision I am acting out now.

Six months have passed since the night we learned about Sirius's death. The new paint on the walls of our house already bears fingerprints, and the familiar clutter is seeping into every corner. The children are getting used to going back and forth between Mom's House and Dad's House, and even seem to enjoy the transitions. Their comings and goings—so wrenching at first—now have the quality of routine.

The children are settled happily into our new home, but Judith Wallerstein continues to wake me up—not every night, but often enough. In her books, she speaks with approval of couples who remained in unhappy marriages for the sake of their children. These couples, she says, "struggled with all the problems that beset modern marriage—infidelity, depression, sexual boredom, loneliness, rejection. Few problems went away as time wore on, but that's not what mattered most to these adults. Given their shared affection and concern for their children, they made parenting their number-one priority. As one woman explained, 'There are two relationships in this marriage. He admires me as a wonderful mother. As a wife, I bore him in every possible way. But our children are wonderful and that's what counts.'"

I try to imagine what life must be like for these people. I envision hushed rooms, heavy drapes, the quiet shutting of doors. The rooms are dark, the colors muted. Only when the children come home do the curtains fly open, and light and color and noise flood the rooms. How do they trudge through every day, not to mention holidays and family vacations? And it may be true that very small children don't notice if their parents are unhappy, but those small children are going to become preteens, teens, and young adults.

In the end, Judith Wallerstein and J. K. Rowling, these two women who loomed so large during the early days of my separation, have completely opposing ideas about what children understand, and how much they can bear.

Many parents I know criticize Rowling for including so much evil and death in books intended for children. Harry Potter's world is not a safe one, and the adults in that world, when they are not evil, are often powerless to protect him. Rowling, once a single mother herself, does not shield her readers from the dark side of life. And I think this is why children love her books so much. Children sense at a very early age that dark forces exist, that bad things happen, and people often do not live happily ever after. They know these things without fully understanding them, and efforts by adults to keep such knowledge from them only give their fears more power. Like other great children's authors, from C. S. Lewis to Roald Dahl to Philip Pullman, Rowling deals directly with these fears, and allows children to wrestle with them on the pages of her books.

Judith Wallerstein, on the other hand, encourages parents to create a fairy tale for children; to keep the nuclear family together, no matter how much duct tape and Krazy Glue it takes to do so. But anyone who has experienced the exquisite misery of a failed relationship could never recommend it as an environment for children.

It has been a hard year for my children, and they show scars. But are they worse off than they would have been had we stayed together?

I'll never know for sure.

Aidan is right of course: Sirius probably won't ever come back to life. But recently the children were listening to *Harry Potter and the Order of the Phoenix* for the second time, and we all noticed something we hadn't before. On first reading, the shock and sadness of Sirius's death obscured the fact that the book has a rather happy ending. It is not a fairy-tale ending: Harry Potter is never going to live happily ever after. But at the end of volume five, J. K. Rowling gives Harry something very precious nonetheless.

In the final scene, Harry is heading home for summer vacation on the Hogwarts train. Since his parents' death, "home" for Harry has been with his Aunt Petunia and Uncle Vernon and their son, Dudley—a family of Muggles who have always treated Harry atrociously. He dreads the summer ahead and the prospect of his aunt and uncle's small-minded cruelty, his cousin's cloddish bullying.

As the Hogwarts train pulls into the station, the Dursley family is there to meet Harry, but another group is present to greet him as well. It is a motley assemblage that waits for him there on the platform: his friend Ron Weasley's parents; a wise and kindly werewolf named Remus Lupin; Mad-Eye Moody, a veteran wizard; and Tonks, a flamboyant young witch. It turns out that they have come to help Harry. They confront the Dursley family right there at the train station, warning that if Harry is mistreated in any way, the family will have to answer to them.

This warning infuriates Uncle Vernon, but the strange and powerful group frightens him, so after some spluttering, he falls silent. Harry is overcome with gratitude for the support of these friends, and so the book ends: "He somehow could not find words to tell them what it meant to him, to see them all ranged there, on his side. Instead he smiled, raised a hand in farewell, turned around, and led the way out of the station toward the sunlit street, with Uncle Vernon, Aunt Petunia, and Dudley hurrying along in his wake."

Harry may have lost his godfather as well as his parents, but it is clear that he still has a refuge in this world—and that refuge is not with his blood relations, the Dursleys. Harry has a different configuration of family, but it is a family nevertheless.

This is what I wish for my children: a sense of belonging in the world, whether their parents are together or not. David and I are trying to build a friendly relationship. Beyond us, the children have a broad constellation of family and friends who care about them, too. It's not perfect, not the nuclear family they were born into, or the happy ending they might have asked for. But maybe it is enough.

When David and I first separated, Dylan would often cry after David dropped him off. When I asked him what was wrong, he always said the same thing: "I miss Dad when I'm with you, and I miss you when I am with Dad." This became his mantra for the separation, a simple, eloquent expression of all that he'd lost, all that he would never have again.

The other day, I asked Dylan how he feels about having two houses.

"I like having two houses," he responded, pondering. "I like your house best when I'm with you, and Dad's house best when I'm with him. But I still miss you both."

Suggestions for Discussion

1. Consider both this piece and "Restoring Basic Values" by Dan Quayle. Discuss how the authors differ in their treatment of divorce and children. Are they similar in any ways? Explain.

2. How does Matthiessen use literature to understand and express her feelings about the divorce? Have you ever used a form of art to understand something difficult in your life?

Suggestion for Writing

Create a new ending for the Harry Potter saga, based on what you know about the series—perhaps one in which fewer of Harry Potter's father figures are ruthlessly killed off. While you are at it, consider changing other outcomes of the story as well; who marries whom, who lives, and what Voldemort's fate is.

PERSONAL WRITING

COLIN POWELL

The Good Soldier

The son of Jamaican immigrant parents, Colin Powell (b. 1937) came from a rough neighborhood in the South Bronx and, after an illustrious military career, became a best-selling author and, in 2001, the nation's first African-American Secretary of State under George W. Bush. After three years in that post, his opposition to the Administration's policies in the war against Iraq led to Powell's resignation. Once considered a possible candidate for President, Powell remains active politically and as a motivational speaker.

When I go to the Middle East or China or wherever my job takes me and I walk into a room, people see a black man. But they also see the American secretary of state and they know that I'm not coming to them as a black man; I'm coming to them as a representative of the American people, as a representative of the president of the United States. I represent all the values of this country and the power of this country, its military power, its economic power and political power, and once we sit down and they get past whatever color I am, they want to do business with me.

Here at home in America, people sometimes ask what is the significance of my being the first African-American secretary of state. I hope it does have significance, particularly to African Americans, and I hope the significance is that it happened in America. It happened in a place where we were once slaves, nothing more than property. It happened in a place where at the time the Constitution was written, we were considered three-fifths of a white person for voting purposes. And it happened in a little over a couple of hundred years. Now that may be a long time by some standards, but by comparison with what's happened in other countries around the world, it's quite remarkable. When you also think that it happened to a guy whose parents just showed up in this country as immigrants off a banana boat back in the 1920s, it's remarkable.

I hope it gives inspiration to African-American youngsters, Peruvian youngsters, and white youngsters who might not have come from a black background but came from a poor background. Back when Desert Storm ended and there was all this celebration, parades everywhere, I went back to the Bronx, where I was raised, and I went to my high school, still in the inner city—and to this day it is bringing along other kids like me. I talked to the kids there, essentially Puerto Rican and black kids who were in the audience, and they were looking at me and they started to ask questions about me being a role model for them. And I said, well, I'm glad that I'm a role model for you, but I want General Schwarzkopf also to be a role model for you. Don't limit yourself by saying, if that black guy can do it, I can do it. If General Schwarzkopf can do it, you can do it, I tell them. Don't limit yourself any longer on the basis of your race, your color, your background, your creed. We've come too far to create our own limitations.

I tell young people a bit of a joke when they say, "Well, gosh, you're the black secretary of state." I say, "No, I'm not. There ain't a white secretary of state somewhere. I'm the secretary of state who is black, you know; there's a difference." I refuse to be limited by my race, and you shouldn't, I tell young people, allow yourself to be limited or stereotyped. Don't use your particular distinction as an excuse for you not to do your best. Take advantage of all the things that have been done for you over these 226 years. I wouldn't be secretary of state if I hadn't done that.

I was raised in a family that never felt constrained by their poverty or by their race. That had nothing to do with anything; we were as good as anyone. And I was raised in a community that had blacks, whites, Puerto Ricans, minority, you name it, we were it, a melting pot of the New York City environment. So I never really knew I was supposed to feel in some way constrained by being an inner-city, public school black kid, the son of immigrants. I just went into the army and I found an organization that said, no, no, no, we've changed, we're ahead of the rest of the society. We don't care if you're black or blue, we only care if you're a good green soldier. And if you do your best, you watch, you'll be recognized. If you don't do your best, you'll be punished. And I started out as a black lieutenant but I became a general who was black.

I want to continue to be a role model for the kids in the neighborhood I grew up in, and for other youngsters in America. Not just a black role model in that stereotypical sense, but an example of what you can achieve if you are willing to work for it. And second, those of us in the African-American community who have been successful financially ought to give some of it back to the community. You can do it through scholarships, through donations, through mentoring, through adopting or sponsoring a school. There are lots of ways to do it, and everything I've just mentioned I have done, or try to do. You don't have to scream and shout about it but just get it done, reach back and help these youngsters who are coming along. And to the extent we have benefited from this society, we can't just walk away from these youngsters.

In fact, so many African Americans have been successful, and have been able to improve their physical station in life—have a nicer neighborhood to live in, a bigger house to live in, fancier cars, nice clothes—that those who get left behind are left further behind than they might have been forty or fifty or sixty years ago. Before integration, the successful people in the community still didn't have anywhere to go, so that success stayed in the community and we had a thriving middle class. You couldn't break out too far. Then integration kind of changed all of that, and for those of us who became successful, it became easier to leave those behind who had not yet gained success, especially those children who needed examples to follow.

The examples were no longer there the way they used to be; the successful people had moved on to some other place. So the kids today, rather than seeing successful middle-class professionals in their neighborhood, are to some extent denied that kind of example. So, then, what example should they follow? They tend to follow people who may not provide them the right example, who may not exert the right kinds of influences. And we've lost something as a result. Those of us who have been successful and have escaped have got to go back.

There are reasons why those of us who are in the black community and who have made it have such a great responsibility. Our youngsters need us more perhaps, for one thing. And our youngsters are still living in a society that is really only one generation removed from racism, discrimination, segregation, and economic deprivation, and we're still suffering from that. It's different in that regard from the way our white counterparts may view their responsibility to youngsters in, say, a poor white community.

We're also living, to some extent, in a society that still sees people by color, much as we would like it to be otherwise. A few of us have been able to rise above that, to be frank. But there are a lot of youngsters walking down the street who get met with, watch out, there's a black kid. There's still that kind of discrimination in our society. Some people would call it racism. There is racism, but I don't call it a kind of discrimination racism; it's just there's a difference there that is part of our legacy, part of our history, that has not yet been overcome. And those of us who have been successful have an obligation to reach back to these youngsters and help them, more so than I think our white brothers. But I tell my white colleagues, you've got to reach down to the black community too. You've got to reach down to any community in need.

I also tell black youngsters, get a white mentor. If there isn't a brother, we'll get you connected up with a white mentor. I had lots of white mentors. Most of my mentors that made me successful in the army were white, and nothing wrong with it. We have to not limit ourselves because of our race or color, and we shouldn't limit ourselves with respect to where we go and get help from. More and more people in the white community are anxious to help those who are less fortunate, and especially those less fortunate in the black community.

I believe the most important thing that I can do, in relation to the black community and in relationship to myself, is to do the job. I have never been driven by ambition. I'm not unambitious—I wouldn't have gotten where I did if I was unambitious—but I'm not driven by that ambition. I'm driven by my desire to do the job. I've always tried to do a good job everywhere I've been. And it's been recognized and that's why I was successful. I try to do the best job I can for people I work for and for the American people, and I try to be a good family guy, as best I can. I try to keep a lot of friends on my side.

The gulf between the two black communities—the middle class and those who have been left behind—need not be permanent, but it's going to take a lot of work to change it. It's going to take a lot of work on the part of both communities, the well-to-do and those who are striving. Those of us who have made it, white and black, need to give back with resources and mentoring. But there's something else we have to give back. We have got to get to our young people and tell them they can be successful. We have to tell them, Rosa Parks did not ride in the back of a bus and Martin Luther King did not die so you could call young girls bad names, so that you could act like a fool, so that you could put stuff up your nose, or so that you could stick up somebody. Now, that is not acceptable. And these people did not die to create these opportunities for you that you refuse to seize. So let me not hear any excuses about why you don't want to go to school or how you go to a bad school. We all went to bad schools at one time or another, but guess what was in that bad school: some education. So don't allow these excuses to keep you from getting what is out there waiting for you if you will seize it.

We have got to teach our young people that as you come along and as you become parents, you have an enormous responsibility for the children you've brought into life. I'm sometimes disturbed by some of the television depictions you see on some of the channels and by some of the shows—and I don't want to get into any particular show—where we pander to this kind of deplorable behavior. If I had ever said these words, or if I had ever talked to an adult that way or ever said anything like this to peers or to anyone, it would not have been tolerated. I would have been told, we don't talk like that in this family. Or as Bill Cosby used to say, "I brought you into this world and I'll take you out!"

We've got to get back to those standards and stop making excuses, saying, I can't do this, I can't do that, this person's down on me, and things like that. Those are not reasons; they're all excuses. We have got to start weaning our youngsters away from this sort of thinking. Most of our youngsters are fine, they're in our universities, they're fine.

I was on the board of Howard University, I was on the board of the United Negro College Fund, another way of giving back, so I know what our youngsters are capable of doing. But there are too many of them who are adopting hedonistic lifestyles. That's simply deplorable and has to be stopped. Too many of our television stations are exploiting this kind of lifestyle and peddling it all over the airways, and other youngsters see it and hear this kind of language and see this kind of dress and this kind of behavior. Our humor has gone from Bill Cosby down to the worst kind, deep in the gutter.

I wear my blackness every day and I use it every day in one way or another, whether it's a check I write for something or a youngster I speak to or a kid I mentor via e-mail. When I was in private life, I was able to do a lot more, whether it was for the College Fund or Howard University or America's Promise, which is a youth campaign I ran. I never said we're going after black kids, but when I went after kids, most of the kids who were in the greatest need were black, and I knew that. With respect to people who may say it's no longer enough to do a good job, that we're not brothers anymore, that we have lost our blackness if we're not teaching in the ghetto at night, I can't spend a lot of time worrying about what people say about me or whether I'm doing enough. I do as much as I can. All of us should do as much as we can and just take whatever compliments or criticism comes with it.

Suggestions for Discussion

1. In response to the statement "Well, gosh, you're the black secretary of state," Powell says, "No I'm not . . . I'm the secretary of state who is black." What does this response tell you about Powell's notion of the importance of race?

2. Why does Powell tell kids that, in addition to himself, he wants General H. Norman Schwarzkopf to be a role model for them as well? What is the significance of this assertion?

Suggestions for Writing

1. Compare Colin Powell's views of race in contemporary America to those expressed by either Cornel West in the essay "On Affirmative Action" or by Dan Quayle in "Restoring Basic Values."

2. How have journalists, political scientists, and historians evaluated Powell's tenure as Secretary of State? Write a paper in which you evaluate the policies that he advocated, his relationship to President George W. Bush and the other members of the administration, and the role he played in recent events in American history.

JUDITH ORTIZ COFER

Casa: A Partial Remembrance of a Puerto Rican Childhood

Judith Ortiz Cofer (b. 1952) is a native of Puerto Rico who immigrated to the United States as a small child. Educated in Florida and Georgia, where she still resides, she attended Oxford University as a Scholar of the English Speaking Union and participated in the prestigious Bread Loaf Writers' Conference at Middlebury College. A teacher of creative writing at the university level, she has received several awards for her poetry, including grants from the Witter Bynner Foundation and the National Endowment for the Arts. Her publications include *The Line of the Sun* (1989), *Silent Dancing* (1990), *The Year of Our Revolution* (1998), *Woman in Front of the Sun: On Becoming a Writer* (2000), and *The Meaning of Consuelo* (2003). This selection was published in 1990.

At three or four o'clock in the afternoon, the hour of *café con leche*, the women of my family gathered in Mamá's living room to speak of important things and retell familiar stories meant to be overheard by us young girls, their daughters. In Mamá's house (everyone called my grandmother Mamá) was a large parlor built by my grandfather to his wife's exact specifications so that it was always cool, facing away from the sun. The doorway was on the side of the house so no one could walk directly into her living room. First they had to take a little stroll through and around her beautiful garden where prize-winning orchids grew in the trunk of an ancient tree she had hollowed out for that purpose. This room was furnished with several mahogany rocking chairs, acquired at the births of her children, and one intricately carved rocker that had passed down to Mamá at the death of her own mother.

It was on these rockers that my mother, her sisters, and my grandmother sat on these afternoons of my childhood to tell their stories, teaching each other, and my cousin and me, what it was like to be a woman, more specifically, a Puerto Rican woman. They talked about life on the island, and life in *Los Nueva Yores*, their way of referring to the United States from New York City to California: the other place, not home, all the same. They told real-life stories though, as I later learned, always embellishing them with a little or a lot of dramatic detail. And they told *cuentos*, the morality and cautionary tales told by the women in our family for generations: stories that became a part of my subconscious as I grew up in two worlds, the tropical island and the cold city, and that would later surface in my dreams and in my poetry.

One of these tales was about the woman who was left at the altar. Mamá liked to tell that one with histrionic intensity. I remember the rise and fall of her voice, the sighs, and her constantly gesturing hands, like two birds swooping through her words. This particular story usually would come up in a conversation as a result of someone mentioning a forthcoming engagement or wedding. The first time I remember hearing it, I was sitting on the floor at Mamá's feet, pretending to read a comic book. I may have been eleven or twelve years old, at that difficult age when a girl was no longer a child who could be ordered to leave the room if the women wanted freedom to take their talk into forbidden zones, nor really old enough to be considered a part of their conclave. I could only sit quietly, pretending to be in another world, while absorbing it all in a sort of unspoken agreement of my status as silent auditor. On this day, Mamá had taken my long, tangled mane of hair into her ever-busy hands. Without looking down at me and with no interruption of her flow of words, she began braiding my hair, working at it with the quickness and determination that characterized all her actions. My mother was watching us impassively from her rocker across the room. On her lips played a little ironic smile. I would never sit still for *her* ministrations, but even then, I instinctively knew that she did not possess Mamá's matriarchal power to command and keep everyone's attention. This was never more evident than in the spell she cast when telling a story.

"It is not like it used to be when I was a girl," Mamá announced. "Then, a man could leave a girl standing at the church altar with a bouquet of fresh flowers in her hands and disappear off the face of the earth. No way to track him down if he was from another town. He could be a married man, with maybe even two or three families all over the island. There was no way to know. And there were men who did this. Hombres with the devil in their flesh who would come to a pueblo, like this one, take a job at one of the haciendas, never meaning to stay, only to have a good time and to seduce the women."

The whole time she was speaking, Mamá would be weaving my hair into a flat plait that required pulling apart the two sections of hair with little jerks that made my eyes water; but knowing how grandmother detested whining and *boba* (sissy) tears, as she called them, I just sat up as straight and stiff as I did at La Escuela San Jose, where the nuns enforced good posture with a flexible plastic ruler they bounced off of slumped shoulders and heads. As Mamá's story progressed, I noticed how my young Aunt Laura lowered her eyes, refusing to meet Mamá's meaningful gaze. Laura was seventeen, in her last year of high school, and already engaged to a boy from another town who had staked his claim with a tiny diamond ring, then left for Los Nueva Yores to make his fortune. They were planning to get married in a year.

Mamá had expressed serious doubts that the wedding would ever take place. In Mamá's eyes, a man set free without a legal contract was a man lost. She believed that marriage was not something men desired, but simply the price they had to pay for the privilege of children and, of course, for what no decent (synonymous with "smart") woman would give away for free.

"María La Loca was only seventeen when it happened to her." I listened closely at the mention of this name. María was a town character, a fat middle-aged woman who lived with her old mother on the outskirts of town. She was to be seen around the pueblo delivering the meat pies the two women made for a living. The most peculiar thing about María, in my eyes, was that she walked and moved like a little girl though she had the thick body and wrinkled face of an old woman. She would swing her hips in an exaggerated, clownish way, and sometimes even hop and skip up to some-one's house. She spoke to no one. Even if you asked her a question, she would just look at you and smile, showing her yellow teeth. But I had heard that if you got close enough, you could hear her humming a tune without words. The kids yelled out nasty things at her, calling her La Loca, and the men who hung out at the bodega playing dominoes sometimes whistled mockingly as she passed by with her funny, outlandish walk. But María seemed impervious to it all, carrying her basket of *pasteles* like a grotesque Little Red Riding Hood through the forest.

María La Loca interested me, as did all the eccentrics and crazies of our pueblo. Their weirdness was a measuring stick I used in my serious quest for a definition of normal. As a Navy brat shuttling between New Jersey and the pueblo, I was constantly made to feel like an oddball by my peers, who made fun of my two-way accent: a Spanish accent when I spoke English, and when I spoke Spanish I was told that I sounded like a *Gringa*. Being the outsider had already turned my brother and me into cultural chameleons. We devel-oped early on the ability to blend into a crowd, to sit and read quietly in a fifth story apartment building for days and days when it was too bitterly cold to play outside, or, set free, to run wild in Mamá's realm, where she took charge of our lives, releasing Mother for a while from the intense fear for our safety that our father's absences instilled in her. In order to keep us from harm when Father was away, Mother kept us under strict surveillance. She even walked us to and from Public School No. 11, which we attended during the months we lived in Paterson, New Jersey, our home base in the states. Mamá freed all three of us like pigeons from a cage. I saw her as my liberator and my model. Her stories were parables from which to glean the *Truth*.

"María La Loca was once a beautiful girl. Everyone thought she would marry the Méndez boy." As everyone knew, Rogelio Méndez was the richest man in town. "But," Mamá continued, knitting my hair with the same inten-sity she was putting into her story, "this *macho* made a fool out of her and ruined her life." She paused for the effect of her use of the word "macho," which at that time had not yet become a popular epithet for an unliberated man. This word had for us the crude and comical connotation of "male of the species," stud; a *macho* was what you put in a pen to increase your stock.

I peeked over my comic book at my mother. She too was under Mamá's spell, smiling conspiratorially at this little swipe at men. She was safe from Mamá's contempt in this area. Married at an early age, an unspotted lamb, she had been accepted by a good family of strict Spaniards whose name was old and respected, though their fortune had been lost long before my birth. In a rocker Papá had painted sky blue sat Mamá's oldest child, Aunt Nena. Mother of three children, stepmother of two more, she was a quiet woman who liked books but had married an ignorant and abusive widower whose main interest in life was accumulating wealth. He too was in the mainland working on his dream of returning home rich and triumphant to buy the *finca* of his dreams. She was waiting for him to send for her. She would leave her children with Mamá for several years while the two of them slaved away in factories. He would one day be a rich man, and she a sadder woman. Even now her life-light was dimming. She spoke little, an aberration in Mamá's house, and she read avidly, as if storing up spiritual food for the long winters that awaited her in Los Nueva Yores without her family. But even Aunt Nena came alive to Mamá's words, rocking gently, her hands over a thick book in her lap.

Her daughter, my cousin Sara, played jacks by herself on the tile porch outside the room where we sat. She was a year older than I. We shared a bed and all our family's secrets. Collaborators in search of answers, Sara and I discussed everything we heard the women say, trying to fit it all together like a puzzle that, once assembled, would reveal life's mysteries to us. Though she and I still enjoyed taking part in boys' games—chase, volleyball, and even *vaqueros,* the island version of cowboys and Indians involving cap-gun battles and violent shoot-outs under the mango tree in Mamá's backyard—we loved best the quiet hours in the afternoon when the men were still at work, and the boys had gone to play serious baseball at the park. Then Mamá's house belonged only to us women. The aroma of coffee perking in the kitchen, the mesmerizing creaks and groans of the rockers, and the women telling their lives in *cuentos* are forever woven into the fabric of my imagination, braided like my hair that day I felt my grandmother's hands teaching me about strength, her voice convincing me of the power of storytelling.

That day Mamá told how the beautiful María had fallen prey to a man whose name was never the same in subsequent versions of the story; it was Juan one time, José, Rafael, Diego, another. We understood that neither the name nor any of the *facts* were important, only that a woman had allowed love to defeat her. Mamá put each of us in María's place by describing her wedding dress in loving detail: how she looked like a princess in her lace as she waited at the altar. Then, as Mamá approached the tragic denouement of her story, I was distracted by the sound of my Aunt Laura's violent rocking. She seemed on the verge of tears. She knew the fable was intended for her. That week she was going to have her wedding gown fitted, though no firm date had been set for the marriage. Mamá ignored Laura's obvious discomfort, digging out a ribbon from the sewing basket she kept by her rocker while describing María's long illness, "a fever that would not break for days." She spoke of a mother's despair: "that woman climbed the church steps on her knees every morning, wore only black as a *promesa* to the Holy Virgin in exchange for her daughter's health." By the time María returned from her honeymoon with death, she was ravished, no longer young or sane. "As you can see, she is almost as old as her mother already," Mamá lamented while tying the ribbon to the ends of my hair, pulling it back with such force that I just knew I would never be able to close my eyes completely again.

"That María's getting crazier every day." Mamá's voice would take a lighter tone now, expressing satisfaction, either for the perfection of my braid, or for a story well told—it was hard to tell. "You know that tune María is always humming?" Carried away by her enthusiasm, I tried to nod, but Mamá still had me pinned between her knees.

"Well, that's the wedding march." Surprising us all, Mamá sang out, "Da, da, dara . . . da, da, dara." Then lifting me off the floor by my skinny shoulders, she would lead me around the room in an impromptu waltz—another session ending with the laughter of women, all of us caught up in the infectious joke of our lives.

Suggestions for Discussion

Relate each of the following quotations to the selection you have just read.

1. "It was on these rockers that my mother, her sisters, and my grandmother sat on these afternoons of my childhood to tell their stories, teaching each other, and my cousin and me, what it was like to be a woman, more specifically, a Puerto Rican woman."

2. "Collaborators in search of answers, Sara and I discussed everything we heard the women say, trying to fit it all together like a puzzle that, once assembled, would reveal life's mysteries to us."

3. "We understood that neither the name nor any of the *facts* were important, only that a woman had allowed love to defeat her."

Suggestions for Writing

1. Children learn much of their culture from eavesdropping on the adult world. Describe a time when you had this experience.

2. Cofer distinguishes between "facts" and "themes." Truth in storytelling has far more to do with one than the other. Write a story in which this is manifest.

∽∾∽∾∽

MOHANDAS K. GANDHI

My Faith in Nonviolence

Mohandas K. Gandhi (1869–1948) is admired throughout the world for his use of nonviolent means to seek the overthrow of British rule of India. Sometimes called Mahatma (or "Great-Souled") Gandhi, the student of Hindu philosophy led an esthetic life, fasting often (for both spiritual and political purposes) and making his own clothes from simple materials. On behalf of the people of India, he fought for relief from widespread economic hardship and for an end to rampant discrimination by caste, gender, and religion. His efforts led to India's liberation from Great

COSTAIN, *Hit Hate*. Acrylic on refrigerator door, 2006. © Costain, Courtesy of the artist. Digital image: © www.foto-lounge.de.

Britain, but he was assassinated by a Hindu radical who believed that his teachings were weakening the nation. Recognized as "The Father of the Nation" in India, his birthday, October 2, is a national holiday in his country of origin and was declared the International Day of Non-Violence by the United Nations General Assembly in 2007. A prolific writer and activist, Mahatma Gandhi's *Collected Works* is a multivolume library that spans 50,000 pages. The following passage was written in 1930.

I have found that life persists in the midst of destruction and, therefore, there must be a higher law than that of destruction. Only under that law would a well-ordered society be intelligible and life worth living. And if that is the law of life, we have to work it out in daily life. Wherever there are jars, wherever you are confronted with an opponent, conquer him with love. In a crude manner I have worked it out in my life. That does not mean that all my difficulties are solved. I have found, however, that this law of love has answered as the law of destruction has never done. In India we have had an ocular demonstration of the operation of this law on the widest scale possible. I do not claim therefore that nonviolence has necessarily penetrated the three hundred millions, but I do claim that it has penetrated deeper than any other message, and in an incredibly short time. We have not been all uniformly nonviolent; and with the vast majority, nonviolence has been a matter of policy. Even so, I want you to find out if the country has not made phenomenal progress under the protecting power of nonviolence.

It takes a fairly strenuous course of training to attain to a mental state of nonviolence. In daily life it has to be a course of discipline, though one may not like it—like, for instance, the life of a soldier. But I agree that, unless there is a hearty cooperation of the mind, the mere outward observance will be simply a mask, harmful both to the man himself and to others. The perfect state is reached only when mind and body and speech are in proper coordination. But it is always a case of intense mental struggle. It is not that I am incapable of anger, for instance, but I succeed on almost all occasions to keep my feelings under control. Whatever may be the result, there is always in me a conscious struggle for following the law of nonviolence deliberately and ceaselessly. Such a struggle leaves one stronger for it. Nonviolence is a weapon of the strong. With the weak it might easily be hypocrisy. Fear and love are contradictory terms. Love is reckless in giving away, oblivious as to what it gets in return. Love wrestles with the world as with the self and ultimately gains a mastery over all other feelings. My daily experience, as of those who are working with me, is that every problem lends itself to solution if we are determined to make the law of truth and nonviolence the law of life. For truth and nonviolence are, to me, faces of the same coin.

The law of love will work, just as the law of gravitation will work, whether we accept it or not. Just as a scientist will work wonders out of various applications of the law of nature, even so a man who applies the law of love with scientific precision can work greater wonders. For the force of nonviolence is infinitely more wonderful and subtle than the material forces of nature, like, for instance, electricity. The men who discovered for us the law of love were greater scientists than any of our modern scientists. Only our explorations have not gone far enough and so it is not possible for everyone to see all its workings. Such, at any rate, is the hallucination, if it is one, under which I am laboring. The more I work at this law the more I feel the delight in life, the delight in the scheme of this universe. It gives me a peace and a meaning of the mysteries of nature that I have no power to describe.

Suggestions for Discussion

1. Why does Gandhi feel it is important to control one's feelings, especially anger?

2. Why does it take strenuous training to become a person of peace?

3. What does Gandhi mean by the "law of love"? Why does he speak of it in scientific and legal terms when it seems to be a spiritual concept? Or a psychological one?

4. Pacifists are often accused of being weak or cowardly. Gandhi argues that they are strong and brave. How does he do this?

5. Look at the image that accompanies this reading. Why might the artist have chosen a baseball player to go with this particular message? Do you see any connection between sports and violence? How might Mohandas Gandhi have reacted to this work of art airbrushed on an old refrigerator door, seeing hate being hit with a baseball bat?

Suggestions for Writing

1. Compare Gandhi's philosophy of nonviolence as he represents it himself to the commentaries on Gandhi and his pacifism as offered by Howard Gardner and Aung San Suu Kyi, whose essays are also included in this text. Write an essay in which you consider the influence of his ideas on other peoples and in other conflicts.

2. The phrase "bread and circuses" originated in ancient Rome, ca. 100, and derives from the Latin *panem et circenses*—a government strategy to entertain people constantly in order to distract them from their everyday business of governing. Think about the role that sports play in society today. Are we still distracted by sports? From what? How do sports keep us content, if they do?

တလတလတလ

JHUMPA LAHIRI

My Hyphenated Identity

Jhumpa Lahiri (b. 1967) was born in London, England, and raised in Rhode Island by traditional Bengali parents. The double identity of her upbringing, her interest in Calcutta, and her Bengali heritage is the impetus for much of her widely admired writing. Her debut work, a collection of nine short stories titled *Interpreter of Maladies* (1999), won the Pulitzer Prize for fiction in 2000, a PEN/Hemingway Award, and other honors. Translated into twenty-nine different languages, it became a best seller in the United States and abroad. Her second book, and first novel, *The Namesake* (2003), was made into a film in 2007. She graduated with multiple master's degrees in English, creative writing, and comparative literature from Boston University, where she also earned a Ph.D. in Renaissance studies. She has taught creative writing at Boston University and the Rhode Island School of Design. In the following passage, Lahiri discusses the challenges of being a second generation immigrant in the United States and how she found balance and peace in her "rich but imperfect" bicultural upbringing.

I have lived in the United States for almost 37 years and anticipate growing old in this country. Therefore, with the exception of my first two years in London, "Indian-American" has been a constant way to describe me. Less constant is my relationship to the term. When I was growing up in Rhode Island in the 1970s I felt neither Indian nor American. Like many immigrant offspring I felt intense pressure to be two things, loyal to the old world and fluent in the new, approved of on either side of the hyphen. Looking back, I see that this was generally the case. But my perception as a young girl was that I fell short at both ends, shuttling between two dimensions that had nothing to do with one another.

At home I followed the customs of my parents, speaking Bengali and eating rice and dal with my fingers. These ordinary facts seemed part of a secret, utterly alien way of life, and I took pains to hide them from my American friends. For my parents, home was not our house in Rhode Island but Calcutta, where they were raised. I was aware that the things they lived for—the Nazrul songs they listened to on the reel-to-reel, the family they missed, the clothes my mother wore that were not available in any store in any mall—were at once as precious and as worthless as an outmoded currency.

I also entered a world my parents had little knowledge or control of: school, books, music, television, things that seeped in and became a fundamental aspect of who I am. I spoke English without an accent, comprehending the language in a way my parents still do not. And yet there was evidence that I was not entirely American. In addition to my distinguishing name and looks, I did not attend Sunday school, did not know how to ice-skate, and disappeared to India for months at a time. Many of these friends proudly called themselves Irish-American or Italian-American. But they were several generations removed from the frequently humiliating process of immigration, so that the ethnic roots they claimed had descended underground whereas mine were still tangled and green. According to my parents I was not American, nor would I ever be no matter how hard I tried. I felt doomed by their pronouncement, misunderstood and gradually defiant. In spite of the first lessons of arithmetic, one plus one did not equal two but zero, my conflicting selves always canceling each other out.

When I first started writing I was not conscious that my subject was the Indian-American experience. What drew me to my craft was the desire to force the two worlds I occupied to mingle on the page as I was not brave enough, or mature enough, to allow in life. My first book was published in 1999, and around then, on the cusp of a new century, the term "Indian-American" has become part of this country's vocabulary. I've heard it so often that these days, if asked about my background, I use the term myself, pleasantly surprised that I do not have to explain further. What a difference from my early life, when there was no such way to describe me, when the most I could do was to clumsily and ineffectually explain.

As I approach middle age, one plus one equals two, both in my work and in my daily existence. The traditions on either side of the hyphen dwell in me like siblings, still occasionally sparring, one outshining the other depending on the day. But like siblings they are intimately familiar with one another, forgiving and intertwined. When my husband and I were married five years ago in Calcutta we invited friends who had never been to India, and they came full of enthusiasm for a place I avoided talking about in my childhood, fearful of what people might say. Around non-Indian friends, I no longer feel compelled to hide the fact that I speak another language. I speak Bengali to my children, even though I lack the proficiency to teach them to read or write the language. As a child I sought perfection and so denied myself the claim to any identity. As an adult I accept that a bicultural upbringing is a rich but imperfect thing.

While I am American by virtue of the fact that I was raised in this country, I am Indian thanks to the efforts of two individuals. I feel Indian not because of the time I've spent in India or because of my genetic composition but rather because of my parents' steadfast presence in my life. They live three hours from my home; I speak to them daily and see them about once a month. Everything will change once they die. They will take certain things with them—conversations in another tongue, and perceptions about the difficulties of being foreign. Without them, the back-and-forth life my family leads, both literally and figuratively, will at last approach stillness. An anchor will drop, and a line of connection will be severed.

I have always believed that I lack the authority my parents bring to being Indian. But as long as they live they protect me from feeling like an impostor. Their passing will mark not only the loss of the people who created me but the loss of a singular way of life, a singular struggle. The immigrant's journey, no matter how ultimately rewarding, is founded on departure and deprivation, but it secures for the subsequent generation a sense of arrival and advantage. I can see a day coming when my American side, lacking the counterpoint India has until now maintained, begins to gain ascendancy and weight. It is in fiction that I will continue to interpret the term "Indian-American," calculating that shifting equation, whatever answers it may yield.

Suggestions for Discussion

1. Consider this statement: "I felt intense pressure to be two things, loyal to the old world and fluent in the new, approved of on either side of the hyphen." What does Lahiri mean by being both loyal and fluent? Have you ever felt pressure to be two contrasting things at once?

2. What was it that drew her to writing? Why was writing an important and useful outlet for her?

3. Why will the eventual loss of her parents mark "the loss of a singular way of life, a singular struggle"? Will the loss of her parents force her into yet another type of identity?

Suggestion for Writing

Compare Lahiri's thoughts on her own double identity to Alfred Lubrano's anxieties about not comfortably being categorized as either working class or middle class but a "straddler."

∽∽∽

NANCY MAIRS

On Being a Cripple

Nancy Mairs (b. 1943) was born in California and received degrees from Wheaton College and the University of Arizona, where she earned her M.F.A. and Ph.D. Her professional career has been spent as an editor, professor, and writer. She writes in a variety of genres, including essays, poetry, autobiography, and fiction. Mairs's books include *In All the Rooms of the Yellow House* (1984), for which she received the Poetry Award from the Western States Art Foundation; *Remembering the Bone House* (1989); *Carnal Acts* (1990); *Voice Lessons* (1994); *Waist-High in the World* (1996); and *A Troubled Guest: Life and Death Stories* (2001). In the selection that follows, from *Plaintext* (1986), Mairs shares the experience of dealing with a chronic, crippling disease in the midst of the demanding richness of personal, family, and professional life.

> *To escape is nothing. Not to escape is nothing.*
>
> —Louise Bogan

The other day I was thinking of writing an essay on being a cripple. I was thinking hard in one of the stalls of the women's room in my office building, as I was shoving my shirt into my jeans and tugging up my zipper. Preoccupied, I flushed, picked up my book bag, took my cane down from the hook, and unlatched the door. So many movements unbalanced me, and as I pulled the door open I fell over backward, landing fully clothed on the toilet seat with my legs splayed in front of me: the old beetle-on-its-back routine. Saturday afternoon, the building deserted, I was free to laugh aloud as I wriggled back to my feet, my voice bouncing off the yellowish tiles from all directions. Had anyone been there with me, I'd have been still and faint and hot with chagrin. I decided that it was high time to write the essay.

First, the matter of semantics. I am a cripple. I choose this word to name me. I choose from among several possibilities, the most common of which are "handicapped" and "disabled." I made the choice a number of years ago, without thinking, unaware of my motives for doing so. Even now, I'm not sure what those motives are, but I recognize that they are complex and not entirely flattering. People—crippled or not—wince at the word "cripple," as they do not at "handicapped" or "disabled." Perhaps I want them to wince.

I want them to see me as a tough customer, one to whom the fates/gods/viruses have not been kind, but who can face the brutal truth of her existence squarely. As a cripple, I swagger.

But, to be fair to myself, a certain amount of honesty underlies my choice. "Cripple" seems to me a clean word, straightforward and precise. It has an honorable history, having made its first appearance in the Lindisfarne Gospel in the tenth century. As a lover of words, I like the accuracy with which it describes my condition: I have lost the full use of my limbs. "Disabled," by contrast, suggests an incapacity, physical or mental. And I certainly don't like "handicapped," which implies that I have deliberately been put at a disadvantage, by whom I can't imagine (my God is not a Handicapper General), in order to equalize chances in the great race of life. These words seem to me to be moving away from my condition, to be widening the gap between word and reality. Most remote is the recently coined euphemism "differently abled," which partakes of the same semantic hopefulness that transformed countries from "undeveloped" to "underdeveloped," then to "less developed," and finally to "developing" nations. People have continued to starve in those countries during the shift. Some realities do not obey the dictates of language.

Mine is one of them. Whatever you call me, I remain crippled. But I don't care what you call me, so long as it isn't "differently abled," which strikes me as pure verbal garbage designed, by its ability to describe anyone, to describe no one. I subscribe to George Orwell's thesis that "the slovenliness of our language makes it easier for us to have foolish thoughts." And I refuse to participate in the degeneration of the language to the extent that I deny that I have lost anything in the course of this calamitous disease; I refuse to pretend that the only differences between you and me are the various ordinary ones that distinguish any one person from another. But call me "disabled" or "handicapped" if you like. I have long since grown accustomed to them; and if they are vague, at least they hint at the truth. Moreover, I use them myself. Society is no readier to accept crippledness than to accept death, war, sex, sweat, or wrinkles. I would never refer to another person as a cripple. It is the word I use to name only myself.

I haven't always been crippled, a fact for which I am soundly grateful. To be whole of limb is, I know from experience, infinitely more pleasant and useful than to be crippled; and if that knowledge leaves me open to bitterness at my loss, the physical soundness I once enjoyed (though I did not enjoy it half enough) is well worth the occasional stab of regret. Though never any good at sports, I was a normally active child and young adult. I climbed trees, played hopscotch, jumped rope, skated, swam, rode my bicycle, sailed. I despised team sports, spending some of the wretchedest afternoons of my life sweaty and humiliated, behind a field-hockey stick and under a basketball hoop. I tramped alone for miles along the bridle paths that webbed the woods behind the house I grew up in. I swayed through countless dim hours in the arms of one man or another under the scattered shot of light from mirrored balls, and gyrated through countless more as Tab Hunter and Johnny Mathis gave way to the Rolling Stones, Creedence Clearwater Revival, Cream. I walked down the aisle. I pushed baby carriages, changed tires in the rain, marched for peace.

When I was twenty-eight I started to trip and drop things. What at first seemed my natural clumsiness soon became too pronounced to shrug off. I consulted a neurologist, who told me that I had a brain tumor. A battery of tests, increasingly disagreeable, revealed no tumor. About a year and a half later I developed a blurred spot in one eye. I had, at last, the episodes "disseminated in space and time" requisite for a diagnosis: multiple sclerosis. I have never been sorry for the doctor's initial misdiagnosis, however. For almost a week, until the negative results of the tests were in, I thought that I was going to die right away. Every day for the past nearly ten years, then, has been a kind of gift. I accept all gifts.

Multiple sclerosis is a chronic degenerative disease of the central nervous system, in which the myelin that sheathes the nerves is somehow eaten away and scar tissue forms in its place, interrupting the nerves' signals. During its course, which is unpredictable and uncontrollable, one may lose vision, hearing, speech, the ability to walk, control of bladder and/or bowels, strength in any or all extremities, sensitivity to touch, vibration, and/or pain, potency, coordination of movements—the list of possibilities is lengthy and yes, horrifying. One may also lose one's sense of humor. That's the easiest to lose and the hardest to survive without.

In the past ten years, I have sustained some of these losses. Characteristic of MS are sudden attacks, called exacerbations, followed by remissions, and these I have not had. Instead, my disease has been slowly progressive. My left leg is now so weak that I walk with the aid of a brace and a cane; and for distances I use an Amigo, a variation on the electric wheelchair that looks rather like an electrified kiddie car. I no longer have much use of my left hand. Now my right side is weakening as well. I still have the blurred spot in my right eye. Overall, though, I've been lucky so far. My world has, of necessity, been circumscribed by my losses, but the terrain left me has been ample enough for me to continue many of the activities that absorb me: writing, teaching, raising children and cats and plants and snakes, reading, speaking publicly about MS and depression, even playing bridge with people patient and honorable enough to let me scatter cards every which way without sneaking a peek.

Lest I begin to sound like Pollyanna, however, let me say that I don't like having MS. I hate it. My life holds realities—harsh ones, some of them—that no right-minded human being ought to accept without grumbling. One of them is fatigue. I know of no one with MS who does not complain of bone-weariness; in a disease that presents an astonishing variety of symptoms, fatigue seems to be a common factor. I wake up in the morning feeling the way most people do at the end of a bad day, and I take it from there. As a result, I spend a lot of time *in extremis* and, impatient with limitation, I tend to ignore my fatigue until my body breaks down in some way and forces rest. Then I miss picnics, dinner parties, poetry readings, the brief visits of old friends from out of town. The offspring of a puritanical tradition of exceptional venerability, I cannot view these lapses without shame. My life often seems a series of small failures to do as I ought.

I lead, on the whole, an ordinary life, probably rather like the one I would have led had I not had MS. I am lucky that my predilections were already solitary, sedentary, and bookish—unlike the world-famous French cellist I have read about, or the young woman I talked with one long afternoon who wanted only to be a jockey. I had just begun graduate school when I found out something was wrong with me, and I have remained, interminably, a graduate student. Perhaps I would not have if I'd thought I had the stamina to return to a full-time job as a technical editor; but I've enjoyed my studies.

In addition to studying, I teach writing courses. I also teach medical students how to give neurological examinations. I pick up freelance editing jobs here and there. I have raised a foster son and sent him into the world, where he has made me two grandbabies, and I am still escorting my daughter and son through adolescence. I go to Mass every Saturday. I am a superb, if messy, cook. I am also an enthusiastic laundress, capable of sorting a hamper full of clothes into five subtly differentiated piles, but a terrible housekeeper. I can do italic writing and, in an emergency, bathe an oil-soaked cat. I play a fiendish game of Scrabble. When I have the time and the money, I like to sit on my front steps with my husband, drinking Amaretto and smoking a cigar, as we imagine our counterparts in Leningrad and make sure that the sun gets down once more behind the sharp childish scrawl of the Tucson Mountains.

This lively plenty has its bleak complement, of course, in all the things I can no longer do. I will never run again, except in dreams, and one day I may have to write that I will never walk again. I like to go camping, but I can't follow George and the children along the trails that wander out of a campsite through the desert or into the mountains. In fact, even on the level I've learned never to check the weather or try to hold a coherent conversation: I need all my attention for my wayward feet. Of late, I have begun to catch myself wondering how people can propel themselves without canes. With only one usable hand, I have to select my clothing with care not so much for style as for ease of ingress and egress, and even so, dressing can be laborious. I can no longer do fine stitchery, pick up babies, play the piano, braid my hair. I am immobilized by acute attacks of depression, which may or may not be physiologically related to MS but are certainly its logical concomitant.

These two elements, the plenty and the privation, are never pure, nor are the delight and wretchedness that accompany them. Almost every pickle that I get into as a result of my weakness and clumsiness—and I get into plenty—is funny as well as maddening and sometimes painful. I recall one May afternoon when a friend and I were going out for a drink after finishing up at school. As we were climbing into opposite sides of my car, chatting, I tripped and fell, flat and hard, onto the asphalt parking lot, my abrupt departure interrupting him in mid-sentence. "Where'd you go?" he called as he came around the back of the car to find me hauling myself up by the door frame. "Are you all right?" Yes, I told him, I was fine, just a bit rattly, and we drove off to find a shady patio and some beer. When I got home an hour or so later, my daughter greeted me with "What have you done to your self?" I looked down. One elbow of my white turtleneck with the green froggies, one knee of my white trousers, one white kneesock were blood-soaked. We peeled off the clothes and inspected the damage, which was nasty enough but not alarming. That part wasn't funny: The abrasions took a long time to heal, and one got a little infected. Even so, when I think of my friend talking earnestly, suddenly, to the hot thin air while I dropped from his view as though through a trap door, I find the image as silly as something from a Marx Brothers movie.

I may find it easier than other cripples to amuse myself because I live propped by the acceptance and the assistance and, sometimes, the amusement of those around me. Grocery clerks tear my checks out of my checkbook for me, and sales clerks find chairs to put into dressing rooms when I want to try on clothes. The people I work with make sure I teach at times when I am least likely to be fatigued, in places I can get to, with the materials I need. My students, with one anonymous exception (in an end-of-the-semester evaluation) have been unperturbed by my disability. Some even like it. One was immensely cheered by the information that I paint my own fingernails; she decided, she told me, that if I could go to such trouble over fine details, she could keep on writing essays. I suppose I became some sort of bright-fingered muse. She wrote good essays, too.

The most important struts in the framework of my existence, of course, are my husband and children. Dismayingly few marriages survive the MS test, and why should they? Most twenty-two- and nineteen-year-olds, like George and me, can vow in clear conscience, after a childhood of chickenpox and summer colds, to keep one another in sickness and in health so long as they both shall live. Not many are equipped for catastrophe: the dismay, the depression, the extra work, the boredom that a degenerative disease can insinuate into a relationship. And our society, with its emphasis on fun and its association of fun with physical performance, offers little encouragement for a whole spouse to stay with a crippled partner. Children experience similar stresses when faced with a crippled parent, and they are more helpless, since parents and children can't usually get divorced. They hate, of course, to be different from their peers, and the child whose mother is tacking down the aisle of a school auditorium packed with proud parents like a Cape Cod dinghy in a stiff breeze jolly well stands out in a crowd. Deprived of legal divorce, the child can at least deny the mother's disability, even her existence, forgetting to tell her about recitals and PTA meetings, refusing to accompany her to stores or church or the movies, never inviting friends to the house. Many do.

But I've been limping along for ten years now, and so far George and the children are still at my left elbow, holding tight. Anne and Matthew vacuum floors and dust furniture and haul trash and rake up dog droppings and button my cuffs and bake lasagne and Toll House cookies with just enough grumbling so I know that they don't have brain fever. And far from hiding me, they're forever dragging me by racks of fancy clothes or through teeming school corridors, or welcoming gaggles of friends while I'm wandering through the house in Anne's filmy pink babydoll pajamas. George generally calls before he brings someone home, but he does just as many dumb thankless chores as the children. And they all yell at me, laugh at some of my jokes, write me funny letters when we're apart—in short, treat me as an ordinary human being for whom they have some use. I think they like me. Unless they're faking . . . .

Faking. There's the rub. Tugging at the fringes of my consciousness always is the terror that people are kind to me only because I'm a cripple. My mother almost shattered me once, with that instinct mothers have—blind, I think, in this case, but unerring nonetheless—for striking blows along the fault-lines of their children's hearts, by telling me, in an attack on my selfishness, "We all have to make allowances for you, of course, because of the way you are." From the distance of a couple of years, I have to admit that I haven't any idea just what she meant, and I'm not sure that she knew either. She was awfully angry. But at the time, as the words thudded home, I felt my worst fear, suddenly realized. I could bear being called selfish: I am. But I couldn't bear the corroboration that those around me were doing in fact what I'd always suspected them of doing, professing fondness while silently putting up with me because of the way I am. A cripple. I've been a little cracked ever since.

Along with this fear that people are secretly accepting shoddy goods comes a relentless pressure to please—to prove myself worth the burdens I impose, I guess, or to build a substantial account of goodwill against which I may write drafts in times of need. Part of the pressure arises from social expectations. In our society, anyone who deviates from the norm had better find some way to compensate. Like fat people, who are expected to be jolly, cripples must bear their lot meekly and cheerfully. A grumpy cripple isn't playing by the rules. And much of the pressure is self-generated. Early on I vowed that, if I had to have MS, by God I was going to do it well. This is a class act, ladies and gentlemen. No tears, no recriminations, no faint-heartedness.

One way and another, then, I wind up feeling like Tiny Tim, peering over the edge of the table at the Christmas goose, waving my crutch, piping down

God's blessing on us all. Only sometimes I don't want to play Tiny Tim. I'd rather be Caliban, a most scurvy monster. Fortunately, at home no one much cares whether I'm a good cripple or a bad cripple as long as I make vichyssoise with fair regularity. One evening several years ago, Anne was reading at the dining-room table while I cooked dinner. As I opened a can of tomatoes, the can slipped in my left hand and juice spattered me and the counter with bloody spots. Fatigued and infuriated, I bellowed, "I'm so sick of being crippled!" Anne glanced at me over the top of her book. "There now," she said, "do you feel better?" "Yes," I said, "yes, I do." She went back to her reading. I felt better. That's about all the attention my scurviness ever gets.

Because I hate being crippled, I sometimes hate myself for being a cripple. Over the years I have come to expect—even accept—attacks of violent self-loathing. Luckily, in general our society no longer connects deformity and disease directly with evil (though a charismatic once told me that I have MS because a devil is in me) and so I'm allowed to move largely at will, even among small children. But I'm not sure that this revision of attitude has been particularly helpful. Physical imperfection, even freed of moral disapprobation, still defies and violates the ideal, especially for women, whose confinement in their bodies as objects of desire is far from over. Each age, of course, has its ideal, and I doubt that ours is any better or worse than any other. Today's ideal woman, who lives on the glossy pages of dozens of magazines, seems to be between the ages of eighteen and twenty-five; her hair has body, her teeth flash white, her breath smells minty, her underarms are dry; she has a career but is still a fabulous cook, especially of meals that take less than twenty minutes to prepare; she does not ordinarily appear to have a husband or children; she is trim and deeply tanned; she jogs, swims, plays tennis, rides a bicycle, sails, but does not bowl; she travels widely, even to out-of-the-way places like Finland and Samoa, always in the company of the ideal man, who possesses a nearly identical set of characteristics. There are a few exceptions. Though usually white and often blonde, she may be black, Hispanic, Asian, or Native American, so long as she is unusually sleek. She may be old, provided she is selling a laxative or is Lauren Bacall. If she is selling a detergent, she may be married and have a flock of strikingly messy children. But she is never a cripple.

Like many women I know, I have always had an uneasy relationship with my body. I was not a popular child, largely, I think now, because I was peculiar: intelligent, intense, moody, shy, given to unexpected actions and inexplicable notions and emotions. But as I entered adolescence, I believed myself unpopular because I was homely: my breasts too flat, my mouth too wide, my hips too narrow, my clothing never quite right in fit or style. I was not, in fact, particularly ugly, old photographs inform me, though I was well off the ideal; but I carried this sense of self-alienation with me into adulthood, where it regenerated in response to the depredations of MS. Even with my brace I walk with a limp so pronounced that, seeing myself on the videotape of a television program on the disabled, I couldn't believe that anything but an inchworm could make progress humping along like that. My shoulders droop and my pelvis thrusts forward as I try to balance myself upright, throwing my frame into a bony S. As a result of contractures, one shoulder is higher than the other and I carry one arm bent in front of me, the fingers curled into a claw. My left arm and leg have wasted into pipe-stems, and I try always to keep them covered. When I think about how my body must look to others, especially to men, to whom I have been trained to display myself, I feel ludicrous, even loathsome.

At my age, however, I don't spend much time thinking about my appearance. The burning egocentricity of adolescence, which assures one that all the world is looking all the time, has passed, thank God, and I'm generally too caught up in what I'm doing to step back, as I used to, and watch myself as though upon a stage. I'm also too old to believe in the accuracy of self-image. I know that I'm not a hideous crone, that in fact, when I'm rested, well dressed, and well made up, I look fine. The self-loathing I feel is neither physically nor intellectually substantial. What I hate is not me but a disease.

I am not a disease.

And a disease is not—at least not singlehandedly—going to determine who I am, though at first it seemed to be going to. Adjusting to a chronic incurable illness, I have moved through a process similar to that outlined by Elizabeth Kübler-Ross in *On Death and Dying*. The major difference—and it is far more significant than most people recognize—is that I can't be sure of the outcome, as the terminally ill cancer patient can. Research studies indicate that, with proper medical care, I may achieve a "normal" life span. And in our society, with its vision of death as the ultimate evil, worse even than decrepitude, the response to such news is, "Oh well, at least you're not going to *die*." Are there worse things than dying? I think that there may be.

I think of two women I know, both with MS, both enough older than I to have served as models. One took to her bed several years ago and has been there ever since. Although she can sit in a high-backed wheelchair, because she is incontinent she refuses to go out at all, even though incontinence pants, which are readily available at any pharmacy, could protect her from embarrassment. Instead, she stays at home and insists that her husband, a small quiet man, a retired civil servant, stay there with her except for a quick weekly foray to the supermarket. The other woman, whose illness was diagnosed when she was eighteen, a nursing student engaged to a young doctor, finished her training, married her doctor, accompanied him to Germany when he was in the service, bore three sons and a daughter, now grown and gone. When she can, she travels with her husband; she plays bridge, embroiders, swims regularly; she works, like me, as a symptomatic-patient instructor of medical students in neurology. Guess which woman I hope to be.

At the beginning, I thought about having MS almost incessantly. And because of the unpredictable course of the disease, my thoughts were always terrified. Each night I'd get into bed wondering whether I'd get out again the next morning, whether I'd be able to see, to speak, to hold a pen between my fingers. Knowing that the day might come when I'd be physically incapable of killing myself, I thought perhaps I ought to do so right away, while I still had the strength. Gradually I came to understand that the Nancy who might one day lie inert under a bedsheet, arms and legs paralyzed, unable to feed or bathe herself, unable to reach out for a gun, a bottle of pills, was not the Nancy I was at present, and that I could not presume to make decisions for that future Nancy, who might well not want in the least to die. Now the only provision I've made for the future Nancy is that when the time comes—and it is likely to come in the form of pneumonia, friend to the weak and the old—I am not to be treated with machines and medications. If she is unable to communicate by then, I hope she will be satisfied with these terms.

Thinking all the time about having MS grew tiresome and intrusive, especially in the large and tragic mode in which I was accustomed to considering my plight. Months and even years went by without catastrophe (at least without one related to MS), and really I was awfully busy, what with George and children and snakes and students and poems, and I hadn't the time, let alone the inclination, to devote myself to being a disease. Too, the richer my life became, the funnier it seemed, as though there were some connection between largesse and laughter, and so my tragic stance began to waver until, even with the aid of a brace and cane, I couldn't hold it for very long at a time.

After several years I was satisfied with my adjustment. I had suffered my grief and fury and terror, I thought, but now I was at ease with my lot. Then one summer day I set out with George and the children across the desert for a vacation in California. Part way to Yuma I became aware that my right leg felt funny. "I think I've had an exacerbation," I told George. "What shall we do?" he asked. "I think we'd better get the hell to California," I said, "because I don't know whether I'll ever make it again." So we went on to San Diego and then to Orange, and up the Pacific Coast Highway to Santa Cruz, across to Yosemite, down to Sequoia and Joshua Tree, and so back over the desert to home. It was a fine two-week trip, filled with friends and fair weather, and I wouldn't have missed it for the world, though I did in fact make it back to California two years later. Nor would there have been any point in missing it, since in MS, once the symptoms have appeared, the neurological damage has been done, and there's no way to predict or prevent that damage.

The incident spoiled my self-satisfaction, however. It renewed my grief and fury and terror, and I learned that one never finishes adjusting to MS. I don't know now why I thought one would. One does not, after all, finish adjusting to life, and MS is simply a fact of my life—not my favorite fact, of course—but as ordinary as my nose and my tropical fish and my yellow Mazda station wagon. It may at any time get worse, but no amount of worry or anticipation can prepare me for a new loss. My life is a lesson in losses. I learn one at a time.

And I had best be patient in the learning, since I'll have to do it like it or not. As any rock fan knows, you can't always get what you want. Particularly when you have MS. You can't, for example, get cured. In recent years researchers and the organizations that fund research have started to pay MS some attention even though it isn't fatal; perhaps they have begun to see that life is something other than a quantitative phenomenon, that one may be very much alive for a very long time in a life that isn't worth living. The researchers have made some progress toward understanding the mechanism of the disease: It may well be an autoimmune reaction triggered by a slow-acting virus. But they are nowhere near its prevention, control, or cure. And most of us want to be cured. Some, unable to accept incurability, grasp at one treatment after another, no matter how bizarre: megavitamin therapy, gluten-free diet, injections of cobra venom, hypothermal suits, lymphocy-topharesis, hyperbaric chambers. Many treatments are probably harmless enough, but none are curative.

The absence of a cure often makes MS patients bitter toward their doctors. Doctors are, after all, the priests of modern society, the new shamans, whose business is to heal, and many an MS patient roves from one to another, searching for the "good" doctor who will make him well. Doctors too think of themselves as healers, and for this reason many have trouble dealing with MS patients, whose disease in its intransigence defeats their aims and mocks their skills. Too few doctors, it is true, treat their patients as whole human beings, but the reverse is also true. I have always tried to be gentle with my doctors, who often have more at stake in terms of ego than I do. I may be frustrated, maddened, depressed by the incurability of my disease, but I am not diminished by it, and they are. When I push myself up from my seat in the waiting room and stumble toward them, I incarnate the limitation of their powers. The least I can do is refuse to press on their tenderest spots.

This gentleness is part of the reason that I'm not sorry to be a cripple. I didn't have it before. Perhaps I'd have developed it anyway—how could I know such a thing?—and I wish I had more of it, but I'm glad of what I have. It has opened and enriched my life enormously, this sense that my frailty and need must be mirrored in others, that in searching for and shaping a stable core in a life wrenched by change and loss, change and loss, I must recognize the same process, under individual conditions, in the lives around me. I do not deprecate such knowledge, however I've come by it.

All the same, if a cure were found, would I take it? In a minute. I may be a cripple, but I'm only occasionally a loony and never a saint. Anyway, in my brand of theology God doesn't give bonus points for a limp. I'd take a cure; I just don't need one. A friend who also has MS startled me once by asking, "Do you ever say to yourself, 'Why me, Lord?'" "No, Michael, I don't," I told him, "because whenever I try, the only response I can think of is 'Why not?'" If I could make a cosmic deal, who would I put in my place? What in my life would I give up in exchange for sound limbs and a thrilling rush of energy? No one. Nothing. I might as well do the job myself. Now that I'm getting the hang of it.

Suggestions for Discussion

1. Why does Mairs prefer the word "crippled" to "handicapped" or "disabled" to describe her condition?

2. How does she characterize the plenty, the privation of her life?

3. What does she mean by "I'd take a cure; I just don't need one"?

Suggestions for Writing

1. Mairs asserts that her multiple sclerosis is only one part of her multifaceted self: "What I hate is not me but a disease. I am not a disease." Write about how people tend instead to identify with things that have happened to them or with aspects of themselves. Use an example from your own experience to support this idea.

2. "My life is a lesson in losses. I learn one at a time." What does this convey about Mairs's attitude toward life? How would you handle a life-long "crisis"?

3. Examine the role of humor as a survival tool. Use examples from the essay and your own experience to explore the topic.

ALFRED LUBRANO

Blue-Collar Roots, White-Collar Dreams

New York native Alfred Lubrano is an award-winning staff reporter for the *Philadelphia Inquirer* and has been a commentator for National Public Radio since 1992. His work has appeared in national magazines and anthologies. A Columbia University graduate and the son of a Brooklyn bricklayer, Lubrano wrote the book *Limbo: Blue-Collar Roots, White-Collar Dreams* (2003), which concerns the class distinctions that separate the working class from the middle class in America. In the following excerpt from *Limbo*, Lubrano focuses on the challenges faced by the upwardly mobile children of the working class.

∾

Blue-Collar Valued

I idealized my dad as a kind of dawn-rising priest of labor, engaged in holy ritual. Up at five every morning, my father made a religion of responsibility. My brother Christopher, who has two degrees from Columbia and is now an executive with the blue-collar sense to make a great white-collar salary, says he always felt safe when he heard Dad stir before him, "as if Pop were taming the day for us." As he aged, my father was expected to put out as if he were decades younger, slipping on machine-washable vestments of khaki cotton without waking my mother. He'd go into the kitchen and turn on the radio to catch the temperature. Bricklayers have an occupational need to know the weather. And because I am my father's son, I can still recite the five-day forecast at any given moment.

My dad wasn't crazy about the bricklayer's life. He had wanted to be a singer and an actor when he was young, but that was frivolous doodling to his immigrant father, who expected money to be coming in, stoking the stove that kept the hearth fires ablaze. Dreams simply were not energy-efficient. After combat duty in Korea, my dad returned home, learned his father-in-law's trade, and acquiesced to a life of backbreaking routine. He says he can't find the black-and-white publicity glossies he once had made. So many limbo folk witnessed the shelving of their blue-collar parents' dreams. Most, like my dad, made the best of it, although a few disappointed people would grow to resent their own children's chances, some Straddlers say.

As kids, Chris and I joked about our father's would-be singing career, wondering where we all would have been had he become rich and famous. His name is Vincent, but everyone calls him Jimmy. So my brother and I dubbed him "Jimmy Vincent," or "Jimmy V. From Across the Sea," a Jerry Vale type with sharper looks and a better set of pipes. As a young man, my father was tall and slender, with large brown eyes and dark hair. He was careful about his appearance, always concerned with pants pleats, pressed shirt cuffs, and the shine on his shoes.

One of our too-close neighbors once told him they liked it when Dad took a shower because of the inevitable tile-enhanced concert he'd provide. When one of my father's sisters died and Pop stopped singing for a while, the neighbor noticed and asked my father what was wrong.

There was a lot about Brooklyn I felt close to. Much about working-class life is admirable and fine. The trick is to avoid glorifying it without painting life in it too darkly. Sure, we lived with a few *cafones*—what some thought of as the low-class losers (there were classes among the working class, too—a pecking order based on taste, dignity, and intelligence). But the very best of blue-collar culture is something I still celebrate in myself and look for in others I meet. The values are an essential defining factor:

A well-developed work ethic, the kind that gets you up early and keeps you locked in until the job is done, regardless of how odious or personally distasteful the task.

A respect for your parents that is nothing short of religious, something I was amazed to find was not shared among the kids with whom I went to college and graduate school.

The need for close contact with extended family—aunts, uncles, and grandparents—each of whom had the authority to whack you in the back of the head should your behavior call for it.

An open and honest manner devoid of hidden agenda and messy subtext. You say something, you mean it.

Other things, too: loyalty; a sense of solidarity with people you live and work with; an understanding and appreciation of what it takes to get somewhere in a hard world where no one gives you a break; a sense of daring; and a physicality that's honest, basic, and attractive. (When I worked for New York *Newsday*, a disgruntled reader had been stalking me and persistently threatening my life. A colleague suggested I get a "goon" to protect me. An editor answered, "Alfred doesn't need a goon. Alfred is a goon.")

We could, between money troubles and family crises, recognize the good in life. Nobody laughs like blue-collar people, who are unashamed to pound the table in gasping recognition of a pure truth, a glaring absurdity, or a sharp irony. I have seen relatives grab onto each other for support in tear-blurred spasms of guffawing that nearly choke them. It's fun to watch.

❧

Class Distinctions and Clashes

Blue-collar origins implant defining characteristics that will cause conflict throughout a life. Straddlers and social scientists can point to specific differences in manner, style, thought, and approach to life that are class-based. Because there's no exact science to this, much comes from observation and opinion. It's still useful to understand, though, because it demonstrates that people think in terms of class all the time. And while it may be hard for them to define precisely, they know class differences when they see them. Interestingly, among Straddlers, resentments toward the middle class are never far below the surface.

"We working-class people have an appreciation for people no matter what they do," asserts Peter Ciotta, director of communications for a $1.6 billion food company in Buffalo. "And we have to outwork people because we have no connections. We're not going to get invited to the party."

James Neal, a Midwest medical malpractice attorney, who woke up at 4 A.M. on his parents' farm each day and went to school stinking of animals, says he takes special delight in facing off against silver-spoon lawyers and doctors because he believes they're so arrogant. "You just don't find a hell of a lot of arrogant working-class people. And blue-collar people say what they mean. In the end, I avoid people with a sense of entitlement. Until you've had hard times, you're not a complete person. And if you've never had them, well, a whole hunk of you is missing."

Struggle, the working class will tell you, is central to blue-collar life and the chief architect of character. Journalist Samme Chittum, a former college instructor who grew up in small-town Illinois, understands that. "The middle class knows what money bestows on you. Not what it can buy, but what it bestows. It's the intangible things—privilege, privacy, immunity from the vagaries of fortune that people who have to struggle are open to. It would be socially immature to be envious of these people; there are so many others in the world whose stack of poker chips is smaller than mine. But white-collar kids did not have to bust their asses for everything they've got. They came equipped with helium balloons to raise them to a higher stratosphere where things just come to you.

"But if you want a dirty job done, give it to me. I will do the hard job. I'll move 50 pieces of furniture up the stairs, take rocks out of the garden. I will push until the job's done or until I fall over. I don't understand letting others do things for you, or spending your social currency to get favors. I have a scorn for that."

The heritage of struggle, as writer and working-class academic Janet Zandy puts it, develops a built-in collectivity in the working class, a sense of people helping each other—you're not going it alone, and you have buddies to watch your back. It's different in the middle class, Zandy and others argue, where the emphasis is on individual achievement and personal ambition. The middle class, my Straddlers would say, rarely had to pay working-class-type dues and were most likely unaware of the help they got—the cultural capital—to ensure their sinecures in life and business.

If you could get through college without having to work at some outside job or take out loans, for example, that says you did not know privation, and that, in turn, says something about you and your class. If your parents gave you the down payment on your house (Straddlers often hate hearing this one), that tells us something about you as well. Straddlers tend to see the family dynamic as struggle, and they learn to accept it. You never expect things to be easy, and you don't whine when they're not. Nothing is promised, so nothing is expected. "My father's goal for me," says Los Angeles Straddler Jeffrey Orridge, a Mattel executive, "was to be able to eat. Not to drive a Mercedes. Just to eat." The working class is told that anything you get you earn by hard work. "Our family was pain and anguish," says Sacramento Straddler Andrea Todd, a freelance magazine writer and editor. "I saw my dad—a fire-fighter—sacrifice his well-being to put food on the table. The middle-class girls I knew didn't see that, didn't know that."

While middle-class kids are allowed some say and voice in their upbringing ("David, would you prefer going to Grandma's or to the park?"), working-class kids develop within a strict, authoritarian world ("David, if you don't come with me to Grandma's right now I'll slap your teeth out!"). Experts say that children raised in authoritarian homes do less well in school than kids from less regimented middle-class environments. Without meaning to, says Hamilton College sociologist Dennis Gilbert, the parent who stresses obedience over curiosity is championing the values of the working class, and helping to keep their kids in it.

Temple University sociologist Annette Lareau did some interesting work in this area, she tells me. Studying 88 African-American and white children from the Northeast and the Midwest who were between the ages of 8 and 10, Lareau was able to see distinct differences in the way working-class and middle-class kids are raised. In fact, she concludes, the importance of class influence in their upbringing was greater even than that of race.

∾

Class Flash Cards: Perceptions are as Real as Origins

I asked Straddlers and working-class studies types to list class-based traits to help understand what the classes look like. Some truly believe class in America is akin to a caste system of different values and outlooks. Ultimately, working-class and middle-class cultures are based on different foundations, says Minnesota psychologist Barbara Jensen, herself a Straddler. The core value of the working class is being part of a like-minded group—a family, a union, or a community, which engenders a strong sense of loyalty. The core value of the middle class is achievement by the individual.

The middle class, Jensen says, is solipsistic, seeing nothing but its own culture. That's made easier by the fact that the middle class literally writes our culture. Movies, books, the news media, and television are creations of the middle class. Working-class people see little of themselves in popular culture. (There are exceptions of course: *Working Girl, Norma Rae, Roseanne.* But by and large, Jensen's observation holds true.) As such, the middle class gets to see complex depictions of itself, while working-class people view mostly stereotypes of themselves.

What else? Jensen provided me with class "flash cards," for lack of a better term—quick observations that separate the workers from the managers, the corner boys from the corner-office boys. Obviously, none of these are hard-and-fast rules. They are traits and tendencies gleaned from observation and study, and are by no means scientific:

Working-class people mistrust eggheads, relying more on intuition, common sense, and luck. The middle class is more analytical, depending on cultivated, logical thinking.

In a social setting, the working class may be more apt to show emotion than the middle class. The working class may be tougher, flashier, and louder.

Working-class people are overawed by doctors and lawyers. The middle class knows how to talk to such folks and realizes they are just as fallible and corrupt as the rest of us.

The middle class is burdened with the pressure to outachieve high-achieving parents. Many working-class families are happy if their kids get and keep a job and avoid being seen on *America's Most Wanted*.

The working class will bowl; the middle class will play racquetball. At Columbia, where physical education was a requirement for graduation, they taught us squash and racquetball, trying to tutor future lawyers and leaders on the finer points of business leisure. I played it like a neighborhood kid, diving into the walls and feeling a sense of accomplishment when I nearly separated my shoulder. I was never that good, because I played too blue-collar, too straight-ahead, and never studied the angles and the corner shots. It was nothing like the stickball, stoopball, and handball we played in Brooklyn. In summer softball games, I used to think I could play center field because our cement parks were so small. Then I moved to Ohio and played in lovely suburban fields, watching ball after ball get by me. I couldn't cover the vast territory, green and endless. I switched to first base.

The working class has traditionally expressed a my-country-right-or-wrong patriotic attitude, while the middle class often has questioned government, Jensen says. The obvious example is the Vietnam War era, when working-class kids died in jungles, and middle-class kids protested on campuses.

There's a greater depth of acquiescence among working-class people, who tend to feel more powerless: You can't fight city hall. The middle class says you can and there's more of a constant striving toward self-hood and becoming something else. The working-class man or woman says, "I am what I am." The middle-class person says, "I have to do this [graduate from college, go to business school, pass the bar] to become who I am."

Regarding racism, everyone is guilty. Minority Straddlers will say the working class is overt in its prejudices, while the middle class is surreptitious, devious, and hypocritical. Ultimately, writes social critic Bell Hooks, blacks fear poor and working-class whites more because, historically, they have acted out their hatred in more violent forms.

The working class works at jobs that bite, maim, and wither. The middle class gets to work indoors at desks. This can be stressful, of course, but as Andrew Levison points out in Fussell's book, office buildings don't implode like coal mines, and professors aren't subjected to industrial noises that destroy their hearing.

Finally, Jensen says, the working class sends out Christmas cards that say, "Love, X." The middle class circulates Christmas newsletters, with proud news of Timmy's adventures in the fourth grade.

Obviously, people are more than just class. We all embody interlocking cultures—ethnicities, races, and genders. We possess different skills and inclinations. Still, imprecise as many of the flash cards are, they do reflect people's perceptions.

In Brooklyn, I used to notice people eyeing each other across the class divide. Older, ethnic working-class women in housedresses would sit on their stoops on summer evenings and watch the single, yuppie women trudge home from Manhattan offices at 8 P.M., carrying their small, Korean-grocer salads in white plastic bags. The old women would laugh, then shake their heads at what they saw as the empty, ascetic lives devoid of children, real food, and steady men. The yuppies, I'm sure, had their own thoughts about overweight, middle-aged women with limited horizons, bad clothes, and inattentive husbands.

Smaller class-based skirmishes go on daily in offices, with janitors, secretaries, and maintenance people on one side, and CEOs, executives, and tech people on the other. It happens everywhere; it happens every day. The perceptions we all have of the other side can have a greater impact than reality.

Suggestions for Discussion

1. What does Lubrano mean by the term "Straddler"?

2. According to Lubrano and the Straddlers cited in this piece, what are the fundamental differences between the classes? Discuss the differences between blue-collar values and white-collar values.

3. How do the Straddlers perceive other people of the middle class? Do they have a right to feel this way? Why, or why not?

Suggestion for Writing

Write an essay comparing Lubrano's analysis of members of the working class in America and John Lennon's description of the British working classes in the song "Working Class Hero" in the Poetry section of the Popular Culture chapter.

ESSAYS

❦❦❦

BENOIT DENIZET-LEWIS

Friends, Friends with Benefits, and the Benefits of the Local Mall

Benoit Denizet-Lewis, who holds both French and U.S. citizenship, is an award-winning journalist and nonfiction writer. He is a contributing American culture writer for the *New York Times Magazine*; he was a senior writer for *Boston Magazine* and a staff writer at the *San Francisco Chronicle*. Benoit's work has also appeared in *Details, ESPN the Magazine, Spin, Out, Salon,* and *JANE.* Educated at Northwestern University, he has taught magazine and nonfiction fiction writing at Tufts University, Emerson College, and Northeastern University. Much of his work takes the form of extensive profiling or expose, and the following piece, published in the *New York Times* in 2004, explores the changing world of relationships.

Jesse wants to meet at Hooters. "It's 40 minutes from where I live," he says, "but trust me, it's worth the drive."

Jesse is 15. Surprisingly, there is no age requirement to dine at Hooters. When I call the restaurant to make sure I'm not aiding and abetting teen delinquency, the woman who picks up seems annoyed I would even ask. "No, we're a family restaurant," she says. So, amid the bronzed, scantily clad waitresses and a boisterous bachelor party, I find Jesse, a high-school sophomore with broad shoulders and messy brown hair peeking out from underneath his baseball cap. Jesse is there with four of his close friends, whom he has arranged for me to meet.

Among them is Caity, a thin, 14-year-old freshman with long blond hair and braces, who says that she is a virgin but that she occasionally "hooks up" with guys. Caity doesn't make clear what she means by "hooking up." The term itself is vague—covering everything from kissing to intercourse—though it is sometimes a euphemism for oral sex, performed by a girl on a boy. Sitting next to Caity is her best friend, Kate, also 14, whom everyone affectionately refers to as the "prude" of the group. Outgoing and

225

attractive, she's had a boyfriend for a couple of months, but they haven't even kissed yet.

In her New England exurban world, where, I was told, oral sex is common by eighth or ninth grade, and where hookups may skip kissing altogether, Kate's predicament strikes her friends, and even herself, as bizarre. "It's retarded," she says, burying her head in Caity's shoulder. "Even my mom thinks it's weird."

Just a few weeks ago, Caity and Kate met a cute boy at the mall. "Me and Kate walked into this store," Caity says, "and this boy saw the shirt Kate was wearing that says, 'Kiss Me, I'm an Amoeba.' So he was, like, 'That's an awesome shirt.' And she was, like, 'Want me to make you one?' So he went and got Sharpies, and she went and got T-shirts, we met back there and then he said to me, 'You want my screen name?' So he wrote it on my arm. He just got his license, so he came up, and we hooked up."

I ask Caity if that's it, or if her hookup might lead to something more. "We might date," she tells me. "I don't know. It's just that guys can get so annoying when you start dating them."

Adam, a 16-year-old sophomore at the end of the table, breaks in, adding that girls, too, can get really annoying when you start dating them. A soccer player with shaggy blond hair and a muscular body, he likes to lift his shirt at inappropriate times (like now, to the Hooters waitress) and scream, "I've had sex!" Adam has had the most hookups of the group—about 10, he estimates.

When he lived in Florida last year, he lost his virginity to a friend who threw a condom at him and ordered him to put it on. "Down in Key West, high-school girls are crazy," Adam said. "Girls were making out with each other on the beach. Lesbians are cool!"

While Adam and Caity denied it, there was a thick fog of sexual intrigue that surrounded their friendship—and a few weeks after our dinner at Hooters, Jesse sent me an online message notifying me of a hookup in the making between Adam and Caity. They were planning to go over to Jesse's house and "mess around." As Jesse explained it, Adam told Caity he didn't want a relationship, and she replied that that was fine, she didn't want one, either.

According to Jesse, Caity set the ground rules. "Caity told me, 'Adam knows he's not going to get in my pants, but I might get into his.' For now they might just make out, but Caity said that if they hang out a lot more, maybe they'll do more." The next day, Jesse messaged me to say that the hookup never materialized. "Everyone got busy. But I'm guessing it still might happen."

I first met Jesse online at facethejury.com, one of many Internet sites popular with high-school and college students, where teenagers can post profiles, exchange e-mail and arrange to hook up. (Though facethejury.com, like many such sites, requires members to be 18, younger teenagers routinely lie about their age.) Over the course of several months spent hanging out and communicating online with nearly 100 high-school students (mostly white, middle- and upper-middle-class suburban and exurban teenagers from the Northeast and Midwest), I heard the same thing: hooking up is more common than dating.

Most of the teenagers I spoke to could think of only a handful of serious couples at their school. One senior in Chicago, who'd been dating the same girl since sophomore year, told me that none of his friends want girlfriends and that he's made to feel like a "loser" because he's in a relationship. As if searching for reassurance, he turned to me and asked, "Do you think I'm a loser?"

The decline in dating and romantic relationships on college campuses has been deplored often enough. By 2001, it had become so pronounced that a conservative group, the Independent Women's Forum, was compelled to take out ads in college papers on the East Coast and in the Midwest pleading with students to "Take Back the Date." But their efforts don't seem to have paid off. The trend toward "hooking up" and "friends with benefits" (basically, friends you hook up with regularly) has trickled down from campuses into high schools and junior highs—and not just in large urban centers. Cellphones and the Internet, which offer teenagers an unparalleled level of privacy, make hooking up that much easier, whether they live in New York City or Boise.

And yet, still, many date. Or sort of, falling out of romantic relationships into hookups and back again. When teenagers do date, they often do so in ways that would be unrecognizable to their parents, or even to their older siblings. A "formal date" might be a trip to the mall with a date and some friends. Teenagers regularly flirt online first, and then decide whether to do so in real life. Dating someone from your school is considered by many to be risky, akin to seeing someone from the office, so teenagers tend to look to nearby schools or towns, whether they're hoping to date or just to hook up.

It's not that teenagers have given up on love altogether. Most of the high-school students I spent time with said they expected to meet the right person, fall in love and marry—eventually. It's just that high school, many insist, isn't the place to worry about that. High school is about keeping your options open. Relationships are about closing them. As these teenagers see it, marriage and monogamy will seamlessly replace their youthful hookup careers sometime in their mid- to late 20's—or, as one high-school boy from Rhode Island told me online, when "we turn 30 and no one hot wants us anymore."

Brian, a 16-year-old friend of Jesse's, put it this way: "Being in a real relationship just complicates everything. You feel obligated to be all, like, couply. And that gets really boring after a while. When you're friends with benefits, you go over, hook up, then play video games or something. It rocks."

ç√∂

Why Valentine's Day Is for Losers

Dating practices and sexual behavior still vary along racial and economic lines, but some common assumptions, particularly about suburban versus urban kids, no longer hold true. Parents often think that teenagers who grow up in cities are more prone to promiscuous sexual behavior than teenagers in the suburbs. But according to a comprehensive study sponsored by the National Institute of Child Health and Development, more suburban 12th graders than urban ones have had sex outside of a romantic relationship (43 percent, compared with 39 percent).

It's unclear just how many teenagers choose hookups or friends with benefits over dating. Many, in fact, go back and forth, and if the distinction between hooking up and dating can seem slippery, that's because one sometimes does lead to the other. But just as often, hooking up is nothing more than what it's advertised to be: a no-strings sexual encounter. Recent studies show that it's not uncommon for high-school students to have sex with someone they aren't dating. A 2001 survey conducted by Bowling Green State University in Ohio found that of the 55 percent of local 11th graders who engaged in intercourse, 60 percent said they'd had sex with a partner who was no more than a friend. That number would perhaps be higher if the study asked about oral sex. While the teen intercourse rate has declined—from 54 percent in 1991 to 47 percent in 2003—this may be partly because teenagers have simply replaced intercourse with oral sex. To a generation raised on MTV, AIDS, Britney Spears, Internet porn, Monica Lewinsky and "Sex and the City," oral sex is definitely not sex (it's just "oral"), and hooking up is definitely not a big deal.

The teenagers I spoke to talk about hookups as matter-of-factly as they might discuss what's on the cafeteria lunch menu—and they look at you in a funny way if you go on for too long about the "emotional" components of sex. But coupled with this apparent disconnection is remarkable frankness about sex, even among friends of the opposite gender. Many teenagers spend a lot of time hanging out in mixed-gender groups (at the mall, at one another's houses), and when they can't hang out in person, they hang out online, asking the questions they might not dare to in real life. While this means that some friendships become sexually charged and lead to "friends with benefits" (one senior from Illinois told me that most of her friends have hooked up with one another), a good number remain platonic.

On Valentine's Day, I was invited to spend the evening with 12 junior and senior friends in an upper-middle-class suburb of Chicago. They were hanging out, eating pizza and watching TV. Not one had a Valentine, and most said they wouldn't have it any other way. Several pointed out that having close friends of the opposite sex makes romantic relationships less essential. Besides, if you feel like something more, there's no need to feign interest in dinner and a movie. You can just hook up or call one of your friends with benefits.

"It would be so weird if a guy came up to me and said, 'Irene, I'd like to take you out on a date,'" said Irene, a tall, outgoing senior. "I'd probably laugh at him. It would be sweet, but it would be so weird!"

Irene and her friends are not nerds. They are attractive and well liked, and most have had at least one romantic relationship. If that experience taught them anything, it's that high school is no place for romantic relationships. They're complicated, messy and invariably painful. Hooking up, when done "right," is exciting, sexually validating and efficient.

"I mean, sometimes you'll go out with a group of friends and meet someone cool, and maybe you'll hang out and hook up, but that's about it," said Irene's friend Marie (who asked me to use her middle name). "There's a few people I know who date, but most of us are like, 'There's no one good to date, we don't need to date, so why date?'"

∾

Once Upon a Time, Before the Internet . . .

The last time American teenagers seemed this uninterested in monogamous, long-term relationships was the 1930's and early 1940's, when high-school popularity was largely equated with social (but not sexual) promiscuity: the "cool kids" had lots of dates with lots of different people, while the "losers" settled down with one person or didn't date at all. This more-the-merrier philosophy played itself out most significantly on the dance floor, where there was nothing more embarrassing for a young woman than to be stuck with the same boy all night.

In her book "From Front Porch to Back Seat: Courtship in 20th-Century America," Beth Bailey, a professor of American Studies at the University of New Mexico, points out that magazine advice columns at the time urged teenagers to keep their options open—and, most important, to appear to be always in demand. Dating was seen as a competition that must never be lost. The advice column in Senior Scholastic, a current-events magazine for high-school students, told girls never to reject any boy outright, because "he may come in handy for an off night." And Ladies Home Journal urged teenagers to be open to blind dates: they "help keep you in circulation. They're good press agents. They even add to your collection."

Bailey found that "going steady," when it was discussed at all before World War II, was often ridiculed by teenagers and the media. Dating a variety of people simultaneously was the key to a good social standing in high school. "These dates had to be highly visible, and with many different people, or they didn't count," Bailey writes.

But the war changed everything. Suddenly, women outnumbered men, and popular women's magazines and advice books scared American girls with dire warnings like "Male shortage . . . It's worse than ever," and "Baldly stated, many girls of your generation will never marry." Young women apparently took up the challenge, because by 1959, 47 percent of brides were under 19, and those who weren't would often report that they had gone to college solely to find a husband.

With marriage occurring at a younger and younger age, teenagers started dating earlier, too. It wasn't uncommon for 13-year-olds to go steady. Bailey cites one 1961 study of a middle-class district in Pennsylvania, in which 40 percent of fifth graders were already dating (for many, this meant holding hands and kissing). One frustrated high-school boy wrote a letter to Senior Scholastic complaining that everyone he knew went steady, and that he was labeled a "playboy" for wanting to date different girls.

By the late 60's and early 70's, the rituals of high-school dating had taken on an almost prehistoric cast. The "rules"—boy calls girl, boy asks girl out, boy drives to girl's house, boy talks to girl's dad, boy takes girl to movies, boy has her home by 11 (or else)—were viewed as restrictive and old-fashioned, not to mention sexist. And that's pretty much how things stood until the Reagan era, when dating made a serious comeback. Many teenagers settled down into a mix of serial dating and going steady—being "popular" often meant having a highly coveted boyfriend or girlfriend. And while parents may have felt, as they typically do, that they didn't always understand teenage culture, most still thought they had a pretty good idea of whom their kids were talking to regularly. "Teens still had to call the home to reach the person they were interested in," Bailey says. "But then came cellphones and the Internet."

∽

Logging On, Tuning Out

It's no coincidence that hooking up has become popular with teenagers just as the Internet has become an integral part of their social lives. Until about five years ago, Internet meeting sites were mostly the domain of gay and lesbian high-school students looking for love, sex or someone to talk to. Today many heterosexual teenagers place personal profiles on meeting sites, usually without their parents' knowledge, and spend hours in chat rooms. (Two of the more popular sites—hotornot.com, with 4.3 million members, and facethejury.com, with 1.2 million—were both launched in late 2000.) And while gay high-school boys frequently advertise that they "don't do hookups" and are only looking for relationships, fewer straight teenagers make that claim—and many make it clear that they're looking for anything but commitment.

"Straight teens have abandoned the rituals of dating, while gay teens have taken them on," says Peter Ian Cummings, the editor of XY, a national magazine for young gay men. The Internet, Cummings says, has made it possible for heterosexual teenagers to act the way "most of straight society assumes gay men act."

The day I spent with Haris and Emcho, two varsity soccer players at a high school in the Chicago area, would seem to bear that out. I'd met Emcho (he asked me to use his nickname) on facethejury.com, where he typically receives high ratings. (Visitors to the site rate personal photos on a scale from 1 to 10, with anything under a 5 meaning, as one teenager told me, "that you should crawl into a hole and die.")

Tall and lanky, with brown hair and a crush-inducing smile, Emcho said there are benefits to being highly rated on a site like facethejury. There was the college girl online who invited Emcho and a friend over to a party at her apartment. "I was online writing my senior paper," Emcho said, "and this girl instant-messages me and says, 'Hey, I saw your picture on facethejury.'" She invited Emcho over that night. They had sex in her bathroom, Emcho told me, and met up a few more times, but he says he cut it off when she started talking about wanting to date him.

Emcho and Haris said they're both partial to "preppy suburban girls." As Haris put it, "City girls are cool, but suburban girls are crazy cool!" (Meaning, Haris explains, that suburban girls are "easier.") Recently, he and Emcho met up with two high-school girls. One girl offered to sneak them all into her house, where she and Emcho hooked up on the floor, while Haris and her friend used the closet.

With so many teenagers online willing to hook up, Emcho and Haris say there's no need to rush a relationship. "A lot of guys get in relationships just so they can get steady [expletive]," Haris told me. "But now that it's easy to get sex outside of relationships, guys don't need relationships."

Last year, there was one girl Emcho really liked who really liked him, but he decided to wait a year or two before beginning a relationship with her. "He's waiting until the well runs dry," Haris said with a smile. It didn't seem to occur to Emcho that the girl might not be available once he's ready.

James Hong, co-founder of the meeting and rating site hotornot.com, which is wildly popular among teenagers, knows that much of his demographic thinks like Emcho and Haris. He says his site purposefully doesn't advertise itself as a dating service (most of its members are under 24). "You'll never see the word 'dating' on our site, because that's much too serious for our demographic," he says. "There are obviously relationships that come from the site, but mostly I think it's a lot of hanging out and hooking up. This demographic doesn't want to appear like they're needy and looking for a relationship."

But the neediness comes through in other ways. Many teenagers are obsessed with how complete strangers view them, and they check their online ratings several times an hour. You have to show enough of your body to entice—washboard abs and cleavage are sure bets—but not enough to have your photo rejected by the site moderators. If your ratings climb high enough, the sites will often feature your profile in their "top girls" or "hottest guys" sections, making some high-school students feel like superstars.

Once there, you're likely to receive hundreds of adoring e-mail messages from teenagers around the country, and many local offers to hang out and hook up. For teenagers who already consider themselves attractive, the sites can be an ego boost. And for teenagers who aren't sure, the sites offer a chance—with the right picture—to feel wanted, too.

But if your ratings are only average, it can be tough. I spoke to several boys with low ratings who tried hard to sound unfazed, but underneath their nonchalance was an obvious hurt. One pouty, brown-haired sophomore in Boston with an average rating called facethejury.com a "whorehouse for people who hate themselves and the way they look, and search for affirmation from the outside." So why is he on it? "Boredom," he told me. "It's also entertaining in a perverse kind of way. I've had four highly overweight women in their late 20's ask to meet me."

There's something surreal about teenagers with online personal profiles and that's especially true when they're 13-year-olds, which is some of what you'll find on buddypic.com. Out of some 50,000 profiles, more than 4,000 are from baby-faced kids around the country. Some lift their shirts in their pictures, showing off their stomachs. Others make it clear what they aren't looking for. "LOTS of piercings, ugly . . . chicks, snitches, teacher's pets, stinky . . . chicks" reads one 13-year-old's "Dislikes" column. His "Likes" column is simpler: "Sexy body, Blonde, Blue eyes . . . good personality, willing to go out of their way to be with me."

Buddypic.com is careful to advertise itself as "fun, clean and real." But on facethejury, "adult" meeting sites are just a click away. The links are advertised alongside teenage profiles, which makes for some eerie echoes between the self-styled photos of teenage members—suggestively posed and airbrushed—and the longstanding conventions of adult erotica. For many teenage boys and some teenage girls, Internet porn, cybersex and real-time cam-to-cam connections exert a strong pull. As one Boston teenager told me, "Who needs the hassle of dating when I've got online porn?" Most of the boys I spoke to said they have access to Internet porn, and many said they started watching it regularly at 12, 13 or 14 years old. Some experts maintain that this kind of exposure is a lot more damaging than sneaking a peek at your dad's Playboy collection. "The Internet gives teen boys the idea that girls are interchangeable sexual objects at their disposal," says Lynn Ponton, a professor of psychiatry at the University of California at San Francisco and the author of "The Sex Lives of Teenagers." "So how can they ever be developmentally ready for a real-life relationship?"

✑

No Pain, All Gain?

Yet for all the resemblance of teenage hookup culture to a 70's singles bar, the old stigmas and prejudices haven't disappeared altogether. Most teenagers who engage in hookups still worry about being discreet. "If you're not careful, by lunch the next day at school, everyone will know," says Irene, the senior from the Chicago suburb. "Some people won't care, but others will, and if it happens too often, it will hurt your reputation."

And girls aren't the only ones who are worried. David, a boyish, brown-haired, 18-year-old varsity basketball player at an all-boys high school in Chicago, said the same thing. Like many male varsity athletes I spoke to, David says he isn't lacking for hookup possibilities. But he tries to be cautious. After all, too much hooking up can ruin any chances for a future relationship—and, like many teenagers, he holds out the possibility of dating if the "perfect" person comes along.

"I've got like five girls in my phone book I can call or text-message who will give it up to me," he says. "But I don't just hook up with anyone. You have to be careful. I have this huge crush on this girl who knows a lot of the girls I know, and I don't want her to find out I hook up a lot and think I'm dirty."

David isn't the only teenager who used the word "dirty" to describe hookups. Inherent in the thinking of many teenagers is the belief that hooking up, while definitely a mainstream activity, is still one that's best kept quiet. And underneath the teenage bravado I heard so often are mixed feelings about an activity that can leave them feeling depressed, confused and guilty.

As much as teenagers like to talk a good game, hooking up isn't nearly as seamless as they'd like it to be, and there are many ways it can go wrong. At the Valentine's Day gathering, Irene and her friends laid out the unwritten etiquette of teenage hookups: if you want it to be a hookup relationship, then you don't call the person for anything except plans to hook up. You don't invite them out with you. You don't call just to say hi. You don't confuse the matter. You just keep it purely sexual, and that way people don't have mixed expectations, and no one gets hurt.

But, invariably, people do. Many teenagers told me they were hurt by hookups—usually because they expected or hoped for more. But they often blamed themselves for letting their emotions get the best of them. The hookups weren't the problem. They were the problem.

When Irene was 15, she hooked up for a while with a boy ("We basically became friends with benefits," she says) who never came around to asking her out officially, as Irene secretly hoped he would. In the end, she was devastated. "Since then, I've become really good at keeping my emotions in check," she says. "I can hook up with a guy and not fall for him."

In fact, many teenagers opt for hookups after a romantic relationship has soured. Boys are less likely to admit this, although Jesse, from New England, isn't afraid to. "I'd usually hook up because I got my heart broken by a girl, and I didn't want to feel like I had lost everything," he said. "So I'd hear that a girl was interested in me, I'd get a ride to her house, we'd hang out and mess around some and I'd leave. Afterward I'd feel dumb, like it wasn't needed. But before you do it, you feel like it's definitely needed."

Melissa, a senior in a high school north of Boston, confessed she'd never had a good relationship. "Dating causes pain," she told me when I first communicated with her online. "It's easier not to get attached. And I realized that if it's O.K. for guys to play the field and have sex with 28,000 people, I should be able to, also."

The day we met in person, Melissa was in a foul mood. Her "friend with benefits" had just broken up with her. "How is that even possible?" she said, sitting, shoulders slumped, in a booth at a diner. "The point of having a friend with benefits is that you won't get broken up with, you won't get hurt. He told me online that he met a girl that he really likes, so now, of course, we can't hook up anymore."

Melissa and the boy used to meet up about once a week. "To be honest, we don't even really like hanging out together," she told me. They met only to have sex. "I go to his house, we sit there and talk for two minutes, then we go at it. Then we sit there again for about 10 minutes, and I go home." (Clearly, for some teenagers, "friends with benefits" is a misnomer. Take away the sex, and they probably wouldn't hang out at all.) Melissa forwarded me one of her online conversations with the boy:

BOY: What are you doing other than not talking to me?

MELISSA: Nothing at all. . . .

BOY: Wow, you're as bored as I am?!? . . .

MELISSA: Booooooooored.

BOY: lol. Yup. Life is good. lol.

MELISSA: Freakin' fantastic. Lemme tell ya.

BOY: I wish you lived like next door. . . . It would be so much easier . . . . Like I don't know about you, but I wanna [expletive].

MELISSA: U always wanna [expletive].

BOY: True.

MELISSA: Haha.

BOY: But that's cuz we've been talking about it and haven't done it. It's built up.

MELISSA: That's bc u haven't picked me up yet silly . . . Well I'm gonna go lay down. U know my number and where I live if things work out soon.

BOY: Hey wait. If I can do you wanna come over?

MELISSA: Sure. So just call me.

BOY: Do you have condoms?

MELISSA: Yes dear.

BOY: Hold on.

MELISSA: I'm holding.

BOY: I can come get you right now if you want.

MELISSA: Um gimme a sec. . . .

BOY: O.K.?? I'll come get you now if you're ready. . . .

MELISSA: But I'm gonna be boring tonite . . . and I'm just telling u I'm not in the mood for nething but str8-up sex.

"I have my friends for my emotional needs, so I don't need that from the guy I'm having sex with," Melissa explained at the time, sounding very much like the "Sex and the City" character Samantha Jones. So why, now that the boy had "broken up" with her, was she feeling so depressed? "It's really stupid, I know," she said, shaking her head. "It's kind of ironic, isn't it? I try to set up a situation where I won't get hurt, and I still manage to get hurt."

On the plus side, there's a new boy who's interested in her. "Problem is, he's annoying," Melissa said. "I liked him before we hooked up. Now I can't stand him. He's so needy, and he won't stop calling." Melissa said she was going to wait until after Valentine's Day to tell him she was not interested. "I want a Valentine's Day present," she said. "After that, I'm just not going to answer my phone." (As it turned out, they broke up before Valentine's Day.)

Like other high-school girls I talked to, Melissa says she doesn't see why boys get to have "all the fun," although during the few months we communicated, it was clear that Melissa's hookups rarely brought her joy. She complained often about being depressed, and her hookups, which she hoped would make her feel better, usually left her feeling worse. But a few days after a hookup, she would have forgotten that they tended to make her miserable, and would tell me excitedly about a new boy she was planning to meet. When that boy failed to show or called to say he was running an hour late, Melissa's spirits would sink—again.

But when I asked Melissa whether she thought hookups worked equally well for girls and boys, she surprised me with her answer. "It's equal," she said. "Everyone is using each other. That's fair."

CHRISTIAN J. MATUSCHEK, *Al lado del Mercado de Sant Josep, Las Ramblas, Barcelona.* C-print, 2005. © Christian J. Matuschek/www.foto-lounge.de.

Girls Just Want to Have Fun?

Ashley, an outgoing junior who is friends with Jesse, met her current boyfriend at a concert in her hometown. Her parents initially balked at the age difference (she's 17, he's 21), but she was quick to reassure them. "People assume that if the guy's older, he's the one making all the moves and using the girl," Ashley told me. "But trust me, I was definitely the aggressor. I got into his pants. He didn't get into mine."

The question of who's in control and who is getting the short end of the stick—whether in dating or hookups—kept cropping up. "Guys who are 16, 17, 18, they're just totally clueless," said Irene, the 17-year-old from the upper-middle-class Chicago suburb. "They'll be like, 'I kind of want you, but now that I have you, I don't really want you anymore, so maybe I should break up with you and have you as a friend with benefits.'" Irene, like many of her high-school friends, has no problem meeting boys who are in college—and the implication is that maybe they offer something high-school boys don't.

So who's hooking up with guys in high school? Freshmen and sophomore girls. "Some senior girls won't even look at us," said one high-school senior from Glenview, another suburb of Chicago, "but underclassmen, they look at us like we're gods. Which, of course, we are, so it works out well." He told me that he regularly hooks up with a sophomore from another school, but he doesn't take her out with his friends. "Until I find someone special, I'm playing the ballfield."

While many girls insist they receive sexual attention during hookups, just as many boys say hookups are mostly about pleasing the guy. Michael Milburn, professor of psychology at the University of Massachusetts, Boston, and co-author of the book "Sexual Intelligence," an examination of sexual beliefs and behaviors in America, says that the boys' take is more accurate. "Most of the time, it's the younger girl performing fellatio on the older boy, with the boy doing very little to pleasure the girl," Milburn says. Some girls told me that guys think it's "nasty" to perform oral sex on a girl. So a lot of girls will just perform oral sex on the guy "and not expect anything in return, because she'll know that he probably thinks it's gross," Irene told me. But her friend Andi pointed out that many girls are themselves insecure about receiving oral sex; they'd rather just have intercourse.

There's a firm belief among many experts on teenage sex that girls, however much they protest to the contrary, are not getting as much pleasure out of hookups as they claim. I was invited to a high school in Boston, where I met with a group of seniors who were debating this very issue. I relayed a conversation I'd had with Marline Pearson, a sociologist who has developed a school curriculum for teenagers called Love U2: Getting Smarter About Relationships, Sex, Babies and Marriage. "In some ways," Pearson said, "I think girls had more power in the 1960's, when they said: 'O.K., you want to get to first base? This is what you have to do.' Today it's: 'O.K., you want to get to third base? Come over.' I'm a feminist, but I think we've put girls back in the dark ages, with very little power."

One girl, a brown-haired senior who says she sometimes hooks up with guys she meets through friends, doesn't feel that she's in the dark ages, or that she's powerless. "If I ask a guy to come over to my house and hook up," she said, "I'm the one benefiting, because I'm the one who wants to . . . . It's not just about pleasing the guy."

Her friend, a well-spoken senior with shaggy brown hair, faded jeans and a T-shirt with the sleeves rolled up to her shoulders, listened quietly as her friends defended a woman's right to hook up. Finally, and with some hesitation, she voiced an unpopular opinion among her friends.

"I feel like women have less power today," she said. "It's not just that the guy often doesn't respect the girl or the girl's sexuality, but the girl sometimes doesn't really respect and validate herself. I have a friend who's

20, and he goes on the Internet and meets 16-year-old girls from the suburbs." He drives out there, she performs oral sex on him and he drives home. "Who has the power there? I think that a lot of the times girls are really self-destructive."

"Well," the first girl said, slightly annoyed, "I don't see why a guy can have a random hookup with a girl and no one questions his motives, but when a girl does it, there's this assumption that she's a girl, so she automatically wants more out of a hookup. When I hook up, I don't want more, and it's not self-destructive. And I enjoy it."

Dr. Drew Pinsky, co-host of "Loveline," a popular, nationally syndicated radio program that has some two million listeners and that was featured on MTV, doesn't buy it. "It's all bravado," he says. "Teens are unwittingly swept up in the social mores of the moment, and it's certainly not some alternative they're choosing to keep from getting hurt emotionally. The fact is, girls don't enjoy hookups nearly as much as boys, no matter what they say at the time. They're only doing it because that's what the boys want."

Wendy Shalit, whose book, "A Return to Modesty," embodies what has been termed "the new chastity," also says she believes that girls are being manipulated, but by a society that tries to convince them that they should act like boys, turning sexual modesty into a sign of weakness or repression—something young women are taught to be embarrassed about. "In the age of the hookup," Shalit writes, "young women confess their romantic hopes in hushed tones, as if harboring some terrible secret."

Those who embrace an abstinence-only sex-education program try to influence teenage behavior by explaining that sexual pleasure requires mutual respect and security. Sarah LaBella works for CareFirst Prevention Services, a group that has taught in junior high and high schools since 1998. One gray, frigid February afternoon, I sat in on a class she was giving to teenage girls in an unremarkable suburban Illinois high school with a view of Dunkin' Donuts.

"Do you want to know the difference between girls and guys?" LaBella asked. Some of the girls listened intently, others doodled or stared blankly out the window. "Guys are like microwaves. You hit the right button, and they're ready to go. We, on the other hand, are ovens. It takes a little while for us to get heated up. You have to preheat us."

Most of the girls smiled, and several laughed. LaBella smiled, too, because if you can make teenagers laugh (with you, not at you), you might get them to actually listen. LaBella, who typically delivers her message to coed classes, knows that some teenagers tune her out between the S.T.D. slide show and the claim that "the best sex" happens only within marriage. But she says that many teenagers listen intently, as if hearing some life-altering wisdom. "We know that most teenagers are never really taught what's involved in making a healthy relationship," she told me after class.

"They're trying to build relationships out of hookups or casual sex, and those relationships do not tend to be fruitful ones."

But are teenagers—and teenage girls in particular—always ill served by choosing hookups over relationships? Jeanette May, co-founder of the Coalition for Positive Sexuality, a grass-roots advocacy and educational organization based in Washington that argues that teenagers should be supported in making their own decisions about safe sex and their sexuality, is one of the few adults I spoke to who doesn't think so. "Often, I think girls, if they are getting as much out of it as the guys, are better served by having sex for their pleasure, without a lot of emotional attachment," she says. "Because they would feel more empowered to practice safe sex, use birth control and avoid sexual interactions that would not benefit them. When girls think they are in love or in a relationship that will lead to love, they're more easily manipulated."

Few adults would take that line. Regardless of which end of the political spectrum they find themselves on, parents and teen-sexuality experts tend to agree on one thing: hooking up is a bad thing for teenagers. They insist that it's bad emotionally and potentially bad physically. Female adolescents ages 15 to 19 have the highest incidence of both gonorrhea and chlamydia, and according to the latest C.D.C. figures, 48 percent of new S.T.D. cases reported in 2000 occurred among 15- to 24-year-olds. Many of the teenagers I talked to told me that no one they know uses condoms during oral sex, only during intercourse.

"Both conservatives and liberals have their respective blinders on when talking about teen sexuality," says Milburn, co-author of "Sexual Intelligence." "I can think of nothing more important than getting in schools and talking about sexual intelligence and healthy relationships, but most conservatives don't want an open and honest discussion about teen sexuality, and they oppose any conversation that doesn't focus on abstinence until marriage. And many liberals will resist any discussion that might touch on the negative consequences of unbridled sexuality. The conversation we need to have with teens is: 'What's the role that sexuality should play in an emotionally healthy person's life? What are the different ways that people can be sexual? What are the potential dangers?'"

◌৸

It's Saturday Night and . . .

For all the efforts to make teenagers aware of the dangers of hookups, many of the high-school students I spoke to shrugged off the idea that hooking up is ultimately a bad thing. As they see it, if they're not going to marry for another 10 years, why not focus on other things (friendships, schoolwork, sports) in high school? And if they're not hurting anyone and not getting anyone pregnant, where is the harm in a little casual fun? The truth is, teenagers may spend less of their time hooking up than adults think they do—for many of them, friendships have become the most important part of their social lives. Kate, Caity and Adam (the group I first met at Hooters with Jesse) often spend weekend nights hanging out together and talking about sex in ways many adults would find difficult to do themselves.

I met up with them again one Saturday evening, as they lounged around a friend's living room. No one was paying much attention to the music video playing on the big-screen TV. Instead, they spent the night talking about music, soccer, their town (and why it's better than the next town over), oral sex (why some people can't do it well), masturbation (whether girls do it, and if so, whether they do it in the shower) and anything else that sprang to mind.

But the big news was that Kate still hadn't kissed her boyfriend. "We talk about it all the time, but it's like whenever we get to a point when we're going to, we don't," Kate said. "I feel like I'm going to have to make the first move, and I don't do first moves!"

"Why don't girls make first moves more often?" asked Brian, Jesse's 16-year-old friend. "It's really annoying."

"Oh, they do if they're drunk!" said Adam (the boy who likes to lift his shirt), sitting on the couch and strumming a guitar.

A lot had happened since I first met Jesse. Through a friend, Adam met a girl he actually would date, except she lived too far away. The biggest development, though, was that Caity and Adam had made out at a concert in front of all their friends. "It was really disgusting," Jesse said. "They did it right in front of everybody. And it was long." Both Adam and Caity dismissed it as a momentary lapse. "It just happened," Caity said. "Nothing serious," Adam said.

The two got to only first base (kissing), which is about the only base that anyone can agree on anymore. "I don't understand the base system at all," Jesse said, lying on the floor and staring at the ceiling. "If making out is first base, what's second base?"

"We need to establish an international base system," Brian said. "Because right now, frankly, no one knows what's up with the bases. And that's a problem."

Jesse nodded in agreement. "First base is obviously kissing," Brian said.

"Obviously," Jesse said.

"But here's the twist," Brian said. "Historically, second base was breasts. But I don't think second base is breasts anymore. I think that's just a given part of first base. I mean, how can you make out without copping a feel?"

"True," Jesse said. "And if third base is oral, what's second base?"

"How does this work for girls?" asked Ashley, the 17-year-old junior. "I mean, are the bases what's been done to you, or what you've done?"

"If it's what base you've gone to with a girl, you go by whoever had more done," Jesse told her.

"But we're girls," Ashley said. "So we've got on bases with guys?"

"Right, but it doesn't matter," Jesse said. "It's not what base you've had done to you, it's what bases you get to."

Kate shook her head. "I'm totally lost."

"See how complicated this is?" Brian said. "Now if someone asks you, 'So, how far did you get with her?' you have to say, 'Well, how do your bases go?'"

Suggestions for Discussion

1. Discuss the difference between today's "hookups" and yesterday's "dating." What reasons does Denizet-Lewis cite for this trend?

2. What are the emotional implications of hookups versus relationships? Do the emotional responses vary and differ between the sexes?

3. What role has the Internet played in changing dating and relationship rituals? Do you see this as problematic? Why or why not?

Suggestion for Writing

Choose one of the questions above and explore the idea in an essay.

CARSON McCULLERS

Loneliness . . . an American Malady

Carson McCullers (1917–1967), a Southern writer, was awarded Guggenheim Fellowships in 1942 and in 1946. Her published works include *The Heart Is a Lonely Hunter* (1940), *Reflections in a Golden Eye* (1941), *The Member of the Wedding* (1946), *The Ballad of the Sad Café* (1951), and *Clock without Hands* (1961). This excerpt from *The Mortgaged Heart* (1971) suggests that the way by which we master loneliness is "to belong to something larger and more powerful than the weak, lonely self."

This city, New York—consider the people in it, the eight million of us. An English friend of mine, when asked why he lived in New York City, said that he liked it here because he could be so alone. While it was my friend's desire to be alone, the aloneness of many Americans who live in cities is an involuntary and fearful thing. It has been said that loneliness is the great American malady. What is the nature of this loneliness? It would seem essentially to be a quest for identity.

To the spectator, the amateur philosopher, no motive among the complex ricochets of our desires and rejections seems stronger or more enduring than the will of the individual to claim his identity and belong. From infancy to death, the human being is obsessed by these dual motives. During our first weeks of life, the question of identity shares urgency with the need for milk. The baby reaches for his toes, then explores the bars of his crib; again and again he compares the difference between his own body and the objects around him, and in the wavering, infant eyes there comes a pristine wonder.

Consciousness of self is the first abstract problem that the human being solves. Indeed, it is this self-consciousness that removes us from lower animals. This primitive grasp of identity develops with constantly shifting emphasis through all our years. Perhaps maturity is simply the history of those mutations that reveal to the individual the relation between himself and the world in which he finds himself.

After the first establishment of identity there comes the imperative need to lose this new-found sense of separateness and to belong to something larger and more powerful than the weak, lonely self. The sense of moral isolation is intolerable to us.

In *The Member of the Wedding* the lonely 12-year-old girl, Frankie Addams, articulates this universal need: "The trouble with me is that for a long time I have just been an *I* person. All people belong to a *We* except me. Not to belong to a *We* makes you too lonesome."

Love is the bridge that leads from the *I* sense to the *We*, and there is a paradox about personal love. Love of another individual opens a new relation between the personality and the world. The lover responds in a new way to nature and may even write poetry. Love is affirmation; it motivates the *yes* responses and the sense of wider communication. Love casts out fear, and in the security of this togetherness we find contentment, courage. We no longer fear the age-old haunting questions: "Who am I?" "Why am I?" "Where am I going?"—and having cast out fear, we can be honest and charitable.

For fear is a primary source of evil. And when the question "Who am I?" recurs and is unanswered, then fear and frustration project a negative attitude. The bewildered soul can answer only: "Since I do not understand 'Who I am,' I only know what I am *not*." The corollary of this emotional incertitude is snobbism, intolerance, and racial hate. The xenophobic individual can only reject and destroy, as the xenophobic nation inevitably makes war.

The loneliness of Americans does not have its source in xenophobia; as a nation we are an outgoing people, reaching always for immediate contacts, further experience. But we tend to seek out things as individuals, alone.

The European, secure in his family ties and rigid class loyalties, knows little of the moral loneliness that is native to us Americans. While the European artists tend to form groups or aesthetic schools, the American artist is the eternal maverick—not only from society in the way of all creative minds, but within the orbit of his own art.

Thoreau took to the woods to seek the ultimate meaning of his life. His creed was simplicity and his *modus vivendi* the deliberate stripping of external life to the Spartan necessities in order that his inward life could freely flourish. His objective, as he put it, was to back the world into a corner. And in that way did he discover "What a man thinks of himself, that it is which determines, or rather indicates, his fate."

On the other hand, Thomas Wolfe turned to the city, and in his wanderings around New York he continued his frenetic and lifelong search for the lost brother, the magic door. He too backed the world into a corner, and as he passed among the city's millions, returning their stares, he experienced "That silent meeting [that] is the summary of all the meetings of men's lives."

Whether in the pastoral joys of country life or in the labyrinthine city, we Americans are always seeking. We wander, question. But the answer waits in each separate heart—the answer of our own identity and the way by which we can master loneliness and feel that at last we belong.

Suggestion for Discussion

How does the author establish the connections between loneliness and identity? Between *I* and *We*? Between lack of a sense of identity and fear? Between fear and hatred or destruction?

Suggestions for Writing

1. Develop or challenge Thoreau's belief, "What a man thinks of himself, that it is which determines, or rather indicates, his fate."

2. Develop an essay in which you argue that country life is or is not more conducive to the development of a sense of self than city life.

Xenophobia—
abnormal fear of
that which is foreign
esp. foreign peoples.

FICTION

KATE CHOPIN

A Respectable Woman

Kate Chopin (1851–1904) was an early feminist who did not begin to write until her late thirties. Her first novel, *At Fault* (1890), was followed by two volumes of short stories, *Bayou Folk* (1894) and *A Night in Acadie* (1897), and her masterpiece, *The Awakening* (1899). The "respectable woman" in this piece, published in 1894, undergoes a metamorphosis after her earlier indifference to her husband's friend.

Mrs. Baroda was a little provoked to learn that her husband expected his friend, Gouvernail, up to spend a week or two on the plantation.

They had entertained a good deal during the winter; much of the time had also been passed in New Orleans in various forms of mild dissipation. She was looking forward to a period of unbroken rest, now, and undisturbed tête-à-tête with her husband, when he informed her that Gouvernail was coming up to stay a week or two.

This was a man she had heard much of but never seen. He had been her husband's college friend; was now a journalist, and in no sense a society man or "a man about town," which were, perhaps, some of the reasons she had never met him. But she had unconsciously formed an image of him in her mind. She pictured him tall, slim, cynical; with eyeglasses, and his hands in his pockets; and she did not like him. Gouvernail was slim enough, but he wasn't very tall nor very cynical; neither did he wear eyeglasses nor carry his hands in his pockets. And she rather liked him when he first presented himself.

But why she liked him she could not explain satisfactorily to herself when she partly attempted to do so. She could discover in him none of those brilliant and promising traits which Gaston, her husband, had often assured her that he possessed. On the contrary, he sat rather mute and receptive before her chatty eagerness to make him feel at home and in face of Gaston's frank and wordy hospitality. His manner was as courteous toward her as the most exacting woman could require; but he made no direct appeal to her approval or even esteem.

Once settled at the plantation he seemed to like to sit upon the wide portico in the shade of one of the big Corinthian pillars, smoking his cigar lazily and listening attentively to Gaston's experience as a sugar planter.

"This is what I call living," he would utter with deep satisfaction, as the air that swept across the sugar field caressed him with its warm and scented velvety touch. It pleased him also to get on familiar terms with the big dogs that came about him, rubbing themselves sociably against his legs. He did not care to fish, and displayed no eagerness to go out and kill grosbecs when Gaston proposed doing so.

Gouvernail's personality puzzled Mrs. Baroda, but she liked him. Indeed, he was a lovable, inoffensive fellow. After a few days, when she could understand him no better than at first, she gave over being puzzled and remained piqued. In this mood she left her husband and her guest, for the most part, alone together. Then finding that Gouvernail took no manner of exception to her action, she imposed her society upon him, accompanying him in his idle strolls to the mill and walks along the batture. She persistently sought to penetrate the reserve in which he had unconsciously enveloped himself.

"When is he going—your friend?" she one day asked her husband. "For my part, he tires me frightfully."

"Not for a week yet, dear. I can't understand; he gives you no trouble."

"No. I should like him better if he did; if he were more like others, and I had to plan somewhat for his comfort and enjoyment."

Gaston took his wife's pretty face between his hands and looked tenderly and laughingly into her troubled eyes. They were making a bit of toilet sociably together in Mrs. Baroda's dressing-room.

"You are full of surprises, ma belle," he said to her. "Even I can never count upon how you are going to act under given conditions." He kissed her and turned to fasten his cravat before the mirror.

"Here you are," he went on, "taking poor Gouvernail seriously and making a commotion over him, the last thing he would desire or expect."

"Commotion!" she hotly resented. "Nonsense! How can you say such a thing? Commotion, indeed! But, you know, you said he was clever."

"So he is. But the poor fellow is run down by overwork now. That's why I asked him here to take a rest."

"You used to say he was a man of ideas," she retorted, unconciliated. "I expected him to be interesting, at least. I'm going to the city in the morning to have my spring gowns fitted. Let me know when Mr. Gouvernail is gone; I shall be at my Aunt Octavie's."

That night she went and sat alone upon a bench that stood beneath a live oak tree at the edge of the gravel walk.

She had never known her thoughts or her intentions to be so confused. She could gather nothing from them but the feeling of a distinct necessity to quit her home in the morning.

Mrs. Baroda heard footsteps crunching the gravel; but could discern in the darkness only the approaching red point of a lighted cigar. She knew it was Gouvernail, for her husband did not smoke. She hoped to remain unnoticed, but her white gown revealed her to him. He threw away his cigar and seated himself upon the bench beside her, without a suspicion that she might object to his presence.

"Your husband told me to bring this to you, Mrs. Baroda," he said, handing her a filmy, white scarf with which she sometimes enveloped her head and shoulders. She accepted the scarf from him with a murmur of thanks, and let it lie in her lap.

He made some commonplace observation upon the baneful effect of the night air at that season. Then as his gaze reached out into the darkness, he murmured, half to himself:

"'Night of south winds—night of the large few stars!
Still nodding night—'"

She made no reply to this apostrophe to the night, which indeed, was not addressed to her.

Gouvernail was in no sense a diffident man, for he was not a self-conscious one. His periods of reserve were not constitutional, but the result of moods. Sitting there beside Mrs. Baroda, his silence melted for the time.

He talked freely and intimately in a low, hesitating drawl that was not unpleasant to hear. He talked of the old college days when he and Gaston had been a good deal to each other; of the days of keen and blind ambitions and large intentions. Now there was left with him, at least, a philosophic acquiescence to the existing order—only a desire to be permitted to exist, with now and then a little whiff of genuine life, such as he was breathing now.

Her mind only vaguely grasped what he was saying. Her physical being was for the moment predominant. She was not thinking of his words, only drinking in the tones of his voice. She wanted to reach out her hand in the darkness and touch him with the sensitive tips of her fingers upon the face or the lips. She wanted to draw close to him and whisper against his cheek—she did not care what—as she might have done if she had not been a respectable woman.

The stronger the impulse grew to bring herself near him, the further, in fact, did she draw away from him. As soon as she could do so without an appearance of too great rudeness, she rose and left him there alone.

Before she reached the house, Gouvernail had lighted a fresh cigar and ended his apostrophe to the night.

Mrs. Baroda was greatly tempted that night to tell her husband—who was also her friend—of this folly that had seized her. But she did not yield to the temptation. Beside being a respectable woman she was a very sensible one; and she knew there are some battles in life which a human being must fight alone.

When Gaston arose in the morning, his wife had already departed. She had taken an early train to the city. She did not return till Gouvernail was gone from under her roof.

There was some talk of having him back during the summer that followed. That is, Gaston greatly desired it; but this desire yielded to his wife's strenuous opposition.

However, before the year ended, she proposed, wholly from herself, to have Gouvernail visit them again. Her husband was surprised and delighted with the suggestion coming from her.

"I am glad, chère amie, to know that you have finally overcome your dislike for him; truly he did not deserve it."

"Oh," she told him, laughingly, after pressing a long, tender kiss upon his lips, "I have overcome everything! you will see. This time I shall be very nice to him."

Suggestions for Discussion

1. How do you learn that Mrs. Baroda is ambivalent about Gouvernail?
2. Why do you think Mrs. Baroda left for the city? What precipitated the move?
3. What details suggest to you that this story was written in an earlier era?
4. What is the significance of the title? Relate it to the theme of the story. Is it used ironically?
5. What are you led to surmise is the relationship of Mrs. Baroda to her husband?
6. What do you think will happen on Gouvernail's next visit? How are you prepared for it?

Suggestion for Writing

Write an essay on Question 4 or 6 above.

POETRY

RUDYARD KIPLING

If...

Joseph Rudyard Kipling (1865–1936) was a novelist, short-story writer, poet, and journalist who won the Nobel Prize for literature in 1907. The Indian-born author is widely known for his children's adventure tales, including *The Jungle Book* (1894), *Kim* (1901), and *Just So Stories* (1902). However, Kipling's reputation has suffered because of his writings about British colonialism, especially his infamous poem *White Man's Burden* (1899). For many critics, foremost among them George Orwell, that poem served to bolster racist attitudes towards nonwhite peoples and advocated the conquest of the developing world by European and American armies. Kipling's defenders argue that his works are brilliantly written, invaluable historical chronicles of life in India during the Victorian period, and more critical and satirical of imperial aims than his arch conservative reputation suggests. Despite Kipling's controversial reputation, his poem *If...* (1895) was voted the most beloved poem in Great Britain one hundred years later, in 1995.

If you can keep your head when all about you
Are losing theirs and blaming it on you,
If you can trust yourself when all men doubt you
But make allowance for their doubting too,
If you can wait and not be tired by waiting,
Or being lied about, don't deal in lies,
Or being hated, don't give way to hating,
And yet don't look too good, nor talk too wise:

If you can dream—and not make dreams your master,
If you can think—and not make thoughts your aim;
If you can meet with Triumph and Disaster
And treat those two impostors just the same;
If you can bear to hear the truth you've spoken
Twisted by knaves to make a trap for fools,
Or watch the things you gave your life to, broken,
And stoop and build 'em up with worn-out tools:

If you can make one heap of all your winnings
And risk it all on one turn of pitch-and-toss,
And lose, and start again at your beginnings
And never breath a word about your loss;
If you can force your heart and nerve and sinew
To serve your turn long after they are gone,
And so hold on when there is nothing in you
Except the Will which says to them: "Hold on!"

If you can talk with crowds and keep your virtue,
Or walk with kings—nor lose the common touch,
If neither foes nor loving friends can hurt you;
If all men count with you, but none too much,
If you can fill the unforgiving minute
With sixty seconds' worth of distance run,
Yours is the Earth and everything that's in it,
And—which is more—you'll be a Man, my son!

Suggestions for Discussion

1. How does Kipling want us to respond to personal disappointment and tragedy? What is the value of this approach? The limitation?

2. How effective is Kipling's pairing of ideas as a poetic and rhetorical technique? Does it make the poem more convincing than it would be otherwise?

3. Critics of this poem see it as promoting an imperialist mindset. What lines in the poem might be imperialistic? What lines might be interpreted differently? Explain.

4. Synthesis: Compare and contrast the philosophy expressed in *If...* to the political views advanced in Kipling's highly controversial poem *White Man's Burden.*

Suggestion for Writing

Synthesis: The film *If...* (1968) satirizes the effect poems such as this had on British educational philosophy and the shaping of the British boarding school system. Watch the film, and consider whether the school administrators are using appropriate means to instill Kipling's values in the students. What role does the film's 1960s counterculture attitude play in the way you view Kipling's Victorian values? Write a paper about the differing values and their interaction in this film. Use Kipling's poem as a source for your argument.

༒༒༒

T. S. ELIOT

The Love Song of J. Alfred Prufrock

Thomas Stearns Eliot (1888–1965) was born in St. Louis, was educated at Harvard University, and studied in Paris and Oxford. He settled in England in 1914 and became a British subject in 1927. His most influential poem, *The Waste Land*, was published in 1922, followed by *The Hollow Men* (1925), *Poems: 1909–1925* (1925), and *Poems: 1909–1935* (1936). His criticism includes *The Use of Poetry and the Use of Criticism* (1933), *Essays Ancient and Modern* (1936), *Notes Toward the Definition of Culture* (1948), and *To Criticize the Critic* (1965). His best-known poetic dramas are *Murder in the Cathedral* (1935), *The Family Reunion* (1939), and *The Cocktail Party* (1950). This dramatic monologue was published in 1917.

> *S'io credesse che mia risposta fosse*
> *A persona che mai tornasse al mondo,*
> *Questa fiamma staria senza piu scosse.*
> *Ma perciocche giammai di questo fondo*
> *Non torno vivo alcun, s'i'odo il vero,*
> *Senza tema d'infamia ti rispondo.*

> ["If I believed that my answer would be to one who would ever return to the world, this flame would shake no more; but since no one ever returns alive from this depth, if what I hear is true, I answer you without fear of infamy."
> —Dante's Inferno, XXVII, 61–66]

Let us go then, you and I,
When the evening is spread out against the sky
Like a patient etherised upon a table;
Let us go, through certain half-deserted streets,
The muttering retreats

Of restless nights in one-night cheap hotels
And sawdust restaurants with oyster-shells:
Streets that follow like a tedious argument
Of insidious intent
To lead you to an overwhelming question . . .
Oh, do not ask, "What is it?"
Let us go and make our visit.

In the room the women come and go
Talking of Michelangelo.

The yellow fog that rubs its back upon the window-panes,
The yellow smoke that rubs its muzzle on the window-panes
Licked its tongue into the corners of the evening,
Lingered upon the pools that stand in drains,
Let fall upon its back the soot that falls from chimneys,
Slipped by the terrace, made a sudden leap,
And seeing that it was a soft October night,
Curled once about the house, and fell asleep.

And indeed there will be time
For the yellow smoke that slides along the street,
Rubbing its back upon the window-panes;
There will be time, there will be time
To prepare a face to meet the faces that you meet;
There will be time to murder and create,
And time for all the works and days of hands
That lift and drop a question on your plate;
Time for you and time for me,
And time yet for a hundred indecisions,
And for a hundred visions and revisions,
Before the taking of a toast and tea.

In the room the women come and go
Talking of Michelangelo.

And indeed there will be time
To wonder, "Do I dare?" and, "Do I dare?"
Time to turn back and descend the stair,
With a bald spot in the middle of my hair—
[They will say: "How his hair is growing thin!"]
My morning coat, my collar mounting firmly to the chin,
My necktie rich and modest, but asserted by a simple pin—
[They will say: "But how his arms and legs are thin!"]
Do I dare
Disturb the universe?
In a minute there is time
For decisions and revisions which a minute will reverse.

For I have known them all already, known them all:—
Have known the evenings, mornings, afternoons,
I have measured out my life with coffee spoons;
I know the voices dying with a dying fall
Beneath the music from a farther room.
So how should I presume?

And I have known the eyes already, known them all—
The eyes that fix you in a formulated phrase,
And when I am formulated, sprawling on a pin,
When I am pinned and wriggling on the wall,
Then how should I begin
To spit out all the butt-ends of my days and ways?
    And how should I presume?

And I have known the arms already, known them all—
Arms that are braceleted and white and bare
[But in the lamplight, downed with light brown hair!]
Is it perfume from a dress
That makes me so digress?
Arms that lie along a table, or wrap about a shawl.
    And should I then presume?
    And how should I begin?

Shall I say, I have gone at dusk through narrow streets
And watched the smoke that rises from the pipes
Of lonely men in shirt-sleeves, leaning out of windows? . . .
    I should have been a pair of ragged claws
Scuttling across the floors of silent seas.

And the afternoon, the evening, sleeps so peacefully!
Smoothed by long fingers,
Asleep . . . tired . . . or it malingers,
Stretched on the floor, here beside you and me.
Should I, after tea and cakes and ices,
Have the strength to force the moment to its crisis?
But though I have wept and fasted, wept and prayed,
Though I have seen my head [grown slightly bald] brought in upon a platter,
I am no prophet—and here's no great matter;
I have seen the moment of my greatness flicker,
And I have seen the eternal Footman hold my coat, and snicker,
And in short, I was afraid.

And would it have been worth it, after all,
After the cups, the marmalade, the tea,
Among the porcelain, among some talk of you and me,
Would it have been worth while,
To have bitten off the matter with a smile,
To have squeezed the universe into a ball
To roll it toward some overwhelming question,
To say: "I am Lazarus, come from the dead.
Come back to tell you all, I shall tell you all"—
If one, settling a pillow by her head,

Should say: "That is not what I meant at all.
That is not it, at all."

And would it have been worth it, after all,
Would it have been worth while,
After the sunsets and the dooryards and the sprinkled streets,
After the novels, after the teacups, after the skirts that trail along the floor—
And this, and so much more?—
It is impossible to say just what I mean!
But as if a magic lantern threw the nerves in patterns on a screen:
Would it have been worth while
If one, settling a pillow or throwing off a shawl,
And turning toward the window, should say:
"That is not it at all,
That is not what I meant, at all."

No! I am not Prince Hamlet, nor was meant to be;
Am an attendant lord, one that will do
To swell a progress, start a scene or two,
Advise the prince; no doubt, an easy tool,
Deferential, glad to be of use,
Politic, cautious, and meticulous;
Full of high sentence, but a bit obtuse;
At times, indeed, almost ridiculous—
Almost, at times, the Fool.

I grow old . . . I grow old . . .
I shall wear the bottoms of my trousers rolled.

Shall I part my hair behind? Do I dare to eat a peach?
I shall wear white flannel trousers, and walk upon the beach.
I have heard the mermaids singing, each to each.

I do not think that they will sing to me.

I have seen them riding seaward on the waves
Combing the white hair of the waves blown back
When the wind blows the water white and black.

We have lingered in the chambers of the sea
By sea-girls wreathed with seaweed red and brown
Till human voices wake us, and we drown.

Suggestions for Discussion

1. Who are "you and I"?

2. What evidence can you find in the structural development of the poem to support the view that one self in the dramatic monologue acts out the conflict

and the other assumes the role of observer? Cite lines from the poem in which shifts in mood and tone occur. How does the poem achieve dramatic unity?

3. Contrast the images of Prufrock's interior world with those of the external world. How does their recurring juxtaposition illuminate the doubleness of the speaker and contribute to tone? How is sensory experience used to convey the circularity of the dialogue with self? Why are the images of the etherized patient, the staircase, winding streets, cat, and fog especially appropriate dramatic symbols of the speaker's state of mind? Trace the use of sea imagery. How does it function differently in the metaphor of the crab and the vision of the mermaids? How do both relate to theme and tone? What do the allusions to John the Baptist, Lazarus, and Hamlet have in common?

4. Distinguish between the dramatic and the lyric elements. How is the mock heroic used to satirize both speaker and society? Study the effects of repetition on rhythm, tone, and meaning. How do the stanzas and the typographical breaks mark the shifts in tone? Discuss the relationship of tone to syntax, refrain, internal rhyme, diction, tempo, and melody. Comment on the irony in the title.

5. How does time function in the poem? How does the shift in tense from present to present perfect and future provide a key to the poem's resolution? What form does the speaker's recognition take? By what means does the poet evoke sympathy for Prufrock, who is psychically impotent to establish an intimate human relationship? To what do you attribute Prufrock's rejection of human encounter? What part does his self-mockery play in our response to him? Does the poem move beyond pathos and self-mockery?

6. In what respect may the poem be viewed as an expression of a search for self?

Suggestions for Writing

1. Write a character study of Prufrock in which you refer directly to the poem.

2. Write a dialogue in which your interior self is counterpointed against your social self or persona.

ANNE SEXTON

Her Kind

Anne Sexton (1928–1974) taught and lectured widely, but she was above all a poet. Recipient of three honorary degrees and numerous fellowships, she was also awarded, among others, the Shelley and Pulitzer

Prizes. Of her many books the best known are *To Bedlam and Part Way Back* (1960), from which the following poem is taken; *All My Pretty Ones* (1962); *Live or Die* (1966); *Transformations* (1971); and *The Death Notebooks* (1974). In "Her Kind," we see another portrayal of the complex and multiple nature of human personality.

I have gone out, a possessed witch,
haunting the black air, braver at night;
dreaming evil, I have done my hitch
over the plain houses, light by light:
lonely thing, twelve-fingered, out of mind.
A woman like that is not a woman, quite.
I have been her kind.

I have found the warm caves in the woods,
filled them with skillets, carvings, shelves,
closets, silks, innumerable goods;
fixed the suppers for the worms and the elves:
whining, rearranging the disaligned.

A woman like that is misunderstood.
I have been her kind.

I have ridden in your car, driver,
waved my nude arms at villages going by,
learning the last bright routes, survivor
where your flames still bite my thigh
and my ribs crack where your wheels wind.
A woman like that is not ashamed to die.
I have been her kind.

Suggestions for Discussion

1. Who is "I" in this poem?

2. What is meant by the phrase "her *kind*?" What *kind* of woman is the speaker relating to? What metaphors does Sexton use to describe the women (or woman?) evoked in this poem? How do these characterizations of womanhood relate to how society has understood and portrayed women?

3. Why is the protagonist described as "not a woman, quite," "misunderstood," "not ashamed to die"?

Suggestions for Writing

1. If you were to think of yourself in terms of a number of different characters or *personae*, what would they be? How would they relate to one another?

2. What are some of the stereotypes our culture has used to describe men? Have these had an impact on how men in our culture behave? Explain.

WILLIAM SHAKESPEARE

William Shakespeare (1564–1616) is generally acknowledged to be the greatest playwright in the English language. He was born in Stratford-upon-Avon, England. By 1592, he had become an actor and playwright in London, and in 1599, he helped establish the famous Globe Theatre. Shakespeare's works include historical plays, such as *Henry IV*, *Henry V*, and *Richard III*; comedies such as *A Midsummer Night's Dream* and *The Taming of the Shrew*; and tragedies such as *Macbeth*, *Hamlet*, *King Lear*, and *Othello*. He also wrote a number of love sonnets, two of which follow. First published in a collected edition of poetry in 1609, Shakespeare's sonnets include poignant musings on love, art, death, and parenthood. Critics believe that these sonnets were written for two mysterious recipients—one a treacherous "dark lady" and the other a beloved young man, although the nature of Shakespeare's relationship to these two figures remains a topic of heated debate in academic circles.

When in Disgrace with Fortune and Men's Eyes

(Sonnet 29)

When, in disgrace with fortune and men's eyes,
I all alone beweep my outcast state,
And trouble deaf heaven with my bootless cries,
And look upon myself and curse my fate;
Wishing me like to one more rich in hope,
Featured like him, like him with friends possessed,
Desiring this man's art, and that man's scope,
With what I most enjoy contented least;
Yet in these thoughts myself almost despising,

Haply I think on thee, and then my state,
Like to the lark at break of day arising
From sullen earth, sings hymns at heaven's gate;
For thy sweet love remembered such wealth brings
That then I scorn to change my state with kings.

Let Me Not to the Marriage of True Minds

(Sonnet 116)

Let me not to the marriage of true minds
Admit impediments. Love is not love
Which alters when it alteration finds,
Or bends with the remover to remove:
Oh, no! it is an ever-fixed mark,
That looks on tempests and is never shaken;
It is the star to every wandering bark,
Whose worth's unknown, although his height be taken.
Love's not Time's fool, though rosy lips and cheeks
Within his bending sickle's compass come;
Love alters not with his brief hours and weeks,
But bears it out even to the edge of doom.
If this be error and upon me proved,
I never writ, nor no man ever loved.

Suggestions for Discussion

1. How does the imagery in each of the sonnets contribute to its unity?

2. How does dramatic understatement at the end of the second of the two sonnets reinforce the theme?

Education

Myths and fairy tales both answer the eternal questions:
What is the world really like? How am I to live my life in it?
How can I truly be myself? The answers given by myths are
definite, while the fairy tale is suggestive; its messages may
imply solutions, but it never spells them out. Fairy tales leave
to the child's fantasizing whether and how to apply to himself what the story reveals about life and human nature.

—BRUNO BETTELHEIM, "The Child's Need for Magic"

Since the 1970s there has been a steep decline in the percentage of students majoring in the liberal arts and sciences, and
an accompanying increase in preprofessional undergraduate
degrees. Business is now by far the most popular undergraduate major . . . In the era of economic constraint before us,
the pressure toward vocational pursuits is likely only to intensify. As a nation, we need to ask more than this from our universities. Higher learning can offer individuals and societies
a depth and breadth of vision absent from the inevitably
myopic present. Human beings need meaning, understanding and perspective as well as jobs. The question should not
be whether we can afford to believe in such purposes in these
times, but whether we can afford not to.

—DREW GILPIN FAUST, "The University's Crisis of Purpose"

MIKEL GLASS

I Once Was Lost

Oil on canvas, 1996

John Pence Gallery, San Francisco, CA

INTRODUCTION

To educate derives from the Latin verb meaning "to lead forth." What education usually leads us from is ignorance. What it leads us *to* is a much more complex question. We begin this section with a Notebook on technology, "multitasking," and modern culture—in this case, how shorter attention spans, hand-held devices, and overscheduled days make people too frantic to concentrate on a single task, and chronically unable to pay attention in a classroom setting, or to have a genuine, undistracted conversation with the person sitting across the table from them at mealtimes. We ask you to consider the extent to which the perspectives presented by Samuel G. Freedman and Maggie Jackson on these issues are accurate or alarmist.

Experience can be a powerful teacher. Anton Chekhov's "The Bet" shows how lived experience can educate us about the issues we face. The classic short story also makes us consider how powerful books are, and how they might influence us, and change the way we view ourselves and the world, should we allow ourselves to be affected by the written word.

Educating our citizens is also seen in this country as a societal duty, and so discussions about the best ways to achieve this can be very public. Those methods—and definitions of what it means to be "educated"—change over time. In fact, it sometimes seems that the more educated we are, the more we argue over what it means to be educated. Assessing how well one is educated is equally difficult. In "The Child's Need for Magic," Bruno Bettelheim posits that fairy tales help children learn to understand the world on their own terms, while Harvard President Drew Gilpin Faust laments the fact that colleges are gradually being transformed into vocational schools for business majors thanks to a bad economy and practical-minded parents.

Some suggest that true education is an examination of mystery, paradox, and the unknown and that examination of the unknown, Lewis Thomas believes, is what makes science engrossing. It is what brings the sciences and the humanities together. True education should not offer students the misleading assumption that all of the "scientific" facts are in and that all of the mysteries have been worked out. Taught with respect for what *is* known *and* what is not, science education can stimulate students to higher-order thinking.

Education is also influenced by cultural and social differences. Gender issues in education and the role of feminism in education and the sciences are explored by Katha Pollitt in "Summers of Our Discontent," while Earl Shorris looks at how high culture is often denied to the poor, and how education can be a source of power and social transformation. His essay features an extensive discussion on Plato's "Allegory of the Cave," an ancient Athenian tract, which is also reprinted here, and which remains a potent metaphor of enlightenment, education, and prophetic transformation.

Finally, poems challenge us to consider how formal education interacts with our creativity, our self-image, and our self-reliance. Langston Hughes's classic "Theme for English B" interrogates the space between teacher expectations and the lives of students, especially African-American students who are trying to define themselves within the educational system.

Where, then, does education lead? Education leads everywhere. Survival of every kind—physical, emotional, psychological—depends on it, but just as important, the fulfillment of our lives depends on it. Ideally, wherever the classrooms, whatever the particular pedagogy, intellectual presuppositions, and politics, education will lead us forth along a road of inquiry, not only toward a better understanding of ourselves and the world around us, but also toward a humane appreciation of our kinship and common causes in a global community.

NOTEBOOK

∽∽∽∽

SAMUEL G. FREEDMAN

New Class(room) War: Teacher versus Technology

New York writer Samuel Freedman, a *New York Times* columnist and author of six nonfiction books, teaches journalism at Columbia University. His writing focuses on issues of religion, race, education, and journalism. His books include *Small Victories* (1990), *Upon This Rock* (1993), *The Inheritance* (1996), *Jew vs. Jew* (2000), *Who She Was: My Search for My Mother's Life* (2005), *Letters to a Young Journalist* (2006), and the upcoming *The Big Game*. A *Times* staff reporter from 1981 to 1987, Freedman has since written the columns "On Education" and "On Religion" for the periodical. He is also a columnist for the *Jerusalem Post*, where he explores issues in American Judaism. His writing has appeared in *Rolling Stone, Salon, USA Today*, and *BeliefNet*, and he has been a featured guest on CNN, NPR, and the *News Hour with Jim Lehrer*. This piece originally appeared in *The New York Times* on November 7, 2007.

Halfway through the semester in his market research course at Roanoke College last fall, only moments after announcing a policy of zero tolerance for cellphone use in the classroom, Prof. Ali Nazemi heard a telltale ring. Then he spotted a young man named Neil Noland fumbling with his phone, trying to turn it off before being caught.

"Neil, can I see that phone?" Professor Nazemi said, more in a command than a question. The student surrendered it. Professor Nazemi opened his briefcase, produced a hammer and proceeded to smash the offending device. Throughout the classroom, student faces went ashen.

"How am I going to call my Mom now?" Neil asked. As Professor Nazemi refused to answer, a classmate offered, "Dude, you can sue."

Let's be clear about one thing. Ali Nazemi is a hero. Ali Nazemi deserves the Presidential Medal of Freedom.

Let's be clear about another thing. The episode in his classroom had been plotted and scripted ahead of time, with Neil Noland part of the charade all along. The phone was an extra of his mother's, its service contract long expired.

Just as fiction can limn truths beyond the grasp of factuality, Professor Nazemi's act of guerrilla theater, which he recounted last week in a telephone interview, attested to the exasperation of countless teachers and professors in the computer era. Their perpetual war of attrition with defiantly inattentive students has escalated from the quaint pursuits of pigtail-pulling, spitball-lobbing and notebook-doodling to a high-tech arsenal of laptops, cellphones, BlackBerries and the like.

The poor schoolmarm or master, required to provide a certain amount of value for your child's entertainment dollar, now must compete with texting, instant-messaging, Facebook, eBay, YouTube, Addictinggames.com and other poxes on pedagogy.

"There are certain lines you shouldn't cross," the professor said. "If you start tolerating this stuff, it becomes the norm. The more you give, the more they take. These devices become an indisposable sort of thing for the students. And nothing should be indisposable. Multitasking is good, but I want them to do more tasking in my class."

To which one can only say: Amen. And add: Too bad the good guy is going to lose.

At age 55, Professor Nazemi stands on the far shore of a new sort of generational divide between teacher and student. This one separates those who want to use technology to grow smarter from those who want to use it to get dumber.

Perhaps there's a nicer way to put it. "The baby boomers seem to see technology as information and communication," said Prof. Michael Bugeja, director of the journalism school at Iowa State University and the author of "Interpersonal Divide: The Search for Community in a Technological Age." "Their offspring and the emerging generation seem to see the same devices as entertainment and socializing."

All the advances schools and colleges have made to supposedly enhance learning—supplying students with laptops, equipping computer labs, creating wireless networks—have instead enabled distraction. Perhaps attendance records should include a new category: present but otherwise engaged.

In the past three years alone, the percentage of college classrooms with wireless service has nearly doubled, to 60 percent from 31 percent, according to the Campus Computing Survey, an annual check by the Campus Computing Project of computer use at 600 colleges. Professor Bugeja's online survey of several hundred Iowa State students found that a majority had used their cellphones, sent or read e-mail, and gone onto social-network sites during class time. A quarter of the respondents admitted they were taking Professor Bugeja's survey while sitting in a different class.

Naturally, there will be many students and no small number of high-tech and progressive-ed apologists ready to lay the blame on boring lessons. One of the great condemnations in education jargon these days, after all, is the "teacher-centered lesson."

"I'm so tired of that excuse," said Professor Bugeja, may he live a long and fruitful life. "The idea that subject matter is boring is truly relative. Boring as opposed to what? Buying shoes on eBay? The fact is, we're not here to entertain. We're here to stimulate the life of the mind."

"Education requires contemplation," he continued. "It requires critical thinking. What we may be doing now is training a generation of air-traffic controllers rather than scholars. And I do know I'm going to lose."

Not, one can only hope, without a fight.

The Canadian company Smart Technologies makes and sells a program called SynchronEyes. It allows a classroom teacher to monitor every student's computer activity and to freeze it at a click. Last year, the company sold more than 10,000 licenses, which range in cost from $779 for one teacher to $3,249 for an entire school.

The biggest problem, said Nancy Knowlton, the company's chief executive officer, is staying ahead of students trying to crack the program's code. "There's an active discussion on the Web, and we're monitoring it," Ms. Knowlton said. "They keep us on our toes."

Scott Carlin, an instructor of teacher interns at Michigan State University, advises his charges to forbid personal use of tech devices in the classroom. Of course he occasionally has to pause in his own lesson to make one of his graduate students stop scrolling through text messages.

"If the students actually found some creative way to use a cellphone or a BlackBerry in a class demonstration, I'd be all for that," Mr. Carlin said in a recent interview, recalling his own years as a middle school and high school teacher. "Or if they could demonstrate how a chat room or AOL instant messenger would help them present a project. But what I found in most cases is that it was just a fancy new way of passing notes."

In the end, as science-fiction writers have prophesied for years, the technology is bound to outwit the fallible human. What teacher or professor can possibly police a room full of determined goof-offs while also delivering an engaging lesson?

I am reminded of a story I heard from an Ivy League junior at a social gathering last year. She and a friend walked into the lecture hall for a class and noticed two young men in a back row surfing Internet pornography sites. They called out and waved to alert the professor.

He stopped his lecture. He turned his eyes to the young women, those would-be whistle-blowers. And as the pornography show proceeded undetected, he chastised them for interrupting.

Suggestions for Discussion

1. What was Nazemi trying to accomplish with his staged destruction of a cell phone?

2. Why does Freedman believe that "the good guy is going to lose" in this generational conflict?

3. According to Freedman, how can technology make people smarter? How can it make them dumber?

4. Why is the argument that "teachers are boring" ultimately a false argument?

Suggestion for Writing

Synthesis: Write a paper responding to both Freedman's article and the following essay by Maggie Jackson, "Distracted: The Erosion of Attention and the Coming Dark Age." Present constructive actions that might be taken in response to these issues.

MAGGIE JACKSON

Distracted: The Erosion of Attention and the Coming Dark Age

Maggie Jackson (b. 1960) is a New York City–based writer known for her examinations of broad social trends, particularly technology's impact on our lives. Currently a columnist for the *Boston Globe*, she has won numerous awards and grants for her work, and her articles have been featured in publications ranging from *The New York Times* and *Gastronomica* to *Utne* and *National Public Radio*. A graduate of the London School of Economics and Yale University—where she studied with John Hersey—Jackson also serves as a senior fellow with the Center for Work-Life Policy in New York. Her books include *What's Happening to Home? Balancing Work, Life and Refuge in the Information Age* (2002), and *Distracted* (2008) from which the following passage is taken.

I am alone inside a glass booth, enveloped in a swirling storm of dialogue snippets, data shards, and clashing storylines. This is a play, for an audience of one. Within the booth is a tiny cybercafe, with a table, two chairs, a fake daisy in a vase, and a Mac computer. Sit down, press a button, and the play begins—disembodied, prerecorded, unshared. Over a soundtrack of clinking dishes and laughing customers, I hear two hushed voices, talking as if from another table. A man and a woman are meeting secretly, worried that their spouses are having a cyber-affair. The Mac comes to life and unfurls an instant message chat: the virtual whispers of the cyber-lovers. I listen and read, as the two couples simultaneously, online and offline, debate whether cyber-love is real, whether harm has been done. "We haven't cheated, if that's what you're thinking," says one. "Then why do I feel guilty?" his virtual lover retorts. The parallel scripts wash over me, clashing and overlapping, competing for my gaze and for my ear.

I listen twice and then try the next booth, and the next. There are six in all, a half dozen playlets, each no more than twelve minutes long, told by and through computers. These are the Technology Plays—six faceless, mechanized dramas of passion, mistrust, and dehumanization, unfolding at the touch of a button. This smorgasbord of experimental theater is on display in the soaring atrium of a college library in upstate New York. Just before the plays are dismantled, I have driven three hours to see them. Here on this dreary campus on a raw November day, I am looking for clues to understanding our own increasingly multilayered, mutable, and virtual world. Are these six mini-plays absurd slices of science fiction or reflections of our own lives of snippets and sound bites? Are they meaningless theatrical peep shows or dramatizations of the real shadows creeping over our lives?

Enter Booth 2, Richard Dresser's *Greetings from the Home Office*. Now I am sitting at an office desk, cast as the new hire in a corporate office that's roiled by a possible accounting scandal. A telephone rings. A frantic woman colleague is calling to say that the boss is covering up his misdoings. The smooth-talking boss telephones next to say that the whistleblower should be ignored; she is his bitter ex-lover. "I'm saying this for your own good," the boss purrs. Rapid-fire calls are punctuated by the interjections of a meddling secretary on an intercom. Ultimately, I'm forced to decide whom to trust, based on incomplete information and faceless relations. It's the age-old game of office politics done blindfolded, execution-style. In another play, *Chip*, a seemingly banal ATM transaction goes wrong when the machine rejects the identity chip allegedly implanted in my finger. The machine and a bank representative on the telephone shout contradictory commands as I hear machine-gun-firing security guards close in. The experience is at once comic and frightening. When the machine orders me not to turn around, I can't help but give a terrified peek over my shoulder. The Technology Plays are equal parts video game, amusement park ride, and high-tech storytelling. Oh-so briefly, you are sent hurtling into fantastical worlds where you are asked to fix what you can't see, decide what you don't understand, relate to those you cannot fully trust. The narratives are fragmented. The experience is disorienting. This is not how we live. Or is it?

I close the door of the last booth and walk back to my car. I've talked to no one all afternoon except a faceless woman whom I called on my cell phone about a technological glitch. (A man wordlessly comes to fix it.) The next day is Thanksgiving. The campus is silent and nearly deserted, with only a few backpack-toting students milling about. In twenty-four hours, most will be gathering with family, as will I. But going forward, I can't shake the lingering unease left by these fragments of plays. They manage to distill in brief much of how we live: tossed and turned by info-floods, pummeled by clashing streams of rapid-fire imagery, floating in limitless cyber-worlds, all while trust and privacy and face-to-face moments slip from our grasp. Twelve-minute plays for a one-minute world. Push the button and the next morsel of "real life" unfolds. Guess again, a soupçon of information will suffice. Do you dare peek over your shoulder? Can you clearly see the way ahead?

We can tap into 50 million Web sites, 1.8 million books in print, 75 million blogs, and other snowstorms of information, but we increasingly seek knowledge in Google searches and Yahoo! headlines that we gulp on the run while juggling other tasks. We can contact millions of people across the globe, yet we increasingly connect with even our most intimate friends and family via instant messaging, virtual visits, and fleeting meetings that are rescheduled a half dozen times, then punctuated when they do occur by pings and beeps and multitasking. Amid the glittering promise of our new technologies and the wondrous potential of our scientific gains, we are nurturing a culture of social diffusion, intellectual fragmentation, sensory detachment. In this new world, something is amiss. And that something is attention.

The premise of this book is simple. The way we live is eroding our capacity for deep, sustained, perceptive attention—the building block of intimacy, wisdom, and cultural progress. Moreover, this disintegration may come at great cost to ourselves and to society. Put most simply, attention defines us and is the bedrock of society. Attention "is the taking possession by the mind, in clear and vivid form, of one out of what seem several simultaneously possible objects or trains of thought," wrote psychologist and philosopher William James in 1890. "It implies withdrawal from some things in order to deal effectively with others, and is a condition which has a real opposite in the confused, dazed, scatter-brained state which in French is called *distraction*, and *Zerstreutheit* in German." James came tantalizingly close to understanding at least one aspect of this mysterious phenomenon whose inner workings eluded philosophers, artists, historians, and scientists for centuries. But today, we know much more about attention, and all that we are learning only serves to underscore its irrefutable importance in life. Attention is an organ system, akin to our respiratory or circulation systems, according to cognitive neuroscientist

Michael Posner. Attention, as James astutely understood, is the brain's conductor, leading the orchestration of our minds. And its various networks are key not only to higher forms of thinking but to our morality and even our very happiness.

Yet increasingly, we are shaped by distraction. James described a clear and vivid possessing of the mind, an ordering, and a withdrawal. We easily recognize that these states of mind are becoming less and less a given in our lives. The seduction of alternative virtual universes, the addictive allure of multitasking people and things, our near-religious allegiance to a constant state of motion: these are markers of a land of distraction, in which our old conceptions of space, time, and place have been shattered. This is why we are less and less able to see, hear, and comprehend what's relevant and permanent, why so many of us feel that we can barely keep our heads above water, and our days are marked by perpetual loose ends. What's more, the waning of our powers of attention is occurring at such a rate and in so many areas of life, that the erosion is reaching critical mass. We are on the verge of losing our capacity as a society for deep, sustained focus. In short, we are slipping toward a new dark age.

A dark age? Certainly, the notion seems so far removed from our techno-miraculous era that the mere mention of the subject appears irresponsibly alarmist. Amid our material riches, abundant information, and creative leaps, how can we be headed toward a time of decline? How can I speak of cultural slippages when we are able to decipher the genome, map the ocean floor, and plumb the depths of the brain to begin understanding something as abstract and intangible as attention? But take a closer look. The parallels between dark ages past and our times are clear and multiplying, and the erosion of attention is the key to understanding why we are on the cusp of a time of widespread cultural and social losses.

Consider first that a dark age is not a one-dimensional time of unending disintegration. Rather, it is a distinct turning point in history, a period of flux that often produces great technological and other gains yet ultimately results in a declining civilization and a desertlike spell of collective forgetting. The medieval era was a fertile time technologically, marked by the invention of eyeglasses, glazed windows, fireplaces, windmills, and stirrups, along with the compass, mechanical clock, and rudder. Yet by the sixth century, all of continental Europe's great libraries not only had disappeared but the *memory* of them was lost to an emerging feudal society, notes Thomas Cahill. After the fall of the mighty Mycenaean Empire in the tenth century BC, the Greeks improved upon the great rowing ships of the time and upon military tactics such as the phalanx. For the first time, the olive was cultivated as a food. Yet overall living standards slipped dramatically, and advances in carving, building, the arts, and farming slipped away as Greece entered a five-hundred-year-long dark age. Beads of amber came to be made of bone. Painted murals and elaborately carved gems gave way to clay modeling. The dead were buried in the crumbling ruins of beautiful buildings. Even writing declined in the time between the waning of the script called "Linear B," and the adoption of an alphabet. A dark age can dazzle if you fail to see the whole. But inexorably, such a time leads to "a culture's dead end."

Chillingly, many of these shifts parallel the current trajectory of our civilization. I'm not arguing that we'll soon be living in wooden huts and burying our dead in ruined landmarks, yet we, too, are in the midst of a time of innovations, flux, and impending decline. Civilization is defined by a "sense of permanence," notes historian Kenneth Clark. "Civilized man, or so it seems to me, must feel that he belongs somewhere in space and time." Consciously doing all we can to free ourselves from the last boundaries of space and time, we are ultimately trading our cultural and societal anchors for an age of glorious freedom, technological innovation—and darkness. As our attentional skills are squandered, we are plunging into a culture of mistrust, skimming, and a dehumanizing merging between man and machine. As we cultivate lives of distraction, we are losing our capacity to create and preserve wisdom and slipping toward a time of ignorance that is paradoxically born amid an abundance of information and connectivity. Our tools transport us, our inventions are impressive, but our sense of perspective and shared vision shrivel. This is why Umberto Eco has called Western society "neomedieval," comparing our own anxious, postliterate, and highly mobile age with the first post-Roman millennium in Europe. The late Jane Jacobs, who wrote the classic *Death and Life of Great American Cities* a generation ago, warned of an impending time of darkness brought on by fatal cracks in various pillars of American society, such as ethics and science. Critic Harold Bloom calls this era a "Dark Age of the Screens."

Although a time of decline may take generations or even centuries to unfold, the first evidence of its shadowy embrace may be seen all around us, if we can rise above the muddle of our days and see clearly. With this in mind, I want to lure you, the reader, into pausing and reflecting on our daily lives and our era. I do not propose to, nor could I, write *The Decline and Fall of the American Empire*, nor could I tackle the enormous political or economic implications of such changes. Nor is this a how-to, although hopefully this book will have a positive impact on a reader's life. Rather, my scope is *how we live and what that means* for our individual and collective futures.

Consider the issue of attention deficit disorder. This is not a book about whether millions of distractible children and adults belong on Ritalin and other stimulants. Yet alongside the voracious debates about the disorder festers a discomfiting realization: this condition, or at least some portion of it, may be exacerbated by the way we are living. With a mixture of self-mockery, perverse pride in our busyness, and real uneasiness, we accept that ADD has spilled far past the confines of the medical world. Educators fret about "vaccinating" children against ADD through better teaching and parenting. A growing roster of defenders venerate the upsides of being attention-deficient. Students pop Adderall and other "wakefulness" pills to focus better on tests. "How do you know you have ADD or a severe case of modern life?" asks Edward Hallowell, a psychiatrist who warns of an epidemic of attention deficit trait. "Everyone these days is super-busy and multitasking and keeping track of more data points than ever. The actual condition is just that—taken to a more extreme level." ADD and ADT are both causes of worry and badges of honor, but above all, they signal disturbing slippages in an asset that we cannot afford to lose.

Not long ago, an old school friend called me. We hadn't talked in years. After hearing about my book, he wanted to get together. E-mails sallied back and forth, like bumper cars bouncing off one another, with no solid hits. After repeated cancellations and postponements, we set a date for lunch. Arriving at his office, I waited while he wound up a meeting, took a phone call, dashed around. (Luckily, I had brought a book.) It was long past noon when we hurried to a coffee shop, where he mentioned that he'd eaten already. I gulped a sandwich, he half-heartedly sipped a soda, then raced back to work. It was all very friendly, yet I stood on the street corner for a few minutes, feeling unsettled. In school, I was studious and he was goofy. But he was never this, well, *diluted.* I thought we were going to catch up. Instead, I got the face-to-face equivalent of an MTV montage. Several times, he uneasily joked about his inability to focus.

We all share the joke. Nearly a third of workers feel they often do not have time to reflect on or process the work they do. More than half typically have to juggle too many tasks simultaneously and/or are so often interrupted that they find it difficult to get work done. One yearlong study found that workers not only switch tasks every three minutes during their workday but that nearly half the time they interrupt themselves. People are so dazed that they have almost no time to reflect on the world around them, much less their futures. Not too long ago, I stood on a New York street corner, watching a businessman who was so busy shouting into a cell phone and hailing a taxi that for some minutes he didn't notice that his colleague already had found a cab and was ready to roll. Speaking at a lunch for forty lawyers in Philadelphia, I talked about our mobile lives, technology's impact on the home, flexible work—and the erosion of focus. They pounced. That was the lightning rod issue: divided, diluted attention. Two hours passed, without a BlackBerry in sight. Finally, the leader of the group tentatively asked, "Is it just me, or is it true that we don't seem to go deeply into anything anymore?" Around the table, heads nodded. "Is all of this really progress?" she wondered.

Is all this progress? We have reason to worry. Kids are the inveterate multitaskers, the technologically fluent new breed that is better suited for the lightning-paced, many-threaded digital world, right? After all, they are bathed in an average of nearly six hours a day of nonprint media content, and a quarter of that time they are using more than one screen, dial, or channel. Nearly a third of fourteen- to twenty-one-year-olds juggle five to eight media while doing homework. Yet for all their tech fluency, kids show less patience, skepticism, tenacity, and skill than adults in navigating the Web, all while overestimating their prowess, studies show. Meanwhile, US fifteen-year-olds rank twenty-fourth out of twenty-nine developed countries on an Organization for Economic Cooperation and Development (OECD) test of problem-solving skills related to analytic reasoning—the sort of skills demanded in today's workforce. Nearly 60 percent of fifteen-year-olds in our country score at or below the most *basic* level of problem solving, which involves using single sources of well-defined information to solve challenges such as plotting a route on a map. Government and other studies show that many US high school students can't synthesize or assess information, express complex thoughts, or analyze arguments. In other words, they often lack the critical thinking skills that are the bedrock of an informed citizenry and the foundation of scientific and other advancements. Is it just a coincidence that they lack the skills nurtured by the brain's executive attention network, the seat of our highest-level powers of focus?

While undoubtedly the reasons for this state of affairs are myriad, what's certain is that we can't be a nation of reflective, analytic problem solvers while cultivating a culture of distraction. I am not alone in wondering how often our children will experience the hard-fought pleasures of plunging deeply into a thought, a conversation, a state of being. Will focusing become a lost art, quaintly exhibited alongside blacksmithing at the historic village? ("Look, honey, that man in twentieth-century costume is doing just one thing!") An executive at a top accounting firm, who was researching the future workforce, confided to me his deep concerns that young workers are less and less able to concentrate, think deeply, or mine a vein of inquiry. Knowledge work can't be done in sound bites, he warned.

And yet again, perhaps it is silly to worry. What if we're all slowly, and with lots of stumbles, learning to adapt to a new world, where multitasking, split-second decision making, information surfing, bullet pointing, and virtual romancing is the new norm? What if our technologies are ushering us into an even more glorious future? Just hang on for the ride! Perhaps the smart folks are creating a new definition of smarts. Those clinging to the power of the word, the mysterious miracles of the human mind and spirit, and a reverence for the sensuality of physical togetherness will be soon left behind!

It's true that our tools are shaping us and teaching us, as they have since man first picked up a stick, sword, or pen. And today's technologies are making us smarter . . . in some ways. We don't yet know whether video games teach us problem-solving, pattern recognition, or how to construct order from chaos, as Steven Johnson and others argue. Early evidence shows that many computer games teach the kind of iconic and spatial skills useful for playing more computer games, and not much more. While some carefully crafted computer-based exercises can and are being powerfully used to educate, many games on the market are simply "training wheels" for improving *computer* literacy, some researchers conclude. Video games also can boost your ability to pay attention to multiple stimuli in your field of vision, a skill useful for driving but not analytical thinking. Limited doses of educational television produce some language, math, and reading gains in young children, but there's no evidence that, as Johnson argues, the growing numbers of sitcom characters or "complexity" of plot lines in adult fare offer us anything more than a diet of loose threads. If crafted well and used wisely, our high-tech tools have the potential to make us smarter, but too often so far they seem to be doing so in narrow ways.

"It's like, instead of writing the whole book, you're just writing the back cover," explained Brendan, age ten. One sultry June day in library class, Brendan was giving me a primer on the difference between a written report—"writing, research, more research, more writing"—and his PowerPoint presentation on piranha fish—"a brief summary." Although Brendan was hardly a boy of few words in person, his slides took bullet points to new heights of brevity. "Habitat. Amazon River. Warm Water. Murky Water. Always Have Food. Lots of Predators," one read. He ticked off the benefits of PowerPoint. It's shorter, animated, fun, and easier, even though you don't learn as much from it. His classmates and other students at a suburban elementary school outside Hartford, Connecticut, agreed with him. They liked PowerPoint's short sentences, bouncing words, the fact that their parents are amazed by the results, and above all, its bright colors. No one wants to read long sentences or too much information, they assured me. Not surprisingly, the information in their presentations was mostly cut and pasted from Web sites. The results? "You get a smattering of information," said the school librarian, whose job is to teach tech skills, not content. "You get a snippet of this and that." When I asked several children about specific words in their slides or why they included a particular and sometimes nonsensical piece of information, most shrugged. "I don't know," they said.

Channeling our thoughts and ideas into outlines and bullet points—is this a new definition of smart? With four hundred million copies in circulation, PowerPoint is the world's most popular presentation tool. Some books get taken off class lists if they don't give good PowerPoint. Many corporate employees, bureaucrats, and military officers hardly dare to make a presentation without it. Proponents, including Microsoft (naturally), argue that in a world of information overload, we need brevity and distillation. PowerPoint's shortcomings stem from people's inexperience with this new tool, they say. But opponents, led by information theorist Edward Tufte, are blistering in their criticism. They say the software shapes thoughts and data into alluringly professional yet narrow and simplistic formats, fostering uninformative and often misleading presentations that discourage creativity or argument. Partly as a result of Tufte's work, NASA blamed its reliance on PowerPoint for a pattern of obfuscation and miscommunication that helped doom the *Challenger* space shuttle. "When presentation becomes its own powerful idea, we diminish our appreciation of complexity," concluded MIT professor Sherry Turkle after studying PowerPoint's use in classrooms. PowerPoint "tells you how to think," quips rock musician David Byrne in "Envisioning Emotional Epistemological Information," a satirical PowerPoint artwork set to his own compositions. "This can be an enjoyable experience."

   PowerPoint doesn't make us dumb, and a judicious use of such slideware likely can help us navigate a world of information overload. I'm not angling for a return to some sort of pastoral, unmechanized Eden in order to halt the erosion of attention. We cannot blame technology for society's ills. Nor can we fall into the opposite and increasingly commonplace trap of blindly trusting that our new tools will automatically usher us into a glorious new age. The tools we are wholeheartedly embracing today are inherently powerful, and we ignore that truth at our peril. You can use a stick for digging potatoes or stabbing your neighbor, so how you use a stick is important, but equally important is the fact that a stick is not a wheel. It's crucial that we better understand how our new high-tech tools, from video games to PowerPoint, may be affecting us. Moreover, our tools reflect the values of our time, so it's no coincidence that PowerPoint is a tool of choice in a world of snippets and sound bites. This is the messy soup that makes up our relation to technology, and explains why technology plays a starring but ultimately subordinate role in this book. Technology is a key to understanding our world, but it is not the full story. Instead, we must ask: how do we want to define progress? We are adapting to a new world, but in doing so are we redefining "smart" to mostly mean twitch speed, multitasking, and bullet points? Are we similarly redefining intimacy and trust? Are we so enamored of our alluring surface gains that we are failing to stem or even notice the deeper, human costs of these "advances"? We may be getting expert at pushing buttons and wiring our thoughts with bells and whistles and tracking two virtual enemies across a screen but losing the skills needed to thrive in an increasingly complex world: deep learning, reasoning, and problem solving. We may be getting better at juggling three people simultaneously over a screen or wire but forgetting that what we need more than ever in a time of growing mistrust and seemingly expendable relations is honesty, unhurried presence, and care.

I think we're beginning to see a time of darkness when, amid a plethora of high-tech connectivity, one-quarter of Americans say they have no close confidante, more than double the number twenty years ago. It's a darkening time when we think togetherness means keeping one eye, hand, or ear on our gadgets, ever ready to tune into another channel of life, when we begin to turn to robots to tend to the sick and the old, when doctors listen to patients on average for just eighteen seconds before interrupting, and when two-thirds of children under six live in homes that keep the television on half or more of the time, an environment linked to attention deficiencies. We should worry when we have the world at our fingertips but half of Americans age eighteen to twenty-four can't find New York state on a map and more than 60 percent can't similarly locate Iraq. We should be concerned when we sense that short-term thinking in the workplace eclipses intellectual pattern making, and when we're staking our cultural memory largely on digital data that is disappearing at astounding rates. We should worry when attention slips through our fingers.

For nothing is more central to creating a flourishing society built upon learning, contentment, caring, morality, reflection, and spirit than attention. As humans, we are formed to pay attention. Without it, we simply would not survive. Just as our respiration or circulatory systems are made up of multiple parts, so attention encompasses three "networks" related to different aspects of awareness, focus, and planning. In a nutshell, "alerting" makes us sensitive to incoming stimuli, while the "orienting" network helps us select information from among the millions of sensations we receive from the world, voluntarily or in reaction to our surroundings. A baby's first job is to hone these skills, which are akin to "awareness" and "focus," respectively. In a class of its own, however, is the executive network, the system of attention responsible for complex cognitive and emotional operations and especially for resolving conflicts between different areas of the brain. (We fire up four separate areas of the brain just to solve a simple word recognition problem, such as coming up with a use for the word *hammer*.) All three networks are crucial and often work together, and without strong skills of attention, we are buffeted by the world and hindered in our capacity to grow and even to enjoy life. People who focus well report feeling less fear, frustration, and sadness day to day, partly because they can literally deploy their attention away from negatives in life. In contrast, attentional problems are one of the main impediments to attaining "flow," the deep sense of contentment that people find when they are stretching themselves to meet a challenge. For example, schizophrenics tend to suffer from *anhedonia*, or literally "lack of pleasure," because they usually are unable to sift stimuli. "Things are coming in too fast," said one patient. "I am attending to everything at once and as a result I do not really attend to anything." Without a symphonic conductor, the music of the brain disintegrates into cacophonic noise.

Attention also tames our inner beast. Primates that receive training in attention become less aggressive. One of attention's highest forms is "effortful control," which involves the ability to shift focus deliberately, engage in planning, and regulate one's impulses. Six- and seven-year-olds who score high in tests of this skill are more empathetic, better able to feel guilt and shame, and less aggressive. Moreover, effortful control is integral to developing a conscience, researchers are discovering. In order to put back the stolen cookie, you must attend to your uneasy feelings, the action itself, and the abstract moral principles—then make the right response. All in all, attention is key to both our free will as individuals and our ability to subordinate ourselves to a greater good. The *Oxford English Dictionary* defines attention as "the act, fact or state of attending or giving heed; earnest direction of the mind," and secondarily as "practical consideration, observant care, notice." The word is rooted in the Latin words *ad* and *tendere*, meaning to "stretch toward," implying effort and intention. Even the phrase "attention span" literally means a kind of bridge, a reaching across in order to widen one's horizons. Attention is not always effortful, but it carries us toward our highest goals, however we define them. A culture that settles for numb distraction cannot shape its future.

This morning, I sat in the library trying to harness my thoughts, but like runaway horses, they would not be reined in. We missed the first birthday of a baby whose parents are two of our closest friends, and I stewed about that for a while. Someone I interviewed for my newspaper column was peeved that an editor hadn't confirmed this evening's photo shoot, and a flurry of e-mails ensued. A man outside my study room made a long, illicit phone call and gestured threateningly when I asked him to stop. The old water pipes hissed in a new, odd way. I have never thought of myself as easily distracted, although I always have had an Olympic capacity for daydreaming, failing to complete my sentences, and slips of the tongue. (Go put on your pajamas, I'll tell my daughter at noon, when I really mean bathing suit.) A friend generously diagnoses me as having "too many words" in my head. But perhaps the ultimate weak spot in my own capacity for focus is that I'm observant and "sensitive"—a label I grew to hate as a child. I notice much of the ceaseless swirl of social intonations, bodily signals, and facial expressions around me. Even in the relative quiet of the library, the world tends to come rushing in, jumbling and splashing about inside me, a restless sea.

Yet isn't that essentially the starting point of attention? Attention is a process of taking in, sorting and shaping, planning, and decision making—a mental and emotional forming and kneading of the bread of life, or, if you prefer, an inner mountain climb. The first two forms of attention—alertness and orienting—allow us to sense and respond to our environment, while the third and highest network of executive attention is needed to make ultimate sense of our world. Our ability to attend is partly genetic, yet also dependent upon a nurturing environment and how willing we are to reach for the highest levels of this skill, just as a naturally gifted athlete who lacks the opportunity, encouragement, and sheer will to practice can never master a sport. Today, our virtual, split-screen, and nomadic era is eroding opportunities for deep focus, awareness, and reflection. As a result, we face a real risk of societal decline. But there is much room for hope, for attention can be trained, taught, and shaped, a discovery that offers the key to living fully in a tech-saturated world. We need not waste our potential for reaching the heights of attention. We don't have to settle for lives mired in detachment, fragmentation, diffusion. A *renaissance of attention* is within our grasp.

I didn't set out to write about attention. I was curious why so many Americans are deeply dissatisfied with life, feeling stressed, and often powerless to shape their futures in a country of such abundant resources. At first, I sought clues in the past, assuming that lessons from the first high-tech era—the heyday of the telegraph, cinema, and railway—could teach us how to better manage our own shifting experiences of space and time. Instead, I discovered that our gadgets are bringing to a climax the changes seeded in these first revolutions. Is this a historical turning point, a "hinge of history," in Thomas Cahill's words? In researching this next question, I discovered stunning similarities between past dark ages and our own era. At the same time, I began studying the astonishing discoveries made just in our own generation about the nature and workings of attention. As I explored these seemingly unrelated threads, I realized that they formed a tapestry: the story of what happens when we allow our powers of attention to slip through our fingers. Realizing this loss is intriguing. Considering the consequences is alarming.

When a civilization wearies, notes Cahill, a confidence based on order and balance is lost, and without such anchors, people begin to return to an era of shadows and fear. Godlike amid our five hundred television channels and three hundred choices of cereal, are we failing to note the creeping arrival of a time of impermanence and uncertainty? Mesmerized by streams of media-borne eye candy and numbed by our faith in technology to cure all ills, are we blind to the realization that our society's progress, in important ways, is a shimmering mirage? Consumed by the vast time and energy simply required to survive the ever-increasing complexity of our systems of living, are we missing the slow extinction of our capacity to think and feel and bond deeply? We just might be too busy, wired, split-focused, and *distracted* to notice a return to an era of shadows and fear.

On the August day in 410 when the Goths brutally sacked Rome, the emperor was at his country house on the Adriatic, attending to his beloved flock of prize poultry. Informed by a servant that Rome had perished, the emperor, Honorius, was stunned. "Rome perished?" he said. "It is not an hour since she was feeding out of my hand." The chamberlain clarified himself. He'd been talking about the city, not the imperial bird of that name. Apocryphal as this story may be, the point is apt. For in the years leading into a dark age, societies often exhibit an inability to perceive or act upon a looming threat, such as a declining resource. Twilight cultures begin to show a preference for veneer and form, not depth and content; a stubborn blindness to the consequences of actions, from the leadership on down. In other words, an epidemic erosion of attention is a sure sign of an impending dark age.

Welcome to the land of distraction.

GUNTER KLÖTZER, *IT-Nomade, 6 August 2000.* © Gunter Klötzer.

Suggestions for Discussion

1. Is Jackson being alarmist and anti-technology? What arguments might best refute her claims about the impossibility of multitasking?

2. What evidence does Jackson present to support her own arguments? How convincing is this evidence? What might people who are often "distracted" in the manner Jackson describes learn from seriously considering her argument?

3. Is it ever acceptable to multitask (a) in a darkened movie theater? (b) during a play or classical music concert? (c) at a weekly religious service? (d) during a funeral? (e) while driving? (f) while performing surgery? (g) while on a date? (h) during sex? Why or why not? How would you feel if your professor asked for the same undivided attention and respect generally offered during some of the above scenarios? How would you reply?

Suggestion for Writing

Under what circumstances is multitasking always acceptable? When is it never acceptable? How might you deal with the gray areas in between? Discuss these ideas in a brief essay.

PERSONAL WRITING

KATHA POLLITT

Summers of Our Discontent

Political analyst, literary critic, and poet Katha Pollitt (b. 1949) is a Harvard-educated New York City native and a leading voice in contemporary liberal feminist thought. Her column for *The Nation*, "Subject to Debate," has tackled issues as varied as abortion, welfare, and the literary canon, and won the National Magazine Award for Columns and Commentary in 2003. Pollitt has appeared in numerous programs on NPR, PBS, CNN, and the BBC. Her writings have appeared in *The New Yorker, The New Republic, Harper's, The Atlantic, Ms., The New York Times*, and the *London Review of Books*, and have garnered her a National Endowment for the Arts grant and a Guggenheim Fellowship. Her poetry is collected in *The Mind-Body Problem* (2009) and *Antarctic Traveler* (1982), winner of the National Book Critics Circle Award. Her essays have been reprinted in *Reasonable Creatures: Essays on Women and Feminism* (1994), *Subject to Debate* (2001), *Virginity or Death! And Other Social and Political Issues of Our Time* (2006), and *Learning to Drive and Other Life Stories* (2007).

As the saying goes, behind every successful woman is a man who is surprised. Harvard president Larry Summers apparently is that man. A distinguished economist who was Treasury Secretary under Clinton, Summers caused a firestorm on January 14 when, speaking from notes at a conference on academic diversity, he argued that tenured women are rare in math and science for three reasons, which he listed in descending order of importance. One, women choose family commitments over the eighty-hour weeks achievement in those fields requires; two, fewer women than men have the necessary genetic gifts; and three, women are discriminated against. Following standard economic theory, Summers largely discounted discrimination: A first-rate woman rejected by one university would surely be snapped up by a rival. We're back to women's lack of commitment and brainpower.

On campus, Summers has lost big—he has had to apologize, appoint a committee and endure many a hairy eyeball from the faculty, and complaints from furious alumnae like me. In the press, he's done much better: Provocative thinker brought down by PC feminist mob! Women *are* dumber! Steven Pinker says so! The *New York Times* even ran a supportive op-ed by Charles Murray without identifying him as the co-author of *The Bell Curve*, the discredited farrago of racist claptrap. While much was made of MIT biologist Nancy Hopkins walking out of his talk—what about free speech, what about Truth?—we heard little about how Summers, who says he only wanted to spark a discussion, has refused to release his remarks. The bold challenger of campus orthodoxy apparently doesn't want the world to know what he actually said.

Do men have an innate edge in math and science? Perhaps someday we will live in a world free of the gender bias and stereo-typing we know exists today both in and out of the classroom, and we will be able to answer that question, if anyone is still asking it. But we know we don't live in a bias-free world now: Girls are steered away from math and science from the moment they are born. The interesting fact is that, thanks partly to antidiscrimination laws that have forced open closed doors, they have steadily increased their performance nonetheless. Most of my Radcliffe classmates remember being firmly discouraged from anything to do with numbers or labs; one was flatly told that women couldn't be physicians—at her Harvard med school interview. Today women obtain 48 percent of BAs in math, 57 percent in biology and agricultural science, half of all places in med school, and they are steadily increasing their numbers as finalists in the Intel high school science contest (fifteen out of forty this year, and three out of four in New York City).

Every gain women have made in the past 200 years has been in the face of experts insisting they couldn't do it and didn't really want to. Biology, now trotted out to "prove" women's incapacity for math and science, used to "prove" that they shouldn't go to college at all. As women progress, the proponents of innate inferiority simply adapt their arguments to explain why further advancement is unlikely. But how can we know that in 2005, any more than we knew it in 1905? I'd like to hear those experts explain this instead: The number of tenure offers to women at Harvard has gone down in each of Summers's three years as president, from nine in thirty-six tenures to three in thirty-two. (The year before his arrival, it was thirteen women out of thirty-six.) Surely women's genes have not deteriorated since 2001?

Whatever they may be in theory, in the workplace, biological incapacity and natural preference are the counters used to defend against accusations of discrimination. Summers argues that competition makes discrimination irrational; that wouldn't hold, though, if an entire field is pervaded with discrimination, if there's a consensus that women don't belong there and if female candidates are judged more harshly by all potential employers. It also doesn't work if the threat of competition isn't so credible: It will be a long time before the Ivies feel the heat from Northwestern, which has improved its profile by hiring the first-rate women they foolishly let go. The history of women and minorities in the workplace shows that vigorous enforcement of antidiscrimination law is what drives progress. Moreover, the competition argument can be turned against Summers: After all, given its prestige and wealth, Harvard could "compete" for women with any university on the planet. So why doesn't it?

This brings us to that eighty-hour week and women's domestic "choices." It's a truism that career ladders are based on the traditional male life plan— he knocks himself out in his 20s and 30s while his wife raises the kids, mends his socks and types his papers. If women had been included from the start, the ladder would look rather different— careers might peak later, taking a semester off to have a baby would not blot your copybook, women would not be expected to do huge amounts of academic service work and then be blamed at tenure time for not publishing more. By treating this work culture as fixed, and women as the problem, Summers lets academia off the hook. Yet Harvard, with its $23 billion endowment, doesn't even offer free daycare to grad students.

There's a ton of research on all the subjects raised by Summers— the socialization of girls; conscious and unconscious gender bias in teaching, hiring and promotion; what makes talented females, like Intel finalists, drop out of science at every stage; what makes motherhood so hard to combine with a career. We are past the day when brilliant women could be expected to sit quietly while a powerful man parades his ignorance of that scholarship and of their experience. It is not "provocative" when the president of Harvard justifies his university's lamentable record by recalling that his toddler daughter treated toy trucks like dolls. It's an insult to his audience. What was his point, anyway? That she'll grow up and flunk calculus? That she'll get a job in a daycare center?

If Summers wants to know why women are underrepresented in math and science, he should do his homework, beginning with Nancy Hopkins's pathbreaking 1999 study of bias against female faculty at MIT. And then he should ask them.

Suggestions for Discussion

1. Why was Pollitt offended by Larry Summers's thesis? Why did she find the media's championing of Summers as a hero of free speech problematic? Was Pollitt's anger understandable?

2. Explain the historical context that Pollitt brings to the discussion. How do Summers's views appear in light of this information?

3. Both Summers and Pollitt arm themselves with statistics. How might one verify the accuracy of these statistics and determine whether those same figures were interpreted correctly?

4. In the wake of the controversy surrounding his speech, Larry Summers resigned and was replaced by Harvard's first female president, Drew Gilpin Faust. Should he have resigned? Why or why not?

Suggestions for Writing

1. According to Pollitt, what is wrong with businesses and universities that judge progress up a "career ladder" by the standards of "the traditional male life plan"? Consider how a change in perception that accommodates a "traditional *female* life plan" might alter the rate of success of women in academia and the workplace. Would this change be completely positive? Support your argument in a brief essay.

2. Synthesis: How does the issue of childhood toys come up in Pollitt's argument? How does her view of toys compare to the views presented by Sherry Turkle, Peggy Orenstein, and Chris Sullentrop in the essays reprinted in this anthology? Use these essays to inform an argument of your own about childhood toys.

ESSAYS

PLATO

The Allegory of the Cave

Translated by Benjamin Jowett, revised by Peter White

Plato (428–348 B.C.), born of a noble family, lived in Athens during troubled political times. After the defeat of Athens in the Peloponnesian War, an autocratic and repressive government replaced the democracy, and it, in turn, was succeeded by a regime more demagogic than democratic. Under this government in 399 B.C., Socrates was prosecuted, tried, and condemned to death for subversive activities. In the *Apology* and *The Crito* (neither of them typical Platonic dialogues), Plato undertook the task of rehabilitating Socrates' reputation. Although the historian Xenophon has provided a somewhat different version of Socrates' trial, Plato's portrait of Socrates explains why he regarded him as the best of men. "The Allegory of the Cave," an excerpt from Plato's masterpiece *The Republic*, is about human ignorance and fear in the face of "change" and "enlightenment" offered by a prophet figure.

SPEAKERS IN THE DIALOGUE:
SOCRATES   GLAUCON

And now, I said, let me show in a figure how far our nature is enlightened or unenlightened:—Behold! human beings living in an underground den, which has a mouth open towards the light and reaching all along the den; here they have been from their childhood, and have their legs and necks chained so that they cannot move, and can only see before them, being prevented by the chains from turning round their heads. Above and behind them a fire is blazing at a distance, and between the fire and the prisoners there is a raised way; and you will see, if you look, a low wall built along the way, like the screen which marionette players have in front of them, over which they show the puppets.

I see.

And do you see, I said, men passing along the wall carrying all sorts of vessels, and statues and figures of animals made of wood and stone and various materials, which appear over the wall? Some of them are talking, others silent.

You have shown me a strange image, and they are strange prisoners.

Like ourselves, I replied; and they see only their own shadows, or the shadows of one another, which the fire throws on the opposite wall of the cave?

True, he said; how could they see anything but the shadows if they were never allowed to move their heads?

And of the objects which are being carried in like manner they would only see the shadows?

Yes, he said.

And if they were able to converse with one another, would they not suppose that they were naming what was actually before them?

Very true.

And suppose further that the prison had an echo which came from the other side, would they not be sure to fancy when one of the passers-by spoke that the voice which they heard came from the passing shadow?

No question, he replied.

To them, I said, the truth would be literally nothing but the shadows of the images.

That is certain.

And now look again, and see what will naturally follow if the prisoners are released and disabused of their error. At first, when any of them is liberated and compelled suddenly to stand up and turn his neck round and walk and look towards the light, he will suffer sharp pains; the glare will distress him, and he will be unable to see the realities of which in his former state he had seen the shadows; and then conceive some one saying to him, that what he saw before was an illusion, but that now, when he is approaching nearer to being and his eye is turned towards more real existence, he has a clearer vision—what will be his reply? And you may further imagine that his instructor is pointing to the objects as they pass and requiring him to name them—will he not be perplexed? Will he not fancy that the shadows which he formerly saw are truer than the objects which are now shown to him?

Far truer.

And if he is compelled to look straight at the light, will he not have a pain in his eyes which will make him turn away to take refuge in the objects of vision which he can see, and which he will conceive to be in reality clearer than the things which are now being shown to him?

True, he said.

And suppose once more, that he is reluctantly dragged up a steep and rugged ascent, and held fast until he is forced into the presence of the sun himself, is he not likely to be pained and irritated? When he approaches the light his eyes will be dazzled, and he will not be able to see anything at all of what are now called realities

Not all in a moment, he said.

He will require to grow accustomed to the sight of the upper world. And first he will see the shadows best, next the reflections of men and other objects in the water, and then the objects themselves; then he will gaze upon the light of the moon and the stars and the spangled heaven; and he will see the sky and the stars by night better than the sun or the light of the sun by day?

Certainly.

Last of all he will be able to see the sun, and not mere reflections of him in the water, but he will see him in his own proper place, and not in another; and he will contemplate him as he is.

Certainly.

He will then proceed to argue that this is he who gives the season and the years, and is the guardian of all that is in the visible world, and in a certain way the cause of all things which he and his fellows have been accustomed to behold?

Clearly, he said, he would first see the sun and then reason about him.

And when he remembered his old habitation, and the wisdom of the den and his fellow-prisoners, do you not suppose that he would felicitate himself on the change, and pity them?

Certainly, he would.

And if they were in the habit of conferring honours among themselves on those who were quickest to observe the passing shadows and to remark which of them went before, and which followed after, and which were together; and who were therefore best able to draw conclusions as to the future, do you think that he would care for such honours and glories, or envy the possessors of them? Would he not say with Homer,

Better to be the poor servant of a poor master, and to endure anything, rather than think as they do and after their manner?

Yes, he said, I think that he would rather suffer anything than entertain these false notions and live in this miserable manner.

Imagine once more, I said, such an one coming suddenly out of the sun to be replaced in his old situation; would he not be certain to have his eyes full of darkness?

To be sure, he said.

And if there were a contest, and he had to compete in measuring the shadows with the prisoners who had never moved out of the den, while his sight was still weak, and before his eyes had become steady (and the time which would be needed to acquire this new habit of sight might be very considerable), would he not be ridiculous? Men would say of him that up he went and down he came without his eyes; and that it was better not even to think of ascending; and if any one tried to loose another and lead him up to the light, let them only catch the offender, and they would put him to death.

No question, he said.

This entire allegory, I said, you may now append, dear Glaucon, to the previous argument; the prison-house is the world of sight, the light of the fire is the sun, and you will not misapprehend me if you interpret the journey upwards to be the ascent of the soul into the intellectual world according to my poor belief, which, at your desire, I have expressed—whether rightly or wrongly God knows. But, whether true or false, my opinion is that in the world of knowledge the idea of good appears last of all, and is seen only with an effort; and, when seen, is also inferred to be the universal author of all things beautiful and right, parent of light and of the lord of light in this visible world, and the immediate source of reason and truth in the intellectual; and that this is the power upon which he who would act rationally either in public or private life must have his eye fixed.

I agree, he said, as far as I am able to understand you.

Moreover, I said, you must not wonder that those who attain to this beatific vision are unwilling to descend to human affairs; for their souls are ever hastening into the upper world where they desire to dwell; which desire of theirs is very natural, if our allegory may be trusted.

Yes, very natural.

And is there anything surprising in one who passes from divine contemplations to the evil state of man, misbehaving himself in a ridiculous manner; if, while his eyes are blinking and before he has become accustomed to the surrounding darkness, he is compelled to fight in courts of law, or in other places, about the images or the shadows of images of justice, and is endeavouring to meet the conceptions of those who have never yet seen absolute justice?

Anything but surprising, he replied.

Any one who has common sense will remember that the bewilderments of the eyes are of two kinds, and arise from two causes, either from coming out of the light or from going into the light, which is true of the mind's eye, quite as much as of the bodily eye; and he who remembers this when he sees any one whose vision is perplexed and weak, will not be too ready to laugh; he will first ask whether that soul of man has come out of the brighter life, and is unable to see because unaccustomed to the dark, or having turned from darkness to the day is dazzled by excess of light. And he will count the one happy in his condition and state of being, and he will pity the other; or, if he have a mind to laugh at the soul which comes from below into the light, there will be more reason in this than in the laugh which greets him who returns from above out of the light into the den.

That, he said, is a very just distinction.

But then, if I am right, certain professors of education must be wrong when they say that they can put a knowledge into the soul which was not there before, like sight into blind eyes.

They undoubtedly say this, he replied.

Whereas, our argument shows that the power and capacity of learning exists in the soul already; and that just as the eye was unable to turn from darkness to light without the whole body, so too the instrument of knowledge can only by the movement of the whole soul be turned from the world of becoming into that of being, and learn by degrees to endure the sight of being, and of the brightest and best of being, or in other words, of the good.

Very true.

And must there not be some art which will effect conversion in the easiest and quickest manner; not implanting the faculty of sight, for that exists already, but has been turned in the wrong direction, and is looking away from the truth?

Yes, he said, such an art may be presumed.

And whereas the other so-called virtues of the soul seem to be akin to bodily qualities, for even when they are not originally innate they can be implanted later by habit and exercise, the virtue of wisdom more than anything else contains a divine element which always remains, and by this conversion is rendered useful and profitable; or, on the other hand, hurtful and useless. Did you never observe the narrow intelligence flashing from the keen eye of a clever rogue—how eager he is, how clearly his paltry soul sees the way to his end; he is the reverse of blind, but his keen eye-sight is forced into the service of evil, and he is mischievous in proportion to his cleverness?

Very true, he said.

But what if there had been a circumcision of such natures in the days of their youth; and they had been severed from those sensual pleasures, such as eating and drinking, which, like leaden weights, were attached to them at their birth, and which drag them down and turn the vision of their souls upon the things that are below—if, I say, they had been released from these impediments and turned in the opposite direction, the very same faculty in them would have seen the truth as keenly as they see what their eyes are turned to now.

Very likely.

Yes, I said; and there is another thing which is likely, or rather a necessary inference from what has preceded, that neither the uneducated and uninformed of the truth, nor yet those who never make an end of their education, will be able ministers of State; not the former, because they have no single aim of duty which is the rule of all their actions, private as well as public; nor the latter, because they will not act at all except upon compulsion, fancying that they are already dwelling apart in the islands of the blest.

Very true, he replied.

Then, I said, the business of us who are the founders of the State will be to compel the best minds to attain that knowledge which we have already shown to be the greatest of all—they must continue to ascend until they arrive at the good; but when they have ascended and seen enough we must not allow them to do as they do now.

What do you mean?

I mean that they remain in the upper world: but this must not be allowed; they must be made to descend again among the prisoners in the den, and partake of their labours and honours, whether they are worth having or not.

But is not this unjust? he said; ought we to give them a worse life, when they might have a better?

You have again forgotten, my friend, I said, the intention of the legislator, who did not aim at making any one class in the State happy above the rest; the happiness was to be in the whole State, and he held the citizens together by persuasion and necessity, making them benefactors of the State, and therefore benefactors of one another; to this end he created them, not to please themselves, but to be his instruments in binding up the State.

True, he said, I had forgotten.

Observe, Glaucon, that there will be no injustice in compelling our philosophers to have a care and providence of others; we shall explain to them that in other States, men of their class are not obliged to share in the toils of politics: and this is reasonable, for they grow up at their own sweet will, and the government would rather not have them. Being self-taught, they cannot be expected to show any gratitude for a culture which they have never received. But we have brought you into the world to be rulers of the hive, kings of yourselves and of the other citizens, and have educated you far better and more perfectly than they have been educated, and you are better able to share in the double duty. Wherefore each of you, when his turn comes, must go down to the general underground abode, and get the habit of seeing in the dark. When you have acquired the habit, you will see ten thousand times better than the inhabitants of the den, and you will know what the several images are, and what they represent, because you have seen the beautiful and just and good in their truth. And thus our State which is also yours will be a reality, and not a dream only, and will be administered in a spirit unlike that of other States, in which men fight with one another about shadows only and are distracted in the struggle for power, which in their eyes is a great good. Whereas the truth is that the State in which the rulers are most reluctant to govern is always the best and most quietly governed, and the State in which they are most eager, the worst.

Quite true, he replied.

And will our pupils, when they hear this, refuse to take their turn at the toils of State, when they are allowed to spend the greater part of their time with one another in the heavenly light?

Impossible, he answered; for they are just men, and the commands which we impose upon them are just; there can be no doubt that every one of them will take office as a stern necessity, and not after the fashion of our present rulers of State.

Yes, my friend, I said; and there lies the point. You must contrive for your future rulers another and a better life than that of a ruler, and then you may have a well-ordered State; for only in the State which offers this, will they rule who are truly rich, not in silver and gold, but in virtue and wisdom, which are the true blessings of life. Whereas if they go to the administration of public affairs, poor and hungering after their own private advantage, thinking that hence they are to snatch the chief good, order there can never be; for they will be fighting about office, and the civil and domestic broils which thus arise will be the ruin of the rulers themselves and of the whole State.

Most true, he replied.

And the only life which looks down upon the life of political ambition is that of true philosophy. Do you know of any other?

Indeed, I do not, he said . . . .

Suggestions for Discussion

1. Does history support the argument that "the people" are often responsible for killing their own greatest champions and advocates? Can you think of prophets who challenged widely accepted "truths," but who were more successful than Socrates' prophet in changing perspectives?

2. According to Socrates, philosophers would make the best rulers. Why? How are philosophers different from the lawyers, businessmen, soldiers, and politicians whom Americans tend to choose as leaders?

3. Plato's allegory is, in part, about how impossible it is to get people to change their minds once they have formed an opinion and reinforced that opinion over time. Have you ever had luck convincing friends, family, colleagues, or opponents to change their minds concerning any matter, large or small? Under what circumstances might you see yourself changing your mind about an important social, political, or religious issue? Under what circumstances might you consider changing your mind about an issue of minor importance, such as what kind of music is best to listen to, or sport is the best, or what the best thing to do on a weekend is?

Suggestions for Writing

1. How does the cave metaphor work as a commentary on education? On politics? On society? Select one area where you think the cave metaphor is useful and write an essay describing how.

2. Synthesis: What role does Plato's "cave" play in Earl Shorris's essay "Education as a Weapon in the Hands of the Restless Poor"? In a brief essay, discuss the importance of Plato's metaphor to Shorris.

EARL SHORRIS

Education as a Weapon in the Hands of the Restless Poor

A contributing editor for *Harper's Magazine* since 1972, Earl Shorris (b. 1936) has written for a variety of periodicals, including *The Nation*, *Atlantic*, and *The New York Times*. He is both founder and chairman of the Advisory Board for the Clemente Course in the Humanities, affiliated with Bard College, which teaches college-level humanities courses to the poor, and a cofounder of the Pan-American Indian Humanities Center at the University of Science and Arts of Oklahoma. His books, fiction and nonfiction, include *The Boots of the Virgin* (1968), *Under the Fifth Sun* (1980), *Death of the Great Spirit* (1972), *The Oppressed Middle: Scenes From Corporate Life* (1981), *Latinos* (1992), *A Nation of Salesmen: The Tyranny of the Market and the Subversion of Culture* (1996), *New American Blues* (1997), *Riches for the Poor: The Clemente Course in the Humanities* (2000), *The Life and Times of Mexico* (2004), and *The Politics of Heaven: America in Fearful Times* (2007). This essay, originally titled "On the uses of a liberal education as a weapon in the hands of the restless poor," appeared in the September 1997 issues of *Harper's*.

Next month I will publish a book about poverty in America, but not the book I intended. The world took me by surprise—not once, but again and again. The poor themselves led me in directions I could not have imagined, especially the one that came out of a conversation in a maximum security prison for women that is set, incongruously, in a lush Westchester suburb fifty miles north of New York City.

I had been working on the book for about three years when I went to the Bedford Hills Correctional Facility for the first time. The staff and inmates had developed a program to deal with family violence, and I wanted to see how their ideas fit with what I had learned about poverty.

Numerous forces—hunger, isolation, illness, landlords, police, abuse, neighbors, drugs, criminals, and racism, among many others—exert themselves on the poor at all times and enclose them, making up a "surround of force" from which, it seems, they cannot escape. I had come to understand that this was what kept the poor from being political and that the absence of politics in their lives was what kept them poor. I don't mean "political" in the sense of voting in an election but in the way Thucydides used the word: to mean activity with other people at every level, from the family to the neighborhood to the broader community to the city-state.

By the time I got to Bedford Hills, I had listened to more than six hundred people, some of them over the course of two or three years. Although my method is that of the *bricoleur*, the tinkerer who assembles a thesis of the bric-a-brac he finds in the world, I did not think there would be any more surprises. But I had not counted on what Viniece Walker was to say.

It is considered bad form in prison to speak of a person's crime, and I will follow that precise etiquette here. I can tell you that Viniece Walker came to Bedford Hills when she was twenty years old, a high school dropout who read at the level of a college sophomore, a graduate of crackhouses, the streets of Harlem, and a long alliance with a brutal man. On the surface Viniece has remained as tough as she was on the street. She speaks bluntly, and even though she is HIV positive and the virus has progressed during her time in prison, she still swaggers as she walks down the long prison corridors. While in prison, Niecie, as she is known to her friends, completed her high school requirements and began to pursue a college degree (psychology is the only major offered at Bedford Hills, but Niecie also took a special interest in philosophy). She became a counselor to women with a history of family violence and a comforter to those with AIDS.

Only the deaths of other women cause her to stumble in the midst of her swaggering step, to spend days alone with the remorse that drives her to seek redemption. She goes through life as if she had been imagined by Dostoevsky, but even more complex than his fictions, alive, a person, a fair-skinned and freckled African-American woman, and in prison. It was she who responded to my sudden question, "Why do you think people are poor?"

We had never met before. The conversation around us focused on the abuse of women. Niecie's eyes were perfectly opaque—hostile, prison eyes. Her mouth was set in the beginning of a sneer.

"You got to begin with the children," she said, speaking rapidly, clipping out the street sounds as they came into her speech.

She paused long enough to let the change of direction take effect, then resumed the rapid, rhythmless speech. "You've got to teach the moral life of downtown to the children. And the way you do that, Earl, is by taking them downtown to plays, museums, concerts, lectures, where they can learn the moral life of downtown."

I smiled at her, misunderstanding, thinking I was indulging her. "And then they won't be poor anymore?"

She read every nuance of my response, and answered angrily, "And they won't be poor *no more.*"

"What you mean is—"

"What I mean is what I said—a moral alternative to the street."

She didn't speak of jobs or money. In that, she was like the others I had listened to. No one had spoken of jobs or money. But how could the "moral life of downtown" lead anyone out from the surround of force! How could a museum push poverty away? Who can dress in statues or eat the past? And what of the political life? Had Niecie skipped a step or failed to take a step? The way out of poverty was politics, not the "moral life of downtown." But to enter the public world, to practice the political life, the poor had first to learn to reflect. That was what Niecie meant by the "moral life of downtown." She did not make the error of divorcing ethics from politics. Niecie had simply said, in a kind of shorthand, that no one could step out of the panicking circumstance of poverty directly into the public world.

Although she did not say so, I was sure that when she spoke of the "moral life of downtown" she meant something that had happened to her. With no job and no money, a prisoner, she had undergone a radical transformation. She had followed the same path that led to the invention of politics in ancient Greece. She had learned to reflect. In further conversation it became clear that when she spoke of "the moral life of downtown" she meant the humanities, the study of human constructs and concerns, which has been the source of reflection for the secular world since the Greeks first stepped back from nature to experience wonder at what they beheld. If the political life was the way out of poverty, the humanities provided an entrance to reflection and the political life. The poor did not need anyone to release them; an escape route existed. But to open this avenue to reflection and politics a major distinction between the preparation for the life of the rich and the life of the poor had to be eliminated.

Once Niecie had challenged me with her theory, the comforts of tinkering came to an end; I could no longer make an homage to the happenstance world and rest. To test Niecie's theory, students, faculty, and facilities were required. Quantitative measures would have to be developed; anecdotal information would also be useful. And the ethics of the experiment had to be considered: I resolved to do no harm. There was no need for the course to have a "sink or swim" character; it could aim to keep as many afloat as possible.

When the idea for an experimental course became clear in my mind, I discussed it with Dr. Jaime Inclán, director of the Roberto Clemente Family Guidance Center in lower Manhattan, a facility that provides counseling to poor people, mainly Latinos, in their own language and in their own community. Dr. Inclán offered the center's conference room for a classroom. We would put three metal tables end to end to approximate the boat-shaped tables used in discussion sections at the University of Chicago of the Hutchins era,[1] which I used as a model for the course. A card table in the back of the room would hold a coffeemaker and a few cookies. The setting was not elegant, but it would do. And the front wall was covered by a floor-to-ceiling blackboard.

Now the course lacked only students and teachers. With no funds and a budget that grew every time a new idea for the course crossed my mind, I would have to ask the faculty to donate its time and effort. Moreover, when Hutchins said, "The best education for the best is the best education

[1]Under the guidance of Robert Maynard Hutchins (1929–1951), the University of Chicago required year-long courses in the humanities, social sciences, and natural sciences for the Bachelor of Arts degree. Hutchins developed the curriculum with the help of Mortimer Adler, among others; the Hutchins courses later influenced Adler's Great Books program.

for us all," he meant it: he insisted that full professors teach discussion sections in the college. If the Clemente Course in the Humanities was to follow the same pattern, it would require a faculty with the knowledge and prestige that students might encounter in their first year at Harvard, Yale, Princeton, or Chicago.

I turned first to the novelist Charles Simmons. He had been assistant editor of *The New York Times Book Review* and had taught at Columbia University. He volunteered to teach poetry, beginning with simple poems, Housman, and ending with Latin poetry. Grace Glueck, who writes art news and criticism for the *New York Times,* planned a course that began with cave paintings and ended in the late twentieth century. Timothy Koranda, who did his graduate work at MIT, had published journal articles on mathematical logic, but he had been away from his field for some years and looked forward to getting back to it. I planned to teach the American history course through documents, beginning with the Magna Carta, moving on to the second of Locke's *Two Treatises of Government,* the Declaration of Independence, and so on through the documents of the Civil War. I would also teach the political philosophy class.

Since I was a naïf in this endeavor, it did not immediately occur to me that recruiting students would present a problem. I didn't know how many I needed. All I had were criteria for selection:

Age: 18–35.
Household income: Less than 150 percent of the Census Bureau's Official Poverty Threshold (though this was to change slightly).
Educational level: Ability to read a tabloid newspaper.
Educational goals: An expression of intent to complete the course.

Dr. Inclán arranged a meeting of community activists who could help recruit students. Lynette Lauretig of The Door, a program that provides medical and educational services to adolescents, and Angel Roman of the Grand Street Settlement, which offers work and training and GED programs, were both willing to give us access to prospective students. They also pointed out some practical considerations. The course had to provide bus and subway tokens, because fares ranged between three and six dollars per class per student, and the students could not afford sixty or even thirty dollars a month for transportation. We also had to offer dinner or a snack, because the classes were to be held from 6:00 to 7:30 P.M.

The first recruiting session came only a few days later. Nancy Mamis-King, associate executive director of the Neighborhood Youth & Family Services program in the South Bronx, had identified some Clemente Course candidates and had assembled about twenty of her clients and their supervisors in a circle of chairs in a conference room. Everyone in the room was black or Latino, with the exception of one social worker and me.

After I explained the idea of the course, the white social worker was the first to ask a question: "Are you going to teach African history?"

"No. We'll be teaching a section on American history, based on documents, as I said. We want to teach the ideas of history so that—"

"You have to teach African history."

"This is America, so we'll teach American history. It we were in Africa, I would teach African history, and if we were in China, I would teach Chinese history."

"You're indoctrinating people in Western culture."

I tried to get beyond her. "We'll study African art," I said, "as it affects art in America. We'll study American history and literature; you can't do that without studying African-American culture, because culturally all Americans are black as well as white, Native American, Asian, and so on." It was no use; not one of them applied for admission to the course.

A few days later Lynette Lauretig arranged a meeting with some of her staff at The Door. We disagreed about the course. They thought it should be taught at a much lower level. Although I could not change their views, they agreed to assemble a group of Door members who might be interested in the humanities.

On an early evening that same week, about twenty prospective students were scheduled to meet in a classroom at The Door. Most of them came late. Those who arrived first slumped in their chairs, staring at the floor or greeting me with sullen glances. A few ate candy or what appeared to be the remnants of a meal. The students were mostly black and Latino, one was Asian, and five were white; two of the whites were immigrants who had severe problems with English. When I introduced myself, several of the students would not shake my hand, two or three refused even to look at me, one girl giggled, and the last person to volunteer his name, a young man dressed in a Tommy Hilfiger sweatshirt and wearing a cap turned sideways, drawled, "Henry Jones, but they call me Sleepy, because I got these sleepy eyes—"

"In our class, we'll call you Mr. Jones."

He smiled and slid down in his chair so that his back was parallel to the floor.

Before I finished attempting to shake hands with the prospective students, a waiflike Asian girl with her mouth half-full of cake said, "Can we get on with it? I'm bored."

I liked the group immediately.

Having failed in the South Bronx, I resolved to approach these prospective students differently. "You've been cheated," I said. "Rich people learn the humanities; you didn't. The humanities are a foundation for getting along in the world, for thinking, for learning to reflect on the world instead of just reacting to whatever force is turned against you. I think the humanities are one of the ways to become political, and I don't mean political in the sense of voting in an election but in the broad sense." I told them Thucydides' definition of politics.

"Rich people know politics in that sense. They know how to negotiate instead of using force. They know how to use politics to get along, to get power. It doesn't mean that rich people are good and poor people are bad. It simply means that rich people know a more effective method for living in this society.

"Do all rich people, or people who are in the middle, know the humanities? Not a chance. But some do. And it helps. It helps to live better and enjoy life more. Will the humanities make you rich? Yes. Absolutely. But not in terms of money. In terms of life.

"Rich people learn the humanities in private schools and expensive universities. And that's one of the ways in which they learn the political life. I think that is the real difference between the haves and have-nots in this country. If you want real power, legitimate power, the kind that comes from the people and belongs to the people, you must understand politics. The humanities will help.

"Here's how it works: We'll pay your subway fare; take care of your children, if you have them; give you a snack or a sandwich; provide you with books and any other materials you need. But we'll make you think harder, use your mind more fully, than you ever have before. You'll have to read and think about the same kinds of ideas you would encounter in a first-year course at Harvard or Yale or Oxford.

"You'll have to come to class in the snow and the rain and the cold and the dark. No one will coddle you, no one will slow down for you. There will be tests to take, papers to write. And I can't promise you anything but a certificate of completion at the end of the course. I'll be talking to colleges about giving credit for the course, but I can't promise anything. If you come to the Clemente Course, you must do it because you want to study the humanities, because you want a certain kind of life, a richness of mind and spirit. That's all I offer you: philosophy, poetry, art history, logic, rhetoric, and American history.

"Your teachers will all be people of accomplishment in their fields," I said, and I spoke a little about each teacher. "That's the course. October through May, with a two-week break at Christmas. It is generally accepted in America that the liberal arts and the humanities in particular belong to the elites. I think you're the elites."

The young Asian woman said, "What are you getting out of this?"

"This is a demonstration project. I'm writing a book. This will be proof, I hope, of my idea about the humanities. Whether it succeeds or fails will be up to the teachers and you."

All but one of the prospective students applied for admission to the course.

I repeated the new presentation at the Grand Street Settlement and at other places around the city. There were about fifty candidates for the thirty positions in the course. Personal interviews began in early September.

Meanwhile, almost all of my attempts to raise money had failed. Only the novelist Starling Lawrence, who is also editor in chief of W. W. Norton, which had contracted to publish the book; the publishing house itself; and a small, private family foundation supported the experiment. We were far short of our budgeted expenses, but my wife, Sylvia and I agreed that the cost was still very low, and we decided to go ahead.

Of the fifty prospective students who showed up at the Clemente Center for personal interviews, a few were too rich (a postal supervisor's son, a fellow who claimed his father owned a factory in Nigeria that employed sixty people) and more than a few could not read. Two home-care workers from Local 1199 could not arrange their hours to enable them to take the course. Some of the applicants were too young: a thirteen-year-old and two who had just turned sixteen.

Lucia Medina, a woman with five children who told me that she often answered the door at the single-room occupancy hotel where she lived with a butcher knife in her hand, was the oldest person accepted into the course. Carmen Quiñones, a recovering addict who had spent time in prison, was the next eldest. Both were in their early thirties.

The interviews went on for days.

Abel Lomas[2] shared an apartment and worked part-time wrapping packages at Macy's. His father had abandoned the family when Abel was born. His mother was murdered by his stepfather when Abel was thirteen. With no one to turn to and no place to stay, he lived on the streets, first in Florida, then back in New York City. He used the tiny stipend from his mother's Social Security to keep himself alive.

After the recruiting session at The Door, I drove up Sixth Avenue from Canal Street with Abel, and we talked about ethics. He had a street tough's delivery, spitting out his ideas in crudely formed sentences of four, five, eight words, strings of blunt declarations, with never a dependent clause to qualify his thoughts. He did not clear his throat with badinage, as timidity teaches us to do, nor did he waste his breath with tact.

"What do you think about drugs?" he asked, the strangely breathless delivery further coarsened by his Dominican accent. "My cousin is a dealer."

"I've seen a lot of people hurt by drugs."

"Your family has nothing to eat. You sell drugs. What's worse? Let your family starve or sell drugs?"

"Starvation and drug addiction are both bad, aren't they?"

"Yes," he said, not "yeah" or "uh-huh" but a precise, almost formal "yes."

[2]Not his real name.

"So it's a question of the worse of two evils? How shall we decide?"

The question came up near Thirty-fourth Street, where Sixth Avenue remains hellishly traffic-jammed well into the night. Horns honked, people flooded into the street against the light. Buses and trucks and taxicabs threatened their way from one lane to the next where the overcrowded avenue crosses the equally crowded Broadway. As we passed Herald Square and made our way north again, I said, "There are a couple of ways to look at it. One comes from Immanuel Kant, who said that you should not do anything unless you want it to become a universal law; that is, unless you think it's what everybody should do. So Kant wouldn't agree to selling drugs *or* letting your family starve."

Again he answered with a formal "Yes."

"There's another way to look at it, which is to ask what is the greatest good for the greatest number: in this case, keeping your family from starvation or keeping tens, perhaps hundreds of people from losing their lives to drugs. So which is the greatest good for the greatest number?"

"That's what I think," he said.

"What?"

"You shouldn't sell drugs. You can always get food to eat. Welfare. Something."

"You're a Kantian."

"Yes."

"You know who Kant is?"

"I think so."

We had arrived at Seventy-seventh Street, where he got out of the car to catch the subway before I turned east. As he opened the car door and the light came on, the almost military neatness of him struck me. He had the newly cropped hair of a cadet. His clothes were clean, without a wrinkle. He was an orphan, a street kid, an immaculate urchin. Within a few weeks he would be nineteen years old, the Social Security payments would end, and he would have to move into a shelter.

Some of those who came for interviews were too poor. I did not think that was possible when we began, and I would like not to believe it now, but it was true. There is a point at which the level of forces that surround the poor can become insurmountable, when there is no time or energy left to be anything but poor. Most often I could not recruit such people for the course; when I did, they soon dropped out.

Over the days of interviewing, a class slowly assembled. I could not then imagine who would last the year and who would not. One young woman submitted a neatly typed essay that said, "I was homeless once, then I lived for some time in a shelter. Right now, I have got my own space granted by the Partnership for the Homeless. Right now, I am living alone, with very limited means. Financially I am overwhelmed by debts. I cannot afford all the food I need . . ."

A brother and sister, refugees from Tashkent, lived with their parents in the farthest reaches of Queens, far beyond the end of the subway line. They had no money, and they had been refused admission by every school to which they had applied. I had not intended to accept immigrants or people who had difficulty with the English language, but I took them into the class.

I also took four who had been in prison, three who were homeless, three who were pregnant, one who lived in a drugged dream-state in which she was abused, and one whom I had known for a long time and who was dying of AIDS. As I listened to them, I wondered how the course would affect them. They had no public life, no place; they lived within the surround of force, moving as fast as they could, driven by necessity, without a moment to reflect. Why should they care about fourteenth-century Italian painting or truth tables or the death of Socrates?

Between the end of recruiting and the orientation session that would open the course, I made a visit to Bedford Hills to talk with Niecie Walker. It was hot, and the drive up from the city had been unpleasant. I didn't yet know Niecie very well. She didn't trust me, and I didn't know what to make of her. While we talked, she held a huge white pill in her hand. "For AIDS," she said.

"Are you sick?"

"My T-cell count is down. But that's neither here nor there. Tell me about the course, Earl. What are you going to teach?"

"Moral philosophy."

"And what does that include?"

She had turned the visit into an interrogation. I didn't mind. At the end of the conversation I would be going out into "the free world"; if she wanted our meeting to be an interrogation, I was not about to argue. I said, "We'll begin with Plato: the *Apology*, a little of the *Crito*, a few pages of the *Phaedo* so that they'll know what happened to Socrates. Then we'll read Aristotle's *Nicomachean Ethics*. I also want them to read Thucydides, particularly Pericles' Funeral Oration in order to make the connection between ethics and politics, to lead them in the direction I hope the course will take them. Then we'll end with *Antigone*, but read as moral and political philosophy as well as drama."

"There's something missing," she said, leaning back in her chair, taking on an air of superiority.

The drive had been long, the day was hot, the air in the room was dead and damp. "Oh, yeah," I said, "and what's that?"

"Plato's Allegory of the Cave. How can you teach philosophy to poor people without the Allegory of the Cave? The ghetto is the cave. Education is the light. Poor people can understand that."

At the beginning of the orientation at the Clemente Center a week later, each teacher spoke for a minute or two. Dr. Inclán and his research assistant, Patricia Vargas, administered the questionnaire he had devised to measure, as best he could, the role of force and the amount of reflection in the lives of the students. I explained that each class was going to be videotaped as another way of documenting the project. Then I gave out the first assignment: "In preparation for our next meeting, I would like you to read a brief selection from Plato's *Republic:* the Allegory of the Cave."

I tried to guess how many students would return for the first class. I hoped for twenty, expected fifteen, and feared ten. Sylvia, who had agreed to share the administrative tasks of the course, and I prepared coffee and cookies for twenty-five. We had a plastic container filled with subway tokens. Thanks to Starling Lawrence, we had thirty copies of Bernard Knox's *Norton Book of Classical Literature*, which contained all of the texts for the philosophy section except the *Republic* and the *Nicomachean Ethics.*

At six o'clock there were only ten students seated around the long table, but by six-fifteen the number had doubled, and a few minutes later two more straggled in out of the dusk. I had written a time line on the blackboard, showing them the temporal progress of thinking—from the role of myth in Neolithic societies to *The Gilgamesh Epic* and forward to the Old Testament, Confucius, the Greeks, the New Testament, the Koran, the *Epic of SonJara*, and ending with Nahuatl and Maya poems, which took us up to the contact between Europe and America, where the history course began. The time line served as context and geography as well as history: no race, no major culture was ignored. "Let's agree," I told them, "that we are all human, whatever our origins. And now let's go into Plato's cave."

I told them that there would be no lectures in the philosophy section of the course; we would use the Socratic method, which is called maieutic dialogue. "'Maieutic' comes from the Greek word for midwifery. I'll take the role of midwife in our dialogue. Now, what do I mean by that? What does a midwife do?"

It was the beginning of a love affair, the first moment of their infatuation with Socrates. Later, Abel Lomas would characterize that moment in his no-nonsense fashion, saying that it was the first time anyone had ever paid attention to their opinions.

Grace Glueck began the art history class in a darkened room lit with slides of the Lascaux caves and next turned the students' attention to Egypt, arranging for them to visit the Metropolitan Museum of Art to see the Temple of Dendur and the Egyptian Galleries. They arrived at the museum on a Friday evening. Darlene Codd brought her two-year-old son. Pearl Lau was late, as usual. One of the students, who had told me how much he was looking forward to the museum visit, didn't show up, which surprised me. Later I learned that he had been arrested for jumping a turnstile in a subway station on his way to the museum and was being held in a prison cell under the Brooklyn criminal courthouse. In the Temple of Dendur, Samantha Smoot asked questions of Felicia Blum, a museum lecturer. Samantha was the student who had burst out with the news, in one of the first sessions of the course, that people in her neighborhood believed it "wasn't no use goin' to school, because the white man wouldn't let you up no matter what." But in a hall where the statuary was of half-human, half-animal female figures, it was Samantha who asked what the glyphs meant, encouraging Felicia Blum to read them aloud, to translate them into English. Toward the end of the evening, Grace led the students out of the halls of antiquities into the Rockefeller Wing, where she told them of the connections of culture and art in Mali, Benin, and the Pacific Islands. When the students had collected their coats and stood together near the entrance to the museum, preparing to leave, Samantha stood apart, a tall, slim young woman, dressed in a deerstalker cap and a dark blue peacoat. She made an exaggerated farewell wave at us and returned to Egypt—her ancient mirror.

Charles Simmons began the poetry class with poems as puzzles and laughs. His plan was to surprise the class, and he did. At first he read the poems aloud to them, interrupting himself with footnotes to bring them along. He showed them poems of love and of seduction, and satiric commentaries on those poems by later poets. "Let us read," the students demanded, but Charles refused. He tantalized them with the opportunity to read poems aloud. A tug-of-war began between him and the students, and the standoff was ended not by Charles directly but by Hector Anderson. When Charles asked if anyone in the class wrote poetry, Hector raised his hand.

"Can you recite one of your poems for us?" Charles said.

Until that moment, Hector had never volunteered a comment, though he had spoken well and intelligently when asked. He preferred to slouch in his chair, dressed in full camouflage gear, wearing a nylon stocking over his hair and eating slices of fresh cantaloupe or honeydew melon.

In response to Charles's question, Hector slid up to a sitting position. "If you turn that camera off," he said. "I don't want anybody using my lyrics." When he was sure the red light of the video camera was off, Hector stood and recited verse after verse of a poem that belonged somewhere in the triangle formed by Ginsberg's *Howl*, the Book of Lamentations, and hip-hop. When Charles and the students finished applauding, they asked Hector to say the poem again, and he did. Later Charles told me, "That kid is the real thing." Hector's discomfort with Sylvia and me turned to ease. He came to our house for a small Christmas party and at other times.

We talked on the telephone about a scholarship program and about what steps he should take next in his education. I came to know his parents. As a student, he began quietly, almost secretly, to surpass many of his classmates.

Timothy Koranda was the most professorial of the professors. He arrived precisely on time, wearing a hat of many styles—part fedora, part Borsalino, part Stetson, and at least one-half World War I campaign hat. He taught logic during class hours, filling the blackboard from floor to ceiling, wall to wall, drawing the intersections of sets here and truth tables there and a great square of oppositions in the middle of it all. After class, he walked with students to the subway, chatting about Zen or logic or Heisenberg.

On one of the coldest nights of the winter, he introduced the students to logic problems stated in ordinary language that they could solve by reducing the phrases to symbols. He passed out copies of a problem, two pages long, then wrote out some of the key phrases on the blackboard. "Take this home with you," he said, "and at out next meeting we shall see who has solved it. I shall also attempt to find the answer."

By the time he finished writing out the key phrases, however, David Iskhakov raised his hand. Although they listened attentively, neither David nor his sister Susana spoke often in class. She was shy, and he was embarrassed at his inability to speak perfect English.

"May I go to blackboard?" David said. "And will see if I have found correct answer to zis problem."

Together Tim and David erased the blackboard, then David began covering it with signs and symbols. "If first man is earning this money, and second man is closer to this town . . .," he said, carefully laying out the conditions. After five minutes or so, he said, "And the answer is: B will get first to Cleveland!"

Samantha Smoot shouted, "That's not the answer. The mistake you made is in the first part there, where it says who earns more money."

Tim folded his arms across his chest, happy. "I shall let you all take the problem home," he said.

When Sylvia and I left the Clemente Center that night, a knot of students was gathered outside, huddled against the wind. Snow had begun to fall, a slippery powder on the gray ice that covered all but a narrow space down the center of the sidewalk. Samantha and David stood in the middle of the group, still arguing over the answer to the problem. I leaned in for a moment to catch the character of the argument. It was even more polite than it had been in the classroom, because now they governed themselves.

One Saturday morning in January, David Howell telephoned me at home. "Mr. Shores," he said, Anglicizing my name, as many of the students did.

"Mr. Howell," I responded, recognizing his voice.

"How you doin', Mr. Shores?"

"I'm fine. How are you?"

"I had a little problem at work."

Uh-oh, I thought, bad news was coming. David is a big man, generally good-humored but with a quick temper. According to his mother, he had a history of violent behavior. In the classroom he had been one of the best students, a steady man, twenty-four years old, who always did the reading assignments and who often made interesting connections between the humanities and daily life. "What happened?"

"Mr. Shores, there's a woman at my job, she said some things to me and I said some things to her. And she told my supervisor I had said things to her, and he called me in about it. She's forty years old and she don't have no social life, and I have a good social life, and she's jealous of me."

"And then what happened?" The tone of his voice and the timing of the call did not portend good news.

"Mr. Shores, she made me so mad, I wanted to smack her up against the wall. I tried to talk to some friends to calm myself down a little, but nobody was around."

"And what did you do?" I asked, fearing this was his one telephone call from the city jail.

"Mr. Shores, I asked myself, 'What would Socrates do?'"

David Howell had reasoned that his coworker's envy was not his problem after all, and he had dropped his rage.

One evening, in the American history section, I was telling the students about Gordon Wood's ideas in *The Radicalism of the American Revolution*. We were talking about the revolt by some intellectuals against classical learning at the turn of the eighteenth century, including Benjamin Franklin's late-life change of heart, when Henry Jones raised his hand.

"If the Founders loved the humanities so much, how come they treated the natives so badly?"

I didn't know how to answer this question. There were confounding explanations to offer about changing attitudes toward Native Americans, vaguely useful references to views of Rousseau and James Fenimore Cooper. For a moment I wondered if I should tell them about Heidegger's Nazi past. Then I saw Abel Lomas's raised hand at the far end of the table. "Mr. Lomas," I said.

Abel said, "That's what Aristotle means by incontinence, when you know what's morally right but you don't do it, because you're overcome by your passions."

The other students nodded. They were all inheritors of wounds caused by the incontinence of educated men; now they had an ally in Aristotle, who had given them a way to analyze the actions of their antagonists.

Those who appreciate ancient history understand the radical character of the humanities. They know that politics did not begin in a perfect world but in a society even more flawed than ours: one that embraced slavery, denied the rights of women, practiced a form of homosexuality that verged on pedophilia, and endured the intrigues and corruption of its leaders. The genius of that society originated in man's re-creation of himself through the recognition of his humanness as expressed in art, literature, rhetoric, philosophy, and the unique notion of freedom. At that moment, the isolation of the private life ended and politics began.

The winners in the game of modern society, and even those whose fortune falls in the middle, have other means to power: they are included at birth. They know this. And they know exactly what to do to protect their place in the economic and social hierarchy. As Allan Bloom, author of the nationally best-selling tract in defense of elitism, *The Closing of the American Mind*, put it, they direct the study of the humanities exclusively at those young people who "have been raised in comfort and with the expectation of ever increasing comfort."

In the last meeting before graduation, the Clemente students answered the same set of questions they'd answered at orientation. Between October and May, students had fallen to AIDS, pregnancy, job opportunities, pernicious anemia, clinical depression, a schizophrenic child, and other forces, but of the thirty students admitted to the course, sixteen had completed it, and fourteen had earned credit from Bard College. Dr. Inclán found that the students' self-esteem and their abilities to divine and solve problems had significantly increased; their use of verbal aggression as a tactic for resolving conflicts had significantly decreased. And they all had notably more appreciation for the concepts of benevolence, spirituality, universalism, and collectivism.

It cost about $2,000 for a student to attend the Clemente Course. Compared with unemployment, welfare, or prison, the humanities are a bargain. But coming into possession of the faculty of reflection and the skills of politics leads to a choice for the poor—and whatever they choose, they will be dangerous: they may use politics to get along in a society based on the game, to escape from the surround of force into a gentler life, to behave as citizens, and nothing more; or they may choose to oppose the game itself. No one can predict the effect of politics, although we all would like to think that wisdom goes our way. That is why the poor are so often mobilized and so rarely politicized. The possibility that they will adopt a moral view other than that of their mentors can never be discounted. And who wants to run that risk?

On the night of the first Clemente Course graduation, the students and their families filled the eighty-five chairs we crammed into the conference room where classes had been held. Robert Martin, associate dean of Bard College, read the graduates' names. David Dinkins, the former mayor of New York City, handed out the diplomas. There were speeches and presentations. The students gave me a plaque on which they had misspelled my name. I offered a few words about each student, congratulated them, and said finally, "This is what I wish for you: May you never be more active than when you are doing nothing . . ." I saw their smiles of recognition at the words of Cato, which I had written on the blackboard early in the course. They could recall again too the moment when we had come to the denouement of Aristotle's brilliantly constructed thriller, the *Nicomachean Ethics*— the idea that in the contemplative life man was most like God. One or two, perhaps more of the students, closed their eyes. In the momentary stillness of the room it was possible to think.

The Clemente Course in the Humanities ended a second year in June 1997. Twenty-eight new students had enrolled; fourteen graduated. Another version of the course will begin this fall in Yucatán, Mexico, using classical Maya literature in Maya.

On May 14, 1997, Viniece Walker came up for parole for the second time. She had served more than ten years of her sentence, and she had been the best of prisoners. In a version of the Clemente Course held at the prison, she had been my teaching assistant. After a brief hearing, her request for parole was denied. She will serve two more years before the parole board will reconsider her case.

A year after graduation, ten of the first sixteen Clemente Course graduates were attending four-year colleges or going to nursing school; four of them had received full scholarships to Bard College. The other graduates were attending community college or working full-time. Except for one: she had been fired from her job in a fast-food restaurant for trying to start a union.

Suggestions for Discussion

1. What is the importance of "reflection" and "the political life" in this article? How does Shorris's program in particular, and the study of humanities in general, foster "reflection" and "the political life"?

2. What were the logistical challenges of launching this teaching program? Why do you believe that Shorris chose the faculty he did, profiled the students the way he did, and fashioned the curriculum in such a way?

3. Why does Shorris believe that middle- and upper-class people would rather pay taxes to fund prison systems than donate funds to education programs such as his? What are the implications of this belief for Shorris?

4. How does the historical photograph taken by F. B. Johnston portray (adult) education? How does this class compare to the classes that Earl Shorris describes teaching?

FRANCES BENJAMIN JOHNSTON, *Geography. Studying the Seasons.* Platinum print, 1900. Digital image © The Museum for Modern Art/licensed by Scala/Art Resource NY.

Suggestions for Writing

1. Have you studied the humanities? Did this study make you feel, as Shorris suggests, liberated, reflective, and political? If not, what did you feel during this study? Explore your own view of "the humanities" and the value of their study in a brief, researched paper.

2. Describe an interaction between professor and student featured in this article that you found particularly interesting. What is significant about this moment?

ᘯᘯᘯ

DREW GILPIN FAUST

The University's Crisis of Purpose

President of Harvard University, Catherine Drew Gilpin Faust (b. 1947) is a historian who writes about the Civil War and the antebellum South. Born in New York and raised in Virginia, Faust comes from a distinguished family lineage that includes business leaders, politicians, and legendary Puritan patriarch Jonathan Edwards. A former dean of the Radcliffe Institute for Advanced Study, Faust is an alumnus of Bryn Mawr College (A.B.) and the University of Pennsylvania (A.M. and Ph.D.). Her books include *A Sacred Circle* (1977), *James Henry Hammond and the Old South* (1982), *The Creation of Confederate Nationalism* (1982), *Southern Stories* (1992), *Mothers of Invention: Women of the Slaveholding South in the American Civil War* (1996), and *This Republic of Suffering* (2008). She began her tenure as Harvard's first female president in 2007, following the resignation of her controversial predecessor Lawrence Summers (see Katha Pollitt's "Summers of Our Discontent" for a discussion of the initiating incident). The following editorial was published in *The New York Times* on September 6, 2009.

The world economic crisis and the election of Barack Obama will change the future of higher education. Even as universities, both public and private, face unanticipated financial constraints, the president has called on them to assist in solving problems from health care delivery to climate change to economic recovery.

American universities have long struggled to meet almost irreconcilable demands: to be practical as well as transcendent; to assist immediate national needs and to pursue knowledge for its own sake; to both add value and question values. And in the past decade and a half, such conflicting and unbounded expectations have yielded a wave of criticism on issues ranging from the cost of college to universities' intellectual quality to their supposed decline into unthinking political correctness. A steady stream of books—among them "Declining by Degrees: Higher Education at Risk" (also a PBS special), edited by Richard H. Hersh and John Merrow; Anthony T. Kronman's "Education's End: Why Our Colleges and Universities Have Given Up on the Meaning of Life"; and Dinesh D'Souza's

"Illiberal Education: The Politics of Race and Sex on Campus"—have delineated what various authors have seen as the failings of higher education.

At the same time, American colleges and universities have remained the envy of the world. A 2005 international ranking included 17 American educational institutions in the top 20, and a recent survey of American citizens revealed that 93 percent of respondents considered our universities one of the country's "most valuable resources."

Such a widespread perception of the value of universities derives in no small part from very pragmatic realities: a college education yields significant rewards. The median earnings for individuals with a B.A. are 74 percent higher than for workers who possess only a high school diploma.

In some respects, this is not new. Education has been central to the American Dream since the time of the nation's founding. But in the years since World War II, it was higher education, not just instruction at the elementary or high school levels, that emerged as necessary for a technologically skilled work force as well as fundamental to cherished values of opportunity. As late as the 1920s, enrollments in the United States stood below 5 percent of the college-age population. They rose to about 15 percent by 1949, in part as a result of the G.I. Bill. They have now reached nearly 60 percent. The United States has pioneered a new postwar era of mass college attendance that has become global in reach.

But today, for all its importance to individual and social prosperity, higher education threatens to become less broadly available. By the end of the 20th century, as Claudia Goldin and Lawrence F. Katz document in "The Race Between Education and Technology," the rate of increase in educational attainment had significantly slowed, and the United States had fallen behind a number of other nations in the percentage of its youth attending college. Goldin and Katz demonstrate how this slowdown is creating a work force with inadequate technological abilities, as well as contributing to rising levels of American inequality.

Escalating college costs have played a significant role in this slowdown, even as universities have substantially expanded their programs of financial aid. So, too, have declining levels of government support.

After World War II, the country witnessed the establishment of a new partnership between Washington and the nation's institutions of higher learning, with the federal government investing in universities as the primary locus for the nation's scientific research. This model now faces significant challenges. Steep federal deficits will combine with diminished university resources to intensify what a 2007 report by the National Academies declared to be a "gathering storm," one that threatened the future of scientific education and research in America. The Obama administration has set a goal of devoting more than 3 percent of gross domestic product to research. One hopes this highly ambitious aspiration can become a reality.

The economic downturn has had what is perhaps an even more worrisome impact. It has reinforced America's deep-seated notion that a college degree serves largely instrumental purposes. The federal government's first effort to support higher education, the Morrill Act of 1862, which established land grant colleges, was intended to advance the "practical education of the industrial classes." A Department of Education report from 2006, "A Test of Leadership: Charting the Future of Higher Education," concentrated on creating a competitive American work force and advancing "our collective prosperity." But even as we as a nation have embraced education as critical to economic growth and opportunity, we should remember that colleges and universities are about a great deal more than measurable utility. Unlike perhaps any other institutions in the world, they embrace the long view and nurture the kind of critical perspectives that look far beyond the present.

Higher education is not about results in the next quarter but about discoveries that may take—and last—decades or even centuries. Neither the abiding questions of humanistic inquiry nor the winding path of scientific research that leads ultimately to innovation and discovery can be neatly fitted within a predictable budget and timetable.

In an assessment of the condition of higher education in the Anglo-American world, "Multiversities, Ideas, and Democracy," George Fallis, a former dean at York University in Toronto, deplores the growing dominance of economic justifications for universities. They conflict, he argues, "with other parts of the multiversity's mission, with . . . narratives of liberal learning, disinterested scholarship and social citizenship." University leaders, he observes, have embraced a market model of university purpose to justify themselves to the society that supports them with philanthropy and tax dollars. Higher education, Fallis insists, has the responsibility to serve not just as a source of economic growth, but as society's critic and conscience.

Universities are meant to be producers not just of knowledge but also of (often inconvenient) doubt. They are creative and unruly places, homes to a polyphony of voices. But at this moment in our history, universities might well ask if they have in fact done enough to raise the deep and unsettling questions necessary to any society.

As the world indulged in a bubble of false prosperity and excessive materialism, should universities—in their research, teaching and writing—have made greater efforts to expose the patterns of risk and denial? Should universities have presented a firmer counterweight to economic irresponsibility? Have universities become too captive to the immediate and worldly purposes they serve? Has the market model become the fundamental and defining identity of higher education?

Since the 1970s there has been a steep decline in the percentage of students majoring in the liberal arts and sciences, and an accompanying increase in preprofessional undergraduate degrees. Business is now by far the most popular undergraduate major, with twice as many bachelor's degrees awarded in this area than in any other field of study. In the era of economic constraint before us, the pressure toward vocational pursuits is likely only to intensify.

As a nation, we need to ask more than this from our universities. Higher learning can offer individuals and societies a depth and breadth of vision absent from the inevitably myopic present. Human beings need meaning, understanding and perspective as well as jobs. The question should not be whether we can afford to believe in such purposes in these times, but whether we can afford not to.

Suggestions for Discussion

1. How does the state of the global economy play into whether or not people attend college, which colleges they attend, and what they major in?

2. What historical perspective does Faust bring to this discussion? How have American colleges "failed" in many ways, while still remaining "the envy of the world"?

3. How might being the president of an "elite" college shape Faust's views of education?

Suggestions for Writing

1. According to Faust, why is it a problem that fewer students are majoring in the arts and humanities, while business majors are increasing? Do you agree with her argument? What might be the advantages, if any, of having many graduates trained in business? What is the difference between studying to prepare for a career and studying to acquire learning?

2. We often assume that an English major will have a harder time finding a good job after graduation than a business major. Examine data from the U.S. Bureau of Labor Statistics (www.bls.gov), *The Chronicle of Higher Education* (chronicle.com), *The Wall Street Journal* (www.wsj.com), *Forbes* (www.forbes.com), and the *Modern Language Association* (www.mla.org) to find out more about whether this assumption is true, and write a paper about what you discover.

෴

LEWIS THOMAS

Humanities and Science

Lewis Thomas (1913–1993) was a physician whose medical career centered on the Sloan Kettering Cancer Care Center in New York, the city of his birth. He wrote for medical journals at the same time that he wrote popular essays to present science and the scientist's view of the world to the lay public. He won the National Book Award in 1974 for *The Lives of a Cell: Notes of a Biology Watcher*. Other collections include *More Notes of a Biology Watcher* (1979), *The Youngest Science: Notes of a Medicine-Watcher* (1983), *Late Night Thoughts on Listening to Mahler's Ninth* (1984), and *The Fragile Species* (1992). In the following essay, from *Late Night Thoughts on Listening to Mahler's Ninth*, Thomas advocates open discussion of what science does not yet know or understand.

Lord Kelvin was one of the great British physicists of the late nineteenth century, an extraordinarily influential figure in his time, and in some ways a paradigm of conventional, established scientific leadership. He did a lot of good and useful things, but once or twice he, like Homer, nodded. The instances are worth recalling today, for we have nodders among our scientific eminences still, from time to time, needing to have their elbows shaken.

On one occasion, Kelvin made a speech on the overarching importance of numbers. He maintained that no observation of nature was worth paying serious attention to unless it could be stated in precisely quantitative terms. The numbers were the final and only test, not only of truth but about meaning as well. He said, "When you can measure what you are speaking about, and express it in numbers, you know something about it. But when you cannot—your knowledge is of a meagre and unsatisfactory kind."

But, as at least one subsequent event showed, Kelvin may have had things exactly the wrong way round. The task of converting observations into numbers is the hardest of all, the last task rather than the first thing to be done, and it can be done only when you have learned, beforehand, a great deal about the observations themselves. You can, to be sure, achieve a very deep understanding of nature by quantitative measurement, but you must know what you are talking about before you can begin applying the numbers for making predictions. In Kelvin's case, the problem at hand was the age of the earth and solar system. Using what was then known about the sources of energy and the loss of energy from the physics of that day, he calculated that neither the earth nor the sun were older than several hundred million years. This caused a considerable stir in biological and geological circles, especially among the evolutionists. Darwin himself was distressed by the numbers; the time was much too short for the theory of evolution. Kelvin's figures were described by Darwin as one of his "sorest troubles."

T. H. Huxley had long been aware of the risks involved in premature extrapolations from mathematical treatment of biological problems. He said, in an 1869 speech to the Geological Society concerning numbers, "This seems to be one of the many cases in which the admitted accuracy of mathematical processes is allowed to throw a wholly inadmissible appearance of authority over the results obtained by them. . . . As the grandest mill in the world will not extract wheat flour from peascods, so pages of formulas will not get a definite result out of loose data."

The trouble was that the world of physics had not moved fast enough to allow for Kelvin's assumptions. Nuclear fusion and fission had not yet been dreamed of, and the true age of the earth could not even be guessed from the data in hand. It was not yet the time for mathematics in this subject.

There have been other examples, since those days, of the folly of using numbers and calculations uncritically. Kelvin's own strong conviction that science could not be genuine science without measuring things was catching. People in other fields of endeavor, hankering to turn their disciplines into exact sciences, beset by what has since been called "physics envy," set about converting whatever they knew into numbers and thence into equations with predictive pretensions. We have it with us still, in economics, sociology, psychology, history, even, I fear, in English-literature criticism and linguistics, and it frequently works, when it works at all, with indifferent success. The risks of untoward social consequences in work of this kind are considerable. It is as important—and as hard—to learn *when* to use mathematics as *how* to use it, and this matter should remain high on the agenda of consideration for education in the social and behavioral sciences.

Of course, Kelvin's difficulty with the age of the earth was an exceptional, almost isolated instance of failure in quantitative measurement in the nineteenth-century physics. The instruments devised for approaching nature by way of physics became increasingly precise and powerful, carrying the field through electromagnetic theory, triumph after triumph, and setting the stage for the great revolution of twentieth-century physics. There is no doubt about it: measurement works when the instruments work, and when you have a fairly clear idea of what it is that is being measured, and when you know what to do with the numbers when they tumble out. The system for gaining information and comprehension about nature works so well, indeed, that it carries another hazard: the risk of convincing yourself that you know everything.

Kelvin himself fell into this trap toward the end of the century. (I don't mean to keep picking on Kelvin, who was a very great scientist; it is just that he happened to say a couple of things I find useful for this discussion.) He stated, in a summary of the achievements of nineteenth-century physics, that it was an almost completed science; virtually everything that needed knowing about the material universe had been learned; there were still a few anomalies and inconsistencies in electromagnetic theory, a few loose ends to be tied up, but this would be done within the next several years. Physics, in these terms, was not a field any longer likely to attract, as it previously had, the brightest and most imaginative young brains. The most interesting part of the work had already been done. Then, within the next decade, came radiation, Planck, the quantum, Einstein, Rutherford, Bohr, and all the rest—quantum mechanics—and the whole field turned over and became a brand-new sort of human endeavor, still now, in the view of many physicists, almost a full century later, a field only at its beginnings.

But even today, despite the amazements that are turning up in physics each year, despite the jumps taken from the smallest parts of nature—particle physics—to the largest of all—the cosmos itself—the impression of science that the public gains is rather like the impression left in the nineteenth-century public mind by Kelvin. Science, in this view, is first of all a matter of simply getting all the numbers together. The numbers are sitting out there in nature, waiting to be found, sorted, and totted up. If only they had enough robots and enough computers, the scientists could go off to the beach and wait for their papers to be written for them. Second of all, what we know about nature today is pretty much the whole story: we are very nearly home and dry. From here on, it is largely a problem of tying up loose ends, tidying nature up, getting the files in order. The only real surprises for the future—and it is about those that the public is becoming more concerned and apprehensive—are the technological applications that the scientists may be cooking up from today's knowledge.

I suggest that the scientific community is to blame. If there are disagreements between the world of the humanities and the scientific enterprise as to the place and importance of science in a liberal-arts education, and the role of science in twentieth-century culture, I believe that the scientists are themselves responsible for a general misunderstanding of what they are really up to.

Over the past half century, we have been teaching the sciences as though they were the same academic collection of cut-and-dried subjects as always, and—here is what has really gone wrong—as though they would always be the same. The teaching of today's biology, for example, is pretty much the same kind of exercise as the teaching of Latin was when I was in high school long ago. First of all, the fundamentals, the underlying laws, the essential grammar, and then the reading of texts. Once mastered, that is that: Latin is Latin and forever after will be Latin. And biology is precisely biology, a vast array of hard facts to be learned as fundamentals, followed by a reading of the texts.

Moreover, we have been teaching science as though its facts were somehow superior to the facts in all other scholarly disciplines, more fundamental, more solid, less subject to subjectivism, immutable. English literature is not just one way of thinking, it is all sorts of ways. Poetry is a moving target. The facts that underlie art, architecture, and music are not really hard facts, and you can change them any way you like by arguing about them, but science is treated as an altogether different kind of learning: an unambiguous, unalterable, and endlessly useful display of data needing only to be packaged and installed somewhere in one's temporal lobe in order to achieve a full understanding of the natural world.

And it is, of course, not like this at all. In real life, every field of science that I can think of is incomplete, and most of them—whatever the record of accomplishment over the past two hundred years—are still in the earliest stage of their starting point. In the fields I know best, among the life sciences, it is required that the most expert and sophisticated minds be capable of changing those minds, often with a great lurch, every few years. In some branches of biology the mind-changing is occurring with accelerating velocities. The next week's issue of any scientific journal can turn a whole field upside down, shaking out any number of immutable ideas and installing new bodies of dogma, and this is happening all the time. It is an almost everyday event in physics, in chemistry, in materials research, in neurobiology, in genetics, in immunology. The hard facts tend to soften overnight, melt away, and vanish under the pressure of new hard facts, and the interpretations of what appear to be the most solid aspects of nature are subject to change, now more than at any other time in history. The conclusions reached in science are always, when looked at closely, far more provisional and tentative than are most of the assumptions arrived at by our colleagues in the humanities.

The running battle now in progress between the sociobiologists and the antisociobiologists is a marvel for students to behold, close up. To observe, in open-mouthed astonishment, the polarized extremes, one group of highly intelligent, beautifully trained, knowledgeable, and imaginative scientists maintaining that all sorts of behavior, animal and human, are governed exclusively by genes, and another group of equally talented scientists saying precisely the opposite and asserting that all behavior is set and determined by the environment, or by culture, and both sides brawling in the pages of periodicals such as *The New York Review of Books*, is an educational experience that no college student should be allowed to miss. The essential lesson to be learned has nothing to do with the relative validity of the facts underlying the argument, it is the argument itself that is the education: we do not yet know enough to settle such questions.

It is true that at any given moment there is the appearance of satisfaction, even self-satisfaction, within every scientific discipline. On any Tuesday morning, if asked, a good working scientist will gladly tell you that the affairs of the field are nicely in order, that things are finally looking clear and making sense, and all is well. But come back again, on another Tuesday, and he may let you know that the roof has just fallen in on his life's work, that all the old ideas—last week's ideas in some cases—are no longer good ideas, that something strange has happened.

It is the very strangeness of nature that makes science engrossing. That ought to be at the center of science teaching. There are more than seven-times-seven types of ambiguity in science, awaiting analysis. The poetry of Wallace Stevens is crystal-clear alongside the genetic code.

I prefer to turn things around in order to make precisely the opposite case. Science, especially twentieth-century science, has provided us with a glimpse of something we never really knew before, the revelation of human ignorance. We have been used to the belief, down one century after another, that we more or less comprehend everything bar one or two mysteries like the mental processes of our gods. Every age, not just the eighteenth century, regarded itself as the Age of Reason, and we have never lacked for explanations of the world and its ways. Now, we are being brought up short, and this has been the work of science. We have a wilderness of mystery to make our way through in the centuries ahead, and we will need science for this but not science alone. Science will, in its own time, produce the data and some of the meaning in the data, but never the full meaning. For getting a full grasp, for perceiving real significance when significance is at hand, we shall need minds at work from all sorts of brains outside the fields of science, most of all the brains of poets, of course, but also those of artists, musicians, philosophers, historians, writers in general.

It is primarily because of this need that I would press for changes in the way science is taught. There is a need to teach the young people who will be doing the science themselves, but this will always be a small minority among us. There is a deeper need to teach science to those who will be needed for thinking about it, and this means pretty nearly everyone else, in hopes that a few of these people—a much smaller minority than the scientific community and probably a lot harder to find—will, in the thinking, be able to imagine new levels of meaning that are likely to be lost on the rest of us.

In addition, it is time to develop a new group of professional thinkers, perhaps a somewhat larger group than the working scientists, who can create a discipline of scientific criticism. We have had good luck so far in the emergence of a few people ranking as philosophers of science and historians and journalists of science, and I hope more of these will be coming along, but we have not yet seen a Ruskin or a Leavis or an Edmund Wilson. Science needs critics of this sort, but the public at large needs them more urgently.

I suggest that the introductory courses in science, at all levels from grade school through college, be radically revised. Leave the fundamentals, the so-called basics, aside for a while, and concentrate the attention of all students on the things that are not known. You cannot possibly teach quantum mechanics without mathematics, to be sure, but you can describe the strangeness of the world opened up by quantum theory. Let it be known, early on, that there are deep mysteries, and profound paradoxes, revealed in their distant outlines, by the quantum. Let it be known that these can be approached more closely, and puzzled over, once the language of mathematics has been sufficiently mastered.

Teach at the outset, before any of the fundamentals, the still imponderable puzzles of cosmology. Let it be known, as clearly as possible, by the youngest minds, that there are some things going on in the universe that lie beyond comprehension, and make it plain how little is known.

Do not teach that biology is a useful and perhaps profitable science; that can come later. Teach instead that there are structures squirming inside all our cells, providing all the energy for living, that are essentially foreign creatures, brought in for symbiotic living a billion or so years ago, the lineal descendants of bacteria. Teach that we do not have the ghost of an idea how they got there, where they came from, or how they evolved to their present structure and function. The details of oxidative phosphorylation and photosynthesis can come later.

Teach ecology early on. Let it be understood that the earth's life is a system of interliving, interdependent creatures, and that we do not understand at all how it works. The earth's environment, from the range of atmospheric gases to the chemical constituents of the sea, has been held in an almost unbelievably improbable state of regulated balance since life began, and the regulation of stability and balance is accomplished solely by the life itself, like the internal environment of an immense organism, and we do not know how *that* one works, even less what it means. Teach that.

Go easy, I suggest, on the promises sometimes freely offered by science. Technology relies and depends on science these days, more than ever before, but technology is nothing like the first justification for doing research, nor is it necessarily an essential product to be expected from science. Public decisions about what to have in the way of technology are totally different problems from decisions about science, and the two enterprises should not be tangled together. The central task of science is to arrive, stage by stage, at a clearer comprehension of nature, but this does not mean, as it is sometimes claimed to mean, a search for mastery over nature. Science may provide us, one day, with a better understanding of ourselves, but never, I hope, with a set of technologies for doing something or other to improve ourselves. I am made nervous by assertions that human consciousness will someday be unraveled by research, laid out for close scrutiny like the workings of a computer, and then, *and then!*

I hope with some fervor that we can learn a lot more than we now know about the human mind, and I see no reason why this strange puzzle should remain forever and entirely beyond us. But I would be deeply disturbed by any prospect that we might use the new knowledge in order to begin doing something about it, to improve it, say. This is a different matter from searching for information to use against schizophrenia or dementia, where we are badly in need of technologies, indeed likely one day to be sunk without them. But the ordinary, everyday, more or less normal human mind is too marvelous an instrument ever to be tampered with by anyone, science or no science.

The education of humanists cannot be regarded as complete, or even adequate, without exposure in some depth to where things stand in the various branches of science, and particularly, as I have said, in the areas of our ignorance. This does not mean that I know how to go about doing it, nor am I unaware of the difficulties involved. Physics professors, most of them, look with revulsion on assignments to teach their subject to poets. Biologists, caught up by the enchantment of their new power, armed with flawless instruments to tell the nucleotide sequences of the entire human genome, nearly matching the physicists in the precision of their measurements of living processes, will resist the prospect of broad survey courses; each biology professor will demand that any student in his path must master every fine detail within that professor's research program. The liberal-arts faculties, for their part, will continue to view the scientists with suspicion and apprehension. "What do the scientists want?" asked a Cambridge professor in Francis Cornford's wonderful *Microcosmographia Academica.* "Everything that's going," was the quick answer. That was back in 1912, and universities haven't much changed.

The worst thing that has happened to science education is that the great fun has gone out of it. A very large number of good students look at it as slogging work to be got through on the way to medical school. Others look closely at the premedical students themselves, embattled and bleeding for grades and class standing, and are turned off. Very few see science as the high adventure it really is, the wildest of all explorations ever undertaken by human beings, the chance to catch close views of things never seen before, the shrewdest maneuver for discovering how the world works. Instead, they become baffled early on, and they are misled into thinking that bafflement is simply the result of not having learned all the facts. They are not told, as they should be told, that everyone else—from the professor in his endowed chair down to the platoons of postdoctoral students in the laboratory all night—is baffled as well. Every important scientific advance that has come in looking like an answer has turned, sooner or later—usually sooner—into a question. And the game is just beginning.

An appreciation of what is happening in science today, and of how great a distance lies ahead for exploring, ought to be one of the rewards of a liberal-arts education. It ought to be a good in itself, not something to be acquired on the way to a professional career but part of the cast of thought needed for getting into the kind of century that is now just down the road. Part of the intellectual equipment of an educated person, however his or her time is to be spent, ought to be a feel for the queernesses of nature, the inexplicable things.

And maybe, just maybe, a new set of courses dealing systematically with ignorance in science might take hold. The scientists might discover in it a new and subversive technique for catching the attention of students driven by curiosity, delighted and surprised to learn that science is exactly as Bush described it: an "endless frontier." The humanists, for their part, might take considerable satisfaction watching their scientific colleagues confess openly to not knowing everything about everything. And the poets, on whose shoulders the future rests, might, late nights, thinking things over, begin to see some meanings that elude the rest of us. It is worth a try.

Suggestions for Discussion

1. Summarize Thomas's complaints about "the impression of science that the public gains."

2. How would he have science taught?

3. What advantages might there be in "a new set of courses dealing systematically with ignorance in science"?

Suggestions for Writing

1. Discuss one or more unanswered questions that you have encountered in your study of science.

2. Tell about an experience in which you had to change your mind because of new information.

BRUNO BETTELHEIM

The Child's Need for Magic

Bruno Bettelheim (1903–1990) was born in Vienna and educated at the University of Vienna. Having survived the Nazi Holocaust, he became an American psychoanalyst and educator and was director of the remarkable University of Chicago Sonia Shankman Orthogenic School from 1944 to 1973. He wrote many penetrating works on parents and children and the significance of the Holocaust. In this excerpt from *The Uses of Enchantment* (1976), the author believes that fairy tales provide answers to the child's pressing questions about his identity and his world.

Myths and fairy stories both answer the eternal questions: What is the world really like? How am I to live my life in it? How can I truly be myself? The answers given by myths are definite, while the fairy tale is suggestive; its messages may imply solutions, but it never spells them out. Fairy tales leave to the child's fantasizing whether and how to apply to himself what the story reveals about life and human nature.

The fairy tale proceeds in a manner which conforms to the way a child thinks and experiences the world; this is why the fairy tale is so convincing to him. He can gain much better solace from a fairy tale than he can from an effort to comfort him based on adult reasoning and viewpoints. A child trusts what the fairy story tells, because its world view accords with his own.

Whatever our age, only a story conforming to the principles underlying our thought processes carries conviction for us. If this is so for adults, who have learned to accept that there is more than one frame of reference for comprehending the world—although we find it difficult if not impossible truly to think in any but our own—it is exclusively true for the child. His thinking is animistic.

Like all preliterate and many literate people, "the child assumes that his relations to the inanimate world are of one pattern with those to the animate world of people: he fondles as he would his mother the pretty thing that pleased him; he strikes the door that has slammed on him." It should be added that he does the first because he is convinced that this pretty thing loves to be petted as much as he does; and he punishes the door because he is certain that the door slammed deliberately, out of evil intention.

As Piaget has shown, the child's thinking remains animistic until the age of puberty. His parents and teachers tell him that things cannot feel and act; and as much as he may pretend to believe this to please these adults, or not to be ridiculed, deep down the child knows better. Subjected to the rational teachings of others, the child only buries his "true knowledge" deeper in his soul and it remains untouched by rationality; but it can be formed and informed by what fairy tales have to say.

To the eight-year-old (to quote Piaget's examples), the sun is alive because it gives light (and, one may add, it does that because it wants to). To the child's animistic mind, the stone is alive because it can move, as it rolls down a hill. Even a twelve-and-a-half-year-old is convinced that a stream is alive and has a will, because its water is flowing. The sun, the stone, and the water are believed to be inhabited by spirits very much like people, so they feel and act like people.

To the child, there is no clear line separating objects from living things; and whatever has life has life very much like our own. If we do not understand what rocks and trees and animals have to tell us, the reason is that we are not sufficiently attuned to them. To the child trying to understand the world, it seems reasonable to expect answers from those objects which arouse his curiosity. And since the child is self-centered, he expects the animal to talk about the things which are really significant to him, as animals do in fairy tales, and as the child himself talks to his real or toy animals. A child is convinced that the animal understands and feels with him, even though it does not show it openly.

Since animals roam freely and widely in the world, how natural that in fairy tales these animals are able to guide the hero in his search which takes him into distant places. Since all that moves is alive, the child can believe that the wind can talk and carry the hero to where he needs to go, as in "East of the Sun and West of the Moon." In animistic thinking, not only animals feel and think as we do, but even stones are alive; so to be turned into stone simply means that the being has to remain silent and unmoving for a time. By the same reasoning, it is entirely believable when previously silent objects begin to talk, give advice, and join the hero on his wanderings. And since everything is inhabited by a spirit similar to all other spirits (namely, that of the child who has projected his spirit into all these things), because of this inherent sameness it is believable that man can change into animal, or the other way around, as in "Beauty and the Beast" or "The Frog King." Since there is no sharp line drawn between living and dead things, the latter, too, can come to life.

When, like the great philosophers, children are searching for the solutions to the first and last questions—"Who am I? How ought I to deal with life's problems? What must I become?"—they do so on the basis of their animistic thinking. But since the child is so uncertain of what his existence consists, first and foremost comes the question "Who am I?"

As soon as a child begins to move about and explore, he begins to ponder the problem of his identity. When he spies his mirror image, he wonders whether what he sees is really he, or a child just like him standing behind this glassy wall. He tries to find out by exploring whether this other child is really, in all ways, like him. He makes faces, turns this way or that, walks away from the mirror and jumps back in front of it to ascertain whether this other one has moved away or is still there. Though only three years old, the child is already up against the difficult problem of personal identity.

The child asks himself: "Who am I? Where did I come from? How did the world come into being? Who created man and all the animals? What is the purpose of life?" True, he ponders these vital questions not in the abstract, but mainly as they pertain to him. He worries not whether there is justice for individual man, but whether *he* will be treated justly. He wonders who or what projects him into adversity, and what can prevent this from happening to him. Are there benevolent powers in addition to his parents? Are his parents benevolent powers? How should he form himself, and why? Is there hope for him, though he may have done wrong? Why has all this happened to him? What will it mean for his future? Fairy tales provide answers to these pressing questions, many of which the child becomes aware of only as he follows the stories.

From an adult point of view and in terms of modern science, the answers which fairy stories offer are fantastic rather than true. As a matter of fact, these solutions seem so incorrect to many adults—who have become estranged from the ways in which young people experience the world—that they object to exposing children to such "false" information. However, realistic explanations are usually incomprehensible to children, because they lack the abstract understanding required to make sense of them. While giving a scientifically correct answer makes adults think they have clarified things for the child, such explanations leave the young child confused, overpowered, and intellectually defeated. A child can derive security only from the conviction that he understands now what baffled him before—never from being given facts which create *new* uncertainties. Even as the child accepts such an answer, he comes to doubt that he has asked the right question. Since the explanation fails to make sense to him, it must apply to some unknown problem—not the one he asked about.

It is therefore important to remember that only statements which are intelligible in terms of the child's existing knowledge and emotional preoccupations carry conviction for him. To tell a child that the earth floats in space, attracted by gravity into circling around the sun, but that the earth doesn't fall to the sun as the child falls to the ground, seems very confusing to him. The child knows from his experience that everything has to rest on something, or be held up by something. Only an explanation based on that knowledge can make him feel he understands better about the earth in space. More important, to feel secure on earth, the child needs to believe that this world is held firmly in place. Therefore he finds a better explanation in a myth that tells him that the earth rests on a turtle, or is held up by a giant.

If a child accepts as true what his parents tell him—that the earth is a planet held securely on its path by gravity—then the child can only imagine that gravity is a string. Thus the parents' explanation has led to no better understanding or feeling of security. It requires considerable intellectual maturity to believe that there can be stability to one's life when the ground on which one walks (the firmest thing around, on which everything rests) spins with incredible speed on an invisible axis; that in addition it rotates around the sun; and furthermore hurtles through space with the entire solar system. I have never yet encountered a prepubertal youngster who could comprehend all these combined movements, although I have known many who could repeat this information. Such children parrot explanations which according to their own experience of the world are lies, but which they must believe to be true because some adult has said so. The consequence is that children come to distrust their own experience, and therefore themselves and what their minds can do for them.

In the fall of 1973, the comet Kohoutek was in the news. At that time a competent science teacher explained the comet to a small group of highly intelligent second- and third-graders. Each child had carefully cut out a paper circle and had drawn on it the course of the planets around the sun; a paper ellipse, attached by a slit to the paper circle, represented the course of the comet. The children showed me the comet moving along at an angle to the planets. When I asked them, the children told me that they were holding the comet in their hands, showing me the ellipse. When I asked how the comet which they were holding in their hands could also be in the sky, they were all nonplussed.

In their confusion, they turned to their teacher, who carefully explained to them that what they were holding in their hands, and had so diligently created, was only a model of the planets and the comet. The children all agreed that they understood this, and would have repeated it if questioned further. But whereas before they had regarded proudly this circle-cum-ellipse in their hands, they now lost all interest. Some crumpled the paper up, others dropped the model in the wastepaper basket. When the pieces of paper had been the comet to them, they had all planned to take the model home to show their parents, but now it no longer had meaning for them.

In trying to get a child to accept scientifically correct explanations, parents all too frequently discount scientific findings of how a child's mind works. Research on the child's mental processes, especially Piaget's, convincingly demonstrates that the young child is not able to comprehend the two vital abstract concepts of the permanence of quantity, and of reversibility—for instance, that the same quantity of water rises high in a narrow receptacle and remains low in a wide one; and that subtraction reverses the process of addition. Until he can understand abstract concepts such as these, the child can experience the world only subjectively.

Scientific explanations require objective thinking. Both theoretical research and experimental exploration have shown that no child below school age is truly able to grasp these two concepts, without which abstract understanding is impossible. In his early years, until age eight or ten, the child can develop only highly personalized concepts about what he experiences. Therefore it seems natural to him, since the plants which grow on this earth nourish him as his mother did from her breast, to see the earth as a mother or a female god, or at least as her abode.

Even a young child somehow knows that he was created by his parents; so it makes good sense to him that, like himself, all men and where they live were created by a superhuman figure not very different from his parents—some male or female god. Since his parents watch over the child and provide him with his needs in his home, then naturally he also believes that something like them, only much more powerful, intelligent, and reliable—a guardian angel—will do so out in the world.

A child thus experiences the world order in the image of his parents and of what goes on within the family. The ancient Egyptians, as a child does, saw heaven and the sky as a motherly figure (Nut) who protectively bent over the earth, enveloping it and them serenely. Far from preventing man from later developing a more rational explanation of the world, such a view offers security where and when it is most needed—a security which, when the time is ripe, allows for a truly rational world view. Life on a small planet surrounded by limitless space seems awfully lonely and cold to a child—just the opposite of what he knows life ought to be. This is why the ancients needed to feel sheltered and warmed by an enveloping mother figure. To depreciate protective imagery like this as mere childish projections of an immature mind is to rob the young child of one aspect of the prolonged safety and comfort he needs.

True, the notion of a sheltering sky-mother can be limiting to the mind if clung to for too long. Neither infantile projections nor dependence on imaginary protectors—such as a guardian angel who watches out for one when one is asleep, or during Mother's absence—offers true security; but as long as one cannot provide complete security for oneself, imaginings and projections are far preferable to no security. It is such (partly imagined) security which, when experienced for a sufficient length of time, permits the child to develop that feeling of confidence in life which he needs in order to trust himself—a trust necessary for his learning to solve life's problems through his own growing rational abilities. Eventually the child recognizes that what he has taken as literally true—the earth as a mother—is only a symbol.

A child, for example, who has learned from fairy stories to believe that what at first seemed a repulsive, threatening figure can magically change into a most helpful friend is ready to believe that a strange child whom he meets and fears may also be changed from a menace into a desirable companion. Belief in the "truth" of the fairy tale gives him courage not to withdraw because of the way this stranger appears to him at first. Recalling how the hero of many a fairy tale succeeded in life because he dared to befriend a seemingly unpleasant figure, the child believes he may work the same magic.

I have known many examples where, particularly in late adolescence, years of belief in magic are called upon to compensate for the person's having been deprived of it prematurely in childhood, through stark reality having been forced on him. It is as if these young people feel that now is their last chance to make up for a severe deficiency in their life experience; or that without having had a period of belief in magic, they will be unable to meet the rigors of adult life. Many young people who today suddenly seek escape in drug-induced dreams, apprentice themselves to some guru, believe in astrology, engage in practicing "black magic," or who in some other fashion escape from reality into daydreams about magic experiences which are to change their life for the better, were prematurely pressed to view reality in an adult way. Trying to evade reality in such ways has its deeper cause in early formative experiences which prevented the development of the conviction that life can be mastered in realistic ways.

What seems desirable for the individual is to repeat in his life span the process involved historically in the genesis of scientific thought. For a long time in his history man used emotional projections—such as gods—born of his immature hopes and anxieties to explain man, his society, and the universe; these explanations gave him a feeling of security. Then slowly, by his own social, scientific, and technological progress, man freed himself of the constant fear for his very existence. Feeling more secure in the world, and also within himself, man could now begin to question the validity of the images he had used in the past as explanatory tools. From there man's "childish" projections dissolved and more rational explanations took their place. This process, however, is by no means without vagaries. In intervening periods of stress and scarcity, man seeks for comfort again in the "childish" notion that he and his place of abode are the center of the universe.

Translated in terms of human behavior, the more secure a person feels within the world, the less he will need to hold on to "infantile" projections— mythical explanations or fairy-tale solutions to life's eternal problems—and the more he can afford to seek rational explanations. The more secure a man is within himself, the more he can afford to accept an explanation which says his world is of minor significance in the cosmos. Once man feels truly significant in his human environment, he cares little about the importance of his planet within the universe. On the other hand, the more insecure a man is in himself and his place in the immediate world, the more he withdraws into himself because of fear, or else moves outward to conquer for conquest's sake. This is the opposite of exploring out of a security which frees our curiosity.

For these same reasons a child, as long as he is not sure his immediate human environment will protect him, needs to believe that superior powers, such as a guardian angel, watch over him, and that the world and his place within it are of paramount importance. Here is one connection between a family's ability to provide basic security and the child's readiness to engage in rational investigations as he grows up.

As long as parents fully believed that Biblical stories solved the riddle of our existence and its purpose, it was easy to make a child feel secure.

The Bible was felt to contain the answers to all pressing questions: the Bible told man all he needed to know to understand the world, how it came into being, and how to behave in it. In the Western world the Bible also provided prototypes for man's imagination. But rich as the Bible is in stories, not even during the most religious of times were these stories sufficient for meeting all the psychic needs of man.

Part of the reason for this is that while the Old and New Testaments and the histories of the saints provided answers to the crucial questions of how to live the good life, they did not offer solutions for the problems posed by the dark sides of our personalities. The Biblical stories suggest essentially only one solution for the asocial aspects of the unconscious: repression of these (unacceptable) strivings. But children, not having their ids in conscious control, need stories which permit at least fantasy satisfaction of these "bad" tendencies, and specific models for their sublimation.

Explicitly and implicitly, the Bible tells of God's demands on man. While we are told that there is greater rejoicing about a sinner who reformed than about the man who never erred, the message is still that we ought to live the good life, and not, for example, take cruel revenge on those whom we hate. As the story of Cain and Abel shows, there is no sympathy in the Bible for the agonies of sibling rivalry—only a warning that acting upon it has devastating consequences.

But what a child needs most, when beset by jealousy of his sibling, is the permission to feel that what he experiences is justified by the situation he is in. To bear up under the pangs of his envy, the child needs to be encouraged to engage in fantasies of getting even someday; then he will be able to manage at the moment, because of the conviction that the future will set things aright. Most of all, the child wants support for his still very tenuous belief that through growing up, working hard, and maturing he will one day be the victorious one. If his present sufferings will be rewarded in the future, he need not act on his jealousy of the moment, the way Cain did.

Like Biblical stories and myths, fairy tales were the literature which edified everybody—children and adults alike—for nearly all of man's existence. Except that God is central, many Bible stories can be recognized as very similar to fairy tales. In the story of Jonah and the whale, for example, Jonah is trying to run away from his superego's (conscience's) demand that he fight against the wickedness of the people of Nineveh. The ordeal which tests his moral fiber is, as in so many fairy tales, a perilous voyage in which he has to prove himself.

Jonah's trip across the sea lands him in the belly of a great fish. There, in great danger, Jonah discovers his higher morality, his higher self, and is wondrously reborn, now ready to meet the rigorous demands of his superego. But the rebirth alone does not achieve true humanity for him: to be a slave neither to the id and the pleasure principle (avoiding arduous tasks by trying to escape from them) nor to the superego (wishing destruction upon the wicked city) means true freedom and higher selfhood. Jonah attains his full humanity only when he is no longer subservient to either institution of his mind, but relinquishes blind obedience to both id and superego and is able to recognize God's wisdom in judging the people of Nineveh not according to the rigid structures of Jonah's superego, but in terms of their human frailty.

Suggestions for Discussion

1. How does Bettelheim distinguish myths from fairy tales? The Bible from fairy tales?

2. Who is Piaget? How has he influenced current thought regarding the way children think and learn?

3. Explain Bettelheim's reference to children as "animistic thinkers." How does this description of them relate to their need for fairy tales?

4. What similarities does the author see between the child and the philosopher? How do they differ?

5. Explain why Bettelheim believes it is a mistake to deprive children of fairy tales. How does he relate their need for fairy tales to the difficulties they have in comprehending scientific ideas?

Suggestions for Writing

1. Using one or more familiar fairy tales, write an essay explaining how magical elements might serve to explain the universe to a child.

2. Write a comparison between a fairy tale and one of the popular children's stories about ordinary life.

FICTION

ANTON CHEKHOV

The Bet

Translated by Constance Garnett

Anton Chekhov (1860–1904), Russian short-story writer and play-wright, practiced medicine briefly before devoting himself to literature. Among his plays are *The Sea Gull* (1896), *Uncle Vanya* (1900), *The Three Sisters* (1901), and *The Cherry Orchard* (1904). His stories, translated by Constance Garnett, were published as *The Tales of Chekhov* (1916–1923).

I

It was a dark autumn night. The old banker was pacing from corner to corner of his study, recalling to his mind the party he gave in the autumn fifteen years before. There were many clever people at the party and much interesting conversation. They talked among other things of capital punishment. The guests, among them not a few scholars and journalists, for the most part disapproved of capital punishment. They found it obsolete as a means of punishment, unfitted to a Christian State and immoral. Some of them thought that capital punishment should be replaced universally by life imprisonment.

"I don't agree with you," said the host. "I myself have experienced neither capital punishment nor life imprisonment, but if one may judge *a priori*, then in my opinion capital punishment is more moral and more humane than imprisonment. Execution kills instantly, life imprisonment kills by degrees. Who is the more humane executioner, one who kills you in a few seconds or one who draws the life out of you incessantly, for years?"

"They're both equally immoral," remarked one of the guests, "because their purpose is the same, to take away life. The State is not God.

It has no right to take away that which it cannot give back, if it should so desire."

Among the company was a lawyer, a young man of about twenty-five. On being asked his opinion, he said:

"Capital punishment and life imprisonment are equally immoral; but if I were offered the choice between them, I would certainly choose the second. It's better to live somehow than not to live at all."

There ensued a lively discussion. The banker who was then younger and more nervous suddenly lost his temper, banged his fist on the table, and turning to the young lawyer, cried out:

"It's a lie. I bet you two millions you wouldn't stick in a cell even for five years."

"If you mean it seriously," replied the lawyer, "then I bet I'll stay not five but fifteen."

"Fifteen! Done!" cried the banker. "Gentlemen, I stake two millions."

"Agreed. You stake two millions, I my freedom," said the lawyer.

So this wild, ridiculous bet came to pass. The banker, who at that time had too many millions to count, spoiled and capricious, was beside himself with rapture. During supper he said to the lawyer jokingly:

"Come to your senses, young man, before it's too late. Two millions are nothing to me, but you stand to lose three or four of the best years of your life. I say three or four, because you'll never stick it out any longer. Don't forget either, you unhappy man, that voluntary is much heavier than enforced imprisonment. The idea that you have the right to free yourself at any moment will poison the whole of your life in the cell. I pity you."

And now the banker, pacing from corner to corner, recalled all this and asked himself:

"Why did I make this bet? What's the good? The lawyer loses fifteen years of his life and I throw away two millions. Will it convince people that capital punishment is worse or better than imprisonment for life? No, no! all stuff and rubbish. On my part, it was the caprice of a well-fed man; on the lawyer's, pure greed of gold."

He recollected further what happened after the evening party. It was decided that the lawyer must undergo his imprisonment under the strictest observation, in a garden wing of the banker's house. It was agreed that during the period he would be deprived of the right to cross the threshold, to see living people, to hear human voices, and to receive letters and newspapers. He was permitted to have a musical instrument, to read books, to write letters, to drink wine, and smoke tobacco. By the agreement he could communicate, but only in silence, with the outside world through a little window specially constructed for this purpose. Everything necessary, books, music, wine, he could receive in any quantity by sending a note through the window. The agreement provided for all the minutest details, which made the confinement strictly solitary, and it obliged the lawyer to remain exactly fifteen years from twelve o'clock of November 14th, 1870 to twelve o'clock of November 14th, 1885. The least attempt on his part to violate the conditions, to escape if only for two minutes before the time freed the banker from the obligation to pay him the two millions.

During the first year of imprisonment, the lawyer, as far as it was possible to judge from his short notes, suffered terribly from loneliness and boredom. From his wing day and night came the sound of the piano. He rejected wine and tobacco. "Wine," he wrote, "excites desires, and desires are the chief foes of a prisoner; besides, nothing is more boring than to drink good wine alone, and tobacco spoils the air in his room." During the first year the lawyer was sent books of a light character; novels with a complicated love interest, stories of crime and fantasy, comedies, and so on.

In the second year the piano was heard no longer and the lawyer asked only for classics. In the fifth year, music was heard again, and the prisoner asked for wine. Those who watched him said that during the whole of that year he was only eating, drinking, and lying on his bed. He yawned often and talked angrily to himself. Books he did not read. Sometimes at nights he would sit down to write. He would write for a long time and tear it all up in the morning. More than once he was heard to weep.

In the second half of the sixth year, the prisoner began zealously to study languages, philosophy, and history. He fell on these subjects so hungrily that the banker hardly had time to get books enough for him. In the space of four years about six hundred volumes were brought at his request. It was while that passion lasted that the banker received the following letter from the prisoner: "My dear gaoler, I am writing these lines in six languages. Show them to experts. Let them read them. If they do not find one single mistake, I beg you to give orders to have a gun fired off in the garden. By the noise I shall know that my efforts have not been in vain. The geniuses of all ages and countries speak in different languages; but in them all burns the same flame. Oh, if you knew my heavenly happiness now that I can understand them!" The prisoner's desire was fulfilled. Two shots were fired in the garden by the banker's order.

Later on, after the tenth year, the lawyer sat immovable before his table and read only the New Testament. The banker found it strange that a man who in four years had mastered six hundred erudite volumes, should have spent nearly a year in reading one book, easy to understand and by no means thick. The New Testament was then replaced by the history of religions and theology.

During the last two years of his confinement the prisoner read an extraordinary amount, quite haphazard. Now he would apply himself to the natural sciences, then he would read Byron or Shakespeare. Notes used to come from him in which he asked to be sent at the same time a book on chemistry, a text-book of medicine, a novel, and some treatise on philosophy or theology. He read as though he were swimming in the sea among broken pieces of wreckage, and in his desire to save his life was eagerly grasping one piece after another.

II

The banker recalled all this, and thought:

"To-morrow at twelve o'clock he receives his freedom. Under the agreement, I shall have to pay him two millions. If I pay, it's all over with me. I am ruined for ever. . . ."

Fifteen years before he had too many millions to count, but now he was afraid to ask himself which he had more of, money or debts. Gambling on the Stock-Exchange, risky speculation, and the recklessness of which he could not rid himself even in old age, had gradually brought his business to decay; and the fearless, self-confident, proud man of business had become an ordinary banker, trembling at every rise and fall in the market.

"That cursed bet," murmured the old man clutching his head in despair. . . . "Why didn't the man die? He's only forty years old. He will take away my last farthing, marry, enjoy life, gamble on the Exchange, and I will look on like an envious beggar and hear the same words from him every day: 'I'm obliged to you for the happiness of my life. Let me help you.' No, it's too much! The only escape from bankruptcy and disgrace—is that the man should die."

The clock had just struck three. The banker was listening. In the house every one was asleep, and one could hear only the frozen trees whining outside the windows. Trying to make no sound, he took out of his safe the key of the door which had not been opened for fifteen years, put on his overcoat, and went out of the house. The garden was dark and cold. It was raining. A damp, penetrating wind howled in the garden and gave the trees no rest. Though he strained his eyes, the banker could see neither the ground, nor the white statues, nor the garden wing, nor the trees. Approaching the garden wing, he called the watchman twice. There was no answer. Evidently the watchman had taken shelter from the bad weather and was now asleep somewhere in the kitchen or the greenhouse.

"If I have the courage to fulfill my intention," thought the old man, "the suspicion will fall on the watchman first of all."

In the darkness he groped for the steps and the door and entered the hall of the garden-wing, then poked his way into a narrow passage and struck a match. Not a soul was there. Some one's bed, with no bedclothes on it, stood there, and an iron stove loomed dark in the corner. The seals on the door that led into the prisoner's room were unbroken.

When the match went out, the old man, trembling from agitation, peeped into the little window.

In the prisoner's room a candle was burning dimly. The prisoner himself sat by the table. Only his back, the hair on his head and his hands were visible. Open books were strewn about on the table, the two chairs, and on the carpet near the table.

Five minutes passed and the prisoner never once stirred. Fifteen years' confinement had taught him to sit motionless. The banker tapped on the window with his finger, but the prisoner made no movement in reply. Then the banker cautiously tore the seals from the door and put the key into the lock. The rusty lock gave a hoarse groan and the door creaked. The banker expected instantly to hear a cry of surprise and the sound of steps. Three minutes passed and it was as quiet inside as it had been before. He made up his mind to enter.

Before the table sat a man, unlike an ordinary human being. It was a skeleton, with tight-drawn skin, with long curly hair like a woman's, and a shaggy beard. The colour of his face was yellow, of an earthy shade; the cheeks were sunken, the back long and narrow, and the hand upon which he leaned his hairy head was so lean and skinny that it was painful to look upon. His hair was already silvering with grey, and no one who glanced at the senile emaciation of the face would have believed that he was only forty years old. On the table, before his bended head, lay a sheet of paper on which something was written in a tiny hand.

"Poor devil," thought the banker, "he's asleep and probably seeing millions in his dreams. I have only to take and throw this half-dead thing on the bed, smother him a moment with the pillow, and the most careful examination will find no trace of unnatural death. But, first, let us read what he has written here."

The banker took the sheet from the table and read:

"Tomorrow at twelve o'clock midnight, I shall obtain my freedom and the right to mix with people. But before I leave this room and see the sun

I think it necessary to say a few words to you. On my own clear conscience and before God who sees me I declare to you that I despise freedom, life, health, and all that your books call the blessings of the world.

"For fifteen years I have diligently studied earthly life. True, I saw neither the earth nor the people, but in your books I drank fragrant wine, sang songs, hunted deer and wild boar in the forests, loved women. . . . And beautiful women, like clouds ethereal, created by the magic of your poets' genius, visited me by night, and whispered to me wonderful tales, which made my head drunken. In your books I climbed the summits of Elbruz and Mont Blanc and saw from there how the sun rose in the morning, and in the evening suffused the sky, the ocean and the mountain ridges with a purple gold. I saw from there how above me lightnings glimmered cleaving the clouds; I saw green forests, fields, rivers, lakes, cities; I heard sirens singing, and the playing of the pipes of Pan; I touched the wings of beautiful devils who came flying to me to speak of God. . . . In your books I cast myself into bottomless abysses, worked miracles, burned cities to the ground, preached new religions, conquered whole countries. . . .

"Your books gave me wisdom. All that unwearying human thought created in the centuries is compressed to a little lump in my skull. I know that I am cleverer than you all.

"And I despise your books, despise all worldly blessings and wisdom. Everything is void, frail, visionary and delusive as a mirage. Though you be proud and wise and beautiful, yet will death wipe you from the face of the earth like the mice underground; and your posterity, your history, and the immorality of your men of genius will be as frozen slag, burnt down together with the terrestrial globe.

"You are mad, and gone the wrong way. You take falsehood for truth and ugliness for beauty. You would marvel if suddenly apple and orange trees should bear frogs and lizards instead of fruit, and if roses should begin to breathe the odour of a sweating horse. So do I marvel at you, who have bartered heaven for earth. I do not want to understand you.

"That I may show you in deed my contempt for that by which you live, I waive the two millions of which I once dreamed as of paradise, and which I now despise. That I may deprive myself of my right to them, I shall come out from here five minutes before the stipulated term, and thus shall violate the agreement."

When he had read, the banker put the sheet on the table, kissed the head of the strange man, and began to weep. He went out of the wing. Never at any other time, not even after his terrible losses on the Exchange, had he felt such contempt for himself as now. Coming home, he lay down on his bed, but agitation and tears kept him a long time from sleeping. . . .

The next morning the poor watchman came running to him and told him that they had seen the man who lived in the wing climb through the window into the garden. He had gone to the gate and disappeared. The banker instantly went with his servants to the wing and established the escape of his prisoner. To avoid unnecessary rumours he took the paper with the renunciation from the table and, on his return, locked it in his safe.

Suggestions for Discussion

1. If you agree that "The Bet" is primarily the lawyer's story, why is our view of the lawyer filtered through the reminiscences and observations of the banker? Why are we permitted to see the lawyer directly only twice? What artistic purposes are served by the use of hearsay and notes and letters, and by the sparseness and flatness of the account of the lawyer's years of confinement?

2. Trace the changes in the lawyer's activities as they mark the development and resolution of the action. What are the implications as to his ultimate fate?

3. How do the shifts in time contribute to suspense and tone?

4. Find examples of irony and paradox.

5. How do you reconcile the lawyer's nihilism with his lyrical assertion that he has known the beauty of earth and love, has seen nature in her glory and tempestuousness, and has achieved wisdom—"All that unwearying human thought created"? What evidence can you find that Chekhov's vision of life extends beyond negation of all values?

Suggestions for Writing

1. Chekhov has said, "When you depict sad or unlucky people and want to touch the reader's heart, try to be colder—it gives their grief, as it were, a background against which it stands out in greater relief. . . . You must be unconcerned when you write pathetic stories . . . the more objective, the stronger will be the effect." Write an evaluation of Chekhov's theories in relation to the characters of the banker and the lawyer, the tone of the story, and its denouement.

2. Write a position paper on the lawyer's (or the banker's) "examined life."

3. Write your own preferred conclusion to "The Bet," or describe the lawyer's next fifteen years, or recount a conversation in which the banker tells his story the next morning.

4. Compare "The Bet" to Malcolm X's "A Homemade Education." Write your observations in an essay.

POETRY

∾∾∾∾

LANGSTON HUGHES

Theme for English B

Langston Hughes (1902–1962), a prominent black poet, was born in Missouri and educated at Lincoln University in Pennsylvania. Often using dialect and jazz rhythms, his work expresses the concerns and feelings of American blacks. His collections of poetry include *The Weary Blues* (1926) and *Shakespeare in Harlem* (1940); his novels include *Not Without Laughter* (1930) and *The Best of Simple* (1950). In "Theme for English B," Hughes clearly expresses the chasm between the races that exists even in the college classroom.

The instructor said,

Go home and write
a page tonight.
And let that page come out of you—
Then, it will be true.

I wonder if it's that simple?
I am twenty-two, colored, born in Winston-Salem.
I went to school there, then Durham, then here
to this college on the hill above Harlem.
I am the only colored student in my class.
The steps from the hill lead down into Harlem,
through a park, then I cross St. Nicholas,
Eighth Avenue, Seventh, and I come to the Y,
the Harlem Branch Y, where I take the elevator
up to my room, sit down, and write this page:

It's not easy to know what is true for you or me
at twenty-two, my age. But I guess I'm what
I feel and see and hear, Harlem, I hear you:
hear you, hear me—we two—you, me, talk on this page.
(I hear New York, too.) Me—who?
Well, I like to eat, sleep, drink, and be in love.

I like to work, read, learn, and understand life.
I like a pipe for a Christmas present,
or records—Bessie, bop, or Bach.
I guess being colored doesn't make me *not* like
the same things other folks like who are other races.
So will my page be colored that I write?
Being me, it will not be white.

But it will be
a part of you, instructor.
You are white—
yet a part of me, as I am a part of you.
That's American.
Sometimes perhaps you don't want to be a part of me.
Nor do I often want to be a part of you.
But we are, that's true!
As I learn from you,
I guess you learn from me—
Although you're older—and white—
and somewhat more free.

This is my page for English B.

Suggestions for Discussion

1. With what details does Hughes convey a strong sense of identity?

2. How does Hughes reveal his feelings about composition, learning, Harlem, his racial background, and his instructor?

Suggestion for Writing

Write an essay in which you attempt to convey some of your feelings about your own background, your likes and dislikes. Try to focus on details as Hughes has done in his poem.

Popular Culture

~~~~~~

Abstinence has never been sexier than it is in Stephenie Meyer's young adult four-book Twilight series. Fans are super hot for Edward, a century-old vampire in a 17-year-old body, who sweeps teenaged Bella, your average human girl, off her feet in a thrilling love story that spans more than 2,000 pages. Fans are enthralled by their tale, which begins when Edward becomes intoxicated by Bella's sweet-smelling blood. By the middle of the first book, Edward and Bella are deeply in love and working hard to keep their pants on, a story line that has captured the attention of a devoted group of fans who obsess over the relationship and delight in Edward's superhuman strength to just say no.

—CHRISTINE SEIFERT, "Bite Me! (Or Don't!): Twilight as
Abstinence Porn"

Fast food is heavily marketed to children and prepared by people who are hardly older than children. This is an industry that both feeds and feeds off the young.

—ERIC SCHLOSSER, "Fast Food Nation"

LI TIANBING

Icone

Hair on canvas, 2000

Courtesy of Galerie Kashya Hildebrand

INTRODUCTION

Popular culture informs, reminds, motivates, sometimes manipulates, and even conditions the average American's life. "Youth" are especially susceptible to the influence of popular culture. They gravitate to its various fads and lures and its attractively imaged standards for appearance and behavior in media advertising, journalism, movies, television, and sports; and are drawn in by its fascinating and ever-beautiful stellar identities. Adults often consider themselves immune to the many popular cultural influences, but that attitude may be delusive. The writings in this section will help you understand the "artifacts" of our culture—and their pervasive influence—with a more analytical eye. In doing so, they will help you become aware of the many potential topics for writing that exist all around you.

The evaluation of popular culture often revolves around matters of taste and value. In the vampire-themed Notebook section, Christine Seifert's critical analysis of the *Twilight* saga considers its rampant popularity, relative literary merit, portrayal of gender roles, and oxymoronic status as "abstinence porn." Meanwhile, filmmaker Guillermo del Toro—who directed the vampire movies *Chronos* and *Blade II* and wrote the vampire novel *The Strain* with collaborator Chuck Hogan—considers the contemporary popularity of vampires in America, thanks not just to the *Twilight* series, but also to TV shows such as *True Blood* and *Buffy the Vampire Slayer*, best-selling "dark romance" novels, and films such as *Let the Right One In* and *30 Days of Night*.

Other popular culture crazes, past and present, are considered in the Essay section. Michael Abernethy condemns sitcoms and commercials that belittle men in "Male-Bashing on TV," while Gloria Steinem writes in praise of the *Wonder Woman* comic books that she collected as a child, which taught her to read and helped inspire her to become a feminist and political activist. Jay Weiner believes that sports have been corrupted by greed and steroids, and lays out how they can be reformed and purified in his article "How to Take Back Sports," while an essay about robot toys considers how the Furby phenomenon changes the way children play and think about what it means to be human.

Other essays ask similar questions about what we value in American popular culture and the effects of these artifacts of this culture on our country's actions and mores. Eric Schlosser, in an excerpt from his bestselling book *Fast Food Nation*, asks us to consider not only the physical, health-centered problems associated with fast food, but also the changes that the mega industry has had on our cultural values. Political commentator Joe Woodard worries that the popularity of tattoos speaks to a society that is becoming less Christian in "Pumped, Pierced, Painted, and Pagan." And because a striking majority of American youths communicate primarily via cell phones and Web sites like Facebook and MySpace (as well as through the chat features of online multiplayer video games), the societal effects of the technological revolution of the past several decades are considered in depth in Steven Levy's article "Facebook Grows Up."

The Poetry selection includes the lyrics to "Working Class Hero," by John Lennon, a song with continuing social relevance, as demonstrated by Green Day's recent re-recording of it. Lennon himself has been reintroduced to a new generation through his digitized appearance with the rest of the Beatles in a new edition of the video game *Rock Band*.

The Fiction selection featured in this chapter, "'What I Did on My Christmas Holidays' By Sally Sparrow," was written as a merchandising tie-in to the British science fiction television series *Doctor Who*. You may want to consider whether the tale, written by series producer and screenwriter Steven Moffat, is merely a product designed to make money from fans, or a genuinely good story about a time-travel paradox that affects the life of a young girl.

This chapter is designed to be accessible and familiar. We hope, however, that it will also challenge you to take seriously topics, such as horror films, that you may not generally take seriously, and to consider the possible bad effects of some things that you may have either taken for granted or developed affection for (tattoos and fast food, for example). In fact, you may find this section more challenging than it appears at first glance.

NOTEBOOK

∾∾∾∾∾

GUILLERMO DEL TORO AND
CHUCK HOGAN

Why Vampires Never Die

Filmmaker Guillermo del Toro is best known for writing and directing a number of visually compelling, psychologically disturbing films including *Pan's Labyrinth* (2006), *Hellboy* (2004), *The Devil's Backbone* (2001), and *Chronos* (1993), which won nine Mexican Academy Awards. Born in Mexico in 1964, del Toro was raised by his zealously religious Catholic grandmother, who tried in vain to discourage his lifelong fascination with monsters. Influenced by H. P. Lovecraft and Jorge Luis Borges, del Toro's films are violent political allegories that condemn imperialism while sensitively portraying children and social outcasts as victims of Fascistic regimes. Similarly, novelist Chuck Hogan is known for writing thrillers that play with genre conventions by including strong romantic subplots, extensive scientific information, and political commentary. Hogan's books include *The Standoff* (1995), *The Blood Artists* (1999), *Prince of Thieves* (2005) and *The Killing Moon* (2008). In addition to collaborating on the *New York Times* article reprinted here, del Toro and Hogan cowrote the vampire novel *The Strain* (2009), the first of a planned trilogy.

Tonight, you or someone you love will likely be visited by a vampire— on cable television or the big screen, or in the bookstore. Our own novel describes a modern-day epidemic that spreads across New York City.

It all started nearly 200 years ago. It was the "Year Without a Summer" of 1816, when ash from volcanic eruptions lowered temperatures around the globe, giving rise to widespread famine. A few friends gathered at the Villa Diodati on Lake Geneva and decided to engage in a small competition to see who could come up with the most terrifying tale—and the two great monsters of the modern age were born.

One was created by Mary Godwin, soon to become Mary Shelley, whose Dr. Frankenstein gave life to a desolate creature. The other monster was less created than fused. John William Polidori stitched together folklore, personal resentment and erotic anxieties into "The Vampyre," a story that is the basis for vampires as they are understood today.

With "The Vampyre," Polidori gave birth to the two main branches of vampiric fiction: the vampire as romantic hero, and the vampire as undead monster. This ambivalence may reflect Polidori's own, as it is widely accepted that Lord Ruthven, the titular creature, was based upon Lord Byron—literary superstar of the era and another resident of the lakeside villa that fateful summer. Polidori tended to Byron day and night, both as his doctor and most devoted groupie. But Polidori resented him as well: Byron was dashing and brilliant, while the poor doctor had a rather drab talent and unremarkable physique.

But this was just a new twist to a very old idea. The myth, established well before the invention of the word "vampire," seems to cross every culture, language and era. The Indian Baital, the Ch'ing Shin in China, and the Romanian Strigoi are but a few of its names. The creature seems to be as old as Babylonia and Sumer. Or even older.

The vampire may originate from a repressed memory we had as primates. Perhaps at some point we were—out of necessity—cannibalistic. As soon as we became sedentary, agricultural tribes with social boundaries, one seminal myth might have featured our ancestors as primitive beasts who slept in the cold loam of the earth and fed off the salty blood of the living.

Monsters, like angels, are invoked by our individual and collective needs. Today, much as during that gloomy summer in 1816, we feel the need to seek their cold embrace.

Herein lies an important clue: in contrast to timeless creatures like the dragon, the vampire does not seek to obliterate us, but instead offers a peculiar brand of blood alchemy. For as his contagion bestows its nocturnal gift, the vampire transforms our vile, mortal selves into the gold of eternal youth, and instills in us something that every social construct seeks to quash: primal lust. If youth is desire married with unending possibility, then vampire lust creates within us a delicious void, one we long to fulfill.

In other words, whereas other monsters emphasize what is mortal in us, the vampire emphasizes the eternal in us. Through the panacea of its blood it turns the lead of our toxic flesh into golden matter.

In a society that moves as fast as ours, where every week a new "blockbuster" must be enthroned at the box office, or where idols are fabricated by consensus every new television season, the promise of something everlasting, something truly eternal, holds a special allure. As a seductive figure, the vampire is as flexible and polyvalent as ever. Witness its slow mutation from the pansexual, decadent Anne Rice creatures to the current permutations—promising anything from chaste eternal love to wild nocturnal escapades—and there you will find the true essence of immortality: adaptability.

Vampires find their niche and mutate at an accelerated rate now—in the past one would see, for decades, the same variety of fiend, repeated in multiple storylines. Now, vampires simultaneously occur in all forms and tap into our every need: soap opera storylines, sexual liberation, noir detective fiction, etc. The myth seems to be twittering promiscuously to serve all avenues of life, from cereal boxes to romantic fiction. The fast pace of technology accelerates its viral dispersion in our culture.

But if Polidori remains the roots in the genealogy of our creature, the most widely known vampire was birthed by Bram Stoker in 1897.

Part of the reason for the great success of his "Dracula" is generally acknowledged to be its appearance at a time of great technological revolution. The narrative is full of new gadgets (telegraphs, typing machines), various forms of communication (diaries, ship logs), and cutting-edge science (blood transfusions)—a mash-up of ancient myth in conflict with the world of the present.

Today as well, we stand at the rich uncertain dawn of a new level of scientific innovation. The wireless technology we carry in our pockets today was the stuff of the science fiction in our youth. Our technological arrogance mirrors more and more the Wellsian dystopia of dissatisfaction, while allowing us to feel safe and connected at all times. We can call, see or hear almost anything and anyone no matter where we are. For most people then, the only remote place remains within. "Know thyself" we do not.

Despite our obsessive harnessing of information, we are still ultimately vulnerable to our fates and our nightmares. We enthrone the deadly virus in the very same way that "Dracula" allowed the British public to believe in monsters: through science. Science becomes the modern man's superstition. It allows him to experience fear and awe again, and to believe in the things he cannot see.

And through awe, we once again regain spiritual humility. The current vampire pandemic serves to remind us that we have no true jurisdiction over our bodies, our climate or our very souls. Monsters will always provide the possibility of mystery in our mundane "reality show" lives, hinting at a larger spiritual world; for if there are demons in our midst, there surely must be angels lurking nearby as well. In the vampire we find Eros and Thanatos fused together in archetypal embrace, spiraling through the ages, undying.

Forever.

Suggestions for Discussion

1. Does the story of the 1816 crafting of the "first" vampire by Polidori help us better understand more recent vampire tales? How?

2. Do you agree that, in our ever-changing society, we feel a need for permanence and that the vampire answers that need? Why or why not?

3. Hogan and del Toro create their own prehistoric myth of a once-cannibalistic human race that settles down to become more civilized. What purpose does that myth serve, and how does it help the authors' thesis? Does it matter if the myth is literally true for it to be an effective part of this article?

4. According to the authors, how is it that "Science becomes the modern man's superstition"?

Suggestions for Writing

1. Synthesis: Compare del Toro and Hogan's treatment of the vampire as a figure of romance, and as taboo sex fantasy, with Christine Seifert's exploration of similar themes in "Bite Me! (Or Don't!): Twilight as Abstinence Porn."

2. Watch a vampire movie or an episode of a vampire television show in the context of this essay by del Toro and Hogan. Discuss how the essay influences your interpretation of what you see. (Some possibilities: *Let the Right One In, 30 Days of Night, Fright Night, The Hunger, Thirst,* John Badham's *Dracula* (1979), *Vampire Hunter D: Bloodlust, Brides of Dracula, Dracula's Daughter, Salem's Lot, The Last Man on Earth, Interview with the Vampire, Subspecies II, The Night Stalker, Near Dark, Nosferatu,* and the more recent *Twilight* series. Television shows include the British series *Ultraviolet,* both the original and the more recent *Dark Shadows, Buffy the Vampire Slayer,* and *The Night Stalker.*)

CHRISTINE SEIFERT

Bite Me! (Or Don't!): Twilight *as Abstinence Porn*

An associate professor of communication at Westminster College in Utah, Christine Seifert (b. 1975) published this analysis of Stephenie Meyer's *Twilight* series in *Bitch Magazine,* a feminist periodical that analyzes the role of women in popular culture, in 2008. The piece has since accumulated more than 400 reader responses on the magazine's Web site, been reprinted in the *Best Sex Writing 2010,* and made Seifert an oft-interviewed expert on "abstinence porn." Born and raised in Fargo,

North Dakota, Seifert is a specialist in composition and rhetoric who has also taught at Salt Lake Community College. Her work analyzing *Twilight* inspired her to write her own, thus far unpublished Young Adult novel, *The Predicted*, a vampire-free tale featuring Seifert's idea of a stronger female heroine.

Abstinence has never been sexier than it is in Stephenie Meyer's young adult four-book *Twilight* series. Fans are super hot for Edward, a century-old vampire in a 17-year-old body, who sweeps teenaged Bella, your average human girl, off her feet in a thrilling love story that spans more than 2,000 pages. Fans are enthralled by their tale, which begins when Edward becomes intoxicated by Bella's sweet-smelling blood. By the middle of the first book, Edward and Bella are deeply in love and working hard to keep their pants on, a story line that has captured the attention of a devoted group of fans who obsess over the relationship and delight in Edward's superhuman strength to just say no.

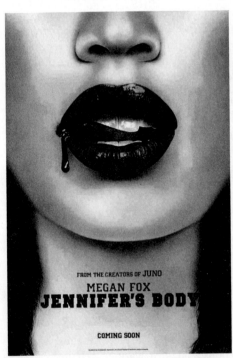

Movie poster for Jennifer's Body. Jennifer's Body, Megan Fox, 2009/TM and © Copyright Fox Atomic. All Rights Reserved/Courtesy Everett Collection

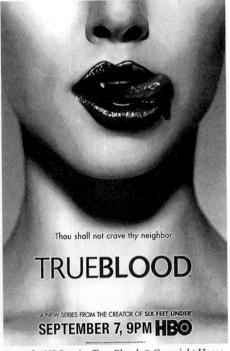

Poster for HBO series, True Blood. © Copyright Home Box Office, Inc.

The *Twilight* series has created a surprising new sub-genre of teen romance: It's abstinence porn, sensational, erotic, and titillating. And in light of all the recent real-world attention on abstinence-only education, it's surprising how successful this new genre is. *Twilight* actually convinces us that self-denial is hot. Fan reaction suggests that in the beginning, Edward and Bella's chaste but sexually charged relationship was steamy precisely because it was unconsummated—kind of like *Cheers,* but with fangs. Despite all the hot "virtue," however, we feminist readers have to ask ourselves if abstinence porn is as uplifting as some of its proponents seem to believe.

Given that teens are apparently still having sex—in spite of virginity rings, abstinence pledges, and black-tie "purity balls"—it might seem that remaining pure isn't doing much for the kids these days anyway. Still, the *Twilight* series is so popular it has done the unthinkable: knocked Harry Potter off his pedestal as prince of the young adult genre. The series has sold more than 50 million copies, and *Twilight* fan fiction, fan sites, and fan blogs crowd the Internet. Scores of fans have made the trek to real-life Forks, Wash., where the series is set. The first of a trilogy of film adaptations of the books, starring Kristen Stewart and Robert Pattinson, was scheduled to hit theaters in time for Christmas.

Nowhere was readers' multigenerational infatuation with Bella and Edward's steamy romance more evident than in their "engagement" party at a Sandy, Utah, Barnes & Noble store. On the evening of August 1, 2008, before the fourth book was released, guests flocked to the store wearing formal wedding attire to celebrate the happy fictional couple. Preteen girls in princess dresses, "My Heart Belongs to Edward" stickers plastered to their faces, posed for photos. Grandmothers in flowing gowns or homemade "I Love Edward" t-shirts stood in line to play *Twilight* trivia. Clever teen boys in Edward costumes fought off ersatz Bellas.

The air in the store was electric as fans broke into two groups: the much smaller group of Jacob fans (Jacob is Bella's best friend who is hopelessly in love with her, but it's a doomed relationship since Jacob is a werewolf, a lifelong enemy of the vamps) and the group of rabid Edward fans. The questions of the night were: Will Edward and Bella finally do it? If so, will the magic be ruined when the abstinence message is gone? But nobody seemed to be asking an even more important question: Has the abstinence message—however unwittingly—undermined feminist sensibilities?

The answers came sooner than expected. After the engagement party, fans rushed home with their copies of *Breaking Dawn,* only to discover that Edward and Bella go all the way in the first few chapters, after they get married, of course. But it seems that in the context of marriage and parenthood (which comes quickly, natch), Edward and now-19-year-old Bella are just like our traditional grandparents. Or the Moral Majority.

Breaking Dawn's Bella is a throwback to a 1950s housewife, except for the fact that Edward has turned her into a vampire. But this act is one of

'50s-esque female self-sacrifice: It's precipitated by Bella's need to let her human self die in order to save their half-vampire baby. Their monstrous offspring is frightening, but what's really frightening is Bella and Edward's honeymoon scene. Edward, lost in his own lust, "makes love" so violently to Bella that she wakes up the next morning covered in bruises, the headboard in ruins from Edward's romp. And guess what? Bella likes it. In fact, she loves it. She even tries to hide her bruises so Edward won't feel bad. If the abstinence message in the previous books was ever supposed to be empowering, this scene, presented early in *Breaking Dawn*, undoes everything.

What's worrisome is that fans are livid about the last book not because of the disturbing nature of Bella and Edward's sexual relationship, but because they consummated it in the first place. Shimmerskin, a poster on the message board Twilightmoms.com, summed it up best for a number of defeated fans: "The first three books were alive with sheer romanticism but I never felt it in [*Breaking Dawn*]. The sweep and scope of a grand love affair in [the first three books] was absent. The brilliantly innocent eroticism that took our breath away was also gone." Some fans are so upset at this loss of "innocence" they've created an online petition demanding answers from Meyer and her publisher, Little, Brown. "We were your faithful fans . . .," the petitioners write. "We are the people that you asked to come along with you on this journey, and we are disappointed."

Perhaps some of this bitter disappointment stems from book four's departure into adult territory, where Bella becomes a traditional—and boring—teenaged mom. The removal of the couple's sexual tension reveals two tepid, unenlightened people. Neither character has much to offer outside the initial high school romance storyline: Bella doesn't have any interesting hobbies, nor is she particularly engaged in the world around her. Her only activity outside her relationship with Edward seems to be cooking dinner for her father. Edward hangs out with his family, but the bulk of his 24 hours a day of wakefulness seems to go to either saving Bella from danger or watching her when she sleeps—you know, that age-old savior/stalker duality. Romantic!

As other feminists like Anna N. on Jezebel.com have pointed out, Edward is a controlling dick, a fact that becomes abundantly clear in the leaked pages of Meyer's first draft of *Midnight Sun*, a retelling of *Twilight* from Edward's perspective. In those pages, available on Meyer's website, Edward imagines what it would be like to kill Bella. "I would not kill her cruelly," he thinks to himself. Ever the gentleman, Edward. His icy calculation of how best to kill Bella is horrifying, and it illustrates the disconnect between the two characters.

By extension, readers who interpreted Edward's reluctance to be near Bella in *Twilight* as evidence of his innocent "crush" on her are forced to recognize that even Edward—the dream guy—is not at all he's cracked up to be. Digging into Edward's mind reinforces the old stereotype that underneath it all, even the best guys are calculating vampires, figuring out how to act on their masculine urges. Edward holds all the power, while Bella—and female readers—romanticizes the perfect man who doesn't exist. It's no wonder that *Midnight Sun* has not been widely released: It would likely spark even greater fan ire.

Such disappointment suggests something about the desire readers have for abstinence messages; it may also suggest readers' belief that, pre-sex, Edward and Bella were the perfect couple. In reality, the abstinence message—wrapped in the genre of abstinence porn—objectifies Bella in the same ways that "real" porn might. The *Twilight* books conflate Bella losing her virginity with the loss of other things, including her sense of self and her very life. Such a high-stakes treatment of abstinence reinforces the idea that Bella is powerless, an object, a fact that is highlighted when we get to the sex scenes in *Breaking Dawn*.

Of course the paradox is that the more Meyer sexualizes abstinence, the more we want Bella and Edward to actually have sex. This paradox becomes extra-convoluted when we find out, in a moment that for some is titillating, for others creepy, that sex could literally equal death for Bella. In one scene in *Twilight*, Bella asks Edward in a roundabout way if they would ever be able to consummate their relationship. Edward responds, "I don't think that . . . that . . . would be possible for us." Bella responds, "Because it would be too hard for you, if I were that . . . close?" Yes, Edward tells her. But more than that he reminds her that she's "soft" and "so fragile" and "breakable." "I could kill you quite easily, Bella, simply by accident."

And it's not just Bella's life that's at stake—it's her very humanity. The closer she and Edward get, the more tempting it is for him to bite her and turn her into a vampire, and the conflation of his vampiric and carnal urges is obvious. As *Midnight Sun* reveals, Edward's bloodlust is every bit as potent as his romantic love. It doesn't take a Freudian to read Edward's pulsating, insistent vampire lips pressed against Bella's pale, innocent neck as an analogy for, well, something else. From clandestine meetings in Bella's bedroom to time spent in a forest clearing, Edward almost always has his lips on Bella's neck—a dangerous activity, as we learn in *Twilight* that "the perfume of [Bella's] skin" is an unbearably erotic and tempting scent for Edward. When they do kiss, Bella often loses control of herself, which means Edward must be ever-vigilant in controlling "his need." After their first kiss, Bella asks if she should give him some room. "No," he tells her, "it's tolerable." He goes on, "I'm stronger than I thought." Bella responds, "I wish I could say the same. I'm sorry."

Fan fiction reveals fans' tacit understanding of the serious dangers of sex and the excitement of it, illustrating that readers have picked up on Meyer's analogy where the sexual penetration of Bella's human body is akin to the vampiric penetration of Bella's skin. One piece of fan fiction was posted to TheTwilightSaga.com on June 22, 2008, before the release of the fourth book, by a particularly ardent fan (hardy'sgirl). In the story, Edward and Bella have gotten married and are on their honeymoon. Edward begins kissing Bella (on her neck, of course), and then begins removing her jeans. Bella, with a pounding heart, asks herself, "Would I really let him go all the way?" Keep in mind that within this story, Bella and Edward are married; waffling about "doing it" with your husband might point to the age and maturity of the writer, but it also taps into the fear of intimacy that Meyer establishes in the books. The fan writer picks up on that fear as she continues her story: As Edward becomes more sexually aroused, he turns into something Bella doesn't recognize, and she begins to fight him. The fan writes:

> Edward had become a monster, that dangerous vampire he held hidden away from me . . . and I was the one about to pay for it . . . he held my arms above my head pinned onto the bed in iron clasps, i was panicking and my breathing was fast. Edward sat up above me . . . and the look in his eyes weren't ones ive ever seen before . . . unless he was about to feed.

The rape fantasy is apparent, of course, but even more salient is the fan writer's subconscious understanding of the theme Meyer has been establishing: that sex is dangerous and men must control themselves. It's a matter of life or death, and ultimately men are in charge.

It's clear from both the books and the fan fiction response to them that Edward has taken on the role of protector of Bella's human blood and chastity, both of which, ironically, are always in peril when Edward is nearby. Bella is not in control of her body, as abstinence proponents would argue; she is absolutely dependent on Edward's ability to protect her life, her virginity, and her humanity. She is the object of his virtue, the means of his ability to prove his self-control. In other words, Bella is a secondary player in the drama of Edward's abstinence.

Reader Shimmerskin again astutely notes, ". . . it's so clever that these books aren't just about sexual abstinence. Edward is fighting two kinds of lust at the same time. Abstaining from human blood has probably been good practice for tamping down his sexual appetites now that he's with Bella. . . ."

It's arguably clever, sure, but it's also a sad commentary on Bella's lack of power. Ultimately, it's a statement of the sexual politics of Meyer's abstinence message: Whether you end up doing the nasty or not doesn't ultimately matter. When it comes to a woman's virtue, sex, identity, or her existence itself, it's all in the man's hands. To be the object of desire, in abstinence porn is not really so far from being the object of desire in actual porn.

Suggestions for Discussion

1. According to Seifert, how "idealized" is the relationship between Edward and Bella in the *Twilight* series? Is it more satisfying than real-life romances? How? What is it about this relationship that fans love? Why are some feminists less happy with the romance?

2. Bella's marriage to Edward bothered both fans and Seifert, but for different reasons. Do you share any of these concerns? Is the married Bella "powerless" and "boring"?

3. Synthesis: Compare Seifert's thoughts on the nature of pornography to those presented by Margaret Atwood in "Pornography" (*Reading Images*). On what might they agree? On what might they disagree?

4. Synthesis: Can the popularity of *Twilight* be seen in part as a reaction to the phenomenon explored by Benoit Denizet-Lewis in "Friends, Friends with Benefits, and the Benefits of the Local Mall" (*Personal Values and Relationships*)?

5. Look at the images accompanying this essay. Describe the images as works of art. Comment on them as advertisements. What emotions do they encourage in the onlooker—a prospective consumer of a product? What kind of gender representation is at work? Are clues offered as to why vampires are so popular in modern America? What might Chuck Hogan, Guillermo del Toro, and Christine Seifert say about such images?

Suggestion for Writing

Synthesis: Feminists have long debated the messages conveyed by traditional fairy tales, comics, and cartoons about the roles of women in society. A number of essays in this collection touch on this subject, including Gloria Steinem's "Wonder Woman," Peggy Orenstein's "What's Wrong with Cinderella?," Constance Matthiessen's "Harry Potter and Divorce Among the Muggles," and Katha Pollitt's "Summers of Our Discontent." Read one or more of these along with Seifert's selection, and write a paper examining how fairy tales and myths about women affect the lives of real women in the real world.

PERSONAL WRITING

~~~~~

MICHAEL ABERNETHY

Male-Bashing on TV

Television reviewer, cultural critic, and queer culture commentator, Michael Abernethy joined the *PopMatters* writing staff in 2000. The Louisville, Kentucky, resident is also a Communication Studies lecturer at Indiana University Southeast, where he teaches political rhetoric and argumentation. This article was originally published in *PopMatters* on January 9, 2003.

Warning for our male readers: The following article contains big words and complex sentences. It might be a good idea to have a woman nearby to explain it to you.

It's been a hard day. Your assistant at work is out with the flu, and there is another deadline fast approaching. Your wife is at a business conference, so you have to pick up your son at daycare, make dinner, clean the kitchen, do a load of laundry, and get Junior to bed before you can settle down on the sofa with those reports you still need to go over.

Perhaps a little comedy will make the work more bearable, you think, so you turn on CBS for a little comedy: *King of Queens; Yes, Dear; Everybody Loves Raymond;* and *Still Standing.* Over the next two hours, you see four male lead characters who are nothing like you. These men are selfish and lazy, inconsiderate husbands, and poor parents.

And the commercials in between aren't any better. Among them: A feminine hygiene ad: Two women are traveling down a lovely country road, laughing and having a great time. But wait. One of them needs to check the freshness of her mini-pad, and, apparently, the next rest area is six states away. A women's voice-over interjects, "It's obvious that the interstate system was designed by men."

A digital camera ad: A young husband walks through a grocery store, trying to match photos in his hand with items on the shelves. Cut to his wife in the kitchen, snapping digital pictures of all the items in the pantry so that hubby won't screw up the shopping.

A family game ad: A dorky guy and beautiful women are playing Trivial Pursuit. He asks her, "How much does the average man's brain weigh?" Her answer: "Not much."

A wine ad: A group of women are sitting around the patio of a beach house, drinking a blush wine. Their boyfriends approach, but are denied refreshment until they have "earned" it by building a sand statue of David.

Welcome to the new comic image of men on TV: incompetence at its worst. Where television used to feature wise and wonderful fathers and husbands, today's comedies and ads often feature bumbling husbands and inept, uninvolved fathers. On *Still Standing*, Bill (Mark Addy) embarrasses his wife Judy (Jamie Gertz) so badly in front of her reading group that she is dropped from the group. On *Everybody Loves Raymond*, Raymond (Ray Romano) must choose between bathing the twin boys or helping his daughter with her homework. He begrudgingly agrees to assist his daughter, for whom he is no help whatsoever.

CBS is not the only guilty party. ABC's *My Wife and Kids* and *According to Jim*, Fox's *The Bernie Mac Show*, *The Simpsons*, *Malcolm in the Middle*, and (the cancelled) *Titus* also feature women who are better organized and possess better relational skills than their male counterparts. While most television dramas tend to avoid gender stereotypes, as these undermine "realism," comic portrayals of men have become increasingly negative. The trend is so noticeable that it has been criticized by men's-rights groups and some television critics.

It has also been studied by academicians Dr. Katherine Young and Paul Nathanson in their book, *Spreading Misandry: The Teaching of Contempt for Men in Popular Culture*. Young and Nathanson argue that in addition to being portrayed as generally unintelligent, men are ridiculed, rejected, and physically abused in the media. Such behavior, they suggest, "would never be acceptable if directed at women." Evidence of this pattern is found in a 2001 survey of 1,000 adults conducted by the Advertising Standards Association in Great Britain, which found that two thirds of respondents thought that women featured in advertisements were "intelligent, assertive, and caring," while the men were "pathetic and silly." The number of respondents who thought men were depicted as "intelligent" was a paltry 14 percent. (While these figures apply to the United Kingdom, comparable advertisements air in the United States.)

Some feminists might argue that for decades women on TV looked mindless and that turnabout is fair play. True, many women characters through the years have had little more to do than look after their families. From the prim housewife whose only means of control over her children was, "Wait 'til your father gets home!" to the dutiful housewife whose husband declares, "My wife: I think I'll keep her," women in the '50s and '60s were often subservient. (This generalization leaves out the unusual someone, like Donna Reed, who produced her own show, on which she was not subservient.)

Then, during the "sexual revolution," TV began to feature independent women who could take care of themselves (Mary and Rhoda on *The Mary Tyler Moore Show*; Julia, Alice, and Flo on *Alice*; Louise and Florence on *The Jeffersons*). So now, 30 years later, you'd think that maybe we'd have come to some parity. Not even.

Granted, men still dominate television, from the newsroom to prime time. And men do plenty on their own to perpetuate the image of the immature male, from Comedy Central's *The Man Show* to the hordes of drunken college boys who show up every year on MTV's *Spring Break*. What's the problem with a few jokes about how dumb men can be? C'mon, can't we take a few jokes?

If only it was just a few. The jokes have become standard fare. Looking at a handful of sitcoms makes the situation seem relatively insignificant, but when those sitcoms are combined with dozens of negative ads which repeat frequently, then a poor image of men is created in the minds of viewers.

According to "Gender Issues in Advertising Language," television portrayals that help create or reinforce negative stereotypes can lead to problems with self-image, self-concept, and personal aspirations. Young men learn that they are expected to screw up, that women will have the brains to their brawn, and that child care is over their heads. And it isn't just men who suffer from this constant parade of dumb men on TV. *Children Now* reports a new study that found that two thirds of children they surveyed describe men on TV as angry and only one third report ever seeing a man on television performing domestic chores, such as cooking or cleaning. There are far too few positive role models for young boys on television.

Moreover, stereotypical male-bashing portrayals undermine the core belief of the feminist movement: equality. Just think: What if the butt of all the jokes took on another identity? Consider the following fictional exchanges:

"It is so hard to get decent employees."

"That's because you keep hiring blacks."

"I just don't understand this project at all."

"Well, a woman explained it to you, so what did you expect?"

"I can't believe he is going out again tonight."

"Oh, please, all Hispanics care about is sex."

All of these statements are offensive and would rightfully be objected to by advocates of fair representation in the media. However, put the word "man" or "men" in place of "blacks," "woman," and "Hispanics" in the above sentences, and they're deemed humorous. Are men who ask to be treated civilly overly sensitive, or are we as justified in our objections as members of NOW, the NAACP, GLAAD, and other groups which protest demeaning television portrayals, whether those portrayals are on sitcoms, dramas, advertisements, or moronic TV like *The Man Show*.

Most of the shows I'm talking about are popular. Maybe that means I am being too sensitive. Yet, many U.S. viewers didn't have a problem with *Amos and Andy* or *I Dream of Jeannie*, both famous for their offensive stereotypes. These shows enjoyed good ratings, but neither concept is likely to be revived anytime soon, as "society" has realized their inappropriateness.

All this is not to say buffoonery—male or female—isn't a comic staple. Barney on *The Andy Griffith Show*, Ted on *The Mary Tyler Moore Show*, and Kramer on *Seinfeld* were all vital characters, but the shows also featured intelligent males. And these clowns were amusing because they were eccentric personalities, not because they were men. The same could be said of many female characters on TV, like *Alice's* Flo, *Friends'* Phoebe, or Karen on *Will and Grace*. Good comedy stems from creative writing and imaginative characterizations, not from degrading stereotypes.

Fortunately, some people are working to change the way television portrays men. J. C. Penney recently ran an ad for a one-day sale, with a father at the breakfast table with his infant crying and throwing things. The father asks the child when his mother will be home. Lana Whited of the *Roanoke Times*, syndicated columnist Dirk Lammers, and the National Men's Resource Center were just a few who objected to this image of an apparently incompetent and uncaring father, one who would let his child cry without making any attempt to calm him. Penney's got the message; their recent holiday ad features a father, mother, and son all happily shopping together.

Few men I know want a return to the "good ol' days." Those generalizations were as unrealistic as the idea that all men are big, slobbering goofballs. Hope lies beyond such simplistic oppositions, in shows like *The Cosby Show* or *Mad About You*, which placed their protagonists on level playing fields. Paul Reiser and Cosby did, on occasion, do moronic things, but so did Helen Hunt and Phylicia Rashad. People—because they are people, not just gendered people—are prone to fall on their faces occasionally.

Undoubtedly, there are men out there who are clones of Ward Cleaver, just as there are men who resemble Al Bundy. But the majority is somewhere in between. We're trying to deal the best we can with the kids, the spouse, the job, the bills, the household chores, and the countless crises that pop up unexpectedly. After all that, when we do get the chance to sit down and relax, it would be nice to turn on the TV and not see ourselves reflected as idiots.

Suggestions for Discussion

1. In your opinion, is Abernethy's assessment of the stereotyping of males on TV accurate? Based on the commercials and television programs you watch, are men portrayed as particularly stupid, lazy, or incompetent?

2. According to Abernethy, how can bad role models on TV have a psychological effect on real-life men?

3. What evidence does Abernethy use to support his claims? He anticipates that some might accuse him of exaggerating, or not being able to take a joke. What is his response?

4. What effect is created when Abernethy substitutes the word "man" in a disparaging remark with "woman," "black," and "Hispanic"? What does the exercise demonstrate? Is there a good counterargument to this point?

5. Synthesis: Several pieces in this collection are by well-known feminist writers (Margaret Atwood, Katha Pollitt, and Peggy Orenstein). How do Abernethy's concerns compare with those of these writers?

Suggestion for Writing

Abernethy complains about the dumb-dad, ex-high-school-jock stereotype of masculinity we see on many sitcoms. What other stereotyped male representations appear in popular culture? Think, for example, of the invincible superhero (*24*'s Jack Bauer, *Batman*), the nerd (*The 40-Year-Old Virgin*, *The Big Bang Theory*), the supportive and gossipy gay friend (*Queer Eye for the Straight Guy*, *Ugly Betty*), the ruthless businessman (*Mad Men*, *The Apprentice*), or the "pretty boy" womanizer (*Nip/Tuck*, *Two and a Half Men*, *How I Met Your Mother*). Consider also the images of male minorities, who are often presented either as dangerous suspects on crime shows, or as wide-eyed goofballs on sitcoms. How do these various stereotypes differ from the one Abernethy presents, and from one another? Are these additional stereotypes equally damaging? Are some "worse" than others? Select one or more of these stereotypes and analyze their potential impact on male (and female) viewers.

GLORIA STEINEM

Wonder Woman

Gloria Steinem (b. 1934), one of the champions of the contemporary women's movement, is an author, a social activist, and a pioneering female journalist and editor who won fame as a critic and proponent of reproductive rights for women. She was a cofounder of *New York Magazine* in 1968 and in the 1970s cofounded *Ms.* magazine, the first national women's magazine run by women. She is also the founder of the Coalition of Labor Union Women, the National Women's Political Caucus, and the Ms. Foundation for Women. Born in Toledo, Ohio,

Steinem enrolled in Smith College in 1952 and studied abroad in Switzerland and India. Some of her books include *The Thousand Indias* (1957), *Outrageous Acts and Everyday Rebellions* (1983), the biography *Marilyn: Norma Jean* (1986), *Revolution from Within* (1992), *and Moving Beyond Words* (1994). In the following essay, Steinem explains how her childhood hero Wonder Woman, an iconic comic book feminist with magical powers and superhuman strength, helped inspire her and fuel her self-esteem during her formative years.

Wonder Woman is the only female super-hero to be published continuously since comic books began—indeed, she is one of the few to have existed at all or to be anything other than part of a male super-hero group— but this may strike many readers as a difference without much distinction. After all, haven't comic books always been a little disreputable? Something that would never have been assigned in school? The answer to those questions is yes, which is exactly why they are important. Comic books have power—including over the child who still lives within each of us—because they are *not* part of the "serious" grown-up world.

I remember hundreds of nights reading comic books under the covers with a flashlight; dozens of car trips while my parents told me I was ruining my eyes and perhaps my mind ("brain-deadeners" was what my mother called them); and countless hours spent hiding in a tree or some other inaccessible spot where I could pore over their pages in sweet freedom. Because my family's traveling meant I didn't go to school regularly until I was about twelve, comic books joined cereal boxes and ketchup labels as the primers that taught me how to read. They were even cheap enough to be the first things I bought on my own—a customer who couldn't see over the countertop but whose dignity was greatly enhanced by making a choice, counting out carefully hoarded coins, and completing a grown-up exchange.

I've always wondered if this seemingly innate drive toward independence in children isn't more than just "a movement toward mastery," as psychologists say. After all, each of us is the result of millennia of environment and heredity, a unique combination that could never happen before—or again. Like a seed that contains a plant, a child is already a unique person; an ancient spirit born into a body too small to express itself, or even cope with the world. I remember feeling the greatest love for my parents whenever they allowed me to express my own will, whether that meant wearing an inappropriate hat for days on end, or eating dessert before I had finished dinner.

Perhaps it's our memories of past competence and dreams for the future that create the need for super-heroes in the first place. Leaping skyscrapers in a single bound, seeing through walls, and forcing people to tell the truth by encircling them in a magic lasso—all would be satisfying fantasies at any age, but they may be psychological necessities when we have trouble tying our shoes, escaping a worldview composed mainly of belts and knees, and getting grownups to *pay attention*.

The problem is that the super-heroes who perform magical feats—indeed, even mortal heroes who are merely competent—are almost always men. A female child is left to believe that, even when her body is as big as her spirit, she will still be helping with minor tasks, appreciating the accomplishments of others, and waiting to be rescued. Of course, pleasure is to be found in all these experiences of helping, appreciating, and being rescued; pleasure that should be open to boys, too. Even in comic books, heroes sometimes work in groups or are called upon to protect their own kind, not just helpless females. But the truth is that a male super-hero is more likely to be vulnerable, if only to create suspense, than a female character is to be powerful or independent. For little girls, the only alternative is suppressing a crucial part of ourselves by transplanting our consciousness into a male character—which usually means a white one, thus penalizing girls of color doubly, and boys of color, too. Otherwise, choices remain limited: in the case of girls, to an "ideal" life of sitting around like a Technicolor clotheshorse, getting into jams with villains, and saying things like, "Oh, Superman! I'll always be grateful to you"; in the case of boys of color, to identifying with villains who may be the only ethnic characters with any power; and in the case of girls of color, to making an impossible choice between parts of their identity. It hardly seems worth learning to tie our shoes.

I'm happy to say that I was rescued from this dependent fate at the age of seven or so; rescued (Great Hera!) by a woman. Not only did she have the wisdom of Athena and Aphrodite's power to inspire love, she was also faster than Mercury and stronger than Hercules. In her all-woman home on Paradise Island, a refuge of ancient Amazon culture protected from nosy travelers by magnetic thought-fields that created an area known to the world as the Bermuda Triangle, she had come to her many and amazing powers naturally. Together with her Amazon sisters, she had been trained in them from infancy and perfected them in Greek-style contests of dexterity, strength, and speed. The lesson was that each of us might have unknown powers within us, if we only believed and practiced them. (To me, it always seemed boring that Superman had bulletproof skin, X-ray vision, and the ability to fly. Where was the contest?) Though definitely white, as were all her Amazon sisters, she was tall and strong, with dark hair and eyes—a relief from the weak, bosomy, blonde heroines of the 1940s.

Of course, this Amazon did need a few fantastic gadgets to help her once she entered a modern world governed by Ares, God of War, not Aphrodite, Goddess of Love: a magic golden lasso that compelled all within its coils to obey her command, silver bracelets that repelled bullets, and an invisible plane that carried her through time as well as space. But she still had to learn how to throw the lasso with accuracy, be agile enough to deflect bullets from her silver-encased wrists, and navigate an invisible plane.

Charles Moulton, whose name appeared on each episode as Wonder Woman's writer and creator, had seen straight into my heart and understood the fears of violence and humiliation hidden there. No longer did I have to pretend to like the "POW!" and "SPLAT!" of boys' comic books, from Captain Marvel to the Green Hornet. No longer did I have nightmares after looking at ghoulish images of torture and murder, bloody scenes made all the more realistic by steel-booted Nazis and fang-toothed Japanese who were caricatures of World War II enemies then marching in every newsreel. (Eventually, the sadism of boys' comic books was so extreme that it inspired Congressional hearings, and publishers were asked to limit the number of severed heads and dripping entrails—a reminder that television wasn't the first popular medium selling sadism to boys.) Best of all, I could stop pretending to enjoy the ridicule, bossing-around, and constant endangering of female characters. In these Amazon adventures, only the villains bought the idea that "masculine" meant aggression and "feminine" meant submission. Only the occasional female accomplice said things like "Girls want superior men to boss them around," and even they were usually converted to the joys of self-respect by the story's end.

This was an Amazon super-hero who never killed her enemies. Instead, she converted them to a belief in equality and peace, to self-reliance, and respect for the rights of others. If villains destroyed themselves, it was through their own actions or some unbloody accident. Otherwise, they might be conquered by force, but it was a force tempered by love and justice.

In short, she was wise, beautiful, brave, and explicitly out to change "a world torn by the hatreds and wars of men."

She was Wonder Woman.

Only much later, when I was in my thirties and modern feminism had begun to explain the political roots of women's status—instead of accepting some "natural" inferiority decreed by biology, God, or Freud—did I realize how hard Charles Moulton had tried to get an egalitarian worldview into comic book form. From Wonder Woman's birth myth as Princess Diana of Paradise Island, "that enlightened land," to her adventures in America disguised as Diana Prince, a be-spectacled army nurse and intelligence officer (a clear steal from Superman's Clark Kent), this female super-hero was devoted to democracy, peace, justice, and "liberty and freedom for all womankind."

One typical story centers on Prudence, a young pioneer in the days of the American Frontier, where Wonder Woman has been transported by the invisible plane that doubles as a time machine. After being rescued from a

Perils of Pauline life, Prudence finally realizes her own worth, and also the worth of all women. "From now on," she says proudly to Wonder Woman, "I'll rely on myself, not on a man." Another story ends with Wonder Woman explaining her own long-running romance with Captain Steve Trevor, the American pilot whose crash-landing on Paradise Island was Aphrodite's signal that the strongest and wisest of all the Amazons must answer the call of a war-torn world. As Wonder Woman says of this colleague whom she so often rescues: "I can never love a dominant man."

The most consistent villain is Ares, God of War, a kind of metavillain who considers women "the natural spoils of war" and insists they stay home as the slaves of men. Otherwise, he fears women will spread their antiwar sentiments, create democracy in the world, and leave him dishonored and unemployed. That's why he keeps trying to trick Queen Hippolyte, Princess Diana's mother, into giving up her powers as Queen of the Amazons, thus allowing him to conquer Paradise Island and destroy the last refuge of ancient feminism. It is in memory of a past time when the Amazons did give in to the soldiers of Ares, and were enslaved by them, that Aphrodite requires each Amazon to wear a pair of cufflike bracelets. If captured and bound by them (as Wonder Woman sometimes is in particularly harrowing episodes), an Amazon loses all her power. Wearing them is a reminder of the fragility of female freedom.

In America, however, villains are marked not only by their violence, but by their prejudice and lust for money. Thomas Tighe, woman-hating industrialist, is typical. After being rescued by Wonder Woman from accidental imprisonment in his own bank vault, he refuses to give her the promised reward of a million dollars. Though the money is needed to support Holliday College, the home of the band of college girls who aid Wonder Woman, Tighe insists that its students must first complete impossible tests of strength and daring. Only after Wonder Woman's powers allow them to meet every challenge does Tighe finally admit: "You win, Wonder Woman! . . . I am no longer a woman hater." She replies: "Then you're the real winner, Mr. Tighe! Because when one ceases to hate, he becomes stronger!"

Other villains are not so easily converted. Chief among them is Dr. Psycho, perhaps a parody of Sigmund Freud. An "evil genius" who "abhors women," the mad doctor's intentions are summed up in this scene-setting preface to an episode called "Battle for Womanhood": "With weird cunning and dark, forbidden knowledge of the occult, Dr. Psycho prepares to change the independent status of modern American women back to the days of the sultans and slave markets, clanking chains and abject captivity. But sly and subtle Psycho reckons without Wonder Woman!"

When I looked into the origins of my proto-feminist super-hero, I discovered that her pseudonymous creator had been a very non-Freudian psychologist named William Moulton Marston. Also a lawyer, businessman, prison reformer, and inventor of the lie-detector test (no doubt the inspiration for Wonder Woman's magic lasso), he had invented Wonder Woman as a heroine for little girls, and also as a conscious alternative to the violence of comic books for boys. In fact, Wonder Woman did attract some boys as readers, but the integrated world of comic book trading revealed her true status: at least three Wonder Woman comic books were necessary to trade for one of Superman. Among the many male super-heroes, only Superman and Batman were to be as long-lived as Wonder Woman, yet she was still a second-class citizen.

Of course, it's also true that Marston's message wasn't as feminist as it might have been. Instead of portraying the goal of full humanity for women and men, which is what feminism has in mind, he often got stuck in the subject/object, winner/loser paradigm of "masculine" versus "feminine," and came up with female superiority instead. As he wrote: "Women represent love; men represent force. Man's use of force without love brings evil and unhappiness. Wonder Woman proves that women are superior to men because they have love in addition to force." No wonder I was inspired but confused by the isolationism of Paradise Island: Did women have to live separately in order to be happy and courageous? No wonder even boys who could accept equality might have felt less than good about themselves in some of these stories: Were there *any* men who could escape the cultural instruction to be violent?

Wonder Woman herself sometimes got trapped in this either/or choice. As she muses to herself: "Some girls love to have a man stronger than they are to make them do things. Do I like it? I don't know, it's sort of thrilling. But isn't it more fun to make a man obey?" Even female villains weren't capable of being evil on their own. Instead, they were hyperfeminine followers of men's commands. Consider Priscilla Rich, the upper-class antagonist who metamorphoses into the Cheetah, a dangerous she-animal. "Women have been submissive to men," wrote Marston, "and taken men's psychology [force without love] as their own."

In those wartime years, stories could verge on a jingoistic, even racist patriotism. Wonder Woman sometimes forgot her initial shock at America's unjust patriarchal system and confined herself to defeating a sinister foreign threat by proving that women could be just as loyal and brave as men in service of their country. Her costume was a version of the Stars and Stripes. Some of her adversaries were suspiciously short, ugly, fat, or ethnic as a symbol of "un-American" status. In spite of her preaching against violence and for democracy, the good guys were often in uniform, and no country but the United States was seen as a bastion of freedom.

But Marston didn't succumb to stereotypes as often as most comic book writers of the 1940s. Though Prudence, his frontier heroine, is threatened by monosyllabic Indians, Prudence's father turns out to be the true villain, who has been cheating the Indians. And the irrepressible Etta Candy, one of Wonder Woman's band of college girls, is surely one of the few fat-girl heroines in comics.

There are other unusual rewards. Queen Hippolyte, for instance, is a rare example of a mother who is good, powerful, and a mentor to her daughter. She founds nations, fights to protect Paradise Island, and is a source of strength to Wonder Woman as she battles the forces of evil and inequality. Mother and daughter stay in touch through a sort of telepathic TV set, and the result is a team of equals who are separated only by experience. In the flashback episode in which Queen Hippolyte succumbs to Hercules, she is even seen as a sexual being. How many girl children grew to adulthood with no such example of a strong, sensual mother—except for these slender stories? How many mothers preferred sons, or believed the patriarchal myth that competition is "natural" between mothers and daughters, or tamed their daughters instead of encouraging their wildness and strength? We are just beginning to realize the sense of anger and loss in girls whose mothers had no power to protect them, or forced them to conform out of fear for their safety, or left them to identify only with their fathers if they had any ambition at all.

Finally, there is Wonder Woman's ability to unleash the power of self-respect within the women around her; to help them work together and support each other. This may not seem revolutionary to male readers accustomed to stories that depict men working together, but for females who are usually seen as competing for the favors of men—especially little girls who may just be getting to the age when girlfriends betray each other for the approval of boys—this discovery of sisterhood can be exhilarating indeed. Women get a rare message of independence, of depending on themselves, not even on Wonder Woman. "You saved yourselves," as she says in one of her inevitable morals at story's end. "I only showed you that you could."

Whatever the shortcomings of William Marston, his virtues became clear after his death in 1947. Looking back at the post-Marston stories I had missed the first time around—for at twelve or thirteen, I thought I had outgrown Wonder Woman and had abandoned her—I could see how little her later writers understood her spirit. She became sexier-looking and more submissive, violent episodes increased, more of her adversaries were female, and Wonder Woman herself required more help from men in order to triumph. Like so many of her real-life sisters in the postwar era of conservatism and "togetherness" of the 1950s, she had fallen on very hard times.

By the 1960s, Wonder Woman had given up her magic lasso, her bullet-deflecting bracelets, her invisible plane, and all her Amazonian powers. Though she still had adventures and even practiced karate, any attractive man could disarm her. She had become a kind of female James Bond, though much more boring because she was denied his sexual freedom. She was Diana Prince, a mortal who walked about in boutique, car-hop clothes and took the advice of a male mastermind named "I Ching."

It was in this sad state that I first rediscovered my Amazon super-hero in 1972. *Ms.* magazine had just begun, and we were looking for a cover story for its first regular issue to appear in July. Since Joanne Edgar and other of its founding editors had also been rescued by Wonder Woman in their childhoods, we decided to rescue Wonder Woman in return. Though it wasn't easy to persuade her publishers to let us put her original image on the cover of a new and unknown feminist magazine, or to reprint her 1940s Golden Age episodes inside, we finally succeeded. Wonder Woman appeared on newsstands again in all her original glory, striding through city streets like a colossus, stopping planes and bombs with one hand and rescuing buildings with the other.

Clearly, there were many nostalgic grown-ups and heroine-starved readers of all ages. The consensus of response seemed to be that if we had all read more about Wonder Woman and less about Dick and Jane, we might have been a lot better off. As for her publishers, they, too, were impressed. Under the direction of Dorothy Woolfolk, the first woman editor of Wonder Woman in all her long history, she was returned to her original Amazon status— golden lasso, bracelets, and all.

One day some months after her rebirth, I got a phone call from one of Wonder Woman's tougher male writers. "Okay," he said, "she's got all her Amazon powers back. She talks to the Amazons on Paradise Island. She even has a Black Amazon sister named Nubia. Now will you leave me alone?"

I said we would.

In the 1970s, Wonder Woman became the star of a television series. As played by Lynda Carter, she was a little blue of eye and large of breast, but she still retained her Amazon powers, her ability to convert instead of kill, and her appeal for many young female viewers. There were some who refused to leave their TV sets on Wonder Woman night. A few young boys even began to dress up as Wonder Woman on Halloween—a true revolution.

In the 1980s, Wonder Woman's story line was revamped by DC Comics, which reinvented its male super-heroes Superman and Batman at about the same time. Steve Trevor became a veteran of Vietnam; he remained a friend, but was romantically involved with Etta Candy. Wonder Woman acquired a Katharine Hepburn–Spencer Tracy relationship with a street-smart Boston detective named Ed Indelicato, whose tough-guy attitude played off Wonder Woman's idealism. She also gained a friend and surrogate mother in Julia Kapatelis, a leading archaeologist and professor of Greek culture at Harvard

University who can understand the ancient Greek that is Wonder Woman's native tongue, and be a model of a smart, caring, single mother for girl readers. Julia's teenage daughter, Vanessa, is the age of many readers and goes through all of their uncertainties, trials, and tribulations, but has the joy of having a powerful older sister in Wonder Woman. There is even Myndi Mayer, a slick Hollywood public relations agent who turns Wonder Woman into America's hero, and is also in constant danger of betraying Diana's idealistic spirit. In other words, there are many of the currents of society today, from single mothers to the worries of teenage daughters and a commercial culture, instead of the simpler plots of America's dangers in World War II.

You will see whether Wonder Woman carries her true Amazon spirit into the present. If not, let her publishers know. She belongs to you.

Since Wonder Woman's beginnings more than a half century ago, however, a strange thing has happened: the Amazon myth has been rethought as archaeological relics have come to light. Though Amazons had been considered figments of the imagination, perhaps the mythological evidence of man's fear of woman, there is a tentative but growing body of evidence to support the theory that some Amazon-like societies did exist. In Europe, graves once thought to contain male skeletons—because they were buried with weapons or were killed by battle wounds—have turned out to hold skeletons of females after all. In the jungles of Brazil, scientists have found caves of what appears to have been an all-female society. The caves are strikingly devoid of the usual phallic design and theme; they feature, instead, the triangular female symbol, and the only cave that does bear male designs is believed to have been the copulatorium, where Amazons mated with males from surrounding tribes, kept only the female children, and returned male infants to the tribe. Such archaeological finds have turned up not only along the Amazon River in Brazil, but at the foot of the Atlas Mountains in northwestern Africa, and on the European and Asiatic sides of the Black Sea.

There is still far more controversy than agreement, but a shared supposition of these myths is this: imposing patriarchy on the gynocracy of prehistory took many centuries and great cruelty. Rather than give up freedom and worship only male gods, some bands of women resisted. They formed all-woman cultures that survived by capturing men from local tribes, mating with them, and raising their girl children to have great skills of body and mind. These bands became warriors and healers who were sometimes employed for their skills by patriarchal cultures around them. As a backlash culture, they were doomed, but they may also have lasted for centuries.

Perhaps that's the appeal of Wonder Woman, Paradise Island, and this comic book message. It's not only a child's need for a lost independence, but an adult's need for a lost balance between women and men, between humans and nature. As the new Wonder Woman says to Vanessa, "Remember your *power*, little sister."

However simplified, that is Wonder Woman's message: Remember Our Power.

Suggestions for Discussion

1. According to Steinem, why are children drawn to comic books and super-heroes? Why are the various character traits of a superhero—including race, age, and gender—important to a young reader of comic books?

2. What kind of morality does the fictional character of Wonder Woman rep-resent? What critical observations does Steinem make about the positive and negative aspects of the heroine?

3. Why did Steinem come into conflict with DC comics over its changes in the characterization of Wonder Woman? How was the issue resolved? In what other ways has the character changed over the years?

4. How do modern superheroines, including Buffy the Vampire Slayer, Xena, Hit Girl, Elastigirl, and Claire Bennet, compare with Wonder Woman? Might Steinem approve of them?

Suggestion for Writing

Think of the fictional character with whom you most strongly identify. Why do you feel such a kinship with a figure that doesn't, in a physical sense, exist in the real world? Do you feel that this character has, in any way, shaped the way you have behaved or viewed yourself or the world around you? Explore the history of your relationship with this character in an essay like the one that Steinem wrote about Wonder Woman.

ESSAYS

STEVEN LEVY

Facebook Grows Up

Senior editor and chief technology correspondent for *Newsweek* magazine, Steven Levy (b. 1951) is the author of six books that explore the
world of technology and its effects on society, including *Hackers: Heroes
of the Computer Revolution* (1984) and *The Perfect Thing: How the iPod
Shuffles Commerce, Culture, and Coolness* (2006). He is hailed as one of
the best interpreters of our technological age, and Levy's pursuit of all
things digital has led one reviewer to comment that he "speaks fluent
geek." In the following article, Levy chronicles the success and future of
the enormously popular Internet networking Web site Facebook.

On Tuesday, July 31, Shara Karasic's world came to a temporary halt.
Facebook was down. She could not follow the fortunes and foibles of her
friends. She could not see if any photos had been posted that were tagged as
including her. She could not even know if anyone had "poked" her (which
is not a sexual act, but just a little cozier way of saying "hey, you" online).
Even though she had the entire Internet to entertain her and connect her,
she felt the loss. "Over the course of those four hours," Karasic says, "I probably tried to get in five or more times."

This would not be surprising if Karasic were a college student. Facebook
is as much a part of campus as finals, iPods and beer—the contemporary
equivalent of jamming several people into a phone booth is squeezing one's
entire social life onto a series of photo shows, news feeds, invitations, friend
requests and status updates on the spare blue-and-white grid of a Facebook
page. Nor would it be remarkable if she were in high school, where millions
of Facebook users, feeling very much like their big brothers and sisters
in college, log on as soon as they toss their books on the bed, forming
outrageously named groups and moving their lunchroom cliques and

locker-room gossip online. Shara Karasic, however, is 40 years old, a Santa Monica, Calif., working mother with a young son. Despite a suspicion that the site was only for college students, she signed on a year ago and found professional people like herself; she quickly got requests to be "friended" from two 40-year-old cousins. And on July 31, when she couldn't get in for a few hours, she realized something: "I'm addicted to Facebook."

Addictions like hers bring joy to the already bursting hearts of the geeky, soon-to-be-loaded executives of Facebook, the hottest tech start-up in Silicon Valley since Sergey and Larry made us feel lucky. Everyone knows that Facebook is the online hangout of just about every college student in the nation as well as the inevitable source of photos of nominees for the Supreme Court in 2038 cavorting in their underwear as youths. But the student population is only a beachhead in the vast ambitions of Facebook. Its people claim that more than half its 35 million active users are not college students, and that by the end of this year less than 30 percent of Facebook users will sport college IDs.

Anything goes in the spirited Facebook world. Just about everybody updates his or her status line with pithy, haiku-ish and often profane precision. For only a dollar you can send a friend a "gift"—an image of a cute item like a polka-dot thong, a champagne glass or sushi. Thousands of groups form daily: sufferers of cancer, conjunctivitis or bad taste. People who scale public buildings in Princeton. Supporters of every politician imaginable. Facebook last year took down the student-only sign and instituted an open-enrollment policy. The idea is that as more people do this— and invite their friends to join the fun—there will be a mass movement to access the world through the interests of, and interests in, the people you know personally. Karel Baloun, an engineer who worked at Facebook until last year, recalls vividly the baldly stated prediction of one of the company's cofounders: "In five years," he said, "we'll have everybody on the planet on Facebook."

That's far from a given: just because older people sign up, there's no evidence yet that it's ubiquitous in their lives the way Facebook is in the school world. Nonetheless, "Facebook has emerged as the 'it' service and company . . . It represents the next logical progression," says former AOL CEO Steve Case (via the messaging system on Facebook, where Case has been digitally hanging out of late; he's even friended Bill Gates). Mark Zuckerberg, the 23-year-old Harvard dropout who started the site, is high tech's new prince. Having turned down a reported $1 billion offer from Yahoo last year—and enduring the taunts of bloggers who predicted that he'd rue the day—Zuckerberg in May took Facebook in a new direction: he opened up the Web site to thousands of developers, who can now unilaterally install applications designed to take advantage of Facebook's people connections. This, along with an astonishing growth rate of 3 percent a week, has triggered a Facebook mania in the Valley. Early investor Peter Thiel, who sits on Facebook's board, believes that a measly billion dollars for this 300-person company spread over three buildings in downtown Palo Alto, Calif., is a risible sum. Instead, he compares Facebook's current price tag to that of MTV, which he values at about seven or eight billion bucks. "Between the two, I'd want to own Facebook," he says. Not that it's for sale. Thiel and other Facebook folk are now talking about an IPO in perhaps two years that would almost certainly be the biggest public offering since Google.

Zuckerberg himself, whose baby-faced looks at 23 would lead any bartender in America to scrutinize his driver's license carefully before serving a mojito, eschews talk about money. It's all about building the company. Speaking with NEWSWEEK between bites of a tofu snack, he is much more interested in explaining why Facebook is (1) not a social-networking site but a "utility," a tool to facilitate the information flow between users and their compatriots, family members and professional connections; (2) not just for college students; and (3) a world-changing idea of unlimited potential. Every so often he drifts back to No. 2 again, just for good measure. But the nub of his vision revolves around a concept he calls the "social graph."

As he describes it, this is a mathematical construct that maps the real-life connections between every human on the planet. Each of us is a node radiating links to the people we know. "We don't own the social graph," he says. "The social graph is this thing that exists in the world, and it always has and it always will. It's really most natural for people to communicate through it, because it's with the people around you, friends and business connections or whatever. What [Facebook] needed to do was construct as accurate of a model as possible of the way the social graph looks in the world. So once Facebook knows who you care about, you can upload a photo album and we can send it to all those people automatically."

Zuckerberg believes that this is what makes Facebook so compelling: as your friends join Facebook, that part of the social graph—the part that matters to you—moves into the digital fast lane and you're getting more out of your connections than you ever could have imagined. (Of course, since your friends on the graph are connected to other people, you have the advantage of seeing *their* friends and expanding your circle.) Unlike services like the giant MySpace—which at more than 70 million users still wins in raw numbers—Facebook is not a place where emerging stand-up comics, hip indie bands and soft-porn starlets try to break out by tagging thousands of people as virtual friends. Zuckerberg even says Facebook isn't intended as a venue to seek out new people, though certainly it's possible to locate promising strangers whose relationship status is "anything I can get." (Proof of concept is Aaron Byrd, who as a Texas-born Harvard senior searched through Facebook networks looking for women named Grace—hey, he likes the name—lighting on a pretty U of Georgia sophomore. First he friended her and then, reader, he married her.)

Still, the Facebook experience is built around people you know, and the center of the page is a News Feed where the stories largely consist of the activities, brief status reports, photo and video postings, and comments from those you have earmarked as friends. Facebook also places ads on the News Feed, so after learning that Sue is out of her relationship and Francis has posted a picture, you may get a "sponsored story" featuring the Geico cavemen. News Feed ads are "well targeted—people like the content," Zuckerberg says, unconvincingly. Facebook also takes in revenue, from banner ads sold by Microsoft, in a partnership that's contracted until 2011.

These were stakes undreamed of when Zuckerberg, a computer-savvy Harvard sophomore who grew up in Westchester County, N.Y., started a site called thefacebook.com in February 2004. The name refers to the yearbook-style booklets of photos and vital statistics that incoming freshmen receive at Harvard. (Late the previous year Zuckerberg had apparently agreed to do some of the computer coding for a different planned social-networking site. The founders of that site, ConnectU, are suing Zuckerberg, charging that the then sophomore intentionally stalled, then took the idea from them. Last month a Massachusetts judge indicated that ConnectU's case might be flimsy, asking the plaintiffs to come up with more evidence than "dorm-room chitchat.")

Zuckerberg's site was an instant success. "It was a pretty bare-bones, uploaded Harvard directory when I signed up on the first day—but it became an immediate distraction," says Olivia Ma, user No. 51, who knew Zuckerberg because he lived in her dorm. "Within a few weeks it seemed the whole school signed up." Indeed, two weeks after its release The Harvard Crimson reported the site had already attracted 4,300 students, faculty, and alumni.

Zuckerberg had done some things very right. "In the Ivy League, where very few incoming freshmen know more than one or two people, the facebook is a really key piece of the social infrastructure," says Danah Boyd, a researcher at the UC Berkeley School of Information. "Zuckerberg made it interactive. It had a slight social stalking element, too. It was addictive, it was juicy—a great way to see what was going on." Another key feature: only those in the Harvard.edu Internet domain could get in. "The fact that you could only see people on your network was crucial," says Boyd. "It let you be in public, but only in the gaze of eyes you want to be public to."

Within days of its release at Harvard, students at other schools were clamoring for their own versions of the site, and by the end of March it was at Stanford, Columbia, and Yale, on its way to capturing the entire college market. But even more extraordinary was the way people used it. Facebook, as it became after a name change, was permeating every aspect of campus social life. Students even came to use its messaging function instead of e-mail.

That spring, Zuckerberg quit school, and he and his partners moved to Silicon Valley, where they met with investor Peter Thiel. "Mark was clearly a brilliant engineer with a great vision for his product," explains Thiel, who kicked in $500,000. "Mark's plan had all the fundamental characteristics you would see in a Google or eBay in the early days of those companies," says

Matt Cohler, an executive who sat in on the meeting and wound up working at Facebook himself.

Later Facebook received $12.7 million in venture-capital money from Accel Partners. (Zuckerberg took this in preference to an investment offer from Don Graham—chairman of NEWSWEEK'S parent, The Washington Post Company—with whom he is friendly.) Accel's Jim Breyer recalls the 2005 dinner that clinched the deal: "I ordered a nice pinot noir and Mark ordered a Sprite, telling me he was underage." Breyer was impressed with Zuckerberg's youthful passion for his product, though he says the investment was controversial within his firm—some colleagues wondered whether social networking was a fad. (The early leader in the field, Friendster, had fizzled.)

Armed with cash (the most recent influx was $25 million in 2006), Facebook began its march beyond colleges, adding high schools in 2005 (no one under 13 is permitted to register) and then "work networks" within corporations in early 2006. By September of last year, anyone could register, and the site's numbers started climbing. That's when Terry Semel, who was then Yahoo's CEO, dangled a billion dollars in front of Zuckerberg—which he blithely ignored.

Zuckerberg's next big move was to fill Facebook with all sorts of applications people could use without leaving the site—programs that took advantage of Facebook's vast social networks. "There are a ton of different ways that people can share information, and rather than trying to develop all those ourselves, we wanted to allow anyone worldwide to create any kind of application," says Zuckerberg. Thousands of developers, from big companies to kids in dorm rooms, instantly began creating applications that piggybacked on Facebook's infrastructure. The new applications could get instant viral distribution, since the News Feed blasts a report to friends every time someone installs a new app (in other words, free promotion). Developers could make money from Facebook-embedded apps by taking ads or selling things—without sharing a penny of the proceeds with Facebook.

For instance, one company took two weeks to create a Facebook version of iLike, a music-recommendation and band-tracking service, and within a month more than doubled its users. A 22-year-old college student stayed up all night to hack a free (though less polished) version of Facebook's $1 graphic "gifts"—and 5 million people downloaded his application.

What does Facebook get from this? If all goes well, much of what people do on the Internet will be accomplished within Facebook. Instead of eBay, you can buy in Facebook's marketplace. Instead of iTunes, there's iLike. In other words, Zuckerberg wants to keep you—student, graduate or graybeard—logged on to Facebook, organizing virtually everything you do via the social graph.

Though some are grumbling about this "walled garden" system's being overly cloistered—and others believe that adding all those applications muddies up Facebook's austere appearance—1 million people a week are flocking to Facebook. And the international push is only beginning. While the site is now available only in English, Zuckerberg says that versions in other languages will appear soon. (Facebook is already the top Web site in Canada, and the geographic network with the most Facebookers is London.)

Still, one big question dogs the company in its attempt to leverage the social graph in the same felicitous—and wildly profitable—way that Google found fame and riches through search. Can Facebook be as much a presence in the life of graduates and geezers as it is to college students? Zuckerberg can't see why not. "Adults still communicate with the people they're connected with."

At this point, though, much of the grammar of the site (as well as much of the first wave of applications) is still tilted toward student life. David Rodnitzky, 35, a San Francisco marketing executive, was having a fine time on Facebook until he installed a widget called "My Questions." Unbeknownst to him, it sent out a query to people on his friend list, specifically: "Do you kiss on the first date?" "Here I was, asking some of my company's venture capitalists, along with some of my guy friends, if they kiss on the first date," says Rodnitzky. "Probably not the best way to interact." Nor is it clear whether grown-ups embrace the new SuperPoke third-party application: instead of a mere poke you can bite, slap, bump, spank, lick, grope or head-butt friends, acquaintances and, uh, business colleagues.

Also, there's a question of whether older people want to interact with fewer or more people as they nestle into their family and work lives. For some, use drops off right after they grab their diplomas; Stephanie Shapiro, 21, a recent Dickinson College grad, has seen her Facebook time drop from up to two hours a day to less than an hour a week. "It's almost an afterthought," she says. It's often one of life's pleasures to lose touch gracefully with people you'd had quite enough of—with a lifetime of Facebook you will have to delete them cruelly if you want to get free. "The social graph will get incredibly meaningless," says Berkeley's Danah Boyd. "Do you really want to be speaking with everyone you ever met?"

Facebook must also deal with persistent privacy concerns. When the company first rolled out the News Feed, and any change on a user's page suddenly began scrolling on the screens of anyone who'd added him or her as a friend, the social graph went bonkers: more than 700,000 people joined a user group called "Students Against Facebook News Feed." The company acted quickly to install privacy controls to let people opt out of the information flow, and the crisis cooled, though Marc Rotenberg of the Electronic Privacy Information Center says that setting privacy preferences is still too complicated. The company says that plenty of protections are built in. "Facebook is about replicating the social restrictions of the offline world," says its chief privacy officer, Chris Kelly. The problem is that Facebook is on the Internet, and it's all too easy to circumvent those and dig up private stuff.

This is all too clear from the experience of political offspring who seem engaged in perpetual competition to embarrass their parents.

Meanwhile, some in the college community—the company's most passionate users—are not happy that Facebook is welcoming swarms of people whose absence was previously appreciated: older people. "Facebook is becoming a different place as it attempts to mass-market itself," says Fred Stutzman, a University of North Carolina grad student who researches social networks. "Do I want to be friends with my uncle?" Robert Putnam, author of *Bowling Alone*, a book about the disconnectedness of contemporary Americans, worries that the site is becoming less useful as it reaches a broader audience and adds applications. "Facebook was originally a classic 'alloy,' bonding the Internet and the real world," he says. But now he says it feels less rooted in real life.

Zuckerberg and his team feel certain that the Facebook idea will trump all these concerns. He's built a superhigh-IQ engineering team (after three years of living on Facebook, top grads desperately want to work there) who drift in late and stay much later at the cheerfully cluttered Palo Alto Facebook headquarters. "Absolutely yes," says Facebook's COO, Owen Van Natta, to the question of whether it will change the world of 30-, 40-, and 50-year-olds the way it has on campus. He then amends the question to conform to the company's new unofficial, and weirdly defensive, motto: it's not just students. "Facebook did not change college life, but it changed the lives of the early adopters . . . many of whom were in college. We're entering a phase where every single day we have more people over 25 entering Facebook than any other demographic. So, absolutely, yes."

Expect a lot of poking.

Suggestions for Discussion

1. What is the ultimate goal that Zuckerberg would like for his site, Facebook? How do you feel about that?

2. Zuckerberg (creator of Facebook) wants to make clear that the site is "not a social networking site but a 'utility,' a tool to facilitate the information flow between users." What does he mean by "utility"? Do you agree?

3. What are the privacy concerns facing the mega-popular site? Discuss.

Suggestion for Writing

Compare and contrast the technological advancements and the implications of using new technology as presented throughout this book. Discuss the pros and cons of the integration of them into society. Consider this essay alongside at least three other technology-themed pieces included here.

$\infty\infty\infty$

JAY WEINER

How to Take Back Sports

A journalist who specializes in sports business and politics, Jay Weiner (b. 1954) has written for the *Minneapolis Star Tribune, ESPN.com, SportsIllustrated.com, MinnPost.com, Business Week, Chronicle of Higher Education*, and the *Christian Science Monitor*, among others. He has covered every Olympics since 1984, and coauthored "College Sports 101" (2009), a study of college sports finances, for the Knight Commission on Intercollegiate Athletics. Weiner's political writing about the Al Franken–Norm Coleman U.S. Senate recount (2008–2009) earned him the Frank Premack Award for journalism, and resulted in a book *This is Not Florida: How Al Franken Won the Minnesota Senate Recount* (2010). The Philadelphia-born writer earned a B.A. from Temple University, and has been a Fellow at the University of Maryland's Specialized Journalism program in Sports Business (1995), and a Policy Fellow at the Humphrey Institute of Public Affairs, 2004. The following article was first published in the January–February 2000 *Utne Reader* as "Sports Centered: Why Our Obsession Has Ruined the Game. And How We Can Save It."

How far back must we go to remember that sports matter? How deeply into our personal and national pasts must we travel to recall that we once cared?

Do we have to return to 1936? Adolf Hitler tried to make the Olympics into a propaganda machine for anti-Semitism and racism. In that case, American track star Jesse Owens, demonstrating that the master race could be mastered at racing, stole Hitler's ideological show. Were not sports a vehicle of significant political substance then?

Or should we return to 1947 and Jackie Robinson? A baseball player integrated our "national pastime" a year before the U.S. Army considered African Americans equal. Robinson's barrier-break may have been largely based on ticket-selling economics for the Brooklyn Dodgers' owners, but didn't sports do something good?

Their fists raised, their dignity palpable, track stars Tommie Smith and John Carlos spread the American black power and student protest movements to the world when they stood on the victory stand at the 1968 Olympics in Mexico City. Politics and sports mixed beautifully then.

Remember when tennis feminist Billie Jean King took on an old fart named Bobby Riggs in 1973, boldly bringing the women's movement to the playing fields? That moment of sports theater stirred up sexual politics as much as any Betty Friedan essay or Miss America bra burning could ever do.

Sports had meaning. And sports were accessible.

Remember when your grandfather or your uncle—maybe your mother—took you to a game when you were a little kid? The hot dog was the best. The crowd was mesmerizing. The colors were bright. The crack of the bat under the summer sun or the autumn chill wrapped around that touchdown run was unforgettable. Back then, some nobody became your favorite player, somebody named Johnny Callison or Hal Greer or Clarence Peaks or Vic Hadfield, someone who sold cars in the off-season and once signed autographs for your father's men's club for a $50 appearance fee. Those "heroes" were working-class stiffs, just like us.

Now you read the sports pages—or, more exactly, the business and crime pages—and you realize you've disconnected from the institution and it from you. Sports is distant. It reeks of greed. Its politics glorify not the majestic drama of pure competition, but a drunken, gambling masculinity epitomized by sports-talk radio, a venue for obnoxious boys on car phones.

How can we reconcile our detachment from corporatized pro sports, professionalized college sports—even out-of-control kids' sports—with our appreciation for athleticism, with our memories? And how, after we sort it all out, can we take sports back?

Part of the problem is that we want sports to be mythological when, in our hearts, we know they aren't. So reclaiming sports requires that we come to grips with our own role in the myth-making. Owens, Robinson, Smith, Carlos, and King played to our highest ideals and so have been enshrined in our sports pantheon. But we've also made heroes of some whose legacies are much less clear-cut. Take Joe Namath, the 1960s quarterback who represented sexual freedom, or BillWalton, the 1970s basketball hippie who symbolized the alienated white suburban Grateful Dead sports antihero. Neither deserves the reverence accorded Owens or Robinson or even King, but both captured the essence of their era. Or how about relief pitcher Steve Howe, who symbolized the evils of drug addiction in the '80s, or Mike Tyson, who currently plays the archetypal angry black male? No less than Tommie Smith and John Carlos, these anti-icons were emblematic of their age.

It may be discomfiting, but it's true: The power of sports and sports heroes to mirror our own aspirations have also contributed to the sorry state of the institution today. The women's sports movement Billie Jean

King helped create proved a great leap forward for female athletes, but it also created a generation of fitness *consumers*, whose appetite for Nikes and Reeboks created a new generation of Asian sweatshops.

Fans applauded the courage of renegade Curt Flood, the St. Louis Cardinals outfielder who in 1969 refused to be traded, arguing that baseball players should be free to play where they want to play. We cheered—all the way to the Supreme Court—his challenge to the cigar-smoking owners' hold on their pinstripe-knickered chattel. Now players can sell their services to the highest bidder, but their astronomical salaries—deserved or not—alienate us from the games as much as the owners' greed.

The greed isn't new, of course. The corporate betrayal of the fan is as traditional as the seventh-inning stretch. The Boston Braves moved to Milwaukee in 1953, and the Dodgers and New York Giants fled to California in 1958, for money, subsidized facilities, and better TV contracts. But what has always been a regrettable by-product of sports has suddenly become its dominant ethos. Our worship of sports and our worship of the buck have now become one and the same. So it shouldn't surprise us that we get the heroes we expect—and maybe deserve.

So how do we as a society reclaim sports from the corporate entertainment behemoth that now controls it? Some modest proposals:

• **Deprofessionalize college and high school sports.** Let's ban college athletic scholarships in favor of financial aid based on need, as for any other student. And let's keep high school athletics in perspective. Why should local news coverage of high school sports exceed coverage given to the band, debating society, or science fair? Sports stars are introduced to the culture of athletic privilege at a very young age.

• **Allow some form of public ownership of professional sports teams.** Leagues and owners ask us to pay for the depreciating asset of a stadium but give us no share of the appreciating asset of a franchise. Lease agreements between teams and publicly financed stadiums should also include enforceable community-involvement clauses.

• **Make sports affordable again.** Sports owners call their games "family entertainment." For whose family? Bill Gates'? Owners whose teams get corporate subsidies should set aside 20 percent of their tickets at prices no higher than a movie admission. And, like any other business feeding at the public trough, they should be required to pay livable wages even to the average schmoes who sell hot dogs.

• **Be conscious of the messages sport is sending.** Alcohol-related advertising should be banned from sports broadcasting. Any male athlete convicted of assaulting a woman should be banned from college and pro sports. Fighting in a sports event should be at least a misdemeanor and maybe a felony, rather than a five-minute stay in the penalty box.

Let's take the sports establishment by its lapels and shake it back toward us. Because even with all the maddening messages of male dominance, black servility, homophobia, corporate power, commercialism, and brawn over brains, sports still play an important role in many lives. When we watch a game, we are surrounded by friends and family. There are snacks and beverages. We sit in awe of the players' remarkable skills. We can't do what they do. They extend our youth. The tension of the competition is legitimate. The drama is high.

And therein lies the essence of modern American sport. It's a good show, albeit bread and circuses. And we just can't give it up. So why not take it back for ourselves as best we can, looking for ways to humanize an institution that mirrors our culture, understanding that those who own sport won't give it up without a fight, knowing that we like it too much to ever just walk away.

Suggestions for Discussion

1. Why does Weiner remind us of major sports events in history? How do his historical references prove that sports "were accessible" and "had meaning"? What forces have changed, and possibly ruined, sports?

2. How effective would each of Weiner's plans to "take sports back" be, in your opinion?

Suggestion for Writing

1. Weiner argues that sports are not mythological. Analyze this argument. Why might the mythologizing of sports help us interpret our past? Our present? The future?

2. Think carefully about one of Weiner's action plans. Write a paper exploring how and why the plan you selected might be implemented. Use research to support your arguments about the obstacles you might confront, the logistics of implementation, and the opportunities that would be created.

SHERRY TURKLE

Cuddling Up to Cyborg Babies

Sherry Turkle, a licensed clinical psychologist and an authority on computers and the Internet, has focused her psychoanalytic studies on the relationship between humans and technology. Turkle has made numerous media appearances, including on NPR, CNN, *Nightline*, and *20/20*. An affiliate member of the Boston Analytic Society and a professor of the Social Studies of Science and Technology at the Massachusetts Institute of Technology, she founded the MIT Initiative on Technology and Self in 2001 and is the research center's director. Turkle received her joint doctorate in sociology and personality psychology from Harvard University in 1976. The National Science Foundation, the Guggenheim Foundation, and the Rockefeller Foundation have all funded her research. Her books include *Psychoanalytic Politics* (1978), *The Second Self: Computers and the Human Spirit* (1984), *Life on the Screen* (1995), and *Simulation and Its Discontents* (2009). This article first appeared in *The UNESCO Courier*, a periodical of the United Nations Educational, Scientific and Cultural Organization, in 2000.

Children have always used their toys and playthings to create models for understanding their world. Fifty years ago, the genius of Swiss psychologist Jean Piaget showed it is the business of childhood to take objects and use how they "work" to construct theories of space, time, number, causality, life and mind. At that time, a child's world was full of things that could be understood in simple, mechanical ways. A bicycle could be understood in terms of its pedals and gears, a windup car in terms of its clockwork springs. Children were able to take electronic devices such as basic radios and (with some difficulty) bring them into this "mechanical" system of understanding.

Revisiting Merlin

But in the early 1980s, a first generation of computer toys changed the traditional story. When children removed the back of their computer toys to "see" how they worked, they found a chip, a battery, and some wires.

Sensing that trying to understand these objects "physically" would lead to a dead end, children tried to use a "psychological" kind of understanding. They asked themselves if the games were conscious, if they had feelings and even if they knew how to "cheat." Earlier objects encouraged children to think in terms of a distinction between the world of psychology and the world of machines, but the computer did not. Its "opacity" encouraged children to see computational objects as psychological machines.

Among the first generation of computational objects was Merlin, which challenged children to games of tic-tac-toe. For children who had only played games with human opponents, reaction to this object was intense. For example, while Merlin followed an optimal strategy for winning tic-tac-toe most of the time, it was programmed to make a slip every once in a while. So when children discovered strategies that allowed them to win and then tried these strategies a second time, they usually would not work. The machine gave the impression of not being "dumb enough" to let down its defences twice. Robert, seven, playing with his friends on the beach, watched his friend Craig perform the "winning trick," but when he tried it, Merlin did not slip up and the game ended in a draw.

Robert, confused and frustrated, threw Merlin into the sand and said, "Cheater. I hope your brains break." He was overheard by Craig and Greg, aged six and eight, who salvaged the by-now very sandy toy and took it upon themselves to set Robert straight. "Merlin doesn't know if it cheats," says Craig. "It doesn't know if you break it, Robert. It's not alive." Greg adds, "It's smart enough to make the right kinds of noises. But it doesn't really know if it loses. And when it cheats it don't even know it's cheating." Jenny, six, interrupts with disdain: "Greg, to cheat you have to know you are cheating. Knowing is part of cheating."

In the early 1980s such scenes were not unusual. Confronted with objects that spoke, strategized and "won," children were led to argue the moral and metaphysical status of machines on the basis of their psychologies: did the machines know what they were doing? Despite Jenny's objections that "knowing is part of cheating," children did come to see computational objects as exhibiting a kind of knowing. By doing so, they recast the Piagetian framework in which a definition of life centred around "moving of one's own accord."

Observing children in the world of the "traditional"—that is noncomputational—objects, Piaget found that at first they considered everything that moved to be alive. Then only things that moved without an outside push or pull. Gradually, children refined the notion to mean "life motions," namely only those things that breathed and grew were taken to be alive.

ᔍ

Motion gives way to emotion

Children broke with this orderly categorization by making distinctions about "machines that think." Their discussions about the computer's aliveness came to centre on what the children perceived as the computer's psychological rather than physical properties. To put it simply, motion gave way to emotion and physics gave way to psychology as criteria for aliveness.

In the 1980s, the computational objects that evoked "artificial life" (the "Sim" series, for example, assigns the task of creating a functioning ecosystem or city) strained that order to the breaking point. Children still tried to impose strategies and categories, but they did so in the manner of theoretical bricoleurs, or tinkerers, making do with whatever materials were at hand and with any theory that fit a prevailing circumstance. When children confronted these new objects and tried to construct a theory about what is alive, we were able to see them cycling through theories of "aliveness."

ᔍ

"Sort of alive" robots

An eleven-year-old named Holly watched a group of robots with "onboard" computational intelligence navigate a maze. As the robots used different strategies to reach their goal, Holly commented on their "personalities" and "cuteness." She finally came to speculate on the robots' "aliveness" and blurted out an unexpected formulation: "It's like Pinocchio [the story of a puppet brought to life]. First Pinocchio was just a puppet. He was not alive at all. Then he was an alive puppet. Then he was an alive boy. A real boy. But he was alive even before he was a real boy. So I think the robots are like that. They are alive like Pinocchio but not like real boys." She cleared her throat and summed up: "They are sort of alive."

Robbie, a ten-year-old who has been given a modem for her birthday, put the emphasis on mobility when she considered whether the creatures she has evolved while creating a virtual ecosystem through the game Sim-Life were alive. "I think they are a little alive in the game, but you cannot save your game [when you turn it off], so that all the creatures you have evolved go away. But if they could figure out how to get rid of that part of the programme so that you would have to save the game and if your modem were on, then they [the creatures] could get out of your computer and go to America Online [an Internet Service Provider]."

The resurfacing of motion (Piaget's classical criterion for how a child decides whether a "traditional" object is alive) is now bound up with notions of a presumed psychology: children are most likely to assume that the creatures in Sim games have a desire to "get out" of the system and evolve in a wider computational world.

Through the 1990s, children still spoke easily about factors which encouraged them to see the "stuff" of computers as the same "stuff" of which life is made. I observed a group of seven-year-olds playing with a set of plastic transformer toys that can take the shape of armoured tanks, robots, or people. The transformers can also be put into intermediate states so that a "robot" arm can protrude from a human form or a human leg from a mechanical tank. Two of the children are playing with the toys, mixing human and machine parts. A third child insists that this is not right. The toys, he says, should not be placed in hybrid states. "You should play them as all tank or all people." An eight-year-old girl comforts the now upset third child. "It's okay to play them when they are in-between. It's all the same stuff," she said, "just yucky computer 'cy-dough-plasm.'"

This comment reflects a cyborg consciousness among today's children: a tendency to see computer systems as "sort of" alive, to fluidly cycle through various explanatory concepts, and to willingly transgress boundaries.

oᴗ

Feelings for Furby

Most recently, the transgressions have involved relationships with "virtual pets" and digital dolls (the first and most popular of these were Tamagotchis and Furbies) which raise new questions about the boundaries of what children consider as life. What these objects have that earlier computational objects did not is that they ask the child for nurturance. They ask the child to assess the object's "state of mind" in order to develop a successful relationship with the object. For example, in order to grow and be healthy, Tamagotchis (imaginary creatures "housed" in small screened devices) need to be fed, cleaned and amused. Going a step further, the furry electronic pets called Furbies simulate learning and loving. They are cuddly, they speak and play games with the child. Furbies add the dimensions of human-like conversation and tender companionship to the mix of what children can anticipate from computational objects. In my research on children and Furbies, I have found that when children play with these new objects they want to know their "state," not to get something "right," but to make the Furbies happy. Children want to understand Furby language, not to "win" in a game over the Furbies, but to have a feeling of mutual recognition. They do not ask how the objects "work," they take the affectively charged toys "at interface value."

In my previous research on children and computer toys, children described the life-like status of machines in terms of their cognitive capacities (the toys could "know" things, "solve" puzzles). In my more recent studies, children describe the new toys, Furbies, as "sort of alive," which reflects their emotional attachments to the toys and their fantasies that the Furby might be emotionally attached to them. When asked whether the Furbies are alive, children tend not to speak about what the toy can do and focus instead on their feelings for the "pet" and how it might feel about them.

∾

Emotional vulnerability

"Well, the Furby is alive for a Furby," says Ron, six. "And you know, something this smart should have arms. It might want to pick up something or hug me." Katherine, age five, asks: "Is it alive? Well, I love it. It's more alive than a Tamagotchi because it sleeps with me. It likes to sleep with me." Jen, age nine, focuses not on what the object offers her, but what she can do for it. "I really like to take care of it. So, I guess it is alive, but it doesn't need to really eat, so it is as alive as you can be if you don't eat. A Furby is like an owl. But it is more alive than an owl because it knows more and you can talk to it. But it needs batteries so it is not an animal. It's not like an animal kind of alive."

Today's children are learning to distinguish between an "animal kind of alive" and a "Furby kind of alive." The category of "sort of alive" becomes increasingly used. Perceived intelligence or "knowing" is another key distinction.

Over the past five decades, research in artificial intelligence has not even come close to creating a machine as intelligent as a person. But it has succeeded in contributing to a certain deflation of our language in terms of how we use the word intelligence. It is now commonplace to talk about intelligent machines when we really are talking about machines that play chess or assess mortgage applications. These feats are wondrous, but intelligence used to mean a great deal more than that. We now face the prospect of a similar deflation of language in talking about affect and emotion. Children talk about an "animal kind of alive" and a "Furby kind of alive." Will they also talk about a "people kind of love" and a "computer kind of love"?

These questions bring us to a different world from the old "AI [artificial intelligence] debates" of the 1960s to 1980s in which researchers argued about whether machines could be "really" intelligent. The old debate was essentialist. The new objects sidestep such arguments about what is inherent in them and play instead on what they evoke in us: when we are asked to care for an object, when this cared-for object thrives and offers us its attention and concern, we experience it as intelligent, but more important, we feel a connection to it. The old AI debates were about the technical abilities of machines. The new ones will be about the emotional vulnerabilities of people.

Suggestions for Discussion

1. What is the significance of Piaget's theory of the role of toys in child development to Turkle's thesis in this article?

2. Are "cyborg babies" alive? Where do you think your opinion about this comes from?

3. How much more will Pinocchio-like toys, such as Furbies, have to evolve before we start considering them "officially alive" and grant them respect and "human" rights?

Suggestion for Writing

Synthesis: Read the essay by David Smith about the future of technology, "2050 and Immortality Is Within Our Grasp." How do Smith's "predictions" compare with the arguments in Turkle's essay? How do you see your own relationship with technology? Do you see the future as positive or negative? Why?

JOE WOODARD

Pumped, Pierced, Painted, and Pagan

Canadian journalist Joe Woodard writes primarily about religious and ethical issues that concern both Canada and the United States but has also covered stories with international scope, including the military interventions in Kosovo and East Timor. Woodard has taught at universities in the United States and Canada and has a Ph.D. in political philosophy from Claremont Graduate University. He has served as the vice president of the Canada Family Action Coalition, a citizens' action group that promotes traditionalist Judeo-Christian morality. Woodard was a regular contributor to the *Alberta Report*, a conservative periodical once affiliated with the religious order Company of the Cross that ceased publication in 2003 and in which the following article originally appeared in 1998.

Plastic surgeon Benjamin Shore was a little flustered last year when a 30-something female patient returned to his office, requesting that her breast implants be redone. A year earlier, he had given her a large set of "double-D cup" saline implants, 500 cubic centimetres or half-a-litre in size. Now she was back, wanting 800 cc implants. "She wasn't an exotic dancer," says the Brampton, Ontario, physician. "She was just a woman who wanted to feel good about herself, and she thought this would do it." But her case also proved to be the last time he cooperated in such an extravagance. "Six months later, she was back, wanting the smaller implants," he recounts. "With all that weight on her chest, whenever she lay on her back, she couldn't breathe."

Though plastic surgeons are voicing some discomfort with the trend, unnaturally large and clearly artificial breasts represent the cutting edge of feminine fashion. The August edition of the fashion magazine *Allure* surveyed American plastic surgeons, asking the age-old question, "what do women want?" And according to the doctors, "women today don't want to look natural but supernatural." The size of the average implant has grown three to four times, and more telling yet, women are voicing a preference for high, round implants, over more anatomically-correct teardrop-shapes. The new ideal has become the gravity-defying "half grapefruit" breast, popularized by the chiselled and sculpted former star of *Baywatch*, Pamela Anderson: absurdly large, firm as a football, and plainly artificial.

The growth of the breast augmentation industry has clearly outstripped the needs of mastectomy patients and women genuinely short-changed by nature. During the Dow-Corning implant fiasco, culminating in the 1992 ban against silicon implants, the market briefly sagged. But the consumer horror stories about scarring and supposed links to diseases like fibromyalgia had less effect than might have been expected. Consumer confidence was restored by the introduction of alternative saline implants, and the procedure's popularity again began to soar. In the past six years, the annual number of breast augmentations has climbed 400%, to over 120,000 in the United States and 10,000 in Canada.

But the desire for unnatural aesthetics is not limited to mammoth mammaries; tattooing, body-piercing and scarification are equally hot trends in body fashion. Experts say all these kinds of cosmetic self-mutilation are unsurprising in our post-Christian culture. In fact, they are the ultimate in retro, a throwback to paganism. Edmontonian Sarai Jorgenson, 23, has accumulated seven tattoos on her breasts, neck, shoulders, back and stomach; and at the moment she has 19 piercings, mostly (though not exclusively) on her face. She wears her naturally blonde hair in green, purple or blue, with black dreadlocks, and people she went to high school with no longer recognize her on the street. She got her first tattoo at 15—a panther she later covered with a butterfly—and her first piercings at 18. "I was a shy person; I had low self-esteem," Ms. Jorgenson recounts. "But I love my body now; I think it's beautiful."

Ms. Jorgenson's first youthful forays into body art may have been hesitant; but her intentions now are fully and confidently thought out. "It's like Rufus Camphausen writes in his book, *The Return of the Tribal*, body art is the recovery of a practice 30,000 years old," she says. "We're simply developing modern medical ways of performing a natural human function." She laughs at the suggestion that her purpose is simply attention-seeking. "Like, I do this so people will insult me on the street?" she guffaws, shaking her array of silver rings. "Like, I want to make it really hard to find a job? No. I do this because I think it's beautiful. I look at the women in *Cosmopolitan*, and they look ridiculous. I look at the women in *Savage* magazine, women who look like me, and I think they're beautiful."

The Edmonton waitress just recently began her next body project, stretching her earlobes and nasal septum, and she has already lengthened her lobes three-quarters of an inch. She has no plans to pump up her breasts, both of which she says are adorned with nipple rings. Some time ago, she tried a little scarification, but like most white people, she cannot form the kinds of "keloid scars" that give scarified black people their "gorgeous" lumpy skin patterns. If scars are out for her, she might eventually try the Hindu practice of tongue-splitting, something just now catching on in Los Angeles. "What I'm doing is, I'm taking what I was born with and making it into what I want it to be," she explains patiently. "These are all just different forms of modifying my body. They're no stranger than steroid muscles or silicon breasts."

"The vast majority of women still want breasts that look natural," Dr. Shore reports. "But in the 1970s, that would have meant 100 cc to 120 cc implants. Today, what's considered natural are 375 cc to 450 cc implants. And I'd say about 10% of [Ontario] women now want them so much bigger than that, and so much higher, they're plainly artificial." Despite feminist claims about male oppression, however, he reports that "less than 1%" of women take such leaps into the unnatural from the prompting of husbands or boyfriends. "In almost every case, this is something the woman herself wants to do for herself," he muses. "I'm amazed whenever I have to say to a woman, that would look unnatural, or that would look artificial, and she still says, 'that's okay, that's what I want.' So I just won't take on those patients anymore."

Calgary plastic surgeon Gregory Waslen thinks that demand for "monster breasts" is largely a geographical phenomenon, oddly prevalent in grapefruit-growing states. "We're not California or Florida here," he argues. "There's always a part of the market that wants something beyond the normal, but I'd guess that's no more than 2% of Alberta patients." In the normal 250 cc to 400 cc (C to D cup) range, breast augmentation now garners a 92% satisfaction rate from its patients, he says. Admittedly, up to 10% of Alberta patients and 50% of American patients subsequently return to their doctors for yet bigger breasts. The trend toward the gargantuan is simply a fad driven by shows like *Baywatch*, in Dr. Waslen's opinion, and it will soon run into its natural upper limit, a limit set by the frequency of "full-figure" backache.

According to the *Allure* survey, however, California's plastic surgeons have some doubts they will be able to hold the line at 1,000 cc implants, or full litre breasts. And magnifying the trend toward the unnatural, a small but growing proportion of women are asking for simultaneous breast implants and the liposuction of their hips, in the attempt to manufacture a body boyishly lean below the ribcage and bovine-bosomy above. They are apparently undeterred by a 3% to 5% complication rate (from internal scarring) for the breast augmentation alone.

New York University psychology professor Paul Vitz, author of *Psychology as Religion*, suspects that monstrous breast augmentation is a fad. However, that sort of fad—cosmetic mutilation—has now been able to enter into the mainstream culture only because of the revival of paganism and the eclipse of the once-dominant Judeo-Christian ethic. "With the exception of [male] circumcision, Orthodox Judaism forbids any alteration of the body, even embalming," he says. "And the Christian tradition has been almost as strict." As the apostle Paul warns in 1 *Corinthians* 3, "Know you not that you are temples of God . . . and if any man defiles the temple of God, him shall God destroy." While modest *pierced* ear studs were traditionally thought permissible, the injunction against "defiling the temple" was understood to forbid everything from tattoos to sexual sterilization.

"There's a different understanding of the body in pagan or animistic cultures," says psychologist Vitz. In Christian cultures, he explains, the physical appetites must be disciplined, but the body is an essential part of human godliness. In pagan cultures, the body is something separate, alien to each person's "inner divinity," yet it belongs entirely to the person or tribe, to do with as they see fit. "As a result, the pagans take a far more extreme and violent attitude toward the domination of the body, as something needing artistic modification or transformation." This "customizing" of the body is not a private activity, however. The tribal group almost always dictates the form of such bodily modifications for anyone who belongs. So the customized bodies are not only painful, but usually highly visible.

"Clearly, all the unnatural breast enhancement today is seeking an effect that is entirely visible," says Dr. Vitz. "Breasts cease to be maternal objects. They even become less and less objects of sexual touch. They've become the 'high kitsch' of an image culture," and primarily signs of status, like the silver rings around an African woman's neck. A century ago, energetic western women might become obsessed with inner moral perfection and fall victim to moral scrupulosity, he continues. Today, however, they seek some vague aesthetic perfection and end up collecting more and more visible abnormalities, like collagen-enhanced lips. "Unnatural breasts aren't the only new cosmetic mutilations," he adds. The new paganism encourages everything from liposuction to body-piercing and scarification.

Tattooing today is almost as common as ear-piercing, says Roman Corkery, an artist with Calgary's "Symbols of Strength" tattoo and body-piercing studio. And as popular as tattooing is, the demand for body piercing has begun to surpass it. "Moms come in with their little 15-year-old daughters, getting little navel rings, then four of their friends come in, then eight more," he marvels. Daily, Mr. Corkery's mid-sized studio averages eight tattoos and a dozen piercings. Body piercing has given tattoos a real race into the mainstream, because its results are less permanent and cheaper. The holes themselves eventually vanish once the jewelry is removed; and piercing runs $20 to $50, while tattoos cost $100 to $500. Scarification and branding, still in the experimental stage in the U.S., have not yet arrived in Alberta.

Good statistics on the growth of these "body arts" are impossible to find, says Caroline Jeffries, owner of the To the Point piercing and Smiling Buddha tattoo studios. But until 15 years ago, Calgary supported only one full-time tattoo parlour; today it boasts a dozen. The first body piercing shop opened in 1991; now there are six. Not accounting for repeat customers, Calgary's 800,000 population may generate as many as 40,000 visits yearly to either sort of establishment.

As tattooing has entered the mainstream, the images of demons, knives and nudes have given way to pictures of dolphins, flowers and Canadian flags, says body artist Corkery. And a high proportion of the women opt for a simple "ankle chain" or "woven armband" pattern. Likewise the majority of piercing enthusiasts opt for multi-earrings or a discreet nose stud. A more adventurous (or randy) minority—roughly 20% of the piercings at "Symbols of Strength"—are on the tongue and 5% to 10% are on the nipples or genitalia. Now available in both Britain and the U.S., but still a fringe interest even there, are the new Teflon and coral "inserts," used primarily to provide "devil's horns" that bond directly onto the customer's skull under the skin.

Anthropologist Claudia Launhardt, who teaches at Trinity Western University in Langley, B.C., agrees that the trend toward cosmetic self-mutilation reflects society's turn toward paganism. The forms of mutilation are consistent with traditional tribal practices the world over. Mutilations can indicate group membership and allegiance, like the tattoos of the Japanese *yakuza* criminal underworld. It can also assert a measure of social dependence. For example, the Manchu Chinese elites of the

19th century bound the feet of female infants almost from birth, partly because small feet were held to be marks of great beauty, but also because it rendered upper-class women almost incapable of walking.

However, there is one crucial difference between traditional tribal mutilations and (at least so far) the modern western equivalents, Prof. Launhardt insists. In tribal societies, the tribe, not the individual, confers the membership, dependence or the status of a particular mutilation.

"Here, so far, what we have is merely fashion or fad, because the individuals decide how they would like to change their bodies," Prof. Launhardt explains. "In a tribal society, the elders or the laws must say whether a warrior, having killed a lion, can now have a particular tattoo, or whether a woman, possessing so many cattle, can wear a certain kind of lip disk. These things are very real and binding marks of a person's status for life." In that sense, breast enhancement is much more tribal than modern body piercing, she argues, because bulbous breasts are an attempt to ape the rich and the famous of Hollywood. In Canada, although medically indicated reconstructive breast surgery is ordinarily covered by medicare, the usual fee for cosmetic work ranges from $4,000 to $4,500.

Cosmetic mutilation has certain repetitive features worldwide that may soon be reproduced in North America. For example, the Haida of the Pacific Northwest, the Kayapo of the Amazon and the Mursi of southern Ethiopia all wore "lip plates," stretching the lower lip either with or without puncturing it. "But the wealth of the material [used in lip plates] was important to the status conveyed, whether it be gold in the Amazon or ivory in Africa." Likewise, from childhood, both the Kikiyu of Africa and the Lao of northern Thailand stretched the necks of their highborn females with silver rings; their necks became so long, they needed the rings to support their heads.

Anthropologist Launhardt adds that in primitive cultures, cosmetic mutilation is often a badge of courage and ability to withstand pain. "Having killed a lion, a Dinka tribesman may be allowed a particular, very painful kind of tattoo," she explains. "Having proven his courage, the tattoo becomes the testimony to the pain he can bear." In North America, however, pain is generally something to be avoided at all costs, so mutilation did not become mainstream until modern anaesthesia made it relatively painless. "As our modern mutilations are made less painful," she predicts, "some people will be driven to find ever more extreme forms of mutilation."

And so they are: body artists in Los Angeles and New York are now experimenting with "skin braiding." Three long strips are cut from the flesh and left attached to the body only at the top. The strips are then braided and reattached at the bottom. The result is supposed to heal as a permanent skin braid.

Medical missionary John Patrick of Ottawa, a fellow of the Centre for Renewal in Public Policy, says that he has seen very little cosmetic mutilation during his many recent trips to central Africa. "Most of that has vanished," he reports. "They're new Christians leaving a pagan tradition, just as we're new pagans, leaving a Christian tradition." Yet he marvels at the rapid resurgence of self-mutilation in the West. "It seems to prove that, even when shorn of all hope, human beings still have a natural sense of the necessity of atonement."

For his part, Calgary plastic surgeon Peter Whidden sees little hope of resisting the invasion of the monster breasts. "I'd agree that, so far, maybe only 2% of the women here want huge, unnatural breasts," he says. "But these fads move north a lot faster than we like to think. There's a burlesque subculture developing, and I don't think we can stop it. Still, after 30 years of practice, I'm not going to start deforming little girls, even if they want me to."

Suggestions for Discussion

1. According to Woodard, how do Pagan and Christian cultures view the human body differently? How does the rise in the popularity of tattoos, breast implants, and body "mutilations" suggest a rise in neo-Paganism?

2. Several cosmetic surgeons who are quoted in the article claim that women who seek "unnaturally" large breast implants do it for their own reasons, not because they feel pressure to undergo the procedure. However, Pamela Anderson's breasts and the popularity of *Baywatch* are mentioned repeatedly in the article as inspiration for the current "balloon" breast craze. To what extent are women choosing to be individuals by getting breast implants? To what extent are they caving in to constant public pressure to conform to a certain kind of "supernatural" beauty?

3. How has Sarai Jorgenson been treated since she has dyed her hair, accumulated an array of body piercings, and covered her torso in tattoos? Does Woodard seem to feel sympathy for her situation and perspective? Do you?

Suggestions for Writing

1. Write an argument responding to the essay.

2. Write a fictionalized dialogue between two or more of the following figures from *The Conscious Reader*: Sarai Jorgenson (who is featured in this article), Peggy Orenstein, Melissa Etheridge, Aung San Suu Kyi, Anya Kamenetz, Margaret Atwood, Katha Pollitt, Peggy Noonan, Gloria Steinem, and Christine Seifert.

CRCRCRCR

ERIC SCHLOSSER

Fast Food Nation

Manhattan-born Eric Schlosser became a correspondent for the *Atlantic Monthly* in 1996, and he has contributed to the *New Yorker* and *Rolling Stone*. His writing addresses controversial topics; *Reefer Madness* (2003) concerns "underground" enterprises such as migrant labor, pornography, and drugs, and more recently he has investigated the American prison system. This selection is taken from *Fast Food Nation* (2001), which attacks the fast food industry and its influence on society.

CR

What We Eat

Over the last three decades, fast food has infiltrated every nook and cranny of American society. An industry that began with a handful of modest hot dog and hamburger stands in southern California has spread to every corner of the nation, selling a broad range of foods wherever paying customers may be found. Fast food is now served at restaurants and drive-throughs, at stadiums, airports, zoos, high schools, elementary schools, and universities, on cruise ships, trains, and airplanes, at K-Marts, Wal-Marts, gas stations, and even at hospital cafeterias. In 1970, Americans spent about $6 billion on fast food; in 2000, they spend more than $110 billion. Americans now spend more money on fast food than on higher education, personal computers, computer software, or new cars. They spend more on fast food than on movies, books, magazines, newspapers, videos, and recorded music—combined.

Pull open the glass door, feel the rush of cool air, walk in, get in line, study the backlit color photographs above the counter, place your order, hand over a few dollars, watch teenagers in uniforms pushing various buttons, and moments later take hold of a plastic tray full of food wrapped in colored paper and cardboard. The whole experience of buying fast food has become so routine, so thoroughly unexceptional and mundane, that it is now taken for granted, like brushing your teeth or stopping for a red light. It has become a social custom as American as a small, rectangular, hand-held, frozen, and reheated apple pie.

This is a book about fast food, the values it embodies, and the world it has made. Fast food has proven to be a revolutionary force in American life; I am interested in it both as a commodity and as a metaphor. What people eat (or don't eat) has always been determined by a complex interplay of social, economic, and technological forces. The early Roman Republic was fed by its citizen-farmers; the Roman Empire, by its slaves. A nation's diet can be more revealing than its art or literature. On any given day in the United States about one-quarter of the adult population visits a fast food restaurant. During a relatively brief period of time, the fast food industry has helped to transform not only the American diet, but also our landscape, economy, workforce, and popular culture. Fast food and its consequences have become inescapable, regardless of whether you eat it twice a day, try to avoid it, or have never taken a single bite.

The extraordinary growth of the fast food industry has been driven by fundamental changes in American society. Adjusted for inflation, the hourly wage of the average U.S. worker peaked in 1973 and then steadily declined for the next twenty-five years. During that period, women entered the workforce in record numbers, often motivated less by a feminist perspective than by a need to pay the bills. In 1975, about one-third of American mothers with young children worked outside the home; today almost two-thirds of such mothers are employed. As the sociologists Cameron Lynne Macdonald and Carmen Sirianni have noted, the entry of so many women into the workforce has greatly increased demand for the types of services that housewives traditionally perform: cooking, cleaning, and child care. A generation ago, three-quarters of the money used to buy food in the United States was spent to prepare meals at home. Today about half of the money used to buy food is spent at restaurants—mainly at fast food restaurants.

The McDonald's Corporation has become a powerful symbol of America's service economy, which is now responsible for 90 percent of the country's new jobs. In 1968, McDonald's operated about one thousand restaurants. Today it has about twenty-eight thousand restaurants worldwide and opens almost two thousand new ones each year. An estimated one out of every eight workers in the United States has at some point been employed by McDonald's. The company annually hires about one million people, more than any other American organization, public or private. McDonald's is the nation's largest purchaser of beef, pork, and potatoes— and the second largest purchaser of chicken. The McDonald's Corporation is the largest owner of retail property in the world. Indeed, the company earns the majority of its profits not from selling food but from collecting rent. McDonald's spends more money on advertising and marketing than any other brand. As a result it has replaced Coca-Cola as the world's most famous brand. McDonald's operates more playgrounds than any other private entity in the United States. It is one of the nation's largest distributors of toys. A survey of American schoolchildren found that 96 percent could identify Ronald McDonald. The only fictional character with a higher degree of recognition was Santa Claus. The impact of McDonald's on the way we live today is hard to overstate. The Golden Arches are now more widely recognized than the Christian cross.

In the early 1970s, the farm activist Jim Hightower warned of "the McDonaldization of America." He viewed the emerging fast food industry as a threat to independent businesses, as a step toward a food economy dominated by giant corporations, and as a homogenizing influence on American life. In *Eat Your Heart Out* (1975), he argued that "bigger is *not* better." Much of what Hightower feared has come to pass. The centralized purchasing decisions of the large restaurant chains and their demand for standardized products have given a handful of corporations an unprecedented degree of power over the nation's food supply. Moreover, the tremendous success of the fast food industry has encouraged other industries to adopt similar business methods. The basic thinking behind fast food has become the operating system of today's retail economy, wiping out small businesses, obliterating regional differences, and spreading identical stores throughout the country like a self-replicating code.

America's main streets and malls now boast the same Pizza Huts and Taco Bells, Gaps and Banana Republics, Starbucks and Jiffy-Lubes, Foot Lockers, Snip N' Clips, Sunglass Huts, and Hobbytown USAs. Almost every facet of American life has now been franchised or chained. From the maternity ward at a Columbia/HCA hospital to an embalming room owned by Service Corporation International—"the world's largest provider of death care services," based in Houston, Texas, which since 1968 has grown to include 3,823 funeral homes, 523 cemeteries, and 198 crematoriums, and which today handles the final remains of one out of every nine Americans—a person can now go from the cradle to the grave without spending a nickel at an independently owned business.

The key to a successful franchise, according to many texts on the subject, can be expressed in one word: "uniformity." Franchises and chain stores strive to offer exactly the same product or service at numerous locations. Customers are drawn to familiar brands by an instinct to avoid the unknown. A brand offers a feeling of reassurance when its products are always and everywhere the same. "We have found out . . . that we cannot trust some people who are nonconformists," declared Ray Kroc, one of the founders of McDonald's, angered by some of his franchisees. "We will make conformists out of them in a hurry . . . The organization cannot trust the individual, the individual must trust the organization."

One of the ironies of America's fast food industry is that a business so dedicated to conformity was founded by iconoclasts and self-made men, by entrepreneurs willing to defy conventional opinion. Few of the people who built fast food empires ever attended college, let alone business school. They worked hard, took risks, and followed their own paths. In many respects, the fast food industry embodies the best and the worst of American capitalism at the start of the twenty-first century—its constant stream of new products and innovations, its widening gulf between rich and poor. The industrialization of the restaurant kitchen has enabled the fast food chains to rely upon a low-paid and unskilled workforce. While a handful of workers manage to rise up the corporate ladder, the vast majority lack full-time employment, receive no benefits, learn few skills, exercise little control over their workplace, quit after a few months, and float from job to job. The restaurant industry is now America's largest private employer, and it pays some of the lowest wages. During the economic boom of the 1990s, when many American workers enjoyed their first pay raises in a generation, the real value of wages in the restaurant industry continued to fall. The roughly 3.5 million fast food workers are by far the largest group of minimum wage earners in the United States. The only Americans who consistently earn a lower hourly wage are migrant farm workers.

A hamburger and french fries became the quintessential American meal in the 1950s, thanks to the promotional efforts of the fast food chains. The typical American now consumes approximately three hamburgers and four orders of french fries every week. But the steady barrage of fast food ads, full of thick juicy burgers and long golden fries, rarely mentions where these foods come from nowadays or what ingredients they contain. The birth of the fast food industry coincided with Eisenhower-era glorifications of technology, with optimistic slogans like "Better Living through Chemistry" and "Our Friend the Atom." The sort of technological wizardry that Walt Disney promoted on television and at Disneyland eventually reached its fulfillment in the kitchens of fast food restaurants. Indeed, the corporate culture of McDonald's seems inextricably linked to that of the Disney empire, sharing a reverence for sleek machinery, electronics, and automation. The leading fast food chains still embrace a boundless faith in science—and as a result have changed not just what Americans eat, but also how their food is made.

The current methods for preparing fast food are less likely to be found in cookbooks than in trade journals such as *Food Technologist* and *Food Engineering*. Aside from the salad greens and tomatoes, most fast food is delivered to the restaurant already frozen, canned, dehydrated, or freeze-dried. A fast food kitchen is merely the final stage in a vast and highly complex system of mass production. Foods that may look familiar have in fact been completely reformulated. What we eat has changed more in the last forty years than in the previous forty thousand. Like Cheyenne Mountain, today's fast food conceals remarkable technological advances behind an ordinary-looking façade. Much of the taste and aroma of American fast food, for example, is now manufactured at a series of large chemical plants off the New Jersey Turnpike.

In the fast food restaurants of Colorado Springs, behind the counters, amid the plastic seats, in the changing landscape outside the window, you can see all the virtues and destructiveness of our fast food nation. I chose Colorado Springs as a focal point for this book because the changes that have recently swept through the city are emblematic of those that fast food—and the fast food mentality—have encouraged throughout the United States. Countless other suburban communities, in every part of the country, could have been used to illustrate the same points. The extraordinary growth of Colorado Springs neatly parallels that of the fast food industry: during the last few decades, the city's population has more than doubled. Subdivisions, shopping malls, and chain restaurants are appearing in the foothills of Cheyenne Mountain and the plains rolling to the east. The Rocky Mountain region as a whole has the fastest-growing economy in the United States, mixing high-tech and service industries in a way that may define America's workforce for years to come. And new restaurants are opening there at a faster pace than anywhere else in the nation.

Fast food is now so commonplace that it has acquired an air of inevitability, as though it were somehow unavoidable, a fact of modern life. And yet the dominance of the fast food giants was no more preordained than the march of colonial split-levels, golf courses, and manmade lakes across the deserts of the American West. The political philosophy that now prevails in so much of the West—with its demand for lower taxes, smaller government, an unbridled free market—stands in total contradiction to the region's true economic underpinnings. No other region of the United States has been so dependent on government subsidies for so long, from the nineteenth-century construction of its railroads to the twentieth-century financing of its military bases and dams. One historian has described the federal government's 1950s highway-building binge as a case study in "interstate socialism"—a phrase that aptly describes how the West was really won. The fast food industry took root alongside that interstate highway system, as a new form of restaurant sprang up beside the new off-ramps. Moreover, the extraordinary growth of this industry over the past quarter-century did not occur in a political vacuum. It took place during a period when the inflation-adjusted value of the minimum wage declined by about 40 percent, when sophisticated mass marketing techniques were for the first time directed at small children, and when federal agencies created to protect workers and consumers too often behaved like branch offices of the companies that were supposed to be regulated. Ever since the administration of President Richard Nixon, the fast food industry has worked closely with its allies in Congress and the White House to oppose new worker safety, food safety, and minimum wage laws. While publicly espousing support for the free market, the fast food chains have quietly pursued and greatly benefited from a wide variety of government subsidies. Far from being inevitable, America's fast food industry in its present form is the logical outcome of certain political and economic choices.

In the potato fields and processing plants of Idaho, in the ranchlands east of Colorado Springs, in the feedlots and slaughterhouses of the High Plains, you can see the effects of fast food on the nation's rural life, its environment, its workers, and its health. The fast food chains now stand atop a huge food-industrial complex that has gained control of American agriculture. During the 1980s, large multinationals—such as Cargill, ConAgra, and IBP—were allowed to dominate one commodity market after another. Farmers and cattle ranchers are losing their independence, essentially becoming hired hands for the agribusiness giants or being forced off the land. Family farms are now being replaced by gigantic corporate farms with absentee owners. Rural communities are losing their middle class and becoming socially stratified, divided between a small, wealthy elite and large numbers of the working poor. Small towns that seemingly belong in a Norman Rockwell painting are being turned into rural ghettos. The hardy, independent farmers whom Thomas Jefferson considered the bedrock of American democracy are a truly vanishing breed. The United States now has more prison inmates than full-time farmers.

The fast food chains' vast purchasing power and their demand for a uniform product have encouraged fundamental changes in how cattle are raised, slaughtered, and processed into ground beef. These changes have made meatpacking—once a highly skilled, highly paid occupation—into the most dangerous job in the United States, performed by armies of poor, transient immigrants whose injuries often go unrecorded and uncompensated. And the same meat industry practices that endanger these workers have facilitated the introduction of deadly pathogens, such as *E. coli* 0157:H7, into America's hamburger meat, a food aggressively marketed to children. Again and again, efforts to prevent the sale of tainted ground beef have been thwarted by meat industry lobbyists and their allies in Congress. The federal government has the legal authority to recall a defective toaster oven or stuffed animal—but still lacks the power to recall tons of contaminated, potentially lethal meat.

I do not mean to suggest that fast food is solely responsible for every social problem now haunting the United States. In some cases (such as the malling and sprawling of the West) the fast food industry has been a catalyst and a symptom of larger economic trends. In other cases (such as the rise of franchising and the spread of obesity) fast food has played a more central role. By tracing the diverse influences of fast food I hope to shed light not only on the workings of an important industry, but also on a distinctively American way of viewing the world.

Elitists have always looked down at fast food, criticizing how it tastes and regarding it as another tacky manifestation of American popular culture. The aesthetics of fast food are of much less concern to me than its impact upon the lives of ordinary Americans, both as workers and consumers. Most of all, I am concerned about its impact on the nation's children. Fast food is heavily marketed to children and prepared by people who are barely older than children. This is an industry that both feeds and feeds off the young. During the two years spent researching this book, I ate an enormous amount of fast food. Most of it tasted pretty good. That is one of the main reasons people buy fast food: it has been carefully designed to taste good. It's also inexpensive and convenient. But the value meals, two-for-one deals, and free refills of soda give a distorted sense of how much fast food actually costs. The real price never appears on the menu.

The sociologist George Ritzer has attacked the fast food industry for celebrating a narrow measure of efficiency over every other human value, calling the triumph of McDonald's "the irrationality of rationality." Others consider the fast food industry proof of the nation's great economic vitality, a beloved American institution that appeals overseas to millions who admire our way of life. Indeed, the values, the culture, and the industrial arrangements of our fast food nation are now being exported to the rest of the world. Fast food has joined Hollywood movies, blue jeans, and pop music as one of America's most prominent cultural exports. Unlike other commodities, however, fast food isn't viewed, read, played, or worn. It enters the body and becomes part of the consumer. No other industry offers, both literally and figuratively, so much insight into the nature of mass consumption.

Hundreds of millions of people buy fast food every day without giving it much thought, unaware of the subtle and not so subtle ramifications of their purchases. They rarely consider where this food came from, how it was made, what it is doing to the community around them. They just grab their tray off the counter, find a table, take a seat, unwrap the paper, and dig in. The whole experience is transitory and soon forgotten. I've written this book out of a belief that people should know what lies behind the shiny, happy surface of every fast food transaction. They should know what really lurks between those sesame-seed buns. As the old saying goes: You are what you eat.

INKA ESSENHIGH, *Shopping.* Oil on linen, 2005. © Inka Essenhigh.

∾

How to Do It

Congress should ban advertising that preys upon children, it should stop subsidizing dead-end jobs, it should pass tougher food safety laws, it should protect American workers from serious harm, it should fight against dangerous concentrations of economic power. Congress should do all those things, but it isn't likely to do any of them soon. The political influence of the fast food industry and its agribusiness suppliers makes a discussion of what Congress should do largely academic. The fast food industry spends millions of dollars every year on lobbying and billions on mass marketing. The wealth and power of the major chains make them seem impossible to defeat. And yet those companies must obey the demands of one group—consumers—whom they eagerly flatter and pursue. As the market for fast food in the United States becomes increasingly saturated, the chains have to compete fiercely with one another for customers. According to William P. Foley II, the chairman of the company that owns Carl's Jr., the basic imperative of today's fast food industry is "Grow or die." The slightest drop in a chain's market share can cause a large decline in the value of its stock. Even the McDonald's Corporation is now vulnerable to the changing whims of consumers. It is opening fewer McDonald's in the United States and expanding mainly through pizza, chicken, and Mexican food chains that do not bear the company name.

The right pressure applied to the fast food industry in the right way could produce change faster than any act of Congress. The United Students Against Sweatshops and other activist groups have brought widespread attention to the child labor, low wages, and hazardous working conditions in Asian factories that make sneakers for Nike. At first, the company disavowed responsibility for these plants, which it claimed were owned by independent suppliers. Nike later changed course, forcing its Asian suppliers to improve working conditions and pay higher wages. The same tactics employed by the antisweatshop groups can be used to help workers much closer to home—workers in the slaughterhouses and processing plants of the High Plains.

As the nation's largest purchaser of beef, the McDonald's Corporation must be held accountable for the behavior of its suppliers. When McDonald's demanded ground beef free of lethal pathogens, the five companies that manufacture its hamburger patties increased their investment in new equipment and microbial testing. If McDonald's were to demand higher wages and safer working conditions for meat-packing workers, its suppliers would provide them. As the nation's largest purchaser of potatoes, McDonald's could also use its clout on behalf of Idaho farmers. And as the second-largest purchaser of chicken, McDonald's could demand changes in the way poultry growers are compensated by their processors. Small increases in the cost of beef, chicken, and potatoes would raise fast food menu prices by a few pennies, if at all. The fast food chains insist that suppliers follow strict specifications regarding the sugar content, fat content, size, shape, taste, and texture of their products. The chains could just as easily enforce a strict code of conduct governing the treatment of workers, ranchers, and farmers.

McDonald's has already shown a willingness to act quickly when confronted with consumer protests. In the late 1960s, African-American groups attacked the McDonald's Corporation for opening restaurants in minority neighborhoods without giving minority businessmen the opportunity to become franchisees. The company responded by actively recruiting African-American franchisees, a move that defused tensions and helped McDonald's penetrate urban markets. A decade ago, environmentalists criticized the chain for the amount of polystyrene waste it generated. At the time, McDonald's served hamburgers in little plastic boxes that were briefly used and then discarded, making it one of the nation's largest purchasers of polystyrene. In order to counter the criticism, McDonald's formed an unusual alliance with the Environmental Defense Fund in August of 1990 and later announced that the chain's hamburgers would no longer be served in polystyrene boxes. The decision was portrayed in the media as the "greening" of McDonald's and a great victory for the environmental movement. The switch from plastic boxes to paper ones did not, however, represent a sudden and profound change in corporate philosophy. It was a response to bad publicity. McDonald's no longer uses polystyrene boxes in the United States—but it continues to use them overseas, where the environmental harms are no different.

Even the anticipation of consumer anger has prompted McDonald's to demand changes from its suppliers. In the spring of 2000, McDonald's informed Lamb Weston and the J. R. Simplot Company that it would no longer purchase frozen french fries made from genetically engineered potatoes. As a result, the two large processors told their growers to stop planting genetically engineered potatoes—and sales of Monsanto's New Leaf, the nation's only biotech potato, instantly plummeted. McDonald's had stopped serving genetically engineered potatoes a year earlier in Western Europe, where the issue of "Frankenfoods" had generated enormous publicity. In the United States, there was relatively little consumer backlash against genetic engineering. Nevertheless, McDonald's decided to act. Just the fear of controversy swiftly led to a purchasing change with important ramifications for American agriculture.

The challenge of overcoming the fast food giants may seem daunting. But it's insignificant compared to what the ordinary citizens, factory workers, and heavy-metal fans of Plauen once faced. They confronted a system propped up by guns, tanks, barbed wire, the media, the secret police, and legions of informers, a system that controlled every aspect of state power—except popular consent. Without leaders or a manifesto, the residents of a small East German backwater decided to seek the freedom of their forefathers. And within months a wall that had seemed impenetrable fell.

Nobody in the United States is forced to buy fast food. The first step toward meaningful change is by far the easiest: stop buying it. The executives who run the fast food industry are not bad men. They are businessmen. They will sell free-range, organic, grass-fed hamburgers if you demand it. They will sell whatever sells at a profit. The usefulness of the market, its effectiveness as a tool, cuts both ways. The real power of the American consumer has not yet been unleashed. The heads of Burger King, KFC, and McDonald's should feel daunted; they're outnumbered. There are three of them and almost three hundred million of you. A good boycott, a refusal to buy, can speak much louder than words. Sometimes the most irresistible force is the most mundane.

Pull open the glass door, feel the rush of cool air, walk inside, get in line, and look around you, look at the kids working in the kitchen, at the customers in their seats, at the ads for the latest toys, study the backlit color photographs above the counter, think about where the food came from, about how and where it was made, about what is set in motion by every single fast food purchase, the ripple effect near and far, think about it. Then place your order. Or turn and walk out the door. It's not too late. Even in this fast food nation, you can still have it your way.

Suggestions for Discussion

1. Some readers might consider Schlosser's argument an overreaction and protest that fast food is reasonably good and a helpful time-saving measure. How does Schlosser anticipate these objections, and how successful is he in building his case against the fast food industry?

2. Has the "McDonaldization" of American society standardized tastes, resulting in a loss of uniqueness and individuality? Place your answer in the context of Schlosser's arguments.

3. Examine Inka Essenhigh's painting *Shopping*, featured in the middle of Schlosser's essay *Fast Food Nation*. What do you see? What is your emotional response to the painting? How does the visual art connect with the essay?

Suggestions for Writing

1. Thoreau's "Reading" recounts his effort to break free of social constraints and assert his individuality. In today's culture of the "Fast Food Nation," how might a similar escape from conformity be attempted?

2. After assessing the problem of fast food in a broad sense, Schlosser suggests a series of steps the American people can take to combat its negative influence. Assess the practicality of these steps in an essay. Do further research.

3. Write a fictional journal entry, set either in present day or sometime in the future, using Essenhigh's work as the accompanying illustration.

FICTION

∽∾∽∾∽

STEVEN MOFFAT

"What I Did on My Christmas Holidays" By Sally Sparrow

A native of Glasgow, Steven Moffat (b. 1961) is an award-winning writer and television producer whose genres of choice are comedy and science fiction. His comedy, like Woody Allen's, often finds inspiration in his own life. Moffat's hit British TV series, *Coupling*, spawned a failed American version deemed "too sexy" for the U.S. viewing audience. Two of his screenplays for the revival of the *Doctor Who* series won Hugo Awards, he wrote *Tintin* for Peter Jackson, and modernized two classic Victorian characters in the TV shows *Jekyll* and *Sherlock*. The following short story originally appeared in the 2006 *Doctor Who Annual* and was later filmed for that series as a BAFTA-winning episode called "Blink."

My name is Sally Sparrow.

I am 12 years old, I have auburn hair, braces you can hardly see, a dent in my left knee from where I fell off a bicycle when I was ten, and parents. I also have a little brother called Tim. My Mum told Mrs Medford that Tim Wasn't Planned, and you can tell because his nose isn't straight and his hair sticks up and I can't believe you'd do all that on purpose. Or his ears.

I am top in English, and Miss Telfer says I have an excellent vocabulary. I have sixteen friends who are mainly girls. I haven't taken much interest in boys yet, because of the noise.

This is the story of the mysterious events that happened to me at my fat Aunt's cottage at Christmas and what I discovered under the wallpaper of my bedroom, which caused me to raise my eyebrows with perplexity.

I was staying at my fat Aunt's cottage because my Mum and Dad had gone on a weekend away. Tim was staying with his friend Rupert (who I don't think was planned either because of his teeth) and I found myself once more in the spare bedroom at my Aunt's cottage in the countryside, which is in Devon.

I love my Aunt's cottage. From her kitchen window you can only see fields, all the way to the horizon, and it's so quiet you can hear water dripping off a leaf from right at the end of the garden. Sometimes, when I lie in bed, I can hear a train far away in the distance and it always fills me with a big sighing feeling, like sadness, only nice. It's good, my bedroom at my aunt's. Really big, with a wardrobe that rattles its hangers when you walk past it and huge yellow flowers on the wallpaper. When I was little I used to sit and stare at those flowers and when no one was looking I'd try to pick them, like they were real flowers. You can still see a little torn bit where I tried to peel one off the wall when I was three, and every time I go into the room, the first thing I do is go straight to that flower and touch it, just remembering and such. I've talked about it with my Dad and we think it might be Nostalgia.

It's because of that flower and the Nostalgia that I first met the Doctor.

It was three days before Christmas. I'd just arrived at my fat Aunt's house, and as usual, I'd hugged her and run straight upstairs to my room, to hang all my clothes in the rattley wardrobe. And as usual I'd gone straight to the torn yellow flower on the wall, and knelt beside it (I'm bigger now) and touched it. But this time, I did something different. I don't know why. I heard my Aunt calling from downstairs that I shouldn't be too long, because she'd cooked my favourite and it was on the table, and usually I'd have run straight down. Maybe it was because I knew she'd want to talk about school and sometimes you don't want to talk about school (sorry, Miss Telfer) especially if you've got braces and frizzy hair and people can be a bit silly about that kind of thing, even if they're supposed to be your friends. Maybe it was because I was thinking about being three, and how much smaller the flowers looked now.

Actually I think it was because Mary Phillips had made up a song about my hair and I was feeling a bit cross and my eyes were all stingy and blurry the way they get when you know you're going to cry if you don't really concentrate. Anyway, my fingers were resting right on the torn bit, and I was thinking about the song, and frizziness and such, and suddenly it was like I just didn't care! And I started to tear the paper a little bit more! Just a tiny bit at first, I just sort of tugged it to see what would happen. And I kept going! And you know sometimes it's like you're in a dream—you're doing something, but it doesn't feel like you're doing it, more like you're just watching? Well, I went right on and peeled the whole flower off the wall. A whole streak of wallpaper and I just ripped it right off!

And then, oh my goodness me! I just stared!

I once read in a story about a girl who got a fright and the writer said she felt her hair stand on end. I thought that was rubbish and would look really stupid, like my brother. I thought the writer was probably making that bit up, because it couldn't happen. But I was wrong. I could feel it happening now, starting up my neck, all cold, then all my scalp just fizzing and tingling.

And here is what was written under the wallpaper. 'Help me, Sally Sparrow'.

I looked closer, trying to work out if it was a trick, and noticed something else. More words, written just under those ones, but still covered by the wallpaper. Well, I thought, I'd already ruined it so I had nothing to lose. As carefully as I could, I tore off another strip. Beneath the words was just a date. 24/12/85.

Twenty years ago, someone in this room, asked for my help. Eight years before I was even born!

'Christmas Eve, 1985? Sorry love, I don't really remember.' My Aunt was frowning at me across the dinner table, trying to think.

'Can you really try, please? It's ever so important. Maybe you had guests, or friends staying or something? Maybe in my room.'

'Well we always had Christmas parties, when your uncle was still alive.'

'He is still alive, he's living in Stoke with Neville.'

'You could check in the shed.'

'Why would he be in the shed, Auntie, he's very happy with—'

'For the photographs.' She was looking at me, all severe now. 'If we had a party we always had photographs. I always keep photographs, I'll have a look around.'

'Thanks, Auntie!'

'What does it matter though? Why so interested?'

I nearly told her, but I knew she'd laugh. Because really, if you think about it, there was only one explanation. Coincidence. There must have been another Sally in the family I'd never heard about, and whoever had written that on the wall twenty years ago, they hadn't meant me, they'd meant her. They'd meant that mysterious other Sally from twenty years ago. I wondered what she was like. I wondered where she was now, and if her hair was frizzy. And I wondered most of all why she'd been kept a dark secret all these many years. Perhaps she'd been horribly murdered for Deadly Reasons!

As I was about to go to bed, I looked hard at my Aunt—the way I do when I'm warning adults not to lie to me—and asked, 'There was another Sally Sparrow, wasn't there, Auntie? I'm not the first, am I?'

My Aunt looked at me really oddly for a moment. I half expected her to stagger back against the mantelpiece, all pale and clutching at her bosom, and ask in quivery tones how I had uncovered the family secret and have terrible rending sobs. But no, she just laughed and said

'No, of course not! One Sally Sparrow is quite enough. Now off to bed with you!'

I lay in my bed but I couldn't sleep! There had to be another Sally, there just had to be. Otherwise someone from twenty years ago was trying to talk to me from under the wallpaper and that was just stupid!

When my Aunt came in to kiss me goodnight (I always pretend to be asleep but I never am) I heard her put something on my bedside table.

As soon as I heard her bedroom door close, I jumped and switched the light on! Maybe this was it! Maybe this was her dark confession—the truth about the other Sally Sparrow, and her Dreadful Fate. Sitting on my bedside table was a box. I gasped horrendously! I wondered how big a box would have to be to contain human remains! I narrowed my eyes shrewdly (and also bravely) and looked at the label on the lid (though I did think labelling murdered human remains would be a bit of an obvious mistake).

The label said 'Photographs 1985'.

The Christmas party ones were right at the bottom, and took me ages to find. They were just the usual kind, lots of people grinning and drinking, and wearing paper hats. My fat Aunt was there, still with Uncle Hugh, and my Mum and Dad too looking all shiny and thin. And then I saw it! My eyebrows raised in perplexity again, slightly higher this time. Because standing right in the middle of one of the photographs was a man with a leather jacket and enormous ears. He was in the middle of a line of grown-ups laughing and dancing, but he was looking right at the camera and holding up a piece of paper like a sign. And on the sign it said 'Help me, Sally Sparrow!'

I gasped in even more amazement. There was another Sally Sparrow and obviously she was taking the photograph. And probably she was a bit deaf, and you had to talk to her with paper signs, because hearing aids hadn't been invented yet.

And then I looked at the next photograph. And that's when everything changed. Suddenly it was like the school bell was ringing in my ears and I could feel my heart thudding in my chest so hard you could probably have seen the buttons bouncing on my pyjamas.

There was the man again, at the back of the photograph, holding up another piece of paper. And this one said 'Look under the wallpaper again.'

As I reached for the wallpaper again my hand was shaking away like when you try to do your homework on the school bus. The next bit of writing was much longer and this is what it said.

'This isn't a dream, and by the way you should never try to do your homework on the school bus. I'm going to prove this is real. Think of a number, any number at all, and then get dressed, find a torch, and see what's carved in the bark of the furthest tree in the garden.'

When people think of a number, they always think of ten, or seven or something. They never think of a really big, stupid one. So I did, I thought of a big, stupid one. Then I halved it. Then I added my age. Then I took away Tim's age. Then I added four, just because I felt like it. And then a few minutes later, I was standing in the garden, shivering, staring at the furthest tree.

And there it was, carved like it had been there forever. No one ever thinks of the number 73. Except me. And the man who had carved the furthest tree in my Aunt's garden twenty years ago.

I sat on my bed for ages, just shaking and wondering what to do now. But it was obvious really. I tore off the next strip of wallpaper. This time, it just said 'Top shelf in the living room, right at the back.'

The top shelf was where my Aunt kept all her videos. She hardly ever watched television, never mind videos, so they were all very dusty. And right at the back, jammed half way down the gap at the back of the shelf, was a tape that looked like it had been there for a long time. And stuck on it, a post-it. It said 'FAO Sally Sparrow'.

I slipped it into the VCR and kept the television volume really low, so as not to wake my Aunt.

And there, grinning like a loon from the television, was the man from the photographs. 'Hello, Sally Sparrow! Any questions?'

He was sitting in my bedroom! Only the walls were bare, and there was a pair of ladders in the middle of the room, like someone was decorating. I could hear party music coming from somewhere downstairs, and I wondered if it was the party in 1985.

'Well, come on, Sally!' the man was saying. 'You've gotta have questions. I would.'

I frowned. Not a lot of point in asking questions when the man you're asking can't hear them!

'Who says I can't hear you?' grinned the man.

I stared! I think I probably gasped. My eyebrows were practically bursting out of the top of my head. It was ridiculous, it was impossible. I hadn't even said that out loud.

'No, you didn't,' said the man, checking on a piece of paper, 'You just thought that.' He glanced at the paper again. 'Oh, and yeah, you did gasp.'

'Who are you?' I blurted.

'That's more like it, now we're cooking. I'm the Doctor. I'm a time traveller and I'm stuck in 1985, and I need your help.'

I had so many questions racing round my head I didn't know which one to pick.

'How did you get stuck?' I said.

'Parked my time machine in your Aunt's shed. Was just locking up, and it . . . well . . . burped.'

'Burped??'

'Yeah, burped. Shot forward twenty years, I hate it when that happens.'

I looked out the window to where my Aunt's shed stood at the end of the garden. And I noticed there was something glowing at the windows. Suddenly, I was just a little bit afraid. 'So it's here then?'

'Exactly. Nip out to your Aunt's shed, you'll find a big blue box, key still in the door. Could just stick around for twenty years and pick it up myself but I don't want it falling into the wrong hands.' He leaned forward to the camera, and his eyes just burned at me. 'And I know you're not the wrong hands, Sally Sparrow. So I want you to fly it back to me!'

I swallowed hard. This was totally freaky.

He glanced at his paper again. 'You've got another question, I think.'

He was right. 'You're just on video tape. How can you hear me??'

He smiled. 'Actually, I can't. Can't hear a thing. I just happen to know everything you and me are gonna say in this whole conversation.'

'How??'

'Cos Mary Phillips made up a song about your hair.'

I could hardly breathe for all the gasping.

'And you punched her, didn't you, Sally Sparrow?

And then you got a punishment?'

My face was burning. How did he know all this?

I hadn't even told my Mum and Dad.

'You got Christmas homework. An essay about what you did over the Christmas holidays.' He grinned.

'And I've got a copy!'

And this is freakiest part of all. Because he held a copy of the actual essay I'm writing right now!!

'I know everything you're gonna ask when you see this tape, cos I've read the essay you wrote about it. That's how I knew what to write on the wall— you'll have to show me exactly where, by the way—and that's how I knew what number you were thinking of.'

'But . . . but . . .' I could hardly think for my mind racing. 'How did you get a copy of my Christmas homework! I haven't even written it yet!!'

'Told you, I'm a time traveller. I got it in the future. From a beautiful woman on a balcony in Istanbul.' He smiled, like it was happy memory. 'She was some sort of spy, I think. Amazing woman! I'd just had a sword fight on the roof with two Sontarans, and she saved me from the second one. Then she gave me your Christmas homework and told me to keep it on me at all times, cos I'd need it one day.' He grinned.

'She was right!'

A spy, in the future, was going to have a copy of my Christmas homework? Talk about pressure!

He was looking at his watch. 'Okay, that's just about time up. Gonna need you to go to the time machine, and fly it here.'

'I can't fly a time machine. I had stabilisers on my bike till I was nine!!'

'Sally, I absolutely know that you can do this. And do you know how?'

'How?'

'Because I've read to the end of the story.' He laughed. 'Also—you hear that noise?'

Coming from the television, a terrible wheezing and groaning.

'What's that?'

He was still grinning.

'That's you!'

Behind the man, a huge blue box just appeared out of thin air. I stared at it. There were words over the door and I squinted closer to read them.

I should've known. He looked like a policeman!

'That's your time machine?'

'Yep. Like it?'

'But who flew it there?'

You could almost get tired of that grin. 'You did!'

The doors on the big blue box were opening. And then the most amazing thing ever. I stepped out of the box!! Me! Sally Sparrow! Another me stepped out of the time machine and waved at the camera.

'Hello, Sally Sparrow, two hours ago!' said the other me. 'It's great in there, you're going to love it. It's bigger on the inside!'

'See?' said the man. "Told you you could fly a time machine.'

'Yeah, it's easy!' said the other Sally,

'It homes in on his watch, anyway. You just have to press the reset button next to the phone.'

'Who told you that?' I asked her.

A frown clouded her face. 'I did,' she said, and looked puzzled.

The man looked a little cross about that.

'Yeah, well before you set off any more time paradoxes . . . Sally Sparrow!' he gave me a Teacher look from the television. 'Go and do your homework!'

'Yeah!' said the other Sally, 'You've got to write the essay before you can fly the time machine. It'll take you about two hours.'

'That's enough, both of you!' said the man, 'Got enough paradoxes going on here, without you pair having a chat!'

'But, listen, it's going to be great!' said the other Sally. And she gave me the biggest, most excited smile ever.

And oh goodness! You can see my braces!

And so here I am, finishing my essay. It's nearly two o'clock in the morning, and in a minute I'll be fetching the shed key from the kitchen drawer and setting off across the garden on the trip of a lifetime.

A big, amazing adventure. And not my last one either, oh no! Just the first of lots and lots, for the rest of my life probably. Suddenly I don't care what my Aunt is going to say about the torn wallpaper or what Mary Phillips thinks about my hair. I'll go back to school after the holidays and just be nice to her, and she can make up all the songs she wants. I'll join in, if it makes her happy.

You see, I know the best thing in the world. I know what's coming. I asked the man one more question before the end of the tape. I asked how a beautiful woman spy in the future could have a copy of my Christmas homework.

'Can't you guess?' he smiled. Not grinned, smiled. 'Her name,' he continued, 'was Sally Sparrow.'

The big blue box is waiting in the shed at the end of the garden. And I've finished my homework.

Suggestions for Discussion

1. The story plays games with time and history, cause and effect. What picture does it paint of time and time travel? Does the story work scientifically or violate its own rules?

2. Moffat is an older man writing with the voice of a young girl. How convincing is his attempt to write in the voice of a different age and gender? Also, is Sally a positive role model for young girls?

3. Sally's aunt lies about her uncle being dead and Sally confronts her about it. What does this lie tell us about her, her aunt, and her family as a whole?

4. What do we learn about the Doctor in this story? His personality? Motivations?

5. This story is British. What parts of the story seem "British"? How hard is it for an American reader to relate to? *Doctor Who* adventures are a phenomenon in England but are only followed by a minority of American readers and television viewers. Why might this be the case?

Suggestions for Writing

1. In a brief essay, compare this story to either "A Place Where Time Stands Still" or "How to Build a Time Machine."

2. In the *Doctor Who* episode "Blink" that is based on this short story, Sally Sparrow is noticeably older, and villains, called the Weeping Angels, are added. To what extent do these alterations and additions change the story's tone, message, and dramatic effect? Write a list of your thoughts on this topic and share them with the class.

POETRY

JOHN LENNON

Working Class Hero

Liverpool native John Lennon (1940–1980) was a member of the Beatles and a cocreator of some of rock's most influential albums, including *Revolver* (1966), *Sgt. Pepper's Lonely Hearts Club Band* (1967), *The White Album* (1968), and *Abbey Road* (1969). The early Beatles were a teen sensation, despite the sophistication of even their earliest compositions; their later work often reflected that of contemporary experimental composers like John Cage. Lennon's whimsical writings were published in *In His Own Write* (1964) and posthumously in *Skywriting by Word of Mouth* (1986). After his marriage to musician Yoko Ono, who was blamed by many for splitting up the Beatles, Lennon enjoyed significant success as a solo artist with songs like "Imagine," "Happy Xmas (War Is Over)," and "Working Class Hero."

As soon as you're born they make you feel small
By giving you no time instead of it all
Till the pain is so big you feel nothing at all
A working class hero is something to be
A working class hero is something to be

They hurt you at home and they hit you at school
They hate you if you're clever and they despise a fool
Till you're so fucking crazy you can't follow their rules
A working class hero is something to be
A working class hero is something to be

When they've tortured and scared you for twenty odd years
Then they expect you to pick a career
When you can't really function you're so full of fear
A working class hero is something to be
A working class hero is something to be

Keep you doped with religion and sex and TV
And you think you're so clever and classless and free
But you're still fucking peasants as far as I can see
A working class hero is something to be
A working class hero is something to be

There's room at the top they are telling you still
But first you must learn how to smile as you kill
If you want to be like the folks on the hill
A working class hero is something to be
A working class hero is something to be
If you want to be a hero well just follow me
If you want to be a hero well just follow me

Suggestions for Discussion

1. When John Lennon writes "As soon as you're born they make you feel small," who is he referring to when he says "they"? Who is the "you" in "you're"?

2. According to the song, why are people who think they are "clever and classless and free" wrong?

3. Why is a working class hero "something to be"? What is the effect of the constant return of this phrase in refrain?

4. What does Lennon mean when he writes, "If you want to be a hero well just follow me"? What is the tone of this final, repeated line?

Suggestions for Writing

1. Write a response song called either "Middle Class Hero" or "Upper Class Hero."

2. Although this song was written in 1970, it was clearly considered relevant to today's society for *Green Day* to release its own version of it in the twenty-first century. Despite all of the changes in society since Lennon wrote the song—technological advancements, 9/11, *American Idol*—what has *not* changed in society to justify the continuing popularity of this song? Write an essay in which this idea is explored.

Art and Society

~~~~~~

Try to describe your experience of music, and you'll quickly reach the limits of words. Music carries us away, and we grope for the grandest terms in our vocabulary just to hint at the marvel of the flight, the incredible marvel, the wonder.

—GLENN KURTZ, "Practicing: A Musician's Guide to Music"

In our time, political speech and writing are largely the defense of the indefensible. Things like the continuation of British rule in India, the Russian purges and deportations, the dropping of the atom bombs on Japan, can indeed be defended, but only by arguments which are too brutal for most people to face, and which do not square with the professed aims of political parties. Thus, political language has to consist of euphemism, question-begging, and sheer cloudy vagueness.

—GEORGE ORWELL, "Politics and the English Language"

MANIT SRIWANICHPOOM

This Bloodless War No. 3

Gelatin silver print, 1997

© Manit Sriwanichpoom

INTRODUCTION

W hat is art, and why should we care about it? Several of the readings in this chapter examine how artists define art and its value, and how artists define themselves, beginning with memoirs by Melissa Etheridge, Ludwig von Beethoven, and Glenn Kurtz. In addition to "defining" music, all of these essays explore the incredible therapeutic power of music. They also address, directly and indirectly, the terrible emptiness of a world without art and music. Incredibly, when Beethoven loses his hearing, he contemplates suicide rather than live without music, but he vows to stay alive so he can continue composing and living for his art, despite his growing deafness. Just as a disability threatens to steal music from Beethoven, the ever-present threat of censorship strives to rob art and music from all society. As defenders of art and music, Charles Taylor and Marilyn Manson decry censorship and refute the arguments most often advanced by moralists and defenders of public safety who believe that all art and music should be "rated G for General Audiences," no matter the cost to culture, education, and enlightenment of the American people as a whole.

The censorship Taylor and Manson decry comes mostly from lawmakers and the demands of consumers, but there are other kinds of censorship besides "concerned parent" initiatives, ratings systems, and FCC regulations about profanity. This section explores the reasons why the importance of the arts has diminished in American society, and why the arts need defending now more than ever. Andrea Frasier protests that artists are often silenced when public funding for the arts is cut, and describes an all-too-common scenario in which art is only produced by "professional" artists, or those who produce art on the side after working a day job as a college faculty member or arts administrator. Roger Rosenblatt's essay is a hymn to the traditional canon of British and American literature, especially nineteenth-century British novels, which are often dismissed as being passé and removed from syllabi because they are long and not multicultural enough. George Orwell warns that the English language has been watered down by legalistic jargon, euphemisms, and advertising lingo in a matter that obscures truth, makes horrific acts seem morally acceptable, and disguises extremist political propaganda as common sense.

Other essays consider how popular culture artifacts might be elevated to the status of art. While many scholars consider cinema a form of popular culture, critic Roger Ebert argues for the value of films that never make it to the American mainstream, demonstrating that movies can be works of

410

art as well as entertaining diversions. In "Bootleg Culture," Pete Rojas explains how modern technology grants the average person the opportunity to remix music, re-edit films, and become artists and editors in their own right, even as copyright protectors try to put an end to such efforts, which they consider a form of piracy.

Willa Cather's work, "The Sculptor's Funeral," is a short story in the Fiction section about how small-town folk have difficulty understanding the artistic temperament, and never truly knew the artist whose funeral they were attending.

Finally, Sonia Sanchez's poem about jazz uses one genre—poetry—that can be both rigidly structured and free-flowing—to describe another that might be similarly defined. This piece, then, enacts the relationship between the arts in ways that fit this chapter's spirit and point: "art" has many meanings.

NOTEBOOK

∾∾∾∾

MELISSA ETHERIDGE

Music as a Safe Haven

Grammy award-winning rock star Melissa Etheridge is a prolific singer and songwriter who came to prominence in the 1990s. A breast cancer survivor, Etheridge famously performed at the 2005 Grammy Awards while still bald from chemotherapy. She has also brought attention to the issue of global warming by performing music for the soundtrack of Al Gore's film *An Inconvenient Truth* and has helped raise money for Hurricane Katrina disaster relief. Her eleven albums include three that went multiplatinum: *Melissa Etheridge* (1988), *Yes I Am* (1993), and *Your Little Secret* (1995). Her 2007 release, *The Awakening*, was nominated for the Gay & Lesbian Alliance Against Defamation (GLAAD) media award.

The one thing that did keep me safe, that gave me a feeling of comfort growing up, was music. Music took me somewhere safe—a place where I was happy and free and comfortable being myself. I knew from a very young age that music was something I wanted to be a part of. It was something that made me feel good and helped me escape to a place where life was how I always dreamed it should be. Where life was like the movies. Fairy-tale endings and unconditional love.

I remember hearing the Beatles for the very first time, in 1964. I was standing in my driveway and putting my ear to our tiny transistor radio. Even with the crackling, barely audible sound that the transistor radio made, I heard "I Want to Hold Your Hand" for the first time, and I thought that I had heard the voice of God. It was the most incredible thing I'd ever heard, and it moved me in a way I had never before experienced. I became obsessed with music.

After that, I had the radio on constantly. Johnny Dohlens, WHB, Kansas City. They played everything on the radio back then. Rock, Pop. Everything. And I'd listen to it all. No judgment. I'd listen to my parents' albums. They had everything from Neil Diamond to the Mamas and the Papas, Bolero to Janis Joplin and Crosby, Stills, Nash, and Young. My sister had much cooler albums like Humble Pie, Led Zeppelin, and George Harrison. Music was complete pleasure. Just like my grandma's white coconut cake. I'd get completely absorbed into it, focused. I'm just completely there and the world goes away.

I'd listen to the music and I'd watch it, too. *The Ed Sullivan Show, The Dick Cavett Show, The Red Skelton Show.* I'd watch all the shows that had live music on them. And I'd watch the people singing the music. Making the music. Mick Jagger. The Beatles. But it was the Archies who were the most influential. I'd watch the Archies and then I'd get the neighborhood kids together, get all the pots and pans out, and do a show in the garage. I never wanted to be Betty or Veronica. I wanted to be Reggie. I always wanted to be Rock and Roll. I drew a big sign that said ARCHIES with a circle around it, put everyone in their place, and then we'd do a show. I was the lead guitarist of course. Jumping up and down with my badminton racquet. We'd play "Sugar, Sugar," Tommy James and the Shondells and Steppenwolf. Every day after school became "Magic Carpet Ride" time.

One day, my father came home with a real guitar for me. I hadn't even been asking for one. He just brought it home. I didn't know that he knew I was playing the badminton racquet. It was a Stella, by Harmony, which is actually a pretty good first guitar for a kid in Kansas. He bought it at Tarbot's Tune Shop in town. I would go down there late in the afternoons after school, and I would see my guitar teacher, Mr. Don Raymond, an old big-band jazz guitarist. I'm sure he had been a fabulous musician in his day, but a tragic accident cut off the fingers on his left hand, right at the knuckles. So he learned to play with his right hand. I was eight years old and it was pretty scary to look at his fingers, or what used to be his fingers, but he was a serious musician and he taught me to be a serious musician and to take my lessons very earnestly. I learned all of the notes on the guitar, one by one, string by string, every day, until I actually learned a song. It was a simple song, but it was the first song I ever learned and pretty soon those notes turned into chords and my chords turned into more songs. Before I knew it, I was playing "I Want to Hold Your Hand" and "Sugar, Sugar." Playing them for real. I was making the music. Not pretending anymore. I realized that once I had learned three basic chords, I could play just about anything. This opened up a whole new world to me—a world where I could perform and create. A world that was mine, that would accept me for who I was. Give me what I wanted. I became inspired and I found some peace in the process. Words began to flow from me and, at age ten, I wrote my first song using three silly little chords: "Don't Let It Fly Away." I rhymed words like *love* with *above*. I rhymed *bus* with *Gus*.

I found solace in my music that I didn't have before I learned to play. I would go into our basement and play my guitar to fill up my loneliness. My mother wouldn't really talk to me, and she wasn't too keen on my playing the guitar. But I played every day. And I would play when we traveled to

Arkansas to visit my grandparents. I dearly loved my grandmother. She had that whole maternal nurturing thing that my mother didn't. She'd open all the drawers in the kitchen, pull out all the tools and the whisks and things. And she'd say, "Just go. Play." She would listen to me play the guitar, those same three chords over and over, and she was actually listening. She'd sit in her living room and listen to me sing and play song after song after song. After a few more trips, Grandma would still listen to me, but from then on, she was lying down in her bed. Unbeknownst to me, she was terribly ill. She had been stricken with cancer of the ovaries and breasts, and eventually her body was so riddled with it, the cancer metastasized everywhere. But she would listen joyfully all the same, lying there in her bed, and I played happily for her. When she would simply tell me that "Grandmother's not feeling well," I knew that it was time to let her get her rest.

My final visit with Grandmother was in the hospital, before she died. My visit needed special arrangements because children under the age of twelve were not allowed in the hospital. But I was this woman's granddaughter and I had showed up, with my guitar, to see my grandmother. I wanted to play my music for her, sing for her—comfort her. The nurses made an exception for me, and I was able to go into her room and sit beside my grandmother on her bed. I sang a new song I had just written—well, more like plagiarized—from a children's book. It was called "The Good Little Sheep." I sang to her with all of the tubes running in and out of her body— and with my grandmother in a state of semiconsciousness.

The Good Little Sheep
The good little sheep run quickly and soft.
Their colors are gray and white.
They follow their leader nose to tail,
For they must be home by night.

I am sure that there were other verses to it—something about wanting to be a good little sheep. For all of her pain, my grandmother still listened. She listened to *me*. And when I was done, she turned to me and said, "When I die, will you put that song in my casket and bury it with me?" I kind of understood what was happening and what was going to happen. I felt a connection with my grandmother that was unique for me at that time in my life. She loved me unconditionally, and she was the only person I felt protected by as a child.

Of course, I couldn't express any of these emotions. I didn't know how. But I remember the feeling when she asked that question, that moment of physical realization that tingles through you when you know something important is happening. But there's no outlet for it. It's a life-and-death moment and I had no idea how to handle it. None of us did. So we don't handle it. We bury it. And move on.

So I looked at my grandmother and said, "Okay." I packed up my guitar and we went home, back to Leavenworth. One night, not too long afterward, I suddenly woke up in the middle of the night and became extremely ill. I stayed home from school that next day, and my mom came home and told me that my grandmother had passed away in the middle of the night. When my grandmother died, it was like everything just went *clunk!* I was in the sixth grade. I had given up being frightened of my sister and all of my raw, unharnessed emotion would, forever forward, be placed into my song writing. All I could think about on our way back to Arkansas for her funeral was her request to be buried with the lyrics to my song. I didn't want to go view her casket. I couldn't face seeing her lifeless body. So I wrote the lyrics down on a piece of paper and gave them to my aunt, who assured me that she would place them in the casket for me. At the funeral and in the limousine, all I could envision in my mind was that piece of paper and those words in her casket with her for all of eternity. I don't remember if I cried. I can't recall seeing my mother cry. We didn't do much crying in my family. That would have been a show of emotion, something we never did.

After the funeral, I wrote what I consider to be my first real song. It came from somewhere in my heart, somewhere in my soul, somewhere that had just been opened up inside of me. It was about a war orphan—something I didn't think that I knew anything about, but the truth is, I knew all too well the feeling of being an orphan. I have felt alone and abandoned during my whole life. The song was called, "Lonely Is a Child."

Lonely Is a Child

Trees are swaying in the wind
Things are so free
But I sit here waiting
For her to come home to me.

Lonely is a child waiting for his mother to come home,
Lonely is a child waiting for his mother, but a mother has he none . . .

When the war came to this land
Many years ago
She disappeared from my sight
And I just want to know
Where is she.

A lot of my earliest songs were sort of sad and lonely. I would write about either the kind of love I never knew, or how I was pining for something or someone who had left me. Even as a teenager. Oh, and there were the typical teenager suicide songs. I was obsessed with dying and writing songs about dying. I went through a phase, around the eighth grade, of telling people that I was terminally ill. It got me attention and sympathy, which was exactly what I was looking for. I would have taken any show of emotion from another person. It's strange to look back. I was never personally thinking of suicide, but I was surely looking to be noticed as a teenager. I can still feel an incredible sadness, a need for emotion, and a sensation of being in my adolescent pain. Things were so bleak in my head that I even went so far as to call a troubled-teen hotline and attend a group therapy class to talk about my dark feelings. I met a girl there whose soul was even angrier and more abused and tortured than mine. She just sat in the corner and didn't talk to anybody. I went home and wrote a song about her. I completely understood that type of darkness and agony. It's an adolescent feeling that can bring on the idea of suicide. I am too ego-driven to have ever gone through with suicide—that's for sure. I guess I just wanted someone to notice me and it came out in the lyrics to the songs I wrote as a teen. One song is called "Stephanie."

Stephanie

Stephanie, oh Stephanie,
What pain do you see?
What's in your eyes?
You sit down, you have a smoke
But never a word have you spoke.
Stephanie, all the lines are dead—
I wish I knew what's goin' on in your head.
Reach out, oh reach out to me.
Oh Stephanie, can't you see—
If you ever need, I am here.
Stephanie, what lingers in the hallway
In the dark corners of your mind?
And the writing that is on the wall—does it say it all?
What will I find?
What key unlocks your door?
What do you tell yourself when
You're crying for more?
But maybe someday when your soul's set free
And the sun beams through, maybe then I may see.
Stephanie, pick up the broken pieces of glass
On your windowsill to the world.
I know inside the dark stormy shell
There's a bright shining beautiful pearl.

I kept playing my guitar and I started to sing for my friends. We would sing and play together. Linda Stuckey and Chris Luevane, who were in my class in school, learned to sing "Lonely Is a Child," and we began to perform as a group. We were so sincere, so sad, and so in the sixth grade. Chris called me up one day all excited about an upcoming talent show at the Leavenworth Plaza. She was certain that we ought to sing in it and so we did. We got up on stage and sang from the deepest part of our sixth-grade hearts. It was incredible. It seemed like thousands of people were watching. There were really about fifty. All the friends and relatives of the people in the talent show, probably. The MC was a man named Bob Hammill. He was a ventriloquist with this Charlie McCarthy sort of doll. He'd do a bit and then introduce the next act. The Shortz Sisters, who sang country music all done up in their spangly country-western gear. The Shroyer Sisters in their little pink outfits, doing their acrobatic act. Very exotic. Back bends and splits and the whole thing.

And then it was our turn. Chris and Linda and I walked out on stage. And I stared out at the audience. It was my first time in front of an audience. My heart was beating so fast. I'm dizzy and I can barely breathe. And then I hit the first note and I play. And Chris and Linda just disappear. There's just me and the audience. And the music. When I finished, there was applause. I walked off stage and it was the most connected I'd ever felt in my entire life. Connected to heart. Connected to want. Connected to experience. It was like a drug. A drug that made me *alive.*

Little Tommy Williams won the talent contest with his rendition of "Okie from Muskogee." But we were finalists and were given a trophy. A very small trophy. Years later, I was presented again with that trophy while visiting Leavenworth for my tenth high school reunion. The trophy is in the photograph on the back of the *Breakdown* album. I keep it in my display case at home, right next to my Grammy Awards.

Soon after the talent contest, Bob Hammill called and told us he was putting together a variety show with some of the other acts from the contest, the Shortz Sisters and the Shroyer Sisters, something he could take around town, perform at old folks' homes, the V.A. center, all the prisons. Prisons have the most enthusiastic audiences: 2,000 people who want to be entertained. You might say they're the ultimate captive audience. Once, we were stuck inside a prison for an hour because there was a stabbing or something, and all the prisoners were locked down. But as soon as it got cleared up, off we went, into the auditorium. It was hilarious, really; these little girls performing for criminals. The Shroyer Sisters in their little leotards doing splits and backbends always got a very enthusiastic response from the inmates.

We played the Kansas State women's prison and I remember standing on stage, staring out at the inmates, and thinking, "What are all these men doing inside a women's prison?" It took a while for me to realize that they *were* women. And once I had that realization, I was curious about them, interested. Not on a conscious level, of course, but there was something going on in that prison that fascinated me.

The Bob Hammill Variety Show was great fun for all of us. It's where I learned how to get up in front of people and perform. No matter where the stage was—local schools, old folks' homes, wherever—I loved it. I loved the attention. I loved the warmth. I loved the appreciation. I loved the spotlight. I felt secure and loved and safe and at home on stage.

The stage became the safest, most rewarding place that I have ever been. I am allowed to open up everything about myself on stage. Being on stage worked so well for me emotionally that, for the longest time, it was all I wanted to do. I would have done anything to do it on as large a scale as I possibly could. Like the movies, it was an escape for me. Performing gave me the ability to hide out and be who I wanted to be, and be loved and feel safe and secure.

Suggestions for Discussion

1. To what extent do you think music is a way for Etheridge to escape from reality? To what extent does she use it to confront reality and her personal pains?

2. Etheridge describes her adolescent fascination with death and her feelings of depression and anger as being common experiences. How universal are her experiences? How did reading about them make you feel? What did you think?

3. Parents today are often so protective of their children, from infancy well through adulthood, that it is difficult to imagine parents allowing their children to perform in public venues like prisons. How might Etheridge's life have been different if she were a fan of music but was neither given a guitar as a present nor allowed to perform publicly for fear of her own safety?

Suggestion for Writing

Compare Etheridge's experiences learning to play the guitar, and the support she garnered from her father and grandmother, to the experiences described by Glenn Kurtz in the essay, titled "Practicing."

MARILYN MANSON

Columbine: Whose Fault Is It?

Born Brian High Warner in Canton, Ohio, Marilyn Manson (b. 1969) cites the "hypocrisy" of the Christian schools he attended as a child in Florida as the inspiration for his self-proclaimed status as the "Antichrist Superstar." His name—a combination drawn from movie superstar Marilyn

Monroe and notorious serial murderer Charles Manson—reflects what Manson suggests is the disturbing dualism of American culture. Manson's eponymous band has been recording since 1990, to both acclaim and disgust. The following article, originally published in *Rolling Stone* magazine, is Manson's response to charges that his music leads to violence, including the horrendous school shootings in Columbine, Colorado.

It is sad to think that the first few people on earth needed no books, movies, games or music to inspire cold-blooded murder. The day that Cain bashed his brother Abel's brains in, the only motivation he needed was his own human disposition to violence. Whether you interpret the Bible as literature or as the final word of whatever God may be, Christianity has given us an image of death and sexuality that we have based our culture around. A half-naked dead man hangs in most homes and around our necks, and we have just taken that for granted all our lives. Is it a symbol of hope or hopelessness? The world's most famous murder-suicide was also the birth of the death icon—the blueprint for celebrity. Unfortunately, for all of their inspiring morality, nowhere in the Gospels is intelligence praised as a virtue.

A lot of people forget or never realize that I started my band as a criticism of these very issues of despair and hypocrisy. The name Marilyn Manson has never celebrated the sad fact that America puts killers on the cover of *Time* magazine, giving them as much notoriety as our favorite movie stars. From Jesse James to Charles Manson, the media, since their inception, have turned criminals into folk heroes. They just created two new ones when they plastered those dipshits Dylan Klebold and Eric Harris' pictures on the front of every newspaper. Don't be surprised if every kid who gets pushed around has two new idols.

We applaud the creation of a bomb whose sole purpose is to destroy all of mankind, and we grow up watching our president's brains splattered all over Texas. Times have not become more violent. They have just become more televised. Does anyone think the Civil War was the least bit civil? If television had existed, you could be sure they would have been there to cover it, or maybe even participate in it, like their violent car chase of Princess Di. Disgusting vultures looking for corpses, exploiting, fucking, filming and serving it up for our hungry appetites in a gluttonous display of endless human stupidity.

When it comes down to who's to blame for the high school murders in Littleton, Colorado, throw a rock and you'll hit someone who's guilty. We're the people who sit back and tolerate children owning guns, and we're the ones who tune in and watch the up-to-the-minute details of what they do with them. I think it's terrible when anyone dies, especially if it is someone you know and love. But what is more offensive is that when these tragedies happen, most people don't really care any more than they would about the season finale of *Friends* or *The Real World*. I was dumbfounded as I watched the media snake right in, not missing a teardrop, interviewing the parents of dead children, televising the funerals. Then came the witch hunt.

Man's greatest fear is chaos. It was unthinkable that these kids did not have a simple black-and-white reason for their actions. And so a scapegoat was needed. I remember hearing the initial reports from Littleton, that Harris and Klebold were wearing makeup and were dressed like Marilyn Manson, whom they obviously must worship, since they were dressed in black. Of course, speculation snowballed into making me the poster boy for everything that is bad in the world. These two idiots weren't wearing makeup, and they weren't dressed like me or like goths. Since Middle America has not heard of the music they did listen to (KMFDM and Rammstein, among others), the media picked something they thought was similar.

Responsible journalists have reported with less publicity that Harris and Klebold were not Marilyn Manson fans—that they even disliked my music. Even if they were fans, that gives them no excuse, nor does it mean that music is to blame. Did we look for James Huberty's inspiration when he gunned down people at McDonald's? What did Timothy McVeigh like to watch? What about David Koresh, Jim Jones? Do you think entertainment inspired Kip Kinkel, or should we blame the fact that his father bought him the guns he used in the Springfield, Oregon, murders? What inspires Bill Clinton to blow people up in Kosovo? Was it something that Monica Lewinsky said to him? Isn't killing just killing, regardless if it's in Vietnam or Jonesboro, Arkansas? Why do we justify one, just because it seems to be for the right reasons? Should there ever be a right reason? If a kid is old enough to drive a car or buy a gun, isn't he old enough to be held personally responsible for what he does with his car or gun? Or if he's a teenager, should someone else be blamed because he isn't as enlightened as an eighteen-year-old?

America loves to find an icon to hang its guilt on. But, admittedly, I have assumed the role of Antichrist; I am the Nineties voice of individuality, and people tend to associate anyone who looks and behaves differently with illegal or immoral activity. Deep down, most adults hate people who go against the grain. It's comical that people are naive enough to have forgotten Elvis, Jim Morrison and Ozzy so quickly. All of them were subjected to the same age-old arguments, scrutiny and prejudice. I wrote a song called "Lunchbox," and some journalists have interpreted it as a song about guns. Ironically, the song is about being picked on and fighting back with my Kiss lunch box, which I used as a weapon on the playground. In 1979, metal lunch boxes were banned because they were considered dangerous weapons in the hands of delinquents. I also wrote a song called "Get Your Gunn." The title is spelled with two n's because the song was a reaction to the murder of

Dr. David Gunn, who was killed in Florida by pro-life activists while I was living there. That was the ultimate hypocrisy I witnessed growing up: that these people killed someone in the name of being "pro-life."

The somewhat positive messages of these songs are usually the ones that sensationalists misinterpret as promoting the very things I am decrying. Right now, everyone is thinking of how they can prevent things like Littleton. How do you prevent AIDS, world war, depression, car crashes? We live in a free country, but with that freedom there is a burden of personal responsibility. Rather than teaching a child what is moral and immoral, right and wrong, we first and foremost can establish what the laws that govern us are. You can always escape hell by not believing in it, but you cannot escape death and you cannot escape prison.

It is no wonder that kids are growing up more cynical; they have a lot of information in front of them. They can see that they are living in a world that's made of bullshit. In the past, there was always the idea that you could turn and run and start something better. But now America has become one big mall, and because of the Internet and all of the technology we have, there's nowhere to run. People are the same everywhere. Sometimes music, movies and books are the only things that let us feel like someone else feels like we do. I've always tried to let people know it's OK, or better, if you don't fit into the program. Use your imagination—if some geek from Ohio can become something, why can't anyone else with the willpower and creativity?

I chose not to jump into the media frenzy and defend myself, though I was begged to be on every single TV show in existence. I didn't want to contribute to these fame-seeking journalists and opportunists looking to fill their churches or to get elected because of their self-righteous finger-pointing. They want to blame entertainment? Isn't religion the first real entertainment? People dress up in costumes, sing songs and dedicate themselves in eternal fandom. Everyone will agree that nothing was more entertaining than Clinton shooting off his prick and then his bombs in true political form. And the news—that's obvious. So is entertainment to blame? I'd like media commentators to ask themselves, because their coverage of the event was some of the most gruesome entertainment any of us have seen.

I think that the National Rifle Association is far too powerful to take on, so most people choose *Doom, The Basketball Diaries* or yours truly. This kind of controversy does not help me sell records or tickets, and I wouldn't want it to. I'm a controversial artist, one who dares to have an opinion and bothers to create music and videos that challenge people's ideas in a world that is watered-down and hollow. In my work I examine the America we live in, and I've always tried to show people that the devil we blame our atrocities on is really just each one of us. So don't expect the end of the world to come one day out of the blue—it's been happening every day for a long time.

Suggestions for Discussion

1. How does Manson respond to the assertion that his music was to blame for the murders at Columbine?

2. What instead does he blame for not only Columbine but also for the majority of the violence in our society? Do you agree? Explain.

3. Do you feel that entertainment is in any way responsible for the violent and cynical state of the world?

Suggestion for Writing

Have you ever been blamed for something that you do not feel responsible for? Write an editorial article like Manson's explaining with convincing evidence why you are not to blame.

CHARLES TAYLOR

The Morality Police

Charles Taylor's political commentaries and writings on film and popular culture have appeared in *Salon*, the *New Yorker*, and *GQ*. A columnist for the Newark *Star-Ledger*, Taylor has also published widely in venues including the *New York Times*, the *Los Angeles Times*, *Newsday*, *Details*, *Dissent*, and the *American Prospect*. He teaches at Columbia University's School of Journalism. The following article was published online in *Slate* on June 11, 2001.

One of the most unbelievable conversations I've ever had took place a few years ago with a friend, a writer, who was in the midst of preparing for a visit from some relatives, including a young cousin of about 10. My friend told me that he'd gone through his house putting away any "inappropriate" material that his cousin might see. We're not talking porn here, or removing [controversial novelist] Henry Miller or [novel] "The Story of O" from the bookshelves, but stashing the copies of [the magazines] "Esquire" and "Entertainment Weekly" in the magazine pile in his living room. Why, I asked, would you feel the need to hide those? Because, my friend explained, they had swear words in them. I pointed out that the worst thing his cousin was likely to see in "Entertainment Weekly" was, as it's so delicately printed in that magazine, "f____," something the boy had certainly already heard in the schoolyard. But my friend wasn't buying. Why, he wanted to know, can't magazine articles be written so that they're suitable for everyone?

∾

A False Assumption

I felt as if I had been asked to justify why water had to be wet. Here was someone who depended for his living on the right to free speech, who wrote as an adult for other adults, who was advocating the false assumption that lies at the core of the censorious impulse: Children need to be protected from vulgarity and obscenity.

At the heart of that argument is the belief that society should be remade for everyone, not just children. Basically, my friend was arguing that all adult discourse should be rendered suitable for kids, that entertainment or writing specifically intended for adults is somehow dangerous and that, as journalists, we should all be required to adhere to a phony "family newspaper" standard.

He didn't come out and say that, of course. He fell back on the protection-of-innocence arguments that censors have used for years and that courts have upheld. There's an understandable impulse behind the desire to protect children, an awareness of their physical fragility, a wish for them to be able to enjoy their childhood and a frustrating sense that out in the world dangers await them that we are powerless to stop. But too often we have lost the ability to distinguish between what's inappropriate for kids and what is actually harmful to them. And, acting on fear and suspicion and assumption, we have, with the best of intentions, created situations that are potentially more harmful to kids and teens than what we want to protect them from.

∾

Children Do Not Need
Extra Protection

The tradition of censorship in the name of the little ones is the subject of Marjorie Heins' new [2001] book, "Not in Front of the Children: 'Indecency,' Censorship, and the Innocence of Youth." Heins, the director of the Free Expression Policy Project at the National Coalition Against Censorship, has essentially written a précis of various legal rulings that have cited the protection of youth as justification for limiting free speech. Heins is blessedly

424   ART AND SOCIETY

clear on the legal ramifications of the obscenity prosecutions she considers. As a lawyer she's adept at pointing out the contradictions, false premises and just plain unconstitutionality of those decisions. . . .

Heins must have realized she was striding into a minefield. Shrewdly—but also, I think, honestly—she focuses on the harm done to children by censorship laws. She questions how children who have been so stringently shielded can be well prepared for life (especially when at age 18—poof!—they magically become "adults"); how, under the Constitution, some citizens can be judged to have fewer free-speech rights than others; and how you can claim to be protecting children if, in the case of birth control or sexual information, you are depriving them of something that, especially with the public health crisis of AIDS, could save their lives. Some parents love to wag their fingers condescendingly at those of us without children who oppose free-speech restrictions. They say, "You'll change your tune when you have kids of your own." But why would anyone wish for a world in which their children would have *fewer* rights?

The notion that words and images and ideas can cause harm to young minds has become such an article of faith that it's hard not to feel a sense of futility when you point out that there is not a shred, not an iota, not an atom of proof that exposure to images or descriptions of sex and violence does children any harm. In the face of people who are certain about the evil Pied Piper effect of the media, insisting on the facts becomes pointless, even though every expert who tries to claim otherwise gives himself or herself away. On May 6 [2001], the Associated Press reported news of an American Psychiatric Association panel on online voyeurism in which a University of Michigan psychiatry professor named Norman Alessi testified that "the potential of seeing hundreds of thousands of such images during adolescence—*I have no idea what that could do. But I can imagine* it must be profound" (emphasis added). God knows psychiatry isn't science, but you'd expect a doctor to be little more circumspect when he has only his imagination to go on.

Yet this is exactly the kind of "data" that Congress swallows whole before coming up with some new way to put the screws to Hollywood. And witnesses who do try to testify to the facts are often treated with contempt. MIT [Massachusetts Institute of Technology] professor Henry Jenkins appeared before the Senate in the hearings that convened in the panicked aftermath of the Columbine killings and found himself to be the only scholar present who didn't take it on faith (because there's no other way to take it) that media violence promotes real violence. Jenkins described a Senate chamber festooned with "hyperbolic and self-parodying" posters and ads for the most violent video games on the market. "Senators," he said, "read them all deadly seriously and with absolute literalness."

◌◌

The Media Get the Facts Wrong

And why wouldn't they? What do senators, what do the most vocal media critics for that matter, know about video games, rock 'n' roll, current movies and television? [Senator] Joe Lieberman admitted to [television show] "Entertainment Weekly" last week [June 2001] that he hasn't seen a movie since going to "Crouching Tiger, Hidden Dragon" just before the Oscars. Think he had a chance to see many during last year's [2001] campaign? Think that will keep him from opening his yap about the sinister effects of media violence....

I have never come across one—not one—critic protesting the perniciousness of media sex and violence who had any sense of irony, or any substantial or direct experience with the way audiences experience sex and violence and the different ways they're portrayed. I know a 16-year-old girl who has seen "The Faculty" [movie] 14 times. Now, I can imagine what Lieberman or Henry Hyde would do with that tidbit—turn it into the story of a teenager obsessed with a movie in which students take up arms against their teachers. The fact is, my friend has seen it repeatedly for the same reason she went to an opening night IMAX [movie theater] screening of [movie] "Pearl Harbor": because she thinks [actor] Josh Hartnett is adorable.

Why we resist facing the facts in this debate is understandable. People don't have to be stupid or corrupt to look at school shootings, or violence in America in general, and feel that *something* has to be responsible. And as someone who spends much of his time looking at pop culture, I won't deny being disturbed by some of the more mindless violence out there, of having felt cut off from an audience that was grooving on mayhem. People feel so overwhelmed by violence that they think there simply must be a connection between media bloodshed and the real thing. But the truth is that violent crime is down in America, and it has been going down for some years now.

Just because I think extreme protectionism is misguided doesn't mean that I think children should be exposed to anything and everything. Parents have to make those decisions for their own kids. And while I sympathize with their frustration over the proliferation of outlets like the Internet, video and cable that makes those decisions more demanding, parents' frustration isn't a good enough reason to limit the First Amendment. It sickened me when I heard stories about parents dragging along their young kids to see [horror movie] "Hannibal." But we see that kind of idiocy even with a damaging movie ratings system in place. Teenagers may be better able to handle material than their younger siblings are, but they too are the target of obscenity laws that don't distinguish between a 6- or 8-year-old and a 14- or 16-year-old.

Some will insist that there have been findings indicating a causal link between violent entertainment and violent behavior. But those studies have profound flaws. Is it really that surprising that toddlers become markedly more rambunctious after being kept in a room watching "The Three Stooges" for five hours? I have some faith in science, and it seems to me that if there really were a cause-and-effect link between real violence and media violence, then it would have been proven by now. At the least, people who believe in that link should work the flaws out of their methodology. . . .

❧

Meddling Parents

Nothing attracts kids' curiosity or spurs their resourcefulness faster than what's forbidden to them. Have a shelf of books or videos you've told your kids are for Mommy and Daddy only? I guarantee you they've perused it. And sure, as kids all of us at one time or another came across things that upset us or confused us or gave us nightmares. I had to stop watching [television series] "Rod Serling's Night Gallery" because it gave me insomnia. And I vividly remember the unsettling mixture of queasiness and thrill in the pit of my stomach in elementary school when a classmate brought in some grainy black-and-white porno photos of a woman giving a man a blow job. But do you know anyone who's been done lasting harm by looking at dirty pictures or watching a violent movie who wasn't already emotionally disturbed to begin with? There's a big difference between wanting to screen what your kids are reading or watching—in other words, nudging them toward good stuff to balance the mountain of available crap—and wanting to keep them in a hermetically sealed bubble that admits nothing of the outside world. The latter approach, which is the "good parenting" at the basis of so many government attempts to restrict kids' access to information, is, at root, an insult to kids, a presumption that they are too stupid or fragile to be given information about the real world.

And of course it's a threat to the civil liberties of the rest of us. Perhaps out of an instinct for the politic, Heins doesn't address the arrogance of parents who think that in order to solve their child-rearing problems, the rest of adult society should have key freedoms curtailed. It's time to put the responsibility for deciding what is and isn't appropriate for children squarely on parents.

I know often this is a question of time. I see how hard it is for friends to balance raising kids with the financial necessity of having two working parents. But parents' convenience isn't a good enough argument for measures that narrow the free-speech rights of adults. . . .

Parents Inconvenienced by the First Amendment

And the granddaddy of all nincompooperies, the Motion Picture Association of America ratings system, originally supposed to protect filmmakers from interference, has instead resulted in studios contractually obligating them to cut their films to what's acceptable for a 17-year-old. Otherwise, they can't avail themselves of crucial newspaper and television advertising. (Many outlets won't accept ads for NC-17 [no one under 17 admitted] films.) The ratings have never been constitutionally challenged. There's no telling how the current Supreme Court would rule on the system, though there's no doubt of its unconstitutionality. The courts have consistently ruled that adult discourse cannot be required to be conducted at a level suitable for children.

A few years ago I got into a heated discussion with some parents over the ratings system. It was startling because it revealed how much some parents believe the rest of us owe them. I argued that ratings should be abolished not only because they were unconstitutional, and have led to de facto censorship, but also because even a cursory glimpse at a review from a critic they trust would give parents better information about the content and tone of a movie. The parents I was talking to seemed outraged that they should have to read a review before deciding whether they would allow their kids to see a movie. Ratings, they insisted—demonstrating that their minds were much more innocent than the ones they were protecting—made sure their kids were only allowed into movies their parents had approved. When I asked why parents couldn't accompany kids to the box office to ensure the same thing, it was as if I had suggested some Herculean task.

I think it's fair to ask how parents who feel that reading a review or driving their kids to a movie theater is too much work ever manage to pull off the greater responsibilities that parenthood entails. What amazed me during this discussion was that the parents seemed completely willing to abandon their responsibility to be informed about the culture their kids were growing up in to some anonymous watchdog. And that willingness makes them much more susceptible to senators who know that calling for decency is always good for political capital, to citizens or religious groups that feel they have the right to make their values the standard for everyone else, to professional witnesses and "experts" who use their degrees and studies the way real-estate swindlers use phony deeds. Sure, it's easier to believe that [movies] "The Matrix" or "The Basketball Diaries" provided blueprints for the Columbine massacre, or that [musician] Eminem is promoting mother raping and homophobia. It's *always* easier not to think.

&

Stunting Kids Intellectually

But fear and ignorance are never a good basis for making any decision. In the broadest terms, this insistence that children see only material that teaches approved values is a way of stunting kids intellectually. It institutionalizes the [former U.S. secretary of education] William Bennett definition of art as a delivery system for little object lessons on virtue.

I'm not saying that art (and even books and movies that may be less than art) has nothing to teach, but what it does teach is the complex and contradictory nature of experience, experience that resists easy judgments. So by making art abide by narrow and vague standards of decency, we're making kids ill-equipped not just to experience art but to experience life.

&

Danger of Keeping Kids Uninformed

And there's a more urgent danger. In the midst of a public health crisis, denying minors access to sexual information is an insane way to "protect" them. Heins cites a 1998 study that puts our teen childbirth rate ahead of all European countries. Even Mexico, a country where the Catholic Church is such a strong presence, offers much more forthright public health information to teens.

By contrast, by the '90s a [conservative activist] Phyllis Schlafly–inspired program called "Sex Respect" had gotten hundreds of thousands of dollars in government grants and was still being taught in one out of eight public schools. "Sex Respect" informed students that the "epidemic" of STDs [sexually transmitted diseases] and teen pregnancy is nature's judgment on the sexually active; that "there's no way to have premarital sex without hurting someone"; that HIV [human immunodeficiency virus] can be contracted through kissing; that premarital sex can lead to shotgun weddings, cervical cancer, poverty, substance abuse, a diminished ability to communicate and death. Heins describes one video in which a student asks an instructor what will happen if he wants to have sex before getting married. The answer: "Well, I guess you'll just have to be prepared to die."

You have to admire the honesty of that response. Because, of course, whether or not they admit it, the people who want to deny teenagers access to sexual information (to say nothing of access to condoms or abortion) are implicitly saying that kids should die rather than have their innocence sullied. It's always a temptation in the culture wars to sound superior, to give in to ridiculing the values and beliefs of others. But some values need to be ridiculed. The people keeping kids in the dark may be articulate and well dressed and prosperous, but the morality they're selling is that of hicks and ignoramuses and yahoos. How many times in the past 80 years has America proved that it hasn't learned one basic lesson: Prohibition doesn't work. The bodies pile up from our war on drugs and still we haven't learned it. How many teenage bodies need to pile up before we apply that lesson to our national preoccupation with decency?

Suggestions for Discussion

1. According to Taylor, how does protecting children from "adult content" take away their rights as Americans, deny them a proper education, and endanger their lives?

2. What is the "Pied Piper" view of popular culture? According to Taylor, what is wrong with trusting politicians over scientists?

3. Why does Taylor think that AIDS, abortion, and sex education are at the heart of the argument over censorship?

Suggestions for Writing

1. The first amendment to the United States Constitution, part of the Bill of Rights, reads: "Congress shall make no law respecting an establishment of religion, or prohibiting the free exercise thereof; or abridging the freedom of speech, or of the press; or the right of the people peaceably to assemble, and to petition the Government for a redress of grievances." How does the argument that Taylor makes about censorship fit into the context of this amendment? Are there limits—or should there be—to "freedom of speech"? Use research to support your argument.

2. Synthesis: Taylor writes in response to the 1999 Columbine shootings, in which twelve high school students and one teacher were massacred by two seniors who then turned their guns on themselves, and to the public outcry over violent media that followed. How does Taylor's reaction to the national crisis compare to Marilyn Manson's in "Columbine: Whose Fault is It?" Write a paper exploring your own opinion about censorship, using these two essays to support your writing.

PERSONAL WRITING

∽∾∽∾∽∾

LUDWIG VAN BEETHOVEN

The Heiligenstadt Testament

German classical composer Ludwig van Beethoven (1770–1827) is one
of the most admired and imitated figures in music history. His Sym-
phonies 3 ("Eroica") and 9 (including "Ode to Joy"), *Fidelio,* the Turkish
March, and the piano compositions "Moonlight Sonata" and "Für Elise"
are among works that have a populist as well as elite appeal. Raised in a
family of musicians from Bonn, Beethoven studied under Haydn and
Salieri and saw his first music published when he was just twelve. After
moving to Vienna in 1792, his business savvy, commanding personal
presence, and widespread fame gained him financial stability in an era
when arts patronage was in decline. Over the course of several decades,
Beethoven developed a highly individualistic and dynamic style that distinguished him from his renowned predecessors Mozart and Haydn.
Despite his professional successes, Beethoven suffered many personal
tragedies, ranging from romantic difficulties with women and a strained
relationship with his nephew to a degenerative hearing condition. As
deafness approached, Beethoven contemplated suicide in the letter
reprinted here, which he wrote to his brothers in 1802.

FOR MY BROTHERS CARL AND — BEETHOVEN

O ye men who regard or declare me to be malignant, stubborn or cynical, how unjust are ye towards me. You do not know the secret cause of my
seeming so. From childhood onward, my heart and mind prompted me to
be kind and tender, and I was ever inclined to accomplish great deeds. But
only think that during the last six years, I have been in a wretched condition, rendered worse by unintelligent physicians. Deceived from year to year
with hopes of improvement, and then finally forced to the prospect of *lasting
infirmity* (which may last for years, or even be totally incurable). Born with
a fiery, active temperament, even susceptive of the diversions of society,
I had soon to retire from the world, to live a solitary life. At times, even,
I endeavoured to forget all this, but how harshly was I driven back by the
redoubled experience of my bad hearing. Yet it was not possible for me to

say to men: Speak louder, shout, for I am deaf. Alas! how could I declare the weakness of a *sense* which in me *ought to be* more acute than in others—a sense which *formerly* I possessed in highest perfection, a perfection such as few in my profession enjoy, or ever have enjoyed; no I cannot do it. Forgive, therefore, if you see me withdraw, when I would willingly mix with you. My misfortune pains me doubly, in that I am certain to be misunderstood. For me there can be no recreation in the society of my fellow creatures, no refined conversations, no interchange of thought. Almost alone, and only mixing in society when absolutely necessary, I am compelled to live as an exile. If I approach near to people, a feeling of hot anxiety comes over me lest my condition should be noticed—for so it was during these past six months which I spent in the country. Ordered by my intelligent physician to spare my hearing as much as possible, he almost fell in with my present frame of mind, although many a time I was carried away by my sociable inclinations. But how humiliating was it, when some one standing close to me heard a distant flute, and I heard *nothing,* or a *shepherd singing,* and again I heard nothing. Such incidents almost drove me to despair; at times I was on the point of putting an end to my life—*art* alone restrained my hand. Oh! it seemed as if I could not quit this earth until I had produced all I felt within me, and so I continued this wretched life—wretched, indeed, with so sensitive a body that a somewhat sudden change can throw me from the best into the worst state. *Patience,* I am told, I must choose as my guide. I have done so—lasting, I hope, will be my resolution to bear up until it pleases the inexorable Parcae to break the thread. Forced already in my 28th year to become a philosopher, it is not easy; for an artist more difficult than for any one else. O Divine Being, Thou who lookest down into my inmost soul, Thou understandest; Thou knowest that love for mankind and a desire to do good dwell therein. Oh, my fellow men, when one day you read this, remember that you were unjust to me, and let the unfortunate one console himself if he can find one like himself, who in spite of all obstacles which nature has thrown in his way, has still done everything in his power to be received into the ranks of worthy artists and men. You, my brothers Carl and —, as soon as I am dead, beg Professor Schmidt, if he be still living, to describe my malady; and annex this written account to that of my illness, so that at least the world, so far as is possible, may become reconciled to me after my death. And now I declare you both heirs to my small fortune (if such it may be called). Divide it honourably and dwell in peace, and help each other. What you have done against me, has, as you know, long been forgiven. And you, brother Carl, I especially thank you for the attachment you have shown towards me of late. My prayer is that your life may be better, less troubled by cares, than mine. Recommend to your children *virtue*; it alone can bring happiness, not money. I speak from experience. It was virtue which bore me up in time of trouble; to her, next to my art, I owe thanks for my not having laid violent hands on myself. Farewell, and love one another. My thanks to all friends, especially *Prince Lichnowski and Professor Schmidt.* I should much like one of you to keep as an heirloom the instruments given to me by Prince L., but let no strife arise between you concerning them; if money should be of more service to you, just sell them. How happy I feel that even when lying in my grave, I may be useful to you.

So let it be. I joyfully hasten to meet death. If it come before I have had opportunity to develop all my artistic faculties, it will come, my hard fate notwithstanding, too soon, and I should probably wish it later—yet even then I shall be happy, for will it not deliver me from a state of endless suffering? Come when thou wilt, I shall face thee courageously—farewell, and when I am dead do not entirely forget me. This I deserve from you, for during my lifetime I often thought of you, and how to make you happy. Be ye so.

LUDWIG VAN BEETHOVEN.

HEILIGENSTADT, *the 6th of October,* 1802.

[Black seal]

[On the fourth side of the great Will sheet.]

"Heiligenstadt, October, 1802, thus I take my farewell of thee—and indeed sadly—yes, that fond hope which I entertained when I came here, of being at any rate healed up to a certain point, must be entirely abandoned. As the leaves of autumn fall and fade, so it has withered away for me; almost the same as when I came here do I go away—even the High courage which often in the beautiful summer days quickened me, that has vanished. O Providence, let me have just one pure day of *joy*; so long is it since true joy filled my heart. Oh when, oh when, oh Divine Being, shall I be able once again to feel it in the temple of nature and of men. Never—no—that would be too hard.

"For my brothers Carl and — to execute after my death."

Suggestions for Discussion

1. Does Beethoven's description of the experience of going deaf move you? Why or why not?

2. Why was it hard for Beethoven to admit his hearing problem? What effect did his hearing loss have on his social life? Why does Beethoven contemplate suicide?

3. What might Beethoven's views teach us about the meaning of art?

Suggestions for Writing

1. Synthesis: Compare Beethoven's discussion of his disability with Nancy Mairs's essay "On Being a Cripple" (*Personal Values and Relationships*). How might Mairs have reacted to Beethoven's letter, had she been the recipient? Whose view seems more compelling to you? Why?

2. Other essayists in this collection explore the therapeutic role of music. Read the selections by Melissa Etheridge and Glenn Kurtz. How do these views compare? What are the points of agreement? Of disagreement? Do you find music therapeutic in your own life?

GLENN KURTZ

Practicing

A writer, college instructor, and musician who currently resides in New York City, Glenn Kurtz's writing has appeared in *Tema Celeste, Artweek,* and *ZYZZYVA.* A graduate of the New England Conservatory–Tufts University double degree program, Kurtz has taught at San Francisco State University, the California College of the Arts, and his alma mater, Stanford University, where he earned a Ph.D. in German Studies and Comparative Literature. The following excerpts from his 2007 book *Practicing: A Musician's Return to Music* concern the importance of practicing any craft and the frustrations that we all encounter when we travel on the path to excellence (if not perfection).

There are two things that people frequently say about practicing that have always puzzled me. The first I must have heard a thousand times as a child from well-meaning friends of my parents. When a kid plays an instrument, adults gush with enthusiasm in an utterly predictable way. No matter how you sound, they say, "How wonderful! How beautiful!" Then they recall their old piano teacher with a laugh, or lament their unfulfilled desire for lessons. For some reason the conversation invariably ends with the cheerful reminder that "practice makes perfect." As a child, I never knew how to respond to this. What can you say, except "thanks" or "I hope so"? As I got a bit older and began to work harder at playing what I heard, the phrase changed in my ears. Now it stung like a criticism: so much practicing—and *still* not perfect? Finally, like all kids who actually practice, I learned to ignore it. "Practice makes perfect" was just something adults said, as if they were perfect already and knew from experience. The next time you hear someone invoke this misleading adage, watch for the knowing nod, followed by an awkward pause. It never fails to end the conversation.

The second phrase that I hear all the time now, as an adult, makes even less sense. When I tell people I practice the guitar, even accomplished professionals—people who spend half of their lives at an office—will ask, "How do you get yourself to sit down every day? It takes such discipline!" This truly puzzles me. As if their work were not also practicing.

For me, sitting down to play has very little to do with discipline. "It isn't just education and discipline that makes one so devoted to work," Rilke wrote in a 1907 letter to his wife, the painter Clara Westhoff, "it is simple joy. It is one's natural sense of well-being, to which nothing else can compare." Love of music brings me to the practice room. Nothing can compare with the joy of playing a Bach fugue. Yet each time I sit down, I grasp only a fragment of what I hear and feel in the notes. Bach's music is better than it can be played, and this taunts and teases and often tortures me. Grasping, shaping these sounds, I breathe faster, I juice up. When the lines intertwine, I feel an exquisite delicacy of expectation: maybe this time I'll get it! Maybe now! Doesn't everyone feel this in relation to something? It doesn't matter if it's your golf swing, playing with your children, baking a cake, or closing a deal. All of this too is practicing. You reach beyond yourself for some imagined beauty. Discipline is just the outward shape of this hopeful desire.

"For the past eighty years I have started each day in the same manner," wrote the cellist Pablo Casals in his memoir, *Joys and Sorrows*. "I go to the piano, and I play two preludes and fugues of Bach. It fills me with awareness of the wonder of life, with a feeling of the incredible marvel of being a human being."

Try to describe your experience of music, and you'll quickly reach the limits of words. Music carries us away, and we grope for the grandest terms in our vocabulary just to hint at the marvel of the flight, the incredible marvel, the wonder. "Each day," Casals continues, "it is something new, fantastic, and unbelievable." I imagine him leaning forward in excitement, a round-faced bald man in his eighties, gesturing with his hands, then meeting my eyes to see if I've understood. Fantastic and unbelievable. The words say little. But yes, I think I understand.

I'm sitting down to practice, and like Casals, I'm grasping for words to equal my experience. Alone in the practice room, I hold my instrument silently. Every day it is the same task, yet something new. I delve down, seeking what hides waiting in the notes, what lies dormant in myself that music brings to life. I close my eyes and listen for the unheard melody in what I've played a hundred times before, the unsuspected openings.

What are the tones, the terms, that unlock music's power, the pleasure and profundity we experience in listening? I begin to play, leaning forward excitedly and grasping for the right notes, my whole body alive with aspiration. Sounds ring out, ripening for a moment in the air, then dying away. I play the same notes again, reaching for more of the sweetness, the bittersweetness they contain and express. And again the sounds ring out, float across the room, and fall still. Each day, with every note, practicing is the same task, this essential human gesture—reaching out for an ideal, for the grandeur of what you desire, and feeling it slip through your fingers.

Practicing music—practicing anything we really love—we are always at the limit of words, striving for something just beyond our ability to express. Sometimes, when we speak of this work, therefore, we make this the goal, emphasizing the pleasure of reaching out. Practicing, writes Yehudi Menuhin, is "the search for ever greater joy in movement and expression. This is what practice is really about." But frequently we experience a darker, harsher mood, aware in each moment of what slips away unattained. Then pleasure seems like nourishment for the journey, but it is not what carries us forward. When musicians speak of this experience, they often stress the labor, warning how difficult a path it is, how lonesome and demanding. The great Spanish guitarist Andrés Segovia cautioned that "it is impossible to feign mastery of an instrument, however skillful the impostor may be." But to attain mastery, if it is possible at all, requires "the stern discipline of life-long practice." For the listener, Segovia says, music might seem effortless or divine. But for the musician it is the product of supreme effort and devotion, the feast at the end of the season.

Like every practicing musician, I know both the joy and the hard labor of practice. *To hear these sounds emerging from my instrument! And to hear them more clearly, more beautifully in my head than my fingers can ever seem to grasp.* Together this pleasure in music and the discipline of practice engage in an endless tussle, a kind of romance. The sense of joy justifies the labor; the labor, I hope, leads to joy. This, at least, is the bargain I quietly make with myself each morning as I sit down. If I just do my work, then pleasure, mastery will follow. Even the greatest artists must make the same bargain. "I was obliged to work hard," Johann Sebastian Bach is supposed to have said. And I want so much to believe him when he promises that "whoever is equally industrious will succeed just as well."

Yet as I wrap my arms around the guitar to play, I also hear another voice whispering in my ears. "Whatever efforts we may make," warned Jean-Jacques Rousseau in his 1767 *Dictionary of Music,* "we must still be born to the art, otherwise our works can never mount above the insipid." In every musician's mind lurks the fear that practicing is merely busywork, that you are either born to your instrument or you are an impostor. Trusting Bach and Segovia, I cling to the belief that my effort will, over time, yield mastery. But this faith sometimes seems naïve, merely a wish. "The capacity for melody is a gift," asserted Igor Stravinsky. "This means that it is not within our power to develop it by study." Practice all you want, Rousseau and Stravinsky say, but you will never become a musician if you don't start out one. Perhaps practice will carry me only so far. Perhaps, as Oscar Wilde put it, "only mediocrities develop."

I shake out my hands. Outside on the street, the morning commute is over. The workday has begun; school is in session. Only tourists pass by my window now, lumbering up the hill in search of Lombard Street, "the crookedest street in the world." I walk down this tourist attraction all the time, a pretty, twisting street festooned with flowers. Now, from my chair, I watch a family cluster around a map, Mom, Dad, and two red-haired teenage boys, each pointing in a different direction. They're just a block from their destination, but they don't know it, lost within sight of their goal. I feel that way every day.

Practicing is striving; practicing is a romance. But practicing is also a risk, a test of character, a threat of deeply personal failure. I warm up my hands and awaken my ears and imagination, developing skill to equal my experience. I listen and concentrate in an effort to make myself better. Yet every day I collide with my limits, the constraints of my hands, my instrument, and my imagination. Each morning when I sit down, I'm bewildered by a cacophony of voices, encouraging and dismissive, joyous and harsh, each one a little tyrant, each one insisting on its own direction. And I struggle to harmonize them, to find my way between them, uncertain whether this work is worth it or a waste of my time.

Everything I need to make music is here, my hands, my instrument, my imagination, and these notes. For most of their lives Segovia, Casals, Bach, and Stravinsky were also just men sitting alone in a room with these same raw materials, looking out the window at people on the street. Like me, they must at times have wondered how to grasp the immensity of music's promise in a few simple notes, how to hold fast to their devotion against a cutting doubt that would kill it.

∾

I sit with the final notes, feeling the surprising shape of this music. I've given everything I can give now, a performance. Perhaps I am my only audience today, and my attention alone makes this a performance and not just playing in my room. But attention changes everything.

I have to laugh in wonder. I've found a new story of practicing, though it is not the one I expected when I sat down this morning. Practicing, I might repeat a note, a section, a whole piece a hundred times, as if I had all the time in the world to play. This bit of pretending allows me to escape the urgency of each instant and improve slowly. Yet each instant *is* urgent, and in the end practicing is a lie. It is a necessary lie—a fiction that suspends time so we may examine and reflect on what we do or who we are—but still a lie.

Music lives only in performance; only then does what we hear become real. Performing reveals everything we are able to show, and yet for this reason, the first time through, we often perform badly. And we yearn so deeply to go back again and correct our mistakes. Few yearnings are as profound in us, because the truth is, we cannot go back. Yet the fiction of practicing makes it *seem* as if we can, and this is enough to change our lives.

Practice lets us grow in our own time, protected from the demands, the vitality and mortality, of each moment. Within the practice-room walls it often seems as if time really does stand still, as if we could always remain protected, practicing and improving forever. This illusion holds transformative power—but also a dangerous seduction. Practice, by itself, is a dream of perfection. Only performing can turn practice into shared life, where our own time may join with others', becoming musical. Yet practicing is the necessary lie that lets us pause to collect ourselves. It is the inner life of performance, the inward turn that allows us to develop, to grow, to move forward having learned.

Suggestions for Discussion

1. Why doesn't Kurtz like the cliché "Practice makes perfect"? What effect does he say it has?

2. For Kurtz, what is one of the main frustrations of live performances?

3. How does Kurtz describe the process of making music in a way that is accessible to nonmusicians? Have readers who are musicians experienced something similar when performing?

Suggestion for Writing

How might Kurtz's writings on the importance of practicing apply to other hobbies, trades, or disciplines? Ponder this idea, and write a brief essay in reflection.

ESSAYS

A N D R E A   F R A S E R

Why I Would Rather Have a Day Job

Performance artist Andrea Fraser (b. 1965) is best known for criticizing museums, arts administrators, and grant-making foundations for being too motivated by profit margins and a fear of backlash from conservatives to support artists and promote genuinely avant-garde art. She is considered a pioneer of the "institutional critique art movement," and has famously impersonated self-important museum tour guides and art gallery saleswomen in live presentations, on video, and in essays. Her often satirical and absurdist tone paradoxically enhances the severity and seriousness of her condemnations. A member of the Art Department faculty at the University of California, Los Angeles, Fraser has given live performances and created installations for museums and institutions across America and Europe, and her work is included in collections in the Tate and the Saatchi Gallery in London, and the Centre Pompidou, Paris. Fraser's essays and performance scripts have appeared in numerous art periodicals, and have been collected in *Museum Highlights* (2005), from which this essay was taken.

"Slashing the American Canvas" was written for a panel on "Support for Elite, Middlebrow, and Vernacular Cultures" at the conference "New Trends in Cultural Policy for the 21st Century" held at the New School University and New York University in the spring of 1998. A revised and expanded version appears below.

I'd like to begin with the observation that, although I'm not the only artist participating in this conference, I do appear to be the only producer of "elite" culture without an institutional affiliation. I mention this not to complain about the conference—and I'd like to thank the organizers for inviting me to participate. I mention it, rather, because it's the most convenient example of the "trends in cultural policy" about which I would like to speak.

One of the major trends in cultural policy in the United States in the past decade has been the decline in direct support for unaffiliated producers

438

of "elite" culture—otherwise known as individual artists. The National Endowment for the Arts' artists fellowship programs, after years of attack by the right, were finally eliminated in 1996. These attacks also had a chilling effect on state arts councils as well as on corporate and foundation support for individual artists. Of the few foundations that provide grants to individual artists, Art Matters Inc., one of the most active and progressive, was recently forced to discontinue its programs largely as a result of lack of support within the foundation community. In addition, what indirect support continues to exist, such as project funding that artists can pursue through the fiscal sponsorship of nonprofit organizations or through participation in institutional programs, is being narrowed by the growing emphasis, in the guidelines of public, foundation, and corporate sponsors, on public education, community development, and community-based engagement with what could be called, in the vocabulary of this panel, "vernacular" cultures.

My point here, however, is not to decry the drying up of funding for individual artists. When one's position on policy corresponds so neatly to one's professional interests, it's a good idea to take a second look at how those interests themselves are being defined.

A good place to start is *American Canvas,* the much discussed National Endowment for the Arts report authored by Gary O. Larson and released by the NEA in October 1997.[1] Based on a series of public forums held in six different U.S. cities, *American Canvas* takes up with a vengeance the notion of the arts serving social needs. It describes "using the arts to build strong communities" and to "promote civic responsibility and good citizenship"; it claims that art "stimulates the economy and attracts tourists, revitalizes neighborhoods and addresses social problems," and finally that art contributes to "a city's 'feel-good' element," making it "more attractive, both to the general public as well as to the business community" (Larson 4, 15, 81–82). The arts, we are told, are about "celebration rather than confrontation" (Larson 14). "No longer restricted solely to the sanctioned arenas of culture, the arts would be literally suffused throughout the civic structure, finding a home in a variety of community service and economic development activities" (Larson 127).

One need not dig deep, however, to find the dark side of the boosterism and uplift. Further into the document, arts professionals are advised to "target" HUD to subsidize what used to be called gentrification: "Artists' housing *can* . . . be used as a community revitalization tool" (Larson 129). And when it's stated that art should be built into "the fabric" of "basic public-sector functions," what's at the top of the list? Crime prevention! Yes, the criminal justice system is "among a number of . . . areas with which the arts community might profitably develop new relations" (Larson 128). We can decorate prisons! And so, the public sector's fastest-growing industry can rescue the one in the most precipitous decline.

This new emphasis on art's utilitarian value in serving social needs, developed to an extreme in *American Canvas,* might be traced back to two basic sources. First, for public and foundation funders, it may relate to the desperateness of those needs within an increasingly impoverished public sector. Second, for public and corporate funders, it may relate to what George Yúdice has called a shift in the strategies of legitimation of cultural sponsorship—and of the sponsors themselves—from one that depends on the symbolic value of culture in generating international or public prestige, to one that banks instead on art's supposed social use value.[2] For corporations, such a move may be an answer to the difficulty of rationalizing phil- anthropic activity as such in an era of mass layoffs and relentless pressure to cut wages and benefits. (This applies less to support for exhibitions, which usually comes out of advertising budgets, than to corporate collecting, which has declined, and to the programs of corporate foundations.) For public funders, and especially for the NEA, the new strategies of legitimation have been linked to the end of the Cold War and, most often, have been seen as a response to the right-wing attacks which charged that the art funded by the endowment is, among other sins, "elitist."

What interests me, however—and what makes these issues relevant to this panel—is less the political or economic conditions of this phenome- non, than its cultural logic. What one finds in *American Canvas* is that this totally instrumentalized vision of arts funding is propped on an equally instrumentalized and purely affirmative vision of "vernacular" culture, one that reduces the latter to the most generalized function of providing for the symbolic integration of communities. The resulting representation does jus- tice to Pierre Bourdieu's characterization of "certain populist exaltations of 'popular culture'" as "the 'pastorals' of our epoch": "a sham inversion of dominant values" that functions to "produce the fiction of a unity of the social world."[3]

I quote *American Canvas:* "The legacy of the future may have a more common, if no less valued, profile. Included will be the art that is woven through the social fabric" (Larson 15).

The "dominant values" to be inverted in *American Canvas* are identified almost exclusively with "specialized, professional" cultural production, which art institutions are criticized for having stressed to the point that art has become "something that we watch other people do, usually highly skilled professionals, rather than something we do ourselves" (Larson 60). Now, the document argues, "the narrow, professional, institutional defi- nition" of the past must be replaced with "a more expansive view," one that includes the "avocational and ethnic, participatory and popular" (Larson 162–63).

While it is strongly implied that such a redefinition justifies a shift of support away from "elite" cultural producers, support for the producers of this "vernacular" culture is never entertained. Why? Because, it can be supposed, their practices, being avocational and amateur, don't require economic support: they are defined, in fact, by their place outside of the relations of recognition and reward, subsidy and institutional sanction which define the places of professional artists within their professional fields. But if the function of cultural policy in relation to "vernacular" culture is not to support its production, what is it? According to the "expansive view" of culture articulated in *American Canvas,* art "is an essential part of the lives of most families. *The problem is that they just don't know it.*" What we must do is "help them recognize, nourish, and value the art they already possess" as well as "the artistic merit of their own creative efforts" (Larson 62, italics added). And why? To reverse the effects of domination imposed by cultural legitimacies? Guess again. Because a "larger, more committed audience for the arts" can "be developed out of a nation of avocational singers, dancers, painters, and musicians." And all this can be achieved without ever "losing sight of the standards of professional excellence that still have a role in providing benchmarks of achievement" (Larson 163).

And so at last we arrive at the ends of support for "vernacular" culture in the vision of cultural policy laid out in *American Canvas.* Its function is not to challenge cultural hierarchies or even the perimeters of "elite" art but, rather, to seduce a greater number into serving as "a larger, more inclusive base of support" for what is, in fact, the same old cultural pyramid. "Avocational and ethnic, participatory and popular" cultural practices are finally described only as raw material to be re-formed by art professionals or, even more insidiously, to be exploited.

Can "vernacular culture" exist within cultural policy as anything other than an object of the discourse and practices of arts professionals—whether administrators or "elite" artists themselves, who are increasingly talking up the roles of cultural mediators? Can it be more that an object of administration, appropriation, or even expropriation (as is suggested in *American Canvas* by the metaphor of taking "stock" of "pockets of creativity" in communities that might have been "overlooked in previous inventories" [Larson 163])?

I don't believe that the answer to this question depends on the definitions of "elite," "middlebrow," and "vernacular" applied to various cultural forms. It depends, rather, on how these terms—or better, the distributions of competence and credit, prestige and power they are often used to describe—relate to the networks through which various cultural forms are passed. What makes cultural institutions or policy "elite" is not the fact that they privilege "elite" culture, but that they privilege modes of appropriation of culture that require rarefied and socially valorized competencies. That these competencies are displaced, in *American Canvas,* from producers and consumers of culture to administrators does nothing to mitigate their "elite" character: if anything, it represents a tendency to consolidate those competencies in administrative functions—functions made all the more important for the newly discovered "needs" they are supposed to satisfy.

American Canvas is not only a product of right-wing attacks on the NEA. It must also be read as a product of the professionalization of the cultural field which has taken place in the past few decades, a process that has coincided with the expansion and increasing rationalization of the intermediary functions of cultural management and administration. That process of professionalization was facilitated, if not made possible, by public sector intervention and subvention. Until the 1960s, a surprising number of the museums were still staffed by "gentlemen curators" or by art connoisseurs who began their careers providing personal consulting services to patrons and trustees. Most art dealers were also wealthy collectors. Foundations were run largely by the relatives and business associates of their founders.

With the establishment of the NEA and state arts councils in the mid-1960s, all this began to change. Public arts administrators and other cultural workers began to develop professional organizations in the space of relative freedom from specific private interests created by the public sector. The professionalization of foundation staff was spurred by the restrictions introduced in the Tax Reform Act of 1969 on the heels of a decade of governmental scrutiny of self-dealing and other abuses by foundations. Tax reform, together with the comparatively progressive social policy of the Johnson era, meant that the old patrons of "elite" culture didn't have as much money to give away—and, with new restrictions on charitable deductions, what they had was getting more expensive to give. Within museums, art professionals used the sudden weakness of private donors, and the increased dependence of museums on newly available public funds, as leverage in their efforts to establish a foothold of professional autonomy from trustees and patrons within their institutions. All of these forces combined to bring about an unprecedented professionalization in the field: beyond peer review panels, there were artists organizations and alternative spaces, unionization drives in cultural institutions, professional associations for arts administrators, arts lobbying groups, training and degree programs in curating and arts administration, art consultants for the expanding ranks of corporate collectors and sponsors, professional art dealers with investor backing, paid as well as voluntary presidents in cultural institutions and managing as well as artistic directors.

At the same time that arts administrators were expanding their autonomy as professionals, at least some of the so-called avant-garde segments of "elite" cultural producers were beginning to recognize the partial and ideological character of their autonomy as artists—of the freedom and independence which supposedly distinguished their activities from those of producers of "middlebrow" and "vernacular" culture. The realization that even the most formally autonomous art was used to serve social, political, and economic interests—often not in spite of but because of its aestheticism—led some artists to the realization that "elite" art is also, in a sense, the "vernacular" culture of a particular patron class, and led a few to see that it existed as the "vernacular" culture of its class of specialized producers as well. This critique of artistic autonomy from within the field of art joined together with struggles for cultural equality outside of it in an effort to redefine what is constituted as legitimate culture within the public sphere defined by nonprofit art institutions.

Within the visual art world, at least, I can say that a large part of the professional autonomy gained by cultural workers since the 1960s was won, not only with the aid of public sector support, but also in the name of the "public"—or publics—newly defined as composed of heterogeneous cultural constituencies: in the name, that is, of struggles for cultural democratization. I found only one reference in *American Canvas* to these struggles—struggles of which, in its call for an expanded view of culture, the document itself is the product. This reference is a quotation from Bernice Johnson Reagon of Sweet Honey in the Rock, and it goes far in explaining why this history would be omitted. "No sooner," she says, "had our efforts begun to result in funding for more complex cultural constituencies . . . than the mainstream institutions themselves began to maneuver to take over the very resources we had, through our lobbying efforts, created" (quoted in Larson 29). In the next sentence, the author of *American Canvas* interprets this phenomenon as a matter of "increased competition." In fact, it is just the opposite: the reassertion of the cultural monopolies of "elite" institutions.

My concern today is that those publics in whose names we pursued professionalization—even and perhaps especially as defined as complex constituencies of popular, participatory, ethnic, and avocational cultures—are being reduced once again to audiences, or even clients, of institutions and their administrators: a form of capital to be invested in the reproduction of what remains a field of "elite" culture, albeit one now defined less by the rarefied and gratuitous forms of its products than by the conditions, at once specialized and professionalized, of their mediation and distribution.[4]

American Canvas is not about the democratization of cultural policy; it's about making public funding safe for arts administrators. The view I take of this is admittedly harsh. The professionalization of the cultural field did indeed provide arts administrators with a greater degree of autonomy: the freedom, for example, to identify constituencies other than a patron class. It also, however, created homologies of interest that can provide stronger motives for responding to the political and economic demands of sponsors than any relative weakness. Let's not forget that, as many commentators have suggested, the attacks on the NEA were successful largely because so many arts administrators capitulated—from the directors of the Corcoran and Artists Space to the chairman of the NEA—sacrificing artists to censorship in exchange for protecting their organizations. And now, adding to the political autonomy left behind in the triage of the "culture wars," *American Canvas* suggests that art's most fundamental form of freedom be forsaken: the freedom from rationalization with respect to specific functions. We are advised to jump to the service of "social needs," gentrifying neighborhoods, decorating prisons, enhancing cities for destination marketers. And why? Not because the demand exists: the function of cultural policy, according to *American Canvas,* is precisely to *produce* such demand. We should work to serve these "needs," rather, to generate, and justify, the funds necessary to maintain, or even expand, the organizations established during the non-profit cultural boom years of the 1970s and '80s—and especially, of course, the most legitimate ones.

Is it really worth it? And, most importantly, for whom?

I, for one, would rather have a day job.

Notes

1. Gary O. Larson, *American Canvas* (Washington, D.C.: National Endowment for the Arts, 1997). For economy's sake, all future references to Larson will appear in parentheses in the text.

2. George Yúdice, "The Privatization of Culture," paper presented at the University of Kansas, Lawrence, November 6, 1997.

3. Pierre Bourdieu and Loïc Wacquant, *An Invitation to Reflexive Sociology* (Chicago: University of Chicago Press, 1992), 83.

4. Once again, I would turn to Bourdieu for a description of this process:

> The constitution of a socially recognized corps of experts . . . which is now coming about through the gradual professionalization of voluntary, philanthropic or political associations, is the paradigmatic form of the process whereby agents tend, with that deep conviction of disinterestedness which is the basis of all missionary zeal, to satisfy their group interests by deploying the legitimate culture with which they have been endowed by the education system to win the acquiescence of the classes excluded from legitimate culture, in producing the need for and the rarity of their class culture.

> Pierre Bourdieu, *Distinction: A Social Critique of the Judgment of Taste,* trans. Richard Nice (Cambridge: Harvard University Press, 1984), 153.

Suggestions for Discussion

1. This essay was originally written as a conference presentation, and Frasier delivered the speech before professionals in the art field. How do you think her criticisms were received by the conference attendees?

2. Why is it significant that there are so few "individual artists" or "unaffiliated producers of elite culture"? What difference does an institutional affiliation make for the artist? For the art? For the audience? For museums and galleries?

3. Synthesis: According to Fraser, what effects have "right-wing attacks on the National Endowment for the Arts" had? How do her views on censorship in elite culture compare to Charles Taylor's views on censorship of the Internet and mass media in "The Morality Police"?

4. Why should people who don't often go to museums or art galleries care at all about what Fraser is talking about?

Suggestions for Writing

1. Synthesis: How do Fraser's concerns about "arts serving social needs" compare and contrast with the ideas presented by Earl Shorris in "Education as a Weapon in the Hands of the Restless Poor" (*Education*)?

2. What relationship between censorship and economics is presented in this essay? Research the issues that Fraser raises—the history, statistics, and ideologies at work—and discuss the extent to which you agree or disagree with her perspective.

GEORGE ORWELL

Politics and the English Language

George Orwell (1903–1950), pseudonym of Eric Arthur Blair, a British writer with socialist sympathies, wrote essays and novels based on his experiences as a British imperial policeman in Burma, as an impoverished writer in Paris and London, and as a volunteer in the republican army in the Spanish Civil War. He served for several years as editor of the magazine of the British Labour Party. Although his essays and letters are considered masterpieces of prose style, he is probably best known for the satirical anti-Communist fable *Animal Farm* (1945) and for the novel *1984,* published in 1949. Orwell conceived a terrifying vision of a future where mechanized language and thought have become the tools of a totalitarian society. This essay, published in April 1946 in *Horizon: A Review of Literature and Art,* examines the link between the deterioration of the English language and the rise of destructive and inhumane political movements.

Most people who bother with the matter at all would admit that the English language is in a bad way, but it is generally assumed that we cannot by conscious action do anything about it. Our civilization is decadent and our language—so the argument runs—must inevitably share in the general collapse. It follows that any struggle against the abuse of language is a sentimental archaism, like preferring candles to electric light or hansom cabs to airplanes. Underneath this lies the half-conscious belief that language is a natural growth and not an instrument which we shape for our own purposes.

Now, it is clear that the decline of a language must ultimately have political and economic causes: it is not due simply to the bad influence of this or that individual writer. But an effect can become a cause, reinforcing the original cause and producing the same effect in an intensified form, and so on indefinitely. A man may take to drink because he feels himself to be a failure, and then fail all the more completely because he drinks. It is rather the same thing that is happening to the English language. It becomes ugly and inaccurate because our thoughts are foolish, but the slovenliness of our language makes it easier for us to have foolish thoughts. The point is that the process is reversible. Modern English, especially written English, is full of bad habits which spread by imitation and which can be avoided if one is willing to take the necessary trouble. If one gets rid of these habits one can think more clearly, and to think clearly is a necessary first step towards political regeneration: so that the fight against bad English is not frivolous and is not the exclusive concern of professional writers. I will come back to this presently, and I hope that by that time the meaning of what I have said here will have become clearer. Meanwhile, here are five specimens of the English language as it is now habitually written.

These five passages have not been picked out because they are especially bad—I could have quoted far worse if I had chosen—but because they illustrate various of the mental vices from which we now suffer. They are a little below the average, but are fairly representative samples. I number them so that I can refer back to them when necessary:

> "(1) I am not, indeed, sure whether it is not true to say that the Milton who once seemed not unlike a seventeenth-century Shelley had not become, out of an experience ever more bitter in each year,

*more alien (sic) to the founder of that Jesuit sect which nothing
could induce him to tolerate."*

Professor Harold Laski (Essay in Freedom of Expression).

*"(2) Above all, we cannot play ducks and drakes with a native
battery of idioms which prescribes such egregious collocations of
vocables as the Basic* put up with *for* tolerate *or* put at a loss *for*
bewilder."

Professor Lancelot Hogben (Interglossa).

*"(3) On the one side we have the free personality: by definition it
is not neurotic, for it has neither conflict nor dream. Its desires, such
as they are, are transparent, for they are just what institutional
approval keeps in the forefront of consciousness; another institutional pattern would alter their number and intensity; there is
little in them that is natural, irreducible, or culturally dangerous.
But* on the other side, *the social bond itself is nothing but the
mutual reflection of these self-secure integrities. Recall the
definition of love. Is not this the very picture of a small academic?
Where is there a place in this hall of mirrors for either personality
or fraternity?"*

Essay on psychology in Politics (New York).

*"(4) All the 'best people' from the gentlemen's clubs, and all the
frantic fascist captains, united in common hatred of Socialism and
bestial horror of the rising tide of the mass revolutionary movement,
have turned to acts of provocation, to foul incendiarism, to medieval
legends of poisoned wells, to legalize their own destruction of
proletarian organizations, and rouse the agitated petty-bourgeoisie
to chauvinistic fervor on behalf of the fight against the revolutionary
way out of the crisis."*

Communist pamphlet.

*"(5) If a new spirit is to be infused into this old country, there is one
thorny and contentious reform which must be tackled, and that is
the humanization and galvanization of the B.B.C. Timidity here
will bespeak cancer and atrophy of the soul. The heart of Britain
may be sound and of strong beat, for instance, but the British lion's
roar at present is like that of Bottom in Shakespeare's* Midsummer
Night's Dream—*as gentle as any sucking dove. A virile new Britain
cannot continue indefinitely to be traduced in the eyes, or rather
ears, of the world by the effete languors of Langham Place, brazenly
masquerading as 'standard English.' When the Voice of Britain is
heard at nine o'clock, better far and infinitely less ludicrous to hear
aitches honestly dropped than the present priggish, inflated,
inhibited, school-ma'amish arch braying of blameless bashful
mewing maidens!"*

Letter in Tribune.

Each of these passages has faults of its own, but, quite apart from avoidable ugliness, two qualities are common to all of them. The first is staleness of imagery: the other is lack of precision. The writer either has a meaning and cannot express it, or he inadvertently says something else, or he is almost indifferent as to whether his words mean anything or not. This mixture of vagueness and sheer incompetence is the most marked characteristic of modern English prose, and especially of any kind of political writing. As soon as certain topics are raised, the concrete melts into the abstract and no one seems able to think of turns of speech that are not hackneyed: prose consists less and less of *words* chosen for the sake of their meaning, and more and more of *phrases* tacked together like the sections of a prefabricated hen-house. I list below, with notes and examples, various of the tricks by means of which the work of prose-construction is habitually dodged:

ॐ

Dying Metaphors

A newly invented metaphor assists thought by evoking a visual image, while on the other hand a metaphor which is technically "dead" (e.g. *iron resolution*) has in effect reverted to being an ordinary word and can generally be used without loss of vividness. But in between these two classes there is a huge dump of worn-out metaphors which have lost all evocative power and are merely used because they save people the trouble of inventing phrases for themselves. Examples are: *Ring the changes on, take up the cudgels for, toe the line, ride roughshod over, stand shoulder to shoulder with, play into the hands of, no axe to grind, grist to the mill, fishing in troubled waters, on the order of the day, Achilles' heel, swan song, hotbed.* Many of these are used without knowledge of their meaning (what is a "rift,"[1] for instance?), and incompatible metaphors are frequently mixed, a sure sign that the writer is not interested in what he is saying. Some metaphors now current have been twisted out of their original meaning without those who use them even being aware of the fact. For example, *toe the line* is sometimes written *tow the line*. Another example is the *hammer and the anvil*, now always used with the implication that the anvil gets the worst of it. In real life it is always the anvil that breaks the hammer, never the other way about: a writer who stopped to think what he was saying would be aware of this, and would avoid perverting the original phrase.

---

[1]Originally *rift* referred to a geological fault or fissure. Now it is commonly used to indicate a breach or estrangement. [Eds.]

༄

Operators or Verbal False Limbs

These save the trouble of picking out appropriate verbs and nouns, and at the same time pad each sentence with extra syllables which give it an appearance of symmetry. Characteristic phrases are: *render inoperative, militate against, make contact with, be subjected to, give rise to, give grounds for, have the effect of, play a leading part (role) in, make itself felt, take effect, exhibit a tendency to, serve the purpose of, etc., etc.* The keynote is the elimination of simple verbs. Instead of being a single word, such as *break, stop, spoil, mend, kill,* a verb becomes a *phrase,* made up of a noun or adjective tacked on to some general-purposes verb such as *prove, serve, form, play, render.* In addition, the passive voice is wherever possible used in preference to the active, and noun constructions are used instead of gerunds (*by examination of* instead of *by examining*). The range of verbs is further cut down by means of the *-ize* and *de-* formation, and the banal statements are given an appearance of profundity by means of the *not un-* formation. Simple conjunctions and prepositions are replaced by such phrases as *with respect to, having regard to, the fact that, by dint of, in view of, in the interests of, on the hypothesis that*; and the ends of sentences are saved from anticlimax by such resounding commonplaces as *greatly to be desired, cannot be left out of account, a development to be expected in the near future, deserving of serious consideration, brought to a satisfactory conclusion,* and so on and so forth.

༄

Pretentious Diction

Words like *phenomenon, element, individual* (as noun), *objective, categorical, effective, virtual, basic, primary, promote, constitute, exhibit, exploit, utilize, eliminate, liquidate,* are used to dress up simple statements and give an air of scientific impartiality to biased judgments. Adjectives like *epoch-making, epic, historic, unforgettable, triumphant, age-old, inevitable, inexorable, veritable,* are used to dignify the sordid processes of international politics, while writing that aims at glorifying war usually takes on an archaic color, its characteristic words being: *realm, throne, chariot, mailed fist, trident, sword, shield, buckler, banner, jackboot, clarion.* Foreign words and expressions such as *cul de sac, ancien régime, deus ex machina, mutatis mutandis, status quo, gleichschaltung, weltanschauung,* are used to give an air of culture and elegance. Except for the useful abbreviations *i.e., e.g.,* and *etc.,* there is no real need for any of the hundreds of foreign phrases now current in English. Bad writers, and especially scientific, political and sociological writers, are nearly always haunted by the notion that Latin or Greek words are grander than Saxon ones, and unnecessary words like *expedite, ameliorate, predict, extraneous, deracinated, clandestine, subaqueous* and hundreds of others constantly gain ground from their Anglo-Saxon opposite numbers.[2] The jargon peculiar to Marxist writing (*hyena, hangman, cannibal, petty bourgeois, these gentry, lacquey, flunkey, mad dog, White Guard,* etc.) consists largely of words and phrases translated from Russian, German or French; but the normal way of coining a new word is to use a Latin or Greek root with the appropriate affix and, where necessary, the *-ize* formation. It is often easier to make up words of this kind (*deregionalize, impermissible, extra-marital, nonfragmentatory* and so forth) than to think up the English words that will cover one's meaning. The result, in general, is an increase in slovenliness and vagueness.

⌘

Meaningless Words

In certain kinds of writing, particularly in art criticism and literary criticism, it is normal to come across long passages which are almost completely lacking in meaning.[3] Words like *romantic, plastic, values, human, dead, sentimental, natural, vitality,* as used in art criticism, are strictly meaningless in the sense that they not only do not point to any discoverable object, but are hardly ever expected to do so by the reader. When one critic writes, "The outstanding feature of Mr. X's work is its living quality," while another writes, "The immediately striking thing about Mr. X's work is its peculiar deadness," the reader accepts this as a simple difference of opinion. If words like *black* and *white* were involved, instead of the jargon words *dead* and *living,* he would see at once that language was being used in an improper way. Many political words are similarly abused. The word *Fascism* has now no meaning except in so far as it signifies "something not desirable." The

---

[2]An interesting illustration of this is the way in which the English flower names which were in use till very recently are being ousted by Greek ones, *snapdragon* becoming *antirrhinum, forget-me-not* becoming *myosotis,* etc. It is hard to see any practical reason for this change in fashion: it is probably due to an instinctive turning-away from the more homely word and a vague feeling that the Greek word is scientific.

[3]Example: "Comfort's catholicity of perception and image, strangely Whitmanesque in range, almost the exact opposite in aesthetic compulsion, continues to evoke that trembling atmospheric accumulative hinting at a cruel, an inexorably serene timelessness. . . . Wrey Gardiner scores by aiming at simple bull's-eyes with precision. Only they are not so simple, and through this contended sadness—runs more than the surface bittersweet of resignation" (*Poetry Quarterly*).

words *democracy, socialism, freedom, patriotic, realistic, justice,* have each of them several different meanings which cannot be reconciled with one another. In the case of a word like *democracy,* not only is there no agreed definition, but the attempt to make one is resisted from all sides. It is almost universally felt that when we call a country democratic we are praising it: consequently the defenders of every kind of regime claim that it is a democracy, and fear that they might have to stop using the word if it were tied down to any one meaning. Words of this kind are often used in a consciously dishonest way. That is, the person who uses them has his own private definition, but allows his hearer to think he means something quite different. Statements like *Marshal Pétain was a true patriot, The Soviet Press is the freest in the world, The Catholic Church is opposed to persecution,* are almost always made with intent to deceive. Other words used in variable meanings, in most cases more or less dishonestly, are: *class, totalitarian, science, progressive, reactionary, bourgeois, equality.*

Now that I have made this catalogue of swindles and perversions, let me give another example of the kind of writing that they lead to. This time it must of its nature be an imaginary one. I am going to translate a passage of good English into modern English of the worst sort. Here is a well-known verse from *Ecclesiastes:*

> "I returned and saw under the sun, that the race is not to the swift, nor the battle to the strong, neither yet bread to the wise, nor yet riches to men of understanding, nor yet favor to men of skill; but time and chance happeneth to them all."

Here it is in modern English:

> "Objective consideration of contemporary phenomena compels the conclusion that success or failure in competitive activities exhibits no tendency to be commensurate with innate capacity, but that a considerable element of the unpredictable must invariably be taken into account."

This is a parody, but not a very gross one. Exhibit (3), above, for instance, contains several patches of the same kind of English. It will be seen that I have not made a full translation. The beginning and ending of the sentence follow the original meaning fairly closely, but in the middle the concrete illustrations—race, battle, bread—dissolve into the vague phrase "success or failure in competitive activities." This had to be so, because no modern writer of the kind I am discussing—no one capable of using phrases like "objective consideration of contemporary phenomena"—would ever tabulate his thoughts in that precise and detailed way. The whole tendency of modern prose is away from concreteness. Now analyze these two sentences a little more closely. The first contains forty-nine words but

452 ART AND SOCIETY

only sixty syllables, and all its words are those of everyday life. The second contains thirty-eight words of ninety syllables: eighteen of its words are from Latin roots, and one from Greek. The first sentence contains six vivid images, and only one phrase ("time and chance") that could be called vague. The second contains not a single fresh, arresting phrase, and in spite of its ninety syllables it gives only a shortened version of the meaning contained in the first. Yet without a doubt it is the second kind of sentence that is gaining ground in modern English. I do not want to exaggerate. This kind of writing is not yet universal, and outcrops of simplicity will occur here and there in the worst-written page. Still, if you or I were told to write a few lines on the uncertainty of human fortunes, we should probably come much nearer to my imaginary sentence than to the one from *Ecclesiastes*.

As I have tried to show, modern writing at its worst does not consist in picking out words for the sake of their meaning and inventing images in order to make the meaning clearer. It consists in gumming together long strips of words which have already been set in order by someone else, and making the results presentable by sheer humbug. The attraction of this way of writing is that it is easy. It is easier—even quicker, once you have the habit—to say *In my opinion it is a not unjustifiable assumption that* than to say *I think*. If you use ready-made phrases, you not only don't have to hunt about for words; you also don't have to bother with the rhythms of your sentences, since these phrases are generally so arranged as to be more or less euphonious. When you are composing in a hurry—when you are dictating to a stenographer, for instance, or making a public speech— it is natural to fall into a pretentious, Latinized style. Tags like *a consideration which we should do well to bear in mind* or *a conclusion to which all of us would readily assent* will save many a sentence from coming down with a bump. By using stale metaphors, similes and idioms, you save much mental effort, at the cost of leaving your meaning vague, not only for your reader but for yourself. This is the significance of mixed metaphors. The sole aim of a metaphor is to call up a visual image. When these images clash—as in *The Fascist octopus has sung its swan song, the jackboot is thrown into the melting pot*—it can be taken as certain that the writer is not seeing a mental image of the objects he is naming; in other words he is not really thinking. Look again at the examples I gave at the beginning of this essay. Professor Laski (1) uses five negatives in fifty-three words. One of these is superfluous, making nonsense of the whole passage, and in addition there is the slip *alien* for *akin*, making further nonsense, and several avoidable pieces of clumsiness which increase the general vagueness. Professor Hogben (2) plays ducks and drakes with a battery which is able to write prescriptions, and, while disapproving of the everyday phrase *put up with*, is unwilling to look *egregious* up in the dictionary and see what it means. (3), if one takes an uncharitable attitude towards it, is simply meaningless: probably one could work out its intended meaning by reading the whole of the article in which it occurs. In (4), the writer knows more or less what he wants to say, but an accumulation of stale phrases chokes him like tea leaves blocking a sink. In (5), words and meaning have almost parted company. People who write in this manner usually have a general emotional meaning—they dislike one thing and want to express solidarity with another—but they are not interested in the detail of what they are saying. A scrupulous writer, in every sentence that he writes, will ask himself at least four questions, thus: What am I trying to say? What words will express it? What image or idiom will make it clearer? Is this image fresh enough to have an effect? And he will probably ask himself two more: Could I put it more shortly? Have I said anything that is avoidably ugly? But you are not obliged to go to all this trouble. You can shirk it by simply throwing your mind open and letting the ready-made phrases come crowding in. They will construct your sentences for you—even think your thoughts for you, to a certain extent—and at need they will perform the important service of partially concealing your meaning even from yourself. It is at this point that the special connection between politics and the debasement of language becomes clear.

In our time it is broadly true that political writing is bad writing. Where it is not true, it will generally be found that the writer is some kind of rebel, expressing his private opinions and not a "party line." Orthodoxy, of whatever color, seems to demand a lifeless, imitative style. The political dialects to be found in pamphlets, leading articles, manifestos, White Papers and the speeches of under-secretaries do, of course, vary from party to party, but they are all alike in that one almost never finds in them a fresh, vivid, home-made turn of speech. When one watches some tired hack on the platform mechanically repeating the familiar phrases—*bestial atrocities, iron heel, bloodstained tyranny, free peoples of the world, stand shoulder to shoulder*—one often has a curious feeling that one is not watching a live human being but some kind of dummy: a feeling which suddenly becomes stronger at moments when the light catches the speaker's spectacles and turns them into blank discs which seem to have no eyes behind them. And this is not altogether fanciful. A speaker who uses that kind of phraseology has gone some distance towards turning himself into a machine. The appropriate noises are coming out of his larynx, but his brain is not involved as it would be if he were choosing his words for himself. If the speech he is making is one that he is accustomed to make over and over again, he may be almost unconscious of what he is saying, as one is when one utters the responses in church. And this reduced state of consciousness, if not indispensable, is at any rate favorable to political conformity.

In our time, political speech and writing are largely the defense of the indefensible. Things like the continuance of British rule in India, the

Russian purges and deportations, the dropping of the atom bombs on Japan, can indeed be defended, but only by arguments which are too brutal for most people to face, and which do not square with the professed aims of political parties. Thus political language has to consist largely of euphemism, question-begging and sheer cloudy vagueness. Defenseless villages are bombarded from the air, the inhabitants driven out into the countryside, the cattle machine-gunned, the huts set on fire with incendiary bullets: this is called *pacification*. Millions of peasants are robbed of their farms and sent trudging along the roads with no more than they can carry: this is called *transfer of population* or *rectification of frontiers*. People are imprisoned for years without trial, or shot in the back of the neck or sent to die of scurvy in Arctic lumber camps: this is called *elimination of unreliable elements*. Such phraseology is needed if one wants to name things without calling up mental pictures of them. Consider for instance some comfortable English professor defending Russian totalitarianism. He cannot say outright, "I believe in killing off your opponents when you can get good results by doing so." Probably, therefore, he will say something like this:

"While freely conceding that the Soviet régime exhibits certain features which the humanitarian may be inclined to deplore, we must, I think, agree that a certain curtailment of the right to political opposition is an unavoidable concomitant of transitional periods, and that the rigors which the Russian people have been called upon to undergo have been amply justified in the sphere of concrete achievement."

The inflated style is itself a kind of euphemism. A mass of Latin words falls upon the facts like soft snow, blurring the outlines and covering up all the details. The great enemy of clear language is insincerity. When there is a gap between one's real and one's declared aims, one turns as it were instinctively to long words and exhausted idioms, like a cuttlefish squirting out ink. In our age there is no such thing as "keeping out of politics." All issues are political issues, and politics itself is a mass of lies, evasions, folly, hatred and schizophrenia. When the general atmosphere is bad, language must suffer. I should expect to find—this is a guess which I have not sufficient knowledge to verify—that the German, Russian and Italian languages have all deteriorated in the last ten to fifteen years, as a result of dictatorship.

But if thought corrupts language, language can also corrupt thought. A bad usage can spread by tradition and imitation, even among people who should and do know better. The debased language that I have been discussing is in some ways very convenient. Phrases like *a not unjustifiable assumption, leaves much to be desired, would serve no good purpose, a consideration which we should do well to bear in mind,* are a continuous temptation, a packet of aspirins always at one's elbow. Look back through this essay, and for certain you will find that I have again and again committed the very faults I am protesting against. By this morning's post I have received a pamphlet dealing with conditions in Germany. The author tells me that he "felt impelled" to write it. I open it at random, and here is almost the first sentence that I see: "(The Allies) have an opportunity not only of achieving a radical transformation of Germany's social and political structure in such a way as to avoid a nationalistic reaction in Germany itself, but at the same time of laying the foundations of a cooperative and unified Europe." You see, he "feels impelled" to write—feels, presumably, that he has something new to say—and yet his words, like cavalry horses answering the bugle, group themselves automatically into the familiar dreary pattern. This invasion of one's mind by ready-made phrases (*lay the foundations, achieve a radical transformation*) can only be prevented if one is constantly on guard against them, and every such phrase anesthetizes a portion of one's brain.

I said earlier that the decadence of our language is probably curable. Those who deny this would argue, if they produced an argument at all, that language merely reflects existing social conditions, and that we cannot influence its development by any direct tinkering with words and constructions. So far as the general tone or spirit of a language goes, this may be true, but it is not true in detail. Silly words and expressions have often disappeared, not through any evolutionary process but owing to the conscious action of a minority. Two recent examples were *explore every avenue* and *leave no stone unturned,* which were killed by the jeers of a few journalists. There is a long list of flyblown metaphors which could similarly be got rid of if enough people would interest themselves in the job; and it should also be possible to laugh the *not un-* formation out of existence,[4] to reduce the amount of Latin and Greek in the average sentence, to drive out foreign phrases and strayed scientific words, and, in general, to make pretentiousness unfashionable. But all these are minor points. The defense of the English language implies more than this, and perhaps it is best to start by saying what it does *not* imply.

To begin with it has nothing to do with archaism, with the salvaging of obsolete words and turns of speech, or with the setting up of a "standard English" which must never be departed from. On the contrary, it is especially concerned with the scrapping of every word or idiom which has outworn its usefulness. It has nothing to do with correct grammar and syntax, which are of no importance so long as one makes one's meaning clear, or with the avoidance of Americanisms, or with having what is called a "good prose style." On the other hand it is not concerned with fake simplicity and

---

[4]One can cure oneself of the *not un-* formation by memorizing this sentence: *A not unblack dog was chasing a not unsmall rabbit across a not ungreen field.*

the attempt to make written English colloquial. Nor does it even imply in every case preferring the Saxon word to the Latin one, though it does imply using the fewest and shortest words that will cover one's meaning. What is above all needed is to let the meaning choose the word and not the other way about. In prose, the worst thing one can do with words is to surrender to them. When you think of a concrete object, you think wordlessly, and then, if you want to describe the thing you have been visualizing you probably hunt about till you find the exact words that seem to fit. When you think of something abstract you are more inclined to use words from the start, and unless you make a conscious effort to prevent it, the existing dialect will come rushing in and do the job for you, at the expense of blurring or even changing your meaning. Probably it is better to put off using words as long as possible and get one's meaning as clear as one can through pictures or sensations. Afterwards one can choose—not simply accept—the phrases that will best cover the meaning, and then switch round and decide what impression one's words are likely to make on another person. This last effort of the mind cuts out all stale or mixed images, all prefabricated phrases, needless repetitions, and humbug and vagueness generally. But one can often be in doubt about the effect of a word or a phrase, and one needs rules that one can rely on when instinct fails. I think the following rules will cover most cases:

i.   Never use a metaphor, simile or other figure of speech which you are used to seeing in print.

ii. Never use a long word where a short one will do.

iii. If it is possible to cut a word out, always cut it out.

iv. Never use the passive where you can use the active.

v.   Never use a foreign phrase, a scientific word, or a jargon word if you can think of an everyday English equivalent.

vi. Break any of these rules sooner than say anything outright barbarous.

These rules sound elementary, and so they are, but they demand a deep change of attitude in anyone who has grown used to writing in the style now fashionable. One could keep all of them and still write bad English, but one could not write the kind of stuff that I quoted in those five specimens at the beginning of this article.

I have not here been considering the literary use of language, but merely language as an instrument for expressing and not for concealing or preventing thought. Stuart Chase[5] and others have come near to claiming that all abstract words are meaningless, and have used this as a pretext for advocating a kind of political quietism. Since you don't know what

---

[5]Writer known for his advocacy of clear writing and clear thinking. [Eds.]

Fascism is, how can you struggle against Fascism? One need not swallow such absurdities as this, but one ought to recognize that the present political chaos is connected with the decay of language, and that one can probably bring about some improvement by starting at the verbal end. If you simplify your English, you are freed from the worst follies of orthodoxy. You cannot speak any of the necessary dialects, and when you make a stupid remark its stupidity will be obvious, even to yourself. Political language—and with variations this is true of all political parties, from Conservatives to Anarchists—is designed to make lies sound truthful and murder respectable, and to give an appearance of solidity to pure wind. One cannot change this all in a moment, but one can at least change one's own habits, and from time to time one can even, if one jeers loudly enough, send some worn-out and useless phrase, some *jackboot, Achilles' heel, hotbed, melting pot, acid test, veritable inferno* or other lump of verbal refuse—into the dustbin where it belongs.

Suggestions for Discussion

1. Do you agree that everything in life is political? Why or why not?

2. Orwell argues that all writing about politics bad writing. Do you agree? When might it be good? What makes political writing defend the indefensible?

3. Why do you think key political terms are often left deliberately vague? What would happen if speakers actually spelled out what they meant by terms such as "democracy," "Fascism," "socialism," and the others Orwell cites?

Suggestions for Writing

1. What are Orwell's six rules of good writing? How might keeping these ideas in mind result in better writing, and make political statements more honest? Does Orwell follow his own rules? Analyze this essay—or one of Orwell's well-known books like *Animal Farm* or *1984*—based on these rules.

2. Select another piece of political writing from this book and analyze it through the lens of Orwell's "Politics and the English Language." Does the essay meet Orwell's criteria? In what way? (Provide examples from the text.) If not, do you find it compelling anyway? Why? (Again, provide specific examples.)

3. Select a provocative piece of political writing from a newspaper, blog, or magazine, or use a video of a political commentary/round-table-discussion show. What would Orwell think of the arguments made and the words chosen? Have "the rules" for political rhetoric changed since Orwell was writing? In what ways?

$\infty\infty\infty$

ROGER EBERT

Great Movies

Roger Ebert (b. 1942) is the well-known film critic who popularized the "Two Thumbs Up," "Two Thumbs Down," and "Split Decision" movie review approach with fellow critic Gene Siskel on the television program they began in 1975, *Siskel and Ebert*. Although Siskel died in 1999, Ebert continues the program (now called *Ebert and Roeper*) with critic Richard Roeper. Ebert began his career as the *Chicago Sun-Times'* resident film critic in 1967 and won a 1975 Pulitzer Prize for criticism. Since 1969, Ebert has lectured on film in the University of Chicago's fine arts program. Each year his reviews are collected in a new edition of *The Movie Yearbook*. His other books include *A Kiss Is Still a Kiss* (1985), *Behind the Phantom's Mask* (1993), and *I Hated, Hated, Hated This Movie* (2000). Ebert was inspired to write the following essay as he neared completion on *The Great Movies* (2002), a book in which he expressed his love for some of the best movies that he has ever seen.

Every other week I visit a film classic from the past and write about it. My "Great Movies" series began in the autumn of 1996 and now reaches a landmark of 100 titles with today's review of Federico Fellini's "8 1/2," which is, appropriately, a film about a film director. I love my job, and this is the part I love the most.

We have completed the first century of film. Too many moviegoers are stuck in the present and recent past. When people tell me that "Ferris Bueller's Day Off" or "Total Recall" are their favorite films, I wonder: Have they tasted the joys of Welles, Bunuel, Ford, Murnau, Keaton, Hitchcock, Wilder or Kurosawa? If they like Ferris Bueller, what would they think of Jacques Tati's "Mr. Hulot's Holiday," also about a strange day of misadventures? If they like "Total Recall," have they seen Fritz Lang's "Metropolis," also about an artificial city ruled by fear?

I ask not because I am a film snob. I like to sit in the dark and enjoy movies. I think of old films as a resource of treasures. Movies have been made for 100 years, in color and black and white, in sound and silence, in wide-screen and the classic frame, in English and every other language. To limit yourself to popular hits and recent years is like being Ferris Bueller but staying home all day.

I believe we are born with our minds open to wonderful experiences, and only slowly learn to limit ourselves to narrow tastes. We are taught to lose our curiosity by the bludgeon-blows of mass marketing, which brainwash us to see "hits," and discourage exploration.

I know that many people dislike subtitled films, and that few people reading this article will have ever seen a film from Iran, for example. And yet a few weeks ago at my Overlooked Film Festival at the University of Illinois, the free kiddie matinee was "Children of Heaven," from Iran. It was a story about a boy who loses his sister's sneakers through no fault of his own, and is afraid to tell his parents. So he and his sister secretly share the same pair of shoes. Then he learns of a footrace where third prize is . . . a pair of sneakers.

"Anyone who can read at the third-grade level can read these subtitles," I told the audience of 1,000 kids and some parents. "If you can't, it's OK for your parents or older kids to read them aloud—just not too loudly."

The lights went down and the movie began. I expected a lot of reading aloud. There was none. Not all of the kids were old enough to read, but apparently they were picking up the story just by watching and using their intelligence. The audience was spellbound. No noise, restlessness, punching, kicking, running down the aisles. Just eyes lifted up to a fascinating story. Afterward, we asked kids up on the stage to ask questions or talk about the film. What they said indicated how involved they had become.

Kids. And yet most adults will not go to a movie from Iran, Japan, France or Brazil. They will, however, go to any movie that has been plugged with a $30 million ad campaign and sanctified as a "box-office winner." Yes, some of these big hits are good, and a few of them are great. But what happens between the time we are 8 and the time we are 20 that robs us of our curiosity? What turns movie lovers into consumers? What does it say about you if you only want to see what everybody else is seeing?

I don't know. What I do know is that if you love horror movies, your life as a filmgoer is not complete until you see "Nosferatu." I know that once you see Orson Welles appear in the doorway in "The Third Man," you will never forget his curious little smile. And that the life and death of the old man in "Ikiru" will be an inspiration every time you remember it.

I have not written any of the 100 Great Movies reviews from memory. Every film has been seen fresh, right before writing. When I'm at home, I often watch them on Sunday mornings. It's a form of prayer: The greatest films are meditations on why we are here. When I'm on the road, there's no telling where I'll see them. I saw "Written on the Wind" on a cold January night at the Everyman Cinema in Hampstead, north of London. I saw "Last Year at Marienbad" on a DVD on my PowerBook while at the Cannes Film Festival. I saw "2001: A Space Odyssey" in 70mm at Cyberfest, the celebration of HAL 9000's birthday, at the University of Illinois. I saw "Battleship Potemkin" projected on a sheet on the outside wall of the Vickers Theater in Three Oaks, Mich., while three young musicians played the score they had written for it. And Ozu's "Floating Weeds" at the Hawaii Film Festival, as part of a shot-by-shot seminar that took four days.

When people asked me where they should begin in looking at classic films, I never knew what to say. Now I can say, "Plunge into these Great Movies, and go where they lead you."

There's a next step. If you're really serious about the movies, get together with two or three friends who care as much as you do. Watch the film all the way through on video. Then start again at the top. Whenever anyone sees anything they want to comment on, freeze the frame. Talk about what you're looking at. The story, the performances, the sets, the locations. The camera movement, the lighting, the composition, the special effects. The color, the shadows, the sound, the music. The themes, the tone, the mood, the style.

There are no right answers. The questions are the point. They make you an active movie watcher, not a passive one. You should not be a witness at a movie, but a collaborator. Directors cannot make the film without you. Together, you can accomplish amazing things. The more you learn, the quicker you'll know when the director is not doing his share of the job. That's the whole key to being a great moviegoer. There's nothing else to it.

Suggestions for Discussion

1. According to Roger Ebert, what happens to our curiosity level as we get older? Why does this happen?

2. How does Ebert make the case for the greatness of certain older movies and foreign films? How persuasive are his arguments?

3. How does Ebert try to deflect the accusation that he is a film snob?

Suggestions for Writing

1. Watch one of the classic motion pictures that Roger Ebert has cited in this essay and test his theory to see if it is, in actuality, a great movie. Were you inclined not to like the film in advance when you heard that it was an older film or a foreign film? Were you surprised by your reaction when you saw it? Are you interested in seeing more of the movies he has mentioned on his list? Write down your reactions to the film and try to

come to a determination about how you evaluate the relative quality of the movies that you have seen in your life.

2. Make a list of your favorite movies. Compare it with other lists of great films, including those compiled by Roger Ebert, by the American Film Institute, and by the users of the Internet Movie Database (www.imdb.com). What aesthetic taste and artistic criteria seem to be at work in the making of these lists? Are there any other observations that can be made about popular taste and scholarly opinion by examining these lists?

ROGER ROSENBLATT

What's That to Us?

Roger Rosenblatt (b. 1940) was born in New York City. He holds graduate degrees from Harvard University and honorary degrees from several other universities. He has been editor of *The New Republic,* columnist for the *Washington Post,* and contributing editor of the *New York Times Magazine.* He has published a number of books and won numerous journalistic honors. In this short essay, he argues that the traditional canon of English literature is, because of its high quality, meaningful for students from many different backgrounds.

The food was wrong. The medicines were wrong. The clothing was wrong. We took the wrong exercise. We learned the wrong trades. We used the wrong words. One of the more irritating parts of growing older is that you come to find out that everything you did in your youth was wrong. Oh, yes. Our education. Our education was terribly wrong.

How gratifying, then, to be sitting in a movie theater and watching *Sense and Sensibility.* I thought "The hell it was"—the "it" being the education of my over-50 generation, which was a literary education, which was an English literary education, composed of the observations of obsolete Europeans. Extreme multiculturalists declare that the travails of a bunch of DWEMs (dead white European males), or in the case of *Sense and Sensibility,* DWEFs, were none of our business. They say that the curriculum ought to allow for every ethnic group to study its own lit. But we studied English lit., which usually consisted of the efforts of oddly costumed people to keep money or get money, so that they could live happily forever, bowing and curtseying to one another, drinking tea, riding horses, and wailing on the moors. "What's that to us?" the multiculturalists want to know. The question is not entirely a stupid one.

In the late 1960s, when the question was born in universities, I was teaching in a distinguished university whose distinguished English department taught not one black American author. The survey course in American literature not only overlooked the more minor writers like Paul Laurence Dunbar and James Weldon Johnson, it did not include indisputably first-class writers like Richard Wright, Ralph Ellison and James Baldwin. A group of black students, upset at this omission, came to me and asked if I would teach them these writers. I told them that I knew as little about the subject as they did, but that I did know how to plumb a text, and if they were willing to attempt the discovery together, I was their man.

We met as a noncredit seminar for a year, and learned much about African-American writers and, in the process, about America. Amiri Baraka/LeRoi Jones said that a black man who emerges from his own room in America's house, knows the whole house. And so my students and I learned a lot about the whole house of our country—I more than they, who had been living in that special room. But the joy of that course, which soon grew into a large lecture course for credit and became part of the curriculum, was that we were studying black writers as an enrichment of the old canon. Indeed, they justified the stability of the old canon by adding a particular experience to the general, which, no matter how remote it might appear, pertained to black and white, and everyone else, together.

Watching *Sense and Sensibility,* I rediscovered the value of the old canon. I was not alone. My fellow audience members were as ethnically diverse as any urban audience in America, yet we sat together—Latinos, Asians, African-Americans, Jews, Irish, Italians, and maybe a few English descendants as well, all laughing and weeping in the right spots at people and circumstances wholly removed from contemporary experience. This was my education, as it was for most of the readers of this magazine (I assume that *Modern Maturity* may not be given to anyone underage; that is, under age 50). Our standard syllabus could certainly have been improved, with such additions as black writers, but it was quite strong at the core.

Up to a few years ago, a literary education meant the reading of such books as *Great Expectations.* Ethnically diverse though we were, we older generations had no trouble seeing ourselves as laboring boys or as haughty wards, living in draughty manses or traipsing about the brooding English hills. American Pips and Estellas came in every color. It was no hardship to project ourselves into the life of an English prince or a pauper or a housekeeper or a mad young man storming about in a storm. It never occurred to us that merely because our forefathers happened to come from the bogs or from the shtetl or from shacks in the South that we could be denied our noble birthright or our place on the British throne.

T hree reasons for this easy acceptance by association occurred to me as I walked out of *Sense and Sensibility.* One was the attitude of the English themselves, they who created English lit. They might be an island, but they saw themselves as the world, and they built up a navy to prove the point. No Englishman ever worried about being out of it. They *were* it—at least until the Empire struck out. The supreme self-confidence that could be so unattractive in international matters, leading, for example, to their remarkable habit of seizing and subjugating every foreign country they landed in, also enabled them in the arts to speak for all human experience with persuasive authority.

Second, they were good; English literature was/is very good stuff. (The reason my lecture course grew from a seminar was that the material we were reading was very good stuff.) Since the English tongue (or a version of it) was also America's, we were bound to go for English literature no matter what it was like. Luckily for us, most of English lit. was the top of the line. Chaucer, Shakespeare, Donne, Marvell, Milton, Swift, Pope, Johnson, Wordsworth, Keats, and George Eliot, and Jane Austen—you don't get much better than those boys and girls. It was no strain at all to accept the English monarchy as one's own, as long as Shakespeare taught it to speak.

But the third reason, which is probably the most important as regards the value of our archaic, out-of-date education, is that we *wanted* to be dead Englishmen; that is, we gladly gave ourselves over to being people other than whom we were. Keats called this capacity in Shakespeare that of "negative capability"—the ability to translate oneself into a character so wholeheartedly that the self was negated. We older-timers were more than happy to negate ourselves to become Heathcliff, Becky Sharp, Ebenezer Scrooge, or the ladies of *Sense and Sensibility* because by that imaginative leap we ourselves entered into the creative process.

The trouble with extreme multiculturalism, to my way of thinking, has nothing at all to do with its content. Books and stories I've read by Bharati Mukherjee, Oscar Hijuelos, N. Scott Momaday, Richard Rodriguez, and Amy Tan, not to mention Wright, Ellison and Baldwin, are as good as anything written about Hampshire manses and Yorkshire moors. The trouble lies in the attitude adopted by people who argue for multicultural education as a political issue. Instead of seeing the value of the self negated, they want the self pampered and pandered to. They want literature to come to them. They have the queer idea that education has self-esteem as its primary purpose. Self-esteem played a part in the black students' approaching me originally, but the pleasure lay in our esteem of the authors. I like the question, "What's that to us?" because the answer was, and should be, "Nothing."

Great writers do not write to make readers feel good about themselves. More often they write to make us feel troubled about ourselves. But they really do not take much account of us at all. They simply, and not at all simply, beckon us to their world. The test of a good book is whether it is worth negating the self to enter it. The excessive individualism that has poisoned America in recent years, and of which extreme multiculturalism is a by-product, has led to the worst of all things in art and educations—dullness. Individualism carried to extremes not only breaks the social contract, it tends to look the same in every manifestation: "I am proud, I am sensitive, I am misunderstood, I am alone."

The touching beauty of the audience in which I sat at *Sense and Sensibility* is that we were not alone. Together we were eager to become that strange remote past we saw on the screen, which was also our strange remote present. We were there; the story was ours. And when, in the end, Edward Ferrars tells Elinor Dashwood that he is not married, as she had feared, but is free to marry her, and Elinor, who has been so brave and "sensible" throughout, bursts into a tearful, joyful laugh, we all left the theater, mounted up, rode home to our estates and felt like queens and kings of the perfectly green hills.

Suggestions for Discussion

1. What is Rosenblatt's defense of the canon of English literature?

2. Explain Rosenblatt's major disagreement with the concept of multiculturalism in relation to literature. What is Rosenblatt's response to the question, "What's that to us?" Explain why you agree or disagree with his response.

3. What conclusion does Rosenblatt draw from his seminar on African-American writers in the 1960s?

Suggestions for Writing

1. Write an essay in which you agree or disagree with Rosenblatt's position on literature.

2. Write an essay explaining the meaning of the term *negative capability*.

∽∾∽∾∽

PETE ROJAS

Bootleg Culture

Freelance journalist and editor-in-chief of the online magazine *Engadget,* Pete Rojas is an authority in the fields of new media, entertainment, and emerging technologies. He has contributed articles to *Wired, Popular Science,* the *Village Voice,* and the *New York Times.* The following article considers the stifling effect that copyright laws have on the cutting-edge and increasingly popular grassroots "bootleg" movement, in which individuals make their own pop songs, music videos, and films from preexisting material and illegally share the results with others through venues such as YouTube.

ROBERT HUBER, *Subway, New York USA.* 1999. © Robert Huber/www.Lookatonline.com.

When the Belgian DJ duo 2ManyDJs were creating their own album of "bootlegs"—hybrid tracks that mix together other people's songs to create new songs that are at once familiar yet often startlingly different—they decided to get permission to use every one of the hundreds of tracks they mashed together. The result: almost a solid year of calling, e-mailing, and faxing dozens and dozens of record labels all over the world. (Creating the album itself only took about a week.) In the end about a third of their requests were turned down, which isn't surprising. Many artists and their labels have become reluctant to allow any sampling of their work unless they are sure the new work will sell enough copies to generate large royalty checks.

What is surprising are the names of some of the artists who turned them down: the Beastie Boys, Beck, Missy Elliott, Chemical Brothers, and M/A/R/R/S—artists whose own careers are based on sampling and who in some cases have been sued in the past for their own unauthorized sampling. For whatever reason these artists decided not to license their material, the net effect is that more entrenched, "legitimate" sampling artists are preventing lesser known, struggling sampling artists from doing what the legitimate artists probably wish they could have done years ago: sample without hindrance to create new works.

Typically consisting of a vocal track from one song digitally superimposed on the instrumental track of another, bootlegs (or "mash-ups," as they are also called) are being traded over the Internet, and they're proving to be a big hit on dance floors across the U.K. and Europe. In just the past couple of years, hundreds if not thousands of these homebrewed mixes have been created, with music fans going wild over such odd pairings as Soulwax's bootleg of Destiny's Child's "Bootylicious" mixed with Nirvana's "Smells Like Teen Spirit," Freelance Hellraiser's mix of Christina Aguilera singing over the Strokes, and Kurtis Rush's pairing of Missy Elliott rapping over George Michael's "Faith." Bootlegs inject an element of playfulness into a pop music scene that can be distressingly sterile.

While there have been odd pairings, match-ups and remixes for decades now, and club DJs have been doing something similar during live sets, the recent explosion in the number of tracks being created and disseminated is a direct result of the dramatic increase in the power of the average home computer and the widespread use on these computers of new software programs like Acid and ProTools. Home remixing is technically incredibly easy to do, in effect turning the vast world of pop culture into source material for an endless amount of slicing and dicing by desktop producers.

So easy, in fact, that bootlegs constitute the first genre of music that truly fulfills the "anyone can do it" promises originally made by punk and, to lesser extent, electronic music. Even punk rockers had to be able write the most rudimentary of songs. With bootlegs, even that low bar for traditional musicianship and composition is obliterated. Siva Vaidhyanthan, an assistant professor of culture and communication at New York University and the author of "Copyrights and Copywrongs," believes that what we're seeing is the result of a democratization of creativity and the demystification of the process of authorship and creativity.

"It's about demolishing the myth that there has to be a special class of creators, and flattening out the creative curve so we can all contribute to our creative environment," says Vaidhyanthan.

The debate over what bootlegs are and what they mean is taking place within the wider context of a culture where turntables now routinely out-sell guitars, teenagers aspire to be Timbaland and the Automator, No. 1 singles rework or sample other records, and DJs have become pop stars in their own right, even surpassing in fame the very artists whose records they spin. Pop culture in general seems more and more remixed—samples and references are permeating more and more of mainstream music, film, and television, and remix culture appears to resonate strongly with consumers. We're at the point where it almost seems unnatural not to quote, reference, or sample the world around us. To the teens buying the latest all-remixes J.Lo album, dancing at a club to an unauthorized two-step white-label remix of the new Nelly single, or even hacking together their own bootleg, recombination—whether legal or not—doesn't feel wrong in the slightest. The difference now is that they have the tools to sample, reference, and remix, allowing them to finally "talk back" to pop culture in the way that seems most appropriate to them.

The recording industry instinctively fears such unauthorized use of copyrighted materials. But instead of sending out cease-and-desist orders, it should be embracing bootlegs. In a world of constantly recycled sounds and images, bootleg culture is no aberration—it's part of the natural evolution of all things digital.

Bootlegs don't contain any specific audible element of originality in the track, in the sense that one can identify any specific original vocal or musical composition created by the remixer. The only original element of a bootleg is the selection and arrangement of the tracks to be blended into a new work. Scottish bootlegger Grant Robson, who goes by the name Grant McSleazy, responsible for such tracks as Missy Elliott versus the Strokes, readily admits this: "There is a creative aspect, because not all songs work well together, but all the lyric writing and music composition has been done for you. You may rearrange the segments of an instrumental/a capella, but that's just production work."

Even so, isn't production work what constitutes most of what goes into crafting most hip-hop, electronic music, and pop these days? Because of this, bootlegs highlight the increasing difficulty in distinguishing between musicians, DJs and producers. Is there really all that much difference, on a technical level, between McSleazy, DJ Shadow, Moby and P. Diddy? Putting aside any qualitative judgments, on one level or another they are all just appropriators of sound. They are all combining elements of other people's works in order to create new ones, in effect challenging the old model of authorship that presupposes that the building blocks of creativity should spill forth directly from the mind of the artist.

Already we've seen that our notion of what makes a song "creative" has widened in the case of hip-hop. Early on, hip-hop—constructed largely with snippets of other songs—faced similar charges that it lacked a creative element. Eventually, because a great deal of arrangement is involved (usually a large number of samples are blended together to create just a single hip-hop track), and because the rapping itself contributes an original element, pop culture at large has found it easier to acknowledge some aspect of originality and creativity within hip-hop. Bootlegs challenge this notion even further, but it is almost inevitable that as they grow in popularity, something similar will happen, and our definition of creativity will expand to accommodate them.

Existing copyright laws mean that, for the most part, this movement will remain underground. Consequently bootlegs may be the first new genre of music that is almost entirely contraband, and most bootlegs now can only be found on a few Web sites or on file-sharing networks like KaZaA and Gnutella. The bootleggers behind these audio mismatches know they will never get permission from the artists they sample and haven't even bothered to try to get it. Though 2ManyDJs tried to go legit and get permission for as many songs as possible, they still were unable to get clearance for a significant number of samples they used on their album—and even the permissions and clearances they do have are so restricted that it will be impossible to release the album in the United States. Despite the tremendous amount of energy poured into these desktop productions, the fact remains that because the original works cut and pasted together are used without the original artists' permission, bootlegs have stayed, well, bootlegs.

While everyone (particularly the companies touting the technologies that make all this possible) predicted a flood of original movies and music spewing forth from the desktops of bedroom auteurs, no one anticipated that large numbers of people would be more interested in using their computers to combine, mash together, or remix other people's work. Sharing one's unauthorized creations via the Net is even easier. It's a dramatic change from just a few years ago, when a bootlegger's sole option would have been to have vinyl or CDs manufactured and then distributed, something that would risk arousing the attention, and legal action, of the record labels of the remixed artists.

This phenomenon hasn't been limited to music: Remixing has begun to infect film as well. Last year copies of a home-edited version of "Star Wars

Episode 1: The Phantom Menace" began circulating on the Internet to widespread acclaim from fans who declared "Star Wars Episode 1.1: The Phantom Edit" the superior of the two versions. It's probably only a matter of time until someone creates a fan edit of "Attack of the Clones." Inspired by the "Phantom" edit, DJ Hupp, a freelance film editor in Sacramento, Calif., has created his own "Kubrick edit" of Spielberg's "A.I." and it is unlikely that his will be the last fan edit we see of a major motion picture.

Such fan edits are also, technically, illegal, but from the perspective of the turntablists, remixers, and home editors at the forefront of the explosion of bootleg culture, copyright laws don't look like anything other than the means by which one group of artists limits the work of another.

Illegality can actually be a large part of the allure of bootlegs. Much underground cultural expression takes place at the margins of the law—rave culture, for example, has its origins in illegal warehouse parties. Using other people's music without permission used to be the point of mash-ups. Back in the '80s and early '90s, when culture-jamming sound collagists like Negativland and the Evolution Control Committee released their first works, mash-ups had a decidedly subversive edge to them. Mash-ups were typically created as statements about pop culture and the media juggernaut that surrounds us, not as fodder for the dance floor. Pasting together elements swiped from the top 40 and placing them together in a new form was supposed to snap us out of what these sonic outlaws saw as our media-induced trance and make a point about copyright in the process.

Traces of that element remain in the bootlegs being made today. One Australian bootlegger, a 26-year-old who goes by the name Dsico, and for legal reasons prefers that his identity be withheld, sees bootlegs as akin to the kitschiness and pastiche of pop art. "The reinterpretation and recontextualization of cultural icons like Britney Spears or the Strokes is fun and good for a laugh. But if I can grab an a cappella track of Mandy Moore and mix it with something like "Roxanne" by the Police, while that juxtaposition may be trite, it still works as a commentary on pop music today."

And at a time when it has become increasingly difficult for pop music to be shocking (witness the mainstream acceptability, however grudging, of Eminem), it may be that the only way to write a transgressive pop song is to flat-out steal it from someone else. In other words, the only way left to shock is not through controversial content, but by subverting the very form and structure of the song itself.

Even though making music out of other people's songs without permission may appear to pose a threat to the business model of the recording industry, killing off this nascent genre may not ultimately be in the industry's best interests. Radio stations in Britain that have played bootlegs have found themselves on the receiving end of cease-and-desist orders. Hip-hop got its start using pre-existing music in innovative and not always legal ways.

It is arguable that had the music industry clamped down on sampling earlier than it did (it wasn't until a 1991 suit against rapper Biz Markie that sampling without permission was established as illegal), the industry's top-selling genre would never have gotten off the ground commercially. Now legendary hip-hop albums, such as Public Enemy's "It Takes a Nation of Millions to Hold Us Back," and the Beastie Boys' "Paul's Boutique," would be impossible to release today.

Just as with every other subcultural movement that has threatened the status quo, the music industry's best response may be to let the genre flourish online and on the margins. So far no one is really making any money from bootlegs—if anything, bootlegs stimulate demand for the original songs. Rather than threaten bootleggers with legal action, a sounder strategy would be to co-opt the scene by skimming the best ones off the top and re-releasing them as "official" bootlegs. This has already produced one No. 1 hit, with Richard X's mash-up of new waver Gary Numan and soul singer Adina Howard. The track follows in the footsteps of DNA's bootleg dance remix of Suzanne Vega's "Tom's Diner," which Vega ended up authorizing and re-releasing to much chart success in 1990.

As computers and software programs get more and more powerful with each passing year, as file-sharing networks make it simple for anyone to share their work with the world, and as it is next to impossible to outlaw digital editing software (which has plenty of legitimate uses), bootlegs and remixes will likely be a part of the cultural landscape for years to come. Bootlegging may even evolve into something of a hobby for tens of thousands of desktop producers who will spend their free time splicing together the latest top 40 hits for kicks, like model-airplane builders. The record industry could even respond by selling its own do-it-yourself bootleg kits, complete with editing software and authorized samples. In a sense bootlegs are music fans' response to the current disposability of pop culture. Effortlessly easy to create, with an infinite number of combinations possible, bootlegs are even more perfectly disposable than the pop songs they combine—by the time the novelty and the cleverness have worn off there will always be new hit singles to mash together.

Eventually recombining and remixing is likely to become so prevalent that it will be all but impossible to even identify the original source of samples, making questions about authorship and origins largely irrelevant, or at least unanswerable. We're already seeing the beginnings of that, like the hip-hop song that samples an older hip-hop song that samples a '70s funk song. Some artists, most notably David Bowie, are already proclaiming the death of authorship altogether. Technology has not only expanded who can create; in blurring the distinction between consumers and producers, these new digital tools are also challenging the very ideas of creativity and authorship. They are forcing us to recognize modes of cultural production that often make it impossible to answer such once simple questions as, Who wrote this song? The cultural landscape that emerges will be a plural space of creation in which it may even become pointless to designate who created exactly what, since everyone will be stealing from and remixing everyone else. The results might be confusing, but it'll probably be a lot more fun and worth listening to than a world where only those with the financial resources to pay licensing fees (e.g., P. Diddy) get to make songs with sampling.

Suggestions for Discussion

1. Rojas asserts that modern copyright laws are so strict that classic albums such as the Beastie Boys' *Paul's Boutique* couldn't be released legally today. He also begins his essay with a story of 2ManyDJs' attempts to release a legal bootleg album that was met with great resistance and, in some ways, failed. How do these anecdotes influence the tone and slant of the article? To what extent do you sympathize with 2ManyDJs? To what extent does this essay encourage "stealing" music?

2. Given how easy it is for anyone with a little knowledge of computers to "steal" songs and films these days, and to remix them, what will be the incentive for future artists to produce truly "original" works when they can no longer expect to make a profit from them, or feel reassured that their work is protected from "tampering"? Furthermore, won't "Bootleg Culture" ultimately collapse when fewer truly "new" songs are released to remix?

3. According to Rojas, the Bootleg movement has traits in common with the Pop Art movement. Where is the overlap? The *Reading Images* chapter of *The Conscious Reader* includes several pieces of Pop Art, such as one by Andy Warhol. How is Pop Art like a remixed piece of music, or like a re-edited movie in the vein of *Star Wars: The Phantom Edit*?

4. Please go back to the beginning of the Rojas essay and examine the accompanying image. How does impersonating Elvis, bringing him to life in the modern era, act as a form of "remixing" music and history? What is it about Elvis, who died more than 30 years ago, that continues to fascinate people? Is impersonating Elvis an act of devotion? An escape? An artistic statement? A form of live theater? Is it a form of copyright infringement? Is there a person, real or fictional, of whom you are a passionate fan? Would you imitate or impersonate your hero?

Suggestion for Writing

Compare this essay to Melissa Etheridge's essay. To what extent is music still a "Safe Haven" in the world of Bootleg Culture? Write your thoughts in a four-paragraph essay.

FICTION

∾∾∾∾

WILLA CATHER

The Sculptor's Funeral

Willa Cather (1873–1947) was born in Virginia and grew up in Nebraska. On leaving the University of Nebraska, where as an undergraduate she had written for a Lincoln newspaper, she worked in Pittsburgh as a reporter and then as a teacher, and she wrote her first collection of stories, *The Troll Garden* (1905). Her works include *My Antonia (1918), A Lost Lady (1923), The Professor's House* (1925), *Death Comes for the Archbishop (1927),* and *Sapphira and the Slave Girl* (1940), which dealt with her native Virginia. In her writing, she celebrated the frontier spirit, whether of art or of action.

PHILLIP DE LOACH, *"Paying Attention to Details"*—*Assemblage #2.* Found objects: metal, wood, paint, 2003. Courtesy of the artist. Digital image: © www.foto-lounge.de.

A group of the townspeople stood on the station siding of a little Kansas town, awaiting the coming of the night train, which was already twenty minutes overdue. The snow had fallen thick over everything; in the pale starlight the line of bluffs across the wide, white meadows south of the town made soft, smoke-coloured curves against the clear sky. The men on the siding stood first on one foot and then on the other, their hands thrust deep into their trousers pockets, their overcoats open, their shoulders screwed up with the cold; and they glanced from time to time toward the southeast, where the railroad track wound along the river shore. They conversed in low tones and moved about restlessly, seeming uncertain as to what was expected of them. There was but one of the company who looked as though he knew exactly why he was there; and he kept conspicuously apart; walking to the far end of the platform, returning to the station door, then pacing up the track again, his chin sunk in the high collar of his overcoat, his burly shoulders drooping forward, his gait heavy and dogged. Presently he was approached by a tall, spare, grizzled man clad in a faded Grand Army suit, who shuffled out from the group and advanced with a certain deference, craning his neck forward until his back made the angle of a jackknife three-quarters open.

"I reckon she's a-goin' to be pretty late agin tonight, Jim," he remarked in a squeaky falsetto. "S'pose it's the snow?"

"I don't know," responded the other man with a shade of annoyance, speaking from out an astonishing cataract of red beard that grew fiercely and thickly in all directions.

The spare man shifted the quill toothpick he was chewing to the other side of his mouth. "It ain't likely that anybody from the East will come with the corpse, I s'pose," he went on reflectively.

"I don't know," responded the other, more curtly than before.

"It's too bad he didn't belong to some lodge or other. I like an order funeral myself. They seem more appropriate for people of some repytation," the spare man continued, with an ingratiating concession in his shrill voice, as he carefully placed his toothpick in his vest pocket. He always carried the flag at the G.A.R. funerals in the town.

The heavy man turned on his heel, without replying, and walked up the siding. The spare man shuffled back to the uneasy group. "Jim's ez full ez a tick, ez ushel," he commented commiseratingly.

Just then a distant whistle sounded, and there was a shuffling of feet on the platform. A number of lanky boys of all ages appeared as suddenly and slimily as eels wakened by the crack of thunder; some came from the waiting-room, where they had been warming themselves by the red stove, or half asleep on the slat benches; others uncoiled themselves from baggage trucks or slid out of express wagons. Two clambered down from the driver's seat of a hearse that stood backed up against the siding. They straightened their

stooping shoulders and lifted their heads, and a flash of momentary anima-
tion kindled their dull eyes at that cold, vibrant scream, the world-wide call
for men. It stirred them like the note of a trumpet; just as it had often stirred
the man who was coming home tonight, in his boyhood.

The night express shot, red as a rocket, from out the eastward marsh
lands and wound along the river shore under the long lines of shivering
poplars that sentineled the meadows, the escaping steam hanging in grey
masses against the pale sky and blotting out the Milky Way. In a moment
the red glare from the headlight streamed up the snow-covered track before
the siding and glittered on the wet, black rails. The burly man with the
dishevelled red beard walked swiftly up the platform toward the approaching train, uncovering his head as he went. The group of men behind him
hesitated, glanced questioningly at one another, and awkwardly followed his
example. The train stopped, and the crowd shuffled up to the express car
just as the door was thrown open, the spare man in the G.A.R. suit thrust-
ing his head forward with curiosity. The express messenger appeared in the
doorway, accompanied by a young man in a long ulster and traveling cap.
"Are Mr. Merrick's friends here?" inquired the young man. The group on
the platform swayed and shuffled uneasily. Philip Phelps, the banker,
responded with dignity: "We have come to take charge of the body. Mr. Merrick's father is very feeble and can't be about."

"Send the agent out here," growled the express messenger, "and tell the
operator to lend a hand."

The coffin was got out of its rough box and down on the snowy
platform. The townspeople drew back enough to make room for it and then
formed a close semicircle about it, looking curiously at the palm leaf which
lay across the black cover. No one said anything. The baggage man stood
by his truck, waiting to get at the trunks. The engine panted heavily, and
the fireman dodged in and out among the wheels with his yellow torch and
long oilcan, snapping the spindle boxes. The young Bostonian, one of the
dead sculptor's pupils who had come with the body, looked about him
helplessly. He turned to the banker, the only one of that black, uneasy, stoop-
shouldered group who seemed enough of an individual to be addressed.

"None of Mr. Merrick's brothers are here?" he asked uncertainly.

The man with the red beard for the first time stepped up and joined the
group. "No, they have not come yet: the family is scattered. The body will be
taken directly to the house." He stooped and took hold of one of the handles of the coffin.

"Take the long hill road up, Thompson, it will be easier on the horses,"
called the liveryman as the undertaker snapped the door of the hearse and
prepared to mount to the driver's seat.

Laird, the red-bearded lawyer, turned again to the stranger: "We didn't
know whether there would be anyone with him or not," he explained. "It's

a long walk, so you'd better go up in the hack." He pointed to a single bat-tered conveyance, but the young man replied stiffly: "Thank you, but I think I will go up with the hearse. If you don't object," turning to the undertaker, "I'll ride with you."

They clambered up over the wheels and drove off in the starlight up the long, white hill toward the town. The lamps in the still village were shining from under the low, snow-burdened roofs; and beyond, on every side, the plains reached out into emptiness, peaceful and wide as the soft sky itself, and wrapped in a tangible, white silence.

When the hearse backed up to a wooden sidewalk before a naked, weather-beaten frame house, the same composite, ill-defined group that had stood upon the station siding was huddled about the gate. The front yard was an icy swamp, and a couple of warped planks, extending from the side-walk to the door, made a sort of rickety footbridge. The gate hung on one hinge, and was opened wide with difficulty. Steavens, the young stranger, noticed that something black was tied to the knob of the front door.

The grating sound made by the casket, as it was drawn from the hearse, was answered by a scream from the house; the front door was wrenched open, and a tall, corpulent woman rushed out bareheaded into the snow and flung herself upon the coffin, shrieking: "My boy, my boy! And this is how you've come home to me!"

As Steavens turned away and closed his eyes with a shudder of unutter-able repulsion, another woman, also tall, but flat and angular, dressed entirely in black, darted out of the house and caught Mrs. Merrick by the shoulders, crying sharply: "Come, come, mother; you mustn't go on like this!" Her tone changed to one of obsequious solemnity as she turned to the banker: "The parlour is ready, Mr. Phelps."

The bearers carried the coffin along the narrow boards, while the under-taker ran ahead with the coffin rests. They bore it into a large, unheated room that smelled of dampness and disuse and furniture polish, and set it down under a hanging lamp ornamented with jingling glass prisms and before a "Rogers group" of John Alden and Priscilla, wreathed with smilax. Henry Steavens stared about him with the sickening conviction that there had been some horrible mistake, and that he had somehow arrived at the wrong destination. He looked painfully about over the clover-green Brus-sels, the fat plush upholstery; among the hand-painted china plaques and panels, and vases, for some mark of identification, for something that might once conceivably have belonged to Harvey Merrick. It was not until he rec-ognized his friend in the crayon portrait of a little boy in kilts and curls hanging above the piano, that he felt willing to let any of these people approach the coffin.

"Take the lid off, Mr. Thompson; let me see my boy's face," wailed the elderly woman between her sobs. This time Steavens looked fearfully, almost beseechingly into her face, red and swollen under its masses of strong, black, shiny hair. He flushed, dropped his eyes, and then, almost incredulously, looked again. There was a kind of power about her face—a kind of brutal handsomeness, even, but it was scarred and furrowed by violence, and so coloured and coarsened by fiercer passions that grief seemed never to have laid a gentle finger there. The long nose was distended and knobbed at the end, and there were deep lines on either side of it; her heavy, black brows almost met across her forehead, her teeth were large and square, and set far apart—teeth that could tear. She filled the room; the men were obliterated, seemed tossed about like twigs in an angry water, and even Steavens felt himself being drawn into the whirlpool.

The daughter—the tall, raw-boned woman in crêpe, with a mourning comb in her hair which curiously lengthened her long face—sat stiffly upon the sofa, her hands, conspicuous for their large knuckles, folded in her lap, her mouth and eyes drawn down, solemnly awaiting the opening of the coffin. Near the door stood a mulatto woman, evidently a servant in the house, with a timid bearing and an emaciated face pitifully sad and gentle. She was weeping silently, the corner of her calico apron lifted to her eyes, occasionally suppressing a long, quivering sob. Steavens walked over and stood beside her.

Feeble steps were heard on the stairs, and an old man, tall and frail, odorous of pipe smoke, with shaggy, unkempt grey hair and a dingy beard, tobacco stained about the mouth, entered uncertainly. He went slowly up to the coffin and stood rolling a blue cotton handkerchief between his hands, seeming so pained and embarrassed by his wife's orgy of grief that he had no consciousness of anything else.

"There, there, Annie, dear, don't take on so," he quavered timidly, putting out a shaking hand and awkwardly patting her elbow. She turned with a cry, and sank upon his shoulder with such violence that he tottered a little. He did not even glance toward the coffin, but continued to look at her with a dull, frightened, appealing expression, as a spaniel looks at the whip. His sunken cheeks slowly reddened and burned with miserable shame. When his wife rushed from the room, her daughter strode after her with set lips. The servant stole up to the coffin, bent over it for a moment, and then slipped away to the kitchen, leaving Steavens, the lawyer, and the father to themselves. The old man stood trembling and looking down at his dead son's face. The sculptor's splendid head seemed even more noble in its rigid stillness than in life. The dark hair had crept down upon the wide forehead; the face seemed strangely long, but in it there was not that beautiful and chaste repose which we expect to find in the faces of the dead. The brows were so drawn that there were two deep lines above the beaked nose, and the chin was thrust forward defiantly. It was as though the strain of life had been so sharp and bitter that death could not at once wholly relax the tension and smooth the countenance into perfect peace—as though he were still guarding something precious and holy, which might even yet be wrested from him.

The old man's lips were working under his stained beard. He turned to the lawyer with timid deference: "Phelps and the rest are comin' back to set up with Harve, ain't they?" he asked. "Thank 'ee, Jim, thank 'ee." He brushed the hair back gently from his son's forehead. "He was a good boy, Jim; always a good boy. He was ez gentle ez a child and the kindest of 'em all—only we didn't none of us ever onderstand him." The tears trickled slowly down his beard and dropped upon the sculptor's coat.

"Martin, Martin. Oh, Martin! come here," his wife wailed from the top of the stairs. The old man started timorously: "Yes, Annie, I'm coming." He turned away, hesitated, stood for a moment in miserable indecision; then reached back and patted the dead man's hair softly, and stumbled from the room.

"Poor old man, I didn't think he had any tears left. Seems as if his eyes would have gone dry long ago. At his age nothing cuts very deep," remarked the lawyer.

Something in his tone made Steavens glance up. While the mother had been in the room, the young man had scarcely seen any one else; but now, from the moment he first glanced into Jim Laird's florid face and bloodshot eyes, he knew that he had found what he had been heartsick at not finding before—the feeling, the understanding that must exist in some one, even here.

The man was red as his beard, with features swollen and blurred by dissipation, and a hot, blazing blue eye. His face was strained—that of a man who is controlling himself with difficulty—and he kept plucking at his beard with a sort of fierce resentment. Steavens, sitting by the window, watched him turn down the glaring lamp, still its jangling pendants with an angry gesture, and then stand with his hands locked behind him, staring down into the master's face. He could not help wondering what link there could have been between the porcelain vessel and so sooty a lump of potter's clay.

From the kitchen an uproar was sounding; when the dining-room door opened, the import of it was clear. The mother was abusing the maid for having forgotten to make the dressing for the chicken salad which had been prepared for the watchers. Steavens had never heard anything in the least like it; it was injured, emotional, dramatic abuse, unique and masterly in its excruciating cruelty, as violent and unrestrained as had been her grief of twenty minutes before. With a shudder of disgust the lawyer went into the dining room and closed the door into the kitchen.

"Poor Roxy's getting it now," he remarked when he came back. "The Merricks took her out of the poorhouse years ago; and if her loyalty would let her, I guess the poor old thing could tell tales that would curdle your blood. She's the mulatto woman who was standing in here a while ago, with her apron to her eyes. The old woman is a fury; there never was anybody like her for demonstrative piety and ingenious cruelty. She made Harvey's life a hell for him when he lived at home; he was so sick ashamed of it. I never could see how he kept himself so sweet."

"He was wonderful," said Steavens slowly, "wonderful; but until tonight I have never known how wonderful."

"That is the true and eternal wonder of it, anyway; that it can come even from such a dung heap as this," the lawyer cried, with a sweeping gesture which seemed to indicate much more than the four walls within which they stood.

"I think I'll see whether I can get a little air. The room is so close I am beginning to feel rather faint," murmured Steavens, struggling with one of the windows. The sash was stuck, however, and would not yield, so he sat down dejectedly and began pulling at his collar. The lawyer came over, loosened the sash with one blow of his red fist and sent the window up a few inches. Steavens thanked him, but the nausea which had been gradually climbing into his throat for the last half hour left him with but one desire—a desperate feeling that he must get away from this place with what was left of Harvey Merrick. Oh, he comprehended well enough now the quiet bitterness of the smile that he had seen so often on his master's lips!

He remembered that once, when Merrick returned from a visit home, he brought with him a singularly feeling and suggestive bas-relief of a thin, faded old woman, sitting and sewing something pinned to her knee; while a full-lipped, full-blooded little urchin, his trousers held up by a single gallus, stood beside her, impatiently twitching her gown to call her attention to a butterfly he had caught. Steavens, impressed by the tender and delicate modelling of the thin, tired face, had asked him if it were his mother. He remembered the dull flush that had burned up in the sculptor's face.

The lawyer was sitting in a rocking-chair beside the coffin, his head thrown back and his eyes closed. Steavens looked at him earnestly, puzzled at the line of the chin, and wondering why a man should conceal a feature of such distinction under that disfiguring shock of beard. Suddenly, as though he felt the young sculptor's keen glance, he opened his eyes.

"Was he always a good deal of an oyster?" he asked abruptly. "He was terribly shy as a boy."

"Yes, he was an oyster, since you put it so," rejoined Steavens. "Although he could be very fond of people, he always gave one the impression of being detached. He disliked violent emotion; he was reflective, and rather distrustful of himself—except, of course, as regarded his work. He was sure-footed enough there. He distrusted men pretty thoroughly and women even more, yet somehow without believing ill of them. He was determined, indeed, to believe the best, but he seemed afraid to investigate."

"A burnt dog dreads the fire," said the lawyer grimly, and closed his eyes. Steavens went on and on, reconstructing that whole miserable boyhood. All this raw, biting ugliness had been the portion of the man whose tastes were refined beyond the limits of the reasonable—whose mind was an exhaustless gallery of beautiful impressions, and so sensitive that the mere shadow of a poplar leaf flickering against a sunny wall would be etched and held there forever. Surely, if ever a man had the magic word in his fingertips, it was Merrick. Whatever he touched, he revealed its holiest secret; liberated it from enchantment and restored to it its pristine loveliness, like the Arabian prince who fought the enchantress spell for spell. Upon whatever he had come in contact with, he had left a beautiful record of the experience—a sort of ethereal signature; a scent, a sound, a colour that was his own.

Steavens understood now the real tragedy of his master's life; neither love nor wine, as many had conjectured; but a blow which had fallen earlier and cut deeper than these could have done—a shame not his, and yet so unescapably his, to hide in his heart from his very boyhood. And without—the frontier warfare; the yearning of a boy, cast ashore upon a desert of newness and ugliness and sordidness, for all that is chastened and old, and noble with traditions.

At eleven o'clock the tall, flat woman in black crêpe entered and announced that the watchers were arriving, and asked them "to step into the dining-room." As Steavens rose, the lawyer said dryly: "You go on—it'll be a good experience for you, doubtless; as for me, I'm not equal to that crowd tonight; I've had twenty years of them."

As Steavens closed the door after him he glanced back at the lawyer, sitting by the coffin in the dim light, with his chin resting on his hand.

The same misty group that had stood before the door of the express car shuffled into the dining room. In the light of the kerosene lamp they separated and became individuals. The minister, a pale, feeble-looking man with white hair and blond chin-whiskers, took his seat beside a small side table and placed his Bible upon it. The Grand Army man sat down behind the stove and tilted his chair back comfortably against the wall, fishing his quill toothpick from his waistcoat pocket. The two bankers, Phelps and Elder, sat off in a corner behind the dinner table, where they could finish their discussion of the new usury law and its effect on chattel security loans. The real estate agent, an old man with a smiling, hypocritical face, soon joined them. The coal and lumber dealer and the cattle shipper sat on opposite sides of the hard coal-burner, their feet on the nickelwork. Steavens took a book from his pocket and began to read. The talk around him ranged through various topics of local interest while the house was quieting down. When it was clear that the members of the family were in bed, the Grand Army man hitched his shoulders and, untangling his long legs, caught his heels on the rounds of his chair.

"S'pose there'll be a will, Phelps?" he queried in his weak falsetto.

The banker laughed disagreeably, and began trimming his nails with a pearl-handled pocketknife.

"There'll scarcely be any need for one, will there?" he queried in his turn.

The restless Grand Army man shifted his position again, getting his knees still nearer his chin. "Why, the ole man says Harve's done right well lately," he chirped.

The other banker spoke up. "I reckon he means by that Harve ain't asked him to mortgage any more farms lately, so as he could go on with his education."

"Seems like my mind don't reach back to a time when Harve wasn't bein' edycated," tittered the Grand Army man.

There was a general chuckle. The minister took out his handkerchief and blew his nose sonorously. Banker Phelps closed his knife with a snap. "It's too bad the old man's sons didn't turn out better," he remarked with reflective authority. "They never hung together. He spent money enough on Harve to stock a dozen cattle farms and he might as well have poured it into Sand Creek. If Harve had stayed at home and helped nurse what little they had, and gone into stock on the old man's bottom farm, they might all have been well fixed. But the old man had to trust everything to tenants and was cheated right and left."

"Harve never could have handled stock none," interposed the cattleman. "He hadn't it in him to be sharp. Do you remember when he bought Sander's mules for eight-year-olds, when everybody in town knew that Sander's father-in-law give 'em to his wife for a wedding present eighteen years before, an' they was full-grown mules then."

Every one chuckled, and the Grand Army man rubbed his knees with a spasm of childish delight.

"Harve never was much account for anything practical, and he shore was never fond of work," began the coal and lumber dealer. "I mind the last time he was home; the day he left, when the old man was out to the barn helpin' his hand hitch up to take Harve to the train, and Cal Moots was patchin' up the fence, Harve, he come out on the step and sings out, in his ladylike voice: 'Cal Moots, Cal Moots! please come cord my trunk.'"

"That's Harve for you," approved the Grand Army man gleefully. "I kin hear him howlin' yet when he was a big feller in long pants and his mother used to whale him with a rawhide in the barn for lettin' the cows get foundered in the cornfield when he was drivin' 'em home from pasture. He killed a cow of mine that-a-way onct—a pure Jersey and the best milker I had, an' the ole man had to put up for her. Harve, he was watchin' the sun set acrost the marshes when the anamile got away; he argued that sunset was oncommon fine."

"Where the old man made his mistake was in sending the boy East to school," said Phelps, stroking his goatee and speaking in a deliberate, judicial tone. "There was where he got his head full of trapesing to Paris and all such folly. What Harve needed, of all people, was a course in some first-class Kansas City business college."

The letters were swimming before Steavens's eyes. Was it possible that these men did not understand, that the palm of the coffin meant nothing to them? The very name of their town would have remained forever buried in the postal guide had it not been now and again mentioned in the world in connection with Harvey Merrick's. He remembered what his master had said to him on the day of his death, after the congestion of both lungs had shut off any probability of recovery, and the sculptor had asked his pupil to send his body home. "It's not a pleasant place to be lying while the world is moving and doing and bettering," he had said with a feeble smile, "but it rather seems as though we ought to go back to the place we came from in the end. The townspeople will come in for a look at me; and after they have had their say I shan't have much to fear from the judgment of God. The wings of the Victory, in there"—with a weak gesture toward his studio—"will not shelter me."

The cattleman took up the comment. "Forty's young for a Merrick to cash in; they usually hang on pretty well. Probably he helped it along with whisky."

"His mother's people were not long-lived, and Harve never had a robust constitution," said the minister mildly. He would have liked to say more. He had been the boy's Sunday-school teacher, and had been fond of him; but he felt that he was not in a position to speak. His own sons had turned out badly, and it was not a year since one of them had made his last trip home in the express car, shot in a gambling house in the Black Hills.

"Nevertheless, there is no disputin' that Harvey frequently looked upon the wine when it was red, also variegated, and it shore made an oncommon fool of him," moralized the cattleman.

Just then the door leading into the parlor rattled loudly and everyone started involuntarily, looking relieved when only Jim Laird came out. His red face was convulsed with anger, and the Grand Army man ducked his head when he saw the spark in his blue, bloodshot eye. They were all afraid of Jim; he was a drunkard, but he could twist the law to suit his client's needs as no other man in all western Kansas could do; and there were many who tried. The lawyer closed the door gently behind him, leaned back against it and folded his arms, cocking his head a little to one side. When he assumed this attitude in the courtroom, ears were always pricked up, as it usually foretold a flood of withering sarcasm.

"I've been with you gentlemen before," he began in a dry, even tone, "when you've sat by the coffins of boys born and raised in this town; and, if I remember rightly, you were never any too well satisfied when you checked them up. What's the matter, anyhow? Why is it that reputable young men are as scarce as millionaires in Sand City? It might almost seem to a stranger that there was some way something the matter with your progressive town. Why did Ruben Sayer, the brightest young lawyer you ever turned out, after he had come home from the university as straight as a die, take to drinking and forge a check and shoot himself? Why did Bill Merrit's son die of the shakes in a saloon in Omaha? Why was Mr. Thomas's son, here, shot in a gambling-house? Why did young Adams burn his mill to beat the insurance companies and go to the pen?"

The lawyer paused and unfolded his arms, laying one clenched fist quietly on the table. "I'll tell you why. Because you drummed nothing but money and knavery into their ears from the time they wore knickerbockers; because you carped away at them as you've been carping here tonight, holding our friends Phelps and Elder up to them for their models, as our grandfathers held up George Washington and John Adams. But the boys, worse luck, were young and raw at the business you put them to; and how could they match coppers with such artists as Phelps and Elder? You wanted them to be successful rascals; they were only unsuccessful ones—that's all the difference. There was only one boy ever raised in this borderland between ruffianism and civilization, who didn't come to grief, and you hated Harvey Merrick more for winning out than you hated all the other boys who got under the wheels. Lord, Lord, how you did hate him! Phelps, here, is fond of saying that he could buy and sell us all out any time he's a mind to; but he knew Harve wouldn't have given a tinker's damn for his bank and all his cattle farms put together; and a lack of appreciation, that way, goes hard with Phelps.

"Old Nimrod, here, thinks Harve drank too much; and this from such as Nimrod and me!

"Brother Elder says Harve was too free with the old man's money—fell short in filial consideration, maybe. Well, we can all remember the very tone in which brother Elder swore his own father was a liar, in the county court; and we all know that the old man came out of that partnership with his son as bare as a sheared lamb. But maybe I'm getting personal, and I'd better be driving ahead at what I want to say."

The lawyer paused a moment, squared his heavy shoulders, and went on: "Harvey Merrick and I went to school together, back East. We were dead in earnest, and we wanted you all to be proud of us some day. We meant to be great men. Even I, and I haven't lost my sense of humour, gentlemen, I meant to be a great man. I came back here to practise, and I found you didn't in the least want me to be a great man. You wanted me to be a shrewd lawyer—oh, yes! Our veteran here wanted me to get him an increase of pension, because he had dyspepsia; Phelps wanted a new country survey that would put the widow Wilson's little bottom farm inside his south line; Elder wanted to lend money at 5 percent a month, and get it collected; old Stark here wanted to wheedle old women up in

Vermont into investing their annuities in real-estate mortgages that are not worth the paper they are written on. Oh, you needed me hard enough, and you'll go on needing me; and that's why I'm not afraid to plug the truth home to you this once.

"Well, I came back here and became the damned shyster you wanted me to be. You pretend to have some sort of respect for me; and yet you'll stand up and throw mud at Harvey Merrick, whose soul you couldn't dirty and whose hands you couldn't tie. Oh, you're a discriminating lot of Christians! There have been times when the sight of Harvey's name in some Eastern paper has made me hang my head like a whipped dog; and, again, times when I liked to think of him off there in the world, away from all this hogwallow, doing his great work and climbing the big, clean upgrade he'd set for himself.

"And we? Now that we've fought and lied and sweated and stolen, and hated as only the disappointed strugglers in a bitter, dead little Western town know how to do, what have we got to show for it? Harvey Merrick wouldn't have given one sunset over your marshes for all you've got put together, and you know it. It's not for me to say why, in the inscrutable wisdom of God, a genius should ever have been called from his place of hatred and bitter waters; but I want this Boston man to know that the drivel he's been hearing here tonight is the only tribute any truly great man could ever have from such a lot of sick, side-tracked, burnt-dog, land-poor sharks as the here-present financiers of Sand City—upon which town may God have mercy!"

The lawyer thrust out his hand to Steavens as he passed him, caught up his overcoat in the hall, and had left the house before the Grand Army man had had time to lift his ducked head and crane his long neck about at his fellows.

Next day Jim Laird was drunk and unable to attend the funeral services. Steavens called twice at his office, but was compelled to start East without seeing him. He had a presentiment that he would hear from him again, and left his address on the lawyer's table; but if Laird found it, he never acknowledged it. The thing in him that Harvey Merrick had loved must have gone underground with Harvey Merrick's coffin; for it never spoke again, and Jim got the cold he died of driving across the Colorado mountains to defend one of Phelps's sons who had got into trouble out there by cutting government timber.

Suggestions for Discussion

1. Discuss the details Cather uses to characterize the small Kansas town to which the dead sculptor's body is brought for burial. Why is Steavens repelled by the furnishings in the house of Merrick's mother?

2. The sculptor's mother is overcome by grief. Steavens is disgusted by her outburst of emotion. Why? Explain how Cather arranges details so that we will agree with Steavens.

3. How does Cather contrast Mrs. Merrick with her daughter? What function do both characters have in the story?

4. Why does Cather portray Jim Laird as a heavy drinker? What is his function in the story?

5. What was the real tragedy of the dead sculptor's life? How had it affected his work?

6. What is the theme of Cather's story? Why does she use the long speech by Laird to express it?

Suggestions for Writing

1. Cather's view of the artist as somehow alienated from his society is illustrated in this story. Write a paper dealing with the issue, using examples of well-known artists. You might make this a research project by investigating the life of Beethoven, Mozart, Baudelaire, or Poe. What about the relation of the artists to society in other cultures, for example, China, India, or Bali?

2. The sculptor has been buried. Imagine the accompanying artwork *"Paying Attention to Detail"*—*Assemblage #2* as being the artist's last work, about to be auctioned off at a well-known auction house. Write an appraisal for this unique piece of art. Be imaginative. Be compelling. Sell the art.

POETRY

SONIA SANCHEZ

A Poem for Ella Fitzgerald

Sonia Sanchez (b. 1934), a poet, playwright, and children's fiction writer, was born in Birmingham, AL, and moved to Harlem at the age of nine. She graduated from Hunter College with a political science degree and did graduate work at New York University before going on to become the first college professor to ever offer a course on African American women writers. She is a retired professor of creative writing and Black American literature at Temple University. She is the author *of I've Been a Woman* (1978), *Homegirls and Handgrenades* (1984), *Under a Soprano Sky* (1987), *Wounded in the House of a Friend* (1995), *Does Your House Have Lions?* (1997), *Like the Singing Coming off the Drums* (1998), and *Shake Loose My Skin* (1999).

when she came on the stage, this Ella
there were rumors of hurricanes and
over the rooftops of concert stages
the moon turned red in the sky,
it was Ella, Ella.
queen Ella had come
and words spilled out
leaving a trail of witnesses smiling
amen—amen—a woman—a woman.

she began
this three agèd woman
nightingales in her throat
and squads of horns came out
to greet her.

streams of violins and pianos
splashed their welcome
and our stained glass silences
our braided spaces

unraveled
opened up
said who's that coming?
who's that knocking at the door?
whose voice lingers on
that stage gone mad with
    perdido. perdido. perdido.
    i lost my heart in toledoooooo.

whose voice is climbing
up this morning chimney
smoking with life
carrying her basket of words
    a tisket a tasket
    my little yellow
    basket—i wrote a
    letter to my mom and
    on the way I dropped it—
    was it red . . . no no no no
    was it green . . . no no no no
    was it blue . . . no no no no
    just a little yellow

voice rescuing razor thin lyrics
from hopscotching dreams.

we first watched her navigating
an apollo stage amid high-stepping
yellow legs

we watched her watching us
shiny and pure woman
sugar and spice woman
her voice a nun's whisper
her voice pouring out
guitar thickened blues,
her voice a faraway horn
questioning the wind,
and she became Ella,
first lady of tongues
Ella cruising our veins
voice walking on water

crossed in prayer,
she became holy
a thousand sermons
concealed in her bones
as she raised them in a
symphonic shudder
carrying our sighs into
her bloodstream.

this voice, chasing the
morning waves,
this Ella-tonian voice soft
like four layers of lace.
 when i die Ella
 tell the whole joint
 please, please, don't talk
 about me when i'm gone . . . .

i remember waiting one nite for her appearance
audience impatient at the lateness
of musicians
I remember it was april
and the flowers ran yellow
the sun downpoured yellow butterflies
and the day was yellow and silent
all of spring held us
in a single drop of blood.

when she appeared on stage
she became Nut arching over us
feet and hands placed on the stage
music flowing from her breasts
she swallowed the sun
sang confessions from the evening stars
made earth divulge her secrets
gave birth to skies in her song
remade the insistent air
and we became anointed found
inside her bop

 bop bop dowa
 bop bop doowaaa
 bop bop dooooowaaaa

Lady. Lady. Lady.
be good. be good
to me.
    to you.   to us all
cuz we just some lonesome babes
in the woods
hey lady. sweetellalady
Lady. Lady. Lady. be gooooood
ELLA ELLA ELLALADY

    be good
       gooooood
          goooooood . . .

Suggestions for Discussion

1. How does Sanchez describe Ella Fitzgerald?
2. What is the significance of the religious symbolism in the poem?

Suggestion for Writing

Were you ever moved to heights of emotion by music? Describe the experience
in a poem.

WALT WHITMAN

Poets to Come

Walt Whitman (1819–1892), regarded by many as the greatest American
poet, was born on Long Island, NY. He was a printer, a journalist, and a
nurse during the Civil War. Strongly influenced by Ralph Waldo Emerson, he published *Leaves of Grass* in 1855 at his own expense and added
sections to new editions over the years. By the time of his death, Whitman had become a major influence on younger poets who were moved
by his experiments in free verse and by his transcendental ideas.

Poets to come! orators, singers, musicians to come!
Not to-day is to justify me and answer what I am for,
But you, a new brood, native, athletic, continental, greater than
    before known,
Arouse! for you must justify me.

I myself but write one or two indicative words for the future,
I but advance a moment only to wheel and hurry back in the darkness.

I am a man who, sauntering along without fully stopping, turns a
    casual look upon you and then averts his face,
Leaving it to you to prove and define it,
Expecting the main things from you.

Suggestions for Discussion

1. How will the "poets to come" justify Whitman?
2. Why does Whitman feel he will "hurry back into darkness"?
3. What "main things" does Whitman expect from the future poets?

Suggestion for Writing

Answer Whitman's call and write a poem that he'd be proud to have inspired you to compose.

Science and Civilization

ᘓᘓᘓ

The conventional wisdom is often wrong. Crime didn't keep soaring in the 1990s, money alone doesn't win elections, and—surprise—drinking eight glasses of water a day has never actually been shown to do a thing for your health. Conventional wisdom is often shoddily formed and devilishly difficult to see through, but it can be done.

—STEVE D. LEVITT AND STEPHEN J. DUBNER
"Freakenomics: The Hidden Side of Everything"

Evolution by natural selection, the central concept of the life's work of Charles Darwin, is a theory. It's a theory about the origin of adaptation, complexity, and diversity among earth's living creatures. If you are skeptical by nature, unfamiliar with the terminology of science, and unaware of the overwhelming evidence, you might even be tempted to say that it's "just" a theory. In the same sense, relativity as described by Albert Einstein is "just" a theory. The notion that earth orbits around the sun rather than vice versa, offered by Copernicus in 1543, is a theory. Continental drift is a theory. The existence, structure, and dynamics of atoms? Atomic theory. Even electricity is a theoretical construct, involving electrons, which are tiny units of charged mass that no one has ever seen. Each of these theories is an explanation that has been confirmed to such a degree, by observation and experiment, that knowledgeable experts accept it as fact.

—DAVID QUAMMEN, "Was Darwin Wrong?"

HAJIME SORAYAMA

Aibo Entertainment Robot (ERS-110)

Various materials, 1999

Digital Image©The Museum of Modern Art

Licensed by SCALA

Art Resource, New York

INTRODUCTION

Scientia, Latin for knowledge, has a particularly strong hold on our consciousness. It is not just an academic discipline but a way of viewing the world—empirically and largely quantitatively—in a search for reliable "knowledge." Indeed, if something has "good science," or lacks it, its "truth" is often judged accordingly. But despite the dominance of science as a worldview, it is not the *only* way of viewing the world. The selections in this section, then, do not merely accept science's epistemological dominance, but debate its predictions, its uses, and even its premises.

For some, science cannot adequately explain the wonders of the universe. Indeed, several works herein seem to address the question: What has "progress" and even science wrought? Affonso Romano de Sant'Anna's poem "Letter to the Dead" slyly suggests that people are essentially the same as they have always been, only now they have computer gadgets to play with instead of bows and arrows. Darker in tone, other pieces consider how the industrialization of the world has ravaged the environment, and the extent to which science might solve problems that technology created. To this end, Nicholas Kristof offers an impassioned jeremiad about global warming, while James Howard Kunstler wonders what the world will be like when our oil-dependent civilization runs out of oil sometime in the frighteningly near future.

For others, science and mathematics are the most effective means of defeating ignorance—which for many scholars includes ideology—and defining a more accurate, nuanced worldview. Steve D. Levitt and Stephen J. Dubner, for example, use statistics to confront emotional and controversial topics such as gun control, abortion, and racism; they suggest that using mathematical formulas, and especially statistics, is a "value-neutral" way of determining what the world is "really" like and a way to avoid seeing the world through a distorted liberal or conservative lens. Consequently, Levitt and Dubner's work is likely to offend ideologues of every stripe.

Another such set of scientific questions comes from various new versions of *human* nature. What does it suggest about human life if we can see beneath its mystery? The ever-controversial debate between evolutionists and creationists is explored in David Quammen's essay. Stephen Jay Gould suggests that the extinction of the dinosaur may have significance for us today, and demonstrates how bad science is ruthlessly debunked, even if it tells a compelling story based on false assumptions.

492

Other essays deal with the future of scientific developments: with Tom Wolfe lamenting the functional death of the space program thanks to budget cuts, and David Smith suggesting that medical advancements made by 2050 might enable human life to be extended indefinitely. The nature of time and time travel is considered in two thematically linked selections. Paul Davies posits the possibility that time travel is feasible in "How to Build a Time Machine," while Alan Lightman's story demonstrates that a scientific, or science fiction, concept may be presented in a beautiful and poetic way, no matter what anti-science romantics might suggest, in the tale of a town in which time slows to a stop.

NOTEBOOK

∾∾∾

DAVID SMITH

2050—And Immortality Is Almost Within Our Grasp

David Smith (b. 1975) is the Africa correspondent for *The Guardian*, covering news, politics, and sports across the whole of Africa. Born in Salford, United Kingdom, Smith now lives in Johannesburg, South Africa, and travels extensively. Previous to this assignment, Smith was a reporter in Iraq and Afghanistan for *The Observer,* and also served as that paper's technology correspondent. He edited Britain's largest student weekly newspaper as a student at the University of Leeds in the late 1990s. The following article was published in *The Observer* on May 22, 2005.

Aeroplanes will be too afraid to crash, yoghurts will wish you good morning before being eaten and human consciousness will be stored on supercomputers, promising immortality for all—though it will help to be rich.

These fantastic claims are not made by a science fiction writer or a crystal ball–gazing lunatic. They are the deadly earnest predictions of Ian Pearson, head of the futurology unit at BT.

"If you draw the timelines, realistically by 2050 we would expect to be able to download your mind into a machine, so when you die it's not a major career problem," Pearson told *The Observer.* "If you're rich enough then by 2050 it's feasible. If you're poor you'll probably have to wait until 2075 or 2080 when it's routine. We are very serious about it. That's how fast this technology is moving: 45 years is a hell of a long time in IT."

Pearson, 44, has formed his mind-boggling vision of the future after graduating in applied mathematics and theoretical physics, spending four years working in missile design and the past 20 years working in optical networks, broadband network evolution and cybernetics in BT's laboratories. He admits his prophecies are both "very exciting" and "very scary."

He believes that today's youngsters may never have to die, and points to the rapid advances in computing power demonstrated last week, when Sony released the first details of its PlayStation 3. It is 35 times more powerful than previous games consoles. "The new PlayStation is 1 percent as powerful as a human brain," he said. "It is into supercomputer status compared to 10 years ago. PlayStation 5 will probably be as powerful as the human brain."

The world's fastest computer, IBM's BlueGene, can perform 70.72 trillion calculations per second (teraflops) and is accelerating all the time. But anyone who believes in the uniqueness of consciousness or the soul will find Pearson's next suggestion hard to swallow. "We're already looking at how you might structure a computer that could possibly become conscious. There are quite a lot of us now who believe it's entirely feasible.

"We don't know how to do it yet but we've begun looking in the same directions, for example at the techniques we think that consciousness is based on: information comes in from the outside world but also from other parts of your brain and each part processes it on an internal sensing basis. Consciousness is just another sense, effectively, and that's what we're trying to design in a computer. Not everyone agrees, but it's my conclusion that it is possible to make a conscious computer with superhuman levels of intelligence before 2020."

He continued: "It would definitely have emotions—that's one of the primary reasons for doing it. If I'm on an aeroplane I want the computer to be more terrified of crashing than I am so it does everything to stay in the air until it's supposed to be on the ground.

"You can also start automating an awful lots of jobs. Instead of phoning up a call centre and getting a machine that says, 'Type 1 for this and 2 for that and 3 for the other,' if you had machine personalities you could have any number of call staff, so you can be dealt with without ever waiting in a queue at a call centre again."

Pearson, from Whitehaven in Cumbria, collaborates on technology with some developers and keeps a watching brief on advances around the world. He concedes the need to debate the implications of progress. 'You need a completely global debate. Whether we should be building machines as smart as people is a really big one. Whether we should be allowed to modify bacteria to assemble electronic circuitry and make themselves smart is already being researched.

"We can already use DNA, for example, to make electronic circuits so it's possible to think of a smart yoghurt some time after 2020 or 2025, where the yoghurt has got a whole stack of electronics in every single bacterium. You could have a conversation with your strawberry yogurt before you eat it."

In the shorter term, Pearson identifies the next phase of progress as "ambient intelligence": chips with everything. He explained: "For example, if you have a pollen count sensor in your car you take some antihistamine before you get out. Chips will come small enough that you can start impregnating them into the skin. We're talking about video tattoos as very, very thin sheets of polymer that you just literally stick on to the skin and they stay there for several days. You could even build in cellphones and connect it to the network, use it as a video phone and download videos or receive emails."

Philips, the electronics giant, is developing the world's first rollable display which is just a millimetre thick and has a 12.5cm screen which can be wrapped around the arm. It expects to start production within two years.

The next age, he predicts, will be that of "simplicity" in around 2013–2015. "This is where the IT has actually become mature enough that people will be able to drive it without having to go on a training course.

"Forget this notion that you have to have one single chip in the computer which does everything. Why not just get a stack of little self-organising chips in a box and they'll hook up and do it themselves. It won't be able to get any viruses because most of the operating system will be stored in hardware which the hackers can't write to. If your machine starts going wrong, you just push a button and it's reset to the factory setting."

Pearson's third age is "virtual worlds" in around 2020. "We will spend a lot of time in virtual space, using high quality, 3D, immersive, computer generated environments to socialise and do business in. When technology gives you a life-size 3D image and the links to your nervous system allow you to shake hands, it's like being in the other person's office. It's impossible to believe that won't be the normal way of communicating."

Suggestions for Discussion

1. How are the prophecies in this article both "very exciting" and "very scary"?

2. What are the ethical dimensions of the technologies being discussed?

3. What social, religious, and political consequences might follow the developments predicted in this article?

Suggestion for Writing

As humans become more cybernetic, and computers become more human, where does humanity end and technology begin? Write an essay in which you consider the scientific, social, moral, religious, and individualistic ramifications of this question.

PAUL DAVIES

How to Build a Time Machine

Astrophysicist Paul Davies has written more than twenty books that are widely praised for making difficult scientific subjects graspable to the general public. Among those works are *The Mind of God: The Scientific Basis for a Rational World* (1992), *About Time: Einstein's Unfinished Revolution* (1995), and *The Fifth Miracle: The Search for the Origin and Meaning of Life* (1999). His 2002 book *How to Build a Time Machine* inspired this article of the same title, which was published in ScientificAmerican.com that same year and summarizes some of the key theories Davies presented in the longer text.

Time travel has been a popular science-fiction theme since H. G. Wells wrote his celebrated novel *The Time Machine* in 1895. But can it really be done? Is it possible to build a machine that would transport a human being into the past or future?

For decades, time travel lay beyond the fringe of respectable science. In recent years, however, the topic has become something of a cottage industry among theoretical physicists. The motivation has been partly recreational—time travel is fun to think about. But this research has a serious side, too. Understanding the relation between cause and effect is a key part of attempts to construct a unified theory of physics. If unrestricted time travel were possible, even in principle, the nature of such a unified theory could be drastically affected.

Our best understanding of time comes from Einstein's theories of relativity. Prior to these theories, time was widely regarded as absolute and universal, the same for everyone no matter what their physical circumstances were. In his special theory of relativity, Einstein proposed that the measured interval between two events depends on how the observer is moving. Crucially, two observers who move differently will experience different durations between the same two events.

The effect is often described using the "twin paradox." Suppose that Sally and Sam are twins. Sally boards a rocket ship and travels at high speed to a nearby star, turns around and flies back to Earth, while Sam stays at home. For Sally the duration of the journey might be, say, one year, but when she returns and steps out of the spaceship, she finds that 10 years have elapsed on Earth. Her brother is now nine years older than she is. Sally and Sam are no longer the same age, despite the fact that they were born on the same day. This example illustrates a limited type of time travel. In effect, Sally has leaped nine years into Earth's future.

ᕦ

Jet Lag

The effect, known as time dilation, occurs whenever two observers move relative to each other. In daily life we don't notice weird time warps, because the effect becomes dramatic only when the motion occurs at close to the speed of light. Even at aircraft speeds, the time dilation in a typical journey amounts to just a few nanoseconds—hardly an adventure of Wellsian proportions. Nevertheless, atomic clocks are accurate enough to record the shift and confirm that time really is stretched by motion. So travel into the future is a proved fact, even if it has so far been in rather unexciting amounts.

To observe really dramatic time warps, one has to look beyond the realm of ordinary experience. Subatomic particles can be propelled at nearly the speed of light in large accelerator machines. Some of these particles, such as muons, have a built-in clock because they decay with a definite half-life; in accordance with Einstein's theory, fast-moving muons inside accelerators are observed to decay in slow motion. Some cosmic rays also experience spectacular time warps. These particles move so close to the speed of light that, from their point of view, they cross the galaxy in minutes, even though in Earth's frame of reference they seem to take tens of thousands of years. If time dilation did not occur, those particles would never make it here.

Speed is one way to jump ahead in time. Gravity is another. In his general theory of relativity, Einstein predicted that gravity slows time. Clocks run a bit faster in the attic than in the basement, which is closer to the center of Earth and therefore deeper down in a gravitational field. Similarly, clocks run faster in space than on the ground. Once again the effect is minuscule, but it has been directly measured using accurate clocks. Indeed, these time-warping effects have to be taken into account in the Global Positioning System. If they weren't, sailors, taxi drivers, and cruise missiles could find themselves many kilometers off course.

At the surface of a neutron star, gravity is so strong that time is slowed by about 30 percent relative to Earth time. Viewed from such a star, events here would resemble a fast-forwarded video. A black hole represents the ultimate time warp; at the surface of the hole, time stands still relative to Earth. This means that if you fell into a black hole from nearby, in the brief interval it took you to reach the surface, all of eternity would pass by in the wider universe. The region within the black hole is therefore beyond the end of time, as far as the outside universe is concerned. If an astronaut could zoom very close to a black hole and return unscathed—admittedly a fanciful, not to mention foolhardy, prospect—he could leap far into the future.

ॐ

My Head Is Spinning

So far I have discussed travel forward in time. What about going backward? This is much more problematic. In 1948 Kurt Gödel of the Institute for Advanced Study in Princeton, N.J., produced a solution of Einstein's gravitational field equations that described a rotating universe. In this universe, an astronaut could travel through space so as to reach his own past. This comes about because of the way gravity affects light. The rotation of the universe would drag light (and thus the causal relations between objects) around with it, enabling a material object to travel in a closed loop in space that is also a closed loop in time, without at any stage exceeding the speed of light in the immediate neighborhood of the particle. Gödel's solution was shrugged aside as a mathematical curiosity—after all, observations show no sign that the universe as a whole is spinning. His result served nonetheless to demonstrate that going back in time was not forbidden by the theory of relativity. Indeed, Einstein confessed that he was troubled by the thought that his theory might permit travel into the past under some circumstances.

Other scenarios have been found to permit travel into the past. For example, in 1974 Frank J. Tipler of Tulane University calculated that a massive, infinitely long cylinder spinning on its axis at near the speed of light could let astronauts visit their own past, again by dragging light around the cylinder into a loop. In 1991 J. Richard Gott of Princeton University predicted that cosmic strings—structures that cosmologists think were created in the early stages of the big bang—could produce similar results. But in the mid-1980s the most realistic scenario for a time machine emerged, based on the concept of a wormhole.

In science fiction, wormholes are sometimes called stargates; they offer a shortcut between two widely separated points in space. Jump through a hypothetical wormhole, and you might come out moments later on the other side of the galaxy. Wormholes naturally fit into the general theory of relativity, whereby gravity warps not only time but also space. The theory allows the analogue of alternative road and tunnel routes connecting two points in space. Mathematicians refer to such a space as multiply connected. Just as a tunnel passing under a hill can be shorter than the surface street, a wormhole may be shorter than the usual route through ordinary space.

The wormhole was used as a fictional device by Carl Sagan in his 1985 novel *Contact*. Prompted by Sagan, Kip S. Thorne and his co-workers at the California Institute of Technology set out to find whether wormholes were consistent with known physics. Their starting point was that a wormhole would resemble a black hole in being an object with fearsome gravity. But unlike a black hole, which offers a one-way journey to nowhere, a wormhole would have an exit as well as an entrance.

ᘇ

In the Loop

For the wormhole to be traversable, it must contain what Thorne termed *exotic matter*. In effect, this is something that will generate antigravity to combat the natural tendency of a massive system to implode into a black hole under its intense weight. Antigravity, or gravitational repulsion, can be generated by negative energy or pressure. Negative-energy states are known to exist in certain quantum systems, which suggests that Thorne's exotic matter is not ruled out by the laws of physics, although it is unclear whether enough antigravitating stuff can be assembled to stabilize a wormhole [see "Negative Energy, Wormholes and Warp Drive," by Lawrence H. Ford and Thomas A. Roman; *Scientific American*, January 2000].

Soon Thorne and his colleagues realized that if a stable wormhole could be created, then it could readily be turned into a time machine. An astronaut who passed through one might come out not only somewhere else in the universe but somewhen else, too—in either the future or the past.

To adapt the wormhole for time travel, one of its mouths could be towed to a neutron star and placed close to its surface. The gravity of the star would slow time near that wormhole mouth, so that a time difference between the ends of the wormhole would gradually accumulate. If both mouths were then parked at a convenient place in space, this time difference would remain frozen in.

Suppose the difference were 10 years. An astronaut passing through the wormhole in one direction would jump 10 years into the future, whereas an astronaut passing in the other direction would jump 10 years into the past. By returning to his starting point at high speed across ordinary space, the second astronaut might get back home before he left. In other words, a closed loop in space could become a loop in time as well. The one restriction is that the astronaut could not return to a time before the wormhole was first built.

A formidable problem that stands in the way of making a wormhole time machine is the creation of the wormhole in the first place. Possibly space is threaded with such structures naturally—relics of the big bang. If so, a supercivilization might commandeer one. Alternatively, wormholes might naturally come into existence on tiny scales, the so-called Planck length, about 20 factors of 10 as small as an atomic nucleus. In principle, such a minute wormhole could be stabilized by a pulse of energy and then somehow inflated to usable dimensions.

᪥

Censored!

Assuming that the engineering problems could be overcome, the production of a time machine could open up a Pandora's box of causal paradoxes. Consider, for example, the time traveler who visits the past and murders his mother when she was a young girl. How do we make sense of this? If the girl dies, she cannot become the time traveler's mother. But if the time traveler was never born, he could not go back and murder his mother.

Paradoxes of this kind arise when the time traveler tries to change the past, which is obviously impossible. But that does not prevent someone from being a part of the past. Suppose the time traveler goes back and rescues a young girl from murder, and this girl grows up to become his mother. The causal loop is now self-consistent and no longer paradoxical. Causal consistency might impose restrictions on what a time traveler is able to do, but it does not rule out time travel per se.

Even if time travel isn't strictly paradoxical, it is certainly weird. Consider the time traveler who leaps ahead a year and reads about a new mathematical theorem in a future edition of *Scientific American.* He notes the details, returns to his own time and teaches the theorem to a student, who then writes it up for *Scientific American.* The article is, of course, the very one that the time traveler read. The question then arises: Where did the information about the theorem come from? Not from the time traveler, because he read it, but not from the student either, who learned it from the time traveler. The information seemingly came into existence from nowhere, reasonlessly.

The bizarre consequences of time travel have led some scientists to reject the notion outright. Stephen W. Hawking of the University of Cambridge has proposed a "chronology protection conjecture," which would outlaw causal loops. Because the theory of relativity is known to permit causal loops, chronology protection would require some other factor to intercede to prevent travel into the past. What might this factor be? One suggestion is that quantum processes will come to the rescue. The existence of a time machine would allow particles to loop into their own past. Calculations hint that the ensuing disturbance would become self-reinforcing, creating a runaway surge of energy that would wreck the wormhole.

Chronology protection is still just a conjecture, so time travel remains a possibility. A final resolution of the matter may have to await the successful union of quantum mechanics and gravitation, perhaps through a theory such as string theory or its extension, so-called M-theory. It is even conceivable that the next generation of particle accelerators will be able to create subatomic wormholes that survive long enough for nearby particles to execute fleeting causal loops. This would be a far cry from Wells's vision of a time machine, but it would forever change our picture of physical reality.

Suggestions for Discussion

1. Describe, in your own words, the concept of "time dilation."
2. According to Davies, a time traveler could *not* kill his own mother as a little girl and prevent his own birth. He could, however, save his young mother's life from a different assassin, thereby ensuring his own birth. Besides the obvious, why is one kind of meddling with the past acceptable and another not?

3. While popular science fiction stories posit time machines made from cars (as in *Back to the Future*) or "phone booths" (the *Bill and Ted* films and *Doctor Who*), what would a *real* time machine be made of? Assuming it is possible, how many years or generations are we away from creating such a device? How practical would such a time travel system be to use?

4. What might be the societal consequences of a publicly known, workable time machine?

Suggestions for Writing

1. Given the limitations imposed upon time travel by a Paul Davies-style time machine, what would be the incentive to time traveling? Write an essay or a short work of fiction in which you explore how and why one might use such a time machine. Adhere to the strict, scientific parameters that Davies lays out in his essay rather than write a science "fantasy" story like *Back to the Future*.

2. Evaluate Steven Moffat's story "'What I Did on My Christmas Holidays' By Sally Sparrow" in terms of Davies's essay. Does Moffat violate the rules and logic of time travel as laid out by Davies, or does the paradox he presents work scientifically?

PERSONAL WRITING

TOM WOLFE

One Giant Leap to Nowhere

Contemporary novelist Tom Wolfe (b. 1931) is widely credited as the inventor of "New Journalism"—an exuberant style that abandoned traditional journalistic objectivity for a more personal view. Wolfe chronicled the turbulent 1960s and 1970s for periodicals such as *New York, Esquire, Harper's Magazine,* and the *New York Herald-Tribune,* and his often controversial books examine contemporary American society, focusing on racial tensions, drug use, sexual politics, Manhattan provincialism, and modern masculinity. Virginia-born and Yale-educated, Wolfe began his writing career as a reporter for a Massachusetts paper, the *Springfield Union,* in 1956. In 1960, he won the Washington Newspaper Guild's foreign news prize for his coverage of Cuba for the *Washington Post.* Credited with coining a number of catchphrases including "the right stuff," "radical chic," and "the Me Generation," Wolfe famously dresses in a white suit and gloves and enjoys the disarming effect his outfit has on people. His books include *The Kandy-Kolored Tangerine-Flake Streamline Baby* (1965), *The Pump House Gang* and *The Electric Kool-Aid Acid Test* (both 1968), *The Painted Word* (1975), *The Right Stuff* (1979), *Bonfire of the Vanities* (serialized in *Rolling Stone Magazine* from 1984 to 1985), *A Man in Full* (1998), *I Am Charlotte Simmons* (2004), and *Back to Blood* (2010). This selection was published as an editorial in *The New York Times* on July 18, 2009.

Well, let's see now . . . That was a small step for Neil Armstrong, a giant leap for mankind and a real knee in the groin for NASA.

The American space program, the greatest, grandest, most Promethean—O.K. if I add "godlike"?—quest in the history of the world, died in infancy at 10:56 p.m. New York time on July 20, 1969, the moment the foot of Apollo 11's Commander Armstrong touched the surface of the Moon.

It was no ordinary dead-and-be-done-with-it death. It was full-blown purgatory, purgatory being the holding pen for recently deceased but still restless souls awaiting judgment by a Higher Authority.

Like many another youngster at that time, or maybe retro-youngster in my case, I was fascinated by the astronauts after Apollo 11. I even dared to dream of writing a book about them someday. If anyone had told me in July 1969 that the sound of Neil Armstrong's small step plus mankind's big one was the shuffle of pallbearers at graveside. I would have averted my eyes and shaken my head in pity. Poor guy's bucket's got a hole in it.

Why, putting a man on the Moon was just the beginning, the prelude, the prologue! The Moon was nothing but a little satellite of Earth. The great adventure was going to be the exploration of the planets . . . Mars first, then Venus, then Pluto. Jupiter, Mercury, Saturn, Neptune and Uranus? NASA would figure out their slots in the schedule in due course. In any case, we Americans wouldn't stop until we had explored the entire solar system. And after that . . . the galaxies beyond.

NASA had long since been all set to send men to Mars, starting with manned fly-bys of the planet in 1975. Wernher von Braun, the German rocket scientist who had come over to our side in 1945, had been designing a manned Mars project from the moment he arrived. In 1952 he published his Mars Project as a series of graphic articles called "Man Will Conquer Space Soon" in Collier's magazine. It created a sensation. He was front and center in 1961 when NASA undertook Project Empire, which resulted in working plans for a manned Mars mission. Given the epic, the saga, the triumph of Project Apollo, Mars would naturally come next. All NASA and von Braun needed was the president's and Congress's blessings and the great adventure was a Go. Why would they so much as blink before saying the word?

Three months after the landing, however, in October 1969, I began to wonder . . . I was in Florida, at Cape Kennedy, the space program's launching facility, aboard a NASA tour bus. The bus's Spielmeister was a tall-fair-and-handsome man in his late 30s . . . and a real piece of lumber when it came to telling tourists on a tour bus what they were looking at. He was so bad, I couldn't resist striking up a conversation at the end of the tour.

Sure enough, it turned out he had not been put on Earth for this job. He was an engineer who until recently had been a NASA heat-shield specialist. A baffling wave of layoffs had begun, and his job was eliminated. It was so bad he was lucky to have gotten this stand-up Spielmeister gig on a tour bus. Neil Armstrong and his two crew mates, Buzz Aldrin and Mike Collins, were still on their triumphal world tour . . . while back home, NASA's irreplaceable team of highly motivated space scientists— irreplaceable!—there were no others! . . . anywhere! . . . You couldn't just run an ad saying, "Help Wanted: Experienced heat-shield expert" . . . the irreplaceable team was breaking up, scattering in nobody knows how many hopeless directions.

∽

How could such a thing happen? In hindsight, the answer is obvious. NASA had neglected to recruit a corps of philosophers.

From the moment the Soviets launched Sputnik I into orbit around the Earth in 1957, everybody from Presidents Eisenhower, Kennedy and Johnson on down looked upon the so-called space race as just one thing: a military contest. At first there was alarm over the Soviets' seizure of the "strategic high ground" of space. They were already up there—right above us! They could now hurl thunderbolts down whenever and wherever they wanted. And what could we do about it? Nothing. *Ka-boom!* There goes Bangor . . . *Ka-boom!* There goes Boston . . . *Ka-boom!* There goes New York . . . Baltimore . . . Washington . . . St. Louis . . . Denver . . . San Jose—blown away!—just like that.

Physicists were quick to point out that nobody would choose space as a place from which to attack Earth. The spacecraft, the missile, the Earth itself, plus the Earth's own rotation, would be traveling at wildly different speeds upon wildly different geometric planes. You would run into the notorious "three body problem" and then some. You'd have to be crazy. The target would be untouched and you would wind up on the floor in a fetal ball, twitching and gibbering. On the other hand, the rockets that had lifted the Soviets' five-ton manned ships into orbit were worth thinking about. They were clearly powerful enough to reach any place on Earth with nuclear warheads.

But that wasn't what was on President Kennedy's mind when he summoned NASA's administrator, James Webb, and Webb's deputy, Hugh Dryden, to the White House in April 1961. The president was in a terrible funk. He kept muttering: "If somebody can just tell me how to catch up. Let's find somebody—anybody . . . There's nothing more important." He kept saying, "We've got to catch up." Catching up had become his obsession. He never so much as mentioned the rockets.

Dryden said that, frankly, there was no way we could catch up with the Soviets when it came to orbital flights. A better idea would be to announce a crash program on the scale of the Manhattan Project, which had produced the atomic bomb. Only the aim this time would be to put a man on the Moon within the next 10 years.

Barely a month later Kennedy made his famous oration before Congress: "I believe that this nation should commit itself to achieving the goal, before this decade is out, of landing a man on the Moon and returning him safely to Earth." He neglected to mention Dryden.

Intuitively, not consciously, Kennedy had chosen another form of military contest, an oddly ancient and archaic one. It was called "single combat."

The best known of all single combats was David versus Goliath. Before opposing armies clashed in all-out combat, each would send forth its "champion," and the two would fight to the death, usually with swords. The victor would cut off the head of the loser and brandish it aloft by its hair.

The deadly duel didn't take the place of the all-out battle. It was regarded as a sign of which way the gods were leaning. The two armies then had it out on the battlefield . . . unless one army fled in terror upon seeing its champion slaughtered. There you have the Philistines when Little David killed their giant, Goliath . . . and cut his head off and brandished it aloft by its hair (1 Samuel 17:1–58). They were overcome by a mad desire to be somewhere else. (The Israelites pursued and destroyed them.)

More than two millenniums later, the mental atmosphere of the space race was precisely that. The details of single combat were different. Cosmonauts and astronauts didn't fight hand to hand and behead one another. Instead, each side's brave champions, including one woman (Valentina Tereshkova), risked their lives by sitting on top of rockets and having their comrades on the ground light the fuse and fire them into space like the human cannonballs of yore.

The Soviets rocketed off to an early lead. They were the first to put an object into orbit around the Earth (Sputnik), the first to put an animal into orbit (a dog), the first to put a man in orbit (Yuri Gagarin). No sooner had NASA put two astronauts (Gus Grissom and Alan Shepard) into 15-minute suborbital flights to the Bahamas—*the Bahamas!—15 minutes!—two miserable little mortar lobs!*—then the Soviets put a second cosmonaut (Gherman Titov) into orbit. He stayed up there for 25 hours and went around the globe 17 times. Three times he flew directly over the United States. The gods had shown which way they were leaning, all right!

❧

At this point, the mental atmospheres of the rocket-powered space race of the 1960s and the sword-clanking single combat of ancient days became so similar you had to ask: Does the human beast ever really change—or merely his artifacts? The Soviet cosmo-champions beat our astro-champions so handily, gloom spread like a gas. Every time you picked up a newspaper you saw headlines with the phrase, SPACE GAP . . . SPACE GAP . . . SPACE GAP . . . The Soviets had produced a generation of scientific geniuses—while we slept, fat and self-satisfied! Educators began tearing curriculums apart as soon as Sputnik went up, introducing the New Math and stressing another latest thing, the Theory of Self-Esteem.

At last, in February 1962, NASA managed to get a man into Earth orbit, John Glenn. You had to have been alive at that time to comprehend the reaction of the nation, practically all of it. He was up for only five hours, compared to Titov's 25, but he was our . . . Protector! Against all odds he had risked his very hide for . . . us!—protected us from our mortal enemy!—struck back in the duel in the heavens!—showed the world that we Americans were born fighting and would never give up! John Glenn made us whole again!

During his ticker-tape parade up Broadway, you have never heard such cheers or seen so many thousands of people crying. Big Irish cops, the classic New York breed, were out in the intersections in front of the world, sobbing, blubbering, boo-hoo-ing, with tears streaming down their faces. John Glenn had protected all of us, cops, too. All tears have to do with protection . . . but I promise not to lay that theory on you now. John Glenn, in 1962, was the last true national hero America has ever had.

There were three more Mercury flights, and then the Gemini series of two-man flights began. With Gemini, we dared to wonder if perhaps we weren't actually pulling closer to the Soviets in this greatest of all single combats. But we held our breath, fearful that the Soviets' anonymous Chief Designer would trump us again with some unimaginably spectacular feat.

Sure enough, the C.I.A. brought in sketchy reports that the Soviets were on the verge of a Moon shot.

NASA entered into the greatest crash program of all time, Apollo. It launched five lunar missions in one year, December 1968 to November 1969. With Apollo 11, we finally won the great race, landing a man on the Moon before the end of this decade and returning him safely to Earth.

Everybody, including Congress, was caught up in the adrenal rush of it all. But then, on the morning after, congressmen began to wonder about something that hadn't dawned on them since Kennedy's oration. What was this single combat stuff—they didn't use the actual term—really all about? It had been a battle for morale at home and image abroad. Fine, O.K., we won, but it had no tactical military meaning whatsoever. And it had cost a fortune, $150 billion or so. And this business of sending a man to Mars and whatnot? Just more of the same, when you got right down to it. How laudable . . . how far-seeing . . . but why don't we just do a Scarlett O'Hara and think about it tomorrow?

And that NASA budget! Now there was some prime pork you could really sink your teeth into! And they don't need it anymore! Game's over, NASA won, congratulations. Who couldn't use some of that juicy meat to make the people happy? It had an ambrosial aroma . . . made you think of re-election. . . .

NASA's annual budget sank like a stone from $5 billion in the mid-1960s to $3 billion in the mid-1970s. It was at this point that NASA's lack of a philosopher corps became a real problem. The fact was, NASA had only one philosopher, Wernher von Braun. Toward the end of his life, von Braun knew he was dying of cancer and became very contemplative. I happened to hear him speak at a dinner in his honor in San Francisco. He raised the question of what the space program was really all about.

It's been a long time, but I remember him saying something like this: Here on Earth we live on a planet that is in orbit around the Sun. The Sun itself is a star that is on fire and will someday burn up, leaving our solar system uninhabitable. Therefore we must build a bridge to the stars, because as far as we know, we are the only sentient creatures in the entire universe. When do we start building that bridge to the stars? We begin as soon as we are able, and this is that time. We must not fail in this obligation we have to keep alive the only meaningful life we know of.

Unfortunately, NASA couldn't present as its spokesman and great philosopher a former high-ranking member of the Nazi Wehrmacht with a heavy German accent.

As a result, the space program has been killing time for 40 years with a series of orbital projects . . . Skylab, the Apollo-Soyuz joint mission, the International Space Station and the space shuttle. These programs have required a courage and engineering brilliance comparable to the manned programs that preceded them. But their purpose has been mainly to keep the lights on at the Kennedy Space Center and Houston's Johnson Space Center—by removing manned flight from the heavens and bringing it very much down to earth. The shuttle program, for example, was actually supposed to appeal to the public by offering orbital tourist rides, only to end in the Challenger disaster, in which the first such passenger, Christa McAuliffe, a schoolteacher, perished.

☙

Forty years! For 40 years, everybody at NASA has known that the only logical next step is a manned Mars mission, and every overture has been entertained only briefly by presidents and the Congress. They have so many more luscious and appealing projects that could make better use of the close to $10 billion annually the Mars program would require. There is another overture even at this moment, and it does not stand a chance in the teeth of Depression II.

"Why not send robots?" is a common refrain. And once more it is the late Wernher von Braun who comes up with the rejoinder. One of the things he most enjoyed saying was that there is no computerized explorer in the world with more than a tiny fraction of the power of a chemical analog computer known as the human brain, which is easily reproduced by unskilled labor.

What NASA needs now is the power of the Word. On Darwin's tongue, the Word created a revolutionary and now well-nigh universal conception of the nature of human beings, or, rather, human beasts. On Freud's tongue, the Word means that at this very moment there are probably several million orgasms occurring that would not have occurred had Freud never lived. Even the fact that he is proved to be a quack has not diminished the power of his Word.

July 20, 1969, was the moment NASA needed, more than anything else in this world, the Word. But that was something NASA's engineers had no specifications for. At this moment, that remains the only solution to recovering NASA's true destiny, which is, of course, to build that bridge to the stars.

Suggestions for Discussion

1. According to Wolfe, what were the roots of the development of the space program? What role did the relationship of the United States to the Soviet Union play? What happened to the program as Cold War tensions eased?

2. Why does Wolfe argue that John Glenn is the "last true national hero America has ever had"?

3. What is the "Bridge to the Stars" argument for continuing the space program?

Suggestion for Writing

Synthesis: If you were responsible for allocating U.S. government funding of the sciences, where would you spend the money? Consider Wolfe's arguments in favor of space-program funding alongside the arguments presented about possible future technologies in the other essays included in this section. Explain what kind of research you believe is most in need of funding, based on the information and arguments you find in this section.

ESSAYS

༺ঙ༻

STEPHEN JAY GOULD

Sex, Drugs, Disasters, and the Extinction of Dinosaurs

The late paleontologist, evolutionary biologist, and Harvard University professor Stephen Jay Gould (1941–2002) is credited with making science popular and accessible by writing a column for *Natural History* magazine for nearly thirty years. His most influential scientific theory, punctuated equilibrium, explained accelerated evolutionary cycles in a manner that modified Charles Darwin's evolutionary theory. A prolific writer, Gould's books include *The Mismeasure of Man* (1981), *Full House: The Spread of Excellence from Plato to Darwin* (1996), and *The Hedgehog, the Fox, and the Magister's Pox* (2003). In addition, his *Natural History* columns were collected in books such as *Ever Since Darwin* (1977), *The Panda's Thumb* (1980), *The Lying Stones of Marrakech* (2000), and *The Flamingo's Smile* (1985), from which the following essay is reprinted.

Science, in its most fundamental definition, is a fruitful mode of inquiry, not a list of enticing conclusions. The conclusions are the consequence, not the essence.

My greatest unhappiness with most popular presentations of science concerns their failure to separate fascinating claims from the methods that scientists use to establish the facts of nature. Journalists, and the public, thrive on controversial and stunning statements. But science is, basically, a way of knowing—in P. B. Medawar's apt words, "the art of the soluble." If the growing corps of popular science writers would focus on *how* scientists develop and defend those fascinating claims, they would make their greatest possible contribution to public understanding.

Consider three ideas, proposed in perfect seriousness to explain that greatest of all titillating puzzles—the extinction of dinosaurs. Since these three notions invoke the primally fascinating themes of our culture—sex, drugs, and violence—they surely reside in the category of fascinating claims. I want to show why two of them rank as silly speculation, while the other represents science at its grandest and most useful.

510

Science works with testable proposals. If, after much compilation and scrutiny of data, new information continues to affirm a hypothesis, we may accept it provisionally and gain confidence as further evidence mounts. We can never be completely sure that a hypothesis is right, though we may be able to show with confidence that it is wrong. The best scientific hypotheses are also generous and expansive: they suggest extensions and implications that enlighten related, and even far distant, subjects. Simply consider how the idea of evolution has influenced virtually every intellectual field.

Useless speculation, on the other hand, is restrictive. It generates no testable hypothesis, and offers no way to obtain potentially refuting evidence. Please note that I am not speaking of truth or falsity. The speculation may well be true; still, if it provides, in principle, no material for affirmation or rejection, we can make nothing of it. It must simply stand forever as an intriguing idea. Useless speculation turns in on itself and leads nowhere; good science, containing both seeds for its potential refutation and implications for more and different testable knowledge, reaches out. But, enough preaching. Let's move on to dinosaurs, and the three proposals for their extinction.

1. Sex: Testes function only in a narrow range of temperature. (Those of mammals hang externally in a scrotal sac because internal body temperatures are too high for their proper function.) A worldwide rise in temperature at the close of the Cretaceous period caused the testes of dinosaurs to stop functioning and led to their extinction by sterilization of males.

2. Drugs: Angiosperms (flowering plants) first evolved toward the end of the dinosaurs' reign. Many of these plants contain psychoactive agents, avoided by mammals today as a result of their bitter taste. Dinosaurs had neither means to taste the bitterness nor livers effective enough to detoxify the substances. They died of massive overdoses.

3. Disasters: A large comet or asteroid struck the earth some 65 million years ago, lofting a cloud of dust into the sky and blocking sunlight, thereby suppressing photosynthesis and so drastically lowering world temperatures that dinosaurs and hosts of other creatures became extinct.

Before analyzing these three tantalizing statements, we must establish a basic ground rule often violated in proposals for the dinosaurs' demise. *There is no separate problem of the extinction of dinosaurs.* Too often we divorce specific events from their wider contexts and systems of cause and effect. The fundamental fact of dinosaur extinction is its synchrony with the demise of so many other groups across a wide range of habitats, from terrestrial to marine.

The history of life has been punctuated by brief episodes of mass extinction. A recent analysis by University of Chicago paleontologists Jack

Sepkoski and Dave Raup, based on the best and most exhaustive tabulation of data ever assembled, shows clearly that five episodes of mass dying stand well above the "background" extinctions of normal times (when we consider all mass extinctions, large and small, they seem to fall in a regular 26-million-year cycle. . . .). The Cretaceous debacle, occurring 65 million years ago and separating the Mesozoic and Cenozoic eras of our geological time scale, ranks prominently among the five. Nearly all the marine plankton (single-celled floating creatures) died with geological suddenness; among marine invertebrates, nearly 15 percent of all families perished, including many previously dominant groups, especially the ammonites (relatives of squids in coiled shells). On land, the dinosaurs disappeared after more than 100 million years of unchallenged domination.

In this context, speculations limited to dinosaurs alone ignore the larger phenomenon. We need a coordinated explanation for a system of events that includes the extinction of dinosaurs as one component. Thus it makes little sense, though it may fuel our desire to view mammals as inevitable inheritors of the earth, to guess that dinosaurs died because small mammals ate their eggs (a perennial favorite among untestable speculations). It seems most unlikely that some disaster peculiar to dinosaurs befell these massive beasts—and that the debacle happened to strike just when one of history's five great dyings had enveloped the earth for completely different reasons.

The testicular theory, an old favorite from the 1940s, had its root in an interesting and thoroughly respectable study of temperature tolerances in the American alligator, published in the staid *Bulletin of the American Museum of Natural History* in 1946 by three experts on living and fossil reptiles—E. H. Colbert, my own first teacher in paleontology; R. B. Cowles; and C. M. Bogert.

The first sentence of their summary reveals a purpose beyond alligators: "This report describes an attempt to infer the reactions of extinct reptiles, especially the dinosaurs, to high temperatures as based upon reactions observed in the modern alligator." They studied, by rectal thermometry, the body temperatures of alligators under changing conditions of heating and cooling. (Well, let's face it, you wouldn't want to try sticking a thermometer under a 'gator's tongue.) The predictions under test go way back to an old theory first stated by Galileo in the 1630s—the unequal scaling of surfaces and volumes. As an animal, or any object, grows (provided its shape doesn't change), surface areas must increase more slowly than volumes—since surfaces get larger as length squared, while volumes increase much more rapidly, as length cubed. Therefore, small animals have high ratios of surface to volume, while large animals cover themselves with relatively little surface.

Among cold-blooded animals lacking any physiological mechanism for keeping their temperatures constant, small creatures have a hell of a time keeping warm—because they lose so much heat through their relatively large surfaces. On the other hand, large animals, with their relatively small surfaces, may lose heat so slowly that, once warm, they may maintain effectively constant temperatures against ordinary fluctuations of climate. (In fact, the resolution of the "hot-blooded dinosaur" controversy that burned so brightly a few years back may simply be that, while large dinosaurs possessed no physiological mechanism for constant temperature, and were not therefore warm-blooded in the technical sense, their large size and relatively small surface area kept them warm.)

Colbert, Cowles, and Bogert compared the warming rates of small and large alligators. As predicted, the small fellows heated up (and cooled down) more quickly. When exposed to a warm sun, a tiny 50-gram (1.76-ounce) alligator heated up one degree Celsius every minute and a half, while a large alligator, 260 times bigger at 13,000 grams (28.7 pounds), took seven and a half minutes to gain a degree. Extrapolating up to an adult 10-ton dinosaur, they concluded that a one-degree rise in body temperature would take eighty-six hours. If large animals absorb heat so slowly (through their relatively small surfaces), they will also be unable to shed any excess heat gained when temperatures rise above a favorable level.

The authors then guessed that large dinosaurs lived at or near their optimum temperatures; Cowles suggested that a rise in global temperatures just before the Cretaceous extinction caused the dinosaurs to heat up beyond their optimal tolerance—and, being so large, they couldn't shed the unwanted heat. (In a most unusual statement within a scientific paper, Colbert and Bogert then explicitly disavowed this speculative extension of their empirical work on alligators.) Cowles conceded that this excess heat probably wasn't enough to kill or even to enervate the great beasts, but since testes often function within a narrow range of temperature, he proposed that this global rise might have sterilized all the males, causing extinction by natural contraception.

The overdose theory has recently been supported by UCLA psychiatrist Ronald K. Siegel. Siegel has gathered, he claims, more than 2,000 records of animals who, when given access, administer various drugs to themselves—from a mere swig of alcohol to massive doses of the big H. Elephants will swill the equivalent of twenty beers at a time, but do not like alcohol in concentrations greater than 7 percent. In a silly bit of anthropocentric speculation, Siegel states that "elephants drink, perhaps, to forget . . . the anxiety produced by shrinking rangeland and the competition for food."

Since fertile imaginations can apply almost any hot idea to the extinction of dinosaurs, Siegel found a way. Flowering plants did not evolve until late in the dinosaurs' reign. These plants also produced an array of aromatic, amino-acid-based alkaloids—the major group of psychoactive agents. Most mammals are "smart" enough to avoid these potential poisons. The alkaloids simply don't taste good (they are bitter); in any case, we mammals have livers happily supplied with the capacity to detoxify them. But, Siegel speculates, perhaps dinosaurs could neither taste the bitterness nor detoxify the substances once ingested. He recently told members of the American Psychological Association: "I'm not suggesting that all dinosaurs OD'd on plant drugs, but it certainly was a factor." He also argued that death by overdose may help explain why so many dinosaur fossils are found in contorted positions. (Do not go gentle into that good night.)

Extraterrestrial catastrophes have long pedigrees in the popular literature of extinction, but the subject exploded again in 1979, after a long lull, when the father-son, physicist-geologist team of Luis and Walter Alvarez proposed that an asteroid, some 10 km in diameter, struck the earth 65 million years ago (comets, rather than asteroids, have since gained favor. . . . Good science is self-corrective).

The force of such a collision would be immense, greater by far than the megatonnage of all the world's nuclear weapons. . . . In trying to reconstruct a scenario that would explain the simultaneous dying of dinosaurs on land and so many creatures in the sea, the Alvarezes proposed that a gigantic dust cloud, generated by particles blown aloft in the impact, would so darken the earth that photosynthesis would cease and temperatures drop precipitously. (Rage, rage against the dying of the light.) The single-celled photosynthetic oceanic plankton, with life cycles measured in weeks, would perish outright, but land plants might survive through the dormancy of their seeds (land plants were not much affected by the Cretaceous extinction, and any adequate theory must account for the curious pattern of differential survival). Dinosaurs would die by starvation and freezing; small, warm-blooded mammals, with more modest requirements for food and better regulation of body temperature, would squeak through. "Let the bastards freeze in the dark," as bumper stickers of our chauvinistic neighbors in sunbelt states proclaimed several years ago during the Northeast's winter oil crisis.

All three theories, testicular malfunction, psychoactive overdosing, and asteroidal zapping, grab our attention mightily. As pure phenomenology, they rank about equally high on the hit parade of primal fascination. Yet one represents expansive science, the others restrictive and untestable speculation. The proper criterion lies in evidence and methodology; we must probe behind the superficial fascination of particular claims.

How could we possibly decide whether the hypothesis of testicular frying is right or wrong? We would have to know things that the fossil record cannot provide. What temperatures were optimal for dinosaurs? Could they avoid the absorption of excess heat by staying in the shade, or in caves? At what temperatures did their testicles cease to function? Were late Cretaceous climates ever warm enough to drive the internal temperatures of dinosaurs close to this ceiling? Testicles simply don't fossilize, and how could we infer their temperature tolerances even if they did? In short, Cowles's hypothesis is only an intriguing speculation leading nowhere. The most damning statement against it appeared right at the conclusion of Colbert, Cowles, and Bogert's paper, when they admitted: "It is difficult to advance any definite arguments against this hypothesis." My statement may seem paradoxical— isn't a hypothesis really good if you can't devise any arguments against it? Quite the contrary. It is untestable and unusable.

Siegel's overdosing has even less going for it. At least Cowles extrapolated his conclusion from some good data on alligators. And he didn't completely violate the primary guideline of citing dinosaur extinction in the context of a general mass dying—for rise in temperature could be the root cause of a general catastrophe, zapping dinosaurs by testicular malfunction and different groups for other reasons. But Siegel's speculation cannot touch the extinction of ammonites or oceanic plankton (diatoms make their own food with good sweet sunlight; they don't OD on the chemicals of terrestrial plants). It is simply a gratuitous, attention-grabbing guess. It cannot be tested, for how can we know what dinosaurs tasted and what their livers could do? Livers don't fossilize any better than testicles.

The hypothesis doesn't even make any sense in its own context. Angiosperms were in full flower ten million years before dinosaurs went the way of all flesh. Why did it take so long? As for the pains of a chemical death recorded in contortions of fossils, I regret to say (or rather I'm pleased to note for the dinosaurs' sake) that Siegel's knowledge of geology must be a bit deficient; muscles contract after death and geological strata rise and fall with motions of the earth's crust after burial—more than enough reason to distort a fossil's pristine appearance.

The impact story, on the other hand, has a sound basis in evidence. It can be tested, extended, refined and, if wrong, disproved. The Alvarezes did not just construct an arresting guess for public consumption. They proposed their hypothesis after laborious geochemical studies with Frank Asaro and Helen Michel had revealed a massive increase of iridium in rocks deposited right at the time of the extinction. Iridium, a rare metal of the platinum group, is virtually absent from indigenous rocks of the earth's crust; most of our iridium arrives on extraterrestrial objects that strike the earth.

The Alvarez hypothesis bore immediate fruit. Based originally on evidence from two European localities, it led geochemists throughout the world to examine other sediments of the same age. They found abnormally high amounts of iridium everywhere—from continental rocks of the western United States to deep sea cores from the South Atlantic.

Cowles proposed his testicular hypothesis in the mid-1940s. Where has it gone since then? Absolutely nowhere, because scientists can do nothing with it. The hypothesis must stand as a curious appendage to a solid study of alligators. Siegel's overdose scenario will also win a few press notices and fade into oblivion. The Alvarezes' asteroid falls into a different category

516 SCIENCE AND CIVILIZATION

altogether, and much of the popular commentary has missed this essential distinction by focusing on the impact and its attendant results, and forgetting what really matters to a scientist—the iridium. If you talk just about asteroids, dust, and darkness, you tell stories no better and no more entertaining than fried testicles or terminal trips. It is the iridium—the source of testable evidence—that counts and forges the crucial distinction between speculation and science.

The proof, to twist a phrase, lies in the doing. Cowles's hypothesis has generated nothing in thirty-five years. Since its proposal in 1979, the Alvarez hypothesis has spawned hundreds of studies, a major conference, and attendant publications. Geologists are fired up. They are looking for iridium at all other extinction boundaries. Every week exposes a new wrinkle in the scientific press. Further evidence that the Cretaceous iridium represents extraterrestrial impact and not indigenous volcanism continues to accumulate. As I revise this essay in November 1984 (this paragraph will be out of date when the book is published), new data include chemical "signatures" of other isotopes indicating unearthly provenance, glass spherules of a size and sort produced by impact and not by volcanic eruptions, and high-pressure varieties of silica formed (so far as we know) only under the tremendous shock of impact.

My point is simply this: Whatever the eventual outcome (I suspect it will be positive), the Alvarez hypothesis is exciting, fruitful science because it generates tests, provides us with things to do, and expands outward. We are having fun, battling back and forth, moving toward a resolution, and extending the hypothesis beyond its original scope. . . .

As just one example of the unexpected, distant cross-fertilization that good science engenders, the Alvarez hypothesis made a major contribution to a theme that has riveted public attention in the past few months—so-called nuclear winter. . . . In a speech delivered in April 1982, Luis Alvarez calculated the energy that a ten-kilometer asteroid would release on impact. He compared such an explosion with a full nuclear exchange and implied that all-out nuclear war might unleash similar consequences.

This theme of impact leading to massive dust clouds and falling temperatures formed an important input to the decision of Carl Sagan and a group of colleagues to model the climatic consequences of nuclear holocaust. Full nuclear exchange would probably generate the same kind of dust cloud and darkening that may have wiped out the dinosaurs. Temperatures would drop precipitously and agriculture might become impossible. Avoidance of nuclear war is fundamentally an ethical and political imperative, but we must know the factual consequences to make firm judgments. I am heartened by a final link across disciplines and deep concerns—another criterion, by the way, of science at its best: A recognition of the very phenomenon that made our evolution possible by exterminating the previously dominant dinosaurs and clearing a way for the evolution of large mammals, including us, might actually help to save us from joining those magnificent beasts in contorted poses among the strata of the earth.

Suggestions for Discussion

1. What distinction does Gould make between good scientific theories and bad ones? What does he feel that science is, in essence? What does he feel it should accomplish?

2. According to Gould, why is it unlikely that a sex-related catastrophe killed the dinosaurs? Why is it unlikely that a drugs-related catastrophe killed the dinosaurs? According to Gould, why is it more likely that a natural disaster-related catastrophe killed the dinosaurs?

3. How has the asteroid theory influenced the development of the nuclear winter theory? Why is the nuclear winter theory important from both scientific and political perspectives?

Suggestion for Writing

New scientific findings and theories concerning dinosaurs and their extinction are advanced each year. What do some of the latest scientific writings in the field posit? Do these writings build upon and further develop Gould's views on the subject? Or have some of his suppositions been corrected or disproved? Write an essay in which you compare recent writings to Gould's essay.

DAVID QUAMMEN

Was Darwin Wrong?

David Quammen (b. 1948) is an award-winning author and naturalist. Although he writes both nonfiction and fiction, he is best known for his nonfiction works on nature and science. For fifteen years, Quammen was a contributing columnist to *Outside* magazine, and he is the author of four works of fiction and eight notable nonfiction titles, including *Monster of God: The Man-Eating Predator in the Jungles of History and the Mind* (2003) and his most recent *The Reluctant Mr. Darwin: An Intimate Portrait of Charles Darwin and the Making of His Theory of Evolution* (2006). He is a graduate of both Yale and Oxford Universities.

While studying literature at Oxford, he was awarded the prestigious Rhodes scholarship and Guggenheim Fellowship and three National Magazine Awards. The following piece appeared in *National Geographic* and traces the creation-versus-evolution controversy while citing scientific evidence for Darwin's theory of natural selection.

Evolution by natural selection, the central concept of the life's work of Charles Darwin, is a theory. It's a theory about the origin of adaptation, complexity, and diversity among Earth's living creatures. If you are skeptical by nature, unfamiliar with the terminology of science, and unaware of the overwhelming evidence, you might even be tempted to say that it's "just" a theory. In the same sense, relativity as described by Albert Einstein is "just" a theory. The notion that Earth orbits around the Sun rather than vice versa, offered by Copernicus in 1543, is a theory. Continental drift is a theory. The existence, structure, and dynamics of atoms? Atomic theory. Even electricity is a theoretical construct, involving electrons, which are tiny units of charged mass that no one has ever seen. Each of these theories is an explanation that has been confirmed to such a degree, by observation and experiment, that knowledgeable experts accept it as fact. That's what scientists mean when they talk about a theory: not a dreamy and unreliable speculation, but an explanatory statement that fits the evidence. They embrace such an explanation confidently but provisionally—taking it as their best available view of reality, at least until some severely conflicting data or some better explanation might come along.

The rest of us generally agree. We plug our televisions into little wall sockets, measure a year by the length of Earth's orbit, and in many other ways live our lives based on the trusted reality of those theories.

Evolutionary theory, though, is a bit different. It's such a dangerously wonderful and far-reaching view of life that some people find it unacceptable, despite the vast body of supporting evidence. As applied to our own species, *Homo sapiens*, it can seem more threatening still. Many fundamentalist Christians and ultra-orthodox Jews take alarm at the thought that human descent from earlier primates contradicts a strict reading of the Book of Genesis. Their discomfort is paralleled by Islamic creationists such as Harun Yahya, author of a recent volume titled *The Evolution Deceit*, who points to the six-day creation story in the Koran as literal truth and calls the theory of evolution "nothing but a deception imposed on us by the dominators of the world system." The late Srila Prabhupada, of the Hare Krishna movement, explained that God created "the 8,400,000 species of life from the very beginning," in order to establish multiple tiers of reincarnation for rising souls. Although souls ascend, the species themselves don't change, he insisted, dismissing "Darwin's nonsensical theory."

Other people too, not just scriptural literalists, remain unpersuaded about evolution. According to a Gallup poll drawn from more than a thousand telephone interviews conducted in February 2001, no less than 45 percent of responding U.S. adults agreed that "God created human beings pretty much in their present form at one time within the last ten thousand years or so." Evolution, by their lights, played no role in shaping us.

Only 37 percent of the polled Americans were satisfied with allowing room for both God and Darwin—that is, divine initiative to get things started, evolution as the creative means. (This view, according to more than one papal pronouncement, is compatible with Roman Catholic dogma.) Still fewer Americans, only 12 percent, believed that humans evolved from other life-forms without any involvement of a god.

The most startling thing about these poll numbers is not that so many Americans reject evolution, but that the statistical breakdown hasn't changed much in two decades. Gallup interviewers posed exactly the same choices in 1982, 1993, 1997, and 1999. The creationist conviction—that God alone, and not evolution, produced humans—has never drawn less than 44 percent. In other words, nearly half the American populace prefers to believe that Charles Darwin was wrong where it mattered most.

Why are there so many antievolutionists? Scriptural literalism can only be part of the answer. The American public certainly includes a large segment of scriptural literalists—but not *that* large, not 44 percent. Creationist proselytizers and political activists, working hard to interfere with the teaching of evolutionary biology in public schools, are another part. Honest confusion and ignorance, among millions of adult Americans, must be still another. Many people have never taken a biology course that dealt with evolution nor read a book in which the theory was lucidly explained. Sure, we've all heard of Charles Darwin, and of a vague, somber notion about struggle and survival that sometimes goes by the catchall label "Darwinism." But the main sources of information from which most Americans have drawn their awareness of this subject, it seems, are haphazard ones at best: cultural osmosis, newspaper and magazine references, half-baked nature documentaries on the tube, and hearsay.

Evolution is both a beautiful concept and an important one, more crucial nowadays to human welfare, to medical science, and to our understanding of the world than ever before. It's also deeply persuasive—a theory you can take to the bank. The essential points are slightly more complicated than most people assume, but not so complicated that they can't be comprehended by any attentive person. Furthermore, the supporting evidence is abundant, various, ever increasing, solidly interconnected, and easily available in museums, popular books, textbooks, and a mountainous accumulation of peer-reviewed scientific studies. No one needs to, and no one should, accept evolution merely as a matter of faith.

Two big ideas, not just one, are at issue: the evolution of all species, as a historical phenomenon, and natural selection, as the main mechanism causing that phenomenon. The first is a question of what happened. The second is a question of how. The idea that all species are descended from common ancestors had been suggested by other thinkers, including Jean-Baptiste Lamarck, long before Darwin published *The Origin of Species* in 1859. What made Darwin's book so remarkable when it appeared, and so influential in the long run, was that it offered a rational explanation of how evolution must occur. The same insight came independently to Alfred Russel Wallace, a young naturalist doing fieldwork in the Malay Archipelago during the late 1850s. In historical annals, if not in the popular awareness, Wallace and Darwin share the kudos for having discovered natural selection.

The gist of the concept is that small, random, heritable differences among individuals result in different chances of survival and reproduction— success for some, death without offspring for others—and that this natural culling leads to significant changes in shape, size, strength, armament, color, biochemistry, and behavior among the descendants. Excess population growth drives the competitive struggle. Because less successful competitors produce fewer surviving offspring, the useless or negative variations tend to disappear, whereas the useful variations tend to be perpetuated and gradually magnified throughout a population.

So much for one part of the evolutionary process, known as anagenesis, during which a single species is transformed. But there's also a second part, known as speciation. Genetic changes sometimes accumulate within an isolated segment of a species, but not throughout the whole, as that isolated population adapts to its local conditions. Gradually it goes its own way, seizing a new ecological niche. At a certain point it becomes irreversibly distinct—that is, so different that its members can't interbreed with the rest. Two species now exist where formerly there was one. Darwin called that splitting-and-specializing phenomenon the "principle of divergence." It was an important part of his theory, explaining the overall diversity of life as well as the adaptation of individual species.

This thrilling and radical assemblage of concepts came from an unlikely source. Charles Darwin was shy and meticulous, a wealthy landowner with close friends among the Anglican clergy. He had a gentle, unassuming manner, a strong need for privacy, and an extraordinary commitment to intellectual honesty. As an undergraduate at Cambridge, he had studied half-heartedly toward becoming a clergyman himself, before he discovered his real vocation as a scientist. Later, having established a good but conventional reputation in natural history, he spent twenty-two years secretly gathering evidence and pondering arguments—both for and against his theory— because he didn't want to flame out in a burst of unpersuasive notoriety. He may have delayed, too, because of his anxiety about announcing a theory that seemed to challenge conventional religious beliefs—in particular, the Christian beliefs of his wife, Emma. Darwin himself quietly renounced Christianity during his middle age, and later described himself as an agnostic. He continued to believe in a distant, impersonal deity of some sort, a greater entity that had set the universe and its laws into motion, but not in a personal God who had chosen humanity as a specially favored species. Darwin avoided flaunting his lack of religious faith, at least partly in deference to Emma. And she prayed for his soul.

In 1859 he finally delivered his revolutionary book. Although it was hefty and substantive at 490 pages, he considered *The Origin of Species* just a quick-and-dirty "abstract" of the huge volume he had been working on until interrupted by an alarming event. (In fact, he'd wanted to title it *An Abstract of an Essay on the Origin of Species and Varieties Through Natural Selection*, but his publisher found that insufficiently catchy.) The alarming event was his receiving a letter and an enclosed manuscript from Alfred Wallace, whom he knew only as a distant pen pal. Wallace's manuscript sketched out the same great idea—evolution by natural selection—that Darwin considered his own. Wallace had scribbled this paper and (unaware of Darwin's own evolutionary thinking, which so far had been kept private) mailed it to him from the Malay Archipelago, along with a request for reaction and help. Darwin was horrified. After two decades of painstaking effort, now he'd be scooped. Or maybe not quite. He forwarded Wallace's paper toward publication, though managing also to assert his own prior claim by releasing two excerpts from his unpublished work. Then he dashed off *The Origin*, his "abstract" on the subject. Unlike Wallace, who was younger and less meticulous, Darwin recognized the importance of providing an edifice of supporting evidence and logic.

The evidence, as he presented it, mostly fell within four categories: biogeography, paleontology, embryology, and morphology. Biogeography is the study of the geographical distribution of living creatures—that is, which species inhabit which parts of the planet and why. Paleontology investigates extinct life-forms, as revealed in the fossil record. Embryology examines the revealing stages of development (echoing earlier stages of evolutionary history) that embryos pass through before birth or hatching; at a stretch, embryology also concerns the immature forms of animals that metamorphose, such as the larvae of insects. Morphology is the science of anatomical shape and design. Darwin devoted sizable sections of *The Origin of Species* to these categories.

Biogeography, for instance, offered a great pageant of peculiar facts and patterns. Anyone who considers the biogeographical data, Darwin wrote, must be struck by the mysterious clustering pattern among what he called "closely allied" species—that is, similar creatures sharing roughly the same body plan. Such closely allied species tend to be found on the same continent (several species of zebras in Africa) or within the same group of oceanic islands (dozens of species of honeycreepers in Hawaii, thirteen species of Galápagos finch), despite their species-by-species preferences for different habitats, food sources, or conditions of climate. Adjacent areas of South America, Darwin noted, are occupied by two similar species of large, flightless birds (the rheas, *Rhea americana* and *Pterocnemia pennata)*, not by ostriches as in Africa or emus as in Australia. South America also has agoutis and viscachas (small rodents) in terrestrial habitats, plus coypus and capybaras in the wetlands, not—as Darwin wrote—hares and rabbits in terrestrial habitats or beavers and muskrats in the wetlands. During his own youthful visit to the Galápagos, aboard the survey ship *Beagle*, Darwin himself had discovered three very similar forms of mockingbird, each on a different island.

Why should "closely allied" species inhabit neighboring patches of habitat? And why should similar habitat on different continents be occupied by species that aren't so closely allied? "We see in these facts some deep organic bond, prevailing throughout space and time," Darwin wrote. "This bond, on my theory, is simply inheritance." Similar species occur nearby in space because they have descended from common ancestors.

Paleontology reveals a similar clustering pattern in the dimension of time. The vertical column of geologic strata, laid down by sedimentary processes over the eons, lightly peppered with fossils, represents a tangible record showing which species lived when. Less ancient layers of rock lie atop more ancient ones (except where geologic forces have tipped or shuffled them), and likewise with the animal and plant fossils that the strata contain. What Darwin noticed about this record is that closely allied species tend to be found adjacent to one another in successive strata. One species endures for millions of years and then makes its last appearance in, say, the middle Eocene epoch; just above, a similar but not identical species replaces it. In North America, for example, a vaguely horselike creature known as *Hyracotherium* was succeeded by *Orohippus*, then *Epihippus*, then *Mesohippus*, which in turn were succeeded by a variety of horsey American critters. Some of them even galloped across the Bering land bridge into Asia, then onward to Europe and Africa. By five million years ago they had nearly all disappeared, leaving behind *Dinohippus*, which was succeeded by *Equus*, the modern genus of horse. Not all these fossil links had been unearthed in Darwin's day, but he captured the essence of the matter anyway. Again, were such sequences just coincidental? No, Darwin argued. Closely allied species succeed one another in time, as well as living nearby in space, because they're related through evolutionary descent.

Embryology too involved patterns that couldn't be explained by coincidence. Why does the embryo of a mammal pass through stages resembling stages of the embryo of a reptile? Why is one of the larval forms of a barnacle, before metamorphosis, so similar to the larval form of a shrimp? Why do the larvae of moths, flies, and beetles resemble one another more than any of them resemble their respective adults? Because, Darwin wrote, "the embryo is the animal in its less modified state" and that state "reveals the structure of its progenitor."

Morphology, his fourth category of evidence, was the "very soul" of natural history, according to Darwin. Even today it's on display in the layout and organization of any zoo. Here are the monkeys, there are the big cats, and in that building are the alligators and crocodiles. Birds in the aviary, fish in the aquarium. Living creatures can be easily sorted into a hierarchy of categories—not just species but genera, families, orders, whole kingdoms—based on which anatomical characters they share and which they don't.

All vertebrate animals have backbones. Among vertebrates, birds have feathers, whereas reptiles have scales. Mammals have fur and mammary glands, not feathers or scales. Among mammals, some have pouches in which they nurse their tiny young. Among these species, the marsupials, some have huge rear legs and strong tails by which they go hopping across miles of arid outback; we call them kangaroos. Bring in modern microscopic and molecular evidence, and you can trace the similarities still further back. All plants and fungi, as well as animals, have nuclei within their cells. All living organisms contain DNA and RNA (except some viruses with RNA only), two related forms of information-coding molecules.

Such a pattern of tiered resemblances—groups of similar species nested within broader groupings, and all descending from a single source—isn't naturally present among other collections of items. You won't find anything equivalent if you try to categorize rocks, or musical instruments, or jewelry. Why not? Because rock types and styles of jewelry don't reflect unbroken descent from common ancestors. Biological diversity does. The number of shared characteristics between any one species and another indicates how recently those two species have diverged from a shared lineage.

That insight gave new meaning to the task of taxonomic classification, which had been founded in its modern form back in 1735 by the Swedish naturalist Carolus Linnaeus. Linnaeus showed how species could be systematically classified, according to their shared similarities, but he worked from creationist assumptions that offered no material explanation for the nested pattern he found. In the early and middle nineteenth century, morphologists such as George Cuvier and Étienne Geoffroy Saint-Hilaire in France and Richard Owen in England improved classification with their meticulous studies of internal as well as external anatomies, and tried to make sense of what the ultimate source of these patterned similarities could be. Not even Owen, a contemporary and onetime friend of Darwin's (later in life they had a bitter falling-out), took the full step to an evolutionary vision before *The Origin of Species* was published. Owen made a major contribution, though, by advancing the concept of homologues—that is, superficially different but fundamentally similar versions of a single organ or trait, shared by dissimilar species.

For instance, the five-digit skeletal structure of the vertebrate hand appears not just in humans and apes and raccoons and bears but also, variously modified, in cats and bats and porpoises and lizards and turtles. The paired bones of our lower leg, the tibia and the fibula, are also represented by homologous bones in other mammals and in reptiles, and even in the long-extinct bird-reptile *Archaeopteryx*. What's the reason behind such varied recurrence of a few basic designs? Darwin, with a nod to Owen's "most interesting work," supplied the answer: common descent, as shaped by natural selection, modifying the inherited basics for different circumstances.

Vestigial characteristics are still another form of morphological evidence, illuminating to contemplate because they show that the living world is full of small, tolerable imperfections. Why do male mammals (including human males) have nipples? Why do some snakes (notably boa constrictors) carry the rudiments of a pelvis and tiny legs buried inside their sleek profiles? Why do certain species of flightless beetle have wings, sealed beneath wing covers that never open? Darwin raised all these questions, and answered them, in *The Origin of Species*. Vestigial structures stand as remnants of the evolutionary history of a lineage.

Today the same four branches of biological science from which Darwin drew—biogeography, paleontology, embryology, morphology—embrace an ever growing body of supporting data. In addition to those categories we now have others: population genetics, biochemistry, molecular biology, and, most recently, the whiz-bang field of machine-driven genetic sequencing known as genomics. These new forms of knowledge overlap one another seamlessly and intersect with the older forms, strengthening the whole edifice, contributing further to the certainty that Darwin was right.

He was right about evolution, that is. He wasn't right about *everything*. Being a restless explainer, Darwin floated a number of theoretical notions during his long working life, some of which were mistaken and illusory. He was wrong about what causes variation within a species. He was wrong about a famous geologic mystery, the parallel shelves along a Scottish valley called Glen Roy. Most notably, his theory of inheritance—which he labeled pangenesis and cherished despite its poor reception among his biologist colleagues—turned out to be dead wrong. Fortunately for Darwin, the correctness of his most famous good idea stood independent of that particular bad idea. Evolution by natural selection represented Darwin at his best—which is to say, scientific observation and careful thinking at its best.

Douglas Futuyma is a highly respected evolutionary biologist, author of textbooks as well as influential research papers. His office, at the University of Michigan, is a long narrow room in the natural sciences building, well stocked with journals and books, including volumes about the conflict between creationism and evolution. I arrived carrying a well-thumbed copy of his own book on that subject, *Science on Trial: The Case for Evolution.* Killing time in the corridor before our appointment, I noticed a blue flyer on a departmental bulletin board, seeming oddly placed there amid the announcements of career opportunities for graduate students. "CREATON VS. EVOLUTION," it said. "A series of messages challenging popular thought with Biblical truth and scientific evidences." A traveling lecturer from something called the Origins Research Association would deliver these messages at a local Baptist church. Beside the lecturer's photo was a drawing of a dinosaur. "Free pizza following the evening service," said a small line at the bottom. Dinosaurs, biblical truth, and pizza: something for everybody.

In response to my questions about evidence, Dr. Futuyma moved quickly through the traditional categories—paleontology, biogeography—and talked mostly about modern genetics. He pulled out his heavily marked copy of the journal *Nature* for February 15, 2001, a historic issue, fat with articles reporting and analyzing the results of the Human Genome Project. Beside it he slapped down a more recent issue of *Nature,* this one devoted to the sequenced genome of the house mouse, *Mus musculus.* The headline of the lead editorial announced: "Human Biology by Proxy." The mouse genome effort, according to *Nature's* editors, had revealed "about thirty thousand genes, with 99 percent having direct counterparts in humans."

The resemblance between our thirty thousand human genes and those thirty thousand mousy counterparts, Futuyma explained, represents another form of homology, like the resemblance between a five-fingered hand and a five-toed paw. Such genetic homology is what gives meaning to biomedical research using mice and other animals, including chimpanzees, which (to their sad misfortune) are our closest living relatives.

No aspect of biomedical research seems more urgent today than the study of microbial diseases. And the dynamics of those microbes within human bodies, within human populations, can only be understood in terms of evolution.

Nightmarish illnesses caused by microbes include both the infectious sort (AIDS, Ebola, SARS) that spread directly from person to person and the sort (malaria, West Nile fever) delivered to us by biting insects or other intermediaries. The capacity for quick change among disease-causing microbes is what makes them so dangerous to large numbers of people and so difficult and expensive to treat. They leap from wildlife or domestic animals into humans, adapting to new circumstances as they go. Their inherent variability allows them to find new ways of evading and defeating human immune systems. By natural selection they acquire resistance to drugs that should kill them. They evolve. There's no better or more immediate evidence supporting the Darwinian theory than this process of forced transformation among our inimical germs.

Take the common bacterium *Staphylococcus aureus*, which lurks in hospitals and causes serious infections, especially among surgery patients. Penicillin, becoming available in 1943, proved almost miraculously effective in fighting staphylococcus infections. Its deployment marked a new phase in the old war between humans and disease microbes, a phase in which humans invent new killer drugs and microbes find new ways to be unkillable. The supreme potency of penicillin didn't last long. The first resistant strains of *Staphylococcus aureus* were reported in 1947. A newer staph-killing drug, methicillin, came into use during the 1960s, but methicillin-resistant strains appeared soon, and by the 1980s those strains were widespread. Vancomycin became the next great weapon against staph, and the first vancomycin-resistant strain emerged in 2002. These antibiotic-resistant strains represent an evolutionary series, not much different in principle from the fossil series tracing horse evolution from *Hyra-cotherium* to *Equus*. They make evolution a very practical problem by adding expense, as well as misery and danger, to the challenge of coping with staph.

The biologist Stephen Palumbi has calculated the cost of treating penicillin-resistant and methicillin-resistant staph infections, just in the United States, at $30 billion a year. "Antibiotics exert a powerful evolutionary force," he wrote last year, "driving infectious bacteria to evolve powerful defenses against all but the most recently invented drugs." As reflected in their DNA, which uses the same genetic code found in humans and horses and hagfish and honeysuckle, bacteria are part of the continuum of life, all shaped and diversified by evolutionary forces.

Even viruses belong to that continuum. Some viruses evolve quickly, some slowly. Among the fastest is HIV, because its method of replicating itself involves a high rate of mutation, and those mutations allow the virus to assume new forms. After just a few years of infection and drug treatment, each HIV patient carries a unique version of the virus. Isolation within one infected person, plus differing conditions and the struggle to survive, forces each version of HIV to evolve independently. It's nothing but a speeded up and microscopic case of what Darwin saw in the Galápagos—except that each human body is an island, and the newly evolved forms aren't so charming as finches or mockingbirds.

Understanding how quickly HIV acquires resistance to antiviral drugs, such as AZT, has been crucial to improving treatment by way of multiple-drug cocktails. "This approach has reduced deaths due to HIV by severalfold since 1996," according to Palumbi, "and it has greatly slowed the evolution of this disease within patients."

Insects and weeds acquire resistance to our insecticides and herbicides through the same process. As we humans try to poison them, evolution by natural selection transforms the population of a mosquito or thistle into a new sort of creature, less vulnerable to that particular poison. So we invent another poison, then another. It's a futile effort. Even DDT, with its ferocious and long-lasting effects throughout ecosystems, produced resistant house flies within a decade of its discovery in 1939. By 1990 more than 500 species (including 114 kinds of mosquitoes) had acquired resistance to at least one pesticide. Based on these undesired results, Stephen Palumbi has commented glumly, "humans may be the world's dominant evolutionary force."

Among most forms of living creatures, evolution proceeds slowly—too slowly to be observed by a single scientist within a research lifetime. But science functions by inference, not just by direct observation, and the inferential sorts of evidence such as paleontology and biogeography are no less cogent simply because they're indirect. Still, skeptics of evolutionary theory ask: Can we see evolution in action? Can it be observed in the wild? Can it be measured in the laboratory?

The answer is yes. Peter and Rosemary Grant, two British-born researchers who have spent decades where Charles Darwin spent weeks, have captured a glimpse of evolution with their long-term studies of beak size among Galápagos finches. William R. Rice and George W. Salt achieved something similar in their lab, through an experiment involving thirty-five generations of the fruit fly *Drosophila melanogaster.* Richard E. Lenski and his colleagues at Michigan State University have done it too, tracking twenty thousand generations of evolution in the bacterium *Escherichia coli.* Such field studies and lab experiments document anagenesis—that is, slow evolutionary change within a single, unsplit lineage. With patience it can be seen, like the movement of a minute hand on a clock.

Speciation, when a lineage splits into two species, is the other major phase of evolutionary change, making possible the divergence between lineages about which Darwin wrote. It's rarer and more elusive even than anagenesis. Many individual mutations must accumulate (in most cases, anyway, with certain exceptions among plants) before two populations become irrevocably separated. The process is spread across thousands of generations, yet it may finish abruptly—like a door going *slam!*—when the last critical changes occur. Therefore it's much harder to witness. Despite the difficulties, Rice and Salt seem to have recorded a speciation event, or very nearly so, in their extended experiment on fruit flies. From a small stock of mated females they eventually produced two distinct fly populations adapted to different habitat conditions, which the researchers judged "incipient species."

After my visit with Douglas Futuyma in Ann Arbor, I spent two hours at the university museum there with Philip D. Gingerich, a paleontologist well-known for his work on the ancestry of whales. As we talked, Gingerich guided me through an exhibit of ancient cetaceans on the museum's second floor. Amid weird skeletal shapes that seemed almost chimerical (some hanging overhead, some in glass cases) he pointed out significant features and described the progress of thinking about whale evolution. A burly man with a broad open face and the gentle manner of a scoutmaster, Gingerich combines intellectual passion and solid expertise with one other trait that's valuable in a scientist: a willingness to admit when he's wrong.

Since the late 1970s Gingerich has collected fossil specimens of early whales from remote digs in Egypt and Pakistan. Working with Pakistani colleagues, he discovered *Pakicetus*, a terrestrial mammal dating from fifty million years ago, whose ear bones reflect its membership in the whale lineage but whose skull looks almost doglike. A former student of Gingerich's, Hans Thewissen, found a slightly more recent form with webbed feet, legs suitable for either walking or swimming, and a long toothy snout. Thewissen called it *Ambulocetus natans*, or the "walking-and-swimming whale." Gingerich and his team turned up several more, including *Rodhocetus balochistanensis*, which was fully a sea creature, its legs more like flippers, its nostrils shifted backward on the snout, halfway to the blowhole position on a modern whale. The sequence of known forms was becoming more and more complete. And all along, Gingerich told me, he leaned toward believing that whales had descended from a group of carnivorous Eocene mammals known as mesonychids, with cheek teeth useful for chewing meat and bone. Just a bit more evidence, he thought, would confirm that relationship. By the end of the 1990s most paleontologists agreed.

Meanwhile, molecular biologists had explored the same question and arrived at a different answer. No, the match to those Eocene carnivores might be close, but not close enough. DNA hybridization and other tests suggested that whales had descended from artiodactyls (that is, even-toed herbivores, such as antelopes and hippos), not from meat-eating mesonychids.

In the year 2000 Gingerich chose a new field site in Pakistan, where one of his students found a single piece of fossil that changed the prevailing view in paleontology. It was half of a pulley-shaped anklebone, known as an astragalus, belonging to another new species of whale. A Pakistani colleague found the fragment's other half. When Gingerich fitted the two pieces together, he had a moment of humbling recognition: The molecular biologists were right. Here was an anklebone, from a four-legged whale dating back forty-seven million years, that closely resembled the homologous anklebone in an artiodactyl. Suddenly he realized how closely whales are related to antelopes.

This is how science is supposed to work. Ideas come and go, but the fittest survive. Downstairs in his office Phil Gingerich opened a specimen drawer, showing me some of the actual fossils from which the display skeletons upstairs were modeled. He put a small lump of petrified bone, no larger than a lug nut, into my hand. It was the famous astragalus, from the species he had eventually named *Artiocetus clavis*. It felt solid and heavy as truth.

Seeing me to the door, Gingerich volunteered something personal: "I grew up in a conservative church in the Midwest and was not taught anything about evolution. The subject was clearly skirted. That helps me understand the people who are skeptical about it. Because I come from that tradition myself." He shares the same skeptical instinct. Tell him that there's an ancestral connection between land animals and whales, and his reaction is: Fine, maybe, but show me the intermediate stages. Like Charles Darwin, the onetime divinity student, who joined that round-the-world voyage aboard the *Beagle* instead of becoming a country parson, and whose grand view of life on Earth was shaped by close attention to small facts, Phil Gingerich is a reverent empiricist. He's not satisfied until he sees solid data. That's what excites him so much about pulling whale fossils out of the ground. In thirty years he has seen enough to be satisfied. For him, Gingerich said, it's "a spiritual experience."

"The evidence is there," he added. "It's buried in the rocks of ages."

Suggestions for Discussion

1. What scientific evidence does Quammen cite to support the theory of evolution?

2. Discuss the results of the 2001 telephone survey that stated that 45 percent of U.S. adults agreed that "God created human beings pretty much in their present form at one time within the last ten thousand years or so." Based on the evidence for evolution, do you feel that number is too high or too low? Explain.

3. Discuss Quammen's reasons for the high numbers of antievolutionists in the United States.

Suggestions for Writing

1. Write an essay discussing your beliefs for or against the theory of evolution.

2. Research and write about the current debate for and against the teaching of evolution versus creationism in schools. Which side do you agree with?

∽∾∽∾∽

NICHOLAS D. KRISTOF

Warm, Warmer, Warmest

A *New York Times* columnist since 1984, Nicholas D. Kristof writes stories with an international scope and has distinguished himself covering politics in China, Japan, and Africa. He and his wife, Sheryl WuDunn, have collaborated on the books *China Wakes* (1995) and *Thunder from the East* (2000), and they jointly earned a Pulitzer Prize in 1990 for their coverage of the historic Tiananmen Square protests of 1989. Kristof won a second Pulitzer in 2006 for risking his life to offer firsthand reporting on the genocide in Darfur. In addition, Kristof has covered President George W. Bush's career since the 2000 presidential campaign and wrote a chapter about Bush for the reference book *The Presidents*. The following 2006 essay concerning global warming appeared in the *New York Times*.

One of the hottest environmental battles has been over oil drilling in the coastal plain of the Arctic National Wildlife Refuge, but the sad reality is that much of the Arctic plain will probably be lost anyway in this century to rising sea levels.

That should be our paramount struggle: to stop global warming. It threatens not only the Arctic plain, but also low-lying areas around the world with 100 million inhabitants. And it could be accelerating because of the three scariest words in climate science: positive feedback loops.

Bear with me now: a positive feedback loop occurs when a small change leads to an even larger change of the same type. For example, a modest amount of warming melts ice in northern climates. But the bare ground absorbs three times as much heat as ground covered by snow or ice, so the change amplifies the original warming. Even more ice melts, more heat is absorbed, and the spiral grows.

That feedback loop is well understood and part of climate models, but others aren't.

IMKE LASS, *Boat cemetery at the former shoreline of the Aral Sea, Muynak, Uzbekistan.* C-print, 1999.
© Imke Lass, www.imkelass.com.

For example, perhaps the biggest single source of uncertainty about whether Lower Manhattan will be underwater in 2100 has to do with the glaciers of Greenland. If Greenland's ice sheet melted completely, that alone—over centuries—would raise the oceans by 23 feet. And those glaciers are dumping much more water into the oceans than they did a decade ago, according to two satellite surveys just published, but the studies disagree on the amounts.

Positive feedback seems to be at work. As a glacier melts a little, the water trickles down to the rock and lubricates the glacier's slide toward the sea. So, because of this and other effects, some of Greenland's glaciers are now, in glacial terms, rocketing toward the sea at 7.5 miles a year.

Here's another positive loop. The Arctic permafrost may hold 14 percent of the world's carbon, but as it melts, some of its carbon dioxide and methane are released, adding to the amount of greenhouse gases. So more permafrost melts.

Likewise, millions of years ago, warming oceans with vast amounts of methane in their depths had great episodes of methane belching, which added to the greenhouse effect then. I don't expect the oceans to burp in the same massive way tomorrow, but if they did, no one would know how to fit those unmannerly oceans into a climate model.

Part of the challenge in modeling climate is that we're already off the charts with greenhouse gases like nitrous oxide, carbon dioxide, and methane. "We've driven them out of the range that has existed for the last one million years," noted James Hansen, NASA's top climate expert. "And the climate has not fully responded to changes that have already occurred."

In fairness, there are also negative feedback loops, which could dampen change. For example, warmer temperatures could mean more snow over Antarctica, implying an initial buildup of the Antarctic ice sheet. The added ice could slow global warming and rising sea levels. But a new study just published in Science Express says that the Antarctic ice sheet is already thinning significantly—raising more alarms and casting doubt on that negative feedback. In any case, it's clear that negative feedback loops in climatology are much less common than positive loops, which amplify change and leave our climate both unstable and vulnerable to human folly.

Still with me?

Look, I know that climate science can be—here's a shock—boring! But it's better for us to slog through it now than for coming generations to slog through the rising waters of, say, Manhattan. It may be more exciting to thump the table about Iraq or torture—or even the preservation of the Arctic National Wildlife Refuge—and those are all hugely important. But global warming may ultimately be the greatest test we face as stewards of our planet. And so far we're failing catastrophically.

"Historians of science will be brutal on us," said Jerry Mahlman, a climate expert at the National Center for Atmospheric Research. "We are right now in a state of deep denial about how severe the problem is. Political people are saying, 'Well, it's not on my watch.' They're ducking for cover, because who's going to tell the American people?"

We know what to do: energy conservation, gas taxes and carbon taxes, more renewable energy sources like wind and solar power, and new (and safe) nuclear power plants. But our political system is paralyzed in the face of what may be the single biggest challenge to our planet.

"Are we an intelligent species or not?" Dr. Mahlman asked. "Right now, the evidence is against it."

Suggestions for Discussion

1. What are "positive feedback loops"? Why are they significant?

2. In the issue of global warming, where does science end and politics begin?

3. Kristof says that governments can curtail the damage currently being done to the environment by conserving energy, raising taxes on gas and carbon, creating new and safe nuclear power plants, and developing wind and solar power energy sources. He says politicians know the importance of taking these steps, but they ignore the issue. Why won't they take action? Would you be eager or upset to see any of these measures taken? Do you see the necessity of these changes? Why or why not?

4. The photograph accompanying Kristof's essay shows the Aral Sea in Uzbekistan. On the Internet, explore what has happened to the Aral Sea. Share your findings in class.

Suggestions for Writing

1. Activists who wish to raise awareness about the dangers of global warming assert that the vast majority of scientists and serious juried scientific journals maintain that global warming is a reality, while news venues such as Fox News often claim that opinion is more divided on the issue, and their commentators question the reliability of the science behind the "panic." How much consensus is there concerning the reality of global warming? Research several scientific articles and studies, using sources checked for reliability by your professor and/or librarian, to determine whether the scientific community is truly as united/divided on the issue as others would portray them to be. Write your findings in essay form, using at least seven cited non-Internet sources.

2. Write an editorial for your local newspaper compiling your findings about the Aral Sea and its fate, and about the difference this has made to the local area and its population. Include your thoughts about how this could or should affect us in our own lives and the lives of generations to come.

3. Write a work of short fiction using Lass's photograph as the starting point or conclusion of your story.

JAMES   HOWARD   KUNSTLER

The Long Emergency

James Howard Kunstler (b. 1948) is a New York author and social critic who warns that dwindling supplies of oil will cause the end of suburban life and industrialization as we know it. The crisis, he believes, needs to be confronted by a revamped railway system and the development of self-sufficient, agrarian communities throughout the world. Kunstler writes regularly about such issues, and about the crumbling, poorly planned infrastructure of the United States, in the *New York Times' Sunday Magazine* and Op-Ed page, and for *Rolling Stone Magazine.* He has also appeared in the documentaries *Radiant City* (2006) and *The End of Suburbia* (2007). His books include *The Wampanaki Tales* (1979), *A Clown in the Moonlight* (1981), *The Geography of Nowhere* (1993), *Home from Nowhere* (1996), *The City in Mind* (2002), *Maggie Darling* (2003), *The Long Emergency* (2005), and *World Made by Hand* (2008). The following is an excerpt from *The Long Emergency.*

A few weeks ago, the price of oil ratcheted above fifty-five dollars a barrel, which is about twenty dollars a barrel more than a year ago. The next day, the oil story was buried on page six of the *New York Times* business section. Apparently, the price of oil is not considered significant news, even when it goes up five bucks a barrel in the span of ten days. That same day, the stock market shot up more than a hundred points because, CNN said, government data showed no signs of inflation. Note to clueless nation: Call planet Earth.

Carl Jung, one of the fathers of psychology, famously remarked that "people cannot stand too much reality." What you're about to read may challenge your assumptions about the kind of world we live in, and especially the kind of world into which events are propelling us. We are in for a rough ride through uncharted territory.

It has been very hard for Americans—lost in dark raptures of nonstop infotainment, recreational shopping and compulsive motoring—to make sense of the gathering forces that will fundamentally alter the terms of everyday life in our technological society. Even after the terrorist attacks of 9/11, America is still sleepwalking into the future. I call this coming time the Long Emergency.

Most immediately we face the end of the cheap-fossil-fuel era. It is no exaggeration to state that reliable supplies of cheap oil and natural gas underlie everything we identify as the necessities of modern life—not to mention all of its comforts and luxuries: central heating, air conditioning, cars, airplanes, electric lights, inexpensive clothing, recorded music, movies, hip-replacement surgery, national defense—you name it.

The few Americans who are even aware that there is a gathering global-energy predicament usually misunderstand the core of the argument. That argument states that we don't have to run out of oil to start having severe problems with industrial civilization and its dependent systems. We only have to slip over the all-time production peak and begin a slide down the arc of steady depletion.

The term "global oil-production peak" means that a turning point will come when the world produces the most oil it will ever produce in a given year and, after that, yearly production will inexorably decline. It is usually represented graphically in a bell curve. The peak is the top of the curve, the halfway point of the world's all-time total endowment, meaning half the world's oil will be left. That seems like a lot of oil, and it is, but there's a big catch: It's the half that is much more difficult to extract, far more costly to get, of much poorer quality and located mostly in places where the people hate us. A substantial amount of it will never be extracted.

The United States passed its own oil peak—about 11 million barrels a day—in 1970, and since then production has dropped steadily. In 2004 it ran just above 5 million barrels a day (we get a tad more from natural-gas condensates). Yet we consume roughly 20 million barrels a day now. That means we have to import about two-thirds of our oil, and the ratio will continue to worsen.

The U.S. peak in 1970 brought on a portentous change in geoeconomic power. Within a few years, foreign producers, chiefly OPEC, were setting the price of oil, and this in turn led to the oil crises of the 1970s. In response, frantic development of non-OPEC oil, especially the North Sea fields of England and Norway, essentially saved the West's ass for about two decades. Since 1999, these fields have entered depletion. Meanwhile, worldwide discovery of new oil has steadily declined to insignificant levels in 2003 and 2004.

Some "cornucopians" claim that the Earth has something like a creamy nougat center of "abiotic" oil that will naturally replenish the great oil fields of the world. The facts speak differently. There has been no replacement whatsoever of oil already extracted from the fields of America or any other place.

Now we are faced with the global oil-production peak. The best estimates of when this will actually happen have been somewhere between now and 2010. In 2004, however, after demand from burgeoning China and India shot up, and revelations that Shell Oil wildly misstated its reserves, and Saudi Arabia proved incapable of goosing up its production despite promises to do so, the most knowledgeable experts revised their predictions and now concur that 2005 is apt to be the year of alltime global peak production.

It will change everything about how we live.

To aggravate matters, American natural-gas production is also declining, at five percent a year, despite frenetic new drilling, and with the potential of much steeper declines ahead. Because of the oil crises of the 1970s, the nuclear-plant disasters at Three Mile Island and Chernobyl and the acid-rain problem, the U.S. chose to make gas its first choice for electric-power generation. The result was that just about every power plant built after 1980 has to run on gas. Half the homes in America are heated with gas. To further complicate matters, gas isn't easy to import. Here in North America, it is distributed through a vast pipeline network. Gas imported from overseas would have to be compressed at minus 260 degrees Fahrenheit in pressurized tanker ships and unloaded (re-gasified) at special terminals, of which few exist in America. Moreover, the first attempts to site new terminals have met furious opposition because they are such ripe targets for terrorism.

Some other things about the global energy predicament are poorly understood by the public and even our leaders. This is going to be a permanent energy crisis, and these energy problems will synergize with the disruptions of climate change, epidemic disease and population overshoot to produce higher orders of trouble.

We will have to accommodate ourselves to fundamentally changed conditions.

No combination of alternative fuels will allow us to run American life the way we have been used to running it, or even a substantial fraction of it. The wonders of steady technological progress achieved through the reign of cheap oil have lulled us into a kind of Jiminy Cricket syndrome, leading many Americans to believe that anything we wish for hard enough will come true. These days, even people who ought to know better are wishing ardently for a seamless transition from fossil fuels to their putative replacements.

The widely touted "hydrogen economy" is a particularly cruel hoax. We are not going to replace the U.S. automobile and truck fleet with vehicles run on fuel cells. For one thing, the current generation of fuel cells is largely designed to run on hydrogen obtained from natural gas. The other way to get hydrogen in the quantities wished for would be electrolysis of water using power from hundreds of nuclear plants. Apart from the dim prospect of our building that many nuclear plants soon enough, there are also numerous severe problems with hydrogen's nature as an element that present forbidding obstacles to its use as a replacement for oil and gas, especially in storage and transport.

Wishful notions about rescuing our way of life with "renewables" are also unrealistic. Solar-electric systems and wind turbines face not only the enormous problem of scale but the fact that the components require substantial amounts of energy to manufacture and the probability that they can't be manufactured at all without the underlying support platform of a fossil-fuel economy. We will surely use solar and wind technology to generate some electricity for a period ahead but probably at a very local and small scale.

Virtually all "biomass" schemes for using plants to create liquid fuels cannot be scaled up to even a fraction of the level at which things are currently run. What's more, these schemes are predicated on using oil and gas "inputs" (fertilizers, weed-killers) to grow the biomass crops that would be converted into ethanol or bio-diesel fuels. This is a net energy loser—you might as well just burn the inputs and not bother with the biomass products. Proposals to distill trash and waste into oil by means of thermal depolymerization depend on the huge waste stream produced by a cheap oil and gas economy in the first place.

Coal is far less versatile than oil and gas, extant in less abundant supplies than many people assume and fraught with huge ecological drawbacks—as a contributor to greenhouse "global warming" gases and many health and toxicity issues ranging from widespread mercury poisoning to acid rain. You can make synthetic oil from coal, but the only time this was tried on a large scale was by the Nazis under wartime conditions, using impressive amounts of slave labor.

If we wish to keep the lights on in America after 2020, we may indeed have to resort to nuclear power, with all its practical problems and eco-conundrums. Under optimal conditions, it could take ten years to get a new generation of nuclear power plants into operation, and the price may be beyond our means. Uranium is also a resource in finite supply. We are no closer to the more difficult project of atomic fusion, by the way, than we were in the 1970s.

The upshot of all this is that we are entering a historical period of potentially great instability, turbulence and hardship. Obviously, geopolitical maneuvering around the world's richest energy regions has already led to war and promises more international military conflict. Since the Middle East contains two-thirds of the world's remaining oil supplies, the U.S. has attempted desperately to stabilize the region by, in effect, opening a big police station in Iraq. The intent was not just to secure Iraq's oil but to modify and influence the behavior of neighboring states around the Persian Gulf, especially Iran and Saudi Arabia. The results have been far from entirely positive, and our future prospects in that part of the world are not something we can feel altogether confident about.

And then there is the issue of China, which, in 2004, became the world's second-greatest consumer of oil, surpassing Japan. China's surging industrial growth has made it increasingly dependent on the imports we are counting on. If China wanted to, it could easily walk into some of these places—the Middle East, former Soviet republics in central Asia—and extend its hegemony by force. Is America prepared to contest for this oil in an Asian land war with the Chinese army? I doubt it. Nor can the U.S. military occupy regions of the Eastern Hemisphere indefinitely, or hope to secure either the terrain or the oil infrastructure of one distant, unfriendly country after another. A likely scenario is that the U.S. could exhaust and bankrupt itself trying to do this, and be forced to withdraw back into our own hemisphere, having lost access to most of the world's remaining oil in the process.

We know that our national leaders are hardly uninformed about this predicament. President George W. Bush has been briefed on the dangers of the oil-peak situation as long ago as before the 2000 election and repeatedly since then. In March, the Department of Energy released a report that officially acknowledges for the first time that peak oil is for real and states plainly that "the world has never faced a problem like this. Without massive mitigation more than a decade before the fact, the problem will be pervasive and will not be temporary."

Most of all, the Long Emergency will require us to make other arrangements for the way we live in the United States. America is in a special predicament due to a set of unfortunate choices we made as a society in the twentieth century. Perhaps the worst was to let our towns and cities rot away and to replace them with suburbia, which had the additional side effect of trashing a lot of the best farmland in America. Suburbia will come to be regarded as the greatest misallocation of resources in the history of the world. It has a tragic destiny. The psychology of previous investment suggests that we will defend our drive-in utopia long after it has become a terrible liability.

Before long, the suburbs will fail us in practical terms. We made the ongoing development of housing subdivisions, highway strips, fried-food shacks and shopping malls the basis of our economy, and when we have to stop making more of those things, the bottom will fall out.

The circumstances of the Long Emergency will require us to down-scale and rescale virtually everything we do and how we do it, from the kind of communities we physically inhabit to the way we grow our food to the way we work and trade the products of our work. Our lives will become profoundly and intensely local. Daily life will be far less about mobility and much more about staying where you are. Anything organized on the large scale, whether it is government or a corporate business enterprise such as Wal-Mart, will wither as the cheap energy props that support bigness fall away. The turbulence of the Long Emergency will produce a lot of economic losers, and many of these will be members of an angry and aggrieved former middle class.

Food production is going to be an enormous problem in the Long Emergency. As industrial agriculture fails due to a scarcity of oil- and gas-based inputs, we will certainly have to grow more of our food closer to where we live, and do it on a smaller scale. The American economy of the mid-twenty-first century may actually center on agriculture, not information, not high tech, not "services" like real estate sales or hawking cheeseburgers to tourists. Farming. This is no doubt a startling, radical idea, and it raises extremely difficult questions about the reallocation of land and the nature of work. The relentless subdividing of land in the late twentieth century has destroyed the contiguity and integrity of the rural landscape in most places. The process of readjustment is apt to be disorderly and improvisational. Food production will necessarily be much more labor-intensive than it has been for decades. We can anticipate the re-formation of a native-born American farm-laboring class. It will be composed largely of the aforementioned economic losers who had to relinquish their grip on the American dream. These masses of disentitled people may enter into quasifeudal social relations with those who own land in exchange for food and physical security.

But their sense of grievance will remain fresh, and if mistreated they may simply seize that land.

The way that commerce is currently organized in America will not survive far into the Long Emergency. Wal-Mart's "warehouse on wheels" won't be such a bargain in a non-cheap-oil economy. The national chain stores' 12,000-mile manufacturing supply lines could easily be interrupted by military contests over oil and by internal conflict in the nations that have been supplying us with ultracheap manufactured goods, because they, too, will be struggling with similar issues of energy famine and all the disorders that go with it.

As these things occur, America will have to make other arrangements for the manufacture, distribution and sale of ordinary goods. They will probably be made on a "cottage industry" basis rather than the factory system we once had, since the scale of available energy will be much lower— and we are not going to replay the twentieth century. Tens of thousands of the common products we enjoy today, from paints to pharmaceuticals, are made out of oil. They will become increasingly scarce or unavailable. The selling of things will have to be reorganized at the local scale. It will have to be based on moving merchandise shorter distances. It is almost certain to result in higher costs for the things we buy and far fewer choices.

The automobile will be a diminished presence in our lives, to say the least. With gasoline in short supply, not to mention tax revenue, our roads will surely suffer. The interstate highway system is more delicate than the public realizes. If the "level of service" (as traffic engineers call it) is not maintained to the highest degree, problems multiply and escalate quickly. The system does not tolerate partial failure. The interstates are either in excellent condition, or they quickly fall apart.

America today has a railroad system that the Bulgarians would be ashamed of. Neither of the two major presidential candidates in 2004 mentioned railroads, but if we don't refurbish our rail system, then there may be no long-range travel or transport of goods at all a few decades from now. The commercial aviation industry, already on its knees financially, is likely to vanish. The sheer cost of maintaining gigantic airports may not justify the operation of a much-reduced air-travel fleet. Railroads are far more energy efficient than cars, trucks or airplanes, and they can be run on anything from wood to electricity. The rail-bed infrastructure is also far more economical to maintain than our highway network.

The successful regions in the twenty-first century will be the ones surrounded by viable farming hinterlands that can reconstitute locally sustainable economies on an armature of civic cohesion. Small towns and smaller cities have better prospects than the big cities, which will probably have to contract substantially. The process will be painful and tumultuous. In many American cities, such as Cleveland, Detroit and St. Louis, that process is already well advanced. Others have further to fall. New York and Chicago face extraordinary difficulties, being oversupplied with gigantic buildings out of scale with the reality of declining energy supplies. Their former agricultural hinterlands have long been paved over. They will be encysted in a surrounding fabric of necrotic suburbia that will only amplify and reinforce the cities' problems. Still, our cities occupy important sites. Some kind of urban entities will exist where they are in the future, but probably not the colossi of twentieth-century industrialism.

Some regions of the country will do better than others in the Long Emergency. The Southwest will suffer in proportion to the degree that it prospered during the cheap-oil blowout of the late twentieth century. I predict that Sunbelt states like Arizona and Nevada will become significantly depopulated, since the region will be short of water as well as gasoline and natural gas. Imagine Phoenix without cheap air conditioning.

I'm not optimistic about the Southeast, either, for different reasons. I think it will be subject to substantial levels of violence as the grievances of the formerly middle class boil over and collide with the delusions of Pentecostal Christian extremism. The latent encoded behavior of Southern culture includes an outsized notion of individualism and the belief that firearms ought to be used in the defense of it. This is a poor recipe for civic cohesion.

The Mountain States and Great Plains will face an array of problems, from poor farming potential to water shortages to population loss. The Pacific Northwest, New England and the Upper Midwest have somewhat better prospects. I regard them as less likely to fall into lawlessness, anarchy or despotism and more likely to salvage the bits and pieces of our best social traditions and keep them in operation at some level.

These are daunting and even dreadful prospects. The Long Emergency is going to be a tremendous trauma for the human race. We will not believe that this is happening to us, that 200 years of modernity can be brought to its knees by a world-wide power shortage. The survivors will have to cultivate a religion of hope—that is, a deep and comprehensive belief that humanity is worth carrying on. If there is any positive side to stark changes coming our way, it may be in the benefits of close communal relations, of having to really work intimately (and physically) with our neighbors, to be part of an enterprise that really matters and to be fully engaged in meaningful social enactments instead of being merely entertained to avoid boredom. Years from now, when we hear singing at all, we will hear ourselves, and we will sing with our whole hearts.

Suggestions for Discussion

1. Why does Kunstler believe we are running out of oil? What problems will this scenario create? What are the problems with alternative fuels, as Kunstler sees them?

2. Why are railroads one of the few forms of transportation that Kunstler deems essential?

3. What do the wars in the Middle East have to do with the situation Kunstler describes?

4. Assuming Kunstler is correct, what actions might be taken now to lessen the terrible effects of the Long Emergency? What hope, if any, does Kunstler offer for the future?

Suggestion for Writing

Using the wide range of information that Kunstler provides as well as your own research, support an argument either for or against Kunstler's claim that suburbia will be remembered as "the greatest misallocation of resources in the history of the world."

STEVEN D. LEVITT AND STEPHEN J. DUBNER

Freakonomics: The Hidden Side of Everything

Steven D. Levitt (b. 1967), the Alvin H. Baum Professor of Economics at the University of Chicago, is best known for his groundbreaking work on the effects of legalized abortion on crime statistics. He has been named in *Time* magazine's list of "100 People Who Shape Our World" and, in 2003, was the recipient of the John Bates Clarke Medal, awarded to an outstanding economist under age forty. Stephen J. Dubner (b. 1963) writes frequently for the *New York Times* and the *New Yorker* and was first published, at age eleven, in *Highlights for Children*. The following excerpt is from the best seller *Freakonomics: A Rogue Economist Explores the Hidden Side of Everything* (2005).

Anyone living in the United States in the early 1990s and paying even a whisper of attention to the nightly news or a daily paper could be forgiven for having been scared out of his skin.

The culprit was crime. It had been rising relentlessly—a graph plotting the crime rate in any American city over recent decades looked like a ski slope in profile—and it seemed now to herald the end of the world as we knew it. Death by gunfire, intentional and otherwise, had become commonplace. So too had carjacking and crack dealing, robbery and rape. Violent crime was a gruesome, constant companion. And things were about to get even worse. Much worse. All the experts were saying so.

The cause was the so-called superpredator. For a time, he was everywhere. Glowering from the cover of newsweeklies. Swaggering his way through foot-thick government reports. He was a scrawny, big-city teenager with a cheap gun in his hand and nothing in his heart but ruthlessness. There were thousands out there just like him, we were told, a generation of killers about to hurl the country into deepest chaos.

In 1995 the criminologist James Alan Fox wrote a report for the U.S. attorney general that grimly detailed the coming spike in murders by teenagers. Fox proposed optimistic and pessimistic scenarios. In the optimistic scenario, he believed, the rate of teen homicides would rise another 15 percent over the next decade; in the pessimistic scenario, it would more than double. "The next crime wave will get so bad," he said, "that it will make 1995 look like the good old days."

Other criminologists, political scientists, and similarly learned forecasters laid out the same horrible future, as did President Clinton. "We know we've got about six years to turn this juvenile crime thing around," Clinton said, "or our country is going to be living with chaos. And my successors will not be giving speeches about the wonderful opportunities of the global economy; they'll be trying to keep body and soul together for people on the streets of these cities." The smart money was plainly on the criminals.

And then, instead of going up and up and up, crime began to fall. And fall and fall and fall some more. The crime drop was startling in several respects. It was ubiquitous, with every category of crime falling in every part of the country. It was persistent, with incremental decreases year after year. And it was entirely unanticipated—especially by the very experts who had been predicting the opposite.

The magnitude of the reversal was astounding. The teenage murder rate, instead of rising 100 percent or even 15 percent as James Alan Fox had warned, fell more than 50 percent within five years. By 2000 the overall murder rate in the United States had dropped to its lowest level in thirty-five years. So had the rate of just about every other sort of crime, from assault to car theft.

Even though the experts had failed to anticipate the crime drop—which was in fact well under way even as they made their horrifying predictions—they now hurried to explain it. Most of their theories sounded perfectly logical. It was the roaring 1990s economy, they said, that helped turn back crime. It was the proliferation of gun control laws, they said. It was the sort of innovative policing strategies put into place in New York City, where murders would fall from 2,245 in 1990 to 596 in 2003.

These theories were not only logical; they were also *encouraging*, for they attributed the crime drop to specific and recent human initiatives. If it was gun control and clever police strategies and better-paying jobs that quelled crime—well then, the power to stop criminals had been within our reach all along. As it would be the next time, God forbid, that crime got so bad.

These theories made their way, seemingly without question, from the experts' mouths to journalists' ears to the public's mind. In short course, they became conventional wisdom.

There was only one problem: they weren't true.

There was another factor, meanwhile, that *had* greatly contributed to the massive crime drop of the 1990s. It had taken shape more than twenty years earlier and concerned a young woman in Dallas named Norma McCorvey.

Like the proverbial butterfly that flaps its wings on one continent and eventually causes a hurricane on another, Norma McCorvey dramatically altered the course of events without intending to. All she had wanted was an abortion. She was a poor, uneducated, unskilled, alcoholic, drug-using twenty-one-year-old woman who had already given up two children for adoption and now, in 1970, found herself pregnant again. But in Texas, as in all but a few states at that time, abortion was illegal. McCorvey's cause came to be adopted by people far more powerful than she. They made her the lead plaintiff in a class-action lawsuit seeking to legalize abortion. The defendant was Henry Wade, the Dallas County district attorney. The case ultimately made it to the U.S. Supreme Court, by which time McCorvey's name had been disguised as Jane Roe. On January 22, 1973, the court ruled in favor of Ms. Roe, allowing legalized abortion throughout the country. By this time, of course, it was far too late for Ms. McCorvey/Roe to have her abortion. She had given birth and put the child up for adoption. (Years later she would renounce her allegiance to legalized abortion and become a pro-life activist.)

So how did *Roe v. Wade* help trigger, a generation later, the greatest crime drop in recorded history?

As far as crime is concerned, it turns out that not all children are born equal. Not even close. Decades of studies have shown that a child born into an adverse family environment is far more likely than other children to become a criminal. And the millions of women most likely to have an abortion in the wake of *Roe v. Wade*—poor, unmarried, and teenage mothers for whom illegal abortions had been too expensive or too hard to get—were often models of adversity. They were the very women whose children, if born, would have been much more likely than average to become criminals.

But because of *Roe v. Wade,* these children *weren't* being born. This power-ful cause would have a drastic, distant effect: years later, just as these unborn children would have entered their criminal primes, the rate of crime began to plummet.

It wasn't gun control or a strong economy or new police strategies that finally blunted the American crime wave. It was, among other factors, the reality that the pool of potential criminals had dramatically shrunk.

Now, as the crime-drop experts (the former crime doomsayers) spun their theories to the media, how many times did they cite legalized abortion as a cause?

Zero.

It is the quintessential blend of commerce and camaraderie: you hire a real-estate agent to sell your home.

She sizes up its charms, snaps some pictures, sets the price, writes a seductive ad, shows the house aggressively, negotiates the offers, and sees the deal through to its end. Sure, it's a lot of work, but she's getting a nice cut. On the sale of a $300,000 house, a typical 6 percent agent fee yields $18,000. Eighteen thousand dollars, you say to yourself: that's a lot of money. But you also tell yourself that you never could have sold the house for $300,000 on your own. The agent knew how to—what's that phrase she used?—"maximize the house's value." She got you top dollar, right?

Right?

A real-estate agent is a different breed of expert than a criminologist, but she is every bit the expert. That is, she knows her field far better than the layman on whose behalf she is acting. She is better informed about the house's value, the state of the housing market, even the buyer's frame of mind. You depend on her for this information. That, in fact, is why you hired an expert.

As the world has grown more specialized, countless such experts have made themselves similarly indispensable. Doctors, lawyers, contractors, stock-brokers, auto mechanics, mortgage brokers, financial planners: they all enjoy a gigantic informational advantage. And they use that advantage to help you, the person who hired them, get exactly what you want for the best price.

Right?

It would be lovely to think so. But experts are human, and humans respond to incentives. How any given expert treats you, therefore, will depend on how that expert's incentives are set up. Sometimes his incentives may work in your favor. For instance: a study of California auto mechanics found they often passed up a small repair bill by letting failing cars pass emissions inspections—the reason being that lenient mechanics are rewarded with repeat business. But in a different case, an expert's incentives may work against you. In a medical study, it turned out that obstetricians in areas with declining birth rates are much more likely to perform cesarean-section deliveries than obstetricians in growing areas—suggesting that, when business is tough, doctors try to ring up more expensive procedures.

It is one thing to muse about experts' abusing their position and another to prove it. The best way to do so would be to measure how an expert treats you versus how he performs the same service for himself. Unfortunately a surgeon doesn't operate on himself. Nor is his medical file a matter of public record; neither is an auto mechanic's repair log for his own car.

Real-estate sales, however, *are* a matter of public record. And real-estate agents often do sell their own homes. A recent set of data covering the sale of nearly 100,000 houses in suburban Chicago shows that more than 3,000 of those houses were owned by the agents themselves.

Before plunging into the data, it helps to ask a question: what is the real-estate agent's incentive when she is selling her own home? Simple: to make the best deal possible. Presumably this is also your incentive when you are selling your home. And so your incentive and the real-estate agent's incentive would seem to be nicely aligned. Her commission, after all, is based on the sale price.

But as incentives go, commissions are tricky. First of all, a 6 percent real-estate commission is typically split between the seller's agent and the buyer's. Each agent then kicks back half of her take to the agency. Which means that only 1.5 percent of the purchase price goes directly into your agent's pocket.

So on the sale of your $300,000 house, her personal take of the $18,000 commission is $4,500. Still not bad, you say. But what if the house was actually worth more than $300,000? What if, with a little more effort and patience and a few more newspaper ads, she could have sold it for $310,000? After the commission, that puts an additional $9,400 in your pocket. But the agent's additional share—her personal 1.5 percent of the extra $10,000—is a mere $150. If you earn $9,400 while she earns only $150, maybe your incentives aren't aligned after all. (Especially when she's the one paying for the ads and doing all the work.) Is the agent willing to put out all that extra time, money, and energy for just $150?

There's one way to find out: measure the difference between the sales data for houses that belong to real-estate agents themselves and the houses they sold on behalf of clients. Using the data from the sales of those 100,000 Chicago homes, and controlling for any number of variables—location, age and quality of the house, aesthetics, and so on—it turns out that a real-estate agent keeps her own home on the market an average often days longer and sells it for an extra 3-plus percent, or $10,000 on a $300,000 house. When she sells her own house, an agent holds out for the best offer; when she sells yours, she pushes you to take the first decent offer that comes along. Like a stockbroker churning commissions, she wants to make deals and make them fast. Why not? Her share of a better offer—$150—is too puny an incentive to encourage her to do otherwise.

Of all the truisms about politics, one is held to be truer than the rest: money buys elections. Arnold Schwarzenegger, Michael Bloomberg, Jon Corzine—these are but a few recent, dramatic examples of the truism at work. (Disregard for a moment the contrary examples of Howard Dean, Steve Forbes, Michael Huffington, and especially Thomas Golisano, who over the course of three gubernatorial elections in New York spent $93 million of his own money and won 4 percent, 8 percent, and 14 percent, respectively, of the vote.) Most people would agree that money has an undue influence on elections and that far too much money is spent on political campaigns.

Indeed, election data show it is true that the candidate who spends more money in a campaign usually wins. But is money the *cause* of the victory?

It might seem logical to think so, much as it might have seemed logical that a booming 1990s economy helped reduce crime. But just because two things are correlated does not mean that one causes the other. A correlation simply means that a relationship exists between two factors—let's call them X and Y—but it tells you nothing about the direction of that relationship. It's possible that X causes Y; it's also possible that Y causes X; and it may be that X and Y are both being caused by some other factor, Z.

Think about this correlation: cities with a lot of murders also tend to have a lot of police officers. Consider now the police/murder correlation in a pair of real cities. Denver and Washington, D.C., have about the same population—but Washington has nearly three times as many police as Denver, and it also has eight times the number of murders. Unless you have more information, however, it's hard to say what's causing what. Someone who didn't know better might contemplate these figures and conclude that it is all those extra police in Washington who are causing the extra murders. Such wayward thinking, which has a long history, generally provokes a wayward response. Consider the folktale of the czar who learned that the most disease-ridden province in his empire was also the province with the most doctors. His solution? He promptly ordered all the doctors shot dead.

Now, returning to the issue of campaign spending: in order to figure out the relationship between money and elections, it helps to consider the incentives at play in campaign finance. Let's say you are the kind of person who might contribute $1,000 to a candidate. Chances are you'll give the money in one of two situations: a close race, in which you think the money will influence the outcome; or a campaign in which one candidate is a sure winner and you would like to bask in reflected glory or receive some future in-kind consideration. The one candidate you *won't* contribute to is a sure loser. (Just ask any presidential hopeful who bombs in Iowa and New Hampshire.) So front-runners and incumbents raise a lot more money than long shots. And what about spending that money? Incumbents and front-runners obviously have more cash, but they only spend a lot of it when they stand a legitimate chance of losing; otherwise, why dip into a war chest that might be more useful later on, when a more formidable opponent appears?

Now picture two candidates, one intrinsically appealing and the other not so. The appealing candidate raises much more money and wins easily. But was it the money that won him the votes, or was it his appeal that won the votes *and* the money?

That's a crucial question but a very hard one to answer. Voter appeal, after all, isn't easy to quantify. How can it be measured?

It can't, really—except in one special case. The key is to measure a candidate against . . . himself. That is, Candidate A today is likely to be similar to Candidate A two or four years hence. The same could be said for Candidate B. If only Candidate A ran against Candidate B in two consecutive elections but in each case spent different amounts of money. Then, with the candidates' appeal more or less constant, we could measure the money's impact.

As it turns out, the same two candidates run against each other in consecutive elections all the time—indeed, in nearly a thousand U.S. congressional races since 1972. What do the numbers have to say about such cases?

Here's the surprise: the amount of money spent by the candidates *hardly matters at all.* A winning candidate can cut his spending in half and lose only 1 percent of the vote. Meanwhile, a losing candidate who doubles his spending can expect to shift the vote in his favor by only that same 1 percent. What really matters for a political candidate is *not* how much you spend; what matters is who you are. (The same could be said—and will be said, in chapter 5—about parents.) Some politicians are inherently attractive to voters and others simply aren't, and no amount of money can do much about it. (Messrs. Dean, Forbes, Huffington, and Golisano already know this, of course.)

And what about the other half of the election truism—that the amount of money spent on campaign finance is obscenely huge? In a typical election period that includes campaigns for the presidency, the Senate, and the House of Representatives, about $1 billion is spent per year—which sounds like a lot of money, unless you care to measure it against something seemingly less important than democratic elections.

It is the same amount, for instance, that Americans spend every year on chewing gum.

This isn't a book about the cost of chewing gum versus campaign spending per se, or about disingenuous real-estate agents, or the impact of legalized abortion on crime. It will certainly address these scenarios and dozens more, from the art of parenting to the mechanics of cheating, from the inner workings of the Ku Klux Klan to racial discrimination on *The Weakest Link*. What this book *is* about is stripping a layer or two from the surface of modern life and seeing what is happening underneath. We will ask a lot of questions, some frivolous and some about life-and-death issues. The answers may often seem odd but, after the fact, also rather obvious. We will seek out these answers in the data—whether those data come in the form of schoolchildren's test scores or New York City's crime statistics or a crack dealer's financial records. (Often we will take advantage of patterns in the data that were incidentally left behind, like an airplane's sharp contrail in a high sky.) It is well and good to opine or theorize about a subject, as humankind is wont to do, but when moral posturing is replaced by an honest assessment of the data, the result is often a new, surprising insight.

Morality, it could be argued, represents the way that people would like the world to work—whereas economics represents how it actually *does* work. Economics is above all a science of measurement. It comprises an extraordinarily powerful and flexible set of tools that can reliably assess a thicket of information to determine the effect of any one factor, or even the whole effect. That's what "the economy" is, after all: a thicket of information about jobs and real estate and banking and investment. But the tools of economics can be just as easily applied to subjects that are more—well, more *interesting*.

This book, then, has been written from a very specific worldview, based on a few fundamental ideas:

Incentives are the cornerstone of modern life. And understanding them—or, often, ferreting them out—is the key to solving just about any riddle, from violent crime to sports cheating to online dating.

The conventional wisdom is often wrong. Crime didn't keep soaring in the 1990s, money alone doesn't win elections, and—surprise—drinking eight glasses of water a day has never actually been shown to do a thing for your health. Conventional wisdom is often shoddily formed and devilishly difficult to see through, but it can be done.

Dramatic effects often have distant, even subtle, causes. The answer to a given riddle is not always right in front of you. Norma McCorvey had a far greater impact on crime than did the combined forces of gun control, a strong economy, and innovative police strategies. So did, as we shall see, a man named Oscar Danilo Blandon, aka the Johnny Appleseed of Crack.

"Experts"—from criminologists to real-estate agents—use their informational advantage to serve their own agenda. However, they can be beat at their own game. And in the face of the Internet, their informational advantage is shrinking every day—as evidenced by, among other things, the falling price of coffins and life-insurance premiums.

Knowing what to measure and how to measure it makes a complicated world much less so. If you learn how to look at data in the right way, you can explain riddles that otherwise might have seemed impossible. Because there is nothing like the sheer power of numbers to scrub away layers of confusion and contradiction.

So the aim of this book is to explore the hidden side of . . . everything. This may occasionally be a frustrating exercise. It may sometimes feel as if we are peering at the world through a straw or even staring into a funhouse mirror; but the idea is to look at many different scenarios and examine them in a way they have rarely been examined. In some regards, this is a strange concept for a book. Most books put forth a single theme, crisply expressed in a sentence or two, and then tell the entire story of that theme: the history of salt; the fragility of democracy; the use and misuse of punctuation. This book boasts no such unifying theme. We did consider, for about six minutes, writing a book that would revolve around a single theme—the theory and practice of applied microeconomics, anyone?—but opted instead for a sort of treasure-hunt approach. Yes, this approach employs the best analytical tools that economics can offer, but it also allows us to follow whatever freakish curiosities may occur to us. Thus our invented field of study: Freakonomics. The sort of stories told in this book are not often covered in Econ. 101, but that may change. Since the science of economics is primarily a set of tools, as opposed to a subject matter, then no subject, however offbeat, need be beyond its reach.

It is worth remembering that Adam Smith, the founder of classical economics, was first and foremost a philosopher. He strove to be a moralist and, in doing so, became an economist. When he published *The Theory of Moral Sentiments* in 1759, modern capitalism was just getting under way. Smith was entranced by the sweeping changes wrought by this new force, but it wasn't only the numbers that interested him. It was the human effect, the fact that economic forces were vastly changing the way a person thought and behaved in a given situation. What might lead one person to cheat or steal while another didn't? How would one person's seemingly innocuous choice, good or bad, affect a great number of people down the line? In Smith's era, cause and effect had begun to wildly accelerate; incentives were magnified tenfold. The gravity and shock of these changes were as overwhelming to the citizens of his time as the gravity and shock of modern life seem to us today.

Smith's true subject was the friction between individual desire and societal norms. The economic historian Robert Heilbroner, writing in *The Worldly Philosophers*, wondered how Smith was able to separate the doings of man, a creature of self-interest, from the greater moral plane in which man operated. "Smith held that the answer lay in our ability to put ourselves in the position of a third person, an impartial observer," Heilbroner wrote, "and in this way to form a notion of the objective . . . merits of a case."

Consider yourself, then, in the company of a third person—or, if you will, a pair of third people—eager to explore the objective merits of interesting cases. These explorations generally begin with the asking of a simple unasked question. Such as: what do schoolteachers and sumo wrestlers have in common?

Suggestions for Discussion

1. How do the authors use economic theory to answer questions that they say range from "frivolous" to "life-and-death"?

2. What do the authors mean when they say "moral posturing"?

3. What are the fundamental ideas the authors have based the book on? Why did they decide to use these as a basis for their book? Choose one of those ideas and discuss it further.

Suggestion for Writing

Pick one of the fundamental ideas and write an essay discussing the larger implications of that idea.

FICTION

ALAN LIGHTMAN

A Place Where Time Stands Still

Alan Lightman (b. 1948) holds a dual appointment in science and humanities at the Massachusetts Institute of Technology, where he teaches science and writing. His novel *Einstein's Dream* was an international best seller and has been translated into more than thirty languages. His science writing reflects his wide-ranging contributions to astrophysics; he has published five essay collections and seven books on science, and his work has appeared in the leading scientific journals. The following selection is from *Einstein's Dream*.

DOUG CURTLER, *Beach Scene, Virginia*. Painted and glazed clay, wood, sand, 1974. Clay work by Doug Curtler, arranged by Martin Johner. Courtesy of the collector Martin Johner. Digital image: © www.foto-lounge.de.

There is a place where time stands still. Raindrops hang motionless in air. Pendulums of clocks float mid-swing. Dogs raise their muzzles in silent howls. Pedestrians are frozen on the dusty streets, their legs cocked as if held by strings. The aromas of dates, mangoes, coriander, cumin are suspended in space.

As a traveler approaches this place from any direction, he moves more and more slowly. His heartbeats grow farther apart, his breathing slackens, his temperature drops, his thoughts diminish, until he reaches dead center and stops. For this is the center of time. From this place, time travels outward in concentric circles—at rest at the center, slowly picking up speed at greater diameters.

Who would make pilgrimage to the center of time? Parents with children, and lovers.

And so, at the place where time stands still, one sees parents clutching their children, in a frozen embrace that will never let go. The beautiful young daughter with blue eyes and blond hair will never stop smiling the smile she smiles now, will never lose this soft pink glow on her cheeks, will never grow wrinkled or tired, will never get injured, will never unlearn what her parents have taught her, will never think thoughts that her parents don't know, will never know evil, will never tell her parents that she does not love them, will never leave her room with the view of the ocean, will never stop touching her parents as she does now.

And at the place where time stands still, one sees lovers kissing in the shadows of buildings, in a frozen embrace that will never let go. The loved one will never take his arms from where they are now, will never give back the bracelet of memories, will never journey far from his lover, will never place himself in danger in self-sacrifice, will never fail to show his love, will never become jealous, will never fall in love with someone else, will never lose the passion of this instant in time.

One must consider that these statues are illuminated by only the most feeble red light, for light is diminished almost to nothing at the center of time, its vibrations slowed to echoes in vast canyons, its intensity reduced to the faint glow of fireflies.

Those not quite at dead center do indeed move, but at the pace of glaciers. A brush of the hair might take a year, a kiss might take a thousand. While a smile is returned, seasons pass in the outer world. While a child is hugged, bridges rise. While a goodbye is said, cities crumble and are forgotten.

And those who return to the outer world . . . Children grow rapidly, forget the centuries-long embrace from their parents, which to them lasted but seconds. Children become adults, live far from their parents, live in their own houses, learn ways of their own, suffer pain, grow old. Children curse their parents for trying to hold them forever, curse time for their own wrinkled skin and hoarse voices. These now old children also want to stop time, but at another time. They want to freeze their own children at the center of time.

Lovers who return find their friends are long gone. After all, lifetimes have passed. They move in a world they do not recognize. Lovers who return still embrace in the shadows of buildings, but now their embraces seem empty and alone. Soon they forget the centuries-long promises, which to them lasted only seconds. They become jealous even among strangers, say hateful things to each other, lose passion, drift apart, grow old and alone in a world they do not know.

Some say it is best not to go near the center of time. Life is a vessel of sadness, but it is noble to live life, and without time there is no life. Others disagree. They would rather have an eternity of contentment, even if that eternity were fixed and frozen, like a butterfly mounted in a case.

Suggestions for Discussion

1. How does Lightman's use of language create a sensory experience of time? Does it evoke a sense of stillness? Movement?

2. Does the narrator portray this "place where time stands still" as positive or negative? Explain.

Suggestions for Writing

1. At the end of the piece, the narrator states, "Life is a vessel of sadness, but it is noble to live life, and without time there is no life." What does this mean in terms of the larger piece? What does this mean to you in your life?

2. Write a paper on the lyrical use of language to depict time and the stillness of it. Discuss how the author's word choice and sentence construction add or detract from the meaning of the piece.

POETRY

∾∾∾∾

AFFONSO ROMANO DE SANT'ANNA

Letter to the Dead

The works of writer, professor, and literary critic Affonso Romano de Sant'Anna (b. 1937) explore the cultural and political landscapes of his native Brazil. His book *Popular Music and Modern Brazilian Poetry* (1978) acknowledges the artistry and influence of popular music lyrics, and in *Loving Cannibalism* (1984), De Sant'Anna offers an analysis of love poetry undertaken from a psychological standpoint. In his 1980 poem "What Kind of Nation Is This?" de Sant'Anna challenged the Brazilian government's policy of censorship, charging that it harmed the national sense of identity. His talent for social commentary is evident in the following poem, translated from the original Portuguese by Mark Strand and published in the *New Yorker* in 2000.

Friends, nothing has changed
in essence.

Wages don't cover expenses,
wars persist without end,
and there are new and terrible viruses,
beyond the advances of medicine.
From time to time, a neighbor
falls dead over questions of love.
There are interesting films, it is true,
and, as always, voluptuous women
seducing us with their mouths and legs,
but in matters of love
we haven't invented a single position that's new.

Some astronauts stay in space
six months or more, testing
equipment and solitude.
In each Olympics new records are predicted
and in the countries social advances and setbacks.
But not a single bird has changed its song
with the times.

We put on the same Greek tragedies,
reread "Don Quixote," and spring
arrives on time each year.

Some habits, rivers, and forests are lost.
Nobody sits in front of his house anymore
or takes in the breezes of afternoon,
but we have amazing computers
that keep us from thinking.

On the disappearance of the dinosaurs
and the formation of galaxies
we have no new knowledge.
Clothes come and go with the fashions.
Strong governments fall, others rise,
countries are divided,
and the ants and the bees continue
faithful to their work.

Nothing has changed in essence.

We sing congratulations at parties,
argue football on street corners,
die in senseless disasters,
and from time to time
one of us looks at the star-filled sky
with the same amazement we had
when we looked at caves.
And each generation, full of itself,
continues to think
that it lives at the summit of history.

Suggestions for Discussion

1. If "nothing has changed in essence" then why does each generation "think that it lives at the summit of history"?

2. Are the narrator's feelings about the continuity of human experience clearly defined or ambivalent?

3. Doesn't de Sant'Anna admit that technology creates change when the narrator notes "we have amazing computers that keep us from thinking"?

Suggestion for Writing

Compare de Sant'Anna's "Letter to the Dead" to Salman Rushdie's "Imagine There's No Heaven." Analyze the effectiveness of this "open letter" technique as a form of persuasive writing.

Freedom and Human Dignity

༄༅༅༅

I am twenty-four years old and I was born into a broke generation. I look around and I see people who have borrowed more than they can ever repay, who can't find a good job, can't save, can't afford basic necessities like health insurance, can't make solid plans. Their credit card bills mount every month, while their lives stall out on the first uphill slope. Born into a century of unimaginable prosperity, in the richest country in the world, those of us between the ages of eighteen and thirty-five have somehow been cheated out of our inheritance.

—ANYA KAMENETZ, "Generation Debt"

We needn't all agree on the issue of homosexuality to believe that the government should treat every citizen alike. If that means living next door to someone of whom we disapprove, so be it. But disapproval needn't mean disrespect. And if the love of two people, committing themselves to each other exclusively for the rest of their lives, is not worthy of respect, then what is?

—ANDREW SULLIVAN, "A Conservative Case for Gay Marriage"

PATTI S. LEVEY

"With Honour" from the series *"Taking Liberty"*

Gelatin silver print, 2002

Copyright © Patti S. Levey

Courtesy of Photo Eye Gallery, Santa Fe, NM

INTRODUCTION

Personal freedom can be defined in many ways: by a government's social contract with its citizens; by those citizens' right to exercise their freedom within legal limits; by the guaranteed equality of all human beings under the law; by the respect at all times for every individual's dignity. All of these definitions are explored—and none are taken for granted—in the readings that follow. Raising complex social and political issues in response to different historical situations spanning hundreds of years, these works offer a detailed introduction to the questions that surround freedom and human dignity.

In Thomas Jefferson's "The Declaration of Independence," we hear a nation declare her sovereign independence from royal tyranny and announce to the world that all men are created equal in the eyes of the body politic and of God, who has endowed them with certain inalienable rights. The Seneca Falls Convention's "Declaration of Sentiments and Resolutions, 1848" is a carbon copy of Jefferson's Declaration in rhetorical structure, political content, and moral focus—with the critical addition that equality before the law applies to "all women" as well. With the Civil War as its backdrop and a cemetery for war dead as its stage, Abraham Lincoln's Gettysburg Address continues to espouse the American principles of liberty and equality—the freedoms upon which this country was founded and in defense of which the Civil War must continue.

But one can argue that the inalienable rights so vigorously declared by Jefferson, reiterated at the Seneca Falls Convention, and defended by Lincoln have not in social, political, and ethical practice been fully accorded to American minorities, particularly Native American Indians and African Americans. In the "Speech on the Signing of the Treaty of Port Elliott, 1855," we hear the dignified, prideful response to President Franklin Pierce from Chief Seattle, a leader of Pacific Northwest Indian tribes who have lost their freedom to live traditionally on their native land. Chief Seattle offers us a glimpse not only into Indians' kinship with the natural world, but also into the abusive aggression of white Manifest Destiny that denied Indians life, liberty, and the pursuit of happiness in their natural world. Also, Martin Luther King, Jr.'s famous "Letter from Birmingham Jail" confirms that, even by the 1960s, freedom and human dignity for black Americans continued to be fugitive in a predominantly white society. Cornel West's essay on "Affirmative Action" similarly argues that the African American struggle for equality is not yet over, and that the fight for Civil Rights did not end with the assassinations of King and Malcolm X.

In matters of political freedom and personal dignity, we would hope to have advanced beyond the practice of autocratic force and fear, and to have overcome racial and gender discrimination and prejudice, abuses of legal and personal power at the expense of other people, and cruel insensitivity based upon sexual preference. But many abuses still obscure those rights that people in a free society presume to have. In the Notebook, issues of economic hardship in contemporary America are explored. Anya Kamenetz and Barbara Ehrenreich discuss contemporary conditions that deprive both young people and working-class people of fulfilling jobs, reasonable salaries that support the cost of living, and affordable housing instead of apartments subdivided ad infinitum until one is forced to live with strangers in order to live. These pieces paint a vivid picture of "the middle-class squeeze" in America, and of a world in which blue-collar workers, unprotected by broken and powerless unions, have no advocate, and no place to go to register complaint about the profoundly unjust condition of their lives.

While some of the most controversial political issues of today are seen as purely "black and white," "liberal" or "conservative," sometimes the most passionate voices raised to address contemporary controversies cannot be easily categorized or dismissed. For example, it is a conservative commentator, Andrew Sullivan, who writes in favor of protecting gay marriage from being banned, while a Roman Catholic writer, Mary Gordon, counterintuitively argues that abortion can sometimes be a moral choice. These essays, like those by Jefferson, King, and Mott, argue for the repeal of laws that limit personal freedom, and for the granting of further political power to disenfranchised individuals. These ideas are as controversial and volatile now as Jefferson's were in his time, but the passing of the ages has not yet taken the sting out of their words, or coated their writings with the sheen of nostalgia.

Although the preservation of freedom and human dignity is a constant struggle, William Faulkner's Nobel Prize award speech strikes an optimistic note: We do have the freedom and we do have the dignity, he says, and we do have the right stuff to "endure and prevail."

NOTEBOOK

ᘖᘖᘖᘖ

ANYA KAMENETZ

Generation Debt

Anya Kamenetz (b. 1980), a New Orleans native and the daughter of
writers Rodger Kamenetz and Moira Crone, has written for the *New York
Times, Washington Post, New York* magazine, *Salon, Slate, The Nation,*
and the *Village Voice.* Her *Village Voice* column, "Generation Debt: The
New Economics of Being Young," was nominated for a 2004 Pulitzer
Prize and led to her widely discussed first book, *Generation Debt: Why
Now Is a Terrible Time to Be Young* (2006).

What would you do if you grew up and realized that everything
America has always promised its children no longer holds true for you?

I am twenty-four years old, and I was born into a broke generation.
I look around and I see people who have borrowed more to go to college
than they can repay, who can't find a good job, can't save, can't afford basic
necessities like health insurance, can't make solid plans. Their credit card
bills mount every month, while their lives stall out on the first uphill slope.
Born into a century of unimaginable prosperity, in the richest country in
the world, those of us between the ages of eighteen and thirty-five have
somehow been cheated out of our inheritance.

I came of age at a precarious moment in American history. I graduated
from Yale in the spring of 2002. During the four years I was in school, the country rode more highs and lows than the Coney Island Cyclone. In 1998 and 1999,
some of my classmates had their own start-ups, making million-dollar deals on
their cell phones between classes. By the turn of the millennium, the NASDAQ
had peaked, the Internet balloon was leaking fast, and a presidential election
decided in the courts shook the timbers of our democracy. Then, in the fall of
my senior year, four days before my twenty-first birthday, came September 11,
2001. My generation was forever marked by a catastrophe, our Pearl Harbor.

The dust of the World Trade Center was still hanging in the air when I
moved to New York to find work as a journalist. Dot-com exuberance had
deflated; the paper millionaires had blown away. The country was struggling
through a long "jobless recovery," and the drums were beating for a new
global war. It was not an auspicious moment to begin a career.

Like many of my peers, I interviewed without success for full-time jobs, and ended up freelancing as a writer and researcher. In the spring of 2004, I began to contribute to a feature series in *The Village Voice* called "Generation Debt: The New Economics of Being Young," conceived and named by executive editor Laura Conaway.

I started talking with dozens of people around my age from different walks of life. At parties, at clubs, at coffee shops, on campuses, at bars, at job-training centers, at political meetings, on Internet message boards, on the street, I'd have the same conversation over and over. I'd say I was writing about the economic obstacles facing young people. "You could write about me," they would respond. Then they would tell me about student loan debt in the tens of thousands of dollars. About working their way through college for six years at $9 an hour. About parents' divorces or job loss that derailed their own dreams. About mounting credit card debt that kept them up at night. Degrees, even advanced degrees, that led nowhere. Long searches for unsatisfying jobs. Layoffs. Underemployment. Flat incomes. No health insurance, no retirement plan, no paid vacation. Unaffordable housing. Moving back in with Mom. Turning thirty with negative savings and no assets. Putting off marriage or kids because they couldn't afford them.

After a few months, I knew that the problem was bigger than a series of articles could describe. I had to write a book to document the full situation, not to mention get answers for my friends and myself. Is student loan debt really that bad? Why has college gotten so expensive? What happened to all the good jobs? Are we really going to do worse than our parents?

Through research, I have realized just how lucky I am. Not only am I one of just a quarter of the young population with a bachelor's degree, I am part of the one-third of four-year college graduates without loan debt. My parents, married for twenty-six years—rare their generation—can give me help if I need it. They raised me in middle-class comfort, but with realistic expectations. Because of them, I spend no more than I earn and pay off my one credit card every month.

Still, I live my life in a Zen-like state of transience. No employer has yet offered me a full-time job with a 401 (k), a paid vacation, or any other benefits beyond the next assignment. I have a savings account but no retirement fund. Settling down seems like an insurmountable achievement; I can't afford preschool fees or a mortgage anywhere near the city where I live and work. People usually suggest graduate school as a means of finding something more permanent, but $40,000 in loans, with no guarantees on the other end, seems like a bad deal to me. In short, I've been taught to expect the world on a plate, but I know that I'll be stuck with the check. If concerns like these are touching my life, they are touching everyone's.

Wait a minute, you say. If things are really going down the tubes for young people, why hasn't anyone noticed? Well, for one thing, money in

America is more private than sex. My friends and I rarely discuss our financial anxieties, so we tend to see our situations as our own fault. "I'm just lazy," an unemployed nineteen-year-old told me. "I don't know why I was so restless," said a twenty-eight-year-old who's held six jobs in eight years.

Not only do we blame ourselves, our elders blame us, too. It makes me really angry to see the Boomers in charge of the media and other powerful institutions attributing the problems young people are going through to nothing more serious than a lack of initiative. Collectively, the mass media have stamped an image of eighteen-to-thirty-four-year-olds as slackers, overgrown children, and procrastinators, as though we're intentionally dragging our heels to avoid reaching adulthood.

In December 2004, *The New York Times* published a roundup of the coinages and catchphrases of the year. Among them was the awkward hybrid "adultescent."

"The adult it describes is too busy playing Halo 2 on his Xbox or watching SpongeBob at his parents' house to think about growing up," wrote John Tierney, a *Times* op-ed columnist. In January 2005, *Time* magazine devoted a cover story, written by Lev Grossman, to "twixters," another ugly neologism. Again, twenty-somethings were portrayed as drifting through "a strange, transitional never-never land between adolescence and adulthood."

Rather than probe the underlying causes of this shift, journalists too often settle for cheap shots. Most articles, books, and TV segments about people my age note economic factors only in passing. The headlines and the titles strike accusatory notes: "Don't Let Boomerang Kids Derail Your Goals"; "It's the Kids—Lock Up the China!" As Tierney concludes: "One common explanation for the rise in adultescence is the cost of housing and education, which has made it harder for young people (especially in places like New York) to afford homes and children. Another explanation is that young adults now enjoy some pleasures of marriage without the consequences." Of course! It's the premarital sex that makes us want to go without full-time jobs or benefits! "But if you ask adultescents why they haven't grown up," Tierney goes on, "they may give you a simple answer: Because they don't have to." How about, because we can't?

This attitude is especially insufferable because it's arguably our elders who are taking far more than their fair share. As Nicholas Kristof, another *Times* op-ed columnist, wrote in May 2005, history will probably call the Boomers "The Greediest Generation": "I fear that we'll be remembered mostly for grabbing resources for ourselves, in such a way that the big losers will be America's children."

Kristof is right. Instead of saving enough for their own retirement, let alone for our future, the Boomers are going into deeper debt than any generation before them. Because of their projected retirement expenses, the entire nation is essentially bankrupt, with a total accumulated funding gap in the federal budget that's greater than our national net worth. Who's going to be around when that bill comes due? Young people.

Add to these material debts the ominous global legacy our parents and grandparents have left for us—environmental degradation, petroleum dependence, climate change, geopolitical instability—and the smugness starts to look downright cruel.

The New York Times might see a typical young man as a baseball-cap-clad schlub on his parents' couch. Well, his father probably just refinanced that house, which has appreciated ten times over since he bought it after graduating from a practically free state university. While the poor kid sits at home, seeking electronic distraction from the bleakness of his emasculated, dependent existence, Dad is rattling down the highway in a brand-new $40,000 SUV that gets twelve miles to the gallon and has a bumper sticker on the back that says, RETIRED—SPENDING MY CHILDREN'S INHERITANCE! Who's immature now?

In all seriousness, I ask my over-thirty-five readers to keep an open mind as they look at the evidence marshaled here that the deck is stacked against the young. If you still can't summon much sympathy, at least consider the country's bottom line. The United States' greatest resource for future prosperity and growth is its human capital, which is a fancy term for educated young people. Our young nation has a robust image of itself as bursting with opportunity and devoted to progress. Each generation is meant to outdo the last. The innovation we rely on comes from a youthful, adventuring spirit of self-reliance and fair play.

And yet the country has retreated from this forward-looking stance into a defensive crouch. It is abandoning its children to struggle, narrowing their opportunities, dampening their boldness by forcing them to put liens on their future to pay for the education they need to make a decent living. Our debt precludes us from taking the kinds of entrepreneurial risks on which American success depends.

As perverse as the current course is, as cruelly as it plays out in the lives of so many young people, I don't think it's America's self-image that is wrong. It's the gulf that has grown between ideal and reality. Mom, Dad, listen up: Things have changed. We're not doing as well as you did. And if something doesn't change soon, it's unlikely that we ever will.

I hope I've made the case here that my generation is not entirely made up of shiftless, walleyed dawdlers lingering in outgrown sandboxes (as depicted on the cover of *Time* magazine). Nor are we simply passive victims of wicked, mustachioed Social Conditions.

The transition to adulthood these days may be more convoluted and difficult. The deck is stacked against us in many ways: economic, social, political, and in the court of public opinion. But it just might turn out that the most striking character trait of Generation Debt—our penchant for outsized dreams—is exactly what we need to turn things around.

Terry, twenty-two, is the younger daughter of Taiwanese immigrants. Her father works in an airport concession; her mother is a clerk in an office. "They are very, very modest people," she says. "Simple. Not professionals. They don't function the best in an English[-language] environment. They had to take the jobs they've taken."

Terry will probably take a total of six years to finish her B.A. in interdisciplinary international development studies, having taken classes at both UCLA and at a community college to save money. When I met up with her at a coffee shop in San Francisco's Richmond neighborhood, she was interning at a global culture magazine, indulging her fascination in multicultural art. She's an irrepressible girl with a nose piercing and a trendy haircut who practices the Brazilian martial art capoeira in her free time. She's considering a career as either a freelance writer or some kind of contemporary art curator. But she's aware that her passions conflict with her parents' program of "study hard, get an education, and make more money than we did."

"I should be having a better future than my parents," Terry says. "They came here and they were able to buy a house. My dad's job's secure, five days a week, unionized, steady paycheck, health care." She knows that in today's job climate, she is unlikely to find the same. And that's not even all she's looking for. "I'm not going to be happy to just have this all-right job. My generation has more desires, which complicates things."

Should Terry shelve her interests and switch her major to accounting, or ask her dad to get her into the airport concession aire's union? Tough questions! They might well be more practical choices, and I've been spending this time telling people to adjust to reality. But I'm still rooting for her to pursue her talents. To do otherwise would be to give up on the America I love, the America of progress and opportunity.

The direction of American history is and must be toward more freedom, not less. Neither I nor any woman I know would want to go back to my mother's day, when her classmates at Smith College were still said to be going for their MRS degrees. Nor do the ethnic minorities and immigrants I have spoken with have any desire to go back to a time when their opportunities were determined by discrimination. This country needs the energy and optimism of young people like Terry if it's going to get things back on track. We need more dreams fulfilled, not dreams deferred.

This book is about economic forces, impersonal as storm winds battering a small fishing boat. I have introduced you to the people behind the numbers: how it feels to hear your mother say she couldn't afford to send your tuition check, or to declare bankruptcy at age twenty-four because of a life-threatening illness, or to sit at your kitchen table and cry over a $700 car repair. No one should have to go through times like these. No more should we keep quiet about it.

ANONYMOUS, *"U.S. Treasury—No Cents."* Carbon copy pasted on wall.
© Christian J. Matuschek/www.foto-lounge.de.

If you feel the same urgency I do about the new economics of being young, I have some suggestions of what to do after you put down this book.

If you're a parent or a concerned older person:

Understand that things have truly changed, and not all your experience in work and life is relevant to ours. Be on the lookout for unthinking attitudes that condescend to young people and blame us for a lack of success or initiative, when the causes are much more complicated.

Start an adult conversation with your kids about money. They should know your hopes and fears and your own financial plans, even as you quiz them about theirs. What kind of example are you setting? Is your retirement plan in order? Is your credit card debt mounting? If you don't have the means to save for college, do you and your children have a Plan B?

Don't be afraid to let your kids take some economic responsibility from an early age. Make sure you teach them about the dangers of credit and debt.

Our government's obligation to the security of young and old alike is a matter of open debate. Understand that as members of a large, aging generation, you have a built-in advantage in this debate, and a disproportionate amount of public resources is already being diverted to your needs.

I know that parents don't need to be told to sacrifice for their children, but consider, as well, that investing in the future will benefit everyone, including you and the people who will take care of you in your old age.

∾

If you're a member of my generation:

Begin a real adult conversation with your parents about money, security, and success. Stop being defensive and start talking positively. Usually, they want to help you and to understand what you're going through.

If you are in college, think about founding a national student PAC. Or start by lobbying your state government for a one-cent sales tax for education and a cap on tuition hikes.

If you're working, join an organization to try to improve your own working conditions and get health care, better wages, or whatever it is you need most. Or start your own.

Yes, the job market sucks. But if the job you personally have sucks, it's ultimately up to you to find something you can live on, and live with. This could mean grad school. It could also mean working hard enough to get promoted, a short course to improve your skills, an internship, an apprenticeship, studying for a real estate license, or bartending a hundred hours a week to save up money to start your own business.

Eventual success could mean adjusting your expectations now. Are you ready to change your lifestyle and exchange some of the anxiety of wanting and buying for the joy of making and doing? Can you cut up your credit cards, consolidate your debt, and start climbing out of that hole? Forget what you've been taught about money, forget placing blame, and start over.

Strike up a conversation with strangers your age, from the next cubicle or in the coffee shop. Talk about the economic problems you have in common, about your trouble getting health insurance, your worry over your credit card debt. Share your frustrations and aspirations.

Ok, so we're ready to start a movement. What should our banners read? How about more public investment in young people, supporting education, job training, entrepreneurship, and child rearing, for a start? Call it human capital development, or the Homeland Security Jobs Act, or No Twenty-Something Left Behind.

Increased government spending on young people ought to appeal to every shade of the political spectrum, because we are in a unique position to repay what we're given. To take just one example, equalizing educational opportunity among whites, blacks, and Hispanics, says Richard Kazis in the book *Double the Numbers*, could add as much as $230 billion to the gross domestic product and raise $80 billion in new tax revenues from higher earners.

Corporate responsibility for companies that both employ and market overwhelmingly to young people is another place to start. Why not ask MTV to pay the interns who give it such invaluable advice on what's "hott"? Why not make McDonald's accountable for how many of its teenage workers rise to management—or graduate high school? Why not require Citibank to offer free financial management classes on college campuses where they market their credit cards?

I want my generation to accomplish all it can, and not only for its own sake. The nation's progress depends on the productivity of the young, and our productivity depends on the education and opportunities available to us. If we get the resources we need now, supporting ourselves, our parents, and eventually our children will be a joyful responsibility, not a hardship. When the people in power today shortchange us, they are really short-changing themselves, and the nation as a whole. It is time for all of us to start living for the future.

Suggestions for Discussion

1. Who and what does the author blame for the increasing debt of young people? How do you feel about this accusation? What do her critics think?

2. What does Kamenetz mean when she says that "money in America is more private than sex"? Do you agree with this statement? If so, why do you think we are so private about our finances? Should it be this way?

3. What suggestions does she offer for both parents and members of "Generation Debt" for improving the situations for our nation's young people?

4. Anya Kamenetz's book was released during a period when the U.S. economy seemed to be strong in certain quarters. Can her observations be

seen as prophetic in light of the Great Recession that followed? How might her observations about the financial woes of young people now be applicable to a broader section of the U.S. populace?

⟋**5.** Consider the artwork accompanying this essay. How does it portray America? Capitalism? What does it say about the economy? The recession? What thoughts and emotions does it inspire in you?

Suggestions for Writing

1. Take Kamenetz's suggestion and write a letter to your local state representative lobbying for a cap on tuition hikes.

2. Write an editorial for your school or local newspaper informing people of the rising financial difficulties for people of "Generation Debt."

BARBARA EHRENREICH

Selling in Minnesota

Author, journalist, and activist (b. 1941) Barbara Ehrenreich is a champion of women's rights, economic justice, peace, and health care reform. The daughter of a Butte, Montana, miner and union organizer, Ehrenreich studied the sciences at Reed College and earned a doctorate from Rockefeller University in cell biology. Her participation in the anti-Vietnam war movement drew her away from science and into activism. She worked first for a nonprofit organization that advocated better health care for the poor of New York City and later became a columnist for *Ms.* and *Mother Jones.* Her writing has appeared in *Time, The Progressive,* the *New York Times, The Atlantic Monthly, The New Republic,* and *Salon.com,* among others. Her books include *For Her Own Good* (1978, with Deirdre English), *Fear of Falling: the Inner Life of the Middle Class* (1989), *Blood Rites* (1997), *This Land is Their Land: Reports from a Divided Nation* (2008), and *Bright-sided: How the Relentless Promotion of Positive Thinking Has Undermined America* (2009). She is best known for the books *Nickel and Dimed: On (Not) Getting By in America* (2001), which explores the plight of the working poor, and *Bait and Switch: The (Futile) Pursuit of the American Dream* (2005) about nearly bankrupt college graduates and beleaguered white-collar workers. The following is an excerpt from *Nickel and Dimed.*

For sheer grandeur, scale, and intimidation value, I doubt if any corporate orientation exceeds that of Wal-Mart. I have been told that the process will take eight hours, which will include two fifteen-minute breaks and one half-hour break for a meal, and will be paid for like a regular shift. When I arrive, dressed neatly in khakis and clean T-shirt, as befits a potential Wal-Mart "associate," I find there are ten new hires besides myself, mostly young and Caucasian, and a team of three, headed by Roberta, to do the "orientating." We sit around a long table in the same windowless room where I was interviewed, each with a thick folder of paperwork in front of us, and hear Roberta tell once again about raising six children, being a "people person," discovering that the three principles of Wal-Mart philosophy were the same as her own, and so on. We begin with a video, about fifteen minutes long, on the history and philosophy of Wal-Mart, or, as an anthropological observer might call it, the Cult of Sam. First young Sam Walton, in uniform, comes back from the war. He starts a store, a sort of five-and-dime; he marries and fathers four attractive children; he receives a Medal of Freedom from President Bush, after which he promptly dies, making way for the eulogies. But the company goes on, yes indeed. Here the arc of the story soars upward unstoppably, pausing only to mark some fresh milestone of corporate expansion. 1992: Wal-Mart becomes the largest retailer in the world. 1997: Sales top $100 billion. 1998: The number of Wal-Mart associates hits 825,000, making Wal-Mart the largest private employer in the nation. Each landmark date is accompanied by a clip showing throngs of shoppers, swarms of associates, or scenes of handsome new stores and their adjoining parking lots. Over and over we hear in voiceover or see in graphic display the "three principles," which are maddeningly, even defiantly, nonparallel: "respect for the individual, exceeding customers' expectations, strive for excellence."

"Respect for the individual" is where we, the associates, come in, because vast as Wal-Mart is, and tiny as we may be as individuals, everything depends on us. Sam always said, and is shown saying, that "the best ideas come from the associates"—for example, the idea of having a "people greeter," an elderly employee (excuse me, associate) who welcomes each customer as he or she enters the store. Three times during the orientation, which began at three and stretches to nearly eleven, we are reminded that this brainstorm originated in a mere associate, and who knows what revolutions in retailing each one of us may propose? Because our ideas are welcome, more than welcome, and we are to think of our managers not as bosses but as "servant leaders," serving us as well as the customers. Of course, all is not total harmony, in every instance, between associates and their servant-leaders. A video on "associate honesty" shows a cashier being caught on videotape as he pockets some bills from the cash register. Drums beat ominously as he is led away in handcuffs and sentenced to four years.

The theme of covert tensions, overcome by right thinking and positive attitude, continues in the twelve-minute video entitled *You've Picked a Great Place to Work*. Here various associates testify to the "essential feeling of family for which Wal-Mart is so well-known," leading up to the conclusion that we don't need a union. Once, long ago, unions had a place in American society, but they "no longer have much to offer workers," which is why people are leaving them "by the droves." Wal-Mart is booming; unions are declining: judge for yourself. But we are warned that "unions have been targeting Wal-Mart for years." Why? For the dues money of course. Think of what you would lose with a union: first, your dues money, which could be $20 a month "and sometimes much more." Second, you would lose "your voice" because the union would insist on doing your talking for you. Finally, you might lose even your wages and benefits because they would all be "at risk on the bargaining table." You have to wonder—and I imagine some of my teenage fellow orientees may be doing so—why such fiends as these union organizers, such outright extortionists, are allowed to roam free in the land.

There is more, much more than I could ever absorb, even if it were spread out over a semester-long course. On the reasonable assumption that none of us is planning to go home and curl up with the "Wal-Mart Associate Handbook," our trainers start reading it out loud to us, pausing every few paragraphs to ask, "Any questions?" There never are. Barry, the seventeen-year-old to my left, mutters that his "butt hurts." Sonya, the tiny African American woman across from me, seems frozen in terror. I have given up on looking perky and am fighting to keep my eyes open. No nose or other facial jewelry, we learn; earrings must be small and discreet, not dangling; no blue jeans except on Friday, and then you have to pay $1 for the privilege of wearing them. No "grazing," that is, eating from food packages that somehow become open; no "time theft." This last sends me drifting off in a sci-fi direction: *And as the time thieves headed back to the year 3420, loaded with weekends and days off looted from the twenty-first century* . . . Finally, a question. The old guy who is being hired as a people greeter wants to know, "What is time theft?" Answer: Doing anything other than working during company time, anything at all. Theft of *our* time is not, however, an issue. There are stretches amounting to many minutes when all three of our trainers wander off, leaving us to sit there in silence or take the opportunity to squirm. Or our junior trainers go through a section of the handbook, and then Roberta, returning from some other business, goes over the same section again. My eyelids droop and I consider walking out. I have seen time move more swiftly during seven-hour airline delays. In fact, I am getting nostalgic about seven-hour airline delays. At least you can read a book or get up and walk around, take a leak.

On breaks, I drink coffee purchased at the Radio Grill, as the in-house fast-food place is called, the real stuff with caffeine, more because I'm concerned about being alert for the late-night drive home than out of any need to absorb all the Wal-Mart trivia coming my way. Now, here's a drug the drug warriors ought to take a little more interest in. Since I don't normally drink it at all—iced tea can usually be counted on for enough of a kick—the coffee has an effect like reagent-grade Dexedrine: my pulse races, my brain overheats, and the result in this instance is a kind of delirium. I find myself overly challenged by the little kindergarten-level tasks we are now given to do, such as affixing my personal bar code to my ID card, then sticking on the punch-out letters to spell my name. The letters keep curling up and sticking to my fingers, so I stop at "Barb," or more precisely, "BARB," drifting off to think of all the people I know who have gentrified their names in recent years—Patsy to Patricia, Dick to Richard, and so forth—while I am going in the other direction. Now we start taking turns going to the computers to begin our CBL, or Computer-Based Learning, and I become transfixed by the HIV-inspired module entitled "Bloodborne Pathogens," on what to do in the event that pools of human blood should show up on the sales floor. All right, you put warning cones around the puddles, don protective gloves, etc., but I can't stop trying to envision the circumstances in which these pools might arise: an associate uprising? a guest riot? I have gone through six modules, three more than we are supposed to do tonight—the rest are to be done in our spare moments over the next few weeks—when one of the trainers gently pries me away from the computer. We are allowed now to leave.

Suggestions for Discussion

1. Why is it significant that the employee orientation for Wal-Mart takes place in a "windowless" room? That the presentation is long and boring? That the participants are assigned "kindergarten-level tasks"?

2. Why does Wal-Mart paint such a negative portrait of labor unions? Does Ehrenreich expect the teenagers watching the presentation to believe Wal-Mart's presentation? Why?

3. Wal-Mart is clearly worried about employees stealing "time" as well as products. Ehrenreich argues that Wal-Mart is, in return, stealing from its "associates." What is Wal-Mart stealing?

4. Have you ever worked for Wal-Mart or known anyone who has? If so, how accurate do you find this article? Is Wal-Mart a "family" work environment?

Suggestions for Writing

1. Synthesis: Ehrenreich's essay, like many others in this collection, is ultimately about class conflict in the United States. Select and read one or more additional texts (for example, Alfred Lubrano's "Blue-Collar Roots,

White-Collar Dreams"; Anya Kamenetz's "Generation Debt"; Earl Shorris's "Education as a Weapon in the Hands of the Restless Poor"; John Lennon's "Working Class Hero"; Oscar Wilde's "The Soul of Man Under Socialism"; Dan Quayle's "Restoring Basic Values"; and Thomas Jefferson's "The Declaration of Independence" and "The Declaration of the Rights of Man"). What points of agreement do you find between Ehrenreich and your additional text(s)? What points of disagreement? Who do you think offers a more realistic portrayal of class conflict in the United States? Why?

2. Ehrenreich's essay was part of *Nickel and Dimed*, which was published in 2001. Wal-Mart has made conscious efforts to improve its public image as an employer since then. It has, for instance, moved to the forefront in environmental technology for its stores. Research Wal-Mart's public relations efforts over the past few years. What kind of changes has Wal-Mart implemented? Do these changes significantly impact their relationship to their employees? Analyze these efforts critically in the context of Ehrenreich's writing.

PERSONAL WRITING

MARTIN LUTHER KING, JR.

Letter from Birmingham Jail

Martin Luther King, Jr. (1929–1968), nearly thirty years after his death by assassination in Memphis, remains the most charismatic leader of the civil rights movement of the 1950s and 1960s. He led sit-ins and demonstrations throughout the South and was founder and president of the Southern Christian Leadership Conference, leader of the 1963 March on Washington, as well as pastor of a large Baptist congregation in Atlanta. King followed the principles of Gandhi and Thoreau in all of his public actions and writings. In 1964 he received the Nobel Peace Prize. His writings include *Strength to Love* (1963) and *Conscience for Change* (1967). The occasion for "Letter from Birmingham Jail" was provided by a public statement by eight Alabama clergymen calling on civil rights leaders to abandon the public demonstrations in Birmingham and press their claims for justice in the courts. The letter, revised and published in *Why We Can't Wait* (1964), is printed here in its original form. King began to write it on the margins of the newspaper in which the public statement by the eight Alabama clergymen appeared. That statement is also printed here.

Public Statement by Eight Alabama Clergymen

(April 12, 1963)

We the undersigned clergymen are among those who, in January, issued "An Appeal for Law and Order and Common Sense," in dealing with racial problems in Alabama. We expressed understanding that honest convictions in racial matters could properly be pursued in the courts, but urged that decisions of those courts should in the meantime be peacefully obeyed.

Since that time there had been some evidence of increased forbearance and a willingness to face facts. Responsible citizens have undertaken to work on various problems which cause racial friction and unrest. In Birmingham, recent public events have given indication that we all have opportunity for a new constructive and realistic approach to racial problems.

However, we are now confronted by a series of demonstrations by some of our Negro citizens, directed and led in part by outsiders. We recognize the natural impatience of people who feel that their hopes are slow in being realized. But we are convinced that these demonstrations are unwise and untimely.

We agree rather with certain local Negro leadership which has called for honest and open negotiation of racial issues in our area. And we believe this kind of facing of issues can best be accomplished by citizens of our own metropolitan area, white and Negro, meeting with their knowledge and experience of the local situation. All of us need to face that responsibility and find proper channels for its accomplishment.

Just as we formerly pointed out that "hatred and violence have no sanction in our religious and political traditions," we also point out that such actions as incite to hatred and violence, however technically peaceful those actions may be, have not contributed to the resolution of our local problems. We do not believe that these days of new hope are days when extreme measures are justified in Birmingham.

We commend the community as a whole, and the local news media and law enforcement officials in particular, on the calm manner in which these demonstrations have been handled. We urge the public to continue to show restraint should the demonstrations continue, and the law enforcement officials to remain calm and continue to protect our city from violence.

We further strongly urge our own Negro community to withdraw support from these demonstrations, and to unite locally in working peacefully for a better Birmingham. When rights are consistently denied, a cause should be pressed in the courts and in negotiations among local leaders, and not in the streets. We appeal to both our white and Negro citizenry to observe the principles of law and order and common sense.

Signed by:

C. C. J. CARPENTER, D.D., LL.D., *Bishop of Alabama*

JOSEPH A. DURICK, D.D., *Auxiliary Bishop, Diocese of Mobile, Birmingham*

RABBI MILTON L. GRAFMAN, *Temple Emanu-El, Birmingham, Alabama*

BISHOP PAUL HARDIN, *Bishop of the Alabama-West Florida Conference of the Methodist Church*

BISHOP NOLAN B. HARMON, *Bishop of the North Alabama Conference of the Methodist Church*

GEORGE M. MURRAY, D.D., LL.D., *Bishop Coadjutor, Episcopal Diocese of Alabama*
EDWARD V. RAMAGE, *Moderator, Synod of the Alabama Presbyterian Church in the United States*
EARL STALLINGS, *Pastor, First Baptist Church, Birmingham, Alabama*

ↄ

Letter from Birmingham Jail

MARTIN LUTHER KING, JR.
Birmingham City Jail
April 16, 1963

Bishop C. C. J. Carpenter
Bishop Joseph A. Durick
Rabbi Milton L. Grafman
Bishop Paul Hardin
Bishop Nolan B. Harmon
The Rev. George M. Murray
The Rev. Edward V. Ramage
The Rev. Earl Stallings

My dear Fellow Clergymen,

While confined here in the Birmingham City Jail, I came across your recent statement calling our present activities "unwise and untimely." Seldom, if ever, do I pause to answer criticism of my work and ideas. If I sought to answer all of the criticisms that cross my desk, my secretaries would be engaged in little else in the course of the day and I would have no time for constructive work. But since I feel that you are men of genuine good will and your criticisms are sincerely set forth, I would like to answer your statement in what I hope will be patient and reasonable terms.

I think I should give the reason for my being in Birmingham, since you have been influenced by the argument of "outsiders coming in." I have the honor of serving as president of the Southern Christian Leadership Conference, an organization operating in every Southern state with headquarters in Atlanta, Georgia. We have some eighty-five affiliate organizations all across the South—one being the Alabama Christian Movement for Human Rights. Whenever necessary and possible we share staff, educational, and financial resources with our affiliates. Several months ago our local affiliate here in Birmingham invited us to be on call to engage in a nonviolent direct action program if such were deemed necessary. We readily consented and when the hour came we lived up to our promises. So I am here, along with several members of my staff, because we were invited here. I am here because

I have basic organizational ties here. Beyond this, I am in Birmingham because injustice is here. Just as the eighth century prophets left their little villages and carried their "thus saith the Lord" far beyond the boundaries of their home town, and just as the Apostle Paul left his little village of Tarsus and carried the gospel of Jesus Christ to practically every hamlet and city of the Graeco-Roman world, I too am compelled to carry the gospel of freedom beyond my particular home town. Like Paul, I must constantly respond to the Macedonian call for aid.

Moreover, I am cognizant of the interrelatedness of all communities and states. I cannot sit idly by in Atlanta and not be concerned about what happens in Birmingham. Injustice anywhere is a threat to justice everywhere. We are caught in an inescapable network of mutuality tied in a single garment of destiny. Whatever affects one directly affects all indirectly. Never again can we afford to live with the narrow, provincial "outside agitator" idea. Anyone who lives inside the United States can never be considered an outsider anywhere in this country.

You deplore the demonstrations that are presently taking place in Birmingham. But I am sorry that your statement did not express a similar concern for the conditions that brought the demonstrations into being. I am sure that each of you would want to go beyond the superficial social analyst who looks merely at effects, and does not grapple with underlying causes. I would not hesitate to say that it is unfortunate that so-called demonstrations are taking place in Birmingham at this time, but I would say in more emphatic terms that it is even more unfortunate that the white power structure of this city left the Negro community with no other alternative.

In any nonviolent campaign there are four basic steps: (1) collection of the facts to determine whether injustices are alive; (2) negotiation; (3) self-purification; and (4) direct action. We have gone through all of these steps in Birmingham. There can be no gainsaying of the fact that racial injustice engulfs this community. Birmingham is probably the most thoroughly segregated city in the United States. Its ugly record of police brutality is known in every section of this country. Its unjust treatment of Negroes in the courts is a notorious reality. There have been more unsolved bombings of Negro homes and churches in Birmingham than any city in this nation. These are the hard, brutal, and unbelievable facts. On the basis of these conditions Negro leaders sought to negotiate with the city fathers. But the political leaders consistently refused to engage in good faith negotiation.

Then came the opportunity last September to talk with some of the leaders of the economic community. In these negotiating sessions certain promises were made by the merchants—such as the promise to remove the humiliating racial signs from the stores. On the basis of these promises

Rev. Shuttlesworth and the leaders of the Alabama Christian Movement for Human Rights agreed to call a moratorium on any type of demonstrations. As the weeks and months unfolded we realized that we were the victims of a broken promise. The signs remained. As in so many experiences of the past we were confronted with blasted hopes, and the dark shadow of a deep disappointment settled upon us. So we had no alternative except that of preparing for direct action, whereby we would present our very bodies as a means of laying our case before the conscience of the local and national community. We were not unmindful of the difficulties involved. So we decided to go through a process of self-purification. We started having workshops on nonviolence and repeatedly asked ourselves the questions, "Are you able to accept blows without retaliating?" "Are you able to endure the ordeals of jail?"

We decided to set our direct action program around the Easter season, realizing that with the exception of Christmas, this was the largest shopping period of the year. Knowing that a strong economic withdrawal program would be the by-product of direct action, we felt that this was the best time to bring pressure on the merchants for the needed changes. Then it occurred to us that the March election was ahead, and so we speedily decided to postpone action until after election day. When we discovered that Mr. Connor was in the run-off, we decided again to postpone so that the demonstrations could not be used to cloud the issues. At this time we agreed to begin our nonviolent witness the day after the run-off.

This reveals that we did not move irresponsibly into direct action. We too wanted to see Mr. Connor defeated; so we went through postponement after postponement to aid in this community need. After this we felt that direct action could be delayed no longer.

You may well ask, "Why direct action? Why sit-ins, marches, etc.? Isn't negotiation a better path?" You are exactly right in your call for negotiation. Indeed, this is the purpose of direct action. Nonviolent direct action seeks to create such a crisis and establish such creative tension that a community that has constantly refused to negotiate is forced to confront the issue. It seeks so to dramatize the issue that it can no longer be ignored. I just referred to the creation of tension as a part of the work of the nonviolent resister. This may sound rather shocking. But I must confess that I am not afraid of the word tension. I have earnestly worked and preached against violent tension, but there is a type of constructive nonviolent tension that is necessary for growth. Just as Socrates felt that it was necessary to create a tension in the mind so that individuals could rise from the bondage of myths and half-truths to the unfettered realm of creative analysis and objective appraisal, we must see the need of having nonviolent gadflies to create the kind of tension in society that will help men rise from the dark depths of prejudice and racism to the majestic heights of understanding and brotherhood. So the purpose of the direct action is to create a situation so crisis-packed that it will inevitably open the door to negotiation. We, therefore, concur with you in your call for negotiation. Too long has our beloved Southland been bogged down in the tragic attempt to live in monologue rather than dialogue.

One of the basic points in your statement is that our acts are untimely. Some have asked, "Why didn't you give the new administration time to act?" The only answer that I can give to this inquiry is that the new administration must be prodded about as much as the outgoing one before it acts. We will be sadly mistaken if we feel that the election of Mr. Boutwell will bring the millennium to Birmingham. While Mr. Boutwell is much more articulate and gentle than Mr. Connor, they are both segregationists dedicated to the task of maintaining the status quo. The hope I see in Mr. Boutwell is that he will be reasonable enough to see the futility of massive resistance to desegregation. But he will not see this without pressure from the devotees of civil rights. My friends, I must say to you that we have not made a single gain in civil rights without determined legal and nonviolent pressure. History is the long and tragic story of the fact that privileged groups seldom give up their privileges voluntarily. Individuals may see the moral light and voluntarily give up their unjust posture; but as Reinhold Niebuhr has reminded us, groups are more immoral than individuals.

We know through painful experience that freedom is never voluntarily given by the oppressor; it must be demanded by the oppressed. Frankly I have never yet engaged in a direct action movement that was "well timed," according to the timetable of those who have not suffered unduly from the disease of segregation. For years now I have heard the word "Wait!" It rings in the ear of every Negro with a piercing familiarity. This "wait" has almost always meant "never." It has been a tranquilizing thalidomide, relieving the emotional stress for a moment, only to give birth to an ill-formed infant of frustration. We must come to see with the distinguished jurist of yesterday that "justice too long delayed is justice denied." We have waited for more than three hundred and forty years for our constitutional and God-given rights. The nations of Asia and Africa are moving with jet-like speed toward the goal of political independence, and we still creep at horse and buggy pace toward the gaining of a cup of coffee at a lunch counter.

I guess it is easy for those who have never felt the stinging darts of segregation to say wait. But when you have seen vicious mobs lynch your mothers and fathers at will and drown your sisters and brothers at whim; when you have seen hate filled policemen curse, kick, brutalize, and even kill your black brothers and sisters with impunity; when you see the vast majority of your twenty million Negro brothers smothering in an air-tight cage of poverty in the midst of an affluent society; when you suddenly find your tongue twisted and your speech stammering as you seek to explain to your six-year-old daughter why she can't go to the public amusement park that has just been advertised on television, and see tears welling up in her little eyes when she is told that Funtown is closed to colored children, and see the depressing clouds of inferiority begin to form in her little mental sky, and see her begin to distort her little personality by unconsciously developing a bitterness toward white people; when you have to concoct an answer for a five-year-old son asking in agonizing pathos: "Daddy, why do white people treat colored people so mean?"; when you take a cross country drive and find it necessary to sleep night after night in the uncomfortable corners of your automobile because no motel will accept you; when you are humiliated day in and day out by nagging signs reading "white" men and "colored"; when your first name becomes "nigger" and your middle name becomes "boy" (however old you are) and your last name becomes "John," and when your wife and mother are never given the respected title "Mrs."; when you are harried by day and haunted by night by the fact that you are a Negro, living constantly at tip-toe stance never quite knowing what to expect next, and plagued with inner fears and outer resentments; when you are forever fighting a degenerating sense of "nobodiness";—then you will understand why we find it difficult to wait. There comes a time when the cup of endurance runs over, and men are no longer willing to be plunged into an abyss of injustice where they experience the bleakness of corroding despair. I hope, sirs, you can understand our legitimate and unavoidable impatience.

You express a great deal of anxiety over our willingness to break laws. This is certainly a legitimate concern. Since we so diligently urge people to obey the Supreme Court's decision of 1954 outlawing segregation in the public schools, it is rather strange and paradoxical to find us consciously breaking laws. One may well ask, "How can you advocate breaking some laws and obeying others?" The answer is found in the fact that there are two types of laws. There are *just* laws and there are *unjust* laws. I would be the first to advocate obeying just laws. One has not only a legal but moral responsibility to obey just laws. Conversely, one has a moral responsibility to disobey unjust laws. I would agree with Saint Augustine that "An unjust law is no law at all."

Now what is the difference between the two? How does one determine when a law is just or unjust? A just law is a man-made code that squares with the moral law or the law of God. An unjust law is a code that is out of harmony with the moral law. To put it in the terms of Saint Thomas Aquinas, an unjust law is a human law that is not rooted in eternal and natural law. Any law that uplifts human personality is just. Any law that degrades human personality is unjust. All segregation statutes are unjust because segregation distorts the soul and damages the personality. It gives the segregator a false sense of superiority and the segregated a false sense of inferiority. To use the words of Martin Buber, the great Jewish philosopher, segregation substitutes an "I-it" relationship for the "I-thou" relationship, and ends up relegating persons to the status of things. So segregation is not only politically, economically, and sociologically unsound, but it is morally wrong and sinful. Paul Tillich has said that sin is separation. Isn't segregation an existential expression of man's tragic separation, an expression of his awful estrangement, his terrible sinfulness? So I can urge men to obey the 1954 decision of the Supreme Court because it is morally right, and I can urge them to disobey segregation ordinances because they are morally wrong.

Let us turn to a more concrete example of just and unjust laws. An unjust law is a code that a majority inflicts on a minority that is not binding on itself. This is *difference* made legal. On the other hand a just law is a code that a majority compels a minority to follow that it is willing to follow itself. This is *sameness* made legal.

Let me give another explanation. An unjust law is a code inflicted upon a minority which that minority had no part in enacting or creating because they did not have the unhampered right to vote. Who can say the legislature of Alabama which set up the segregation laws was democratically elected? Throughout the state of Alabama all types of conniving methods are used to prevent Negroes from becoming registered voters and there are some counties without a single Negro registered to vote despite the fact that the Negro constitutes a majority of the population. Can any law set up in such a state be considered democratically structured?

These are just a few examples of unjust and just laws. There are some instances when a law is just on its face but unjust in its application. For instance, I was arrested Friday on a charge of parading without a permit. Now there is nothing wrong with an ordinance which requires a permit for a parade, but when the ordinance is used to preserve segregation and to deny citizens the First Amendment privilege of peaceful assembly and peaceful protest, then it becomes unjust.

I hope you can see the distinction I am trying to point out. In no sense do I advocate evading or defying the law as the rabid segregationist would do. This would lead to anarchy. One who breaks an unjust law must do it *openly, lovingly* (not hatefully as the white mothers did in New Orleans when they were seen on television screaming "nigger, nigger, nigger") and with a willingness to accept the penalty. I submit that an individual who breaks a law that conscience tells him is unjust, and willingly accepts the penalty by staying in jail to arouse the conscience of the community over its injustice, is in reality expressing the very highest respect for law.

Of course there is nothing new about this kind of civil disobedience. It was seen sublimely in the refusal of Shadrach, Meshach, and Abednego to obey the laws of Nebuchadnezzar because a higher moral law was involved. It was practiced superbly by the early Christians who were willing to face hungry lions and the excruciating pain of chopping blocks, before submitting to certain unjust laws of the Roman Empire. To a degree academic freedom is a reality today because Socrates practiced civil disobedience.

We can never forget that everything Hitler did in Germany was "legal" and everything the Hungarian freedom fighters did in Hungary was "illegal." It was "illegal" to aid and comfort a Jew in Hitler's Germany. But I am sure that, if I had lived in Germany during that time, I would have aided and comforted my Jewish brothers even though it was illegal. If I lived in a communist country today where certain principles dear to the Christian faith are suppressed, I believe I would openly advocate disobeying those antireligious laws.

I must make two honest confessions to you, my Christian and Jewish brothers. First I must confess that over the last few years I have been gravely disappointed with the white moderate. I have almost reached the regrettable conclusion that the Negroes' great stumbling block in the stride toward freedom is not the White Citizens' "Counciler" or the Ku Klux Klanner, but the white moderate who is more devoted to "order" than to justice; who prefers a negative peace which is the absence of tension to a positive peace which is the presence of justice; who constantly says "I agree with you in the goal you seek, but I can't agree with your methods of direct action"; who paternalistically feels that he can set the timetable for another man's freedom; who lives by the myth of time and who constantly advises the Negro to wait until a "more convenient season." Shallow understanding from people of good will is more frustrating than absolute misunderstanding from people of ill will. Lukewarm acceptance is much more bewildering than outright rejection.

I had hoped that the white moderate would understand that law and order exist for the purpose of establishing justice, and that when they fail to do this they become the dangerously structured dams that block the flow of social progress. I had hoped that the white moderate would understand that the present tension in the South is merely a necessary phase of the transition from an obnoxious negative peace, where the Negro passively accepted his unjust plight, to a substance-filled positive peace, where all men will respect the dignity and worth of human personality. Actually, we who engage in nonviolent direct action are not the creators of tension. We merely bring to the surface the hidden tension that is already alive. We bring it out in the open where it can be seen and dealt with. Like a boil that can never be cured as long as it is covered up but must be opened with all its pus-flowing ugliness to the natural medicines of air and light, injustice must likewise be exposed, with all of the tension its exposing creates, to the light of human conscience and the air of national opinion before it can be cured.

In your statement you asserted that our actions, even though peaceful, must be condemned because they precipitate violence. But can this assertion be logically made? Isn't this like condemning the robbed man because his possession of money precipitated the evil act of robbery? Isn't this like condemning Socrates because his unswerving commitment to truth and his philosophical delvings precipitated the misguided popular mind to make him drink the hemlock? Isn't this like condemning Jesus because His unique God consciousness and never-ceasing devotion to His will precipitated the evil act of crucifixion? We must come to see, as federal courts have consistently affirmed, that it is immoral to urge an individual to withdraw his efforts to gain his basic constitutional rights because the quest precipitates violence. Society must protect the robbed and punish the robber.

I had also hoped that the white moderate would reject the myth of time. I received a letter this morning from a white brother in Texas which said: "All Christians know that the colored people will receive equal rights eventually, but is it possible that you are in too great of a religious hurry? It has taken Christianity almost 2,000 years to accomplish what it has. The teachings of Christ take time to come to earth." All that is said here grows out of a tragic misconception of time. It is the strangely irrational notion that there is something in the very flow of time that will inevitably cure all ills. Actually time is neutral. It can be used either destructively or constructively. I am coming to feel that the people of ill will have used time much more effectively than the people of good will. We will have to repent in this generation not merely for the vitriolic words and actions of the bad people, but for the appalling silence of the good people. We must come to see that human progress never rolls in on wheels of inevitability. It comes through the tireless efforts and persistent work of men willing to be co-workers with God, and without this hard work time itself becomes an ally of the forces of social stagnation.

We must use time creatively, and forever realize that the time is always ripe to do right. Now is the time to make real the promise of democracy, and transform our pending national elegy into a creative psalm of brotherhood. Now is the time to lift our national policy from the quicksand of racial injustice to the solid rock of human dignity.

You spoke of our activity in Birmingham as extreme. At first I was rather disappointed that fellow clergymen would see my nonviolent efforts as those of the extremist. I started thinking about the fact that I stand in the middle of two opposing forces in the Negro community. One is a force of complacency made up of Negroes who, as a result of long years of oppression, have been so completely drained of self-respect and a sense of "some-bodiness" that they have adjusted to segregation, and of a few Negroes in the middle class who, because of a degree of academic and economic security, and because at points they profit by segregation, have unconsciously become insensitive to the problems of the masses. The other force is one of bitterness and hatred and comes perilously close to advocating violence. It is expressed in the various black nationalist groups that are springing up over the nation, the largest and best known being Elijah Muhammad's Muslim movement. This movement is nourished by the contemporary frustration over the continued existence of racial discrimination. It is made up of people who have lost faith in America, who have absolutely repudiated Christianity, and who have concluded that the white man is an incurable "devil." I have tried to stand between these two forces saying that we need not follow the "do-nothingism" of the complacent or the hatred and despair of the black nationalist. There is the more excellent way of love and nonviolent protest. I'm grateful to God that, through the Negro church, the dimension of nonviolence entered our struggle. If this philosophy had not emerged I am convinced that by now many streets of the South would be flowing with floods of blood. And I am further convinced that if our white brothers dismiss us as "rabble rousers" and "outside agitators"—those of us who are working through the channels of nonviolent direct action—and refuse to support our nonviolent efforts, millions of Negroes, out of frustration and despair, will seek solace and security in black nationalist ideologies, a development that will lead inevitably to a frightening racial nightmare.

Oppressed people cannot remain oppressed forever. The urge for freedom will eventually come. This is what has happened to the American Negro. Something within has reminded him of his birthright of freedom; something without has reminded him that he can gain it. Consciously and unconsciously, he has been swept in by what the Germans call the *Zeitgeist*, and with his black brothers of Africa, and his brown and yellow brothers of Asia, South America, and the Caribbean, he is moving with a sense of cosmic urgency toward the promised land of racial justice. Recognizing this vital urge that has engulfed the Negro community, one should readily understand public demonstrations. The Negro has many pent-up resentments and latent frustrations. He has to get them out. So let him march sometime; let him have his prayer pilgrimages to the city hall; understand why he must have sit-ins and freedom rides. If his repressed emotions do not come out in these nonviolent ways, they will come out in ominous expressions of violence. This is not a threat; it is a fact of history. So I have not said to my people, "Get rid of your discontent." But I have tried to say that this normal and healthy discontent can be channeled through the creative outlet of nonviolent direct action. Now this approach is being dismissed as extremist. I must admit that I was initially disappointed in being so categorized.

But as I continued to think about the matter I gradually gained a bit of satisfaction from being considered an extremist. Was not Jesus an extremist in love? "Love your enemies, bless them that curse you, pray for them that despitefully use you." Was not Amos an extremist for justice—"Let justice roll down like waters and righteousness like a mighty stream." Was not Paul an extremist for the gospel of Jesus Christ—"I bear in my body the marks of the Lord Jesus." Was not Martin Luther an extremist—"Here I stand; I can do none other so help me God." Was not John Bunyan an extremist—"I will stay in jail to the end of my days before I make a butchery of my conscience." Was not Abraham Lincoln an extremist—"This nation cannot survive half slave and half free." Was not Thomas Jefferson an extremist—"We hold these truths to be self evident that all men are created equal." So the question is not whether we will be extremist but what kind of extremist will we be. Will we be extremists for hate or will we be extremists for love? Will we be extremists for the preservation of injustice—or will we be extremists for the cause of justice? In that dramatic scene on Calvary's hill three men were crucified. We must never forget that all three were crucified for the same crime—the crime of extremism. Two were extremists for immorality, and thus fell below their environment. The other, Jesus Christ, was an extremist for love, truth, and goodness, and thereby rose above His environment. So, after all, maybe the South, the nation, and the world are in dire need of creative extremists.

I had hoped that the white moderate would see this. Maybe I was too optimistic. Maybe I expected too much. I guess I should have realized that few members of a race that has oppressed another race can understand or appreciate the deep groans and passionate yearnings of those that have been oppressed, and still fewer have the vision to see that injustice must be rooted out by strong, persistent, and determined action. I am thankful, however, that some of our white brothers have grasped the meaning of this social revolution and committed themselves to it. They are still all too small in quantity, but they are big in quality. Some like Ralph McGill, Lillian Smith, Harry Golden, and James Dabbs have written about our struggle in eloquent, prophetic, and understanding terms. Others have marched with us down nameless streets of the South. They have languished in filthy, roach-infested jails, suffering the abuse and brutality of angry policemen who see them as "dirty nigger lovers." They, unlike so many of their moderate brothers and sisters, have recognized the urgency of the moment and sensed the need for powerful "action" antidotes to combat the disease of segregation.

Let me rush on to mention my other disappointment. I have been so greatly disappointed with the white Church and its leadership. Of course there are some notable exceptions. I am not unmindful of the fact that each of you has taken some significant stands on this issue. I commend you, Rev. Stallings, for your Christian stand on this past Sunday, in welcoming Negroes to your worship service on a nonsegregated basis. I commend the Catholic leaders of this state for integrating Springhill College several years ago.

But despite these notable exceptions I must honestly reiterate that I have been disappointed with the Church. I do not say that as one of those negative critics who can always find something wrong with the Church. I say it as a minister of the gospel, who loves the Church; who was nurtured in its bosom; who has been sustained by its spiritual blessings and who will remain true to it as long as the cord of life shall lengthen.

I had the strange feeling when I was suddenly catapulted into the leadership of the bus protest in Montgomery several years ago that we would have the support of the white Church. I felt that the white ministers, priests, and rabbis of the South would be some of our strongest allies. Instead, some have been outright opponents, refusing to understand the freedom movement and misrepresenting its leaders; all too many others have been more cautious than courageous and have remained silent behind the anesthetizing security of stained glass windows.

In spite of my shattered dreams of the past, I came to Birmingham with the hope that the white religious leadership of the community would see the justice of our cause and, with deep moral concern, serve as the channel through which our just grievances could get to the power structure. I had hoped that each of you would understand. But again I have been disappointed.

I have heard numerous religious leaders of the South call upon their worshippers to comply with a desegregation decision because it is the law, but I have longed to hear white ministers say follow this decree because integration is morally right and the Negro is your brother. In the midst of blatant injustices inflicted upon the Negro, I have watched white churches stand on the sideline and merely mouth pious irrelevancies and sanctimonious trivialities. In the midst of a mighty struggle to rid our nation of racial and economic injustice, I have heard so many ministers say, "Those are social issues with which the Gospel has no real concern," and I have watched so many churches commit themselves to a completely otherworldly religion which made a strange distinction between body and soul, the sacred and the secular.

So here we are moving toward the exit of the twentieth century with a religious community largely adjusted to the status quo, standing as a tail light behind other community agencies rather than a headlight leading men to higher levels of justice.

I have travelled the length and breadth of Alabama, Mississippi, and all the other Southern states. On sweltering summer days and crisp autumn mornings I have looked at her beautiful churches with their spires pointing heavenward. I have beheld the impressive outlay of her massive religious education buildings. Over and over again I have found myself asking: "Who worships here? Who is their God? Where were their voices when the lips of Governor Barnett dripped with words of interposition and nullification? Where were they when Governor Wallace gave the clarion call for defiance and hatred? Where were their voices of support when tired, bruised, and weary Negro men and women decided to rise from the dark dungeons of complacency to the bright hills of creative protest?"

Yes, these questions are still in my mind. In deep disappointment, I have wept over the laxity of the Church. But be assured that my tears have been tears of love. There can be no deep disappointment where there is not deep love. Yes, I love the Church; I love her sacred walls. How could I do otherwise? I am in the rather unique position of being the son, the grandson, and the great grandson of preachers. Yes, I see the Church as the body of Christ. But, oh! How we have blemished and scarred that body through social neglect and fear of being nonconformists.

There was a time when the Church was very powerful. It was during that period when the early Christians rejoiced when they were deemed worthy to suffer for what they believed. In those days the Church was not merely a thermometer that recorded the ideas and principles of popular opinion; it was a thermostat that transformed the mores of society. Wherever the early Christians entered a town the power structure got disturbed and immediately sought to convict them for being "disturbers of the peace" and "outside agitators." But they went on with the conviction that they were a "colony of heaven" and had to obey God rather than man. They were small in number but big in commitment. They were too God-intoxicated to be "astronomically intimidated." They brought an end to such ancient evils as infanticide and gladiatorial contest.

Things are different now. The contemporary Church is so often a weak, ineffectual voice with an uncertain sound. It is so often the archsupporter of the status quo. Far from being disturbed by the presence of the Church, the power structure of the average community is consoled by the Church's silent and often vocal sanction of things as they are.

But the judgment of God is upon the Church as never before. If the Church of today does not recapture the sacrificial spirit of the early Church, it will lose its authentic ring, forfeit the loyalty of millions, and be dismissed as an irrelevant social club with no meaning for the twentieth century. I am meeting young people every day whose disappointment with the Church has risen to outright disgust.

Maybe again I have been too optimistic. Is organized religion too inextricably bound to the status quo to save our nation and the world? Maybe I must turn my faith to the inner spiritual Church, the church within the Church, as the true *ecclesia* and the hope of the world. But again I am thankful to God that some noble souls from the ranks of organized religion have broken loose from the paralyzing chains of conformity and joined us as active partners in the struggle for freedom. They have left their secure congregations and walked the streets of Albany, Georgia, with us. They have gone through the highways of the South on torturous rides for freedom. Yes, they have gone to jail with us. Some have been kicked out of their churches and lost the support of their bishops and fellow ministers. But they have gone with the faith that right defeated is stronger than evil triumphant. These men have been the leaven in the lump of the race. Their witness has been the spiritual salt that has preserved the true meaning of the Gospel in these troubled times. They have carved a tunnel of hope through the dark mountain of disappointment.

I hope the Church as a whole will meet the challenge of this decisive hour. But even if the Church does not come to the aid of justice, I have no despair about the future. I have no fear about the outcome of our struggle in Birmingham, even if our motives are presently misunderstood. We will reach the goal of freedom in Birmingham and all over the nation, because the goal of America is freedom. Abused and scorned though we may be, our destiny is tied up with the destiny of America. Before the pilgrims landed at Plymouth, we were here. Before the pen of Jefferson etched across the pages of history the majestic words of the Declaration of Independence, we were here. For more than two centuries our foreparents labored in this country without wages; they made cotton "king"; and they built the homes of their masters in the midst of brutal injustice and shameful humiliation—and yet out of a bottomless vitality they continued to thrive and develop. If the inexpressible cruelties of slavery could not stop us, the opposition we now face will surely fail. We will win our freedom because the sacred heritage of our nation and the eternal will of God are embodied in our echoing demands.

I must close now. But before closing I am impelled to mention one other point in your statement that troubled me profoundly. You warmly commended the Birmingham police force for keeping "order" and "preventing violence." I don't believe you would have so warmly commended the police force if you had seen its angry violent dogs literally biting six unarmed, nonviolent Negroes. I don't believe you would so quickly commend the policemen if you would observe their ugly and inhuman treatment of Negroes here in the city jail; if you would watch them push and curse old Negro women and young Negro girls; if you would see them slap and kick old Negro men and young Negro boys; if you will observe them, as they did on two occasions, refuse to give us food because we wanted to sing our grace together. I'm sorry that I can't join you in your praise for the police department.

It is true that they have been rather disciplined in their public handling of the demonstrators. In this sense they have been rather publicly "nonviolent." But for what purpose? To preserve the evil system of segregation. Over the last few years I have consistently preached that nonviolence demands that the means we use must be as pure as the ends we seek. So I have tried to make it clear that it is wrong to use immoral means to attain moral ends. But now I must affirm that it is just as wrong, or even more so, to use moral means to preserve immoral ends. Maybe Mr. Connor and his policemen have been rather publicly nonviolent, as Chief Pritchett was in Albany, Georgia, but they have used the moral means of nonviolence to maintain the immoral end of flagrant racial injustice. T. S. Eliot has said that there is no greater treason than to do the right deed for the wrong reason.

I wish you had commended the Negro sit-inners and demonstrators of Birmingham for their sublime courage, their willingness to suffer, and their amazing discipline in the midst of the most inhuman provocation. One day the South will recognize its real heroes. They will be the James Merediths, courageously and with a majestic sense of purpose, facing jeering and hostile mobs and the agonizing loneliness that characterizes the life of the pioneer. They will be old, oppressed, battered Negro women, symbolized in a seventy-two year old woman of Montgomery, Alabama, who rose up with a sense of dignity and with her people decided not to ride the segregated buses, and responded to one who inquired about her tiredness with ungrammatical profundity: "My feets is tired, but my soul is rested." They will be young high school and college students, young ministers of the gospel and a host of the elders, courageously and nonviolently sitting in at lunch counters and willingly going to jail for conscience sake. One day the South will know that when these disinherited children of God sat down at lunch counters they were in reality standing up for the best in the American dream and the most sacred values in our Judeo-Christian heritage, and thus carrying our whole nation back to great wells of democracy which were dug deep by the founding fathers in the formulation of the Constitution and the Declaration of Independence.

Never before have I written a letter this long (or should I say a book?). I'm afraid that it is much too long to take your precious time. I can assure you that it would have been much shorter if I had been writing from a comfortable desk, but what else is there to do when you are alone for days in the dull monotony of a narrow jail cell other than write long letters, think strange thoughts, and pray long prayers?

If I have said anything in this letter that is an overstatement of the truth and is indicative of an unreasonable impatience, I beg you to forgive me. If I have said anything in this letter that is an understatement of the truth and is indicative of my having a patience that makes me patient with anything less than brotherhood, I beg God to forgive me.

I hope this letter finds you strong in the faith. I also hope that circumstances will soon make it possible for me to meet each of you, not as an integrationist or a civil rights leader, but as a fellow clergyman and a Christian brother. Let us all hope that the dark clouds of racial prejudice will soon pass away and the deep fog of misunderstanding will be lifted from our fear-drenched communities and in some not too distant tomorrow the radiant stars of love and brotherhood will shine over our great nation with all of their scintillating beauty.

Yours for the cause of
Peace and Brotherhood
MARTIN LUTHER KING, JR.

Suggestions for Discussion

1. What is the rhetorical tone of King's letter? How does he achieve that tone? List and explain a half-dozen examples.

2. How does King deal with the eight clergymen's accusation that the demonstrators are "outsiders"?

3. In the letter King refers to a number of enemies of integration; for example, Eugene "Bull" Connor, Albert Bantwell, Ross R. Barnett, George C. Wallace, and Laurie Pritchett. Identify these people and explain their role in the fight against integration.

4. How does King answer the charge that his actions, though peaceful, are dangerous because they lead to violence?

5. What are King's objections to the white churches' response to the fight for integration? What are his objections to white moderates?

Suggestions for Writing

1. Write an essay in which you comment on King's statement: "I submit that an individual who breaks a law that conscience tells him is unjust, and willingly accepts the penalty by staying in jail to arouse the conscience of the community over its injustice, is in reality expressing the very highest respect for the law."

2. Write a paper in which you explain King's use of the examples of Nazi Germany and Communist-controlled Hungary to defend his fight for civil rights.

3. Write a paper in which you agree or disagree with King's assessment of white moderates. Give explicit examples to support your position.

4. King calls his movement a viable alternative to black complacency, or acceptance of the status quo, and to the militant opposition of the black nationalists. Write a paper evaluating his assessment.

5. Write a paper in which you evaluate the civil rights movement of King's day in terms of the present. To what extent did his movement succeed? Fail?

ESSAYS

~~~~~

THOMAS JEFFERSON

The Declaration of Independence

The Continental Congress, assembled in Philadelphia in 1776, delegated to Thomas Jefferson (1743–1826) the task of writing a declaration of independence from Great Britan, which the Congress amended and adopted on July 4 of that year. In its theory as well as in its style, the Declaration of Independence is a typical eighteenth-century view of man's place in society, which included the right to overthrow a tyrannical ruler. After the Revolution, Jefferson was elected governor of Virginia and, in 1801, he was elected the third president of the United States. He was the father of what became known as "Jeffersonian democracy," which exceeded the democracy then advocated by either George Washington or Jefferson's rival, Alexander Hamilton. After leaving the presidency, he founded the University of Virginia as a place where truth could assert itself in free competition with other ideas.

When in the course of human events, it becomes necessary for one people to dissolve the political bands which have connected them with another, and to assume among the powers of the earth, the separate and equal station to which the Laws of Nature and of Nature's God entitle them, a decent respect to the opinions of mankind requires that they should declare the causes which impel them to the separation.

We hold these truths to be self-evident, that all men are created equal, that they are endowed by their Creator with certain inalienable rights, that among these are life, liberty, and the pursuit of happiness. That to secure these rights, governments are instituted among men, deriving their just powers from the consent of the governed. That whenever any form of government becomes destructive of these ends, it is the right of the people to alter or to abolish it, and to institute new government, laying its foundation on such principles and organizing its powers in such form, as to them shall seem most likely to effect their safety and happiness. Prudence, indeed, will dictate that governments long established should not be changed for light and transient causes; and accordingly all experience hath shown, that

590

mankind are more disposed to suffer, while evils are sufferable, than to right themselves by abolishing the forms to which they are accustomed. But when a long train of abuses and usurpations, pursuing invariably the same object, evinces a design to reduce them under absolute despotism, it is their right, it is their duty, to throw off such government, and to provide new guards for their future security. Such has been the patient sufferance of these Colonies; and such is now the necessity which constrains them to alter their former systems of government. The history of the present King of Great Britain is a history of repeated injuries and usurpations, all having in direct object the establishment of an absolute tyranny over these States. To prove this, let facts be submitted to a candid world.

He has refused his assent to laws, the most wholesome and necessary for the public good.

He has forbidden his Governors to pass laws of immediate and pressing importance, unless suspended in their operation till his assent should be obtained; and when so suspended, he has utterly neglected to attend to them.

He has refused to pass other laws for the accommodation of large districts of people, unless those people would relinquish the right of representation in the legislature, a right inestimable to them and formidable to tyrants only.

He has called together legislative bodies at places unusual, uncomfortable, and distant from the depository of their public records, for the sole purpose of fatiguing them into compliance with his measures.

He has dissolved representative houses repeatedly, for opposing with manly firmness his invasions on the rights of the people.

He has refused for a long time, after such dissolutions, to cause others to be elected; whereby the legislative powers, incapable of annihilation, have returned to the people at large for their exercise; the State remaining in the meantime exposed to all the dangers of invasion from without and convulsions within.

He has endeavoured to prevent the population of these states; for that purpose obstructing the laws for naturalization of foreigners; refusing to pass others to encourage their migration hither, and raising the conditions of new appropriations of lands.

He has obstructed the administration of justice, by refusing his assent to laws for establishing judiciary powers.

He has made judges dependent on his will alone, for the tenure of their offices, and the amount and payment of their salaries.

He has erected a multitude of new offices, and sent hither swarms of officers to harass our people, and eat out their substance.

He has kept among us, in times of peace, standing armies without the consent of our legislatures.

He has affected to render the military independent of and superior to the civil power.

He has combined with others to subject us to a jurisdiction foreign of our constitution, and unacknowledged by our laws; giving his assent to their acts of pretended legislation:

For quartering large bodies of armed troops among us:

For protecting them, by a mock trial, from punishment for any murders which they should commit on the inhabitants of these States:

For cutting off our trade with all parts of the world:

For imposing taxes on us without our consent:

For depriving us in many cases of the benefits of trial by jury:

For transporting us beyond seas to be tried for pretended offences:

For abolishing the free system of English laws in a neighbouring Province, establishing therein an arbitrary government, and enlarging its boundaries so as to render it at once an example and fit instrument for introducing the same absolute rule into these Colonies:

For taking away our Charters, abolishing our most valuable laws, and altering fundamentally the forms of our governments:

For suspending our own legislatures, and declaring themselves invested with power to legislate for us in all cases whatsoever.

He has abdicated government here, by declaring us out of his protection and waging war against us.

He has plundered our seas, ravaged our coasts, burnt our towns, and destroyed the lives of our people.

He is at this time transporting large armies of foreign mercenaries to complete the works of death, desolation, and tyranny, already begun with circumstances of cruelty and perfidy scarcely paralleled in the most barbarous ages, and totally unworthy the head of a civilized nation.

He has constrained our fellow citizens taken captive on the high seas to bear arms against their country, to become the executioners of their friends and brethren, or to fall themselves by their hands.

He has excited domestic insurrections amongst us, and has endeavoured to bring on the inhabitants of our frontiers, the merciless Indian savages, whose known rule of warfare, is an undistinguished destruction of all ages, sexes, and conditions.

In every stage of these oppressions we have petitioned for redress in the most humble terms: our repeated petitions have been answered only by repeated injury. A prince whose character is thus marked by every act which may define a tyrant is unfit to be the ruler of a free people.

Nor have we been wanting in attention to our British brethren. We have warned them from time to time of attempts by their legislature to extend an unwarrantable jurisdiction over us. We have reminded them of the circumstances of our emigration and settlement here. We have appealed to their native justice and magnanimity, and we have conjured them by the ties of our common kindred to disavow these usurpations, which would inevitably interrupt our connections and correspondence. They too have been deaf to the voice of justice and of consanguinity. We must, therefore, acquiesce in the necessity, which denounces our separation, and hold them, as we hold the rest of mankind, enemies in war, in peace friends.

We, therefore, the Representatives of the United States of America, in General Congress assembled, appealing to the Supreme Judge of the world for the rectitude of our intentions, do, in the name, and by authority of the good people of these Colonies, solemnly publish and declare, That these United Colonies are, and of right ought to be, Free and Independent States; that they are absolved from all allegiance to the British Crown, and that all political connection between them and the state of Great Britain, is and ought to be totally dissolved; and that as Free and Independent States, they have full power to levy war, conclude peace, contract alliances, establish commerce, and to do all other acts and things which Independent States may of right do. And for the support of this declaration, with a firm reliance on the protection of Divine Providence, we mutually pledge to each other our lives, our fortunes, and our sacred honor.

Suggestions for Discussion

1. What is the basis for Jefferson's belief that "all men are created equal"?

2. In the eighteenth century, the notion of the "divine right" of kings was still popular. How does Jefferson refute that notion?

3. Discuss the list of tyrannical actions that Jefferson attributes to the King of Great Britain. Account for the order in which he lists them.

4. This essay has been called a "model of clarity and precision." Explain your agreement with this statement. How does Jefferson balance strong feeling with logical argument?

Suggestion for Writing

Jefferson asserts that "all men are created equal," and yet he does not include black slaves as equals. In Jefferson's *Autobiography*, he wrote that a clause "reprobating the enslaving the inhabitants of Africa" was omitted in the final draft "in complaisance to South Carolina and Georgia." Was Jefferson merely opportunistic in agreeing to strike this clause? Write an essay in which you relate the ideas of the Declaration to the ideas in Lincoln's Gettysburg Address. Show how one set of ideas leads to the other.

ᐯᐯᐯᐯᐯ

The Declaration of the Rights of Man

Soon after the fall of the Bastille on July 14, 1789, a day celebrated in France as July 4th is celebrated in the United States, the French National Assembly was asked to provide a declaration that would correspond to the American Declaration of Independence. The Assembly appointed a committee of five to draft the document. After several weeks of debate and compromise, the completed declaration was approved and proclaimed on August 27, 1789. Although a number of phrases resemble the American model, the Declaration of the Rights of Man is derived more particularly from the English Bill of Rights of 1689. Ironically, the basis for democratic government embodied in this document was to be subverted by a leader of the new republic who would declare himself Emperor. This leader was Napoléon Bonaparte, and he ruled from 1804 until 1815.

The representatives of the French people, gathered in the National Assembly, believing that ignorance, neglect, and disdain of the rights of men are the sole causes of public misfortunes and of the corruption of governments, have resolved to set forth, in solemn declaration, the natural, inalienable, and sacred rights of men, in order that this Declaration, held always before the members of the body social, will forever remind them of their rights and duties; that the acts of legislative and executive power, always identifiable with the ends and purposes of the whole body politic, may be more fully respected; that the complaints of citizens, founded henceforth on simple and incontrovertible principles, may be turned always to the maintaining of the Constitution and to the happiness of all.

The National Assembly therefore recognizes and declares, in the presence and under the auspices of the Supreme Being, the following rights of Man and of citizen:

1. Men are born and will remain free and endowed with equal rights. Social distinctions can be based only upon usefulness to the common weal.

2. The end and purpose of all political groups is the preservation of the natural and inalienable rights of Man. These rights are Liberty, the Possession of Property, Safety, and Resistance to Oppression.

3. The principle of all sovereignty will remain fundamentally in the State. No group and no individual can exercise authority which does not arise expressly from the State.

4. Liberty consists in being able to do anything which is not harmful to another or to others; therefore, the exercise of the natural rights of each individual has only such limits as will assure to other members of society the enjoyment of the same rights. These limits can be determined only by the Law.

5. The Law has the right to forbid only such actions as are harmful to society. Anything not forbidden by the Law can never be forbidden; and none can be forced to do what the Law does not prescribe.

6. The Law is the expression of the will of the people. All citizens have the right and the duty to concur in the formation of the Law, either in person or through their representatives. Whether it punishes or whether it protects, the Law must be the same for all. All citizens, being equal in the eyes of the Law, are to be admitted equally to all distinctions, ranks, and public employment, according to their capacities, and without any other discrimination than that established by their individual abilities and virtues.

7. No individual can be accused, arrested, or detained except in cases determined by the Law, and according to the forms which the Law has prescribed. Those who instigate, expedite, execute, or cause to be executed any arbitrary or extralegal prescriptions must be punished; but every citizen called or seized through the power of the Law must instantly obey. He will render himself culpable by resisting.

8. The Law should establish only those penalties which are absolutely and evidently necessary, and none can be punished except through the power of the Law, as already established and proclaimed for the public good and legally applied.

9. Every individual being presumed innocent until he has been proved guilty, if it is considered necessary to arrest him, the Law must repress with severity any force which is not required to secure his person.

10. None is to be persecuted for his opinions, even his religious beliefs, provided that his expression of them does not interfere with the order established by the Law.

11. Free communication of thought and opinion is one of the most precious rights of Man; therefore, every citizen can speak, write, or publish freely, except that he will be required to answer for the abuse of such freedom in cases determined by the Law.

12. The guarantee of the rights of Man and of the citizen makes necessary a Public Force and Administration; this Force and Administration has

therefore been established for the good of all, and not for the particular benefit of those to whom it has been entrusted.

13. For the maintaining of this Public Force and Administration, and for the expense of administering it, a common tax is required; it must be distributed equally among the people, in accordance with their ability to pay.

14. All citizens have the right and duty to establish, by themselves or by their representatives, the requirements of a common tax, to consent to it freely, to indicate its use, and to determine its quota, its assessment, its collection, and its duration.

15. Society has the right and duty to demand from every public servant an accounting of his administration.

16. No society in which the guarantee of rights is not assured nor the distinction of legal powers determined can be said to have a constitution.

17. The possession of property being an inviolable and sacred right, none can be deprived of it, unless public necessity, legally proved, clearly requires the deprivation, and then only on the necessary condition of a previously established just reparation.

Suggestions for Discussion

1. What is the major purpose of setting forth the principles enunciated in this declaration?

2. The declaration refers to a "Supreme Being." Why did not the writers of the declaration refer simply to God?

3. How do the seventeen "rights of Man and of citizen" define the relationship between the individual person and the state?

4. How does the declaration define the function of the law and of the state?

5. How does the declaration propose to guarantee freedom of speech?

6. Can you explain why the declaration says that the possession of property is an "inviolable and sacred right"? How does this statement basically differ from modern revolutionary thought?

7. On what principles is this declaration based?

Suggestions for Writing

1. Write an essay about the similarities and differences between this declaration and both the United States Declaration of Independence and the Bill of Rights of the United States Constitution.

2. Examine the English Bill of Rights of 1689 and write an essay in which you explain the close relationship between the French and English declarations.

༼༽༼༽

ELIZABETH CADY STANTON AND LUCRETIA COFFIN MOTT

Seneca Falls Convention

On July 19–20, 1848, around two hundred delegates (women and men) representing suffragist, abolitionist, and temperance groups met in Seneca Falls, NY, at a convention to discuss women's rights. The Declaration of Sentiments and Resolutions was written by Elizabeth Cady Stanton and Lucretia Coffin Mott, assisted by the delegates present. The first major document that sought to define the issues and goals of the nineteenth-century women's movement, it was modeled after the Declaration of Independence to suggest the natural line of development from the American Revolution. Consequently, it stated women's demands for legal, political, economic, and social equality. The only resolution that created an objection was the one on women's suffrage, but after debate it too was included. Sixty-eight women and thirty-two men signed the declaration.

When, in the course of human events, it becomes necessary for one portion of the family of man to assume among the people of the earth a position different from that which they have hitherto occupied, but one to which the laws of nature and of nature's God entitle them, a decent respect to the opinions of mankind requires that they should declare the causes that impel them to such a course.

We hold these truths to be self-evident: that all men and women are created equal; that they are endowed by their Creator with certain inalienable rights; that among these are life, liberty, and the pursuit of happiness; that to secure these rights governments are instituted, deriving their just powers from the consent of the governed. Whenever any form of government becomes destructive of these ends, it is the right of those who suffer from it to refuse allegiance to it, and to insist upon the institution of a new government, laying its foundation on such principles, and organizing its powers in such form, as to them shall seem most likely to effect their safety and happiness. Prudence, indeed, will dictate that governments long established should not be changed for light and transient causes; and accordingly all experience hath shown that mankind are more disposed to suffer, while evils are sufferable, than to right themselves by abolishing the forms to which they were accustomed. But when a long train of abuses and usurpations, pursuing invariably the same object, evinces a design to reduce them under absolute despotism, it is their duty to throw off such government, and to provide new guards for their future security. Such has been the patient sufferance of the women under this goverment, and such is now the necessity which constrains them to demand the equal station to which they are entitled.

The history of mankind is a history of repeated injuries and usurpations on the part of man toward woman, having in direct object the establishment of an absolute tyranny over her. To prove this, let facts be submitted to a candid world.

He has never permitted her to exercise her inalienable right to the elective franchise.

He has compelled her to submit to laws, in the formation of which she had no voice.

He has withheld from her rights which are given to the most ignorant and degraded men—both natives and foreigners.

Having deprived her of this first right of a citizen, the elective franchise, thereby leaving her without representation in the halls of legislation, he has oppressed her on all sides.

He has made her, if married, in the eye of the law, civilly dead.

He has taken from her all right in property, even to the wages she earns.

He has made her, morally, an irresponsible being, as she can commit many crimes with impunity, provided they be done in the presence of her husband. In the covenant of marriage, she is compelled to promise obedience to her husband, he becoming to all intents and purposes, her master—the law giving him power to deprive her of her liberty, and to administer chastisement.

He has so framed the laws of divorce, as to what shall be the proper causes, and in case of separation, to whom the guardianship of the children shall be given, as to be wholly regardless of the happiness of women—the law, in all cases, going upon a false supposition of the supremacy of man, and giving all power into his hands.

After depriving her of all rights as a married woman, if single, and the owner of property, he has taxed her to support a government which recognizes her only when her property can be made profitable to it.

He has monopolized nearly all the profitable employments, and from those she is permitted to follow, she receives but a scanty remuneration. He closes against her all the avenues to wealth and distinction which he considers most honorable to himself. As a teacher of theology, medicine, or law, she is not known.

He has denied her the facilities for obtaining a thorough education, all colleges being closed against her.

He allows her in Church, as well as State, but a subordinate position, claiming Apostolic authority for her exclusion from the ministry, and, with some exceptions, from any public participation in the affairs of the Church.

He has created a false public sentiment by giving to the world a different code of morals for men and women, by which moral delinquencies which exclude women from society, are not only tolerated, but deemed of little account in man.

He has usurped the prerogative of Jehovah himself, claiming it as his right to assign for her a sphere of action, when that belongs to her conscience and to her God.

He has endeavored, in every way that he could, to destroy her confidence in her own powers, to lessen her self-respect, and to make her willing to lead a dependent and abject life.

Now, in view of this entire disfranchisement of one-half the people of this country, their social and religious degradation—in view of the unjust laws above mentioned, and because women do feel themselves aggrieved, oppressed, and fraudulently deprived of their most sacred rights, we insist that they have immediate admission to all the rights and privileges which belong to them as citizens of the United States.

In entering upon the great work before us, we anticipate no small amount of misconception, misrepresentation, and ridicule; but we shall use every instrumentality within our power to effect our object. We shall employ agents, circulate tracts, petition the State and National legislatures, and endeavor to enlist the pulpit and the press in our behalf. We hope this Convention will be followed by a series of Conventions embracing every part of the country.

Whereas, The great precept of nature is conceded to be, that "man shall pursue his own true and substantial happiness." Blackstone in his Commentaries remarks, that this law of Nature being coeval with mankind, and dictated by God himself, is of course superior in obligation to any other. It is binding over all the globe, in all countries and at all times; no human laws are of any validity if contrary to this, and such of them as are valid, derive all their force, and all their validity, and all their authority, mediately and immediately, from this original; therefore,

Resolved, That such laws as conflict, in any way, with the true and substantial happiness of woman, are contrary to the great precept of nature and of no validity, for this is "superior in obligation to any other."

Resolved, That all laws which prevent woman from occupying such a station in society as her conscience shall dictate, or which place her in a position inferior to that of man, are contrary to the great precept of nature, and therefore of no force or authority.

Resolved, That woman is man's equal—was intended to be so by the Creator, and the highest good of the race demands that she should be recognized as such.

Resolved, That the women of this country ought to be enlightened in regard to the laws under which they live, that they may no longer publish their degradation by declaring themselves satisfied with their present position, nor their ignorance, by asserting that they have all the rights they want.

Resolved, That inasmuch as man, while claiming for himself intellectual superiority, does accord to woman moral superiority, it is pre-eminently his duty to encourage her to speak and teach, as she has an opportunity, in all religious assemblies.

Resolved, That the same amount of virtue, delicacy, and refinement of behavior that is required of woman in the social state, should also be required of man, and the same transgressions should be visited with equal severity on both man and woman.

Resolved, That the objection of indelicacy and impropriety, which is so often brought against woman when she addresses a public audience, comes with a very ill-grace from those who encourage, by their attendance, her appearance on the stage, in the concert, or in feats of the circus.

Resolved, That woman has too long rested satisfied in the circumscribed limits which corrupt customs and a perverted application of the Scriptures have marked out for her, and that it is time she should move in the enlarged sphere which her great Creator has assigned her.

Resolved, That it is the duty of the women of this country to secure to themselves their sacred right to the elective franchise.

Resolved, That the equality of human rights results necessarily from the fact of the identity of the race in capabilities and responsibilities.

Resolved, therefore, That, being invested by the Creator with the same capabilities, and the same consciousness of responsibility for their exercise, it is demonstrably the right and duty of woman, equally with man, to promote every righteous cause by every righteous means; and especially in regard to the great subjects of morals and religion, it is self-evidently her right to participate with her brother in teaching them, both in private and in public, by writing and by speaking, by any instrumentalities proper to be used, and in any assemblies proper to be held; and this being a self-evident truth growing out of the divinely implanted principles of human nature, any custom or authority adverse to it, whether modern or wearing the hoary sanction of antiquity, is to be regarded as a self-evident falsehood, and at war with mankind.

Resolved, That the speedy success of our cause depends upon the zealous and untiring efforts of both men and women, for the overthrow of the monopoly of the pulpit, and for the securing to woman an equal participation with men in the various trades, professions, and commerce.

Suggestions for Discussion

1. Compare the Declaration of Independence with the Seneca Falls declaration and discuss their parallel structure. Note particularly the basis, the "whereas" statement, for the resolutions that follow.

2. Examine and discuss the preliminary list of grievances that lead to the need for the resolutions.

3. How might a contemporary declaration on the rights of women differ from this one? What other resolutions might appear at a similar convention today?

4. Why was there objection to women's suffrage?

5. The convention was attended by abolitionists and members of the temperance movement. How were these causes compatible with a convention on women's rights?

Suggestions for Writing

1. Write a paper comparing the Declaration of Independence with the Seneca Falls declaration. What was missing from the first of these declarations?

2. Write a paper in which you discuss how a contemporary convention might stress different grievances. Be specific. Try to write some contemporary resolutions.

ABRAHAM LINCOLN

The Gettysburg Address

Abraham Lincoln (1809–1865), the sixteenth president of the United States, is generally regarded, along with Thomas Jefferson, to be one of the greatest American prose stylists. On November 19, 1863, he traveled to Gettysburg in southern Pennsylvania to dedicate the cemetery for the soldiers killed there the previous July. The simple words he composed form the most famous speech ever delivered in America. A close reading reveals why it continues to hold meaning for Americans today.

Four score and seven years ago our fathers brought forth on this continent, a new nation, conceived in Liberty, and dedicated to the proposition that all men are created equal.

Now we are engaged in a great civil war, testing whether that nation, or any nation so conceived and so dedicated, can long endure. We are met on a great battlefield of that war. We have come to dedicate a portion of that field, as a final resting place for those who here gave their lives that that nation might live. It is altogether fitting and proper that we should do this.

But, in a larger sense, we cannot dedicate—we cannot consecrate—we cannot hallow—this ground. The brave men, living and dead, who struggled here, have consecrated it, far above our poor power to add or detract. The world will little note nor long remember what we say here, but it can never forget what they did here. It is for us the living, rather, to be dedicated here to the unfinished work which they who fought here have thus far so nobly advanced. It is rather for us to be here dedicated to the great task remaining before us—that from these honored dead we take increased devotion to that cause for which they gave the last full measure of devotion—that we here highly resolve that these dead shall not have died in vain—that this nation, under God, shall have a new birth of freedom—and that government of the people, by the people, for the people, shall not perish from the earth.

Suggestions for Discussion

1. How is the proposition "that all men are created equal" related to the issues of the Civil War?

2. Why does Lincoln not simply begin his speech "Eighty-seven years ago"? What would he lose in tone if he had done so?

3. In paragraph three, Lincoln says, "The world will little note, nor long remember what we say here." How do you account for the fact that he was wrong? Why did he make this statement? What function does it serve?

4. How does Lincoln use the verbs *dedicate, consecrate, hallow*? Could one easily change the order of these words?

5. How does Lincoln connect the first paragraph of his speech to the last?

6. What was the "unfinished work" of the soldiers who died at the Battle of Gettysburg?

Suggestion for Writing

Write an essay in which you relate the power of this speech to the simplicity of its language.

WILLIAM FAULKNER

Nobel Prize Award Speech

William Faulkner (1897–1962) lived most of his life in Oxford, Mississippi. After a year at the University of Mississippi, he joined the Royal Canadian Air Force, eager to participate in World War I. His novels set in the fictional Yoknapatawpha County, Mississippi, include *The Sound and the Fury* (1929), *Light in August* (1932), *Absalom, Absalom!* (1936), and *The Hamlet* (1940). In his speech accepting the Nobel Prize for Literature in 1949, Faulkner states his belief in the significance and dignity of humankind and the need for the writer to reassert the universal truths of "love and honor and pity and pride and compassion and sacrifice."

I feel that this award was not made to me as a man but to my work—a life's work in the agony and sweat of the human spirit, not for glory and least of all for profit, but to create out of the materials of the human spirit something which did not exist before. So this award is only mine in trust. It will not be difficult to find a dedication for the money part of it commensurate with the purpose and significance of its origin. But I would like to do the same with the acclaim too, by using this moment as a pinnacle from which I might be listened to by the young men and women already dedicated to the same anguish and travail, among whom is already that one who will some day stand here where I am standing.

Our tragedy today is a general and universal physical fear so long sustained by now that we can even bear it. There are no longer problems of the spirit. There is only the question: When will I be blown up? Because of this, the young man or woman writing today has forgotten the problems of the human heart in conflict with itself which alone can make good writing because only that is worth writing about, worth the agony and the sweat.

He must learn them again. He must teach himself that the basest of all things is to be afraid; and, teaching himself that, forget it forever, leaving no room in his workshop for anything but the old verities and truths of the heart, the old universal truths lacking which any story is ephemeral and doomed—love and honor and pity and pride and compassion and sacrifice. Until he does so, he labors under a curse. He writes not of love but of lust, of defeats in which nobody loses anything of value, of victories without hope and, worst of all, without pity or compassion. His griefs grieve on no universal bones, leaving no scars. He writes not of the heart but of the glands.

Until he relearns these things, he will write as though he stood alone and watched the end of man. I decline to accept the end of man. It is easy enough to say that man is immortal simply because he will endure; that when the last ding-dong of doom has clanged and faded from the last worthless rock hanging tideless in the last red and dying evening, that even then there will still be one more sound: that of his puny inexhaustible voice, still talking. I refuse to accept this. I believe that man will not merely endure: he will prevail. He is immortal, not because he alone among creatures has an inexhaustible voice but because he has a soul, a spirit capable of compassion and sacrifice and endurance. The poet's, the writer's, duty is to write about these things. It is his privilege to help man endure by lifting his heart, by reminding him of the courage and honor and hope and pride and compassion and pity and sacrifice which have been the glory of his past. The poet's voice need not merely be the record of man, it can be one of the props, the pillars to help him endure and prevail.

Suggestions for Discussion

1. Do you agree with Faulkner's optimistic statement about man's ability to "endure and prevail"? Explain.

2. Do you think Faulkner's speech too brief for a major occasion such as the Nobel Prize Awards? Explain your answer.

3. Discuss whether or not man still lives in that state of general and universal physical fear to which Faulkner refers.

Suggestions for Writing

1. Summarize your own opinions about man's ability to survive the challenges of the next hundred years.

2. Prepare a formal speech in which you accept an international prize for literature or some other accomplishment.

CRWRW

CHIEF SEATTLE

Speech on the Signing of the Treaty of Port Elliott

Chief Seattle (1786–1866) of the Suquamish and Dewamish tribes, was a significant figure among Native Americans of the Pacific Northwest. The city of Seattle was named in his honor. He was one of several chiefs in the Northwest who maintained peaceful relations with the continually encroaching white settlers. This speech, translated by a doctor named Henry Smith, acknowledges the defeat of the Native Americans and their willingness to live on a reservation in the state of Washington, provided that the American government agrees to treat them humanely and to respect the differences in their culture.

Yonder sky that has wept tears of compassion upon my people for centuries untold, and which to us appears changeless and eternal, may change. Today is fair. Tomorrow may be overcast with clouds. My words are like the stars that never change. Whatever Seattle says the great chief at Washington can rely upon with as much certainty as he can upon the return of the sun or the seasons. The White Chief says that Big Chief at Washington sends us greetings of friendship and goodwill. That is kind of him for we know he has little need of our friendship in return. His people are many. They are like the grass that covers vast prairies. My people are few. They resemble the scattering trees of a storm-swept plain. The great, and—I presume—good, White Chief sends us word that he wishes to buy our lands but is willing to allow us enough to live comfortably. This indeed appears just, even generous, for the Red Man no longer has rights that he need respect, and the offer may be wise also, as we are no longer in need of an extensive country. . . . I will not dwell on, nor mourn over, our untimely decay, nor reproach our paleface brothers with hastening it, as we too may have been somewhat to blame.

Youth is impulsive. When our young men grow angry at some real or imaginary wrong, and disfigure their faces with black paint, it denotes that their hearts are black, and then they are often cruel and relentless, and our old men and old women are unable to restrain them. Thus it has ever been. Thus it was when the white men first began to push our forefathers westward. But let us hope that the hostilities between us may never return.

We would have everything to lose and nothing to gain. Revenge by young men is considered gain, even at the cost of their own lives, but old men who stay at home in times of war, and mothers who have sons to lose, know better.

Our good father at Washington—for I presume he is now our father as well as yours, since King George has moved his boundaries further north—our great good father, I say, sends us word that if we do as he desires he will protect us. His brave warriors will be to us a bristling wall of strength, and his wonderful ships of war will fill our harbors so that our ancient enemies far to the northward—the Hydas and Tsimpsians—will cease to frighten our women, children, and old men. Then in reality will he be our father and we his children. But can that ever be? Your God is not our God! Your God loves your people and hates mine. He folds his strong and protecting arms lovingly about the paleface and leads him by the hand as a father leads his infant son—but He has forsaken His red children—they really are his. Our God, the Great Spirit, seems also to have forsaken us. Your God makes your people wax strong every day. Soon they will fill the land. Our people are ebbing away like a rapidly receding tide that will never return. The white man's God cannot love our people or He would protect them. They seem to be orphans who can look nowhere for help. How then can we be brothers? How can your God become our God and renew our prosperity and awaken in us dreams of returning greatness? If we have a common heavenly father He must be partial—for He came to his paleface children. We never saw Him. He gave you laws but He had no word for His red children whose teeming multitudes once filled this vast continent as stars fill the firmament. No; we are two distinct races with separate origins and separate destinies. There is little in common between us.

To us the ashes of our ancestors are sacred and their resting place is hallowed ground. You wander far from the graves of your ancestors and seemingly without regret. Your religion was written upon tables of stone by the iron finger of your God so that you could not forget. The Red Man could never comprehend nor remember it. Our religion is the traditions of our ancestors—the dreams of our old men, given them in solemn hours of night by the Great Spirit; and the visions of our sachems; and it is written in the hearts of our people.

Your dead cease to love you and the land of their nativity as soon as they pass the portals of the tomb and wander way beyond the stars. They are soon forgotten and never return. Our dead never forget the beautiful world that gave them being.

Day and night cannot dwell together. The Red Man has ever fled the approach of the White Man, as the morning mist flees before the morning sun. However, your proposition seems fair and I think that my people will accept it and will retire to the reservation you offer them. Then we will dwell apart in peace, for the words of the Great White Chief seem to be the words of nature speaking to my people out of dense darkness.

It matters little where we pass the remnant of our days. They will not be many. A few more moons; a few more winters—and not one of the descendants of the mighty hosts that once moved over this broad land or lived in happy homes, protected by the Great Spirit, will remain to mourn over the graves of a people once more powerful and hopeful than yours. But why should I mourn at the untimely fate of my people? Tribe follows tribe, and nation follows nation, like the waves of the sea. It is the order of nature, and regret is useless. Your time of decay may be distant, but it will surely come, for even the White Man whose God walked and talked with him as friend with friend, cannot be exempt from the common destiny. We may be brothers after all. We will see.

We will ponder your proposition, and when we decide we will let you know. But should we accept it, I here and now make this condition that we will not be denied the privilege without molestation of visiting at any time the tombs of our ancestors, friends and children. Every part of this soil is sacred in the estimation of my people. Every hillside, every valley, every plain and grove, has been hallowed by some sad or happy event in days long vanished. . . . The very dust upon which you now stand responds more lovingly to their footsteps than to yours, because it is rich with the blood of our ancestors and our bare feet are conscious of the sympathetic touch. . . . Even the little children who lived here and rejoiced here for a brief season will love these somber solitudes and at eventide they greet shadowy returning spirits. And when the last Red Man shall have perished, and the memory of my tribe shall have become a myth among the White Men, these shores will swarm with the invisible dead of my tribe, and when your children's children think themselves alone in the field, the store, the shop, upon the highway, or in the silence of the pathless woods, they will not be alone. . . . At night when the streets of your cities and villages are silent and you think them deserted, they will throng with the returning hosts that once filled and still love this beautiful land. The White Man will never be alone.

Let him be just and deal kindly with my people, for the dead are not powerless. Dead, did I say? There is no death, only a change of worlds.

Suggestions for Discussion

1. Discuss the figurative language that Chief Seattle uses in the speech. How are similes and metaphors used to characterize white settlers and Native Americans?

2. What is the tone of the speech? How does its tone fit Chief Seattle's purposes?

3. Experts have argued that this translation by Dr. Smith reflects a stereotypical picture of the Native American. What examples can you find in support of this claim? Why might this have occurred despite Dr. Smith's fluency in tribal languages?

4. Identify some ironic aspects of the speech. How might Americans of the mid-nineteenth century have responded to Chief Seattle's predictions?

Suggestions for Writing

1. Chief Seattle's speech refers to Native American enemies from whom he expects the government to protect his tribes. Write a short research paper in which you explain who those enemies were and the grounds for their enmity.

2. Write a paper comparing and contrasting the poetic nature of this speech with that of the Gettysburg Address. How do the two speeches reflect not only the differences between the two speakers and the occasions for their speeches but cultural differences as well?

3. Chief Seattle converted to Christianity in the 1830s. Does this speech reflect his conversion? Write a paper in which you contrast the fact of his conversion with what he says about God in the speech.

CORNEL WEST

On Affirmative Action

Professor of Religion and African American Studies at Princeton, Cornel West (b. 1953) is an American philosopher and scholar. He is the winner of a National Book Award and has received over twenty honorary degrees. West's work draws from a mixture of influences, including the African American Baptist Church, transcendentalism, socialism, and pragmatism. He is a prolific writer and the author of the contemporary classic *Race Matters* published in 1993. West's work is most concerned with issues of politics, religion, and race. He has been involved in such events as the Million Man March, Russell Simmons's Hip-Hop Summit, and he was advisor to Al Sharpton's presidential campaign in 2004. West also appears as one of the elders on the council of Zion in the films *The Matrix Reloaded* and *The Matrix Revolutions.*

Today's affirmative-action policy is not the appropriate starting point for a substantive debate on affirmative action. Instead, we must begin with the larger historical and moral context of the recent controversy. Why was the policy established in the first place? What were the alternatives? Who questioned its operation, and when? How did it come about that a civil rights initiative in the 1960s is viewed by many as a civil rights violation in the 1990s? Whose civil rights are we talking about? Is there a difference between a right and an expectation? What are the limits of affirmative action? What would the consequences be if affirmative action disappeared in America?

ॐ

The Aim of Affirmative Action

The vicious legacy of white supremacy—institutionalized in housing, education, health care, employment and social life—served as the historical context for the civil rights movement in the late 1950s and 1960s. Affirmative action was a *weak* response to this legacy. It constituted an imperfect policy conceded by a powerful political, business and educational establishment in light of the pressures of organized citizens and the disturbances of angry unorganized ones.

The fundamental aim of affirmative action was to put a significant dent in the tightly controlled networks of privileged white male citizens who monopolized the good jobs and influential positions in American society. Just as Catholics and Jews had earlier challenged the white Anglo-Saxon Protestant monopoly of such jobs and positions, in the 1960s blacks and women did also. Yet since the historical gravity of race and gender outweighs that of religion and ethnicity in American society, the federal government had to step in to facilitate black and female entry into the U.S. mainstream and malestream. This national spectacle could not but prove costly under later, more hostile circumstances.

The initial debate focused on the relative lack of fairness, merit and public interest displayed by the prevailing systems of employment and education, principally owing to arbitrary racist and sexist exclusion. In the 1960s, class-based affirmative action was not seriously considered, primarily because it could easily have been implemented in such a way as to perpetuate exclusion, especially given a labor movement replete with racism and sexism. Both Democratic and Republican administrations supported affirmative action as the painful way of trying to create a multiracial democracy in which women and people of color were not second-class citizens. Initially, affirmative action was opposed by hard-line conservatives, usually the same ones who opposed the civil rights movement led by Dr. Martin Luther King, Jr. Yet the pragmatic liberals and conservatives prevailed.

∾

The Neoconservative Opposition

The rise of the neoconservatives unsettled this fragile consensus. By affirming the principle of equality of opportunity yet trashing any mechanism that claimed to go beyond merit, neoconservatives drove a wedge between civil rights and affirmative action. By claiming that meritocratic judgments trump egalitarian efforts to produce tangible results, neoconservatives cast affirmative-action policies as reverse racism and the major cause of racial divisiveness and low black self-esteem in the workplace and colleges.

Yet even this major intellectual and ideological assault did not produce a wholesale abandonment of affirmative action on behalf of business, political and educational elites. The major factor that escalated the drive against affirmative action was the shrinking job possibilities—along with stagnating and declining wages—that were squeezing the white middle class. Unfortunately, conservative leaders seized this moment to begin to more vociferously scapegoat affirmative action and to seek its weakening or elimination.

Their first move was to define affirmative action as a program for "unqualified" women and, especially, black people. Their second move was to cast affirmative action as "un-American," a quota system for groups rather than a merit system for individuals. The third move was to claim that antidiscrimination laws are enough, given the decline or end of racism among employers. The latest move has been to soothe the agonized consciences of liberals and conservatives by trying to show that black people are genetically inferior to whites in intelligence; hence, nothing can be done.

The popularity—distinct from the rationality—of these moves has created a climate in which proponents of affirmative action are on the defensive. Even those of us who admit the excesses of some affirmative-action programs—and therefore call for correcting, not eliminating, them—give aid and comfort to our adversaries. This reality reveals just how far the debate has moved in the direction of the neoconservative and conservative perceptions in the country. It also discloses that we need far more than weak policies like affirmative action to confront the legacies of white supremacy and corporate power in the United States—legacies visible in unemployment and underemployment, unaffordable health care and inadequate child care, dilapidated housing and decrepit schools for millions of Americans, disproportionately people of color, women and children.

The idea that affirmative action violates the rights of fellow citizens confuses a right with an expectation. We all have a right to be seriously and fairly considered for a job or position. But calculations of merit, institutional benefit and social utility produce the results. In the past, those who were never even considered had their rights violated; in the present, those who are seriously and fairly considered yet still not selected do not have their rights violated but rather have their expectations frustrated.

For example, if Harvard College receives more than ten thousand applications for fourteen hundred slots in the freshman class and roughly four thousand meet the basic qualifications, how does one select the "worthy" ones? Six thousand applicants are already fairly eliminated. Yet twenty-six hundred still will not make it. When considerations of factors other than merit are involved, such as whether candidates are the sons or daughters of alumni, come from diverse regions of the country or are athletes, no one objects. But when racial diversity is involved, the opponents of affirmative action yell foul play. Yet each class at Harvard remains about 5 to 7 percent black—far from a black takeover. And affirmative action bears the blame for racial anxiety and division on campus in such an atmosphere. In short, neoconservatives and conservatives fail to see the subtle (and not so subtle) white-supremacist sensibilities behind their "color-blind" perspectives on affirmative action.

∾

The Limits of Affirmative Action

Yet it would be myopic of progressives to make a fetish of affirmative action. As desirable as those policies are—an insight held fast by much of corporate America except at the almost lily-white senior-management levels—they will never ameliorate the plight and predicament of poor people of color. More drastic and redistributive measures are needed in order to address their situations, measures that challenge the maldistribution of wealth and power and that will trigger cultural renewal and personal hope.

If affirmative action disappears from the American scene, many blacks will still excel and succeed. But the larger signal that sends will be lethal for the country. It is a signal that white supremacy now has one less constraint and black people have one more reason to lose trust in the promise of American democracy.

Suggestions for Discussion

1. What was the original aim of affirmative action at its inception? How has that aim been changed and shaped throughout the years? According to West, who or what is responsible for the change?

2. Discuss in depth what West calls the "neoconservative opposition." What is this group's position against affirmative action?

3. What might the consequences be if affirmative action is eliminated?

Suggestion for Writing

In a personal essay, discuss the modern implications of race relations and the idea of historical amnesia. What role does this amnesia play in race relations today?

ANDREW SULLIVAN

A Conservative Case for Gay Marriage

British-born political commentator Andrew Sullivan (b. 1963) is a journalist and author who moved to America in 1984. His HIV-positive status, which he publicly revealed in 1996, prevented him from seeking U.S. citizenship until immigration laws were changed in 2009. Self-described as "a loyal Tory" with "center-right" views who does not fit comfortably in either the Republican or Democratic parties, Sullivan has written his political commentary blog *The Daily Dish* since 2000. Formerly a senior editor at the *New Republic* (serving between 1991 and 1996), Sullivan's work has been published by *The Atlantic, Time Magazine*, the *Sunday Times*, London, and the *New York Times Magazine*. He is the author of *Virtually Normal: An Argument about Homosexuality* (1995), *Love Undetectable* (1998), *The Conservative Soul: How We Lost It, How to Get It Back* (2006), and *Intimations Pursued* (2007). He has also edited the book *Same-Sex Marriage: Pro and Con* (1997). Culturally and religiously Roman Catholic, Sullivan nevertheless disagrees with the Vatican's position on homosexuality. He married Aaron Tone in Massachusetts in 2007. The following essay appeared in the *New Republic* on August 28, 1989.

Last month in New York, a court ruled that a gay lover had the right to stay in his deceased partner's rent-control apartment because the lover qualified as a member of the deceased's family. The ruling deftly annoyed almost everybody. Conservatives saw judicial activism in favor of gay rent control: three reasons to be appalled. Chastened liberals (such as the *New York Times*

Andrew Sullivan, "Here Comes the Groom: A (Conservative) Case for Gay Marriage," the *New Republic*, August 28, 1989. Reprinted by permission.

editorial page), while endorsing the recognition of gay relationships, also worried about the abuse of already stretched entitlements that the ruling threatened. What neither side quite contemplated is that they both might be right, and that the way to tackle the issue of unconventional relationships in conventional society is to try something both more radical and more conservative than putting courts in the business of deciding what is and is not a family. That alternative is the legalization of civil gay marriage.

The New York rent-control case did not go anywhere near that far, which is the problem. The rent-control regulations merely stipulated that a "family" member had the right to remain in the apartment. The judge ruled that to all intents and purposes a gay lover is part of his lover's family inasmuch as a "family" merely means an interwoven social life, emotional commitment, and some level of financial interdependence.

It's a principle now well established around the country. Several cities have "domestic partnership" laws, which allow relationships that do not fit into the category of heterosexual marriage to be registered with the city and qualify for benefits that up till now have been reserved for straight married couples. San Francisco, Berkeley, Madison, and Los Angeles all have legislation, as does the politically correct Washington, D.C. suburb, Takoma Park. In these cities, a variety of interpersonal arrangements qualify for health insurance, bereavement leave, insurance, annuity and pension rights, housing rights (such as rent-control apartments), adoption and inheritance rights. Eventually, according to gay lobby groups, the aim is to include federal income tax and veterans' benefits as well. A recent case even involved the right to use a family member's accumulated frequent-flier points. Gays are not the only beneficiaries; heterosexual "live-togethers" also qualify.

There's an argument, of course, that the current legal advantages extended to married people unfairly discriminate against people who've shaped their lives in less conventional arrangements. But it doesn't take a genius to see that enshrining in the law a vague principle like "domestic partnership" is an invitation to qualify at little personal cost for a vast array of entitlements otherwise kept crudely under control.

To be sure, potential DPs have to prove financial interdependence, shared living arrangements, and a commitment to mutual caring. But they don't need to have a sexual relationship or even closely mirror old-style marriage. In principle, an elderly woman and her live-in nurse could qualify. A couple of uneuphemistically confirmed bachelors could be DPs. So could two close college students, a pair of seminarians, or a couple of frat buddies. Left as it is, the concept of domestic partnership could open a Pandora's box of litigation and subjective judicial decision-making about who qualifies. You either are or are not married; it's not a complex question. Whether you are in a "domestic partnership" is not so clear.

More important, the concept of domestic partnership chips away at the prestige of traditional relationships and undermines the priority we give them. This priority is not necessarily a product of heterosexism. Consider heterosexual couples. Society has good reason to extend legal advantages to heterosexuals who choose the formal sanction of marriage over simply living together. They make a deeper commitment to one another and to society; in exchange, society extends certain benefits to them. Marriage provides an anchor, if an arbitrary and weak one, in the chaos of sex and relationships to which we are all prone. It provides a mechanism for emotional stability, economic security, and the healthy rearing of the next generation. We rig the law in its favor not because we disparage all forms of relationships other than the nuclear family, but because we recognize that not to promote marriage would be to ask too much of human virtue. In the context of the weakened family's effect upon the poor, it might also invite social disintegration. One of the worst products of the New Right's "family values" campaign is that its extremism and hatred of diversity has disguised this more measured and more convincing case for the importance of the marital bond.

The concept of domestic partnership ignores these concerns, indeed directly attacks them. This is a pity, since one of its most important objectives—providing some civil recognition for gay relationships—is a noble cause and one completely compatible with the defense of the family. But the way to go about it is not to undermine straight marriage; it is to legalize old-style marriage for gays.

The gay movement has ducked this issue primarily out of fear of division. Much of the gay leadership clings to notions of gay life as essentially outsider, antibourgeois, radical. Marriage, for them, is co-optation into straight society. For the Stonewall[1] generation, it is hard to see how this vision of conflict will ever fundamentally change. But for many other gays—my guess, a majority—while they don't deny the importance of rebellion twenty years ago and are grateful for what was done, there's now the sense of a new opportunity. A need to rebel has quietly ceded to a desire to belong. To be gay and to be bourgeois no longer seems such an absurd proposition. Certainly since AIDS, to be gay and to be responsible has become a necessity.

Gay marriage squares several circles at the heart of the domestic partnership debate. Unlike domestic partnership, it allows for recognition of gay relationships, while casting no aspersions on traditional marriage. It merely asks that gays be allowed to join in. Unlike domestic partnership, it doesn't open up avenues for heterosexuals to get benefits without the responsibilities of marriage, or a nightmare of definitional litigation. And unlike domestic

---

[1]The Stonewall Inn was a gay bar in New York City. When the police closed it in June 1966, the gays did not submit (as they had done in the past) but attacked the police. The event is regarded as a turning point in gay history. (All notes are by the editors.)

partnership, it harnesses to an already established social convention the yearnings for stability and acceptance among a fast-maturing gay community.

Gay marriage also places more responsibilities upon gays: It says for the first time that gay relationships are not better or worse than straight relationships, and that the same is expected of them. And it's clear and dignified. There's a legal benefit to a clear, common symbol of commitment. There's also a personal benefit. One of the ironies of domestic partnership is that it's not only more complicated than marriage, it's more demanding, requiring an elaborate statement of intent to qualify. It amounts to a substantial invasion of privacy. Why, after all, should gays be required to prove commitment before they get married in a way we would never dream of asking of straights?

Legalizing gay marriage would offer homosexuals the same deal society now offers heterosexuals: general social approval and specific legal advantages in exchange for a deeper and harder-to-extract-yourself-from commitment to another human being. Like straight marriage, it would foster social cohesion, emotional security, and economic prudence. Since there's no reason gays should not be allowed to adopt or be foster parents, it could also help nurture children. And its introduction would not be some sort of radical break with social custom. As it has become more acceptable for gay people to acknowledge their loves publicly, more and more have committed themselves to one another for life in full view of their families and their friends. A law institutionalizing gay marriage would merely reinforce a healthy social trend. It would also, in the wake of AIDS, qualify as a genuine public health measure. Those conservatives who deplore promiscuity among some homosexuals should be among the first to support it. Burke[2] could have written a powerful case for it.

The argument that gay marriage would subtly undermine the unique legitimacy of straight marriage is based upon a fallacy. For heterosexuals, straight marriage would remain the most significant—and only legal—social bond. Gay marriage could only delegitimize straight marriage if it were a real alternative to it, and this is clearly not true. To put it bluntly, there's precious little evidence that straights could be persuaded by any law to have sex with—let alone marry—someone of their own sex. The only possible effect of this sort would be to persuade gay men and women who force themselves into heterosexual marriage (often at appalling cost to themselves and their families) to find a focus for their family instincts in a more personally positive environment. But this is clearly a plus, not a minus: Gay marriage could both avoid a lot of tortured families and create the possibility for many happier ones. It is not, in short, a denial of family values. It's an extension of them.

---

[2]Edmund Burke (1729–97), conservative British politician.

Of course, some would claim that any legal recognition of homosexuality is a de facto attack upon heterosexuality. But even the most hardened conservatives recognize that gays are a permanent minority and aren't likely to go away. Since persecution is not an option in a civilized society, why not coax gays into traditional values rather than rail incoherently against them?

There's a less elaborate argument for gay marriage: It's good for gays. It provides role models for young gay people who, after the exhilaration of coming out, can easily lapse into short-term relationships and insecurity with no tangible goal in sight. My own guess is that most gays would embrace such a goal with as much (if not more) commitment as straights. Even in our society as it is, many lesbian relationships are virtual textbook cases of monogamous commitment. Legal gay marriage could also help bridge the gulf often found between gays and their parents. It could bring the essence of gay life—a gay couple—into the heart of the traditional straight family in a way the family can most understand and the gay off-spring can most easily acknowledge. It could do as much to heal the gay-straight rift as any amount of gay rights legislation.

If these arguments sound socially conservative, that's no accident. It's one of the richest ironies of our society's blind spot toward gays that essentially conservative social goals should have the appearance of being so radical. But gay marriage is not a radical step. It avoids the mess of domestic partnership: it is humane; it is conservative in the best sense of the word. It's also practical. Given the fact that we already allow legal gay relationships, what possible social goal is advanced by framing the law to encourage those relationships to be unfaithful, undeveloped, and insecure?

Suggestions for Discussion

1. In what ways does Sullivan suggest that gay marriage would be "good for gays"? Do you agree? Why?

2. Sullivan also suggests that current domestic partnership laws are flawed and harmful to the traditional institution of marriage. In what ways? Do you agree?

3. Finally, Sullivan argues that gay marriage would protect the institution of marriage and extend family values, rather than undermining them. Do you agree?

4. Synthesis: Sullivan describes the New Right's "family values" campaign as encouraging "extremism" and "hatred of diversity." Dan Quayle's "Restoring Basic Values" speech is, in many ways, the cornerstone of this campaign. Read that essay and consider whether you think it can be interpreted as a prejudiced statement. Ask yourself the same question about Sullivan's essay.

Suggestions for Writing

1. Are you in favor of or against the legalization of marriage between two individuals of the same gender? Explore the current legal situation of gay marriage in the United States, where some states permit it, some states recognize marriages performed legally in other states, and some states make such a union illegal. Make sure you also understand the federal Defense of Marriage Act and its relationship to state laws. Read about current legal cases involving gay marriage (in 2010, such cases were being argued in California and Massachusetts). Now support your own opinion with your research.

2. Robert Mapplethorpe, who died of AIDS in 1989, explored sexual taboos as well as the expressive power of cautiously controlled form and shape with his stark and evocative (and for some critics, simply provocative) imagery. Consider his photograph of Ken and Robert in terms of race and sexuality. Pay close attention to Ken's closed eyes. Follow Robert's gaze beyond the frame of the photograph. Notice how close these faces are to each other, and their positions one in front of the other. Think about the photo in terms of "the male body," "dominance," and "marginalization." Pick one of these as a theme and write an essay about it.

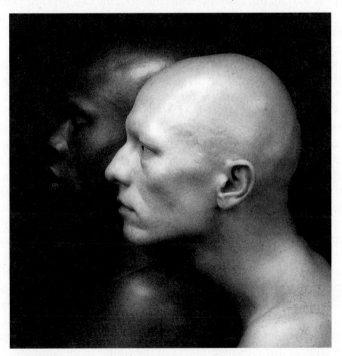

ROBERT MAPPLETHORPE, *Ken Moody and Robert Sherman*. Gelatin silver print, 1984. © The Robert Mapplethorpe Foundation/Art and Commerce.

CRᴀᴗᴄᴗᴄᴗ

MARY GORDON

A Moral Choice

Mary Gordon (b. 1949) was born on Long Island, NY, and educated at Barnard College and the University of Syracuse. She has taught English at Dutchess County Community College, Amherst College, and Barnard College and has published short stories, poems, and novels that have received critical and popular success. Among her works are *Final Payments* (1978); *The Company of Women* (1981); *Men and Angels* (1985); *The Other Side* (1989); a collection of stories, *Temporary Shelter* (1990); *The Rest of Life* (1993); and *Spending: A Utopian Divertimento* (1998). Her recent works include *Joan of Arc: Penguin Lives* (2000), *Seeing Through Places: Reflections on Geography and Identity* (2000), and *Pearl* (2005). In this essay, published in 1990, she calls for clear definitions of the moral issues surrounding abortion and explains why she has taken a pro-choice position.

I am having lunch with six women. What is unusual is that four of them are in their seventies, two of them widowed, the other two living with husbands beside whom they've lived for decades. All of them have had children. Had they been men, they would have published books and hung their paintings on the walls of important galleries. But they are women of a certain generation, and their lives were shaped around their families and personal relations. They are women you go to for help and support. We begin talking about the latest legislative act that makes abortion more difficult for poor women to obtain. An extraordinary thing happens. Each of them talks about the illegal abortions she had during her young womanhood. Not one of them was spared the experience. Any of them could have died on the table of whatever person (not a doctor in any case) she was forced to approach, in secrecy and in terror, to end a pregnancy that she felt would blight her life.

I mention this incident for two reasons: first as a reminder that all kinds of women have always had abortions; second because it is essential that we remember that an abortion is performed on a living woman who has a life in which a terminated pregnancy is only a small part. Morally speaking, the decision to have an abortion doesn't take place in a vacuum. It is connected to other choices that a woman makes in the course of an adult life.

Anti-choice propagandists paint pictures of women who choose to have abortions as types of moral callousness, selfishness, or irresponsibility. The woman choosing to abort is the dressed-for-success yuppie who gets rid of her baby so that she won't miss her Caribbean vacation or her chance for promotion. Or she is the feckless, promiscuous ghetto teenager who couldn't bring herself to just say no to sex. A third, purportedly kinder, gentler picture has recently begun to be drawn. The woman in the abortion clinic is there because she is misinformed about the nature of the world. She is having an abortion because society does not provide for mothers and their children, and she mistakenly thinks that another mouth to feed will be the ruin of her family, not understanding that the temporary truth of family unhappiness doesn't stack up beside the eternal verity that abortion is murder. Or she is the dupe of her husband or boyfriend, who talks her into having an abortion because a child will be a drag on his life-style. None of these pictures created by the anti-choice movement assumes that the decision to have an abortion is made responsibly, in the context of a morally lived life, by a free and responsible moral agent.

ॐ

The Ontology of the Fetus

How would a woman who habitually makes choices in moral terms come to the decision to have an abortion? The moral discussion of abortion centers on the issue of whether or not abortion is an act of murder. At first glance it would seem that the answer should follow directly upon two questions: Is the fetus human? and Is it alive? It would be absurd to deny that a fetus is alive or that it is human. What would our other options be—to say that it is inanimate or belongs to another species? But we habitually use the terms "human" and "live" to refer to parts of our body—"human hair," for example, or "live red-blood cells"—and we are clear in our understanding that the nature of these objects does not rank equally with an entire personal existence. It then seems important to consider whether the fetus, this alive human thing, is a *person*, to whom the term "murder" could sensibly be applied. How would anyone come to a decision about something so impalpable as personhood? Philosophers have struggled with the issue of personhood, but in language that is so abstract that it is unhelpful to ordinary people making decisions in the course of their lives. It might be more productive to begin thinking about the status of the fetus by examining the language and customs that surround it. This approach will encourage us to focus on the choosing, acting woman, rather than the act of abortion—as if the act were performed by abstract forces without bodies, histories, attachments.

This focus on the acting woman is useful because a pregnant woman has an identifiable, consistent ontology, and a fetus takes on different ontological identities over time. But common sense, experience, and linguistic usage point clearly to the fact that we habitually consider, for example, a seven-week-old fetus to be different from a seven-month-old one. We can tell this by the way we respond to the involuntary loss of one as against the other. We have different language for the experience of the involuntary expulsion of the fetus from the womb depending upon the point of gestation at which the experience occurs. If it occurs early in the pregnancy, we call it a miscarriage; if late, we call it a stillbirth.

We would have an extreme reaction to the reversal of those terms. If a woman referred to a miscarriage at seven weeks as a stillbirth, we would be alarmed. It would shock our sense of propriety; it would make us uneasy; we would find it disturbing, misplaced—as we do when a bag lady sits down in a restaurant and starts shouting, or an octogenarian arrives at our door in a sailor suit. In short, we would suspect that the speaker was mad. Similarly, if a doctor or a nurse referred to the loss of a seven-month-old fetus as a miscarriage, we would be shocked by that person's insensitivity: could she or he not understand that a fetus that age is not what it was months before?

Our ritual and religious practices underscore the fact that we make distinctions among fetuses. If a woman took the bloody matter—indistinguishable from a heavy period—of an early miscarriage and insisted upon putting it in a tiny coffin and marking its grave, we would have serious concerns about her mental health. By the same token, we would feel squeamish about flushing a seven-month-old fetus down the toilet—something we would quite normally do with an early miscarriage. There are no prayers for the matter of a miscarriage, nor do we feel there should be. Even a Catholic priest would not baptize the issue of an early miscarriage.

The difficulties stem, of course, from the odd situation of a fetus's ontology: a complicated, differentiated, and nuanced response is required when we are dealing with an entity that changes over time. Yet we are in the habit of making distinctions like this. At one point we know that a child is no longer a child but an adult. That this question is vexed and problematic is clear from our difficulty in determining who is a juvenile offender and who is an adult criminal and at what age sexual intercourse ceases to be known as statutory rape. So at what point, if any, do we on the pro-choice side say that the developing fetus is a person, with rights equal to its mother's?

The anti-choice people have one advantage over us; their monolithic position gives them unity on this question. For myself, I am made uneasy by third-trimester abortions, which take place when the fetus could live outside the mother's body, but I also know that these are extremely rare and often performed on very young girls who have had difficulty comprehending the realities of pregnancy. It seems to me that the question of late abortions should be decided case by case, and that fixation on this issue is a deflection from what is most important: keeping early abortions, which are in the majority by far, safe and legal. I am also politically realistic enough to suspect that bills restricting late abortions are not good-faith attempts to make distinctions about the nature of fetal life. They are, rather, the cynical embodiments of the hope among anti-choice partisans that technology will be on their side and that medical science's ability to create situations in which younger fetuses are viable outside their mothers' bodies will increase dramatically in the next few years. Ironically, medical science will probably make the issue of abortion a minor one in the near future. The RU-486 pill, which can induce abortion early on, exists, and whether or not it is legally available (it is not on the market here, because of pressure from anti-choice groups), women will begin to obtain it. If abortion can occur through chemical rather than physical means, in the privacy of one's home, most people not directly involved will lose interest in it. As abortion is transformed from a public into a private issue, it will cease to be perceived as political; it will be called personal instead.

∿

An Equivocal Good

But because abortion will always deal with what it is to create and sustain life, it will always be a moral issue. And whether we like it or not, our moral thinking about abortion is rooted in the shifting soil of perception. In an age in which much of our perception is manipulated by media that specialize in the sound bite and the photo op, the anti-choice partisans have a twofold advantage over us on the pro-choice side. The pro-choice moral position is more complex, and the experience we defend is physically repellent to contemplate. None of us in the pro-choice movement would suggest that abortion is not a regrettable occurrence. Anti-choice proponents can offer pastel photographs of babies in buntings, their eyes peaceful in the camera's gaze. In answer, we can't offer the material of an early abortion, bloody, amorphous in a paper cup, to prove that what has just been removed from the woman's body is not a child, not in the same category of being as the adorable bundle in an adoptive mother's arms. It is not a pleasure to look at the physical evidence of abortion, and most of us don't get the opportunity to do so.

The theologian Daniel Maguire, uncomfortable with the fact that most theological arguments about the nature of abortion are made by men who have never been anywhere near an actual abortion, decided to visit a clinic and observe abortions being performed. He didn't find the experience easy, but he knew that before he could in good conscience make a moral judgment on abortion, he needed to experience through his senses what an aborted fetus is like: he needed to look at and touch the controversial entity. He held in his hand the bloody fetal stuff; the eight-week-old fetus fit in the palm of his hand, and it certainly bore no resemblance to either of his two children when he had held them moments after their birth. He knew at that point what women who have experienced early abortions and miscarriages know: that some event occurred, possibly even a dramatic one, but it was not the death of a child.

Because issues of pregnancy and birth are both physical and metaphorical, we must constantly step back and forth between ways of perceiving the world. When we speak of gestation, we are often talking in terms of potential, about events and objects to which we attach our hopes, fears, dreams, and ideals. A mother can speak to the fetus in her uterus and name it; she and her mate may decorate a nursery according to their vision of the good life; they may choose for an embryo a college, a profession, a dwelling. But those of us who are trying to think morally about pregnancy and birth must remember that these feelings are our own projections onto what is in reality an inappropriate object. However charmed we may be by an expectant father's buying a little football for something inside his wife's belly, we shouldn't make public policy based on such actions, nor should we force others to live their lives conforming to our fantasies.

As a society, we are making decisions that pit the complicated future of a complex adult against the fate of a mass of cells lacking cortical development. The moral pressure should be on distinguishing the true from the false, the real suffering of living persons from our individual and often idiosyncratic dreams and fears. We must make decisions on abortion based on an understanding of how people really do live. We must be able to say that poverty is worse than not being poor, that having dignified and meaningful work is better than working in conditions of degradation, that raising a child one loves and has desired is better than raising a child in resentment and rage, that it is better for a twelve-year-old not to endure the trauma of having a child when she is herself a child.

When we put these ideas against the ideas of "child" or "baby," we seem to be making a horrifying choice of life-style over life. But in fact we are telling the truth of what it means to bear a child, and what the experience of abortion really is. This is extremely difficult, for the object of the discussion is hidden, changing, potential. We make our decisions on the basis of approximate and inadequate language, often on the basis of fantasies and fears. It will always be crucial to try to separate genuine moral concern from phobia, punitiveness, superstition, anxiety, a desperate search for certainty in an uncertain world.

One of the certainties that is removed if we accept the consequences of the pro-choice position is the belief that the birth of a child is an unequivocal good. In real life we act knowing that the birth of a child is not always a good thing: people are sometimes depressed, angry, rejecting, at the birth of a child. But this is a difficult truth to tell; we don't like to say it, and one of the fears preyed on by anti-choice proponents is that if we cannot look at the birth of a child as an unequivocal good, then there is nothing to look toward. The desire for security of the imagination, for typological fixity, particularly in the area of "the good," is an understandable desire. It must seem to some anti-choice people that we on the pro-choice side are not only murdering innocent children but also murdering hope. Those of us who have experienced the birth of a desired child and felt the joy of that moment can be tempted into believing that it was the physical experience of the birth itself that was the joy. But it is crucial to remember that the birth of a child itself is a neutral occurrence emotionally: the charge it takes on is invested in it by the people experiencing or observing it.

ॐ

The Fear of Sexual Autonomy

These uncertainties can lead to another set of fears, not only about abortion but about its implications. Many anti-choice people fear that to support abortion is to cast one's lot with the cold and technological rather than with the warm and natural, to head down the slippery slope toward a brave new world where handicapped children are left on mountains to starve and the old are put out in the snow. But if we look at the history of abortion, we don't see the embodiment of what the anti-choice proponents fear. On the contrary, excepting the grotesque counterexample of the People's Republic of China (which practices forced abortion), there seems to be a real link between repressive anti-abortion stances and repressive governments. Abortion was banned in Fascist Italy and Nazi Germany; it is illegal in South Africa and in Chile. It is paid for by the governments of Denmark, England, and the Netherlands, which have national health and welfare systems that foster the health and well-being of mothers, children, the old, and the handicapped.

Advocates of outlawing abortion often refer to women seeking abortion as self-indulgent and materialistic. In fact these accusations mask a discomfort with female sexuality, sexual pleasure, and sexual autonomy. It is possible for a woman to have a sexual life unriddled by fear only if she can be confident that she need not pay for a failure of technology or judgment (and who among us has never once been swept away in the heat of a sexual moment?) by taking upon herself the crushing burden of unchosen motherhood.

It is no accident, therefore, that the increased appeal of measures to restrict maternal conduct during pregnancy—and a new focus on the physical autonomy of the pregnant woman—have come into public discourse at precisely the time when women are achieving unprecedented levels of economic and political autonomy. What has surprised me is that some of this new anti-autonomy talk comes to us from the left. An example of this new discourse is an article by Christopher Hitchens that appeared in *The Nation* last April, in which the author asserts his discomfort with abortion. Hitchens's tone is impeccably British: arch, light, we're men of the left.

> Anyone who has ever seen a sonogram or has spent even an hour with a textbook on embryology knows that the emotions are not the deciding factor. In order to terminate a pregnancy, you have to still a heartbeat, switch off a developing brain, and whatever the method, break some bones and rupture some organs. As to whether this involves pain on the "Silent Scream" scale, I have no idea. The "right to life" leadership, again, has cheapened everything it touches.

"It is a pity," Hitchens goes on to say, "that . . . the majority of feminists and their allies have stuck to the dead ground of 'Me Decade' possessive individualism, an ideology that has more in common than it admits with the prehistoric right, which it claims to oppose but has in fact encouraged." Hitchens proposes, as an alternative, a program of social reform that would make contraception free and support a national adoption service. In his opinion, it would seem, women have abortions for only two reasons: because they are selfish or because they are poor. If the state will take care of the economic problems and the bureaucratic messiness around adoption, it remains only for the possessive individuals to get their act together and walk with their babies into the communal Utopia of the future. Hitchens would allow victims of rape or incest to have free abortions, on the grounds that since they didn't choose to have sex, the women should not be forced to have the babies. This would seem to put the issue of volition in a wrong and telling place. To Hitchens's mind, it would appear, if a woman chooses to have sex, she can't choose whether or not to have a baby. The implications of this are clear. If a woman is consciously and volitionally sexual, she should be prepared to take her medicine. And what medicine must the consciously sexual male take? Does Hitchens really believe, or want us to believe, that every male who has unintentionally impregnated a woman will be involved in the lifelong responsibility for the upbringing of the engendered child? Can he honestly say that he has observed this behavior—or, indeed, would want to see it observed—in the world in which he lives?

ᘇ

Real Choices

It is essential for a moral decision about abortion to be made in an atmosphere of open, critical thinking. We on the pro-choice side must accept that there are indeed anti-choice activists who take their position in good faith. I believe, however, that they are people for whom childbirth is an emotionally overladen topic, people who are susceptible to unclear thinking because of their unrealistic hopes and fears. It is important for us in the pro-choice movement to be open in discussing those areas involving abortion which are nebulous and unclear. But we must not forget that there are some things that we know to be undeniably true. There are some undeniable bad consequences of a woman's being forced to bear a child against her will. First is the trauma of going through a pregnancy and giving birth to a child who is not desired, a trauma more long-lasting than that experienced by some (only some) women who experience an early abortion. The grief of giving up a child at its birth—and at nine months it is a child whom one has felt move inside one's body—is underestimated both by anti-choice partisans and by those for whom access to adoptable children is important. This grief should not be forced on any woman—or, indeed, encouraged by public policy.

We must be realistic about the impact on society of millions of unwanted children in an overpopulated world. Most of the time, human beings have sex not because they want to make babies. Yet throughout history sex has resulted in unwanted pregnancies. And women have always aborted. One thing that is not hidden, mysterious, or debatable is that making abortion illegal will result in the deaths of women, as it has always done. Is our historical memory so short that none of us remember aunts, sisters, friends, or mothers who were killed or rendered sterile by septic abortions? Does no one in the anti-choice movement remember stories or actual experiences of midnight drives to filthy rooms from which aborted women were sent out, bleeding, to their fate? Can anyone genuinely say that it would be a moral good for us as a society to return to those conditions?

Thinking about abortion, then, forces us to take moral positions as adults who understand the complexities of the world and the realities of human suffering, to make decisions based on how people actually live and choose, and not on our fears, prejudices, and anxieties about sex and society, life and death.

Suggestions for Discussion

1. What is the function of the personal episode Mary Gordon uses in the opening paragraph of the essay?

2. What reasons for abortion do anti-choice people ascribe to those who want abortions? What are Gordon's responses to those reasons?

3. How does Gordon deal with the issue of whether a fetus is live and human? Is her discussion of this issue valid or persuasive? Do you agree with the distinctions she makes between the terms "miscarriage" and "stillbirth"?

4. What does Gordon mean by the term "the ontology of the fetus"? How does this term become crucial to her argument in favor of choice?

5. For the author, what are the real moral choices surrounding a woman's decision to have an abortion? How complex does she believe the issue to be?

6. Gordon objects to the positions of the political left and right on this issue. Explain.

Suggestions for Writing

1. Write a paper in which you argue for or against Gordon's position on abortion. Summarize her argument and try to agree or disagree with it by reference to the points she makes.

2. Look at the last three paragraphs of Gordon's essay. Do you agree or disagree with her conclusions? Write an essay in which you state your position clearly and concretely.

FICTION

E D W I D G E   D A N T I C A T

Selection from Breath, Eyes, Memory

Edwidge Danticat (b. 1969) is a Haitian-born author who immigrated to the United States at age 12 and published her first writings at 14. A winner of a James Michener Fellowship, Danticat was also nominated for the National Book Award in 1995 for her short-story collection *Krik? Krak!* Among her other books are *Farming of Bones* (1998), *After the Dance* (2002), *Behind the Mountains* (2002), and *The Dew Breaker* (2004). Danticat earned a bachelor's degree in literature from Barnard College and a master of fine arts degree from Brown University. Her graduate thesis was published as *Breath, Eyes, Memory* and includes the following controversial passage.

I asked my grandmother if I could cook supper for us that night.

Tante Atie offered to take me to a private vendor where food was cheaper than the *maché.* She put the leeches in some clean water and we started down the road.

"What are you making for us?" she asked.

"Rice, black beans, and herring sauce," I said.

"Your mother's favorite meal."

"That's what we cooked most often."

We followed a footpath off the road, down to a shallow stream. An old mule was yanking water vines from the edge of the stream while baby crabs freely dashed around its nostrils.

A woman filled a calabash a few feet from where my sandals muddied the water. Tante Atie chatted with the women as she went by. Some young girls were sitting barechested in the water, the sun casting darker shadows into their faces. Their hands squirted blackened suds as they pounded their clothes with water rocks.

A dusty footpath led us to a tree-lined cemetery at the top of the hill. Tante Atie walked between the wooden crosses, collecting the bamboo skeletons of fallen kites. She stepped around the plots where empty jars, conch shells, and marbles served as grave markers.

"Walk straight," said Tante Atie, "you are in the presence of family."

She walked around to each plot, and called out the names of all those who had been buried there. There was my great-grandmother, Beloved Martinelle Brigitte. Her sister, My First Joy Sophilus Gentille. My grandfather's sister, My Hope Atinia Ifé, and finally my grandfather, Charlemagne Le Grand Caco.

Tante Atie named them all on sight.

"Our family name, Caco, it is the name of a scarlet bird. A bird so crimson, it makes the reddest hibiscus or the brightest flame trees seem white. The Caco bird, when it dies, there is always a rush of blood that rises to its neck and the wings, they look so bright, you would think them on fire."

From the cemetery, we took a narrow footpath to the vendor's hut. On either side of us were wild grasses that hissed as though they were full of snakes.

We walked to a whitewashed shack where a young woman sold rice and black beans from the same sisal mat where she slept with her husband.

In the yard, the husband sat under the shade of a straw parasol with a pipe in his mouth and a demijohn at his feet. He was pounding small nails into leather straps and thin layers of polished wood to make sandals.

The hammering echoed in my head until I reached the cane fields. The men were singing about a woman who flew without her skin at night, and when she came back home, she found her skin peppered and could not put it back on. Her husband had done it to teach her a lesson. He ended up killing her.

I was surprised how fast it came back. The memory of how everything came together to make a great meal. The fragrance of the spices guided my fingers the way no instructions or measurements could.

The men in this area, they insist that their women are virgins and have ten fingers.

According to Tante Atie, each finger had a purpose. It was the way she had been taught to prepare herself to become a woman. Mothering. Boiling. Loving. Baking. Nursing. Frying. Healing. Washing. Ironing. Scrubbing. It wasn't her fault, she said. Her ten fingers had been named for her even before she was born. Sometimes, she even wished she had six fingers on each hand so she could have two left for herself.

I rushed back and forth between the iron pots in the yard. The air smelled like spices that I had not cooked with since I'd left my mother's home two years before.

I usually ate random concoctions: frozen dinners, samples from global cookbooks, food that was easy to put together and brought me no pain. No memories of a past that at times was cherished and at others despised.

By the time we ate, the air was pregnant with rain. Thunder groaned in the starless sky while the lanterns flickered in the hills.

"Well done," Tante Atie said after her fourth serving of my rice and beans.

My grandmother chewed slowly as she gave my daughter her bottle.

"If the wood is well carved," said my grandmother, "it teaches us about the carpenter. Atie, you taught Sophie well."

Tante Atie was taken off guard by my grandmother's compliment. She kissed me on the forehead before taking the dishes to the yard to wash. Then, she went into the house, took her notebook, and left for her lesson with Louise.

My grandmother groaned her disapproval. She pulled out a small pouch and packed pinches of tobacco powder into her nose. She inhaled deeply, stuffing more and more into her nostrils.

She had a look of deep concern on her face, as her eyes surveyed the evening clouds.

"*Tandé.* Do you hear anything?" she asked.

There was nothing but the usual night sounds: birds finding their ways in the dark, as they shuffled through the leaves.

Often at night, there were women who travelled long distances, on foot or on mare, to save the car fare to Port-au-Prince.

I strained my eyes to see beyond the tree shadows on the road.

"There is a girl going home," my grandmother said. "You cannot see her. She is far away. Quite far. It is not the distance that is important. If I hear a girl from far away, there is an emotion, something that calls to my soul. If your soul is linked with someone, somehow you can always feel when something is happening to them."

"Is it Tante Atie, the girl on the road?"

"*Non.* It is really a girl. A younger woman."

"Is the girl in danger?"

"That's why you listen. You should hear young feet crushing wet leaves. Her feet make a *swish-swash* when they hit the ground and when she hurries, it sounds like a whip chasing a mule."

I listened closely, but heard no whip.

"When it is dark, all men are black," she said. "There is no way to know anything unless you apply your ears. When you listen, it's *kòm si* you had deafness before and you can hear now. Sometimes you can't fall asleep because the sound of someone crying keeps you awake. A whisper sounds like a roar to your ears. Your ears are witness to matters that do not concern you. And what is worse, you cannot forget. Now, listen. Her feet make a *swish* sound and when she hurries it's like a whip in the wind."

I tried, but I heard no whip.

"It's the way old men cry," she said. "Grown brave men have a special way they cry when they are afraid."

She closed her eyes and lowered her head to concentrate.

"It is Ti Alice," she said.

"Who is Ti Alice?"

"The young child in the bushes, it is Ti Alice. Someone is there with her."

"Is she in danger?"

My grandmother tightened her eyelids.

"I know Ti Alice," she said. "I know her mother."

"Why is she in the bushes?"

"She must be fourteen or fifteen years now."

"Why is she out there?"

"She is rushing back to her mother. She was with a friend, a boy."

I thought I heard a few hushed whispers.

"I think I hear a little," I said, rocking my daughter with excitement.

"Ti Alice and the boy, they are bidding one another goodbye, for the night."

My grandmother wrapped her arms around her body, rocking and cradling herself.

"What is happening now?" I asked.

"Her mother is waiting for her at the door of their hut. She is pulling her inside to test her."

The word sent a chill through my body.

"She is going to test to see if young Alice is still a virgin," my grandmother said. "The mother, she will drag her inside the hut, take her last small finger and put it inside her to see if it goes in. You said the other night that your mother tested you. That is what is now happening to Ti Alice."

I have heard it compared to a virginity cult, our mothers' obsession with keeping us pure and chaste. My mother always listened to the echo of my urine in the toilet, for if it was too loud it meant that I had been deflowered. I learned very early in life that virgins always took small steps when they walked. They never did acrobatic splits, never rode horses or bicycles. They always covered themselves well and, even if their lives depended on it, never parted with their panties.

The story goes that there was once an extremely rich man who married a poor black girl. He had chosen her out of hundreds of prettier girls because she was untouched. For the wedding night, he bought her the whitest sheets and nightgowns he could possibly find. For himself, he bought a can of thick goat milk in which he planned to sprinkle a drop of her hymen blood to drink.

Then came their wedding night. The girl did not bleed. The man had his honor and reputation to defend. He could not face the town if he did not have a blood-spotted sheet to hang in his courtyard the next morning. He did the best he could to make her bleed, but no matter how hard he tried, the girl did not bleed. So he took a knife and cut her between her legs to get some blood to show. He got enough blood for her wedding gown and sheets, an unusual amount to impress the neighbors. The blood kept flowing like water out of the girl. It flowed so much it wouldn't stop. Finally, drained of all her blood, the girl died.

Later, during her funeral procession, her blood-soaked sheets were paraded by her husband to show that she had been a virgin on her wedding night. At the grave site, her husband drank his blood-spotted goat milk and cried like a child.

I closed my eyes upon the images of my mother slipping her hand under the sheets and poking her pinky at a void, hoping that it would go no further than the length of her fingernail.

Like Tante Atie, she had told me stories while she was doing it, weaving elaborate tales to keep my mind off the finger, which I knew one day would slip into me and condemn me. I had learned to *double* while being *tested*. I would close my eyes and imagine all the pleasant things that I had known. The lukewarm noon breeze through our bougainvillea. Tante Atie's gentle voice blowing over a field of daffodils.

There were many cases in our history where our ancestors had *doubled*. Following in the *vaudou* tradition, most of our presidents were actually one body split in two: part flesh and part shadow. That was the only way they could murder and rape so many people and still go home to play with their children and make love to their wives.

After my marriage, whenever Joseph and I were together, I *doubled*.

"The testing? Why do the mothers do that?" I asked my grandmother.

"If a child dies, you do not die. But if your child is disgraced, you are disgraced. And people, they think daughters will be raised trash with no man in the house."

"Did your mother do this to you?"

"From the time a girl begins to menstruate to the time you turn her over to her husband, the mother is responsible for her purity. If I give a soiled daughter to her husband, he can shame my family, speak evil of me, even bring her back to me."

"When you tested my mother and Tante Atie, couldn't you tell that they hated it?"

"I had to keep them clean until they had husbands."

"But they don't have husbands."

"The burden was not mine alone."

"I hated the tests," I said. "It is the most horrible thing that ever happened to me. When my husband is with me now, it gives me such nightmares that I have to bite my tongue to do it again."

"With patience, it goes away."

"No Grandmè Ifé, it does not."

"Ti Alice, she has passed her examination."

The sky reddened with a sudden flash of lightning. "Now you have a child of your own. You must know that everything a mother does, she does for her child's own good. You cannot always carry the pain. You must liberate yourself."

We walked to my room and put my daughter down to sleep.

"I will go soon," I told my grandmother, "back to my husband."

"It is better," she said. "It is hard for a woman to raise girls alone."

She walked into her room, took her statue of Erzulie, and pressed it into my hand.

"My heart, it weeps like a river," she said, "for the pain we have caused you."

I held the statue against my chest as I cried in the night. I thought I heard my grandmother crying too, but it was the rain slowing down to a mere drizzle, tapping on the roof.

The next morning, I went jogging, along the road, through the cemetery plot, and into the hills. The sun had already dried some of the puddles from the drizzle the night before.

Along the way, people stared at me with puzzled expressions on their faces. *Is this what happens to our girls when they leave this place?* They become such frightened creatures that they run like the wind, from nothing at all.

Suggestions for Discussion

1. What does the family name, Caco, mean? Is the name symbolic?

2. What relationships exist between the women of each generation in the Caco family?

3. How has the narrator changed since she first left home?

4. What is the story of the rich man who married the poor black girl? Why does this story, and the "testing" of Ti Alice, resonate so strongly with the narrator?

5. How are the men of Haiti depicted in this story?

Suggestion for Writing

Write an essay commenting on the lives of the women in this story alongside the feminist manifesto "The Seneca Falls Convention."

POETRY

༄༅༄

REYNOLDS PRICE

Tom, Dying of AIDS

Macon, NC, native Reynolds Price (b. 1933) has taught at his alma mater, Duke University, since 1958, and has published more than thirty volumes of fiction, drama, essays, poetry, and translations. Nineteen-sixty-two saw the publication of his first novel, *A Long and Happy Life*, which won the William Faulkner Award and has never been out of print. Some of his more recent works include *Kate Vaiden* (which won the National Book Critics Circle Award in 1986), *A Singular Family* (1999), *A Serious Way of Wondering* (2003), and *The Good Priest's Son* (2005).

In seven years you took my picture
A thousand times—in New York mainly
Ringed by gawkers, muggers, geeks—
And you as high as any bystander:
Lobbing me jokes like booby-trapped balls,
Tying your limbs in sheepshank knots
To break my pose and make me yield
Or asking me questions God will blush
To ask at Judgment. I'd laugh and answer;
You'd click and brush my hair aside
Or turn to a geek, "Ain't this boy
Fine?"
    I always came out
Looking like me. Others complained
(Nobody likes the you you like), but
You agreed—*It's you. I just* found *you.*
    Today I hear you're nearly lost,

Under a hundred pounds, eyes out,
Hid from all you saw and served.
    But Tom, I find you—see you still
In parks, up alleys, wrenching your face,
Your wiry limbs, into clowns and monkeys:
Finding me.

Suggestions for Discussion

1. What snapshots are taken in this poem?

2. What is the difference between an image summoned purely by memory and one that has been immortalized by film?

3. Does the poem inspire the reader to feel empathy for pepole with AIDS? Does it make the reader feel vulnerable to contracting HIV/AIDS? How do the emotions evoked by this poem compare to those evoked by AIDS awareness advertisements promoted by the French organization AIDES (which may be found online through a Google image search)?

Suggestion for Writing

Write a poem in honor of a friend you have not seen in many years but for whom you still have strong sentimental feelings.

MATTHEW ARNOLD

Dover Beach

Matthew Arnold (1822–1888), son of Thomas Arnold, the famous head-master of Rugby (a British public school), was first a poet, but he later abandoned poetry to become a lecturer, a critic of life and literature, and an inspector of schools. His *Collected Poems* appeared in 1869, *Essays in Criticism* in 1865 and 1888, *Culture and Anarchy* in 1869, *Friendships Garland* in 1879, and *Mixed Essays* in 1879. In "Dover Beach," the speaker at a moment of emotional crisis, talking to one he loves, raises the question of whether humans can find any peace or joy or release from pain in a world of conflict.

The sea is calm tonight.
The tide is full, the moon lies fair
Upon the straits; on the French coast the light
Gleams and is gone; the cliffs of England stand,
Glimmering and vast, out in the tranquil bay.
Come to the window, sweet is the night-air!

Only, from the long line of spray
Where the sea meets the moon-blanched land,
Listen! you hear the grating roar
Of pebbles which the waves draw back, and fling,
At their return, up the high strand,
Begin, and cease, and then again begin,
With tremulous cadence slow, and bring
The eternal note of sadness in.

Sophocles long ago
Heard it on the Aegean, and it brought
Into his mind the turbid ebb and flow
Of human misery; we
Find also in the sound a thought,
Hearing it by this distant northern sea.
The Sea of Faith
Was once, too, at the full, and round earth's shore
Lay like the folds of a bright girdle furled.
But now I only hear
Its melancholy, long, withdrawing roar,
Retreating, to the breath
Of the night-wind, down the vast edges drear
And naked shingles of the world.

Ah, love, let us be true
To one another! for the world, which seems
To lie before us like a land of dreams,
So various, so beautiful, so new,
Hath really neither joy, nor love, nor light,
Nor certitude, nor peace, nor help for pain;
And we are here as on a darkling plain
Swept with confused alarms of struggle and flight,
Where ignorant armies clash by night.

Suggestions for Discussion

1. How does the sea symbolize modern life?
2. What is the speaker seeking, and what values does he affirm? Exercise your imagination and rewrite this poem from the perspective of the beach as it regards the speaker.

TAHA MUHAMMAD ALI

Revenge

Taha Muhammad Ali is one of the leading poets on the Palestine literary scence. He was born in the Galilee village of Saffariya, which was destroyed in the 1948 war. He settled in Nazareth, where—when not reading and writing—he has run a souvenir shop ever since. Peter Cole (who translated this poem with Yahya Hijazi and Gabriel Levin) is a poet and translator from Hebrew and Arabic. He lives in Jerusalem. In 2007, he was named a Mac Arthur Foundation Fellow.

At times . . . I wish
I could meet in a duel
the man who killed my father
and razed our home,
expelling me
into
a narrow country.
And if he killed me,
I'd rest at last,
and if I were ready—
I would take my revenge!

But if it came to light,
when my rival appeared,
that he had a mother
waiting for him,
or a father who'd put
his right hand over

the heart's place in his chest
whenever his son was late
even by just a quarter-hour
for a meeting they'd set—
then I would not kill him,
even if I could.

Likewise . . . I
would not murder him
if it were soon made clear
that he had a brother or sisters
who loved him and constantly longed to see him.
Or if he had a wife to greet him
and children who
couldn't bear his absence
and whom his gifts would thrill.
Or if he had
friends or companions,
neighbors he knew
or allies from prison
or a hospital room,
or classmates from his school . . .
asking about him
and sending him regards.

But if he turned
out to be on his own—
cut off like a branch from a tree—
without a mother or father,
with neither a brother nor sister,
wifeless, without a child,
and without kin or neighbors or friends,
colleagues or companions,
then I'd add not a thing to his pain
within that aloneness—
not the torment of death,
and not the sorrow of passing away.
Instead I'd be content
to ignore him when I passed him by
on the street—as I
convinced myself
that paying him no attention
in itself was a kind of revenge.

Suggestions for Discussion

1. "Revenge" begins with a list of crimes committed against the narrator by a particular person. What does the reader initially expect to happen by the end of the poem? Is any revenge, ultimately, either sought or achieved? Explain.

2. The speaker posits many different kinds of lives for his tormentor. He conjures images of different friends and family members and imagines different slices of life with his enemy at the center. What effect do these images have on the reader of the poem? What is the speaker doing to himself by imagining, so vividly, the life of the man who killed his father?

3. To the extent that the poem might frustrate reader expectations, would a word in place of "revenge" better describe what occurs in the poem?

4. This poem famously inspired a strongly positive emotional reaction from the attendees at the Dodge Poetry Festival. What accounts for this poem's ability to inspire Americans to such an extent?

Suggestion for Writing

Would it be accurate to suggest that Taha Muhammad Ali expresses an idea in poetry that Joseph Williams and Greg Colomb express in essay form in "Argument, Critical Thinking, and Rationality"? All three writers advocate putting yourself in the shoes of the person you are clashing with. Consider the difficulties of empathy, especially in cases in which there is a history of pain, conflict, and disaster. How do Ali, Williams, and Colomb suggest overcoming anger and the desire for revenge? Write an essay comparing the two.

Globalism, Nationalism, and Cultural Identity

From this arises the question whether it is better to be loved more than feared, or feared more than loved. The reply is, that one ought to be both feared and loved, but as it is difficult for the two to go together, it is much safer to be feared than loved, if one of the two has to be wanting.

—NICCOLO MACHIAVELLI, "Of Cruelty and Clemency, and Whether It Is Better to Be Loved or Feared"

It is not power that corrupts but fear. Fear of losing power corrupts those who wield it and fear of the scourge of power corrupts those who are subject to it.

—AUNG SAN SUU KYI, "Freedom from Fear"

Batmobama and Robiden
Oil painting on canvas, 2008
www.paulrichmondstudio.com

INTRODUCTION

❧❧❧❧

The nations of our "global village" have never been more unified—and never more divided. Never have information and ideas spread as quickly as they do now—but never have lines of productive communication broken down as completely as they seem to have in our world of terrorism and suspicion. Globalization makes us wonder about the value of maintaining separate cultural identities, while, at the same time, nationalism seems fiercer than ever, demanding that we wrap ourselves in our country's values, mores, and traditions. This chapter explores this rich and inscrutable interaction of related ideas.

The Notebook section brings together a cluster of essays that explore the most shared public memory of our era, the September 11 attacks, and the wars in Afghanistan and Iraq that followed. In the speech he made accepting a Nobel Peace Prize in 2009, President Barack Obama defends his decision to escalate the scope of the American military campaign in Afghanistan even as he promises to follow the examples of his heroes, Gandhi and Martin Luther King, and do his best to make the world a more just and peaceful place. Providing another perspective, Anthony Shadid's "Legacy of the Prophet" attempts to explain (not justify) why some Islamics have continued to praise Osama bin Ladin, and despise all that is imperialist and exploitative about American foreign policy. In "The Next War," General Wesley K. Clark looks at the current campaigns in the Middle East with the unusual perspective of a left-leaning military man, and warns that a future war against Iran might not be easy to win.

In a similar fashion, works by Native American writers Sherman Alexie and Sarah Littlecrow-Russell honor the memory of whole tribes, communities, and nations that have been slaughtered and subjugated by imperial aims, and ask us to consider the perspectives of the adversaries of the American military, past and present, as well as the lasting consequences of invasion, conquest, and subjugation.

Other authors in this chapter also move beyond nationalism. Niccolo Machiavelli's classic statement, "Of Cruelty and Clemency, and Whether It Is Better to Be Loved or Feared" is included, adding *realpolitik* and power to the mix of perspectives on leadership. Voices such as Mohandas Gandhi (see the selection in *Personal Values and Relationships*), Howard Gardner, and Aung San Suu Kyi offer alternatives to Machiavelli, suggesting that hope, peaceful protests, and a global perspective are the best ways to ensure international harmony and prevent wars and human rights abuses. And, in a nineteenth-century essay that couldn't feel more relevant to today, social satirist Oscar Wilde considers the possibility that individual freedoms would be better preserved by a socialist society than by capitalist Britain and America, since both countries promote high profits for the few, hard menial work for the many, and conformity of dress, behavior, and opinion for all.

Over the past several years, a global debate about religion and society has raged, with secularists on one side arguing that religion is the primary cause of global ignorance, bigotry, and war, and religious figures on another claiming that religion is a civilizing force, as well as the source of all moral codes and revelation concerning the meaning of life. Paired essays featured in the Personal Writing section represent the two perspectives in this debate: Chris Hedges argues that organized religion can be freed from its dangerously fundamentalist adherents by the enlightened pious, while Salman Rushdie argues that religion is fundamentally oppressive and a millstone around the neck of social progress.

Two other related essays show examples of liberal and conservative editorial writing in prominent American publications. In an editorial written for the *Wall Street Journal*, Ronald-Reagan-speechwriter Peggy Noonan calls for a new kind of Republican Party that is less angry and more thoughtful, and better equipped to challenge the smilingly extremist agenda of the twenty-first century Democratic Party. In a *Newsweek* editorial, liberal cultural commentator Anna Quindlen looks broadly at immigration and suggests that newcomers enrich American society, not drag it down. These pieces are representative of the kinds of columns that are published every day online and in print, and can give students a sense of how issues are debated in the popular media today.

Together, the voices in this chapter provide a rich cacophony of opinions that examine how identity is formed, from the individual to the global. The writers examine the influences of identity from the perspective of both "ordinary" individual and leader as they explore what may finally be the most important issue of our new century: how to survive as one of many on this globe.

NOTEBOOK

BARACK OBAMA

A Just and Lasting Peace

The first African American to be elected president of the United States, Barack Hussein Obama II (b. 1961) is the country's forty-fourth chief executive. Obama first garnered national attention in 2004, during his successful bid to become the junior United States senator from Illinois, and following his inspiring keynote address at the Democratic National Convention. He later spent two years campaigning for the presidency, first in Democratic primaries against Hillary Clinton, and later, in the 2008 general election, against Republican John McCain. Born in Hawaii, Obama spent several childhood years in Indonesia with his mother and stepfather, but was raised primarily by his grandparents in Honolulu. His mixed Kenyan and American heritage as well as his years in Indonesia, where he witnessed extensive suffering, engendered in Obama a multicultural worldview described in his best-selling memoir, *Dreams from My Father* (1995). Obama earned degrees from Columbia University and Harvard Law School where, in 1990, he became the first African-American editor of the *Harvard Law Review*. Relocating to Chicago, Obama served as a community organizer, taught constitutional law at the University of Chicago, and was elected to three terms in the Illinois Senate. His *Audacity of Hope* (2006) laid out Obama's political philosophy. In 2009, President Obama was awarded the Nobel Peace Prize—a controversial choice, since he was overseeing two wars, and the award seemed significantly premature to many. What follows is the text of Obama's acceptance speech, delivered on December 10, 2009, at the Oslo City Hall in Norway.

Your Majesties, Your Royal Highnesses, Distinguished Members of the Norwegian Nobel Committee, citizens of America, and citizens of the world:

I receive this honor with deep gratitude and great humility. It is an award that speaks to our highest aspirations—that for all the cruelty and hardship of our world, we are not mere prisoners of fate. Our actions matter, and can bend history in the direction of justice.

And yet I would be remiss if I did not acknowledge the considerable controversy that your generous decision has generated. In part, this is because I am at the beginning, and not the end, of my labors on the world stage. Compared to some of the giants of history who have received this prize—Schweitzer and King; Marshall and Mandela—my accomplishments are slight. And then there are the men and women around the world who have been jailed and beaten in the pursuit of justice; those who toil in humanitarian organizations to relieve suffering; the unrecognized millions whose quiet acts of courage and compassion inspire even the most hardened of cynics. I cannot argue with those who find these men and women—some known, some obscure to all but those they help—to be far more deserving of this honor than I.

But perhaps the most profound issue surrounding my receipt of this prize is the fact that I am the Commander-in-Chief of a nation in the midst of two wars. One of these wars is winding down. The other is a conflict that America did not seek; one in which we are joined by forty-three other countries—including Norway—in an effort to defend ourselves and all nations from further attacks.

Still, we are at war, and I am responsible for the deployment of thousands of young Americans to battle in a distant land. Some will kill. Some will be killed. And so I come here with an acute sense of the cost of armed conflict—filled with difficult questions about the relationship between war and peace, and our effort to replace one with the other.

These questions are not new. War, in one form or another, appeared with the first man. At the dawn of history, its morality was not questioned; it was simply a fact, like drought or disease—the manner in which tribes and then civilizations sought power and settled their differences.

Over time, as codes of law sought to control violence within groups, so did philosophers, clerics, and statesmen seek to regulate the destructive power of war. The concept of a "just war" emerged, suggesting that war is justified only when it meets certain preconditions: if it is waged as a last resort or in self-defense; if the forced used is proportional, and if, whenever possible, civilians are spared from violence.

For most of history, this concept of just war was rarely observed. The capacity of human beings to think up new ways to kill one another proved inexhaustible, as did our capacity to exempt from mercy those who look different or pray to a different God. Wars between armies gave way to wars between nations—total wars in which the distinction between combatant and civilian became blurred. In the span of thirty years, such carnage would twice engulf this continent. And while it is hard to conceive of a cause more just than the defeat of the Third Reich and the Axis powers, World War II was a conflict in which the total number of civilians who died exceeded the number of soldiers who perished.

In the wake of such destruction, and with the advent of the nuclear age, it became clear to victor and vanquished alike that the world needed institutions to prevent another World War. And so, a quarter century after the United States Senate rejected the League of Nations—an idea for which Woodrow Wilson received this Prize—America led the world in constructing an architecture to keep the peace: a Marshall Plan and a United Nations, mechanisms to govern the waging of war, treaties to protect human rights, prevent genocide, and restrict the most dangerous weapons.

In many ways, these efforts succeeded. Yes, terrible wars have been fought, and atrocities committed. But there has been no Third World War. The Cold War ended with jubilant crowds dismantling a wall. Commerce has stitched much of the world together. Billions have been lifted from poverty. The ideals of liberty, self-determination, equality and the rule of law have haltingly advanced. We are the heirs of the fortitude and foresight of generations past, and it is a legacy for which my own country is rightfully proud.

A decade into a new century, this old architecture is buckling under the weight of new threats. The world may no longer shudder at the prospect of war between two nuclear superpowers, but proliferation may increase the risk of catastrophe. Terrorism has long been a tactic, but modern technology allows a few small men with outsized rage to murder innocents on a horrific scale.

Moreover, wars between nations have increasingly given way to wars within nations. The resurgence of ethnic or sectarian conflicts; the growth of secessionist movements, insurgencies, and failed states; have increasingly trapped civilians in unending chaos. In today's wars, many more civilians are killed than soldiers; the seeds of future conflict are sewn, economies are wrecked, civil societies torn asunder, refugees amassed, and children scarred.

I do not bring with me today a definitive solution to the problems of war. What I do know is that meeting these challenges will require the same vision, hard work, and persistence of those men and women who acted so boldly decades ago. And it will require us to think in new ways about the notions of just war and the imperatives of a just peace.

We must begin by acknowledging the hard truth that we will not eradicate violent conflict in our lifetimes. There will be times when nations—acting individually or in concert—will find the use of force not only necessary but morally justified.

I make this statement mindful of what Martin Luther King said in this same ceremony years ago—"Violence never brings permanent peace. It solves no social problem: it merely creates new and more complicated ones." As someone who stands here as a direct consequence of Dr. King's life's work, I am living testimony to the moral force of nonviolence. I know there is nothing weak—nothing passive—nothing naïve—in the creed and lives of Gandhi and King.

But as a head of state sworn to protect and defend my nation, I cannot be guided by their examples alone. I face the world as it is, and cannot stand idle in the face of threats to the American people. For make no mistake: evil does exist in the world. A nonviolent movement could not have halted Hitler's armies. Negotiations cannot convince al Qaeda's leaders to lay down their arms. To say that force is sometimes necessary is not a call to cynicism—it is a recognition of history; the imperfections of man and the limits of reason.

I raise this point because in many countries there is a deep ambivalence about military action today, no matter the cause. At times, this is joined by a reflexive suspicion of America, the world's sole military superpower.

Yet the world must remember that it was not simply international institutions—not just treaties and declarations—that brought stability to a post–World War II world. Whatever mistakes we have made, the plain fact is this: the United States of America has helped underwrite global security for more than six decades with the blood of our citizens and the strength of our arms. The service and sacrifice of our men and women in uniform has promoted peace and prosperity from Germany to Korea, and enabled democracy to take hold in places like the Balkans. We have borne this burden not because we seek to impose our will. We have done so out of enlightened self-interest—because we seek a better future for our children and grandchildren, and we believe that their lives will be better if other peoples' children and grandchildren can live in freedom and prosperity.

So yes, the instruments of war do have a role to play in preserving the peace. And yet this truth must coexist with another—that no matter how justified, war promises human tragedy. The soldier's courage and sacrifice is full of glory, expressing devotion to country, to cause and to comrades in arms. But war itself is never glorious, and we must never trumpet it as such.

So part of our challenge is reconciling these two seemingly irreconcilable truths—that war is sometimes necessary, and war is at some level an expression of human feelings. Concretely, we must direct our effort to the task that President Kennedy called for long ago. "Let us focus," he said, "on a more practical, more attainable peace, based not on a sudden revolution in human nature but on a gradual evolution in human institutions."

What might this evolution look like? What might these practical steps be?

To begin with, I believe that all nations—strong and weak alike—must adhere to standards that govern the use of force. I—like any head of state— reserve the right to act unilaterally if necessary to defend my nation. Nevertheless, I am convinced that adhering to standards strengthens those who do, and isolates—and weakens—those who don't.

The world rallied around America after the 9/11 attacks, and continues to support our efforts in Afghanistan, because of the horror of those senseless attacks and the recognized principle of self-defense. Likewise, the world recognized the need to confront Saddam Hussein when he invaded Kuwait—a consensus that sent a clear message to all about the cost of aggression.

Furthermore, America cannot insist that others follow the rules of the road if we refuse to follow them ourselves. For when we don't, our action can appear arbitrary, and undercut the legitimacy of future intervention—no matter how justified.

This becomes particularly important when the purpose of military action extends beyond self-defense or the defense of one nation against an aggressor. More and more, we all confront difficult questions about how to prevent the slaughter of civilians by their own government, or to stop a civil war whose violence and suffering can engulf an entire region.

I believe that force can be justified on humanitarian grounds, as it was in the Balkans, or in other places that have been scarred by war. Inaction tears at our conscience and can lead to more costly intervention later. That is why all responsible nations must embrace the role that militaries with a clear mandate can play to keep the peace.

America's commitment to global security will never waiver. But in a world in which threats are more diffuse, and missions more complex, America cannot act alone. This is true in Afghanistan. This is true in failed states like Somalia, where terrorism and piracy is joined by famine and human suffering. And sadly, it will continue to be true in unstable regions for years to come.

The leaders and soldiers of NATO countries—and other friends and allies—demonstrate this truth through the capacity and courage they have shown in Afghanistan. But in many countries, there is a disconnect between the efforts of those who serve and the ambivalence of the broader public. I understand why war is not popular. But I also know this: the belief that peace is desirable is rarely enough to achieve it. Peace requires responsibility. Peace entails sacrifice. That is why NATO continues to be indispensable. That is why we must strengthen UN and regional peacekeeping, and not leave the task to a few countries. That is why we honor those who return home from peacekeeping and training abroad to Oslo and Rome; to Ottawa and Sydney; to Dhaka and Kigali—we honor them not as makers of war, but as wagers of peace.

Let me make one final point about the use of force. Even as we make difficult decisions about going to war, we must also think clearly about how we fight it. The Nobel Committee recognized this truth in awarding its first prize for peace to Henry Dunant—the founder of the Red Cross, and a driving force behind the Geneva Conventions.

Where force is necessary, we have a moral and strategic interest in binding ourselves to certain rules of conduct. And even as we confront a vicious adversary that abides by no rules, I believe that the United States of America must remain a standard bearer in the conduct of war. That is what makes us different from those whom we fight. That is a source of our strength. That is why I prohibited torture. That is why I ordered the prison at Guantanamo Bay closed. And that is why I have reaffirmed America's commitment to abide by the Geneva Conventions. We lose ourselves when we compromise the very ideals that we fight to defend. And we honor those ideals by upholding them not just when it is easy, but when it is hard.

I have spoken to the questions that must weigh on our minds and our hearts as we choose to wage war. But let me turn now to our effort to avoid such tragic choices, and speak of three ways that we can build a just and lasting peace.

First, in dealing with those nations that break rules and laws, I believe that we must develop alternatives to violence that are tough enough to change behavior—for if we want a lasting peace, then the words of the international community must mean something. Those regimes that break the rules must be held accountable. Sanctions must exact a real price. Intransigence must be met with increased pressure—and such pressure exists only when the world stands together as one.

One urgent example is the effort to prevent the spread of nuclear weapons, and to seek a world without them. In the middle of the last century, nations agreed to be bound by a treaty whose bargain is clear: all will have access to peaceful nuclear power; those without nuclear weapons will forsake them; and those with nuclear weapons will work toward disarmament. I am committed to upholding this treaty. It is a centerpiece of my foreign policy. And I am working with President Medvedev to reduce America and Russia's nuclear stockpiles.

But it is also incumbent upon all of us to insist that nations like Iran and North Korea do not game the system. Those who claim to respect international law cannot avert their eyes when those laws are flouted. Those who care for their own security cannot ignore the danger of an arms race in the Middle East or East Asia. Those who seek peace cannot stand idly by as nations arm themselves for nuclear war.

The same principle applies to those who violate international law by brutalizing their own people. When there is genocide in Darfur; systematic rape in Congo; or repression in Burma—there must be consequences. And the closer we stand together, the less likely we will be faced with the choice between armed intervention and complicity in oppression.

This brings me to a second point—the nature of the peace that we seek. For peace is not merely the absence of visible conflict. Only a just peace based upon the inherent rights and dignity of every individual can truly be lasting.

It was this insight that drove drafters of the Universal Declaration of Human Rights after the Second World War. In the wake of devastation, they recognized that if human rights are not protected, peace is a hollow promise.

And yet all too often, these words are ignored. In some countries, the failure to uphold human rights is excused by the false suggestion that these are Western principles, foreign to local cultures or stages of a nation's development. And within America, there has long been a tension between those who describe themselves as realists or idealists—a tension that suggests a stark choice between the narrow pursuit of interests or an endless campaign to impose our values.

I reject this choice. I believe that peace is unstable where citizens are denied the right to speak freely or worship as they please; choose their own leaders or assemble without fear. Pent up grievances fester, and the suppression of tribal and religious identity can lead to violence. We also know that the opposite is true. Only when Europe became free did it finally find peace. America has never fought a war against a democracy, and our closest friends are governments that protect the rights of their citizens. No matter how callously defined, neither America's interests—nor the world's—are served by the denial of human aspirations.

So even as we respect the unique culture and traditions of different countries, America will always be a voice for those aspirations that are universal. We will bear witness to the quiet dignity of reformers like Aung San Suu Kyi; to the bravery of Zimbabweans who cast their ballots in the face of beatings; to the hundreds of thousands who have marched silently through the streets of Iran. It is telling that the leaders of these governments fear the aspirations of their own people more than the power of any other nation. And it is the responsibility of all free people and free nations to make clear to these movements that hope and history are on their side.

Let me also say this: the promotion of human rights cannot be about exhortation alone. At times, it must be coupled with painstaking diplomacy. I know that engagement with repressive regimes lacks the satisfying purity of indignation. But I also know that sanctions without outreach—and condemnation without discussion—can carry forward a crippling status quo. No repressive regime can move down a new path unless it has the choice of an open door.

In light of the Cultural Revolution's horrors, Nixon's meeting with Mao appeared inexcusable—and yet it surely helped set China on a path where millions of its citizens have been lifted from poverty, and connected to open societies. Pope John Paul's engagement with Poland created space not just for the Catholic Church, but for labor leaders like Lech Walesa. Ronald Reagan's efforts on arms control and embrace of perestroika not only improved relations with the Soviet Union, but empowered dissidents throughout Eastern Europe. There is no simple formula here. But we must try as best we can to balance isolation and engagement; pressure and incentives, so that human rights and dignity are advanced over time.

Third, a just peace includes not only civil and political rights—it must encompass economic security and opportunity. For true peace is not just freedom from fear, but freedom from want.

It is undoubtedly true that development rarely takes root without security; it is also true that security does not exist where human beings do not have access to enough food, or clean water, or the medicine they need to survive. It does not exist where children cannot aspire to a decent education or a job that supports a family. The absence of hope can rot a society from within.

And that is why helping farmers feed their own people—or nations educate their children and care for the sick—is not mere charity. It is also why the world must come together to confront climate change. There is little scientific dispute that if we do nothing, we will face more drought, famine and mass displacement that will fuel more conflict for decades. For this reason, it is not merely scientists and activists who call for swift and forceful action—it is military leaders in my country and others who understand that our common security hangs in the balance.

Agreements among nations. Strong institutions. Support for human rights. Investments in development. All of these are vital ingredients in bringing about the evolution that President Kennedy spoke about. And yet, I do not believe that we will have the will, or the staying power, to complete this work without something more—and that is the continued expansion of our moral imagination; an insistence that there is something irreducible that we all share.

As the world grows smaller, you might think it would be easier for human beings to recognize how similar we are; to understand that we all basically want the same things; that we all hope for the chance to live out our lives with some measure of happiness and fulfillment for ourselves and our families.

And yet, given the dizzying pace of globalization, and the cultural leveling of modernity, it should come as no surprise that people fear the loss of what they cherish about their particular identities—their race, their tribe, and perhaps most powerfully their religion. In some places, this fear has led to conflict. At times, it even feels like we are moving backwards. We see it in Middle East, as the conflict between Arabs and Jews seems to harden. We see it in nations that are torn asunder by tribal lines.

Most dangerously, we see it in the way that religion is used to justify the murder of innocents by those who have distorted and defiled the great religion of Islam, and who attacked my country from Afghanistan. These extremists are not the first to kill in the name of God; the cruelties of the Crusades are amply recorded. But they remind us that no Holy War can ever be a just war. For if you truly believe that you are carrying out divine will, then there is no need for restraint—no need to spare the pregnant mother, or the medic, or even a person of one's own faith. Such a warped view of religion is not just incompatible with the concept of peace, but the purpose of faith—for the one rule that lies at the heart of every major religion is that we do unto others as we would have them do unto us.

Adhering to this law of love has always been the core struggle of human nature. We are fallible. We make mistakes, and fall victim to the temptations of pride, and power, and sometimes evil. Even those of us with the best intentions will at times fail to right the wrongs before us.

But we do not have to think that human nature is perfect for us to still believe that the human condition can be perfected. We do not have to live in an idealized world to still reach for those ideals that will make it a better place. The nonviolence practiced by men like Gandhi and King may not have been practical or possible in every circumstance, but the love that they preached—their faith in human progress—must always be the North Star that guides us on our journey.

For if we lose that faith—if we dismiss it as silly or naïve; if we divorce it from the decisions that we make on issues of war and peace—then we lose what is best about humanity. We lose our sense of possibility. We lose our moral compass.

Like generations have before us, we must reject that future. As Dr. King said at this occasion so many years ago, "I refuse to accept despair as the final response to the ambiguities of history. I refuse to accept the idea that the 'isness' of man's present nature makes him morally incapable of reaching up for the eternal 'oughtness' that forever confronts him."

So let us reach for the world that ought to be—that spark of the divine that still stirs within each of our souls. Somewhere today, in the here and now, a soldier sees he's outgunned but stands firm to keep the peace. Somewhere today, in this world, a young protestor awaits the brutality of her government, but has the courage to march on. Somewhere today, a mother facing punishing poverty still takes the time to teach her child, who believes that a cruel world still has a place for his dreams.

Let us live by their example. We can acknowledge that oppression will always be with us, and still strive for justice. We can admit the intractability of depravation, and still strive for dignity. We can understand that there will be war, and still strive for peace. We can do that—for that is the story of human progress; that is the hope of all the world; and at this moment of challenge, that must be our work here on Earth.

Suggestions for Discussion

1. How does Obama wrestle with the concept of a "just war"? How are his views of specific conflicts, such as World War II and the war in Afghanistan, shaped by the notion of a "just war"? Why does he maintain that "No holy war can ever be a just war"?

2. In what three ways does Obama suggests that "a just and lasting peace" might be built?

3. How does Obama define the tension between Americans "who describe themselves as realists or idealists"? Why does he reject the choice between the two perspectives?

4. Why does Obama characterize climate change as a national security issue?

5. Synthesis: At least two other selections in this collection explore the state of religion in the modern world (Hedges, "The Ten Commandments in America," and Rushdie, "Imagine There's No Heaven," both in *Globalism, Nationalism, and Cultural Identity*). How would you compare their views to those of Obama?

6. Synthesis: Consider this speech in light of Anthony Shadid's "Legacy of the Prophet." How might the figures quoted in that essay respond to Obama's speech?

Suggestions for Writing

1. Synthesis: Examine the selections in this book by Gandhi, Martin Luther King, and Aung San Suu Kyi. To what extent are the ideas they express evident in Obama's speech—especially in the passages where he invokes their names? To what extent does Obama deviate from their philosophies? Write an essay comparing and contrasting these views.

2. How are Obama's views on American national security and on America's role in the international community similar to those of his predecessor, President George W. Bush? How are they different? Research speeches by Bush, including his 2005 inauguration address and post-9/11 address on September 20, 2001, to make sure you understand Bush's ideas. Use specific references both from Obama's Nobel address and from Bush's speeches to support your conclusions.

ANTHONY SHADID

Legacy of the Prophet

Anthony Shadid is a foreign correspondent for the *Washington Post*. His coverage of the Iraq war earned him the 2004 Pulitzer Prize for International Reporting and provided the basis for his book *Night Draws Near: Iraq's People in the Shadow of America's War* (2005). This selection is from the second edition of *Legacy of the Prophet* (2000, 2002), Shadid's exploration of contemporary Islamic politics and its ties to American foreign policy.

His words came suddenly, delivered with righteousness. His concern was Osama bin Ladin. "A hero, that's the feeling of the people right now, that he's fighting to save the Muslim world," Mohammed Abdullah said. "When he dies, he'll be a martyr." His sentiments, unadulterated by sensitivity, left me with a sense I had felt often as a journalist in the Muslim world. In October 2001, as smoke continued to rise from the rubble of the World Trade Center and the ugly gash in the Pentagon lay bare, I traveled to Cairo, one of the Muslim world's greatest cities, to cover one aspect of a story that, by then, had become sadly familiar to me. Off and on, for nearly ten years, I had reported and written about the attacks, the strife and the bombings that had come to define, for much of the world, the face of political Islam. Similar circumstances brought me here again, and much remained familiar. There was grief at the shedding of innocents' blood in the attacks of September 11 and over the death of more innocents in the war that followed in Afghanistan. There was disbelief at the spectacle that terrorism can unleash. And, no less troubling, there was the same misunderstanding, the same yawning gulf in perceptions that seemed to follow the scars left by the attacks.

Abdullah, I soon learned, was not alone in his beliefs. To the young men that had gathered around me at a sprawling bus stop in Cairo, their beards suggesting a fervent devotion, the Saudi militant exiled in Afghanistan was a symbol of an embattled religion, the very personification of the men's own frustrations at a faith overwhelmed by an omnipotent West. Their issue was justice, or a lack of it. Bin Ladin, they said, spoke of defending Palestinians, of ending sanctions on Iraq, of curtailing near-total U.S. sway over the region. An older man in a white peasant gown spoke up, raising his voice over the square's circus of vendors hawking fruit and buses barreling down the street, their exhaust stirring the dust carried by Egypt's desert winds. "He's a man who defends his rights," the man insisted, as others nodded in agreement. "If someone tries to hit me, I have to defend myself. He's defending his land, his religion, his rights and himself."

How had we reached this point? As I stood amid Cairo's thriving chaos, I began to think about the divide that made two cultures, both defined to a great extent by religion, almost incomprehensible to each other. Many Muslims, whose disenchantment with the United States evoked an almost nihilist disdain, seemed to cast bin Ladin as militant rather than terrorist, dissident rather than executioner. His defiance of the West had assumed the mantle of heroic resistance. The world's affairs here were defined not by liberty, not by freedom, but instead by justice, a concept that takes on greater importance to those without it. To the men at the bus stop, the United States and, by default, the West were the instruments for depriving justice across the Muslim world, a vast territory embracing one billion people who make up a majority in some forty-five countries.

Passions were no less ardent in the West. The attacks of September 11 were the latest, most persuasive evidence of modern-day Islam's seeming penchant for senseless butchery. Before much of the world, and in a frighteningly short time, one of history's most sublime prophetic messages had become a faith defined not by the omnipotence of God and the need for generosity and justice but by a darker, more menacing side of human nature. Lost were memories of Islam's proud past: the Ottoman Empire's centuries of glory, Arab accomplishments in mathematics, astronomy and medicine, the conquests of an Islamic army whose domain stretched from Central Asia to southwestern France and Islam's heritage in preserving, tailoring and then transmitting Greek philosophy to medieval Europe. Instead, a new legacy had evolved in our lifetimes, and the messages of Islamic militants scrawled in blood were poised to leave a more lasting impression. The result, it seems, is yet another repetition of the fear, misunderstanding and hostility that have defined relations between Islam and the West since before Pope Urban II launched the crusades to liberate the Holy Land in the eleventh century.

From 1979 on, U.S. policy toward the Muslim world has been dangerous and remarkably flawed. Typically, it has been content to view political Islam as inherently threatening or as a target of sometimes cynical opportunity. The approach has helped bring about nearly two decades of enmity with Iran and conflict with Sudan. In Saudi Arabia, our blind support for the monarchy—and, by default, its corruption and repression—has cultivated an Islamic opposition that today threatens both U.S. troops and access to the world's largest oil reserves. U.S. policy toward Israel and the Palestinian authority has inflamed activists there, embroiling the United States in a conflict that need not be our own. In distant Afghanistan, on the cultural and political periphery of the Muslim world, the United States opportunistically armed and supported militias that drew on Islam to fight the Soviet Union in the 1980s. Today, many of those same militants are sworn enemies of America. Bin Ladin, of course, became their most influential graduate.

There is an alternative, one that will require a particular element of courage in the wake of the attacks of September 11 and the war in Afghanistan. The United States and the West face a strategic choice, and that choice will go far in determining the course of politics in much of the Muslim world. Egypt again may be enlightening. Since the Arab world's largest country signed a peace treaty with Israel in 1979, the United States has acted as its patron, wielding substantial, almost colonial, influence over its internal and foreign affairs. This influence, however, has not entailed pressure on its authoritarian government to enact democratic reform. Both Egypt and the United States recognize that such changes, in time, would give rise to an already popular Islamic current in Egypt's political life. That policy is shortsighted and clearly untenable. Repression has already failed in Iran and is soon to fail in the Persian Gulf and in countries like Egypt, where time and again the government has failed to stamp out the substantial support political Islam enjoys, giving rise instead to a generation of militants whose exploits still scar New York, Washington, Luxor, Islamabad and beyond. That leaves one viable alternative: The West must encourage democracy in places like Egypt with the realization that it is, in effect, encouraging Islamism by making room for its growth. It means governments might be elected that have no love for the United States. On the other hand, America's support for those same movements—the Center Party, for instance—could bring forth a new relationship in which U.S. policy and political Islam find common ground. To do so, the West must take further steps in ending the isolation of traditional enemies, giving countries like Iran an opportunity to evolve into more democratic states. In nations like Turkey, Jordan, Kuwait and Yemen, where democratic Islamic movements are now emerging or already in place, the United States must seek to make clear that their assumption of power is not in itself an adverse development. The choice is not sentimental, and without question, the risk of such policies is great. But the potential benefits are myriad—stability in an oil-rich region, democracy in authoritarian countries, a more viable weapon against the scourge of terrorism and the first step in ending a cultural conflict that, today more than ever, threatens to escalate. Both sides must take the journey together.

Suggestions for Discussion

1. How does Shadid present the different perspectives of the West and the Islamic world? Do you think he is successful in creating sympathy for both?

2. What factors does Shadid cite as causes for the rift between the American and Muslim cultures? Explain why you do or do not agree with his assessment, and cite other factors that might be responsible for encouraging conflict.

3. Why do you think Shadid puts so much effort into describing the bus stop scene in Cairo?

Suggestion for Writing

Contrasts Shadid's idea of America's role in world politics with the viewpoint presented by Wesley Clark in the next reading, "The Next War." Which vision of foreign policy do you find more persuasive? Cite specific arguments used by both authors.

$\infty\infty$

W E S L E Y   K .   C L A R K

The Next War

Four-star general and NATO's former Supreme Allied Commander, Europe, Wesley Clark (b. 1944) led the allied military forces to victory in the Kosovo War in 1999. Born in Chicago and raised in Arkansas, Clark graduated first in his class from West Point and was awarded a Rhodes Scholarship to Oxford University in 1966, where he earned a master's degree in politics, philosophy, and economics. In 2000, he retired from the military after thirty-four years of service and became an investment banker, author, and political commentator. A populist "Draft Clark" movement inspired Clark to stand as a Democratic candidate for president of the United States in 2003 and run against President George W. Bush, but Senator John Kerry ultimately won the nomination. Clark founded and organizes the political activist group WesPac, is a fellow at the Burkle Center for International Relations at UCLA, and has written several books, including *A Time to Lead: For Duty, Honor and Country*. He wrote the following editorial, originally published in the *Washington Post* on September 16, 2007, about Operation Iraqi Freedom.

The next war.

It's always looming. But has our military learned the right lessons from this one to fight it and win?

Testifying before Congress last week, Gen. David H. Petraeus appeared commanding, smart, and alive to the challenges that his soldiers face in Iraq. But he also embodied what the Iraq conflict has come to represent: an embattled, able, courageous military at war, struggling to maintain its authority and credibility after 4 1/2 years of a "cakewalk" gone wrong.

Petraeus will not be the last general to find himself explaining how a military intervention has misfired and urging skeptical lawmakers to believe that the mission can still be accomplished. For the next war is always looming, and so is the urgent question of whether the U.S. military can adapt in time to win it.

Today, the most likely next conflict will be with Iran, a radical state that America has tried to isolate for almost 30 years and that now threatens to further destabilize the Middle East through its expansionist aims, backing of terrorist proxies such as the Lebanese group Hezbollah and Hamas in Gaza and the West Bank, and far-reaching support for radical Shiite militias in Iraq. As Iran seems to draw closer to acquiring nuclear weapons, almost every U.S. leader—and would-be president—has said that it simply won't be permitted to reach that goal.

Think another war can't happen? Think again. Unchastened by the Iraq fiasco, hawks in Vice President Cheney's office have been pushing the use of force. It isn't hard to foresee the range of military options that policymakers face.

The next war would begin with an intense air and naval campaign. Let's say you're planning the conflict as part of the staff of the Joint Chiefs. Your list of targets isn't that long—only a few dozen nuclear sites—but you can't risk retaliation from Tehran. So you allow 21 days for the bombardment, to be safe; you'd aim to strike every command-and-control facility, radar site, missile site, storage site, airfield, ship and base in Iran. To prevent world oil prices from soaring, you'd have to try to protect every oil and gas rig, and the big ports and load points. You'd need to use B-2s and lots of missiles up front, plus many small amphibious task forces to take out particularly tough targets along the coast, with manned and unmanned air reconnaissance. And don't forget the Special Forces, to penetrate deep inside Iran, call in airstrikes and drag the evidence of Tehran's nuclear ambitions out into the open for a world that's understandably skeptical of U.S. assertions that yet another Gulf rogue is on the brink of getting the bomb.

But if it's clear how a war with Iran would start, it's far less clear how it would end. How might Iran strike back? Would it unleash Hezbollah cells across Europe and the Middle East, or perhaps even inside the United States? Would Tehran goad Iraq's Shiites to rise up against their U.S. occupiers? And what would we do with Iran after the bombs stopped falling? We certainly could not occupy the nation with the limited ground forces we have left. So what would it be: Iran as a chastened, more tractable government? As a chaotic failed state? Or as a hardened and embittered foe?

Iran is not the only country where the next war with the United States might erupt. Consider the emergence of a new superpower (or at least a close competitor with the United States). China's shoot-down of an old Chinese satellite in January was a wake-up call about the risks inherent in America's reliance on space. The next war could also come from somewhere unexpected; if you'd told most Americans in August 2001 that the United States would be invading Afghanistan within weeks, they'd have called you crazy.

Any future U.S. wars will undoubtedly be shaped by the experiences in Iraq and Afghanistan, however painful that might be. Every military refights the last war, but good militaries learn lessons from the past. We'd better get them right, and soon. Here, the lesson from Iraq and Afghanistan couldn't be more clear: Don't ever, ever go to war unless you can describe and create a more desirable end state. And doing so takes a whole lot more than just the use of force.

The lessons from past conflicts aren't always obvious. After the demoralizing loss in Vietnam, the United States went high-tech, developing whole classes of new tanks, ships and fighter planes and new operational techniques to defeat then-enemy no. 1—the Soviets. We also junked the doctrine of counterinsurgency warfare, which we're trying to relearn in Iraq.

After the 1991 Persian Gulf War, the U.S. military embarked upon another wave of high-tech modernization—and paid for it by cutting ground forces, which were being repeatedly deployed to peacekeeping operations in places such as Haiti, Bosnia, and Kosovo. Instead of preparing for more likely, low-intensity conflicts, we were still spoiling for the "big fight," focusing on such large conventional targets as Kim Jong Il's North Korea and Saddam Hussein's Iraq—and now we lack adequate ground forces. Bulking up these forces, perhaps by as many as 100,000 more active troops, and refitting and recovering from Iraq could cost $70 billion to $100 billion.

Somehow, in the past decade or two, we began to think of ourselves as "warriors." There was an elemental purity to this mindset, a kill-or-be-killed simplicity that drove U.S. commanders to create a leaner force based on more basic skills—the kind that some generals thought were lacking in Vietnam and in the early years of the all-volunteer military. Now, in an age when losing hearts and minds can mean losing a war, we find ourselves struggling in Iraq and Afghanistan to impart the sort of cultural sensitivities that were second nature to an earlier generation of troops trained to eat nuoc mam with everything and sit on the floor during their tours in Vietnam.

One of the most important lessons from the wars in Iraq and Afghanistan—and Vietnam, for that matter—is that we need to safeguard our troops. The U.S. public is more likely to sour on a conflict when it sees the military losing blood, not treasure. So to keep up our staying power, our skill in hunting and killing our foes has to be matched by our care in concealing and protecting our troops. Three particularly obvious requirements are body armor, mine-resistant vehicles, and telescopic and night sights for every weapon. But these things are expensive for a military that has historically been enamored of big-ticket items such as fighter planes, ships and missiles. Many of us career officers understood these requirements after Vietnam, but we couldn't shift the Pentagon's priorities enough to save the lives of forces sent to Iraq years later.

That brings us to the military's leaders. We need generals who are well-educated, flexible and culturally adept men and women—not just warriors, not just technicians. Why aren't more military leaders sent to top schools such as Princeton, the way Petraeus was, or given opportunities to earn Ph.D.s, as did Defense Secretary Robert M. Gates's military assistant, Lt. Gen. Peter Chiarelli? For years, Congress has whacked away at military-education budgets, thereby driving gifted officers from the top-flight graduate schools where they could have honed their analytical skills and cultural awareness.

Still, let's not be too hard on ourselves. As an institution, the U.S. Armed Forces stand head and shoulders above any other military in skill, equipment and compassion, and its leaders are able, conscientious, and loyal.

But shame on political leaders who would hide behind their top generals. It was hard not to catch a whiff of that during last week's hearings. The Constitution, however, is not ambivalent about where the responsiblity for command lies—the president is the commander in chief.

Surely here is where some of the most salient lessons from recent wars lie: in forcing civilian leaders to shoulder their burdens of ultimate responsibility and in demanding that generals unflinchingly offer their toughest, most seasoned, advice. Gen. Tommy R. Franks embarked on the 2001 Afghanistan operation without a clear road map for success, or even a definition of what victory would look like. Somehow, that was good enough for him and his bosses. So Osama bin Laden slunk away, the Taliban was allowed to regroup, and Afghanistan is now mired deep in trouble and sinking fast.

In Iraq, President Bush approved war-fighting plans that hadn't incorporated any of the vital 1990s lessons from Haiti, Bosnia, or Kosovo; worse, then-Defense Secretary Donald H. Rumsfeld fought doing so. Nation-building, however ideologically repulsive some may find it, is a capability that a superpower sometimes needs.

At the same time, the United States' top generals must understand that their duty is to win, not just to get along. They must have the insight and character to demand the resources necessary to succeed—and have the guts to either obtain what they need or to resign. If they get their way and still don't emerge victorious, they must be replaced. That is the lot they accepted when they pinned on those four shiny silver stars.

Above all else, we Americans must understand that the goal of war is to achieve a specific purpose for the nation. In this respect, the military is simply a tool of statecraft, one that must work in tandem with diplomacy, economic suasion, intelligence, and other instruments of U.S. power. How tragic it is to see old men who are unwilling to talk to potential adversaries but seem so ready to dispatch young people to fight and die.

So, steady as we go. We need to tweak our force structure, hone our leadership, and learn everything we can about how to do everything better. But the big lesson is simply this: War is the last, last, last resort. It always brings tragedy and rarely brings glory. Take it from a general who won: The best war is the one that doesn't have to be fought, and the best military is the one capable and versatile enough to deter the next war in the first place.

Suggestions for Discussion

1. Does Clark make a convincing case when he states that Iran is the next country with which we are most likely to go to war? Why does he say that we may find ourselves surprised when we discover our next military enemy?

2. Clark outlines a possible military strategy for defeating Iran in combat. However, what possible terrible scenarios might occur even if America does defeat Iran in war?

3. Why does Clark say it was a mistake for Americans in the military to think of themselves as "warriors"? According to Clark, why are education and cultural sensitivity important to soldiers and the U.S. military leadership?

4. How might Wesley Clark react to the essay "Columbine: Whose Fault Is it?" by Marilyn Manson?

Suggestions for Writing

1. Clark's argument cannot be easily caricatured as "pro-war" or "anti-war." It is what Joseph Williams and Grey Colomb might call a nuanced argument. Nevertheless, his message is clear. Summarize and restate it without distorting it or evaluating it to demonstrate that you grasp the subtleties of his argument.

2. Once you have successfully summarized Clark's argument, write a response.

3. Watch enough footage of General Petraeus's testimony before Congress of September 10, 2007, to develop an informed opinion about it. What are your reactions to it? Research some other editorials and statements of politicians and military strategists who also reacted to the testimony at the time. Write an essay in which you evaluate who has done the fairest analysis of Petraeus's report.

HOWARD GARDNER

Leading Beyond the Nation-State

Howard Gardner (b. 1943) is a professor of education at the Harvard Graduate School of Education and codirector of Harvard Project Zero, a long-term study of human intellectual and creative development. He is the author of more than twenty books, including *Frames of Mind: The Theory of Multiple Intelligences* (1985), *Creating Minds* (1993), *The Disciplined Mind: Beyond Facts and Standardized Tests* (2000), and *Intelligence Reframed* (2000). In this selection, from *Changing Minds* (2004), Gardner profiles three leaders who have exerted positive influences through persuasive storytelling.

Although relatively few positions exist for leaders of entities larger than a single nation, the topic is well worth exploring in any effort to understand how minds are changed. Sometimes, such a transnational position has a predetermined constituency; for example, the secretary-general of the United Nations or the head of the World Health Organization. The leader of the Catholic Church, or of other religious bodies, may well have influence that extends beyond a single land. And indeed, Pope John Paul II stands out among the popes of recent times because he has exerted influence not only over the members of his far-flung church but also, in some matters, over non-Catholics as well. Far more than his immediate predecessors, with the exception of John XXIII, John Paul II has been able both to fashion stories about political and personal values and to embody them in the impressive life that he has lived. Pope John XXIII, operating in the 1960s, was an avowedly simple pastor who called for a liberalization of the church and a decentralization of power; in partial reaction two decades later, John Paul II embraced the traditional conservative values of the church and located the reins of power squarely within the Vatican. At the same time, however, John Paul II is the most traveled and international of Popes, one who has forged a special tie with the young of different lands, and one who has been credited with an indispensable role in the collapse of Communism in Eastern Europe.

On rare occasions, individuals with neither vast armies nor vast congregations have succeeded in exerting influence well beyond national boundaries. Like the successful leaders of nations that we've already examined, they have done so because of the persuasiveness of their stories and the steadfastness with which they have reinforced those stories through their manner of living. In the twentieth century, three men stand out as exemplars in this category: Mohandas (Mahatma) Gandhi, Nelson Mandela, and Jean Monnet.

Perhaps the most well-known is Gandhi. Growing up in undistinguished surroundings in late-nineteenth-century colonial India, Gandhi spent time in England as a young man and then lived for twenty years in South Africa. There he was horrified by the mistreatment by European colonizers of Indians and other "colored persons": he read widely in philosophy and religion; and he became involved in various protests. Returning to his native India at the start of the World War I, Gandhi perfected methods of satyagraha—peaceful (nonviolent) protest (or resistance). Alongside his devoted countrymen, Gandhi led a series of strikes and protest marches, destined to throw into sharp relief the differences between the brutal English masters—who sought to hold power at any cost—and the nonbelligerent Indians. These protests were choreographed to underscore the nobility of the native cause and the reasonableness with which Indians were striving to express their goals. Gandhi's overt message was: "We do not seek to make war or shed blood. We only want to be treated as fellow human beings. Once we have achieved the status of equals, we have no further claims."

In one sense, Gandhi's message could not have been simpler: It can be traced back to Christ and to other religious leaders. Yet, it also clashed with an entrenched counterstory: that one can only attain an equal status vis-à-vis one's colonizers if—like the United States in the late eighteenth century or South America in the early nineteenth century—one is willing to go to war. Moreover, Gandhi did not only have a simple linguistic message; he also developed an integrated program of prayer, fasting, and facing one's opponents without weapons, even willing to do so until death. His embodiment of the message could not have been more dramatic; it went well beyond verbal expression, to include a whole range of evocative formats, such as his squatting on the ground and operating a simple machine for spinning cloth.

Gandhi's story reverberated around the world. While annoying some (Churchill memorably disparaged him as that "half-naked fakir"), it inspired many leaders and ordinary citizens—ranging from Martin Luther King Jr. in the American South in the early 1960s, to the students who rallied for greater democracy in Tiananmen Square in Beijing in 1989.

Like Gandhi, Nelson Mandela embodied a message that resonated on a level far beyond the borders of his own South Africa. Indeed, of all the leaders in recent years, Mandela is widely considered one of the most impressive and influential. A lawyer by training, Mandela became actively involved in resistance as part of the African National Congress. At first, he embraced nonviolent resistance, but after a series of frustrating and degrading encounters, he joined a paramilitary group. Narrowly escaping death by combat or judicial sentence, Mandela was imprisoned for twenty-seven years. Although such an experience would likely have demoralized, radicalized, or marginalized most other persons—especially since it occurred at middle age, often considered the apogee of an individual's personal power—imprisonment seemed only to fortify Mandela. On his release, he rejected any effort to engage in armed conflict; instead he worked with his political opponent F.W. de Klerk to set up democratic institutions, and in 1994 he went on to win the presidency of a post-apartheid South Africa.

Rather than seeking revenge against his opponents and jailers, Mandela called for reconciliation. He was convinced—and was able to convince others—that South Africa could not function as a society unless it could put its wrenching history behind it. Under the leadership of Nobel Peace Prize winner Archbishop Desmond Tutu, Mandela convened a Commission of Truth and Reconciliation. The Gandhian idea behind this commission was that it would seek to establish what actually happened during the years of apartheid but would not attempt to sit in ultimate judgment. The truth having been established as well as it could be, citizens of varying persuasions could come to terms with the past and commit their future energies to the buildup of a new and more fully representative society. A master of nonverbal as well as verbal forms, Mandela asked his one-time jailer to sit in the first row during his presidential inaugural ceremony.

Mandela succeeded in changing the minds not only of millions of his otherwise diverse fellow citizens but equally of millions of observers around the world—few of whom would have predicted that South Africa could become a new nation without decades of bloodshed. Ideas like the Commission on Truth and Reconciliation have traveled across national boundaries. The tipping points for Mandela's success entail both his exemplary behavior after his release from jail and the willingness of the entrenched South African leadership to negotiate with him—both examples reflecting Mandela's personal resonance, among other things.

A third figure of global importance worked largely behind the scenes; the French economist and diplomat Jean Monnet, born in 1888. When his comfortable life was shattered by the events of World War I, Monnet—a careful and reflective student of history—pondered why it was necessary for European countries to continue to go to war, as they had intermittently since the time of Charlemagne more than a thousand years before. He began to work toward the creation of institutions that could bring about a united Europe. After the trauma of World War I, the collapse of the League of Nations, the rise of fascism, and the unprecedented warfare of World War II, a lesser person would have concluded that attempts to build a European community were futile. Monnet, however, was a firm believer in his own oft-repeated slogan: "I regard every defeat (or every challenge) as an opportunity." Amid the physical and psychological ruins of war-torn Europe, Monnet envisioned—and proceeded to sow—the seeds of a larger European polity.

Like Gandhi and Mandela, Monnet had been pursuing his mission for half a century and was well into his seventies by the time of his greatest impact. During the post–World War II period, he played a catalytic role in setting up a number of institutions, including the European Coal and Steel Community, the Action Committee of the United States of Europe, and the European common market. He was opposed nearly every step of the way, most notably by General Charles de Gaulle, the charismatic advocate of French autonomy, and by other nationalists of the Thatcher stripe. Yet while de Gaulle may have prevailed with the French electorate in the 1960s, Monnet's vision has ultimately triumphed on the Continent. After Monnet's death in 1979, the European Union was well launched, the euro was adopted in twelve countries, and, as of this writing, the United States of Europe are closer to a reality than at any time since the Napoleonic era.

Unlike a president, a pope, or the leader of an international organization such as the United Nations, neither Gandhi, nor Mandela, nor Monnet had a dedicated, guaranteed audience. They had to create their constituencies from scratch, with neither financial inducements nor coercive political weapons. They had to identify and speak to an opposition that held power: leaders of South Africa and colonial India, in Gandhi's case; the defenders of apartheid in Mandela's case; and the entrenched national interests of Europe in Monnet's case. At the same time they had to address and convince a lay constituency. Neither Gandhi nor Mandela could have led the fight for independence without an "army" of ordinary followers, who, in the extreme, were prepared to die nonviolently for their cause. And while Monnet worked significantly behind the scenes in the manner of what I term an "indirect" leader, his vision of Europe ultimately has had to triumph at the ballot box. Indeed, it has still not triumphed in nations such as Switzerland and Norway, which (surprisingly) remain outside of the Union.

As leaders addressing heterogeneous audiences, these men had available only the weapons of persuasion and embodiment. They had to tell their stories over and over again, tell them well, and embody their stories in appropriate life actions and evocative symbolic elements. They had to recognize, acknowledge, and ultimately undermine the regnant counterstories. And it is here that they showed their genius.

Hard as it is to mobilize a heterogeneous audience, the established way of doing so is to fashion and articulate a story that is serene in its simplicity. Indeed, the bitter lesson of the first half of the twentieth century is that the simplest and most awful stories generally triumph: The goal of politics is to attain power and to use it toward selfish ends; Might makes right; The state is all-powerful—one must do what it says or perish. These simple stories led to the triumph of terrifying "isms" of the left and the right: fascism, nazism, bolshevism, communism. One might even say that the hateful policies of Hitler, Mussolini, Tojo, Lenin, Stalin, and Mao Zedong convinced the majority of their countrymen; their popularity only waned when military defeat was imminent or starvation threatened. It appeared that in most of the world's nations, these "isms" were more appealing than democracy. Churchill well described this enigma in his oft-quoted comment that "democracy is the worst form of Government except for all those other forms that have been tried from time to time."

Gandhi, Mandela, and Monnet did not, however, take the easy way out. They did not just tell a simple, familiar story more effectively. Rather, they took on a far more daunting task: to develop a new story, tell it well, embody it in their lives, and help others understand why it deserves to triumph over the simpler counterstory. Moreover, they drew continually and imaginatively on several other levers of mind change: reason, multiple modes of representation, and resonance with the experiences of those whom they sought to influence. At the same time, they attempted to mollify the resistances that they encountered; they took advantage of real world events; and they marshaled whatever resources they had at their disposal. On a personal note,

GLOBALISM, NATIONALISM, AND CULTURAL IDENTITY

these three men are my own chosen heroic leaders. They took a more complex, less familiar story, a story that was more "inclusive," and succeeded in giving that story life in institutions that continued beyond their own moments in the limelight.

Suggestions for Discussion

1. How does Gardner distinguish Gandhi, Mandela, and Monnet from leaders with guaranteed audiences, such as presidents and popes?

2. What qualities do Gardner's "chosen heroic leaders" share, and in what ways are they different?

3. What are the various forms of expression—both verbal and nonverbal—employed by Gandhi, Mandela, and Monnet? Cite at least one specific example for each.

Suggestion for Writing

Compare in an essay Gardner's ideas about leadership with the philosophy of Niccolò Machiavelli's "Of Cruelty and Clemency."

PERSONAL WRITING

CHRIS HEDGES

The Ten Commandments
in America

Chris Hedges (b. 1956), who was part of the *New York Times* journalistic team that won the 2002 Pulitzer Prize for its coverage of global terrorism, has worked for *The Christian Science Monitor*, National Public Radio, *The Dallas Morning News*, and *The New York Times*. He spent over two decades of his career as a foreign correspondent for Central America, Africa, the Middle East, and the Balkans. Hedges was an early critic of the Bush administration's plan to invade and occupy Iraq and has written several books on war and religion, including *War is a Force That Gives Us Meaning* (2002), *What Every Person Should Know About War* (2003), and *American Fascists: The Christian Right and the War on America* (2007).

The 10 Commandments

You shall have no other gods before me.

You shall not make for yourself a graven image, or any likeness of anything that is in heaven above, or that is in the earth beneath, or that is in the water under the earth; you shall not bow down to them, or serve them.

You shall not take the name of the Lord your God in vain.

Remember the sabbath day, to keep it holy.

Honor your father and your mother.

You shall not kill.

You shall not commit adultery.

You shall not steal.

You shall not bear false witness against your neighbor.

You shall not covet your neighbor's house.

The commandments are a list of religious edicts, according to passages in Exodus and Deuteronomy, given to Moses by God on Mount Sinai. The first four are designed to guide the believer toward a proper relationship with God. The remaining six deal with our relations with others. It is these final six commands that are given the negative form of "You Shall Not. . . ." Only two of the commandments, the prohibitions against stealing and murder, are incorporated into our legal code. Protestants, Catholics and Jews have compiled slightly different lists, but the core demands of the commandments remain the same. Muslims, while they do not list the commandments in the Koran, honor the laws of Moses, whom they see as a prophet.

The commandments are one of the earliest attempts to lay down rules and guidelines to sustain community. The commandments include the most severe violations and moral dilemmas in human life, although these violations often lie beyond the scope of the law. They were for the ancients, and are for us, the rules that, when honored, hold us together and when dishonored lead to alienation, discord and violence.

The commandments choose us. We are rarely able to choose them. We do not, however hard we work to insulate ourselves, ultimately control our fate. We cannot save ourselves from betrayal, theft, envy, greed, deception and murder, nor always from the impulses that propel us to commit these acts. These violations, often committed without warning, can leave deep, lifelong wounds. Most of us wrestle profoundly with at least one of these violations.

My renewed fascination with the depth and breadth of the commandments came shortly after I returned to New York City after nearly two decades as a foreign correspondent who covered conflicts in Latin America, Africa, the Middle East and the former Yugoslavia. I was unsure of where I was headed. I had lost the emotional and physical resiliency that allowed me to cope in war. I was plagued by memories I wanted to forget, waking suddenly in the middle of the night, my sleep shattered by visions of gunfire and death. I felt alienated from those around me, unaccustomed to the common language and images imposed by popular culture, unable to communicate the pain and suffering I had witnessed, not much interested in building a career.

We lived in a tiny apartment in Manhattan. My son and daughter shared a bedroom. The monthly mortgage payments plunged me into debt. I had, in the past, rarely seen or spoken with editors, who were hundreds or thousands of miles away. I was uncomfortable in the newsroom. My solace came in walking the streets of the city after taking my son and daughter to school. I started early one morning at the very bottom of Manhattan. I walked eighty blocks uptown, peering into some shops, ignoring others, brushing past the mix of races and nationalities, listening to the variety of language and the din of the streets. These mosaics comforted me. There are too many differences in New York to force iron conformity. I had reported from over fifty countries. The narrow definitions of race, religion and nation had been broadened and erased by friendship and experience, by the recognition that those we sometimes find alien and strange often reflect back to us parts of ourselves we do not understand.

The Brooklyn Academy of Music was showing a ten-part series called The Decalogue. "The Decalogue" is the classical name of the 10 Commandments. "Deka-," in Greek, means ten. "Logos" means saying or speech. The director, I read in the announcement, was the Polish filmmaker Krzysztof Kieslowski who had made a trilogy called *White, Blue and Red*. The Decalogue films, each about an hour and based on one of the commandments, were to be shown two at a time over five consecutive weeks. I saw them on Sunday nights, taking the subway to Brooklyn, its cars rocking and screeching along the tracks in the darkened tunnels. The theater was rarely more than half full.

The films were quiet, subtle and often opaque. It was sometimes hard to tell which commandment was being addressed. The characters never spoke about the commandments directly. They were too busy, as we all are, coping with the duress of life. The stories presented the lives of ordinary people confronted by extraordinary events. All lived in a Warsaw housing complex, many of them neighbors, reinforcing the notion of our being on a common voyage, yet also out of touch with the pain and dislocation of those around us. The commandments, Kieslowski understood, were not dusty relics of another age, but spoke in important ways to the human predicament.

He dealt with the core violations raised by the commandments. He freed the commandments from the clutter of piety. The promiscuous woman portrayed in the film about adultery was not married. She had a series of carnal relationships. Adultery, for the director, was at its deepest level sex without love. The father in the film about honoring our parents was not the biological father. Yet the biological mother was absent in the daughter's life. Parenting, Kieslowski understood, is not defined by blood or birth or gender. It is defined by commitment, fidelity and love.

I knew the commandments. I had learned them at Sunday school, listened to sermons based on the commandments from my father's pulpit and studied them as a seminarian. But watching Kieslowski turn them into living, breathing entities gave them a new resonance.

"For 6,000 years these rules have been unquestionably right," Kieslowski said of the commandments. "And yet we break them every day. We know what we should do, and yet we fail to live as we should. People feel that something is wrong in life. There is some kind of atmosphere that makes people turn now to other values. They want to contemplate the basic questions of life, and that is probably the real reason for wanting to tell these stories."

In eight of the films there was a brief appearance by a young man, solemn and silent. Kieslowski said he did not know who he was. Perhaps he was an angel or Christ. Perhaps he represented the divine presence who observed with profound sadness the tragedy and folly we humans commit against others and ourselves.

"He's not very pleased with us," the director said.

When our lives are shattered by tragedy, suffering and pain, or when we express or feel the ethereal and overwhelming power of love, we confront the mystery of good and evil. Voices across time and cultures have struggled to transmit and pay homage to this mystery, what it means for our lives and our place in the cosmos. No human being, no nation, no religion, has been chosen by God to be the sole interpreter of mystery. All cultures struggle to give words to the experience of the transcendent. This is the most powerful testament to the reality of God. It is a reminder that all of us find God not in what we know, but in what we cannot comprehend and cannot see.

These voices, whether in the teachings of the Buddha, the writings of Latin poets or the pages of the Koran, are part of our common struggle as human beings to acknowledge the eternal and the sacred. Nearly every religion has set down an ethical and moral code that is strikingly similar to the 10 Commandments. The Eightfold Path, known within Buddhism as the Wheel of Law, forbids murder, unchastity, theft, falsehood and, especially, covetous desire. The sacred syllable "Om" for Hindus, said or sung before and after prayers, ends with a fourth sound beyond the range of human hearing. This sound is called the "sound of silence." It is also called "the sound of the universe." It is in the repetition of the Sacred Syllable that Hindus try to go beyond thought, to reach the stillness and silence that constitutes God. These are all constructs that the biblical writers would have recognized.

The more we listen to the voices of others, voices unlike our own, the more we remain open to the transcendent forces that save us from idolatry. The more we listen to ourselves, the more we create God in our own image until God becomes a tawdry idol that looks and speaks like us. The power of the commandments is found not in the writings of theologians, although I read and admire some, but in the pathos of human life, including lives that are very unlike our own. All states and nations work to pervert religions into civic religions, ones where the goals of the state become the goals of the divine. This is increasingly true in the United States. But once we believe we understand the will of God and can act as agents of God we become dangerous, a menace to others and a menace to ourselves. We forget that we do not understand. We forget to listen.

In 1983, I was in a United Nations camp for Guatemalan refugees in Honduras. Those in the camp had fled fighting. Most had seen family members killed. The refugees, when I arrived on a dreary January afternoon, were decorating the tents and wooden warehouses with colored paper. They told me they would celebrate the flight of Mary, Joseph and the infant Jesus to Egypt to escape the slaughter ordered by Herod of the children.

Why, I asked one of the peasants, was this an important day?

"It was on this day that Christ became a refugee," he answered.

I knew this Bible passage by heart. I had heard my father read it every year. But until that moment, standing in a muddy refugee camp with a man who may not have been able to read, I did not understand it. This passage meant one thing to me and another to parents who had swept children into their arms and fled to escape death. The commandments can only be understood in moments when they are no longer abstractions. Scholarship, especially biblical scholarship, divorced from experience is narrow, self-absorbed and frequently irrelevant. I learned more about this passage from a Salvadoran farmer than I ever could have from a theologian.

This book is about the lives of people, including myself, who have struggled on a deep and visceral level with one of the commandments. It came out of a series I wrote for *The New York Times*. Some of the stories in the series made it into the book, some did not. Those I write about, from Bishop George Packard, the former platoon leader in Vietnam, to R. Foster Winans, who went to prison for insider trading, cope with lives that have been turned upside down by an intense and overpowering experience with one of the commandments. There is nothing abstract about the commandments to those who know the sting of their violation or have neglected their call. It is this power I want to impart.

The commandments guide us toward relationships built on trust rather than fear. Only through trust can there be love. Those who ignore the commandments diminish the possibility of love, the single force that keeps us connected, whole and saved from physical and psychological torment. A life where the commandments are routinely dishonored becomes a life of solitude, guilt, anger and remorse. The wars I covered from Central America to Yugoslavia were places where the sanctity and respect for human life, that which the commandments protect, were ignored. Bosnia, with its rape camps, genocide, looting, razing of villages, its heady intoxication with violence, power and death, illustrated, like all wars, what happens when societies thrust the commandments aside.

The commandments do not protect us from evil. They protect us from committing evil. The commandments are designed to check our darker impulses, warning us that pandering to impulses can have terrible consequences. "If you would enter life," the Gospel of Matthew reads, "keep the commandments" (Matthew 19:17). The commandments hold community together. It is community that gives our lives, even in pain and grief, a healing solidarity. It is fealty to community that frees us from the dictates of our idols, idols that promise us fulfillment through the destructive impulses of constant self-gratification. The commandments call us to reject and defy powerful forces that can rule our lives and to live instead for others, even if this costs us status and prestige and wealth. The commandments show us how to avoid being enslaved, how to save us from ourselves. They lead us to love, the essence of life.

The German philosopher Ludwig Wittgenstein said, "Tell me 'how' you seek and I will tell you 'what' you are seeking." We are all seekers, even if we do not always know what we are looking to find. We are all seekers, even if we do not always know how to frame the questions. This is what the commandments do for us. In those questions, even more than the answers, we find hope in the strange and contradictory fragments of our lives.

Suggestions for Discussion

1. How does Hedges modernize the Ten Commandments? How does he adapt them to be relevant for today's society?

2. Where does Hedges believe that God is found?

3. What is the importance of listening? What happens when we forget to listen?

4. Hedges suggests that the "commandments can only be understood in moments when they are no longer abstractions." What does he mean by this? At what points can the Commandments move beyond the level of abstraction?

5. What part do the Commandments play in constructing a sense of community?

Suggestions for Writing

1. Choose one of the Ten Commandments and write two paragraphs about what it could mean in your modern life.

2. Summarize Hedges's essay about the modernity of the Ten Commandments. Discuss how this essay has increased your understanding of the decree, or how it has further complicated your perspective.

SALMAN RUSHDIE

Imagine There's No Heaven

After publishing *The Satanic Verses* in 1988, novelist Salman Rushdie (b. 1947) was the subject of a *fatwa*, or death threat, for blasphemy by the Islamic fundamentalist leader of Iran, the Ayatollah Khomeini. The Bombay-born author lived in hiding and under guard for many years, considered a hero by many for his refusal to retract the novel. More recently Rushdie has emerged and begun living a public life again, although the *fatwa* has never officially been lifted. His controversial works have won critical praise for their dense beauty and philosophical brilliance. The Cambridge educated author's other books include *Grimus* (1975), the Booker-Prize-winning *Midnight's Children* (1981), *Shame* (1983), *Haroun and the Sea of Stories* (1990), *Homelands* (1991), *The Moor's Last Sigh* (1995), *The Ground Beneath Her Feet* (1999), *Shalimar The Clown* (2005), and *The Enchantress of Florence* (2008). Anticipating the occasion of the birth of the world's six-billionth citizen in 1997, the United Nations asked Rushdie, among others, to write open letters to the newborn. Rushie's contribution, reprinted here, was typically controversial, alarming the then-U.N. Secretary-General Kofi Annan, and once again placing Rushdie at the center of heated debates about organized religion and freedom of speech.

Dear Little Six Billionth Living Person,

As the newest member of a notoriously inquisitive species, it probably won't be too long before you start asking the two sixty-four thousand dollar questions with which the other 5,999,999,999 of us have been wrestling for some time: How did we get here? And, now that we are here, how shall we live?

Oddly—as if six billion of us weren't enough to be going on with—it will almost certainly be suggested to you that the answer to the question of origins requires you to believe in the existence of a further, invisible, ineffable Being "somewhere up there," an omnipotent creator whom we poor limited creatures are unable even to perceive, much less to understand. That is, you will be strongly encouraged to imagine a heaven with at least one god in residence. This sky-god, it's said, made the universe by churning its matter in a giant pot. Or he danced. Or he vomited Creation out of himself. Or he simply called it into being, and lo, it Was. In some of the more interesting creation stories, the single mighty sky-god is subdivided into many lesser forces— junior deities, *avatars*, gigantic metamorphic "ancestors" whose adventures create the landscape, or the whimsical, wanton, meddling, cruel pantheons of the great polytheisms, whose wild doings will convince you that the real engine of creation was lust: for infinite power, for too-easily-broken human bodies, for clouds of glory. But it's only fair to add that there are also stories which offer the message that the primary creative impulse was, and is, love.

Many of these stories will strike you as extremely beautiful and, therefore, seductive. Unfortunately, however, you will not be required to make a purely literary response to them. Only the stories of "dead" religions can be appreciated for their beauty. Living religions require much more of you. So you will be told that belief in "your" stories and adherence to the rituals of worship that have grown up around them must become a vital part of your life in the crowded world. They will be called the heart of your culture, even of your individual identity. It is possible that they may, at some point, come to feel inescapable, not in the way that the truth is inescapable, but in the way that a jail is. They may at some point cease to feel like the texts in which human beings have tried to solve a great mystery, and feel, instead, like the pretexts for other properly anointed human beings to order you around. And it's true that human history is full of the public oppression wrought by the charioteers of the gods. In the opinion of religious people, however, the private comfort that religion brings more than compensates for the evil done in its name.

As human knowledge has grown, it has also become plain that every religious story ever told about how we got here is quite simply wrong. This, finally, is what all religions have in common. They didn't get it right. There was no celestial churning, no maker's dance, no vomiting of galaxies, no snake or kangaroo ancestors, no Valhalla, no Olympus, no six-day conjuring trick followed by a day of rest. Wrong, wrong, wrong. But here's something genuinely odd. The wrongness of the sacred tales hasn't lessened the zeal of the devout. If anything, the sheer out-of-step zaniness of religion leads the religious to insist ever more stridently on the importance of blind faith.

As a result of this faith, by the way, it has proved impossible in many parts of the world to prevent the human race's numbers from swelling alarmingly. Blame the overcrowded planet at least partly on the misguidedness of the race's spiritual guides. In your own lifetime, you may well witness the arrival of the nine billionth world citizen. If you're Indian (and there's a one-in-six chance that you are) you will be alive when, thanks to the failure of family planning schemes in that poor, God-ridden land, its population surges past China's. And "too many people are being born as a result, in part, of religious strictures against birth control, then too many people are also dying because religious culture, by refusing to face the facts of human sexuality, also refuses to fight against the spread of sexually transmitted diseases.

There are those who say that the great wars of the new century will once again be wars of religion, jihads, and crusades, as they were in the Middle Ages. Even though, for years now, the air has been full of the battle-cries of the faithful as they turn their bodies into God's bombs, and the screams of their victims too, I have not wanted to believe this theory, or not in the way most people mean it.

I have long argued that Samuel Huntington's "clash of civilizations" theory is an oversimplification: that most Muslims have no interest in taking part in religious wars, that the divisions in the Muslim world run as deep as the things it has in common (just take a look at the Sunni-Shia conflict in Iraq if you doubt the truth of this). There's very little resembling a common Islamic purpose to be found. Even after the non-Islamic Nato fought a war for the Muslim Kosovar Albanians, the Muslim world was slow in coming forward with much-needed humanitarian aid.

The real wars of religion, I have argued, are the wars religions unleash against ordinary citizens within their "sphere of influence." They are wars of the godly against the largely defenseless: American fundamentalists against pro-choice doctors, Iranian mullahs against their country's Jewish minority, the Taliban against the people of Afghanistan, Hindu fundamentalists in Bombay against that city's increasingly fearful Muslims.

And the real wars of religion are also the wars religions unleash against unbelievers, whose unbearable unbelief is re-characterized as an offense, as a sufficient reason for their eradication.

But as time has passed I have been obliged to recognize a harsh truth: that the mass of so-called ordinary Muslims seems to have bought into the paranoid fantasies of the extremists and seems to spend more of its energy in mobilizing against cartoonists, novelists, or the Pope than in condemning, disenfranchising, and expelling the fascistic murderers in their midst. If this silent majority allows a war to be waged in its name, then it does, finally, become complicit in that war.

So perhaps a war of religion is beginning, after all, because the worst of us are being allowed to dictate the agenda to the rest of us, and because the fanatics, who really mean business, are not being opposed strongly enough by "their own people."

And if that is so, then the victors in such a war must not be the closed-minded, marching into battle with, as ever, God on their side. To choose unbelief is to choose mind over dogma, to trust in our humanity instead of all these dangerous divinities. So, how did we get here? Don't look for the answer in "sacred" storybooks. Imperfect human knowledge maybe be a bumpy, pot-holed street, but it's the only road to wisdom worth taking. Virgil, who believed that the apiarist Aristaeus could spontaneously generate new bees from the rotting carcass of a cow, was closer to a truth about origins than all the revered old books.

The ancient wisdoms are modern nonsenses. Live in your own time, use what we know, and as you grow up, perhaps the human race will finally grow up with you and put aside childish things.

As the song says, *It's easy if you try.*

As for morality, the second great question—how to live? what is right action, and what wrong?—it comes down to your willingness to think for yourself. Only you can decide if you want to be handed down the law by priests and accept that good and evil are somehow external to ourselves. To my mind religion, even at its most sophisticated, essentially infantilizes our ethical selves by setting infallible moral Arbiters and irredeemably immoral Tempters above us: the eternal parents, good and bad, light and dark, of the supernatural realm.

How, then, are we to make ethical choices without a divine rulebook or judge? Is unbelief just the first step on the long slide into the brain-death of cultural relativism, according to which many unbearable things—female circumcision, to name just one—can be excused on culturally specific grounds, and the universality of human rights, too, can be ignored?

(This last piece of moral unmaking finds supporters in some of the world's most authoritarian régimes, and also, unnervingly, on the op-ed pages of the *Daily Telegraph.*)

Well, no, it isn't, but the reasons for saying so aren't clear cut. Only hard-line ideology is clear cut. Freedom, which is the word I use for the secular-ethical position, is inevitably fuzzier. Yes, freedom is that space in which contradiction can reign; it is a never-ending debate. It is not in itself the answer to the question of morals but the conversation about that question.

And it is much more than mere relativism because it is not merely a never-ending talk-shop but a place in which choices are made, values defined and defended. Intellectual freedom, in European history, has mostly meant freedom from the restraints of the Church, not the state. This is the battle Voltaire was fighting, and it's also what all six billion of us could do for ourselves, the revolution in which each of us could play our small, six-billionth part: once and for all, we could refuse to allow priests, and the fictions on whose behalf they claim to speak, to be the policemen of our liberties and behavior. Once and for all, we could put the stories back into the books, put the books back on the shelves, and see the world undogmatized and plain.

Imagine there's no heaven, my dear Six Billionth, and at once the sky's the limit.

Suggestions for Discussion

1. According to Rushdie, what was the original intention of creation myths? How has that changed over time? How has the emergence of scientific knowledge about the earth challenged the accuracy of such stories?

2. Why does Rushdie question the concept of the "clash of civilizations"? Instead, what kind of holy war does he envision is occurring now? Which side does Rushdie want to win? Why?

3. What are Rushdie's concerns regarding world population and health issues?

Suggestions for Writing

1. Rushdie denies the notion that a world without God is a world of anarchy, moral relativism, and evil. What evidence does he use to support his argument? Do you agree with it? Write a paper either agreeing or disagreeing with Rushdie, supporting your position with examples or evidence from your own research.

2. Synthesis: Compare and contrast Rushdie's letter to Chris Hedges' "The Ten Commandments in America" and/or Oscar Wilde's "The Soul of Man Under Socialism."

ESSAYS

PEGGY NOONAN

The Case for Getting Off Base

Currently a columnist for the *Wall Street Journal*, Peggy Noonan
(b. 1950) is best known for serving as a speech writer and special assistant to President Ronald Reagan in the 1980s. Noonan's work included
some of the most memorable and oft-quoted addresses of the Reagan-
Bush administration, including Reagan's commemoration of the forti-
eth anniversary of D-Day, his famous address consoling the nation after
the destruction of the Space Shuttle Challenger, and George H. W. Bush's
pledge to create "a kinder, gentler nation." She has written eight books,
including *What I Saw at the Revolution* (1990), *Life, Liberty and the Pursuit of Happiness* (1994), *Simply Speaking* (1998), *The Case Against
Hillary Clinton* (2000), *When Character Was King* (2001), *A Heart, a
Cross and a Flag* (2003), *John Paul the Great* (2005), and *Patriotic Grace*
(2008). Noonan began as a writer and producer for CBS News in New
York and WEEI Radio in Boston. She served as a consultant on the television series *The West Wing* from 2000 to 2002 and is a frequent commentator on a variety of television news and opinion shows. Although
she is a long-time Republican, Noonan's freewheeling criticisms of
George W. Bush and Sarah Palin have drawn the wrath of some conservatives. She remains a central voice in the reconstituting of the Republican Party in the aftermath of Barack Obama's presidential victory, and
this *WSJ* article, from June 12, 2009, is an example of her perspective.

In America almost everybody has a base, not only political parties. Businesses do, and public figures, and Web sites. We attempt to quantify to the
nth degree everybody's numbers, ratings, page views. These tell us how big
a base is and, roughly, who is in it.

"The base" is a great if largely unspoken preoccupation in broad segments of our public life. In fact we have developed baseitis. Is this good?

What occasions the question is the USA Today story this week on a
Gallup poll saying nearly half the country's Republicans and Republican-
leaners can't come up with a name when asked who their party's leader is.

675

Of those who could think of a name, 10% said Rush Limbaugh, 10% Newt Gingrich, 9% Dick Cheney. Among Democrats, on the other hand, 83% could think of a leader of their party. Most of them said it was President Obama. This makes sense, yes?

The poll was a source of, or excuse for, interparty needling (the base likes that) and faux sympathy on cable news (their base likes that too.) What no one notes is the poll makes no sense, or rather makes so much sense that it's not news.

The Democrats have a leader. He's the president. When a party has a president, he's the leader.

Parties out of power, almost by definition, are in search of one. When parties do not hold the White House and Congress they are, of necessity, retooling and reshaping themselves. Leaders of various party factions, being humans in politics and therefore bearing within themselves unsleeping little engines of ambition (that's what Billy Herndon said lay inside his friend, unassuming prairie lawyer Abe Lincoln) will jostle each other for place.

The last time the Republican Party was in this position was 1977–78, after Watergate and the 1976 victory of Jimmy Carter. The Republicans then had no leader of the party, or rather there were a number of leaders: Rep. John Anderson was a leading moderate, Howard Baker was in the Senate, and Rep. Jack Kemp was a promising conservative. Out West, Ronald Reagan, nearing 70, was writing commentaries and contemplating a third presidential run.

No one knew what would happen, who would rise.

The last time Democrats were in this position was eight years ago, when they'd lost the presidency and Congress. Who exactly was the Democratic leader at that time? Teddy Kennedy had the liberals' heart but he was going nowhere, Al Gore was in Europe growing a beard, Bill Clinton was out getting rich. Hillary Clinton was settling into New York. There was no leader. But there were people coming up in the states, including a state senator from Chicago named Barack Obama.

Everything changes, life is movement, leaders take time to emerge. Nationally our parties have produced both stasis and surprise.

What is different now, and it really is different, is that assisting and complicating the Republican process is something that didn't exist in 1977 and was only a nascent force in 2000, and that is the conservative media infrastructure. The Republican Party has never re-formed itself while such a thing existed. The infrastructure changes things just by being.

For the Republicans it's not all good news.

The good part is big: Absent a compelling leader with an actual vision of the future, conservative media (I speak here of the highly popular radio shows) lend a sense of dynamism to what used to be called Republican thought. Their hosts talk, explain, lead, providing information and arguments that in the past were unnoticed, unmentioned, uncovered. This has given an air of vitality, of presence, to Republican views.

But it constitutes a challenge to the party, too. Republican National Committee chairman Michael Steele learned this three months ago, when he said Rush Limbaugh was angry. Mr. Steele felt forced to grovel in apology because Rush is more powerful than he is. When Michael Steele gets up in the morning, 20 million people don't wait to hear his opinion. Rush made him look weak. That's not an especially good look when you're trying to rebuild a party.

Conservatives talking only to conservatives is like liberals talking only to liberals. A certain unreality can be enforced. It can encourage a false sense of momentum and dominance when you have an audience of millions saying, "You got that right, buddy."

More voters have declared themselves independents since Mr. Obama came into the presidency. He is popular and admired, but America remains in play. The White House knows this; it's why it is so keen and deadly in its political outreach and media operations. They're never not on the case. They know they can't afford to be.

And they're always presenting themselves as smiling centrists.

The commitment and focus of the Obama political/media operation is connected to the Democrats' knowledge that their position is strong but not fully secure. They aren't just trying to win, they're not only trying to hold on, they're trying to create a new Democratic majority built more or less along the fundamental lines of FDR's New Deal: a new, activist government; a fairer playing field; less inequity; the federal government as friend, goalie, coach and, in some cases, team owner. This isn't quite centrism, and yet they portray it as such, while using the conservative media infrastructure as a foil. The Democratic message on the Republicans has gone from "the party of no" to "the party of angry white men." If they get away with it, it will be in part because angry talkers in the conservative media infrastructure too often leave themselves open to the charge.

Both conservative media and liberal media are alike in that they have to keep the ratings up, or the numbers up, or the hits. If they lose audience, they can lose everything from clout to ad revenue. Because they have to keep the numbers up, they have to keep it hot, which actually has some effect on the national conversation. The mainstream media is only too happy to headline it when a radio talker says Sonia Sotomayor is a dope. The radio talker may be doing it to play to his base, but the mainstream media does it to show that Republicans are mean, thick and angry.

On left and right, on cable and radio, political hosts see gain in hyping the story, agitating and exciting their listeners. All of this creates a circular, self-enclosed world in which it gets hotter and hotter and tighter and tighter. (I remember when the liberals of the Democratic Party were like this, in the '80s. They talked only to themselves, and reinforced each other's views. It took them years to recover.)

Must the Obama administration micromanage General Motors, institute a new health-care system, and institute a new energy regime? Must they mow down the opposition, shutting them out of the development of important bills? Well, the base likes this.

Can the radio host or the freelance policy maker calm down, become less polar and more thoughtful (yawn)? That would leave his base turning the dial and maybe going elsewhere. Can the big left-wing and right-wing Web sites commit apostasy, rethink issues? In general, bases don't like that.

Everyone is looking to the base, the sliver, their piece of the pie, their slice of the demo. You wonder sometimes as you watch: Who's looking out for the country?

Suggestions for Discussion

1. Who is Noonan's chief audience for this article? What is her tone?

2. Whether you are a business or a political party, what are the pros and cons of catering to your "base"? What, according to Noonan, is "the case for getting off base"?

3. What is Noonan's assessment of conservative news commentary shows on radio and television? Does her assessment match yours?

4. How does Noonan's depiction of the core values represented by the Republican Party compare to those expressed by Dan Quayle in "Restoring Basic Values" (reprinted in this text)?

Suggestion for Writing

Consider the final question Noonan asks at the end of her article. How might she answer her own question? How might conservatives in the Republican Party? How might liberals in the Democratic Party? How would you answer the question? Support your views with examples.

NICCOLÒ MACHIAVELLI

Of Cruelty and Clemency, and Whether It Is Better to Be Loved or Feared

Niccolò Machiavelli (1469–1527) was a Florentine statesman. His best-known work, *The Prince*, written in 1513, is an astute analysis of the contemporary political scene. The work was first translated into English in 1640. This selection from *The Prince*, translated by Luigi Ricci and revised by E. R. P. Vincent, explains by examples from history why the prince must rely on the fear he creates rather than the love he might generate. Machiavelli explains also why the prince, though causing fear, must avoid incurring hatred.

Proceeding to the other qualities before named, I say that every prince must desire to be considered merciful and not cruel. He must, however, take care not to misuse this mercifulness. Cesare Borgia was considered cruel, but his cruelty had brought order to the Romagna, united it, and reduced it to peace and fealty. If this is considered well, it will be seen that he was really much more merciful than the Florentine people, who, to avoid the name of cruelty, allowed Pistoia to be destroyed. A prince, therefore, must not mind incurring the charge of cruelty for the purpose of keeping his subjects united and faithful; for, with a very few examples, he will be more merciful than those who, from excess of tenderness, allow disorders to arise, from whence spring bloodshed and rapine; for these as a rule injure the whole community, while the executions carried out by the prince injure only individuals. And of all princes, it is impossible for a new prince to escape the reputation of cruelty, new states being always full of dangers. Wherefore Virgil through the mouth of Dido says:

Res dura, et regni novitas me talia cogunt
  Moliri, et late fines custode tueri.*

Nevertheless, he must be cautious in believing and acting, and must not be afraid of his own shadow, and must proceed in a temperate manner with prudence and humanity, so that too much confidence does not render him incautious, and too much diffidence does not render him intolerant.

From this arises the question whether it is better to be loved more than feared, or feared more than loved. The reply is, that one ought to be both feared and loved, but as it is difficult for the two to go together, it is much safer to be feared than loved, if one of the two has to be wanting. For it may be said of men in general that they are ungrateful, voluble dissemblers, anxious to avoid danger, and covetous of gain; as long as you benefit them, they are entirely yours; they offer you their blood, their goods, their life, and their children, as I have before said, when the necessity is remote; but when it approaches, they revolt. And the prince who has relied solely on their words,

---

*Our harsh situation and the newness of our kingdom compel me to contrive such measure: and to guard our territory far and wide. (Dido offers this explanation to the newly landed Trojans of why her guards received them with hostile and suspicious measures.)

without making other preparations, is ruined; for the friendship which is gained by purchase and not through grandeur and nobility of spirit is bought but not secured, and at a pinch is not to be expended in your service. And men have less scruple in offending one who makes himself loved than one who makes himself feared; for love is held by a chain of obligation which, men being selfish, is broken whenever it serves their purpose; but fear is maintained by a dread of punishment which never fails.

Still, a prince should make himself feared in such a way that if he does not gain love, he at any rate avoids hatred; for fear and the absence of hatred may well go together, and will be always attained by one who abstains from interfering with the property of his citizens and subjects or with their women. And when he is obliged to take the life of anyone, let him do so when there is proper justification and manifest reason for it; but above all he must abstain from taking the property of others, for men forget more easily the death of their father than the loss of their patrimony. Then also pretexts for seizing property are never wanting, and one who begins to live by rapine will always find some reason for taking the goods of others, whereas causes for taking life are rarer and more fleeting.

But when the prince is with his army and has a large number of soldiers under his control, then it is extremely necessary that he should not mind being thought cruel; for without this reputation he could not keep an army united or disposed to any duty. Among the noteworthy actions of Hannibal is numbered this, that although he had an enormous army, composed of men of all nations and fighting in foreign countries, there never arose any dissension either among them or against the prince, either in good fortune or in bad. This could not be due to anything but his inhuman cruelty, which together with his infinite other virtues, made him always venerated and terrible in the sight of his soldiers, and without it his other virtues would not have sufficed to produce that effect. Thoughtless writers admire on the one hand his actions, and on the other blame the principal cause of them.

And that it is true that his other virtues would not have sufficed may be seen from the case of Scipio (famous not only in regard to his own times, but all times of which memory remains), whose armies rebelled against him in Spain, which arose from nothing but his excessive kindness, which allowed more licence to the soldiers than was consonant with military discipline. He was reproached with this in the senate by Fabius Maximus, who called him a corrupter of the Roman militia. Locri having been destroyed by one of Scipio's officers was not revenged by him, nor was the insolence of that officer punished, simply by reason of his easy nature; so much so, that some one wishing to excuse him in the senate, said that there were many men who knew rather how not to err, than how to correct the errors of others. This disposition would in time have tarnished the fame and glory of Scipio had he persevered in it under the empire, but living under the rule of the senate this harmful quality was not only concealed but became a glory to him.

I conclude, therefore, with regard to being feared and loved, that men love at their own free will, but fear at the will of the prince, and that a wise prince must rely on what is in his power and not on what is in the power of others, and he must only contrive to avoid incurring hatred, as has been explained.

Suggestions for Discussion

1. How does Machiavelli show that Cesare Borgia, known for his cruelty, was more merciful than the people of Florence?

2. Explain the use of the quotation from Virgil.

3. Explain Machiavelli's argument that the prince cannot rely on the love of his subjects.

4. What attitudes does Machiavelli express when he says that "men forget more easily the death of their father than the loss of their patrimony"?

5. Compare and contrast the actions of Scipio and Hannibal. How does Machiavelli explain their actions to prove his point about the need of the prince to inspire fear?

Suggestion for Writing

Write an essay in which you comment on the ideas in this selection that may be brilliant but not admirable. What aspects of life does the author ignore? Why? Why does this selection not express the concern for freedom and human dignity that characterizes most of the selections in this section?

A U N G   S A N   S U U   K Y I

Freedom from Fear

Aung San Suu Kyi (b. 1945), a pro-democracy activist and the rightfully elected Prime Minister of Burma (a.k.a. Myanmar), has spent more than twelve years under house arrest by the nation's ruling military junta. Her involvement with Burma's pro-democracy movement began in opposition to a repressive, socialist government, but an even more violent regime, the SLORC, seized control of the country in 1988, slaughtering thousands in the process. Suu Kyi has opposed them ever since. A Buddhist who believes in nonviolent resistance to oppressive forces, Suu Kyi modeled her rebellion after the passive resistance of Mohandas Gandhi and her father Aung San's efforts to free Burma from British control during the 1940s. Suu Kyi won the Nobel Peace Prize in 1991 while under house arrest. In 1972, Suu Kyi met her husband, a Tibetan scholar named Michael Aris, while she was studying abroad at Oxford University. They had two children together but were separated when she was placed under house arrest. Aris died of prostate cancer in 1999 while they were apart. Suu Kyi authored the books *Aung San of Burma: A Biographical Portrait by His Daughter* (1991), *Letters from Burma* (1998), *The Voice of Hope* (1998), and *Freedom from Fear and Other Writings* (1995), from which this essay was reprinted.

It is not power that corrupts but fear. Fear of losing power corrupts those who wield it and fear of the scourge of power corrupts those who are subject to it. Most Burmese are familiar with the four *a-gati*, the four kinds of corruption. *Chanda-gati*, corruption induced by desire, is deviation from the right path in pursuit of bribes or for the sake of those one loves. *Dosa-gati* is taking the wrong path to spite those against whom one bears ill will, and *moha-gati* is aberration due to ignorance. But perhaps the worst of the four is *bhaya-gati*, for not only does *bhaya*, fear, stifle and slowly destroy all sense of right and wrong, it so often lies at the root of the other three kinds of corruption.

Just as *chanda-gati*, when not the result of sheer avarice, can be caused by fear of want or fear of losing the goodwill of those one loves, so fear of being surpassed, humiliated or injured in some way can provide the impetus for ill will. And it would be difficult to dispel ignorance unless there is freedom to pursue the truth unfettered by fear. With so close a relationship between fear and corruption it is little wonder that in any society where fear is rife corruption in all forms becomes deeply entrenched.

Public dissatisfaction with economic hardships has been seen as the chief cause of the movement for democracy in Burma, sparked off by the student demonstrations of 1988. It is true that years of incoherent policies, inept official measures, burgeoning inflation and falling real income had turned the country into an economic shambles. But it was more than the difficulties of eking out a barely acceptable standard of living that had eroded the patience of a traditionally good-natured, quiescent people—it was also the humiliation of a way of life disfigured by corruption and fear. The students were protesting not just against the death of their comrades but against the denial of their right to life by a totalitarian regime which deprived the present of meaningfulness and held out no hope for the future. And because the students' protests articulated the frustrations of the people at large, the demonstrations quickly grew into a nationwide movement. Some of its keenest supporters were businessmen who had developed the skills and the contacts necessary not only to survive but to prosper within the system. But their affluence offered them no genuine sense of security or fulfilment, and they could not but see that if they and their fellow citizens, regardless of economic status, were to achieve a worthwhile existence, an accountable administration was at least a necessary if not a sufficient condition. The people of Burma had wearied of a precarious state of passive apprehension where they were 'as water in the cupped hands' of the powers that be.

Emerald cool we may be
As water in cupped hands
But oh that we might be
As splinters of glass
In cupped hands.

Glass splinters, the smallest with its sharp, glinting power to defend itself against hands that try to crush, could be seen as a vivid symbol of the spark of courage that is an essential attribute of those who would free themselves from the grip of oppression. Bogyoke Aung San regarded himself as a revolutionary and searched tirelessly for answers to the problems that beset Burma during her times of trial. He exhorted the people to develop courage: 'Don't just depend on the courage and intrepidity of others. Each and every one of you must make sacrifices to become a hero possessed of courage and intrepidity. Then only shall we all be able to enjoy true freedom.'

The effort necessary to remain uncorrupted in an environment where fear is an integral part of everyday existence is not immediately apparent to those fortunate enough to live in states governed by the rule of law. Just laws do not merely prevent corruption by meting out impartial punishment to offenders. They also help to create a society in which people can fulfil the basic requirements necessary for the preservation of human dignity without recourse to corrupt practices. Where there are no such laws, the burden of upholding the principles of justice and common decency falls on the ordinary people. It is the cumulative effect of their sustained effort and steady endurance which will change a nation where reason and conscience are warped by fear into one where legal rules exist to promote man's desire for harmony and justice while restraining the less desirable destructive traits in his nature.

In an age when immense technological advances have created lethal weapons which could be, and are, used by the powerful and the unprincipled to dominate the weak and the helpless, there is a compelling need for a closer relationship between politics and ethics at both the national and international levels. The Universal Declaration of Human Rights of the United Nations proclaims that 'every individual and every organ of society' should strive to promote the basic rights and freedoms to which all human beings regardless of race, nationality or religion are entitled. But as long as there are governments whose authority is founded on coercion rather than on the mandate of the people, and interest groups which place short-term profits above long-term peace and prosperity, concerted international action to protect and promote human rights will remain at best a partially realized ideal. There will continue to be arenas of struggle where victims of oppression have to draw on their own inner resources to defend their inalienable rights as members of the human family.

The quintessential revolution is that of the spirit, born of an intellectual conviction of the need for change in those mental attitudes and values which shape the course of a nation's development. A revolution which aims merely at changing official policies and institutions with a view to an improvement in material conditions has little chance of genuine success. Without a revolution of the spirit, the forces which produced the iniquities of the old order would continue to be operative, posing a constant threat to the process of reform and regeneration. It is not enough merely to call for freedom, democracy and human rights. There has to be a united determination to persevere in the struggle, to make sacrifices in the name of enduring truths, to resist the corrupting influences of desire, ill will, ignorance and fear.

Saints, it has been said, are the sinners who go on trying. So free men are the oppressed who go on trying and who in the process make themselves fit to bear the responsibilities and to uphold the disciplines which will maintain a free society. Among the basic freedoms to which men aspire that their lives might be full and uncramped, freedom from fear stands out as both a means and an end. A people who would build a nation in which strong, democratic institutions are firmly established as a guarantee against state-induced power must first learn to liberate their own minds from apathy and fear.

Always one to practise what he preached, Aung San himself constantly demonstrated courage—not just the physical sort but the kind that enabled him to speak the truth, to stand by his word, to accept criticism, to admit his faults, to correct his mistakes, to respect the opposition, to parley with the enemy and to let people be the judge of his worthiness as a leader. It is for such moral courage that he will always be loved and respected in Burma—not merely as a warrior hero but as the inspiration and conscience of the nation. The words used by Jawaharlal Nehru to describe Mahatma Gandhi could well be applied to Aung San: 'The essence of his teaching was fearlessness and truth, and action allied to these, always keeping the welfare of the masses in view.'

Gandhi, that great apostle of non-violence, and Aung San, the founder of a national army, were very different personalities, but as there is an inevitable sameness about the challenges of authoritarian rule anywhere at any time, so there is a similarity in the intrinsic qualities of those who rise up to meet the challenge. Nehru, who considered the instillation of courage in the people of India one of Gandhi's greatest achievements, was a political modernist, but as he assessed the needs for a twentieth-century movement for independence, he found himself looking back to the philosophy of ancient India: 'The greatest gift for an individual or a nation . . . was *abhaya*, fearlessness, not merely bodily courage but absence of fear from the mind.'

Fearlessness may be a gift but perhaps more precious is the courage acquired through endeavour, courage that comes from cultivating the habit of refusing to let fear dictate one's actions, courage that could be described as 'grace under pressure'—grace which is renewed repeatedly in the face of harsh, unremitting pressure.

Within a system which denies the existence of basic human rights, fear tends to be the order of the day. Fear of imprisonment, fear of torture, fear of death, fear of losing friends, family, property or means of livelihood, fear of poverty, fear of isolation, fear of failure. A most insidious form of fear is that which masquerades as common sense or even wisdom, condemning as foolish, reckless, insignificant or futile the small, daily acts of courage which help to preserve man's self-respect and inherent human dignity. It is not easy for a people conditioned by the iron rule of the principle that might is right to free themselves from the enervating miasma of fear. Yet even under the most crushing state machinery courage rises up again and again, for fear is not the natural state of civilized man.

The wellspring of courage and endurance in the face of unbridled power is generally a firm belief in the sanctity of ethical principles combined with a historical sense that despite all setbacks the condition of man is set on an ultimate course for both spiritual and material advancement. It is his capacity for self-improvement and self-redemption which most distinguishes man from the mere brute. At the root of human responsibility is the concept of perfection, the urge to achieve it, the intelligence to find a path towards it, and the will to follow that path if not to the end at least the distance needed to rise above individual limitations and environmental impediments. It is man's vision of a world fit for rational, civilized humanity which leads him to dare and to suffer to build societies free from want and fear. Concepts such as truth, justice and compassion cannot be dismissed as trite when these are often the only bulwarks which stand against ruthless power.

Suggestions for Discussion

1. According to Aung San Suu Kyi, what are the four kinds of corruption? Which is the worst, and why?

2. What fuels the movement for democracy in Burma?

3. What do people in a just society not understand about life under a corrupt regime?

4. What forces hinder the global quest for human rights and for an end to oppressive dictatorships?

5. How is "freedom from fear" both a means and an end?

6. What does Aung San Suu Kyi mean when she warns of a fear that "masquerades as common sense or wisdom"?

Suggestions for Writing

1. After reading this essay and the selection by Machiavelli, write a dialogue between the two authors in which they debate issues related to fear, political power, freedom, and a just society.

2. View the film *Beyond Rangoon*, which includes a segment featuring the character of Aung San Suu Kyi. How is she portrayed in this film? Does this portrayal seem to fit the woman who wrote this essay?

3. Research the recent monk-led uprisings in Burma. How is the democracy movement faring of late?

OSCAR WILDE

The Soul of Man under Socialism

Irish playwright, poet, and author Oscar Wilde (1854–1900) is best known for novels like *The Picture of Dorian Gray* (1891), plays including *The Importance of Being Earnest* (1895) and *An Ideal Husband* (1895), and poems including "Ballad of Reading Gaol" (1898) and "De Profundis" (1905). A pacifist and social reformer whose writings were often as witty as they were politically subversive, the flamboyant Wilde was a controversial figure in Victorian England. Although married and a father of two, Wilde had several homosexual relationships that were publicly exposed by the Marquis of Queensbury, the disapproving father of one of Wilde's lovers, Lord Alfred Douglas. Wilde was brought to trial for homosexuality, found guilty of "gross indecency," and sentenced to two years in prison. The hard labor he did while in Reading Gaol (jail) destroyed his health, and he died shortly after his release. It took several decades for the public scandal surrounding Wilde to fade and for his works to be loved once again. Although Wilde's works have traditionally been interpreted as merely lighthearted and escapist, essays such as

"The Soul of Man Under Socialism" (1891) are now considered both serious *and* funny political tracts, and his body of work as a whole is being reassessed.

The chief advantage that would result from the establishment of Socialism is, undoubtedly, the fact that Socialism would relieve us from that sordid necessity of living for others which, in the present condition of things, presses so hardly upon almost everybody. In fact, scarcely any one at all escapes.

Now and then, in the course of the century, a great man of science, like Darwin; a great poet, like Keats; a fine critical spirit, like M. Renan; a supreme artist, like Flaubert, has been able to isolate himself, to keep himself out of reach of the clamorous claims of others, to stand "under the shelter of the wall," as Plato puts it, and so to realize the perfection of what was in him, to his own incomparable gain, and to the incomparable and lasting gain of the whole world. These, however, are exceptions. The majority of people spoil their lives by an unhealthy and exaggerated altruism—are forced, indeed, so to spoil them. They find themselves surrounded by hideous poverty, by hideous ugliness, by hideous starvation. It is inevitable that they should be strongly moved by all this. The emotions of man are stirred more quickly than man's intelligence; and, as I pointed out some time ago in an article on the function of criticism, it is much more easy to have sympathy with suffering than it is to have sympathy with thought. Accordingly, with admirable though misdirected intentions, they very seriously and very sentimentally set themselves to the task of remedying the evils that they see. But their remedies do not cure the disease: they merely prolong it. Indeed, their remedies are part of the disease.

They try to solve the problem of poverty, for instance, by keeping the poor alive; or, in the case of a very advanced school, by amusing the poor.

But this is not a solution: it is an aggravation of the difficulty. The proper aim is to try and reconstruct society on such a basis that poverty will be impossible. And the altruistic virtues have really prevented the carrying out of this aim. Just as the worst slave-owners were those who were kind to their slaves, and so prevented the horror of the system being realized by those who suffered from it, and understood by those who contemplated it, so, in the present state of things in England, the people who do most harm are the people who try to do most good; and at last we have had the spectacle of men who have really studied the problem and know the life—educated men who live in the East-End—coming forward and imploring the community to restrain its altruistic impulses of charity, benevolence and the like. They do so on the ground that such charity degrades and demoralizes. They are perfectly right. Charity creates a multitude of sins.

There is also this to be said. It is immoral to use private property in order to alleviate the horrible evils that result from the institution of private property. It is both immoral and unfair.

Under Socialism all this will, of course, be altered. There will be no people living in fetid dens and fetid rags, and bringing up unhealthy, hunger-pinched children in the midst of impossible and absolutely repulsive surroundings. The security of society will not depend, as it does now, on the state of the weather. If a frost comes we shall not have a hundred thousand men out of work, tramping about the streets in a state of disgusting misery, or whining to their neighbours for alms, or crowding round the doors of loathsome shelters to try and secure a hunch of bread and a night's unclean lodging. Each member of the society will share in the general prosperity and happiness of the society, and if a frost comes no one will practically be anything the worse.

Upon the other hand, Socialism itself will be of value simply because it will lead to Individualism.

Socialism, Communism, or whatever one chooses to call it, by converting private property into public wealth, and substituting cooperation for competition, will restore society to its proper condition of a thoroughly healthy organism, and ensure the material well-being of each member of the community. It will, in fact, give Life its proper basis and its proper environment. But for the full development of Life to its highest mode of perfection something more is needed. What is needed is Individualism. If the Socialism is Authoritarian; if there are Governments armed with economic power as they are now with political power; if, in a word, we are to have Industrial Tyrannies, then the last state of man will be worse than the first. At present, in consequence of the existence of private property, a great many people are enabled to develop a certain very limited amount of Individualism. They are either under no necessity to work for their living, or are enabled to choose the sphere of activity that is really congenial to them and gives them pleasure. These are the poets, the philosophers, the men of science, the men of culture—in a word, the real men, the men who have realized themselves, and in whom all Humanity gains a partial realization. Upon the other hand, there are a great many people who, having no private property of their own, and being always on the brink of sheer starvation, are compelled to do the work of beasts of burden, to do work that is quite uncongenial to them, and to which they are forced by the peremptory, unreasonable, degrading Tyranny of want. These are the poor, and amongst them there is no grace of manner, or charm of speech, or civilization, or culture, or refinement in pleasures, or joy of life. From their collective force Humanity gains much in material prosperity. But it is only the material result that it gains, and the man who is poor is in himself absolutely of no importance. He is merely the infinitesimal atom of a force that, so far from regarding him, crushes him: indeed, prefers him crushed, as in that case he is far more obedient.

Of course, it might be said that the Individualism generated under conditions of private property is not always, or even as a rule, of a fine or wonderful type, and that the poor, if they have not culture and charm, have still many virtues. Both these statements would be quite true. The possession of private property is very often extremely demoralizing, and that is, of course, one of the reasons why Socialism wants to get rid of the institution. In fact, property is really a nuisance. Some years ago people went about the country saying that property has duties. They said it so often and so tediously that, at last, the Church has begun to say it. One hears it now from every pulpit. It is perfectly true. Property not merely has duties, but has so many duties that its possession to any large extent is a bore. It involves endless claims upon one, endless attention to business, endless bother. If property had simply pleasures we could stand it; but its duties make it unbearable. In the interest of the rich we must get rid of it. The virtues of the poor may be readily admitted, and are much to be regretted. We are often told that the poor are grateful for charity. Some of them are, no doubt, but the best amongst the poor are never grateful. They are ungrateful, discontented, disobedient and rebellious. They are quite right to be so. Charity they feel to be a ridiculously inadequate mode of partial restitution, or a sentimental dole, usually accompanied by some impertinent attempt on the part of the sentimentalist to tyrannize over their private lives. Why should they be grateful for the crumbs that fall from the rich man's table? They should be seated at the board, and are beginning to know it. As for being discontented, a man who would not be discontented with such surroundings and such a low mode of life would be a perfect brute. Disobedience, in the eyes of any one who has read history, is man's original virtue. It is through disobedience that progress has been made, through disobedience and through rebellion. Sometimes the poor are praised for being thrifty. But to recommend thrift to the poor is both grotesque and insulting. It is like advising a man who is starving to eat less. . . . Man should not be ready to show that he can live like a badly fed animal. He should decline to live like that, and should either steal or go on the rates, which is considered by many to be a form of stealing. As for begging, it is safer to beg than to take, but it is finer to take than to beg. No: a poor man who is ungrateful, unthrifty, discontented and rebellious is probably a real personality, and has much in him. He is at any rate a healthy protest. As for the virtuous poor, one can pity them, of course, but one cannot possibly admire them. They have made private terms with the enemy, and sold their birthright for very bad pottage. They must also be extraordinarily stupid. I can quite understand a man accepting laws that protect private property, and admit of its accumulation, as long as he himself is able under those conditions to realize some form of beautiful and intellectual life. But it is almost incredible to me how a man whose life is marred and made hideous by such laws can possibly acquiesce in their continuance.

However, the explanation is not really difficult to find. It is simply this. Misery and poverty are so absolutely degrading, and exercise such a paralysing effect over the nature of men, that no class is ever really conscious of its own suffering. They have to be told of it by other people, and they often entirely disbelieve them. What is said by great employers of labour against agitators is unquestionably true. Agitators are a set of interfering, meddling people, who come down to some perfectly contented class of the community and sow the seeds of discontent amongst them. That is the reason why agitators are so absolutely necessary. Without them, in our incomplete state, there would be no advance towards civilization. Slavery was put down in America, not in consequence of any action on the part of the slaves, or even any express desire on their part that they should be free. It was put down entirely through the grossly illegal conduct of certain agitators in Boston and elsewhere, who were not slaves themselves, nor owners of slaves, nor had anything to do with the question really. It was, undoubtedly, the Abolitionists who set the torch alight, who began the whole thing. And it is curious to note that from the slaves themselves they received, not merely very little assistance, but hardly any sympathy even; and when at the close of the war the slaves found themselves free, found themselves indeed so absolutely free that they were free to starve, many of them bitterly regretted the new state of things. To the thinker, the most tragic fact in the whole of the French Revolution is not that Marie Antoinette was killed for being a queen, but that the starved peasant of the Vendee voluntarily went out to die for the hideous cause of feudalism.

It is clear, then, that no Authoritarian Socialism will do. For, while under the present system a very large number of people can lead lives of a certain amount of freedom and expression and happiness, under an industrial–barrack system, or a system of economic tyranny, nobody would be able to have any such freedom at all. It is to be regretted that a portion of our community should be practically in slavery, but to propose to solve the problem by enslaving the entire community is childish. Every man must be left quite free to choose his own work. No form of compulsion must be exercised over him. If there is, his work will not be good for him, will not be good in itself, and will not be good for others. And by work I simply mean activity of any kind.

I hardly think that any Socialist, nowadays, would seriously propose that an inspector should call every morning at each house to see that each citizen rose up and did manual labour for eight hours. Humanity has got beyond that stage, and reserves such a form of life for the people whom, in a very arbitrary manner, it chooses to call criminals. But I confess that many of the socialistic views that I have come across seem to me to be tainted with ideas of authority, if not of actual compulsion. Of course authority and compulsion are out of the question. All association must be quite voluntary. It is only in voluntary association that man is fine.

But it may be asked how Individualism, which is now more or less dependent on the existence of private property for its development, will benefit by the abolition of such private property. The answer is very simple. It is true that, under existing conditions, a few men who have had private means of their own, such as Byron, Shelley, Browning, Victor Hugo, Baudelaire, and others, have been able to realize their personality more or less completely. Not one of these men ever did a single day's work for hire. They were relieved from poverty. They had an immense advantage. The question is whether it would be for the good of Individualism that such an advantage should be taken away. Let us suppose that it is taken away. What happens then to Individualism? How will it benefit?

It will benefit in this way. Under the new conditions Individualism will be far freer, far finer and far more intensified than it is now. I am not talking of the great imaginatively-realized Individualism of such poets as I have mentioned, but of the great actual Individualism latent and potential in mankind generally. For the recognition of private property has really harmed Individualism, and obscured it, by confusing a man with what he possesses. It has led Individualism entirely astray. It has made gain not growth its aim. So that man thought that the important thing was to have, and did not know that the important thing is to be. The true perfection of man lies, not in what man has, but in what man is. Private property has crushed true Individualism, and set up an Individualism that is false. It has debarred one part of the community from being individual by starving them. It has debarred the other part of the community from being individual, by putting them on the wrong road and encumbering them. Indeed, so completely has man's personality been absorbed by his possessions that the English law has always treated offences against a man's property with far more severity than offences against his person, and property is still the test of complete citizenship. The industry necessary for the making of money is also very demoralizing. In a community like ours, where property confers immense distinction, social position, honour, respect, titles, and other pleasant things of the kind, man, being naturally ambitious, makes it his aim to accumulate this property, and goes on wearily and tediously accumulating it long after he has got far more than he wants, or can use, or enjoy, or perhaps even know of. Man will kill himself by overwork in order to secure property, and really, considering the enormous advantages that property brings, one is hardly surprised. One's regret is that society should be constructed on such a basis that man has been forced into a groove in which he cannot freely develop what is wonderful, and fascinating, and delightful in him—in which, in fact, he misses the true pleasure and joy of living. He is also, under existing conditions, very insecure. An enormously wealthy merchant may be—often is—at every moment of his life at the mercy of things that are not under his control. If the wind blows an extra point or so, or the weather suddenly changes, or some trivial thing happens, his ship may go down, his speculations may go wrong, and he finds himself a poor man, with his social position quite gone. Now, nothing should be able to harm a man except himself. Nothing should be able to rob a man at all. What a man really has, is what is in him. What is outside of him should be a matter of no importance.

With the abolition of private property, then, we shall have true, beautiful, healthy Individualism. Nobody will waste his life in accumulating things and the symbols for things. One will live. To live is the rarest thing in the world. Most people exist, that is all.

It is a question whether we have ever seen the full expression of a personality, except on the imaginative plane of art. In action, we never have. Caesar, says Mommsen, was the complete and perfect man. But how tragically insecure was Caesar! Wherever there is a man who exercises authority, there is a man who resists authority. Caesar was very perfect, but his perfection travelled by too dangerous a road. Marcus Aurelius was the perfect man, says Renan. Yes; the great emperor was a perfect man. But how intolerable were the endless claims upon him! He staggered under the burden of the empire. He was conscious how inadequate one man was to bear the weight of that Titan and too vast orb. What I mean by a perfect man is one who develops under perfect conditions; one who is not wounded, or worried, or maimed, or in danger. Most personalities have been obliged to be rebels. Half their strength has been wasted in friction. Byron's personality, for instance, was terribly wasted in its battle with the stupidity, and hypocrisy, and Philistinism of the English. Such battles do not always intensify strength: they often exaggerate weakness. Byron was never able to give us what he might have given us. Shelley escaped better. Like Byron, he got out of England as soon as possible. But he was not so well known. If the English had had any idea of what a great poet he really was, they would have fallen on him with tooth and nail, and made his life as unbearable to him as they possibly could. But he was not a remarkable figure in society, and consequently he escaped, to a certain degree. Still, even in Shelley the note of rebellion is sometimes too strong. The note of the perfect personality is not rebellion but peace.

It will be a marvellous thing—the true personality of man—when we see it. It will grow naturally and simply, flower-like, or as a tree grows. It will not be at discord. It will never argue or dispute. It will not prove things. It will know everything. And yet it will not busy itself about knowledge. It will have wisdom. Its value will not be measured by material things. It will have nothing. And yet it will have everything, and whatever one takes from it, it will still have, so rich will it be. It will not be always meddling with others, or asking them to be like itself. It will love them because they will be different. And yet while it will not meddle with others it will help all, as a beautiful thing helps us, by being what it is. The personality of man will be very wonderful. It will be as wonderful as the personality of a child.

In its development it will be assisted by Christianity, if men desire that; but if men do not desire that, it will develop none the less surely. For it will not worry itself about the past, nor care whether things happened or did not happen. Nor will it admit any laws but its own laws; nor any authority but its own authority. Yet it will love those who sought to intensify it, and speak often of them. And of these Christ was one.

"Know Thyself" was written over the portal of the antique world. Over the portal of the new world, "Be Thyself" shall be written. And the message of Christ to man was simply "Be thyself." That is the secret of Christ.

When Jesus talks about the poor he simply means personalities, just as when he talks about the rich he simply means people who have not developed their personalities. Jesus moved in a community that allowed the accumulation of private property just as ours does, and the gospel that he preached was not that in such a community it is an advantage for a man to live on scanty, unwholesome food, to wear ragged, unwholesome clothes, to sleep in horrid, unwholesome dwellings, and a disadvantage for a man to live under healthy, pleasant and decent conditions. Such a view would have been wrong there and then, and would of course be still more wrong now and in England; for as man moves northwards the material necessities of life become of more vital importance, and our society is infinitely more complex, and displays far greater extremes of luxury and pauperism than any society of the antique world. What Jesus meant was this. He said to man, "You have a wonderful personality. Develop it. Be your self. Don't imagine that your perfection lies in accumulating or possessing external things. Your perfection is inside of you. If only you could realize that, you would not want to be rich. Ordinary riches can be stolen from a man. Real riches cannot. In the treasury-house of your soul, there are infinitely precious things, that may not be taken from you. And so, try so to shape your life that external things will not harm you. And try also to get rid of personal property. It involves sordid preoccupation, endless industry, continual wrong. Personal property hinders Individualism at every step." It is to be noted that Jesus never says that impoverished people are necessarily good, or wealthy people necessarily bad. That would not have been true. Wealthy people are, as a class, better than impoverished people, more moral, more intellectual, more well-behaved. There is only one class in the community that thinks more about money than the rich, and that is the poor. The poor can think of nothing else. That is the misery of being poor. What Jesus does say is that man reaches his perfection, not through what he has, not even through what he does, but entirely through what he is. And so the wealthy young man who comes to Jesus is represented as a thoroughly good citizen, who has broken none of the laws of his state, none of the commandments of his religion. He is quite respectable, in the ordinary sense of that extraordinary word. Jesus says to him, "You should give up private property. It hinders you from realizing your perfection. It is a drag upon you. It is a burden. Your personality does not need it. It is within you, and not outside of you, that you will find what you really are, and what you really want." To his own friends he says the same thing. He tells them to be themselves, and not to be always worrying about other things. What do other things matter? Man is complete in himself. When they go into the world, the world will disagree with them. That is inevitable. The world hates Individualism. But that is not to trouble them. They are to be calm and self-centred. If a man takes their cloak, they are to give him their coat, just to show that material things are of no importance. If people abuse them, they are not to answer back. What does it signify? The things people say of a man do not alter a man. He is what he is. Public opinion is of no value whatsoever. Even if people employ actual violence, they are not to be violent in turn. That would be to fall to the same low level. After all, even in prison, a man can be quite free. His soul can be free. His personality can be untroubled. He can be at peace. And, above all things, they are not to interfere with other people or judge them in any way. Personality is a very mysterious thing. A man cannot always be estimated by what he does. He may keep the law, and yet be worthless. He may break the law, and yet be fine. He may be bad, without ever doing anything bad. He may commit a sin against society, and yet realize through that sin his true perfection.

There was a woman who was taken in adultery. We are not told the history of her love, but that love must have been very great; for Jesus said that her sins were forgiven her, not because she repented, but because her love was so intense and wonderful. Later on, a short time before his death, as he sat at a feast, the woman came in and poured costly perfumes on his hair. His friends tried to interfere with her, and said that it was an extravagance, and that the money that the perfume cost should have been expended on charitable relief of people in want, or something of that kind. Jesus did not accept that view. He pointed out that the material needs of Man were great and very permanent, but that the spiritual needs of Man were greater still, and that in one divine moment, and by selecting its own mode of expression, a personality might make itself perfect. The world worships the woman, even now, as a saint.

Yes; there are suggestive things in Individualism. Socialism annihilates family life, for instance. With the abolition of private property, marriage in its present form must disappear. This is part of the programme. Individualism accepts this and makes it fine. It converts the abolition of legal restraint into a form of freedom that will help the full development of personality, and make the love of man and woman more wonderful, more beautiful, and more ennobling. Jesus knew this. He rejected the claims of family life, although they existed in his day and community in a very marked form. "Who is my mother? Who are my brothers?" he said, when he was told that they wished to speak to him. When one of his followers asked leave to go and bury his father, "Let the dead bury the dead," was his terrible answer. He would allow no claim whatsoever to be made on personality.

And so he who would lead a Christlike life is he who is perfectly and absolutely himself. He may be a great poet, or a great man of science; or a young student at a University, or one who watches sheep upon a moor; or a maker of dramas, like Shakespeare, or a thinker about God, like Spinoza; or a child who plays in a garden, or a fisherman who throws his nets into the sea. It does not matter what he is, as long as he realizes the perfection of the soul that is within him. All imitation in morals and in life is wrong. Through the streets of Jerusalem at the present day crawls one who is mad and carries a wooden cross on his shoulders. He is a symbol of the lives that are marred by imitation. Father Damien was Christlike when he went out to live with the lepers, because in such service he realized fully what was best in him. But he was not more Christlike than Wagner, when he realized his soul in music; or than Shelley, when he realized his soul in song. There is no one type for man. There are as many perfections as there are imperfect men. And while to the claims of charity a man may yield and yet be free, to the claims of conformity no man may yield and remain free at all.

Individualism, then, is what through Socialism we are to attain to. As a natural result the State must give up all idea of government. It must give it up because, as a wise man once said many centuries before Christ, there is such a thing as leaving mankind alone; there is no such thing as governing mankind. All modes of government are failures. Despotism is unjust to everybody, including the despot, who was probably made for better things. Oligarchies are unjust to the many, and ochlocracies are unjust to the few. High hopes were once formed of democracy; but democracy means simply the bludgeoning of the people by the people for the people. It has been found out. I must say that it was high time, for all authority is quite degrading. It degrades those who exercise it, and degrades those over whom it is exercised. When it is violently, grossly and cruelly used, it produces a good effect, by creating, or at any rate bringing out, the spirit of revolt and Individualism that is to kill it. When it is used with a certain amount of kindness, and accompanied by prizes and rewards, it is dreadfully demoralizing. People, in that case, are less conscious of the horrible pressure that is being put on them, and so go through their lives in a sort of coarse comfort, like petted animals, without ever realizing that they are probably thinking other people's thoughts, living by other people's standards, wearing practically what one may call other people's second-hand clothes, and never being themselves for a single moment. "He who would be free," says a fine thinker, "must not conform." And authority, by bribing people to conform, produces a very gross kind of over-fed barbarism amongst us.

With authority, punishment will pass away. This will be a great gain— a gain, in fact, of incalculable value. As one reads history, not in the expurgated editions written for schoolboys and passmen, but in the original authorities of each time, one is absolutely sickened, not by the crimes that the wicked have committed, but by the punishments that the good have inflicted; and a community is infinitely more brutalized by the habitual employment of punishment, than it is by the occasional occurrence of crime. It obviously follows that the more punishment is inflicted the more crime is produced, and most modern legislation has clearly recognized this, and has made it its task to diminish punishment as far as it thinks it can. Wherever it has really diminished it, the results have always been extremely good. The less punishment, the less crime. When there is no punishment at all, crime will either cease to exist, or if it occurs, will be treated by physicians as a very distressing form of dementia, to be cured by care and kindness. For what are called criminals nowadays are not criminals at all. Starvation, and not sin, is the parent of modern crime. That indeed is the reason why our criminals are, as a class, so absolutely uninteresting from any psychological point of view. They are not marvellous Macbeths and terrible Vautrins. They are merely what ordinary, respectable, commonplace people would be if they had not got enough to eat. When private property is abolished there will be no necessity for crime, no demand for it; it will cease to exist. Of course all crimes are not crimes against property, though such are the crimes that the English law, valuing what a man has more than what a man is, punishes with the harshest and most horrible severity, if we except the crime of murder, and regard death as worse than penal servitude, a point on which our criminals, I believe, disagree. But though a crime may not be against property, it may spring from the misery and rage and depression produced by our wrong system of property-holding, and so, when that system is abolished, will disappear. When each member of the community has sufficient for his wants, and is not interfered with by his neighbour, it will not be an object of any interest to him to interfere with any one else. Jealousy, which is an extraordinary source of crime in modern life, is an emotion closely bound up with our conceptions of property, and under Socialism and Individualism will die out. It is remarkable that in communistic tribes jealousy is entirely unknown.

Now as the State is not to govern, it may be asked what the State is to do. The State is to be a voluntary association that will organize labour, and be the manufacturer and distributor of necessary commodities. The State is to make what is useful. The individual is to make what is beautiful. And as I have mentioned the word labour, I cannot help saying that a great deal of nonsense is being written and talked nowadays about the dignity of manual labour. There is nothing necessarily dignified about manual labour at all, and most of it is absolutely degrading. It is mentally and morally injurious to man to do anything in which he does not find pleasure, and many forms of labour are quite pleasureless activities, and should be regarded as such. To sweep a slushy crossing for eight hours on a day when the east wind is blowing is a disgusting occupation. To sweep it with mental, moral or physical dignity seems to me to be impossible. To sweep it with joy would be appalling. Man is made for something better than disturbing dirt. All work of that kind should be done by a machine.

And I have no doubt that it will be so. Up to the present, man has been, to a certain extent, the slave of machinery, and there is something tragic in the fact that as soon as man had invented a machine to do his work he began to starve. This, however, is, of course, the result of our property system and our system of competition. One man owns a machine which does the work of five hundred men. Five hundred men are, in consequence, thrown out of employment, and having no work to do, become hungry and take to thieving. The one man secures the produce of the machine and keeps it, and has five hundred times as much as he should have, and probably, which is of much more importance, a great deal more than he really wants. Were that machine the property of all, every one would benefit by it. It would be an immense advantage to the community. All unintellectual labour, all monotonous, dull labour, all labour that deals with dreadful things, and involves unpleasant conditions, must be done by machinery. Machinery must work for us in coal mines, and do all sanitary services, and be the stoker of steamers, and clean the streets, and run messages on wet days, and do anything that is tedious or distressing. At present machinery competes against man. Under proper conditions machinery will serve man. There is no doubt at all that this is the future of machinery, and just as trees grow while the country gentleman is asleep, so while Humanity will be amusing itself, or enjoying cultivated leisure—which, and not labour, is the aim of man—or making beautiful things, or reading beautiful things, or simply contemplating the world with admiration and delight, machinery will be doing all the necessary and unpleasant work. The fact is, that civilization requires slaves. The Greeks were quite right there. Unless there are slaves to do the ugly, horrible, uninteresting work, culture and contemplation become almost impossible. Human slavery is wrong, insecure and demoralizing. On mechanical slavery, on the slavery of the machine, the future of the world depends. And when scientific men are no longer called upon to go down to a depressing East-End and distribute bad cocoa and worse blankets to starving people, they will have delightful leisure in which to devise wonderful and marvellous things for their own joy and the joy of everyone else. There will be great storages of force for every city, and for every house if required, and this force man will convert into heat, light or motion, according to his needs. Is this Utopian? A map of the world that does not include Utopia is not worth even glancing at, for it leaves out the one country at which Humanity is always landing. And when Humanity lands there, it looks out, and, seeing a better country, sets sail. Progress is the realization of Utopias.

Now, I have said that the community by means of organization of machinery will supply the useful things, and that the beautiful things will be made by the individual. This is not merely necessary, but it is the only possible way by which we can get either the one or the other. An individual who has to make things for the use of others, and with reference to their wants and their wishes, does not work with interest, and consequently cannot put into his work what is best in him. Upon the other hand, whenever a community or a powerful section of a community, or a government of any kind, attempts to dictate to the artist what he is to do, Art either entirely vanishes, or becomes stereotyped, or degenerates into a low and ignoble form of craft. A work of art is the unique result of a unique temperament. Its beauty comes from the fact that the author is what he is. It has nothing to do with the fact that other people want what they want. Indeed, the moment that an artist takes notice of what other people want, and tries to supply the demand, he ceases to be an artist, and becomes a dull or an amusing craftsman, an honest or a dishonest tradesman. He has no further claim to be considered as an artist. Art is the most intense mode of Individualism that the world has known. I am inclined to say that it is the only real mode of Individualism that the world has known. Crime, which, under certain conditions, may seem to have created Individualism, must take cognizance of other people and interfere with them. It belongs to the sphere of action. But alone, without any reference to his neighbours, without any interference, the artist can fashion a beautiful thing; and if he does not do it solely for his own pleasure, he is not an artist at all.

It will, of course, be said that such a scheme as is set forth here is quite unpractical, and goes against human nature. This is perfectly true. It is unpractical, and it goes against human nature. This is why it is worth carrying out, and that is why one proposes it. For what is a practical scheme? A practical scheme is either a scheme that is already in existence, or a scheme that could be carried out under existing conditions. But it is exactly the existing conditions that one objects to; and any scheme that could accept these conditions is wrong and foolish. The conditions will be done away with, and human nature will change. The only thing that one really knows about human nature is that it changes. Change is the one quality we can predicate of it. The systems that fail are those that rely on the permanency of human nature, and not on its growth and development. The error of Louis XIV was that he thought human nature would always be the same. The result of his error was the French Revolution. It was an admirable result. All the results of the mistakes of governments are quite admirable.

It is to be noted also that Individualism does not come to man with any sickly cant about duty, which merely means doing what other people want because they want it; or any hideous cant about self-sacrifice, which is merely a survival of savage mutilation. In fact, it does not come to man with any claims upon him at all. It comes naturally and inevitably out of man. It is the point to which all development tends. It is the differentiation to which all organisms grow. It is the perfection that is inherent in every mode of life, and towards which every mode of life quickens. And so Individualism exercises no compulsion over man. On the contrary, it says to man that he should suffer no compulsion to be exercised over him. It does not try to force people to be good. It knows that people are good when they are let alone. Man will develop Individualism out of himself. Man is now so developing Individualism. To ask whether Individualism is practical is like asking whether Evolution is practical. Evolution is the law of life, and there is no evolution except towards Individualism. Where this tendency is not expressed, it is a case of artificially arrested growth, or of disease, or of death.

Individualism will also be unselfish and unaffected. It has been pointed out that one of the results of the extraordinary tyranny of authority is that words are absolutely distorted from their proper and simple meaning, and are used to express the obverse of their right signification. What is true about Art is true about Life. A man is called affected, nowadays, if he dresses as he likes to dress. But in doing that he is acting in a perfectly natural manner. Affectation, in such matters, consists in dressing according to the views of one's neighbour, whose views, as they are the views of the majority, will probably be extremely stupid. Or a man is called selfish if he lives in a manner that seems to him most suitable for the full realization of his own personality; if, in fact, the primary aim of his life is self-development. But this is the way in which every one should live. Selfishness is not living as one wishes to live, it is asking others to live as one wishes to live. And unselfishness is letting other people's lives alone, not interfering with them. Selfishness always aims at creating around it an absolute uniformity of type. Unselfishness recognizes infinite variety of type as a delightful thing, accepts it, acquiesces in it, enjoys it. It is not selfish to think for oneself. A man who does not think for himself does not think at all. It is grossly selfish to require of one's neighbour that he should think in the same way, and hold the same opinions. Why should he? If he can think, he will probably think differently. If he cannot think, it is monstrous to require thought of any kind from him. A red rose is not selfish because it wants to be a red rose. It would be horribly selfish if it wanted all the other flowers in the garden to be both red and roses. Under Individualism people will be quite natural and absolutely unselfish, and will know the meanings of the words, and realize them in their free, beautiful lives. Nor will men be egotistic as they are now. For the egotist is he who makes claims upon others, and the Individualist will not desire to do that. It will not give him pleasure. When man has realized Individualism, he will also realize sympathy and exercise it freely and spontaneously. Up to the present man has hardly cultivated sympathy at all. He has merely sympathy with pain, and sympathy with pain is not the highest form of sympathy. All sympathy is fine, but sympathy with suffering is the least fine mode. It is tainted with egotism. It is apt to become morbid. There is in it a certain element of terror for our own safety. We become afraid that we ourselves might be as the leper or as the blind, and that no man would have care of us. It is curiously limiting, too. One should sympathize with the entirety of life, not with life's sores and maladies merely, but with life's joy and beauty and energy and health and freedom. The wider sympathy is, of course, the more difficult. It requires more unselfishness. Anybody can sympathize with the sufferings of a friend, but it requires a very fine nature—it requires, in fact, the nature of a true Individualist—to sympathize with a friend's success. In the modern stress of competition and struggle for place, such sympathy is naturally rare, and is also very much stifled by the immoral ideal of uniformity of type and conformity to rule which is so prevalent everywhere, and is perhaps most obnoxious in England.

Sympathy with pain there will, of course, always be. It is one of the first instincts of man. The animals which are individual, the higher animals that is to say, share it with us. But it must be remembered that while sympathy with joy intensifies the sum of joy in the world, sympathy with pain does not really diminish the amount of pain. It may make man better able to endure evil, but the evil remains. Sympathy with consumption does not cure consumption; that is what Science does. And when Socialism has solved the problem of disease, the area of the sentimentalists will be lessened, and the sympathy of man will be large, healthy, and spontaneous. Man will have joy in the contemplation of the joyous lives of others.

For it is through joy that the Individualism of the future will develop itself. Christ made no attempt to reconstruct society, and consequently the Individualism that he preached to man could be realized only through pain or in solitude. The ideals that we owe to Christ are the ideals of the man who abandons society entirely, or of the man who resists society absolutely. But man is naturally social. Even the Thebaid became peopled at last. And though the cenobite realizes his personality, it is often an impoverished personality that he so realizes. Upon the other hand, the terrible truth that pain is a mode through which man may realize himself exercised a wonderful fascination over the world. Shallow speakers and shallow thinkers in pulpits and on platforms often talk about the world's worship of pleasure, and whine against it. But it is rarely in the world's history that its ideal has been one of joy and beauty. The worship of pain has far more often dominated the world. Medievalism, with its saints and martyrs, its love of self-torture, its wild passion for wounding itself, its gashing with knives and its whipping with rods—Medievalism is real Christianity, and the medieval Christ is the real Christ. When the Renaissance dawned upon the world, and brought with it the new ideals of beauty of life and the joy of living, men could not understand Christ. Even Art shows us that. The painters of the Renaissance drew Christ as a little boy playing with another boy in a palace or a garden, or lying back in his mother's arms, smiling at her, or at a flower, or at a bright bird; or as a noble stately figure moving nobly through the world; or as a wonderful figure rising in a sort of ecstasy from death to life. Even when they drew him crucified they drew him as a beautiful God on whom evil men had inflicted suffering. But he did not preoccupy them much. What delighted them was to paint the men and women whom they admired, and to show the loveliness of this lovely earth. They painted many religious pictures—in fact, they painted far too many, and the monotony of type and motive is wearisome, and was bad for art. It was the result of the authority of the public in art-matters, and is to be deplored. But their soul was not in the subject. Raphael was a great artist when he painted his portrait of the Pope. When he painted his Madonnas and infant Christs, he is not a great artist at all. Christ had no message for the Renaissance, which was wonderful because it brought an ideal at variance with his, and to find the presentation of the real Christ we must go to medieval art. There, he is one maimed and marred; one who is not comely to look on, because Beauty is a joy; one who is not in fair raiment, because that may be a joy also: he is a beggar who has a marvellous soul; he is a leper whose soul is divine; he needs neither property nor health; he is a God realizing his perfection through pain.

The evolution of man is slow. The injustice of men is great. It was necessary that pain should be put forward as a mode of self-realization. Even now, in some places in the world, the message of Christ is necessary. No one who lived in modern Russia could possibly realize his perfection except by pain. A few Russian artists have realized themselves in Art, in a fiction that is medieval in character, because its dominant note is the realization of men through suffering. But for those who are not artists, and to whom there is no mode of life but the actual life of fact, pain is the only door to perfection. A Russian who lives happily under the present system of government in Russia mast either believe that man has no soul, or that, if he has, it is not worth developing. A Nihilist who rejects all authority, because he knows authority to be evil, and who welcomes all pain, because through that he realizes his personality, is a real Christian. To him the Christian ideal is a true thing.

And yet, Christ did not revolt against authority. He accepted the imperial authority of the Roman Empire and paid tribute. He endured the ecclesiastical authority of the Jewish Church, and would not repel its violence by any violence of his own. He had, as I said before, no scheme for the reconstruction of society. But the modern world has schemes. It proposes to do away with poverty and the suffering that it entails. It desires to get rid of pain and the suffering that pain entails. It trusts to Socialism and to Science as its methods. What it aims at is an Individualism expressing itself through joy. This Individualism will be larger, fuller, lovelier than any Individualism has ever been. Pain is not the ultimate mode of perfection. It is merely provisional and a protest. It has reference to wrong, unhealthy, unjust surroundings. When the wrong, and the disease and the injustice are removed, it will have no further place. It will have done its work. It was a great work, but it is almost over. Its sphere lessens every day.

Nor will man miss it. For what man has sought for is, indeed, neither pain nor pleasure, but simply Life. Man has sought to live intensely, fully, perfectly. When he can do so without exercising restraint on others, or suffering it ever, and his activities are all pleasurable to him, he will be saner, healthier, more civilized, more himself. Pleasure is Nature's test, her sign of approval. When man is happy, he is in harmony with himself and his environment. The new Individualism, for whose service Socialism, whether it wills it or not, is working, will be perfect harmony. It will be what the Greeks sought for, but could not, except in Thought, realize completely, because they had slaves, and fed them; it will be what the Renaissance sought for, but could not realize completely, except in Art, because they had slaves, and starved them. It will be complete, and through it each man will attain to his perfection. The new Individualism is the new Hellenism.

—1891

Suggestions for Discussion

1. According to Wilde, how does capitalism undercut freedom and individuality?

2. How do poor people suffer in a capitalist society? How do rich people suffer?

3. Why does Wilde believe socialism will lead to individuality? What distinction does Wilde make between "authoritarian Socialism" and the socialism of Jesus Christ?

4. How does Wilde tie his political and economic theories to Darwin's theories of evolution?

5. Synthesis: How do you think Wilde would react to Earl Shorris's "Education as a Weapon in the Hands of the Restless Poor"? Why?

Suggestions for Writing

1. Wilde suggests that humans have been the "slave of machinery." Do you agree? Do you see technology as a boon or an obstacle to human fulfillment?

How might technology be used to create a better world? Using Wilde's essay as your context, write about the relationship of humans and technology.

2. Synthesis: Compare Wilde's portrayal of the lessons of Jesus Christ to those in the essays by Salman Rushdie and Chris Hedges. Write a paper in which you consider these three models of Christ and Christianity.

ᘄᘄᘄ

A N N A   Q U I N D L E N

Immigration: Newcomers by Numbers

American author, journalist, and opinion columnist Anna Quindlen (b. 1952) won the Pulitzer Prize for commentary in 1992 for her *New York Times* column "Public or Private." She began her writing career at an early age when she was hired by the *New York Post* after graduating from Barnard College. Since leaving journalism in 1995 to become a full-time author, she has written seven works of nonfiction, two children's books, and five novels, including *Black and Blue* (1998) and *Rise and Shine* (2006). Her novel *One True Thing* (1997) was made into a film starring Meryl Streep and Renee Zellweger. Quindlen has also written a biweekly column for *Newsweek* since 1999. In the following piece, Quindlen weighs in on our nation's heated immigration debate. She argues for immigration saying, "America has become a nation dependent on the presence of newcomers, both those with green cards and those without."

Some people talk about immigration in terms of politics, some in terms of history. But the crux of the matter is numbers. The Labor Department says that immigrants make up about 15 percent of the work force. It's estimated that a third of those are undocumented workers, or what those who want to send them back to where they came from call "illegals."

The Pew Hispanic Center estimates that one in four farmhands in the United States is an undocumented immigrant, and that they make up a significant portion of the people who build our houses, clean our office buildings and prepare our food.

All the thundering about policing the border and rounding up those who have slipped over it ignores an inconvenient fact: America has become a nation dependent on the presence of newcomers, both those with green cards and those without. Mayor Michael Bloomberg of New York testified before a Senate committee that they are a linchpin of his city's economy. The current and former chairmen of the Federal Reserve have favored legal accommodations for undocumented workers because of their salutary effect on economic growth—and the downturn that could follow their departure. Business leaders say agriculture, construction, meatpacking and other industries would collapse without them.

Last year the town of Hazleton, Pa., became known for the most draconian immigration laws in the country, laws making English the official city language, levying harsh fines against landlords who rent to undocumented immigrants and revoking the business permit of anyone who employs them. There was a lot of public talk about crime and gangs and very little about hard work in local factories and new businesses along the formerly moribund Wyoming Street. In that atmosphere, those with apartments to let and jobs to fill could be excused if they avoided any supplicant with an accent. Oh, the mayor and his supporters insisted that the laws were meant only to deal with those here illegally but the net effect was to make all Latinos feel unwelcome.

When the law was struck down by a federal judge, there was rejoicing among Hazleton's immigrants, but some said an exodus had already begun. Longtime residents seemed to think that was just fine. This is part of a great historical continuum—the Germans once derided the Irish, and the Irish trashed the Italians—but it is a shortsighted approach. Economists say immigrants buying starter homes will keep the bottom from falling out of the housing market in the years ahead. Latinos are opening new businesses at a rate three times faster than the national average. If undocumented immigrants were driven out of the work force, there would be a domino effect: prices of things ranging from peaches to plastering would rise. Nursing homes would be understaffed. Hotel rooms wouldn't get cleaned.

Sure, it would be great if everyone were here legally, if the immigration service weren't such a disaster that getting a green card is a life's work. It would be great if other nations had economies robust enough to support their citizens so leaving home wasn't the only answer. But at a certain point public policy means dealing not only with how things ought to be but with how they are. Here's how they are: these people work the jobs we don't want, sometimes two and three jobs at a time. They do it on the cheap, which is tough, so that their children won't have to, which is good. They use services like hospitals and schools, which is a drain on public coffers, and they pay taxes, which contribute to them.

Immigration is never about today, always about tomorrow, an exercise in that thing some native-born Americans seem to have lost the knack for: deferred gratification. It's the young woman in New York City who splits family translation duties with her two siblings. Her parents showed extraordinary courage in leaving all that was familiar and coming to a place where they couldn't even read the street signs. Does it matter if they don't speak English when they have children who aced the SAT verbal section and were educated in the Ivy League? It's the educated man who arrived in the Washington, D.C., area and took a job doing landscaping, then found work as a painter, then was hired to fix up an entire apartment complex by someone who liked his work ethic. He started his own business and wound up employing others. Does it matter that he arrived in this country with no work visa if he is now bolstering the nation's economy?

The city of Hazleton says yes. And if towns like Hazleton, whose aging populations were on the wane before the immigrants arrived, succeed in driving newcomers away, those who remain will find themselves surrounded by empty storefronts, deserted restaurants and houses that will not sell. It's the civic equivalent of starving to death because you don't care for the food. But at least everyone involved can tell themselves their town wasted away while they were speaking English.

YASIRIS MARTINEZ, *Ritter Street.* Gelatin silver printer, 2006. Courtesy of the artist.

Suggestions for Discussion

1. Do you agree with Quindlen? Is America a nation dependent on the presence of newcomers? Why or why not?

2. Quindlen writes this article as an editorial piece. How does this help her argument? Detract from it?

3. Take a close look at the photograph by Yasiris Martinez on the previous page. What do you think is its focus? What is the center of attention for you? For the photographer? For the people being photographed? Share your views in class.

Suggestions for Writing

1. Rewrite the article as a nonbiased piece of journalism. How does this change the argument and the outcome?

2. Focus on the eyes of the child resting on the mother's arm in the photo. What do you think the child sees? Create a short narrative from the child's point of view.

FICTION

∾∾∾∾∾

SHERMAN ALEXIE

What You Pawn I Will Redeem

Sherman Alexie (b. 1966) was born fifty miles northwest of Spokane, Washington, on the Spokane Indian Reservation. Born hydrocephalic, he endured a series of brain surgeries as an infant, and doctors predicted that mental disabilities would follow, but instead Alexie taught himself to read when he was three and excelled throughout his school years. Fainting spells in anatomy class led him to change his college major from pre-med to American studies, and he has since published seven novels, ten collections of poetry, and numerous short stories. He adapted his novel *The Lone Ranger and Tonto Fistfight in Heaven* (1993) into a screenplay for the movie *Smoke Signals.* (1999) His novel *The Absolutely True Diary of a Part-Time Indian* won a 2007 National Book Award. The following story won the 2005 O. Henry Prize.

∾

Noon

One day you have a home and the next you don't, but I'm not going to tell you my particular reasons for being homeless, because it's my secret story, and Indians have to work hard to keep secrets from hungry white folks.

I'm a Spokane Indian boy, an Interior Salish, and my people have lived within a one-hundred-mile radius of Spokane, Washington, for at least ten thousand years. I grew up in Spokane, moved to Seattle twenty-three years ago for college, flunked out within two semesters, worked various blue- and bluer-collar jobs for many years, married two or three times, fathered two or three kids, and then went crazy. Of course, "crazy" is not the official definition of my mental problem, but I don't think "asocial disorder" fits it, either, because that makes me sound like I'm a serial killer or something. I've never hurt another human being, or at least not physically. I've broken a few hearts in my time, but we've all done that, so I'm nothing special in that regard. I'm a boring heartbreaker, at that, because I've never abandoned one woman for another. I never dated or married more than one woman at a time. I didn't break hearts into pieces overnight. I broke them slowly and carefully. I didn't set any land-speed records running out the door. Piece by piece, I disappeared. And I've been disappearing ever since. But I'm not going to tell you any more about my brain or my soul.

I've been homeless for six years. If there's such a thing as being an effective homeless man, I suppose I'm effective. Being homeless is probably the only thing I've ever been good at. I know where to get the best free food. I've made friends with restaurant and convenience-store managers who let me use their bathrooms. I don't mean the public bathrooms, either. I mean the employees' bathrooms, the clean ones hidden in the back of the kitchen or the pantry or the cooler. I know it sounds strange to be proud of, but it means a lot to me, being truthworthy enough to piss in somebody else's clean bathroom. Maybe you don't understand the value of a clean bathroom, but I do.

Probably none of this interests you. I probably don't interest you much. Homeless Indians are everywhere in Seattle. We're common and boring, and you walk right on by us, with maybe a look of anger or disgust or even sadness at the terrible fate of the noble savage. But we have dreams and families. I'm friends with a homeless Plains Indian man whose son is the editor of a big-time newspaper back east. That's his story, but we Indians are great storytellers and liars and mythmakers, so maybe that Plains Indian hobo is a plain old everyday Indian. I'm kind of suspicious of him, because he describes himself only as Plains Indian, a generic term, and not by a specific tribe. When I asked him why he wouldn't tell me exactly what he is, he said, "Do any of us know exactly what we are?" Yeah, great, a philosophizing Indian. "Hey," I said, "you got to have a home to be that homely." He laughed and flipped me the eagle and walked away. But you probably want to know more about the story I'm really trying to tell you.

I wander the streets with a regular crew, my teammates, my defenders, and my posse. It's Rose of Sharon, Junior, and me. We matter to one another if we don't matter to anybody else. Rose of Sharon is a big woman, about seven feet tall if you're measuring overall effect, and about five feet tall if you're talking about the physical. She's a Yakama Indian of the Wishram variety, junior is a Colville, but there are about 199 tribes that make up the Colville, so he could be anything. He's good-looking, though, like he just stepped out of some "Don't Litter the Earth" public-service advertisement. He's got those great big cheekbones that are like planets, you know, with little moons orbiting around them. He gets me jealous, jealous, and jealous. If you put Junior and me next to each other, he's the Before Columbus Arrived Indian, and I'm the After Columbus Arrived Indian. I am living proof of the horrible damage that colonialism has done to us Skins. But I'm not going to let you know how scared I sometimes get of history and its ways. I'm a strong man, and I know that silence is the best way of dealing with white folks.

This whole story started at lunchtime, when Rose of Sharon, Junior, and I were panning the handle down at Pike Place Market. After about two hours of negotiating, we earned five dollars, good enough for a bottle of fortified courage from the most beautiful 7–Eleven in the world. So we headed over that way, feeling like warrior drunks, and we walked past this pawnshop I'd never noticed before. And that was strange, because we Indians have built-in pawnshop radar. But the strangest thing was the old powwow-dance regalia I saw hanging in the window.

"That's my grandmother's regalia," I said to Rose of Sharon and Junior.

"How do you know for sure?" Junior asked.

I didn't know for sure, because I hadn't seen that regalia in person ever. I'd seen only photographs of my grandmother dancing in it. And that was before somebody stole it from her fifty years ago. But it sure looked like my memory of it, and it had all the same colors of feathers and beads that my family always sewed into their powwow regalia.

"There's only one way to know for sure," I said.

So Rose of Sharon, Junior, and I walked into the pawnshop and greeted the old white man working behind the counter.

"How can I help you?" he asked.

"That's my grandmother's powwow regalia in your window," I said. "Somebody stole it from her fifty years ago, and my family has been look-ing for it ever since."

The pawnbroker looked at me like I was a liar. I understood. Pawnshops are filled with liars.

"I'm not lying," I said. "Ask my friends here. They'll tell you."

"He's the most honest Indian I know," Rose of Sharon said.

"All right, honest Indian," the pawnbroker said. "I'll give you the bene-fit of the doubt. Can you prove it's your grandmother's regalia?"

Because they don't want to be perfect, because only God is perfect, Indian people sew flaws into their powwow regalia. My family always sewed one yellow bead somewhere on their regalia. But we always hid it where you had to search hard to find it.

"If it really is my grandmother's," I said, "there will be one yellow bead hidden somewhere on it."

"All right, then," the pawnbroker said. "Let's take a look."

He pulled the regalia out of the window, laid it down on his glass counter, and we searched for that yellow bead and found it hidden beneath the armpit.

"There it is," the pawnbroker said. He didn't sound surprised. "You were right. This is your grandmother's regalia."

"It's been missing for fifty years," Junior said.

"Hey, Junior," I said. "It's my family's story. Let me tell it."

"All right," he said. "I apologize. You go ahead."

"It's been missing for fifty years," I said.

"That's his family's sad story," Rose of Sharon said. "Are you going to give it back to him?"

"That would be the right thing to do," the pawnbroker said. "But I can't afford to do the right thing. I paid a thousand dollars for this. I can't give away a thousand dollars."

"We could go to the cops and tell them it was stolen," Rose of Sharon said.

"Hey," I said to her, "don't go threatening people."

The pawnbroker sighed. He was thinking hard about the possibilities.

"Well, I suppose you could go to the cops," he said. "But I don't think they'd believe a word you said."

He sounded sad about that. Like he was sorry for taking advantage of our disadvantages.

"What's your name?" the pawnbroker asked me.

"Jackson," I said.

"Is that first or last?" he asked.

"Both."

"Are you serious?"

"Yes, it's true. My mother and father named me Jackson Jackson. My family nickname is Jackson Squared. My family is funny."

"All right, Jackson Jackson," the pawnbroker said. "You wouldn't happen to have a thousand dollars, would you?"

"We've got five dollars total," I said.

"That's too bad," he said and thought hard about the possibilities. "I'd sell it to you for a thousand dollars if you had it. Heck, to make it fair, I'd sell it to you for nine hundred and ninety-nine dollars. I'd lose a dollar. It would be the moral thing to do in this case. To lose a dollar would be the right thing."

"We've got five dollars total," I said again.

"That's too bad," he said again and thought harder about the possibilities. "How about this? I'll give you twenty-four hours to come up with nine hundred and ninety-nine dollars. You come back here at lunchtime tomorrow with the money, and I'll sell it back to you. How does that sound?"

"It sounds good," I said.

"All right, then," he said. "We have a deal. And I'll get you started. Here's twenty bucks to get you started."

He opened up his wallet and pulled out a crisp twenty-dollar bill and gave it to me. Rose of Sharon, Junior, and I walked out into the daylight to search for nine hundred and seventy-four more dollars.

∾

1:00 P.M.

Rose of Sharon, Junior, and I carried our twenty-dollar bill and our five dollars in loose change over to the 7-Eleven and spent it to buy three bottles of imagination. We needed to figure out how to raise all that money in one day. Thinking hard, we huddled in an alley beneath the Alaska Way Viaduct and finished off those bottles one, two, and three.

∾

2:00 P.M.

Rose of Sharon was gone when I woke. I heard later she had hitchhiked back to Toppenish and was living with her sister on the reservation.

Junior was passed out beside me, covered in his own vomit, or maybe somebody else's vomit, and my head hurt from thinking, so I left him alone and walked down to the water. I loved the smell of ocean water. Salt always smells like memory.

When I got to the wharf, I ran into three Aleut cousins who sat on a wooden bench and stared out at the bay and cried. Most of the homeless Indians in Seattle come from Alaska. One by one, each of them hopped a big working boat in Anchorage or Barrow or Juneau, fished his way south to Seattle, jumped off the boat with a pocketful of cash to party hard at one of the highly sacred and traditional Indian bars, went broke and broker, and has been trying to find his way back to the boat and the frozen north ever since.

These Aleuts smelled like salmon, I thought, and they told me they were going to sit on that wooden bench until their boat came back.

"How long has your boat been gone?" I asked.

"Eleven years," the elder Aleut said.

I cried with them for a while.

"Hey," I said. "Do you guys have any money I can borrow?"

They didn't.

∾

3:00 P.M.

I walked back to Junior. He was still passed out. I put my face down near his mouth to make sure he was breathing. He was alive, so I dug around in his blue-jean pockets and found half a cigarette. I smoked it all the way down and thought about my grandmother.

Her name was Agnes, and she died of breast cancer when I was fourteen. My father thought Agnes caught her tumors from the uranium mine on the reservation. But my mother said the disease started when Agnes was walking back from the powwow one night and got run over by a motorcycle. She broke three ribs, and my mother said those ribs never healed right, and tumors always take over when you don't heal right.

Sitting beside Junior, smelling the smoke and salt and vomit, I wondered if my grandmother's cancer had started when somebody stole her powwow regalia. Maybe the cancer started in her broken heart and then leaked out into her breasts. I know it's crazy, but I wondered if I could bring my grandmother back to life if I bought back her regalia.

I needed money, big money, so I left Junior and walked over to the Real Change office.

∾

4:00 P.M.

"Real Change is a multifaceted organization that publishes a newspaper, supports cultural projects that empower the poor and homeless, and mobilizes the public around poverty issues. Real Change's mission is to organize, educate, and build alliances to create solutions to homelessness and poverty. They exist to provide a voice to poor people in our community."

I memorized Real Change's mission statement because I sometimes sell the newspaper on the streets. But you have to stay sober to sell it, and I'm not always good at staying sober. Anybody can sell the newspaper. You buy each copy for thirty cents and sell it for a dollar and keep the net profit.

"I need one thousand four hundred and thirty papers," I said to the Big Boss.

"That's a strange number," he said. "And that's a lot of papers."

"I need them."

The Big Boss pulled out the calculator and did the math. "It will cost you four hundred and twenty-nine dollars for that many," he said.

"If I had that kind of money, I wouldn't need to sell the papers."

"What's going on, Jackson-to-the-Second-Power?" he asked. He is the only one who calls me that. He is a funny and kind man.

I told him about my grandmother's powwow regalia and how much money I needed to buy it back.

"We should call the police," he said.

"I don't want to do that," I said. "It's a quest now. I need to win it back by myself."

"I understand," he said. "And to be honest, I'd give you the papers to sell if I thought it would work. But the record for most papers sold in a day by one vendor is only three hundred and two."

"That would net me about two hundred bucks," I said.

The Big Boss used his calculator. "Two hundred and eleven dollars and forty cents," he said.

"That's not enough," I said.

"The most money anybody has made in one day is five hundred and twenty-five. And that's because somebody gave Old Blue five hundred dollar bills for some dang reason. The average daily net is about thirty dollars."

"This isn't going to work."

"No."

"Can you lend me some money?"

"I can't do that," he said. "If I lend you money, I have to lend money to everybody."

"What can you do?"

"I'll give you fifty papers for free. But don't tell anybody I did it."

"Okay," I said.

He gathered up the newspapers and handed them to me. I held them to my chest. He hugged me. I carried the newspapers back toward the water.

5:00 P.M.

Back on the wharf, I stood near the Bainbridge Island Terminal and tried to sell papers to business commuters walking onto the ferry.

I sold five in one hour, dumped the other forty-five into a garbage can, and walked into the McDonald's, ordered four cheeseburgers for a dollar each, and slowly ate them.

After eating, I walked outside and vomited on the sidewalk. I hated to lose my food so soon after eating it. As an alcoholic Indian with a busted stomach, I always hope I can keep enough food in my stomach to stay alive.

6:00 P.M.

With one dollar in my pocket, I walked back to Junior. He was still passed out, so I put my ear to his chest and listened for his heartbeat. He was alive, so I took off his shoes and socks and found one dollar in his left sock and fifty cents in his right sock. With two dollars and fifty cents in my hand, I sat beside Junior and thought about my grandmother and her stories.

When I was sixteen, my grandmother told me a story about World War II. She was a nurse at a military hospital in Sydney, Australia. Over the course of two years, she comforted and healed U.S. and Australian soldiers.

One day, she tended to a wounded Maori soldier. He was very dark-skinned. His hair was black and curly, and his eyes were black and warm. His face with covered with bright tattoos.

"Are you Maori?" he asked my grandmother.

"No," she said. "I'm Spokane Indian. From the United States."

"Ah, yes," he said. "I have heard of your tribes. But you are the first American Indian I have ever met."

"There's a lot of Indian soldiers fighting for the United States," she said. "I have a brother still fighting in Germany, and I lost another brother on Okinawa."

"I am sorry," he said. "I was on Okinawa as well. It was terrible." He had lost his legs to an artillery attack.

"I am sorry about your legs," my grandmother said.

"It's funny, isn't it?" he asked.

"What's funny?"

"How we brown people are killing other brown people so white people will remain free."

"I hadn't thought of it that way."

"Well, sometimes I think of it that way. And other times, I think of it the way they want me to think of it. I get confused."

She fed him morphine.

"Do you believe in heaven?" he asked.

"Which heaven?" she asked.

"I'm talking about the heaven where my legs are waiting for me."

They laughed.

"Of course," he said, "my legs will probably run away from me when I get to heaven. And how will I ever catch them?"

"You have to get your arms strong," my grandmother said. "So you can run on your hands."

They laughed again.

Sitting beside Junior, I laughed with the memory of my grandmother's story. I put my hand close to Junior's mouth to make sure he was still breathing. Yes, Junior was alive, so I took his two dollars and fifty cents and walked to the Korean grocery store over in Pioneer Square.

❧

7:00 P.M.

In the Korean grocery store, I bought a fifty-cent cigar and two scratch lottery tickets for a dollar each. The maximum cash prize was five hundred dollars a ticket. If I won both, I would have enough money to buy back the regalia.

I loved Kay, the young Korean woman who worked the register. She was the daughter of the owners and sang all day.

"I love you," I said when I handed her the money.

"You always say you love me," she said.

"That's because I will always love you."

"You are a sentimental fool."

"I'm a romantic old man."

"Too old for me."

"I know I'm too old for you, but I can dream."

"Okay," she said. "I agree to be a part of your dreams, but I will only hold your hand in your dreams. No kissing and no sex. Not even in your dreams."

"Okay," I said. "No sex. Just romance."

"Good-bye, Jackson Jackson, my love, I will see you soon."

I left the store, walked over to Occidental Park, sat on a bench, and smoked my cigar all the way down.

Ten minutes after I finished the cigar, I scratched my first lottery ticket and won nothing. So I could win only five hundred dollars now, and that would be just half of what I needed.

Ten minutes later, I scratched my other lottery ticket and won a free ticket, a small consolation and one more chance to win money.

I walked back to Kay.

"Jackson Jackson," she said. "Have you come back to claim my heart?"

"I won a free ticket," I said.

"Just like a man," she said. "You love money and power more than you love me."

"It's true," I said. "And I'm sorry it's true."

She gave me another scratch ticket, and I carried it outside. I liked to scratch my tickets in private. Hopeful and sad, I scratched that third ticket and won real money. I carried it back inside to Kay.

"I won a hundred dollars," I said.

She examined the ticket and laughed. "That's a fortune," she said and counted out five twenties. Our fingertips touched as she handed me the money. I felt electric and constant.

"Thank you," I said and gave her one of the bills.

"I can't take that," she said. "It's your money."

"No, it's tribal. It's an Indian thing. When you win, you're supposed to share with your family."

"I'm not your family."

"Yes, you are."

She smiled. She kept the money. With eighty dollars in my pocket, I said good-bye to my dear Kay and walked out into the cold night air.

ↄ

8:00 P.M.

I wanted to share the good news with Junior. I walked back to him, but he was gone. I later heard he had hitchhiked down to Portland, Oregon, and died of exposure in an alley behind the Hilton Hotel.

ↄ

9:00 P.M

Lonely for Indians, I carried my eighty dollars over to Big Heart's in South Downtown. Big Heart's is an all-Indian bar. Nobody knows how or why Indians migrate to one bar and turn it into an official Indian bar. But Big Heart's has been an Indian bar for twenty-three years. It used to be way up on Aurora Avenue, but a crazy Lummi Indian burned that one down, and the owners moved to the new location, a few blocks south of Safeco Field.

I walked inside Big Heart's and counted fifteen Indians, eight men and seven women. I didn't know any of them, but Indians like to belong, so we all pretended to be cousins.

"How much for whiskey shots?" I asked the bartender, a fat white guy.

"You want the bad stuff or the badder stuff?"

"As bad as you got."

"One dollar a shot."

I laid my eighty dollars on the bar top.

"All right," I said. "Me and all my cousins here are going to be drinking eighty shots. How many is that apiece?"

"Counting you," a woman shouted from behind me, "that's five shots for everybody."

I turned to look at her. She was a chubby and pale Indian sitting with a tall and skinny Indian man.

"All right, math genius," I said to her and then shouted for the whole bar to hear. "Five drinks for everybody!"

All of the other Indians rushed the bar, but I sat with the mathematician and her skinny friend. We took our time with our whiskey shots.

"What's your tribe?" I asked them.

"I'm Duwamish," she said. "And he's Crow."

"You're a long way from Montana," I said to him.

"I'm Crow," he said. "I flew here."

"What's your name?" I asked them.

"I'm Irene Muse," she said. "And this is Honey Boy."

She shook my hand hard, but he offered his hand like I was supposed to kiss it. So I kissed it. He giggled and blushed as well as a dark-skinned Crow can blush.

"You're one of them two-spirits, aren't you?" I asked him.

"I love women," he said. "And I love men."

"Sometimes both at the same time," Irene said.

We laughed.

"Man," I said to Honey Boy. "So you must have about eight or nine spirits going on inside of you, enit?"

"Sweetie," he said, "I'll be whatever you want me to be."

"Oh, no," Irene said. "Honey Boy is falling in love."

"It has nothing to do with love," he said.

We laughed.

"Wow," I said. "I'm flattered, Honey Boy, but I don't play on your team."

"Never say never," he said.

"You better be careful," Irene said. "Honey Boy knows all sorts of magic. He always makes straight boys fall for him."

"Honey Boy," I said, "you can try to seduce me. And Irene, you can try with him. But my heart belongs to a woman named Kay."

"Is your Kay a virgin?" Honey Boy asked.

We laughed.

We drank our whiskey shots until they were gone. But the other Indians bought me more whiskey shots because I'd been so generous with my money. Honey Boy pulled out his credit card, and I drank and sailed on that plastic boat.

After a dozen shots, I asked Irene to dance. And she refused. But Honey Boy shuffled over to the jukebox, dropped in a quarter, and selected Willie Nelson's "Help Me Make It Through the Night." As Irene and I sat at the table and laughed and drank more whiskey, Honey Boy danced a slow circle around us and sang along with Willie.

"Are you serenading me?" I asked him.

He kept singing and dancing.

"Are you serenading me?" I asked him again.

"He's going to put a spell on you," Irene said.

I leaned over the table, spilling a few drinks, and kissed Irene hard. She kissed me back.

∾

10:00 P.M.

Irene pushed me into the women's bathroom, into a stall, shut the door behind us, and shoved her hand down my pants. She was short, so I had to lean over to kiss her. I grabbed and squeezed her everywhere I could reach, and she was wonderfully fat, and every part of her body felt like a large, warm, and soft breast.

∞

Midnight

Nearly blind with alcohol, I stood alone at the bar and swore I'd been standing in the bathroom with Irene only a minute ago.

"One more shot!" I yelled at the bartender.

"You've got no more money!" he yelled.

"Somebody buy me a drink!" I shouted.

"They've got no more money!"

"Where's Irene and Honey Boy?"

"Long gone!"

∞

2:00 A.M.

"Closing time!" the bartender shouted at the three or four Indians still drinking hard after a long hard day of drinking. Indian alcoholics are either sprinters or marathon runners.

"Where's Irene and Honey Bear?" I asked.

"They've been gone for hours," the bartender said.

"Where'd they go?"

"I told you a hundred times, I don't know."

"What am I supposed to do?"

"It's closing time. I don't care where you go, but you're not staying here."

"You are an ungrateful bastard. I've been good to you."

"You don't leave right now, I'm going to kick your ass."

"Come on, I know how to fight."

He came for me. I don't remember what happened after that.

∞

4:00 A.M.

I emerged from the blackness and discovered myself walking behind a big warehouse. I didn't know where I was. My face hurt. I touched my nose and decided it might be broken. Exhausted and cold, I pulled a plastic tarp from a truck bed, wrapped it around me like a faithful lover, and fell asleep in the dirt.

6:00 A.M.

Somebody kicked me in the ribs. I opened my eyes and looked up at a white cop.

"Jackson," said the cop. "Is that you?"

"Officer Williams," I said. He was a good cop with a sweet tooth. He'd given me hundreds of candy bars over the years. I wonder if he knew I was diabetic.

"What the hell are you doing here?" he asked.

"I was cold and sleepy," I said. "So I laid down."

"You dumb-ass, you passed out on the railroad tracks."

I sat up and looked around. I was lying on the railroad tracks. Dockworkers stared at me. I should have been a railroad-track pizza, a double Indian pepperoni with extra cheese. Sick and scared, I leaned over and puked whiskey.

"What the hell's wrong with you?" Officer Williams asked. "You've never been this stupid."

"It's my grandmother," I said. "She died."

"I'm sorry, man. When did she die?"

"1972."

"And you're killing yourself now?"

"I've been killing myself ever since she died."

He shook his head. He was sad for me. Like I said, he was a good cop.

"And somebody beat the hell out of you," he said. "You remember who?"

"Mr. Grief and I went a few rounds."

"It looks like Mr. Grief knocked you out."

"Mr. Grief always wins."

"Come on," he said, "let's get you out of here."

He helped me stand and led me over to his squad car. He put me in the back. "You throw up in there," he said, "and you're cleaning it up."

"That's fair," I said.

He walked around the car and sat in the driver's seat. "I'm taking you over to detox," he said.

"No, man, that place is awful," I said. "It's full of drunk Indians."

We laughed. He drove away from the docks.

"I don't know how you guys do it," he said.

"What guys?" I asked.

"You Indians. How the hell do you laugh so much? I just picked your ass off the railroad tracks, and you're making jokes. Why the hell do you do that?"

"The two funniest tribes I've ever been around are Indians and Jews, so I guess that says something about the inherent humor of genocide."

We laughed.

"Listen to you, Jackson. You're so smart. Why the hell are you on the streets?"

"Give me a thousand dollars, and I'll tell you."

"You bet I'd give you a thousand dollars if I knew you'd straighten up your life."

He meant it. He was the second-best cop I'd ever known.

"You're a good cop," I said.

"Come on, Jackson," he said. "Don't blow smoke up my ass."

"No, really, you remind me of my grandfather."

"Yeah, that's what you Indians always tell me."

"No, man, my grandfather was a tribal cop. He was a good cop. He never arrested people. He took care of them. Just like you."

"I've arrested hundreds of scumbags, Jackson. And I've shot a couple in the ass."

"It don't matter. You're not a killer."

"I didn't kill them. I killed their asses. I'm an ass-killer."

We drove through downtown. The missions and shelters had already released their overnighters. Sleepy homeless men and women stood on corners and stared up at the gray sky. It was the morning after the night of the living dead.

"Did you ever get scared?" I asked Officer Williams.

"What do you mean?"

"I mean, being a cop, is it scary?"

He thought about that for a while. He contemplated it. I liked that about him.

"I guess I try not to think too much about being afraid," he said. "If you think about fear, then you'll be afraid. The job is boring most of the time. Just driving and looking into dark corners, you know, and seeing nothing. But then things get heavy. You're chasing somebody or fighting them or walking around a dark house and you just know some crazy guy is hiding around a corner, and hell yes, it's scary."

"My grandfather was killed in the line of duty," I said.

"I'm sorry. How'd it happen?"

I knew he'd listen closely to my story.

"He worked on the reservation. Everybody knew everybody. It was safe. We aren't like those crazy Sioux or Apache or any of those other warrior tribes. There's only been three murders on my reservation in the last hundred years."

"That is safe."

"Yeah, we Spokane, we're passive, you know? We're mean with words. And we'll cuss out anybody. But we don't shoot people. Or stab them. Not much, anyway."

"So what happened to your grandfather?"

"This man and his girlfriend were fighting down by Little Falls."

"Domestic dispute. Those are the worst."

"Yeah, but this guy was my grandfather's brother. My great-uncle."

"Oh, no."

"Yeah, it was awful. My grandfather just strolled into the house. He'd been there a thousand times. And his brother and his girlfriend were all drunk and beating on each other. And my grandfather stepped between them just like he'd done a hundred times before. And the girlfriend tripped or something. She fell down and hit her head and started crying. And my grandfather knelt down beside her to make sure she was all right. And for some reason, my great-uncle reached down, pulled my grandfather's pistol out of the holster, and shot him in the head."

"That's terrible. I'm sorry."

"Yeah, my great-uncle could never figure out why he did it. He went to prison forever, you know, and he always wrote these long letters. Like fifty pages of tiny little handwriting. And he was always trying to figure out why he did it. He'd write and write and write and try to figure it out. He never did. It's a great big mystery."

"Do you remember your grandfather?"

"A little bit. I remember the funeral. My grandmother wouldn't let them bury him. My father had to drag her away from the grave."

"I don't know what to say."

"I don't, either."

We stopped in front of the detox center.

"We're here," Officer Williams said.

"I can't go in there," I said.

"You have to."

"Please, no. They'll keep me for twenty-four hours. And then it will be too late."

"Too late for what?"

I told him about my grandmother's regalia and the deadline for buying it back.

"If it was stolen," he said, "then you need to file reports. I'll investigate it myself. If that thing is really your grandmother's, I'll get it back for you. Legally."

"No," I said. "That's not fair. The pawnbroker didn't know it was stolen. And besides, I'm on a mission here. I want to be a hero, you know? I want to win it back like a knight."

"That's romantic crap."

"It might be. But I care about it. It's been a long time since I really cared about something."

Officer Williams turned around in his seat and stared at me. He studied me.

"I'll give you some money," he said. "I don't have much. Only thirty bucks. I'm short until payday. And it's not enough to get back the regalia. But it's something."

"I'll take it," I said.

"I'm giving it to you because I believe in what you believe. I'm hoping, and I don't know why I'm hoping it, but I hope you can turn thirty bucks into a thousand somehow."

"I believe in magic."

"I believe you'll take my money and get drunk on it."

"Then why are you giving it to me?"

"There ain't no such thing as an atheist cop."

"Sure there is."

"Yeah, well, I'm not an atheist cop."

He let me out of the car, handed me two fives and a twenty, and shook my hand. "Take care of yourself, Jackson," he said. "Stay off the railroad tracks."

"I'll try," I said.

He drove away. Carrying my money, I headed back toward the water.

8:00 A.M.

On the wharf, those three Aleut men still waited on the wooden bench.

"Have you seen your ship?" I asked.

"Seen a lot of ships," the elder Aleut said. "But not our ship."

I sat on the bench with them. We sat in silence for a long time. I wondered whether we would fossilize if we sat there long enough.

I thought about my grandmother. I'd never seen her dance in her regalia. More than anything, I wished I'd seen her dance at a powwow.

"Do you guys know any songs?" I asked the Aleuts.

"I know all of Hank Williams," the elder Aleut said.

"How about Indian songs?"

"Hank Williams is Indian."

"How about sacred songs?"

"Hank Williams is sacred."

"I'm talking about ceremonial songs, you know, religious ones. The songs you sing back home when you're wishing and hoping."

"What are you wishing and hoping for?"

"I'm wishing my grandmother was still alive."

"Every song I know is about that."

"Well, sing me as many as you can."

The Aleuts sang their strange and beautiful songs. I listened. They sang about my grandmother and their grandmothers. They were lonely for the cold and snow. I was lonely for everybody.

❦

10:00 A.M.

After the Aleuts finished their last song, we sat in silence. Indians are good at silence.

"Was that the last song?" I asked.

"We sang all the ones we could," the elder Aleut said. "All the others are just for our people."

I understood. We Indians have to keep our secrets. And these Aleuts were so secretive that they didn't refer to themselves as Indians.

"Are you guys hungry?" I asked.

They looked at one another and communicated without talking.

"We could eat," the elder Aleut said.

❦

11:00 A.M.

The Aleuts and I walked over to Mother's Kitchen, a greasy diner in the International District. I knew they served homeless Indians who'd lucked in to money.

"Four for breakfast?" the waitress asked when we stepped inside.

"Yes, we're very hungry," the elder Aleut said.

She sat us in a booth near the kitchen. I could smell the food cooking. My stomach growled.

"You guys want separate checks?" the waitress asked.

"No, I'm paying for it," I said.

"Aren't you the generous one," she said.

"Don't do that," I said.

"Do what?" she asked.

"Don't ask me rhetorical questions. They scare me."

She looked puzzled, and then she laughed.

"Okay, Professor," she said. "I'll only ask you real questions from now on."

"Thank you."

"What do you guys want to eat?"

"That's the best question anybody can ask anybody," I said.

"How much money you got?" she asked.

"Another good question," I said. "I've got twenty-five dollars I can spend. Bring us all the breakfast you can, plus your tip."

She knew the math.

"All right, that's four specials and four coffees and fifteen percent for me."

The Aleuts and I waited in silence. Soon enough, the waitress returned and poured us four coffees, and we sipped at them until she returned again with four plates of food. Eggs, bacon, toast, hash-brown potatoes. It is amazing how much food you can buy for so little money.

Grateful, we feasted.

∾

Noon

I said farewell to the Aleuts and walked toward the pawnshop. I later heard the Aleuts had waded into the saltwater near Dock 47 and disappeared. Some Indians said the Aleuts walked on the water and headed north. Other Indians saw the Aleuts drown. I don't know what happened to them.

I looked for the pawnshop and couldn't find it. I swear it wasn't located in the place where it had been before. I walked twenty or thirty blocks looking for the pawnshop, turned corners and bisected intersections, looked up its name in the phone books, and asked people walking past me if they'd ever heard of it. But that pawnshop seemed to have sailed away from me like a ghost ship. I wanted to cry. Right when I'd given up, when I turned one last corner and thought I might die if I didn't find that pawnshop, there it was, located in a space I swore it hadn't been filling up a few minutes before.

I walked inside and greeted the pawnbroker, who looked a little younger than he had before.

"It's you," he said.

"Yes, it's me," I said.

"Jackson Jackson."

"That is my name."

"Where are your friends?"

"They went traveling. But it's okay. Indians are everywhere."

"Do you have my money?"

"How much do you need again?" I asked and hoped the price had changed.

"Nine hundred and ninety-nine dollars."

It was still the same price. Of course it was the same price. Why would it change?

"I don't have that," I said.

"What do you have?"

"Five dollars."

I set the crumpled Lincoln on the countertop. The pawnbroker studied it.

"Is that the same five dollars from yesterday?"

"No, it's different."

He thought about the possibilities.

"Did you work hard for this money?" he asked.

"Yes," I said.

He closed his eyes and thought harder about the possibilities. Then he stepped into his back room and returned with my grandmother's regalia.

"Take it," he said and held it out to me.

"I don't have the money."

"I don't want your money."

"But I wanted to win it."

"You did win it. Now, take it before I change my mind."

Do you know how many good men live in this world? Too many to count!

I took my grandmother's regalia and walked outside. I knew that solitary yellow bead was part of me. I knew I was that yellow bead in part. Outside, I wrapped myself in my grandmother's regalia and breathed her in. I stepped off the sidewalk and into the intersection. Pedestrians stopped. Cars stopped. The city stopped. They all watched me dance with my grandmother. I was my grandmother, dancing.

Suggestions for Discussion

1. How is Jackson's grandmother's regalia a link to the family's past? Is there any truth to the line "I wondered whether I could bring my grandmother back to life if I bought back her regalia"?

2. Why does Jackson's search for the $999.00 to buy back the regalia become a quest? Why is he so intent on winning it back?

3. Why does the pawnshop owner give him the regalia for five dollars in the end? Why does he say that Jackson won it? What did he do that was worthy of gaining it back? Think of the ways Jackson uses his money throughout the day.

4. How do the characters in this story regard alcohol? What motivates the central character to drink?

Suggestions for Writing

1. After reading the story, have you gained any insight on what it means to give and receive? Write two paragraphs discussing the importance of giving and receiving in your life.

2. In the story, the main character makes it his mission to reconnect with his past and his grandmother through her stolen regalia. Do you have any family heirlooms that are representative of your family's bond? Write a short story that uses these elements of family and reconnection. Use Alexie's story as a model for your own.

POETRY

S A R A   L I T T L E C R O W - R U S S E L L

Apology to the Wasps

DOROTHE SCHRÖDER, *Untitled*. Digital photograph, 2008. Courtesy of the artist.

A journalist, poet, and political activist, Sara Littlecrow- Russell has made a career of opposing domestic violence and advocating for the rights of Native American women. In addition to being a prolific writer, she is a law scholar and volunteer lawyer who specializes in domestic law and social change. She has written *The Indigenous Women's Health Book: Within the Sacred Circle* and the upcoming poetry collection *Eagle Feathers across a Crow Wing*. Her poems have appeared in the periodicals the *Massachusetts Review*, *American Indian Quarterly*, *Race Traitor*, *U.S. Latino Review*, and in the anthologies *Sister Nations: Native American Women Writing on*

Community and *Touched by Eros*. The following poem is simultaneously an environmentalist and a military parable.

Terrorized by your stings,
I took out biochemical weapons
And blasted your nest
Like it was a third world country.
I was the United States Air Force.
It felt good to be so powerful
Until I saw your family
Trailing shredded wings,
Staggering on disintegrating legs,
Trying desperately to save the eggs
You had stung to protect.

Suggestions for Discussion

1. Why does the poet wait until the end of the poem to reveal why the wasp terrorized the speaker with stings? What is the effect of withholding that information? What moral is revealed when the reason for the stings is finally made clear?

2. How might this poem have ended differently if the narrator knew about the eggs before deciding to gas the nest?

3. Is this an animal rights poem? Explain.

4. The narrator says "I was the United States Air Force" and describes the wasp nest as "a third world country." What level of meaning is added to the poem if the reader is to take this comparison literally? If the speaker is the Air Force, then what is the wasp?

Suggestion for Writing

Write a poem from the perspective of the dying wasp.

WILFRED OWEN

Dulce et Decorum Est

Wilfred Owen (1893–1918) was born in Shropshire, England, and educated at Birkenhead Institute. Among the most celebrated of the English war poets, he was killed in action in World War I. Another war poet,

Siegfried Sassoon, collected Owen's poems, which were first published in 1920. Other collections followed, as did critical studies and memoirs. From *The Complete Poems and Fragments of Wilfred Owen*, published in 1984, comes "Dulce et Decorum Est" (taken from Horace's statement, "It is sweet and fitting to die for one's country"); it opposes vivid and devastating images of the casualties of war with statements of sentimental patriotism. It shows war as the ultimate insult to human dignity.

Bent double, like old beggars under sacks,
Knock-kneed, coughing like hags, we cursed through sludge,
Till on the haunting flares we turned our backs,
And towards our distant rest began to trudge.
Men marched asleep. Many had lost their boots,
But limped on, blood-shod. All went lame, all blind;
Drunk with fatigue; deaf even to the hoots
Of gas-shells dropping softly behind.

Gas! Gas! Quick, boys!—An ecstasy of fumbling,
Fitting the clumsy helmets just in time,
But someone still was yelling out and stumbling
And flound'ring like a man in fire or lime.—
Dim through the misty panes and thick green light,
As under a green sea, I saw him drowning.
In all my dreams before my helpless sight
He plunges at me, guttering, choking, drowning.

If in some smothering dreams, you too could pace
Behind the wagon that we flung him in,
And watch the white eyes writhing in his face,
His hanging face, like a devil's sick of sin,
If you could hear, at every jolt, the blood
Come gargling from the froth-corrupted lungs
Bitter as the cud

Of vile, incurable sores on innocent tongues,—
My friend, you would not tell with such high zest
To children ardent for some desperate glory,
The old lie: *Dulce et decorum est*
Pro patria mori.

Suggestions for Discussion

1. In the first two stanzas, Owen presents two connected scenes of war. How are these two stanzas related to the final one?

2. Discuss the use of irony in the poem. Show why Owen uses the quotation from Horace.

3. Examine the series of images that Owen uses to describe war. Do they progress through the poem? Show why one cannot interchange the first two stanzas.

4. Find Brian Turner's poem "Here, Bullet," which was written during the war in Iraq. Discuss the similarities and differences between the two poems.

Suggestion for Writing

Owen's picture of the destruction of lives constitutes a poetic statement against war. Does this poem lead you to a belief in pacifism? Are there "just" and "unjust" wars? Try to sort out your attitudes and write an essay explaining under what conditions, if any, you might be willing to fight for your country. Support your statements with detailed arguments.

GLOSSARY

Abstraction, levels of   Distinguished in two ways: in the range between the general and the specific and in the range between the abstract and the concrete.

A general word refers to a class, genus, or group; a specific word refers to a member of that group. *Ship* is a general word, but *ketch, schooner, liner,* and *tugboat* are specific. The terms *general* and *specific* are relative, however, not absolute. On the one hand, *ketch* is more specific than *ship,* because a ketch is a kind of ship. But on the other hand, *ketch* is more general than *Tahiti ketch,* because a Tahiti ketch is a kind of ketch.

The distinction between the abstract and the concrete also is relative. Ideas, qualities, and characteristics that do not exist by themselves are abstract; physical things such as *house, shoes,* and *horse* are concrete. Concrete words can range not only further into the specific (*bungalow, moccasin,* and *stallion*) but also back toward the general (*domicile, clothing,* and *horses*). These distinctions between the abstract and the concrete and between the general and the specific do not imply that good writing should be specific and concrete and that poor writing is general and abstract. Most good writing constantly moves from the general to the specific and from the abstract to the concrete as the situation demands.

Allusion   Reference to a familiar person, place, or thing, whether real or imaginary: Woodrow Wilson or Zeus evoke leadership and male power, Siam or Atlantis evoke exotic locales, kangaroo or phoenix evoke a comtemplation of the wonder of wildlife. The allusion is an economical way to evoke an atmosphere, a historical era, or an emotion.

Analogy   In exposition, usually a comparison of some length in which the unknown is explained in terms of the known, the unfamiliar in terms of the familiar, the remote in terms of the immediate.

In argument, an analogy consists of a series of likenesses between two or more dissimilar things, demonstrating that they are either similar or identical in other respects; however, these types of analogies can be flawed, because two things alike in many respects are not necessarily alike in all (for example, lampblack and diamonds are both pure carbon; they differ only in their

crystal structure). Although analogy never *proves* anything, its dramatic quality, its assistance in establishing tone, and its vividness make it one of the
writer's most valuable techniques.

Analysis   A method of exposition by logical division, applicable to anything that
can be divided into component parts: an object, such as an automobile or a
watch; an institution, such as a college; or a process, such as mining coal or
writing a poem. These parts or processes may be described technically and fac-
tually or impressionistically and selectively. In the latter method, the parts are
organized in relation to a single governing idea so that the mutually supporting function of each of the components in the total structure becomes clear to
the reader. For example, the actors, director, script, music score, and special
effects are all part of a whole motion picture. Parts may be explained in terms
of their characteristic function. Analysis may also be concerned with the connection of events; for example, given this condition or series of conditions, what
effects will follow? For example, if a country in a recession, with high taxes and
high unemployment, goes to war, what will happen to the economy?

Argument   Often contains the following parts: the *proposition,* an assertion that
leads to the issue; the *issue,* what the writer is attempting to prove and the
question on which the whole argument rests; and the *evidence,* the facts and
opinions that the author offers as testimony. The evidence can be ordered
deductively, by proceeding logically from certain premises and reaching a conclusion, or *inductively,* by generalizing from several instances and drawing a
conclusion. Informal arguments frequently make greater use of the methods
of exposition than they do of formal logic—for example, employing statistics, scientific theorems, or laws to further their case. See Analogy, Deductive
Reasoning, and Inductive Reasoning.

It is possible to distinguish between argument and persuasion by the
means (argument appeals to reason; persuasion, to emotions) or the ends
(argument can change a mind; persuasion can lead to action). These distinctions, however, are more academic than functional, for in practice, argument
and persuasion are not discrete entities. Yet the proof in argument rests
largely upon the objectivity of evidence; the proof in persuasion, upon the
heightened use of language.

Assumption   That part of an argument that is unstated because it is either taken
for granted by the reader and writer or it is undetected by them. For example,
authors are not always aware of their prejudices or gaps in knowledge, and it
hurts their arguments when these flaws go undetected. When the reader consciously disagrees with an assumption, the writer has misjudged his audience
by assuming what the reader refuses to concede. An example of this is a writer,
who assumes that British men are stuffy and sexist, writes an essay that British
men (and those who disagree with the notion that all members of a single
group can be described as all alike) are unlikely to agree with or enjoy.

Audience   For the writer, his expected readers. When the audience is unknown, and the subject matter is closely related to the writer's opinions, preferences, attitudes, and tastes, then the writer's relationship to his audience is his relationship to himself. The writer who distrusts the intelligence of his audience or adapts his material to what he assumes are the tastes and interests of his readers has disguised his authorial voice to the point where it is hard for the reader to feel as close a kinship with him as with a writer with more confessional and less commercialized (or mediated) style.

"It is now necessary to warn the writer that his concern for the reader must be pure; he must sympathize with the reader's plight (most readers are in trouble about half the time) but never seek to know his wants. The whole duty of a writer is to please and satisfy himself, and the true writer always plays to an audience of one. Let him start sniffing the air, or glancing at the Trend Machine, and he is as good as dead although he may make a nice living." Strunk and White, *The Elements of Style* (Macmillan).

On the other hand, when the audience is known (a college class, for example), and the subject matter is factual information, the writer should consider the education, interests, and tastes of her audience. Unless she keeps a definite audience in mind, the beginner is apt to shift levels of usage, employ inappropriate diction, and lose the readers if she does not appeal to any of their interests.

Cause and Effect   A seemingly simple method of development in which a connection is drawn between an event and its trigger. However, because of the philosophical difficulties surrounding causality, the writer should be cautious in ascribing causes. For the explanation of most effects, it is probably safer to proceed in a sequential order, using transitional words to indicate the order of the process. For example, it is a fact that the American Civil War followed the election of President Lincoln, but it is not necessarliy true to say that the election of Lincoln caused the Civil War.

Classification   The division of a whole into the classes that compose it, or the placement of a subject into its appropriate whole. See Analysis and Definition.

Coherence   Literally, a sticking together; therefore, the joining or linking of one point to another. It is the writer's obligation to make clear to the reader the relationship of sentence to sentence and paragraph to paragraph. There are several ways to do this. A writer can achieve coherence by putting the parts in a sequence that is meaningful and relevant—logical sequence, chronological order, order of importance. Or a writer can obtain coherence between parts by using transitional words—*but, however, yet*—to inform the reader that what is to follow contrasts with what went before; and *furthermore, moreover, in addition to* continue or expand what went before.

Another basic way of achieving coherence is to enumerate ideas to remind the reader of the development—*first, second, third*. A more subtle transition is to repeat at the beginning of a paragraph a key word or idea from the end of the preceding paragraph. Such a transition reminds readers of what has gone before and simultaneously prepares them for what is to come.

Comparison and Contrast   The presentation of a subject by indicating similarities between two or more things (comparison) or by indicating differences (contrast). Often comparison and contrast are used in definition and other methods of exposition.

Concreteness   See Abstraction, levels of.

Connotation   All that the word suggests or implies in addition to its literal meaning. For example, the word "odor" technically can suggest any scent, but common usage has led the listener to assume that it means (or connotes) a foul smell.

Contrast   See Comparison and Contrast.

Coordination   Elements of similar importance in similar grammatical construction. More important elements should be placed in grammatically dominant positions. This arrangement makes writing easier to understand and enjoy because the work is organized logically and flows. See Parallelism and Subordination.

Deductive Reasoning   In logic, the application of a generalization to a particular; in rhetoric, development that moves from the general to the specific.

Definition   In logic, the placing of the word to be defined in a general class and then showing how it differs from other members of the class. In rhetoric, the meaningful extension (usually enriched by the use of detail, concrete illustration, anecdote, metaphor) of a logical definition to answer fully, clearly, and often implicitly the question "What is—?"

Denotation   The literal meaning of a word. See Connotation.

Description   Presenting factual information about an object or experience (objective description); or reporting the impression or evaluation of an object or experience (subjective description). Most description combines the two purposes. For example, *It was a frightening night*: an evaluation with which others might disagree; *The wind blew the shingles off the north side of the house and drove the rain under the door*: two facts about which there can be little disagreement.

Diction   Style as determined by choice of words. Good diction is characterized by accuracy and appropriateness to subject matter; weak diction, by the use of inappropriate, vague, or trite words. The relationship between the kinds of words a writer selects and his subject matter in large part determines tone. The deliberate use of inappropriate diction is a frequent device of satire.

Discourse, forms of   Traditionally, exposition, argument, description, and narration. See entries under each. These four kinds of traditional discourse are rarely found in a pure form. Argument and exposition may be interfused in the most complex fashion. Exposition often employs narration and description for purposes of illustration. In an effective piece of writing, the use of more than one form of discourse is never accidental; it always serves the author's central purpose.

Emphasis   The arrangement of the elements in a piece of writing so that the important meanings occur in structurally important parts of the work. Repetition, order of increasing importance, exclamation points, rhetorical questions, and figures of speech are all devices to achieve emphasis.

Evidence   That part of argument or persuasion that involves proof. It usually takes the form of facts, particulars deduced from general principles, or opinions of authorities.

Exposition   That form of discourse that explains or informs. Most papers required of college students are expository. The methods of exposition presented in *The Conscious Reader* are identification, definition, classification, illustration, comparison and contrast, and analysis. See separate entries in the glossary.

Figure of Speech   A form of expression in which the meanings of words are extended beyond the literal. The common figures of speech are metaphor, simile, and analogy.

Generalization   A broad conception or principle derived from particulars. Often, simply a broad statement. See Abstraction, levels of.

Grammar   A systematic description of a language. The organizing principle of a language that gives it shape and provides rules for proper usage.

Identification   A process preliminary to definition of a subject. For the writer, it is that important period preliminary to writing when, wrestling with inchoate glimmerings, she begins to select and shape her materials. As a method of exposition, it brings the subject into focus by describing it.

Illustration   A particular member of a class used to explain or dramatize a class, a type, a thing, a person, a method, an idea, or a condition. The idea explained may be either stated or implied. For purposes of illustration, the individual member of a class must be a fair representation of the distinctive qualities of the class. The use of illustrations, examples, and specific instances adds to the concreteness and vividness of writing. See Narration.

Image   A word or statement that makes an appeal to the senses—sense impressions. Thus, there are visual images, auditory images, and so on. Because the most direct experience of the world is through the senses, writing that uses unexpected examples of sense impressions can be unusually effective.

Inductive Reasoning   In logic, the formulation of a conclusion after the observation of an adequate number of particular instances; in rhetoric, the development of an idea or concept that moves from the particular to the general.

Intention   The reason a piece of writing was first written—its goal. For example, some works are written to convince; others, to entertain; others, to teach; and others, to provoke thought or action. It is often wise to try to determine a work's intent to best understand your reaction to it.

Irony   At its simplest, involves a discrepancy between literal and intended meaning; at its most complex, it involves an utterance more meaningful (and usually meaningful in a different way) to the listener than to the speaker. For example, the audience understands Oedipus' remarks about discovering the murderer of the king in a way Oedipus himself cannot understand. The satirist frequently feigns the inability to grasp the full implications of his own remarks.

Issue   Limiting the general proposition to the precise point on which the argument rests. Defeating this point—the issue—defeats the argument. Typically the main proposition of an argument will raise at least one issue for discussion and controversy.

Limitation of Subject   Restriction of the subject to one centralizing subject or idea that can be adequately developed with reference to audience and purpose.

Metaphor   An implied comparison between two things that are seemingly different; a compressed analogy. Effectively used, metaphors increase clarity, interest, vividness, and concreteness.

Narration   A form of discourse that tells a story. If a story is significant in itself, and the particulars appeal to the imagination, it is *narration*. If a story illustrates a point in exposition or argument, it is *illustrative narration*. If a story outlines a process step by step, the particulars appealing to the understanding, it is *expository narration*.

Organization, methods of   Varies with the form of discourse. Exposition uses in part, in whole, or in combination the organizational methods identification, definition, classification, illustration, comparison and contrast, and analysis. Argument and persuasion often use the method of organization of inductive or deductive reasoning, or analogy. Description is often organized around a dominant idea or object. Narration, to give two examples, may be organized chronologically or in terms of point of view.

Paradox   An assertion or sentiment seemingly self-contradictory, or opposed to common sense, that may yet be true. For example, Thomas Jefferson was a slave owner who wrote that "all men are created equal."

Paragraph   A division of writing that serves to discuss one topic or one aspect of a topic. The central thought is either implied or expressed in a topic sentence, and the rest of the paragraph describes that thought. Most pieces of writing are composed of several paragraphs that are organized in some coherent scheme. See Coherence.

Parallelism   Elements of similar rhetorical importance in similar grammatical patterns. See Coordination.

Parody   Mimicking the language and style of another in a gently humorous or critical style. For example, the Austin Powers movies faithfully recreate characters, scenes, and dialogue from the James Bond films—the better to mock James Bond. The same technique is used in literature when Mark Twain writes like James Fenimore Cooper in order to illustrate why he feels that Cooper is a poor novelist.

Perspective   The vantage point chosen by the writer to achieve his purpose, his strategy. It is reflected in his close scrutiny of, or distance from, his subject; his objective representation or subjective interpretation of it. For example, a writer describing a football game may objectively describe both teams' feelings and actions fairly, or subjectively cast one team as heroic and another as villainous. See Diction, Purpose, Tone.

Persuasion   A rhetorical technique that often uses heightened language designed to appeal to the emotions or prompt the listener to take action. See Argument.

Point of View   In description, the position from which the observer looks at the object described; in narration, the person who sees the action, who tells the story; in exposition, the ideological starting point of the composition. First person or third person are the most commonly used points of view.

Proposition   See Argument.

Purpose   What the writer wants to accomplish with a particular piece of writing.

Rhetoric   The art of using language effectively.

Rhetorical Question   A question asked to induce thought and to provide emphasis rather than to evoke an answer.

Rhythm   In poetry and prose, patterned emphasis.

Satire   The attempt to effect reform by exposing an object to laughter. For example, Charles Dickens convinced the government to pass laws protecting children by satirizing in his novels a Victorian England that mistreated the young. Satire makes frequent recourse to irony, wit, ridicule, and parody. It is usually classified under such categories as social satire, personal satire, and literary satire.

Style   "The essence of a sound style is that it cannot be reduced to rules—that it is a living and breathing thing, with something of the demoniacal in it— that it fits its proprietor tightly and yet ever so loosely, as his skin fits him. It is, in fact, quite as securely an integral part of him as that skin is. . . . In brief, a style is always the outward and visible symbol of a man, and it cannot be anything else." H. L. Mencken, from *On Style.*

   "Young writers often suppose that style is a garnish for the meat of prose, a sauce by which a dull dish is made palatable. Style has no such separate entity; it is nondetachable, unfilterable. The beginner should approach style warily, realizing that it is himself he is approaching, no other; and he should begin by turning resolutely away from all devices that are popularly believed to indicate style—all mannerisms, tricks, adornments. The approach to style is by way of plainness, simplicity, orderliness, sincerity." Strunk and White from *The Elements of Style* (Macmillan).

Subordination   Less important rhetorical elements in grammatically subordinate positions. See Coordination and Parallelism.

Syllogism   In formal logic, a deductive argument in three steps: a major premise, a minor premise, and a conclusion. The major premise states a quality of a class (All men are mortal); the minor premise states that X is a member of the class (Socrates is a man); the conclusion states that the quality of a class is also a quality of a member of the class (Socrates is mortal). In rhetoric, the full syllogism is rarely used; instead, one of the premises is usually omitted. "You can rely on her; she is independent" is an abbreviated syllogism. Major premise: Independent people are reliable; minor premise: She is independent; conclusion: She is reliable. Constructing the full syllogism frequently reveals flaws in reasoning, such as the above, which has an error in the major premise.

Symbol   A concrete image that suggests a meaning beyond itself. For example, a cross symbolizes Christianity; a peace symbol symbolizes the hippie movement of the 1960s; and a dove often symbolizes purity, divinity, or peace.

Tone   The manner in which the writer communicates his feelings or ideas about the materials he is presenting. Diction is the most obvious means of establishing tone. Satire and connotation are others. See Diction.

Topic Sentence   The thesis that the paragraph as a whole develops, encapsulated in one concise statement. Some paragraphs do not have topic sentences, but the thesis is implied through tone or arrangement of relevant information.

Transition   The linking together of sentences, paragraphs, and larger parts of the composition to achieve coherence by making logical connections (thematic and/or grammatical) between them. See Coherence.

Unity   The relevance of selected material to the central theme of an essay. See Coherence.

CREDITS

AUTHOR AND
TITLE INDEX

ART INDEX